תשנ"ו 5756

LEARN TORAH WITH...

1995-1996 TORAH ANNUAL

A COLLECTION OF THE YEAR'S BEST TORAH

EDITED BY RABBI STUART KELMAN
AND JOEL LURIE GRISHAVER

ALEF DESIGN GROUP

ISBN# 1-881283-30-5

ALEF DESIGN GROUP • 4423 FRUITLAND AVENUE, LOS ANGELES, CA 90058
(800) 845–0662 • (323) 582-1200 • (323) 585–0327 FAX
E-MAIL <MISRAD@TORAHAURA.COM>

MANUFACTURED IN THE UNITED STATES OF AMERICA

Learn Torah With...

Back in the 70's, before the computer entered the classroom, the new educational technique was the 'learning center.' These 'centers' were to be tailored to each student, making individualization the primary objective of this new type of education. Students simply worked on their own, quietly (for the most part) in well designed work-stations. They seldom came together. When they did, teachers began to report that their communication skills with others were lacking. While they could handle learning on their own, their ability to be part of a discussion was less than adequate. They could focus on themselves but had great difficulty learning from each other.

Now comes the computer and asks the same questions: can an individual user find community on the Net? Is there a social convention that develops as a result of interactive communication, and most importantly, can this technology be employed in the study of Torah?

This is our second volume of LTW. More and more we find that our project of bringing Torah from a variety of perspectives to our readers has created a community in which it is not only permitted, but encouraged to present different and divergent points of view. What we have found is that this cyber-community has begun to develop its own language and its own grammar and its own interaction patterns. Throughout the year, the communication ebbs and flows. Sometimes, the parashiot provide fertile ground for interpretation; others may be harder to comment on. Summertime, another variable, seems to be rather quiet. But that is precisely the point: we and you have been able to create a vibrant, organic community all centered around textual analysis and reflection. The strength of this ongoing dialogue lies in the ability of the learner to take this work seriously and to be passionately committed to the study of Torah as a (if not 'the') primary life value.

This book is actually a record of an ongoing discussion. Turn it yet again. The conversation continues!

Stuart Kelman and Joel Grishaver
Hanukkah, 5759

Learn Torah With...The Book

Reviewed by David Ellenson

For the past two decades, Joel Grishaver—the iconoclastic founder of the publications company Torah Aura—and Stuart Kelman—currently rabbi of Conservative congregation Netivot Shalom in Berkeley—have been recognized as two of the most creative figures on the American Jewish educational scene. Frequently, they have worked together to guide and enhance the Jewish education, spirituality, and identity of countless numbers of Jews in diverse venues on this continent. Their innovative curricula have brought Judaism alive to persons in synagogue, camp, day school, Hebrew school, and retreat settings. Their common interests and collaborative efforts have coalesced once again and *Learn Torah With...The Book* is the latest fruit of their joint ventures.

Subtitled, "1994-1995 Torah Annual: A Collection of the Year's Best Torah," *Learn Torah With...The Book* is a work of commentary on each of the fifty-four *parshiyot* in the Torah. Authorship of the principal commentary rotates from portion to portion and the authors themselves comprise a virtual Who's Who of American Judaism. Rachel Adler, Robert Alter, Bradley Artson, Elliot Dorff, Eleazer Finkelman, Everett Fox, Tamar Frankiel, Art Green, David Kraemer, Harold Kushner, Lawrence Kushner, Danny Landes, Richard Levy, Deborah Lipstadt, Janet Marder, Carol Meyers, Jacob Milgrom, Jo Milgrom, Jacob Neusner, Gunther Plaut, Nahum Sarna, Zalman Schachter-Shalomi, Harold Schulweis, Chaim Seidler-Feller, Danny Siegel, Joseph Telushkin, Savina Teubal, Jeffrey Tigay, Burton Visotzky, Arthur Waskow, David Wolpe, and Sheldon Zimmerman only constitute a partial listing of the many persons whose words of Torah are found in this book.

Learn Torah With... The Book is taken from the electronic publication issued each week during 1994-1995 by Torah Aura, the sister company of Alef Design Group. Grishaver and Kelman were convinced that the presence of the computer in the lives of so many

American Jews provided a unique opportunity for the dissemination of Torah learning. They invited all the persons listed above, as well as the many others whom space constraints preclude me from mentioning in this review, to offer a commentary on a single Torah portion. Their aim was to provide access to the wisdom of Torah from a wide variety of perspectives to subscribers on the world-wide computer web. *Learn Torah With...* gathers these commentaries into book form.

When Grishaver and Kelman initiated this project, they also asked their subscribers to offer their own thoughts on each commissioned commentary, and they invited their subscribers to offer their own insights into the portion itself. The results of these efforts have also been included in *Learn Torah With...* and have been published along with each invited commentary under the title **Davar A<u>h</u>er**. In addition, the editors provide a synopsis of the major events and figures contained in each Torah portion.

The level of commentary offered in this volume—as would be expected from such a distinguished group of contributors—is remarkably rich and insightful. Each major commentator, without exception, has something significant to say and the insights provided in the **Davar A<u>h</u>er** column are frequently just as rewarding—sometimes even more so! This is significant, for as the late Rabbi Joseph Soloveitchik once observed in a description he offered concerning the phenomenology of Talmud study, Jewish textual learning can be envisioned as an ongoing conversation. Rabbi Soloveitchik stated that when he sat down to study a traditional text he was surrounded by persons old and young, past and present. Tannaim and Amoraim, medieval rabbis, his immediate forebears, and his contemporary students—all of them were present and their voices included through their commentaries on the text. Such conversation received official sanction—it was canonized—through the variegated commentaries contained in the printed editions of rabbinic Bibles—*Mikraot Gedolot*—and Talmud as well as all Jewish legal codes. Rabbi Soloveitchik observed that the dialogue embodied in such commentaries reflected a Jewish veneration of holy texts and in his view this constituted the defining hallmark of Jewish study. For the heremeneutical art of commentary linked communities and generations in a seamless web that transcended time and place. The voices collected in *Learn Torah With...* continue in this tradition.

Learn Torah With... consistently displays a fidelity to the dialogical nature Rabbi Soloveitchik defined as characteristic of Jewish textual *lernen*. On each page of *Learn Torah With...*, the multiplicity of commentators and supra-commentators, by citing insights from the past and providing viewpoints from the present, forge community and direct Jews towards the future. In this way, *Learn Torah With...* situates itself within a Jewish literary heritage that has always viewed the written page as an opportunity and occasion for engagement and discussion with the past. The book indicates that computer technology need not be condemned as subverting traditional textual learning. Its pages demonstrate that the elemental rhythms of traditional Jewish learning and conversation can be and have been nurtured in the medium of cyberspace.

Learn Torah With... is valuable from another perspective as well. In an age of increasing denominational and sectarian division within the Jewish world, the editors have consciously and purposefully sought out and gathered contributors who range across the spectrum of Jewish life. In each Torah portion, Jews of all types attempt to engage with Torah and they seek to find a match between the words—the paradigm—contained in Torah and the present. They turn its words over and over again, demonstrating that Torah remains a font of living waters—*mayim ḫayyim*—for the Jewish people. To such study denominational affiliation is monumentally irrelevant. For the Torah is the common inheritance of all Israel. Grishaver and Kelman have performed a vital—one might say sacred—service to the Jewish people in organizing and facilitating this enterprise and conceptualizing and executing this book. As Torah, it speaks to all Jews. We should not only be stimulated and moved by its words and insights. We should also look forward to subsequent volumes.

Table of Contents

Devarim/Deuteronomy 325

בראשית

Bereshit

השמים ואת הארץ

Parashat Bereshit

Genesis 1.1–6.8

Richard Elliott Friedman

RICHARD ELLIOTT FRIEDMAN IS THE AUTHOR OF *THE DISAPPEARANCE OF GOD: A DIVINE MYSTERY*, PUBLISHED IN OCTOBER, 1995, BY LITTLE, BROWN, AND OF *WHO WROTE THE BIBLE?* HE IS THE KATZIN PROFESSOR OF JEWISH CIVILIZATION AT THE UNIVERSITY OF CALIFORNIA, SAN DIEGO. HE RECEIVED A DOCTORATE IN HEBREW BIBLE AT HARVARD, HELD VISITING POSTS AT OXFORD AND CAMBRIDGE, AND PARTICIPATED IN THE EXCAVATIONS OF BIBLICAL JERUSALEM. HE IS CURRENTLY WRITING *INTRODUCTION TO THE HEBREW BIBLE* FOR THE ANCHOR BIBLE.

As we begin the second year of these weekly commentaries, it is worth noting the significance of the practice of returning immediately to *Bereshit* after completing the reading of Deuteronomy. It conveys the point, with each new reading of the Torah, that the Torah (and the entire Bible) is a whole, that our concern is with the totality as well as the individual parts. That may seem obvious, but it is easy to lose sight of because we are used to studying the text in small units.

The weekly reading is only a few chapters in length; then the rabbi is constrained by time to comment on only a small portion of that reading—as we are in *Learn Torah With...* Likewise, in Bible study groups and in Hebrew and Sunday school classes, we usually deal with a single verse or story. We would do well to learn from Rashi, who never lost sight of the whole while making comments on the parts. His commentary implicitly reminds us at its outset that the word *Tanakh* stands for a whole composed of parts, for in commenting on Genesis 1.1 Rashi brings in citations from all parts of the Bible: from Torah (Genesis and Exodus), the Prophets (Isaiah, Jeremiah, Hosea, and Amos), and the Writings (Psalms and Proverbs). (And he did it without a concordance, let alone a computer.) Even the seemingly obvious fact that Jews study the weekly readings in order, rather than com-

---

דָּבָר אַחֵר DAVAR AHER (Another Insight). IN THE BEGINNING...[GEN. 1.1]. I appreciated Richard Elliott Friedman's wisdom in evoking the ways in which knowledge of the whole Torah, and indeed the whole *Tanakh*, enriches each part of it. But I would like to open up another dimension, one that has to do with being seven years old and learning *humash* for the first time as a student at a Hebrew day school. Because we were learning it in Hebrew, a new and uncertain language for most of us, the pace was very slow: one year for part of Genesis and the next year for the rest of it.

Even relatively brief episodes could get dragged out. I can remember having no idea what fate awaited Sodom when we learned about Lot settling there after his quarrel with Abram, and not knowing whether

בראשית ברא אלהים את

menting on whatever passage one chooses each week, reinforces the notion that, even as we focus on the component, our concern ultimately is with the full narrative, with continuity—with context.

Some things change dramatically over the course of the Hebrew Bible's story: from an undefined divine-human relationship in *parashat Bereshit* to a series of covenants in the books that follow; from a depiction of all humankind in Genesis 1.11 to a focus specifically on Israel for many books thereafter; from explicit depiction of divine power in Genesis 1 to divine hiddenness in Ezra, Nehemiah, and Esther. And as the face of God becomes more hidden through the course of the narrative, humans grow up and must take ever more responsibility for their world.

When I go to a movie or play I prefer to know as little as possible about its story in advance. Few of us are able to come to the Bible that way. It is simply too well known. But few of us experience our knowledge of things that come later in the Bible as spoiling *Bereshit* for us the way it might spoil Agatha Christie's *The Mousetrap* to know that the one who did it is the policeman. (Sorry.) When we read the difficult account of the divine beings and the human women in Genesis 6, which results in the deity's setting a 120-year limit on human life [Gen. 6.3], we gain rather than lose something by knowing that the Torah will end with an announcement that Moses lived the maximum and died at the age of 120 [Deut. 34.7]. (Let's save the well-known exceptions like Noah and Methusaleh for another year.)

SYNOPSIS: *In this sidrah the world is created in seven days, Eve and Adam have a growthful encounter in the Garden of Eden, Cain murders Abel, and the first ten generations pass.*

RASHI OF THE WEEK:

יוֹם אֶחָד YOM EHAD [Day One] [Gen. 1.5]. Why is this day numbered "Day One" while most of the other days are "the second day," "the third day," etc? To show us that the first day was the Day of there being only "One." On Day One God, alone, was the sole force in the Universe. On the second day God divided between the heavens and also divided the heavenly realm and created angels. This is explained in Bereshit Rabbah 3.8. After Day One God was not the only heavenly voice that people might hear.

Rebekah's scheme would work when she set Jacob up to deceive Isaac. Most of all, I can remember the mounting tension through the repeated visits of Jacob's sons to Egypt as I wondered whether they would ever find out that this Egyptian official who behaved in such strange ways towards them was the brother they had treated so cruelly, and then the moment of release when he finally tells them *"Ani Yosef,"* "I AM JOSEPH". The layers of association and meaning came later, but part of what I bring to these stories as we come back to them each year is the memory of reading them as a child, not knowing how they would turn out.

My Christian friends have deep associations with New Testament parables; others find all of life laid out before them in Greek myths. But none of these parables or myths speaks to me in the way that the stories in the *Tanakh* do, and I think a large part of the reason for that is my experience of learning these stories as a young child. For me, this experience is what makes the stories in the *Tanakh* ours in a way that other stories are not. On Simhat Torah these thoughts help me remember why it so important to teach Torah to our children. **Robert Chodos, <leischod@nic.wat.hookup.net>**

Likewise, we can have a richer appreciation of the story of Cain and Abel if we know that fratricide will become a recurring theme—Jacob and Esau, Joseph and his brothers, Abimelekh and his brothers, Absalom and Amnon, the woman of Tekoa's story of two brothers—culminating, presumably, in Solomon's execution of his brother Adonijah and thus establishing the stability of the Davidic line on the throne of Israel. It is no longer just a tale of Cain's fate; it is rather an introduction and first installment in an ongoing, agonizing biblical treatment of the envies, rivalries, and affections of siblings.

And we can better understand humankind's loss of the tree of life as the price of gaining knowledge of good and bad if we know that later, in the book of Proverbs, the highest form of knowledge of good and bad in the Bible—wisdom—will be characterized this way: "*It is a Tree of Life!*" [Prov. 3.18]. The garden of Eden and the tree of life are not destroyed; they are rendered inaccessible. The initial Divine–human alienation that is marked by the eviction from paradise, therefore, is not necessarily to be understood as final. The possibility of human return to a condition in which the creator is so close as to be perceived as walking among humans in the breeze of the day [Gen. 3.8] is left open. Cherubs guard the path back to the tree of life, but this, too, can be understood better if one knows what is coming: Golden cherubs will spread their wings over the ark and its contents inside the temple. The cherubs keep watch over the path to the tree of life, and their images symbolically keep watch over the keys to the path back: covenant, Torah, knowledge, wisdom.

In last year's commentary on *Parashat Bereshit* I emphasized the point—common in biblical scholarship since the work of Erich Auerbach—that the Bible is rich in background, that the events in

---

Bereshit

דָּבָר אַחֵר DAVAR AHER. And there was evening and there was morning, a second day. [Gen. 1.8]. Purposeful repetition and artful omission are a crafty duo that illuminate our texts. "It is Very Good" that not everything God created in Genesis 1 is "good." I take my class through a careful reading, asking them to note what is repeated and what is omitted. The obvious ones: Day 2 doesn't get a "good" mark. Day 3 gets a double portion of "good." (Why Tuesday is a good day for weddings in Jewish folkways becomes obvious.) When everything is done it all gets a "very good." But we note that on Day 6, although the land animals are "good," the mysterious omission is that Adam (the generic earthling) is not "good." Let's do a horizontal exercise. Let's see what's wrong with Day 2.

בראשית ברא אלהים את השמים ואת הארץ

Parashat Bereshit form an essential substratum for all that follows in the Bible's story. Every biblical scene will be laden—artistically, theologically, psychologically, spiritually—with all that has come before. The broad concern with the earth that is established in the first parashah will remain. So when the story narrows to a singular Divine relationship with Abraham, it will still be with the ultimate aim that this will be "A BLESSING TO ALL THE FAMILIES OF THE EARTH" [Gen. 12.3]. This year I want to add the opposite point: that one also has a finer sense of what is happening in each biblical episode, starting with the creation, if one reads it with consciousness of what is coming.

The sabbath is set in the very structure of the universe, but for most readers the sabbath draws its significance here in Genesis 2.1–3 not only from its being a feature of the creation but from the readers' knowledge that it is to be a prime commandment later, one of the Ten Commandments, and will be identified as the *sign* of the relationship between God and the Israelites [Ex. 31.16–17]. Just try to read about the seventh day in Genesis 2 without thinking about what Shabbat means later.

One of the most remarkable results of having a sense of the *Tanakh* as a whole when one reads the parts is this: one can experience the overwhelming irony of God's judging everything to be "good" in Genesis 1 when so much will go wrong later. The deity notes on every working day that what was created in that day is good (except on Monday, which strikes me as appropriate; anyway, we are compensated because GOD SAW THAT IT WAS GOOD twice on Tuesday). And at the end of the six days God observes that everything is, as the old translations say, EXCEEDING GOOD [Gen. 1.31]. But before we are even out of *Parashat Bereshit* we read that God begins to see THAT HUMAN EVIL WAS GREAT IN THE EARTH [Gen. 6.5]. Above all, the struggle between God and humans will recur and unfold powerfully, painfully. The day in which the humans are created is declared to be "good", but that condition will end very soon. No biblical hero or heroine will be unequivocally perfect. Individuals and nations, Israel and all of humankind will be pictured in conflict with the Creator in the great majority of the text that will follow. *Parashat Bereshit* is a portent of this coming theme, which is arguably the central story of the *Tanakh,* for its first chapter contains the creation of humans, divinely dubbed "good", and its last verses [Gen. 6.6ff.] contain the sad report that God "repented" making the humans on the earth. If one knows the course of this development in the Hebrew Bible, one can feel the irony of the account of creation, and one can feel the profound sadness of the account of the Divine decision to erase the human and animal lives from the earth's surface.

Maybe the omission of טוֹב (*tov*), "GOOD," in Day 2 will say something about the omission of "GOOD" for Adam. Maybe טוֹב "*tov*" means something more than "good." We reread Day 2. God creates a firmament (רָקִיעַ *rakiya*: like "a lid on a pot"; the root means "to hammer metal"). The image is that the firmament is a kind of ceiling with storage units. It keeps the upper waters up there (and the snow, hail, and wind). But in the meantime, down here, water covers everything; the lower waters are not contained. That is the condition of the earth when Day 2 ends.

Only in Day 3 does God gather up the waters in one place so the dry land can appear. At that point God sees that it is good. It seems that "operation water" was not finished on Day 2. Aha! Could it be that "*tov*" can also mean finished, complete? Then the artful omission of "*tov*" for Adam can mean that we are not a finished creation. Is that good news or bad news?

If we were finished, fully programmed like the animals, life would be so simple...and dull. We are the least programmed of all creation and therefore have the greatest capacity to exercise will, to learn, to create, and to change; and as it says in the *tachlis* footnotes, תְּשׁוּבָה *tshuvah* (change) is never out of fashion or out of season.
Jo Milgrom, Jerusalem.

Bereshit

It would be a shame to end this commentary on such a sorrowful note, and fortunately we don't have to, for *Parashat Bereshit* itself ends not with the deity's mournful statement that "I REGRET THAT I MADE THEM" [Gen. 6.7], but rather with a point of hope that Noah found favor in the Divine sight: "BUT NOAH FOUND FAVOR WITH THE LORD" [Gen. 6.8]. And once again, this note that there can be hope for humankind based on the acts of righteous individuals can be enriched and appreciated more if one reads it with consciousness of how the Hebrew Bible's story ends. In the latest installment in the narrative, the book of Nehemiah, God does not speak, there are no extraordinary reports of miracles, no angels, dreams, talking animals, or *urim* and *tummim;* but humans, now having to live without these things, behave better and appear to be more committed to the Torah than perhaps any other generation in the Bible. Nehemiah ends by asking his God to "REMEMBER ME FOR GOOD" [Neh. 13.31]. The fact that the Hebrew Bible's story concludes with the word "good" is an exquisite, hopeful bookend to the opening chapter of Genesis, in which everything starts out "good". As we start to read the Torah's first chapter anew this week, we will read it better if we keep this in mind. ■

דָּבָר אַחֵר DAVAR AHER. AND THE ETERNAL GOD SAID: "IT IS NOT GOOD THAT THE EARTHLING SHOULD BE ALONE; I WILL MAKE HIM A HELP THAT FITS WITH HIM" [Gen. 2.18]. In this Torah portion we learn about the making of a helpmate for Adam. This reading is located in Genesis 2.18–23. The passage contains the following ideas: God's realization that man should not be alone; the formation of every beast of the field and fowl of the air; the naming of the animals by Adam; and the separation of Adam into man and woman.

Some questions about the aspect upon which I am focusing are: (1) Why did God create the animals? (2) Why did God ask Adam to name them instead of God doing so? and (3) Why did God want Adam to experience not finding a helpmate among all the other animals?

"Why did God create the animals?" Because God thought it was not good for the man to be alone and wanted him to have a helpmate. However, Adam realized that none of the animals were good to be his mate, and they all had mates except for him. But there could also be a deeper reading of this passage. Maybe this story is in the Torah to show that Adam, the original human being, was much more than just animal, that by our nature we yearn for human company and communion with God.

This leads to an interpretation of the second question, "Why did God ask Adam to name the animals instead of God?" One interpretation is that God tried to prove to the angels that man was superior to them. An ancient Jewish legend tells us that to prove this point, God asked the angels to name the animals, but

Joel Lurie Grishaver

Joel Lurie Grishaver is the Creative Chairperson of Torah Aura Productions and the Co-Editor of *Learn Torah With...*

A Midrash on Genesis 4.10–16

The Eternal said to him: "From now on, anyone who slays Cain—before seven generations have been established—will be punished." And God put a mark on Cain so whoever met Cain would know not to kill him. Cain went from before God's face. He settled in the land of Nod (*which means* "wandering"), East of Eden [Gen. 4.15–6]. That should have been the end of it. Cain had blown it. God had done the vengeance thing, and the scene should have faded to black.

That's what it always did when they told it in Hebrew school. Cain becomes a fugitive, wanders the earth like Dr. Richard Kimble, working as a bartender one week, an elementary school janitor the next. He gets to do a good deed or two. Then his identity is discovered and he has to run. Despite the good deeds, no one is seriously going to believe that he saw a one-armed man fleeing from the scene of the crime. The story was not supposed to have a happy ending.

Looking down, we follow a pool of blood through the trampled wheat. It leads to Abel's head. He is dead. We continue a few inches along the ground, see the bloody rock. The wheat is deep yellow. The blood red stands out. There has been dialogue. Now there is silence, Cain walks away. He leaves the field. He leaves his home. He walks completely off the location for Hebrew creation. He is now on his own.

Meanwhile in Iran, as the story goes, Gayomart had died. From his grave a fruit tree grew. Then the fruit tree separated into Mashya, the first man, and Mashyane, the first woman. The two of

---

they could not. He then sent the animals to Adam to see what he would call them. Adam succeeded in naming all the animals, thus demonstrating superior intelligence, or at least advanced knowledge of zoology, at that point a very young science.

But there is also a deeper interpretation that has to do with human nature. In the ancient world, to know something's inner name was to know its nature...have power over it. By having Adam give names to the animals, God is again showing us in this story that the human being is more than an animal. Unlike the animals, we have the power of speech. By giving the animals their names we show our dominion over them. And just as God has dominion over us and treats us with love and compassion, we have to treat animals with love and compassion.

Finally, in reference to question 3, "Why did God want Adam to experience not finding a helpmate in all the animals?" Adam had to experience his own

them mated, and after fifty years of fertility difficulties (but that's another myth) they produced children. After a lot of personal growth and valuable experience Cain met and courted one of the first people of the Zoroastrian cultural area. CAIN KNEW HIS WOMAN. SHE GAVE BIRTH TO A SON. SHE GOT PREGNANT AND GAVE BIRTH TO ENOCH. HE BUILT A TOWN AND CALLED THE NAME OF THE TOWN LIKE THE NAME OF HIS SON, ENOCH [Gen. 4.17].

Meanwhile, all over the world, the children of first people of each religion and culture began wandering, meeting and mingling with the people and truths of other cultural areas. So the children who thought they came from Ra in Egypt courted the offspring of those who thought that they came from the clay dolls made by mother earth in Madagascar.

Those who thought they came from the union of Luonnatar (the virgin daughter of the goddess Ilma of Finland) and a male duck left home. They met and mingled with those who believed they were the descendants of the first people molded out of the ground of West Africa by Olorun and Orisha Nla.

Those who thought their origin was in the union of Yin and Yang in China, who believed that they evolved through the giant Pangu who grew at the rate of ten feet a day, also left their home. Such is human nature. Some married and lived with the descendants of those in Japan who believed that they grew from the heavenly union of Izanagi and Izanami and their struggles. Others met and married those of the Iroquois nation who thought that a chief's daughter fell down a hole in the world along with a tree and, after getting the advice of the great turtle, birthed the first people. Her descendants knew that she was the mother of all life. And they met and mingled and built new lives with those who descended from other mothers of all life.

Bereshit

loneliness in order to understand his need for a mate. In an ancient Jewish legend we are told that the original human being was created male and female, just as the Torah says, but then it adds more detail: One side of the human was male and one side was female, implying that they could never see or meet each other. This legend also tells us that Eve was not created from Adam's rib, but from Adam's side. God placed the human being, which is what the Hebrew word Adam means, into a deep sleep, and split Adam into Adam and Eve.

For me, one of the most interesting implications of this legend is the new image of the first human being that I have in my mind as I read my Torah portion. As I see Adam naming the animals I see a human being that is both male and female, not only male. My main teaching about my Torah portion is that everyone has another half, meaning that no

God works in mysterious ways. As it is written: LISTEN: THESE ARE BUT THE OUTSKIRTS OF GOD'S HIGHWAYS. WE HEAR JUST A SMALL WHISPER. NO ONE CAN UNDERSTAND THE THUNDER OF GOD'S POWER [Job 26.14]. Each of us in our own ways is Cain, needing to leave home in order to make one of our own. Each of us is the child of a mother of all life. ■

---

one should be alone. The story of creation gives new meaning in my own life by giving me a sense of where I came from. The idea of Adam searching for another half, separated from its partner and looking for a fitting helpmate, reminds me of my own father looking for his other half. The passage helps me to understand his not finding his other half with my birth mother. It also helps me to understand how his marriage to Lori, my adopted mom, reflects how God feels that one should not be alone and how we all have our own halves perfectly fit for ourselves.

I realize from my Torah portion that we human beings are created lonely, created with the need to find human company and, most especially, a mate. We are taught that we are not animals and won't find ultimate human meaning or happiness in just following our animal nature. I know that life can be tough, and not everyone finds their mate, at least not in their first marriage. Somehow I sense that my dad and mom hope I won't find my mate for about another thirty-five years. **Heath Adam Gibson, Bar Mitzvah, Ohr HaTorah, Los Angeles, CA.**

דָּבָר אַחֵר DAVAR AHER. **CAIN SAID TO THE ETERNAL, "MY PUNISHMENT IS TOO GREAT."** [Gen. 4.14]. The Cain story is disturbing not only for the violence, which is the first human interaction (after sex and birth) outside of the garden of Eden; it is disturbing because there's no hopeful ending. Cain has struck out. He is alienated from his nature (a sedentary farmer, he is now forced to wander), from his work (the earth is cursed because of this crime), and from God [I HIDE FROM YOUR FACE, Gen. 4.14]. Where is his rehabilitation, if we are to learn something from this story? I direct the reader to the most healing modern midrash I have found to date, an article called *The Evolution of the Blemished Priest* by Jonathan Omer-man, published in the premier edition of *New Traditions*. (Alas, I do not have the date.) Essentially Omer-man says that the mark of Cain (the Bible artfully omits identifying what exactly that mark is) is his obsession with his evil deed, his blemish. We are all blemished, incomplete, as we learned in Genesis 1.

Omer-man continues: If your illness, your handicap, your evil deed takes over your life, in a sense you become the blemish. The blemish becomes the core around which everything else orbits. Omer-man asks how we can see God in our blemished state. How can we get on with our lives after the disaster? Midrash keeps the Bible endlessly contemporary. **Jo Milgrom, Jerusalem.**

דָּבָר אַחֵר DAVAR AHER.
IN THE BEGINNING... [GEN. 1.1].
This unsigned "Midrash" has been drifting around the Internet for the past year (at least); our first copy came from Janice Tytell.

In the beginning there was the computer. And God said

%>Let there be light!

#Enter user id.

%>God

#Enter password.

%>Omniscient

#Password incorrect. Try again.

%>Omnipotent

#Password incorrect. Try again.

%>Technocrat

#And God logged on at 12:01:00 AM, Sunday, March 1.

%>Let there be light!

#Unrecognizable command. Try again.

%>Create light

#Done.

%>Run heaven and earth

#And God created day and night. And God saw there were 0 errors.

#And God logged off at 12:02:00 AM, Sunday, March 1.

#Approx. funds remaining: $92.50.

Bereshit

#And God logged on at 12:01:00 AM, Monday, March 2.

%>Let there be firmament in the midst of water and light

#Unrecognizable command. Try again.

%>Create firmament

#Done.

%>Run firmament

#And God divided the waters. And God saw there were 0 errors.

#And God logged off at 12:02:00 AM, Monday, March 2.

#Approx. funds remaining: $84.60.

#And God logged on at 12:01:00 AM, Tuesday, March 3.

%>Let the waters under heaven be gathered together unto one place and let the dry land appear and

#Too many characters in specification string. Try again.

%>Create dry_land

#Done.

%>Run firmament

#And God divided the waters. And God saw there were 0 errors.

#And God logged off at 12:02:00 AM, Tuesday, March 3.

> #Approx. funds remaining: $65.00.

#And God logged on at 12:01:00 AM, Wednesday, March 4.

%>Create lights in the firmament to divide the day from the night

#Unspecified type. Try again.

%>Create sun_moon_stars

#Done.

%>Run sun_moon_stars

#And God divided the waters. And God saw there were 0 errors.

#And God logged off at 12:02:00 AM, Wednesday, March 4.

#Approx. funds remaining: $54.00.

#And God logged on at 12:01:00 AM, Thursday, March 5.

%>Create fish

#Done.

%>Create fowl

#Done.

%>Run fish, fowl

#And God created the great sea monsters and every living creature that creepeth wherewith the waters swarmed after its kind and every winged fowl after its kind. And God saw there were 0 errors.

#And God logged off at 12:02:00 AM, Thursday, March 5.

#Approx. funds remaining: $45.00.

#And God logged on at 12:01:00 AM, Friday, March 6.

%>Create cattle

#Done.

%>Create creepy_things

#Done.

%>Now let us make man in our image

#Unspecified type. Try again.

%>Create man

#Done.

%>Be fruitful and multiply and replenish the earth and subdue it and have dominion over the fish of the sea and over the fowl of the air and over every living thing that creepeth upon the earth

#Too many command operands. Try again.

%>Run multiplication

#Execution terminated. 6 errors.

%>Insert breath

#Done.

%>Run multiplication

#Execution terminated. 5 errors.

%>Move man to garden of Eden

#File garden of Eden does not exist.

%>Create garden.edn

#Done.

%>Move man to garden.edn

#Done.

%>Run multiplication

#Execution terminated. 4 errors.

%>Copy woman from man

#Done.

%>Run multiplication

#Execution terminated. 3 errors.

%>Insert woman into man

#Illegal parameters. Try again.

%>Insert man into woman

#Done.

%>Run multiplication

#Execution terminated. 2 errors.

%>Create desire

#Done.

%>Run multiplication

#And God saw man and woman being fruitful and multiplying in garden.edn

#Warning: No time limit on this run. 1 errors.

%>Create freewill

#Done.

%>Run freewill

#And God saw man and woman being fruitful and multiplying in garden.edn

#Warning: No time limit on this run. 1 errors.

%>Undo desire

#Desire cannot be undone once freewill is created.

%>Destroy freewill

#Freewill is an inaccessible file and cannot be destroyed.

#Enter replacement, cancel, or ask for help.

%>Help

#Desire cannot be undone once freewill is created.

#Freewill is an inaccessible file and cannot be destroyed.

#Enter replacement, cancel, or ask for help.

%>Create tree-of-knowledge

#And God saw man and woman being fruitful and multiplying in garden.edn

#Warning: No time limit on this run. 1 errors.

%>Create good, evil

#Done.

%>Activate evil

#And God saw he had created shame.

#Warning system error in sector E95. Man and woman not in garden.edn.

#1 errors.

%>Scan garden.edn for man, woman

#Search failed.

%>Delete shame

#Shame cannot be deleted once evil has been activated.

%>Destroy freewill

#Freewill is an inaccessible file and cannot be destroyed.

#Enter replacement, cancel, or ask for help.

%>Stop

#Unrecognizable command. Try again

%>Break

%>Break

%>Break

#ATTENTION ALL USERS *** ATTENTION ALL USERS: COMPUTER GOING DOWN FOR REGULAR DAY OF MAINTENANCE AND REST IN FIVE MINUTES. PLEASE LOG OFF.

%>Create new world

#You have exceeded your allocated file space. You must destroy old files before new ones can be created.

%>Destroy earth

#Destroy earth: Please confirm.

%>Destroy earth confirmed

#COMPUTER DOWN *** COMPUTER DOWN. SERVICES WILL RESUME SUNDAY, MARCH 8 AT 6:00 AM. YOU MUST SIGN OFF NOW.

#And God logged off at 11:59:59 PM, Friday, March 6.

#Approx. funds remaining: $0.00.

Parashat Noah
Genesis 6.8–11.32

Arthur Waskow

ARTHUR WASKOW IS A PATHFINDER OF ALEPH: ALLIANCE FOR JEWISH RENEWAL. HE FOUNDED AND DIRECTS THE SHALOM CENTER, A DIVISION OF ALEPH THAT FOCUSES ON JEWISH THOUGHT AND PRACTICE TO PROTECT AND HEAL THE EARTH. SINCE 1969, WASKOW HAS BEEN ONE OF THE LEADING CREATORS OF THEORY, PRACTICE, AND INSTITUTIONS FOR THE MOVEMENT FOR JEWISH RENEWAL. HE FOUNDED AND EDITS THE JOURNAL *NEW MENORAH* AND IS THE AUTHOR OF *THE FREEDOM SEDER* (HENRY HOLT & CO., 1970); *GODWRESTLING* (SCHOCKEN, 1978); *SEASONS OF OUR JOY* (BANTAM, 1982; REVISED ED., BEACON, 1991); *THESE HOLY SPARKS: THE REBIRTH OF THE JEWISH PEOPLE* (HARPER AND ROW, 1983); *DOWN-TO-EARTH JUDAISM: FOOD, MONEY, SEX, AND THE REST OF LIFE* (WILLIAM MORROW, 1995) AND *GODWRESTLING, ROUND TWO: ANCIENT WISDOM, FUTURE PATHS* (JEWISH LIGHTS, 1995).

Haftorah for the Rainbow Covenant

[Blessed are You, the Breath of Life, Who makes of every human throat a shofar for the breathing of Your truth.]

You, My people, burnt in fire,
still staring blinded
by the flame and smoke,
that rose from Auschwitz and from Hiroshima.

You, My people,
Battered by the earthquakes
of a planet in convulsion.

You, My people,
Drowning in the flood of words and images
That beckon you to eat and eat,
to drink and drink,
to fill and overfill
your bellies
at the tables of
the gods of wealth and power.

You, My people,
Drowning in the flood of words and images
that poured unceasing on your eyes and ears,
drown out My words of Torah,
My visions of the earth made whole.

Be comforted.

I have for you a mission full of joy,
I call you to a task of celebration.

I call you to make from fire not an all-consuming blaze,

דָּבָר אַחֵר DAVAR AHER. THIS IS THE FAMILY-HISTORY OF NOAH. [Gen. 6.9]. I have always felt badly for poor Noah. He is the only person in the world—his family notwithstanding—chosen by God to survive. The opening sentence of the Torah reading contains two pieces of information: (1) Noah was a righteous person in his generation, and (2) אֶת-הָאֱלֹהִים הִתְהַלֶּךְ-נֹחַ. *Et ha-Elohim hit-haLekh-Noah,* NOAH WALKED WITH GOD. He must have been quite an individual, yet traditional commentators through the centuries look at this lone survivor of total devastation and shrug.

Noah is never allowed to enjoy his accomplishments, for he is always compared to Abraham. Noah is called "RIGHTEOUS FOR HIS GENERATION." The commentators tell us that if Noah had lived in the generation of Abraham, he would have been

But the light in which all beings
see each other fully,
All different,
All bearing One Spark,
I call you to light a flame to see
more clearly,
That the earth and all who live as
part of it,
Are not for burning,
A flame to see
the rainbow
in the many-colored faces
of all life.

I call you,
I, the Breath of Life,
Within you and beyond,
Among you and beyond,
That One Who breathes from
redwood into grizzly,
That One Who breathes from
human into swamp grass,
That One Who breathes the great
pulsations of the galaxies,
In every breath you breathe Me,
In every breath, I breathe you.

I call you,
In every croak of every frog I call
you,
In every rustle of each leaf,
each life,
I call you,
In the wailings of the wounded
earth,
I call you.

I call you to a peoplehood
renewed,
I call you to reweave the fabric of
your folk
and so to join in healing
the weave of life upon your
planet,
I call you to a journey of seven
generations.

For seven generations past
the earth has not been able to
make Shabbos,
And so in your own generation
You tremble on the verge of
Flood,
Your air is filled with poison,

---

totally ignored! Moreover, with regard to Noah we are told that he WALKED WITH GOD, whereas with Abraham the Torah tells us God said, הִתְהַלֵּךְ לְפָנַי (*hit-haLakh l'Fanai*) WALK BEFORE ME [Gen. 17.1]. It is, say the rabbis of the Talmud, like a parent who has two children, one mature and the other a child. To the first child the parent says, "You can go on ahead," while to the young child the parent says, "Stay at my side" [*Bereshit Rabbah* 30.10].

In the Talmud Rabbi Berekhya asks why Noah did not at least pray for his generation to do תְּשׁוּבָה *tshuvah* and be saved. Apparently Noah's piety did not extend to a concern about the welfare of others. We have no report of his going out to warn the people around him that a terrible flood was about to destroy them.

SYNOPSIS: *Flood. Covenant. Post-flood abominations. Geneology. Tower of Babel.*

RASHI OF THE WEEK: *At the end of the Rainbow Covenant God says:* "AND IT WILL BE WHEN I CLOUD THE EARTH WITH CLOUDS, THAT THE BOW SHALL BE SEEN IN THE CLOUDS" [GEN. 9.14]. This means "When it arises in My mind to bring darkness and destruction on the earth." *Because clouds are a symbol of the Divine shadow. Then God says:* "AND I WILL REMEMBER MY COVENANT IS (1) BETWEEN ME, (2) BETWEEN YOU, AND (3) AND BETWEEN EVERY LIFE FORCE" (Gen. 9.15). *Why are there three parties to this contract? God says:* This is a contract between (1) ELOHIM, my higher *Midat ha-Din* (my Justice side), and (2) YOU. Otherwise it would have just said "BETWEEN ME AND BETWEEN ALL LIFE." But this is the midrash that *this extra clause reveals—* "When my *Midat ha-Din* comes to accuse YOU, to hold you responsible *for your actions,* I will see the sign and remember *my covenant with* EVERY LIFE FORCE." *Adam Badik once said God is MPD—this is one of the times that it is very good. This balancing of urges and higher purposes is another way we are created in the Divine image.*

The rain, the seas, with poison,
The earth hides arsenals of
poisonous fire,
Seeds of light surcharged with fatal
darkness,
The ice is melting,
The seas are rising,
The air is dark with smoke and
rising heat.

And so—I call you to carry to all
peoples,
the teaching that for seven
generations,
the earth and all her earthlings
learn to rest.

I call you once again,
To speak for Me,
To speak for Me because I have no
voice,
To speak the Name of the One who
has no Name,
To speak for all the Voiceless of the
planet.

Who speaks for the redwood and
the rock,
the lion and the beetle?

My Breath I blow through you into
a voicing,
Speak for the redwood and the
rock,
the lion and the beetle.

I call you to a task of joy,
For seven generations,
this is what I call for you to do.

To make once more the seasons of
your joy
into celebrations of the seasons of
the earth,
To welcome with your candles the
dark of moon and sun,
To bless with careful chewing
the fruits of every tree,
For when you meet to bless
the rising juice of life
in every tree trunk
I am the Tree of Life.

To live seven days in the open,
windy huts,
And call out truth to all who live
beside you,
You are part of the weave and
breath of life,

Noah

Nor are we told that he pleaded with them to change their evil ways and to save themselves. Noah, it appears, was more concerned with his own safety and survival than he was with the survival of his friends and neighbors.

The comparisons continue through the ages as the question is asked, Why did Noah not protest when God informed him that the world is to be destroyed? After all, Abraham argued with God when the cities of Sodom and Gomorrah were to be annihilated.

A further indictment comes from the commentator who argues that Noah really had no faith, doubting what God had told him. Noah could not believe that such a destruction would take place. Therefore, he kept the information to himself rather than sharing it with others. Instead of warning them—giving

You cannot make walls to wall it out.
I call you to a covenant between the generations,
That when you gather for a blessing of your children
as they take on the tasks of new tomorrows,
You say to them, they say to you,
That you are all My prophets,
Come to turn the hearts of parents
and of children toward each other,
Lest My earth be smashed in utter desolation.

I call you
To eat what
I
call
kosher
Food that springs from an earth you do not poison,
Oil that flows from an earth you do not drain,
Paper that comes from an earth you do not slash,
Air that comes from an earth you do not choke.

I call you to speak
to all the peoples,
all the rulers.

I call you to walk forth before all nations,
to pour out water that is free of poison
and call them all to clean and clarify the rains of winter.

I call you to beat your willows on the earth
and shout its healing to all peoples.

I call on you to call on all the peoples
to cleanse My Breath, My air
from all the gases
that turn My earth into a furnace.

I call you to light the colors of the Rainbow,
To raise once more before all eyes
That banner of the covenant between Me,
and all the children of Noah and Naamah,
and all that lives and breathes upon the Earth,
So that
never again,
all the days of the earth, shall
sowing and harvest,
cold and heat,
summer and winter,
day and night,
ever cease!

I call you to love the Breath of Life,

For love is the fire

That blazes in the Rainbow. ■

---

them a chance to appeal to God or to build their own arks—he said nothing.

Some commentators, like me, are bothered that Noah is not given his due. A fascinating midrash tells us that Noah—and God—did, indeed, give the generation of the flood a chance to change their ways. God tells Noah: עֲשֵׂה לְךָ תֵּבַת עֲצֵי-גֹפֶר (*Asay l'kha Teyvat Atzay-Gofer*) "MAKE FOR YOURSELF AN ARK OF CEDAR WOOD" [Gen. 6.14]. The midrash tells us that Noah went out and planted cedar trees, and from these trees came the wood to make the ark. How long does it take for a forest to grow? It took Noah 120 years—three entire generations—before he could build the ark. His neighbors constantly asked him, "Why these cedars?" Noah would reply, "The Holy One is about to bring a flood upon the world, and God told me to build an ark so that I and my family might escape." His neighbors and friends mocked him and ridiculed him.

In the meantime he watered the cedars, and they kept growing. Young and old continued to ask him, "What are you doing?" Noah always gave the same reply and always received the same ridicule. Finally, he cut the cedars down, and as he sawed them into planks he was again asked, "What are you doing?" He replied, "I am doing what I said I would do," even as he continued to warn the generation of the flood. When they did not change their ways even then, the Holy One allowed the flood to come. [*Tanhuma, Noah* 5.]

What is clear from all sources is that Noah's righteousness has nothing to do with Abraham. The debate is simply whether Noah listened to God and did exactly what he was told without question, or if Noah worked with God to do something that might change the world. To be a "righteous" person one must take action that might make a difference in the world. Just as we should not

Rabbi Patricia Karlin-Neumann

PATRICIA KARLIN-NEUMANN IS THE RABBI FOR TEMPLE ISRAEL IN ALAMEDA, CALIFORNIA. SHE HAS SERVED AS A HILLEL DIRECTOR AT THE CLAREMONT COLLEGES AND UCLA. SHE LIVES IN THE BAY AREA WITH HER HUSBAND, GEORGE (A BIOLOGIST AND TEACHER OF TAI CHI), AND THEIR CHILDREN, CHANA ELIZA AND ZEV MICHAEL.

This was a wet year. In the Sierras the snow pack was heavy. In late spring, as the snow melted, creeks became rivers; waterfalls and cascades were abundant in places they had not been in many years. Later in the summer, when the water was less prodigious, it was possible to see more clearly the effect of its power—rocks worn smooth from the rushing water, deep round potholes formed by eddies, sand wiped clean by the constant flow. The earth transformed by water.

In the story of the flood the earth is transformed by water in a more mythic and dramatic way. The maftir of *Bereshit*, the parashah of creation, gives an indication of the undoing. Adonai said, "I WILL BLOT OUT FROM THE EARTH THE MEN WHOM I CREATED—MEN TOGETHER WITH BEASTS, CREEPING THINGS, AND BIRDS OF THE SKY, FOR I REGRET THAT I MADE THEM" [Gen. 6.7]. It would have been quite straightforward for God to destroy the humans alone. But through human agency the earth itself had become corrupt. The word earth, *eretz*, appears ten times in this section before God's promise to establish the first covenant [Gen. 6.18]. It is not just humans who will experience the flood, but the very earth—indeed, all of creation—will be transformed.

The language of the story of the flood is similar to and the reverse of the language of *Bereshit*. The flood itself is called מַבּוּל *mabbul*—a word found only in the context of this catastrophe. Nahum Sarna suggests that מַבּוּל *mabbul* is a technical term meaning that the heavenly part of the original cosmic

---

Noah

compare two children, so, too, righteousness can never be a matter of comparison. **Rabbi Rick Sherwin, Beth El Congregation, Phoenix, AZ.**

דָּבָר אַחֵר DAVAR AHER. THIS IS THE FAMILY-HISTORY OF NOAH. [Gen. 6.9]. This is a midrash, another version of the Noah story. [*Yalhut Shimoni* 1,42.]

Noah was supposed to be the Messiah. It had been written in the primordial Torah that Noah was supposed to be the Messiah. (Like the Messiah, he was born without the need for *brit milah*; like the Messiah, his "middle name" was Menahem.) Noah hit the ground running. All through his life he did the right things when everyone else did the wrong things. All through his life he tried to change people by helping them, by showing them the ethical way to do things, and even by telling them that what they were doing was wrong. Noah tried to be a teacher and a saint and a

ocean was allowed to fall upon the earth, in effect reuniting the primordial waters that had been separated at the creation. The rhythm of nature established in Genesis 1.14 is suspended during the *mabbul*, only to be reestablished after the flood in Genesis 8.22. The Divine blessing to be fruitful and multiply given to Adam is interrupted by the *mabbul* but restated to Noah. And the first covenant in the Torah follows this blessing.

What is going on here? Some have suggested that the flood was an expression of divine rage. In Peter Pitzele's provocative and thoughtful book *Our Fathers' Wells* he describes the God of the flood as a "playwright who destroys his play in a fit of pique and after his characters have taken on a life of their own and repel the creator's moral sense." But the promise of a covenant, the involvement of the earth, the intricate weaving of the elements of creation suggest that God was doing something more intentional and more enduring.

In the description of the מַבּוּל *mabbul* a scant three lines are devoted to the destruction of all flesh [Gen. 7.21–23]. Yet we read in great detail of the journey of the water, its sources, its levels, its duration. We read of how the waters lifted the ark, floated the ark, submerged the mountains. The earth was immersed in water as if, teaches Rabbi Chaim Seidler-Feller, the *mabbul* became a giant mikvah—surrounding the earth, purifying it, renewing it. Rather than the *mabbul* as the ultimate destruction, the *mabbul* is the ultimate cleansing. Just as one enters the mikvah with every part of one's body open to its waters, so the great mikvah of the *mabbul* touched all the earth, even to the highest mountains, immersing and transforming it.

It is as if God said, "Take two." Following the mikvah is the resumption of natural time [Gen. 8.22], the blessing for fertility [Gen. 9.1], and the creation of the first covenant [Gen. 9.8ff.]. Indeed, it is the very covenant, whose sign in a bow hung up in the clouds, a bow no longer to be shot against the earth and humanity, that confirms this purification. It is as if the bow will now hold up the clouds, preventing them from unleashing the water that had covered the earth. God has entered into a new relationship with humanity and the earth. There will not be another *mabbul*. Now it is up to us to protect the earth that has been purified on our behalf. ■

---

friend all rolled up in one. But this did no good. A messiah can't bring redemption unless people work with him. Instead, the people picked on Noah and his family and went out of their way to be mean to him.

Noah started to build the ark. It took a long time, more than a hundred years—I don't remember the exact number. But every day people would come along and make fun of him. They said, "Noah, who can't finish anything, is going to finish this? Ridiculous!" They laughed. They tagged the ark with rude and crude graffiti. And every day he went back and built and talked and got ignored and put up with the abuse. [*Yalhut Shimoni* 1,42.]

That is more or less where the midrash ends officially (as far as I know), but I think I know the rest of the story. The closer the ark got to being finished, the worse things got. When the animals came on board it became dangerous to go outside. Noah took to preaching from the top of the ark while people threw things at him. Each day he would try to find a good person or two to help out—to be saved by joining in the saving of the world. God said anyone who did תִּקּוּן עוֹלָם *tikkun olam* (world saving) would be saved. But no one would help. Noah would sneak out of the ark in a costume and try to find someone secretly doing good. He found no one. Even the children were mean. One night on the way back to the ark he was discovered, stripped naked, and beaten. He picked up his clothes. He dressed himself. He walked back to the ark crying. "I just want to help them help themselves—and there is nothing I can do!"

He flung himself down on his bed. The rest of his family joined him. They cried together about the loneliness and the pain. They cried about the hurt—and about the failure. Their

Noah

small room at the bottom of the ark was filled with tears. While they were crying God closed the door to the ark. Noah and his family cried. The heavens opened, and rain began to fall. That is how the flood began. That is why no one else was saved. How do you feel about that Noah?

There is also a midrash [*Pirke d'Rabbi Eliezer* 23] that Og the King of Bashan clung onto the side of the ark when the flood waters were rising and found a way to hang on. Noah punched a hole in the side of the ark and fed him every day throughout the whole flood. **Joel Lurie Grishaver, <joel@torahaura.com>**

דָּבָר אַחֵר DAVAR AHER. AND THE RAIN WAS UPON THE EARTH FORTY DAYS AND FORTY NIGHTS [Gen. 7.12]. It's easy to see the connection between the liturgical embellishment to the *Amidah* מַשִּׁיב הָרוּחַ וּמוֹרִיד הַגָּשֶׁם *Mashiv ha-Ruah u'Morid ha-Gashem*, "THE ONE WHO CAUSES THE WINDS/SPIRITS TO BLOW AND THE RAIN TO FALL"—added to the *Gevurot* from Shemini Atzeret—and in the year cycle, the Torah cycle *Parashat Noah* is read after this reading is begun. A second level regarding this connection requires comment. Perhaps it is also a plea to God (given the anticipated cleansing waters of the flood) "to enliven our spirit and bring down the saving waters." **Rabbi Kerry M. Olitzky, Hebrew Union College—Jewish Institute of Religion, <Olitzky@huc.edu>**

דָּבָר אַחֵר DAVAR AHER. AND THE RAIN WAS UPON THE EARTH FORTY DAYS AND FORTY NIGHTS [Gen. 7.12]. Regarding Rabbi Olitzky's comment on the prayers for rain and *Parashat Noah*: In addition to the Shemini Atzeret prayer and the change that follows in the second בְּרָכָה *brakhah* of the *Amidah*, we also make another change in the בְּרָכָה *brakhah* of the daily prayers, from "Bestow dew for a blessing" to "Bestow dew and rain for a blessing." This change, however, we don't make until 7 Heshvan. Most commentators hold that the flood rains in Noah's time began on 17 Heshvan. We are perhaps modifying our prayer for rain to make sure that we ask the rain to come FOR A BLESSING, lest we be reminded too much of Noah's fate. **Tamar Frankiel, <AR410@lafn.org>**

דָּבָר אַחֵר DAVAR AHER. AND GOD BLOTTED OUT THE ENTIRE SPECIES FROM THE EARTH, AND NOAH REMAINED ALONE. [Gen. 7.23]. ***PARASHAT NOAH AS HOME ALONE*:** Noah just does not quite make it. In spite of the fact that he almost singlehandedly saved the world, fed it, and cultivated a new lease on life for an otherwise obliterated planet, he hardly gets the fame and recognition that his decedents Abraham, Isaac, and Jacob receive. In fact, Noah's biography is summed up in this week's reading, "AND HE BLOTTED OUT THE ENTIRE SPECIES FROM THE EARTH, AND NOAH REMAINED ALONE" [Gen. 7.23].

Noah leads the lonely existence of the sole survivor, and his place in history (especially in Jewish history) is hardly monumental. What is the flaw that limits Noah to less than patriarchal stature? Why isn't the sole savior of humanity counted with the great acclamation that is bestowed upon our forefathers? Why is Noah not considered the first, if not the foremost, of our forefathers?

Despite overt differences between Abraham and Noah, there is one small similarity that would seemingly link the two leaders—they both planted. In Genesis 9.21 the Torah tells us, "AND NOAH THE MAN OF THE EARTH PLANTED A VINEYARD. HE DRANK OF THE WINE AND BECAME DRUNK." In Genesis 21.33 we read, "AND ABRAHAM PLANTED AN ESHEL IN BEER-SHEBA." Rashi points out that there are conflicting views as to the exact interpretation of "eshel." Some say he planted an orchard intending to feed hungry wayfarers. Others explain that an eshel is an inn, that Abraham built a lodge for travelers to rest. No matter which interpretation appeals to you, the stark contrast between Noah and Abraham is obvious. Abraham plants for others, Noah for himself. Abraham's goal in life was to educate, nurture, and teach other people about Ha-Shem. Noah, on the other hand, spent more than a century building an ark and was not able to recruit a single passenger. He leaves the ark and gets drunk—lost in his own world.

One of America's largest kosher confectioners was a major supporter of Beth Medrash Gevoah, the Yeshiva ad Kollel founded by the late Rabbi Aaron Kotler and led for twenty years by his late son Rabbi Shneur Kotler. At one major national function the industrialist had the occasion to introduce Rabbi Shneur. He did so in a most unique manner. "Actually," he proclaimed, "the Reb Shneur and I have much in common. We both went to *heder* in Europe, survived the war, and now we both run major institutions. We provide the public with an excellent product, of that is both sweet and enjoyable. Many people stand in line to speak to me, and many people wait in line to speak to the good rabbi. We both are well known and try to offer our advice as we help others. However, there is one major difference between us." The magnate paused and smiled. "I make lollipops, and Rabbi Kotler makes men. We all produce. The question that we all must ask ourselves is 'Who are we producing for?' Are we generating fruit that will be used to benefit mankind, or are we providing ourselves with fruit for self-indulgence?"

Noah had the opportunity to save many more than he did. He could have been the father of mankind and perhaps, as a man who had direct contact with the Creator, could have replaced Abraham as the founder of Judaism. Despite his personal greatness and an ability to overcome the terrible tide of corruption and immorality that condemned his generation, Noah still did not take advantage of a momentous opportunity. He was not able to nurture and save his generation. "AND NOAH REMAINED ALONE." He became drunk. Abraham planted an orchard of generosity. He flourished. Abraham made men; Noah made wine. **Rabbi Mordechai Kamenetzky, Yeshiva of South Shore, <Ateres@aol.com>**

דָּבָר אַחֵר DAVAR AHER. THIS IS THE FAMILY-HISTORY OF NOAH [Gen. 6.9]. When God decided to destroy the world, I think this was the worst state God had ever been in. Rabbi Patricia Karlin-Neumann points out the severe words God used:

וַיֹּאמֶר יהוה אֶמְחֶה אֶת-הָאָדָם אֲשֶׁר-
בָּרָאתִי מֵעַל פְּנֵי הָאֲדָמָה מֵאָדָם עַד-
בְּהֵמָה עַד-רֶמֶשׂ וְעַד-עוֹף הַשָּׁמָיִם
כִּי נִחַמְתִּי כִּי עֲשִׂיתִם.

Va-Yomer Adonai Emhe et ha-Adam Asher Barati Ma'al P'nei ha-Adamah m'Adam Ad B'hama Ad Remes v'Ad Of ha-Shamayim Ki n'Hamti Ki Asitim.

"I WILL BLOT OUT FROM THE EARTH THE MEN WHOM I CREATED—MEN TOGETHER WITH BEASTS, CREEPING THINGS, AND BIRDS OF THE SKY, FOR I REGRET THAT I MADE THEM" [Gen. 6–7].

I think that God didn't even give a second thought before wiping away the earth. God was so outraged that God just destroyed. I would give credit to God here for destroying the evil. But why destroy the good, too? If I were God, I'd plan better whom to destroy and whom to save.

So God was determined to destroy the world and chose Noah to be the leader of all the survivors. But why Noah? Was Noah a righteous man? If Noah were living now, the answer would be "of course not." But in the earth's corrupt state of being, he was then considered a righteous man. (I learned this point from Rabbi Philip Lazowski.)

A convincing reason that Noah was not a righteous man is the following: Noah did obey God, but he did not really care for others. He was definitely not a prophet, because he

Noa<u>h</u>

didn't argue with the people or even bring the message to them. Noah did not really try to make them believe.

But is righteousness a fixed value? Do you have to do a certain number of mitzvot? Or not be involved with bad things—like drugs? I don't think this is the case. I think righteousness may vary in different circumstances. Take Oscar Schindler, for instance. He was a German gentile and not particularly righteous in his personal life. But during the Holocaust he saved Jewish lives by hiring Jews to work in his factory. So while he was not sacrificing his life, he did help Jews avoid the concentration camps.

God chose Noah to be the leader of the "surviving creation." God told Noah to build an ark made out of gopher wood. Noah was told to take his wife, their sons, and their sons' wives. He also had to take two of every kind of animal. But in chapter 7, verse 2, it says: "OF EVERY CLEAN BEAST THOU SHALT TAKE TO THEE SEVEN PLUS SEVEN, EACH WITH HIS MATE". In Biblical terms, "clean" means animals fit for sacrifice. Wouldn't that be impossible? The ark is only 300 cubits long. Imagine: fourteen bulls? I think that the number two seems more correct, for the practical space and for equality. I don't think God would divide the animals like that. I think God just told Noah to take two of every kind, one male and one female.

In conclusion, I think that Noah was a good leader, but definitely not a righteous one. Definitely not one to trust your life with. I do not think that righteousness is decided by how many mitzvot you do, or by how many lives you save. It all depends on what's happening around you. For instance, it's harder to be one good person when the circumstances around you are all bad. I also feel a little frightened of the power God has, and how it was executed so very long ago. **Micha Effron, grade 7, Solomon Schecter Day School, West Hartford, CT.**

לך לך מארצך ממולדך

Brit Milah

"SUCH SHALL BE THE COVENANT BETWEEN ME AND YOU AND YOUR OFFSPRING TO FOLLOW WHICH YOU SHALL KEEP: EVERY MALE AMONG YOU SHALL BE CIRCUMCISED." AND GOD SAID TO ABRAHAM, "AS FOR YOUR WIFE SARAI, YOU SHALL NOT CALL HER SARAI, BUT HER NAME SHALL BE CALLED SARAH. I WILL BLESS HER, INDEED I WILL GIVE YOU A SON BY HER. I WILL BLESS HER SO THAT SHE SHALL GIVE RISE TO NATIONS; RULERS OF PEOPLES SHALL ISSUE FROM HER" [Gen. 17.9-16].

Perhaps no commandment in the Torah is more difficult, more divisive, more perplexing than circumcision. Is it possible for feminism to save it, to inject into this male covenantal ceremony some sense of shared meaning other than lame jokes and awkward silences? Perhaps, if we allow ourselves the power of modern midrash and expand our understanding of symbolism and metaphor in the ceremony.

Scholars all agree that circumcision may be one of the most ancient tribal practices we have recorded. We know from biblical and other sources that the Egyptians, Ammonites, Edomites, and Moabites all practiced it. Among most it was done at marriage or puberty, as a "sacrifice" to insure fertility. (The ancient link between removing the foreskin and marriage may be established in the biblical account of Zipporah and Moses, when in Exodus 4.25, after circumcising their son to ward off supernatural danger, she flings the foreskin, presumably at her hus-

Parashat Lekh-Lekha

Genesis 12.1–13.18

Rabbi Elyse Goldstein

RABBI ELYSE GOLDSTEIN IS THE DIRECTOR OF KOLEL: A CENTRE FOR LIBERAL JEWISH LEARNING IN TORONTO, AN ADULT YESHIVA OF THE REFORM MOVEMENT.

דָּבָר אַחֵר DAVAR AHER: ON ELYSE GOLDSTEIN. Elyse Goldstein's work is as brilliant, insightful, and informative as usual, and, in this case, goes one step too far for me. She writes: "In our society, male violence is still the norm based on phallic authority and the fear that the phallus can instill. It is the male organ that needs 'bloodletting' and not the female." Here, I think, she makes two errors—and therefore creates bad "post-modern" (informed by feminism) faux Torah.

The first error is the classic "radical feminist assumption" that masculinity and evil are inherently connected. The logical extension of that thinking is that universal castration would bring redemption. This is bad Jewish thinking, which understands that women have their own shadows. For the rabbis, masculinity was often expressed in the metaphor of the מִדַּת-הַדִּין *Midat ha-Din*, the male

band, and cries, "YOU ARE A BRIDEGROOM OF BLOOD—חֲתַן-דָּמִים *Hatan-damim*—TO ME.") What is significant in the Hebrew manifestation of circumcision is the move from adult to infant. Thus the connotations of sexuality and fertility are now expanded by levels of spirituality.

The foreskin is the extra piece that defiles, is fruitless, non-useful. Like the "uncircumcised" fruit of trees that cannot be eaten for the first three years (called עָרְלָה *orlah*—the same word as for foreskin), the foreskin is unripe. The foreskin taints, as Ibn Ezra comments on Genesis 17.5: "BLESSED IS GOD…WHO COMMANDED ABRAHAM TO CIRCUMCISE BEFORE SARAH GOT PREGNANT, THAT HIS SEED MIGHT BE PURIFIED."

Women and the Commandment

But what of Sarah? If the cutting of the genitals was meant to insure fertility, then surely women—for whom fertility is the guarantor of status—should have to undergo something similar. And if this mark was a sign of restrained sexuality, as I will suggest later, then it is even more striking that the ultimate assurance of female sexual restraint—clitorectomy—is not commanded, sanctioned, or even mentioned. Sarah shares in the blessing but does not have to sacrifice physically for it. If Abraham's circumcision will signal new fertility, then Sarah's name change signals the end of her barrenness. As he will be the progenitor of multitudes, so will she.

Going from שָׂרַי *Sarai* to שָׂרָה Sarah entails dropping one letter—the י *yud*—and replacing it with another—the ה *hey*. This change was not seen as arbitrary by the commentators. The Hebrew letter *hey* with the accent of "ah" underneath is a symbol of the feminine ending, as in, for example, יַלְדָּה *yaldah* (girl) or נַעֲרָה *na'arah* (young woman). The commentator Kli Yakar suggests, "Before this episode Sarai was barren, not able

---

Lekh Lekha

tendency for rule making and boundary setting. The feminine was expressed as the מִדַּת-הָרַחֲמִים *Midat ha-Rahamin*, the female tendency toward intimacy and connection. The classic midrash on Genesis 2.4 [*Bereshit Rabbah* 12.15] teaches that God's nature resembles a monarch standing with two pitchers, always seeking the right balance between these two opposite traits. We, of course, are always seeking to imitate and maximize the degree to which we are God-like—and should stand seeking equal balance, too. The classic midrashim and folk stories about Lilith, in contradistinction to her reinvention by feminists, are ones in which Lilith smothers infants in the crib and strangles bridegrooms on the eve of their marriages. The shadow of the feminine, of the desire for intimacy, is smothering—it

to give birth, like a man. The masculine י *yud* was exchanged for the feminine ה *hey*. All Jewish women, now in that Sarah-lineage, are automatically covenanted."

I am deeply indebted to the research and thought of Gary Shapiro for another possibility. In his article "Sealed in Our Flesh" in the journal of the Pardes Institute he asks, "Could it be that women are considered already circumcised?" In the Talmud [*Avodah Zara* 27a] the question of whether women may perform a *brit milah* arises. Rabbi Yohanan says yes. To understand this controversial answer Rashi does a word play on Genesis 17.13, where it says, "SURELY ONE MUST BE CIRCUMCISED" to read "one who is circumcised must circumcise." Women are considered ones who have been circumcised! Why? Perhaps simply by virtue of being Jewish, simply by virtue of being members of "the tribe." Or perhaps physically—through their blood, through their womb, or by the very fact of their anatomy being already open, exposed and uncovered, as the penis is after the foreskin is removed.

Thus male circumcision makes men more "feminine," not more masculine—by removing the foreskin and "opening up" or revealing the genitals. Women bleed monthly from their genitals and do not die. They experience the power of life and death themselves every month. Men get to do it just once, at a "like woman" moment. As Zalman Schacter-Shalomi wrote: "Taking my child to the *bris*...is a death that is not fatal."

Women do have a *brit* inscribed in their flesh as an everlasting covenant: covenantal blood not just once, at eight days, but every month. Wouldn't it be possible for girl children not only to be named at eight days or at birth but to be "brought into the covenant" at

---

is radical jealous and the inability to individuate. This explains the universe where women both steal babies because of loneliness and drive their own children into the water to drown them because they cannot care for them. The penis is not the root of all evil.

The second mistake is projecting the past onto the future and denying women their coequal destiny. Just because women were kept out of positions of power previously, and therefore had no ability to abuse power, I have Freudian faith that their envy of "phallic authority" will lead to feminine uses and abuses of power as they assume their coequal places. Power and pride is far more corrupting than "the male organ." **Joel Lurie Grishaver, <Gris@TorahAura.com>**

SYNOPSIS: *God commands and Abram & Company to go to Eretz Yisrael. They have an Egypt experience. Lot leaves. Abram fights the War of the Kings, then receives the Covenant of the Pieces. Hagar gives birth to Ishmael. God renews the covenant with the mitzvah of circumcision.*

RASHI OF THE WEEK:

Sometimes you need to read more than one Rashi to get the point. First we learn: AND ABRAM WAS VERY כָּבֵד *kaved* [Gen. 13.2]. "Kaved" usually means heavy or honored; here it means that he was weighted down with many possessions because he was rich. Then we learn: AND HE WENT לְמַסָּעָיו *L'MASA'AV* FROM THE NEGEV TO BETH EL [Gen. 13.3]. מַסָּעָיו *Masa'av* literally means "his journeys." The word seems redundant. So it must teach us something else. It means that when Abram returned from Egypt to Canaan, even though he now had money, he did not change his stopping points. He stayed at the same inns that he used on the way there. This teaches us that it is דֶּרֶךְ אֶרֶץ *derekh eretz* (menschy) not to change inns.

דָּבָר אַחֵר DAVAR AHER: Now that he had money, he stopped and paid each of his debts. In other words, Abram was menschy about using his new wealth!

menstruation? Since at the *brit milah* one of the prayers said assures us that "in your blood you will live," for women, that life-giving blood is menstrual. The same blessing could be said, now with new meaning!

Men and the Commandment: The Male Birth Experience

Women already know the incredible bonding moment that occurs through the act of giving birth. From our own body comes forth new life, born in blood, a primordial encounter with creation itself. No matter how sensitive, how involved, how sympathetic, a man can never physically participate in that mystical encounter. Or can he?

Myriel Crowley Eykamp, in an article entitled "Born and Born Again: Ritual Rebirth by Males," suggests that nearly every religious culture in the world—Eastern and Western—has some sort of initiation ceremony where there is "a reappropriation or taking over of the birthing act by the male priest.... One must not only be born again, but born again of the male." Ritual rebirth by males is almost a universal religious phenomena. On one side, that can prove universal religious misogyny, but on another level it can prove the universal deep longing by men to be birthers themselves. Many religions enact this through water. We enact it through blood, parallel to the blood of the actual birth.

While that reappropriation can be seen as threatening to women, we can also reexamine it from a spiritual viewpoint. If we see childbirth as a metaphor for nurturing and caring in a relationship, males can experience that firsthand. If a father "gives birth" at least symbolically to his child, he is taking equal responsibility as a giver of life. Of course, we will need

---

Lekh Lekha

דָּבָר אַחֵר DAVAR A<u>H</u>ER. The Eternal said to Abram, "Go you forth from your land" [Gen. 12.1]. The other way to tell the Abraham story is from the viewpoint of the children, Isaac and Ishmael. There is a notion in the Zohar that the ultimate test of Abraham is also a test of both Isaac and Ishmael, that there is something חָסֵר *<u>h</u>aser*, missing, in the generation of Abraham that will only be completed by the future reconciliation of Abraham's children. This is the story of the children of Abraham, what they have been missing, and what they are teaching their fathers, all the Abrahams, Avrahams, and Ibrahims of our past.

Abraham sees that which was missing in his generation in his last vision. When it became time for Abraham to die he ascended to the highest heaven and to the top of the chariot of Ezekiel, which was covered with the dew of light. From there he saw into the future, and he knew the secrets of human minds of the past and future. He saw and

rebirthing through the father for girl children as well.

Since I had three sons who were so closely bonded with me through birth, I wanted to let go and allow them to enter the world of men. I am often confused and angered by that world, but at their *bris*, I was convinced it was a safe world, a world of male sexuality defined and limited.

Men and the Commandment: Male Sexuality Defined and Limited

Circumcision as a symbol of disciplined sexuality is not wholly new. Already Maimonides in the *Guide to the Perplexed* II:49 saw the rite as reducing sexuality to a manageable level. It is today that we sorely need this idea repromulgated. Jewish views of sexuality teach that sexual pleasure is mutual, that force is violence and not love, and that human sexual encounters must be based on sanctity and not strength. Therefore, we can suggest that circumcision functions not only as ritual initiation but also as the communal setting of boundaries to male sexuality.

Zalman Schachter-Shalomi writes, "Perhaps something destructive and 'macho' gets refined by a *bris*, directing a man away from pure instinct and toward prudent judgment.... Maybe Freud was right about the dominating power of the libido: if so, it makes sense to take that absolute power away from the penis.... So much of what happens in sex is covenantal. Perhaps this is why covenant has to be imposed on this organ from the very start."

We cut the organ that can symbolize love or terror, endearment or violence, in a public ceremony. It is as if we say to this child, "We who are gathered here charge you: as your father used his organ in love to produce you, so you too are expected to sanctify yourself, to restrain the power of your maleness." That message, at least in theory, rejects an unbridled masculinity.

For me, that is why an equivalent ceremony for girls of drawing blood, from whatever place suggested, does not inspire. Do women need a בְּרִית *brit* of blood? In our society, male violence is still the norm based on phallic authority and the fear that the phallus can instill. It is the male organ that needs "bloodletting" and not the female. Can those few drops of covenantal blood be seen as כַּפָּרָה *kappara*—atonement—as is most sacrificial blood in the Torah? Let it be seen as the "offering" of Jewish men toward the cleansing of violence in a patriarchal world. Let men teach men—father to son—of vulnerability, of exposure. Let it be seared into their consciousness through their flesh for *tikkun olam*—a safe, new world. ■

---

understood everything. He saw both the generations of Isaac and the generations of Ishmael, his sons, whom he loved. He understood that all that had happened to him happened to his descendants.

Lekh-Lekha, Abraham heard: "TO LEAVE YOUR COUNTRY, YOUR KINDRED, YOUR FATHER'S HOUSE, AND GO TO A LAND THAT I WILL SHOW YOU"—and break the chain of inherited enmity. From atop Ezekiel's chariot Abraham, dressed in hand-me-down celestial garments, received his last vision, and in it he saw the reconciliation missing in his generation, the perfect handshake of his descendants Isaac and Ishmael. Just as Abraham had left his father's house, he sees the children of Isaac and Ishmael leave their fathers' house of enmity. *Lekh-Lekha*, they heard/OUT OF YOUR COUNTRY/ came those words/AWAY FROM YOUR KINDRED/they hear again/TO A LAND THAT I WILL SHOW YOU/And from atop Ezekiel's chariot, Abraham whispered: Amen. **James Stone Goodman, <Stavisker@aol.com>**

דָּבָר אַחֵר DAVAR A<u>H</u>ER. **THE ETERNAL SAID TO ABRAM, "GO YOU FORTH FROM YOUR LAND, FROM YOUR BIRTHPLACE, AND FROM YOUR FATHER'S HOUSE—TO THE LAND THAT I WILL SHOW YOU"** [Gen. 12.1]. OK, I did what You told me to do. I left my parents' home, moved away from the city where I grew up, and have little to do with the alien culture of my youth. Truth be told, I couldn't wait to get away from there anyhow. I was suffocating in that environment—way too empty for me. I heard Your call a long time ago. The echo of its mes-

Rabbi Bradley Shavit Artson

Rabbi Bradley Shavit Artson is the Executive vice-president of the Board of Rabbis of Southern California, Mission Viejo, and is the author of *It's A Mitzvah! Step by Step to Jewish Living* (Behrman House).

Lekh Lekha

Moral Misers: Let It Shine!

Notice how it's easier to criticize from a distance than it is to make a positive difference. Sitting in a comfortable chair in the safety of our suburban homes, we peruse the newspapers and comment on the "obvious" solution, even though that solution seems to have escaped the attention of everyone else in the world. Almost everyone succumbs to the temptation to solve the world's problems.

But notice how few are the people who volunteer at the local hospital, for the AIDS walk, or at a nearby synagogue. We all love to criticize the experts, love to sound wise and insightful at a dinner party or social gathering, but the idea of spending time with the homeless, the elderly shut-ins, or the critically ill paralyzes us in our inaction. Abraham, in that regard, was not so different from the rest of us. In *Parashat Lekh-Lekha* Abram is a comfortable gentleman. He is married and at the center of a thriving clan. He probably sounded off at festival gatherings about what was wrong with Ur and how it should be fixed, but generally he minded his own business.

In *Midrash Bereshit Rabbah* Rabbi Berekiah compares him to "a vial of myrrh closed with a tight-fitting lid and lying in a corner, so that its fragrance was not disseminated." It isn't hard to guess Rabbi Berekiah's estimation of a bottle of perfume that is so tightly sealed that no one can smell it at all. And it isn't hard to extrapolate his opinion of people who are well-off, well-

---

sage, still reverberating in my ears, is what pushed me forward during those difficult early years. When I think about it, I have to admit that I rushed through many of them before I was prepared to slow down and take the time necessary to actually hear what You had always been trying to tell me. I even ran off to Israel, thinking that I could hear the message more clearly there. In Israel there were special moments, piercing glimpses of awe-inspiring possibility and holy potential. Yet with the noise of those Egged buses you can't hear much of anything in Israel, let alone make room for הֶגְיוֹן לִבִּי *hegyon libi*, the meditations of my heart.

לֶךְ-לְךָ **Lekh Lekha.** According to the tradition, Abraham destroyed the idols in his father's Terah shop. I tried to take advantage of his working-class reality. True, that makes me more sensitive to those around me, but it seems insuffi-

educated, and full of opinions, yet who somehow never seem to find the time to apply their opinions in a practical way. Good advice on how to live, if sealed into a cozy corner, doesn't do the world any good. At the height of Abram's comfort and self-absorption. God shattered his complacency forever. With one forceful call God forced Abram to abandon his posturing and lectures, and to apply his wisdom to helping his fellow human beings. "GO FORTH FROM YOUR NATIVE LAND, AND FROM YOUR FATHER'S HOUSE, TO THE LAND THAT I WILL SHOW YOU." Without even knowing where his involvement would lead, Abraham shifted his focus from editorializing to activism—working on behalf of morality, God, and other people. Rabbi Berekiah shrewdly notes that the sealed perfume, "once it was taken up, disseminated its fragrance. Similarly, the Holy Blessed One said to Abraham, 'Travel from place to place and your name will become great in the world.'" Perfume gains value by sharing its rich fragrance with all who can smell it.

A wise education, moral balance, or physical strength are worthwhile to the extent that they translate into action on behalf of building a better world. Rather than hoarding our viewpoints and our energy, we become rich to the extent that we share them with others. There is nothing so glorious, nothing so rewarding, and nothing so needed as reaching out to a needy stranger. In caring for an anonymous creature in the image of God we uncover a new reflection of God's precious love, and we illumine our own lives by the light of that beauty. And we make someone else's life a little more pleasant, too. ■

---

cient and rather limiting. Would that he could hear Your call as well.

לֶךְ-לְךָ **LEKH LEKHA.** As soon as I read those words the first time, a flush of familiarity rushed through me. Those were my words, my call. They belong not to Abraham alone, but to all like me who seek Your face. I have to admit that when I first heard Your voice, I couldn't figure out where it was coming from—and I was a bit afraid of admitting that I heard it in the first place. I tried not listening to it, then responded to it in rather general ways: community service, social action, political activity, environmental protest, the typical activities of a Kennedy-era youth.

לֶךְ-לְךָ **LEKH LEKHA.** It took me and my parents—and everyone else when I told them—by surprise. After all, I was the kid who hated religious school, who couldn't sit still in the synagogue, who devised every scheme to unnerve the rabbi (and I was usually rather innovative and quite successful at it). I think that I was the only child for whom my rabbi had a personal countdown calendar, marking off the days until I dropped out of Sunday school. No follow-up calls encouraging confirmation for me. He'd accept the dropout statistic on my behalf. It was worth the solitude that my absence provided.

לֶךְ-לְךָ **LEKH LEKHA.** Keep going. Not out, but in: inside of self, to the interior of self, suggest some of our teachers. That's precisely where I have been heading, preoccupied with interior landscapes, hoping that I might better hear Your voice by listening to my own.

אֶל-הָאָרֶץ אֲשֶׁר אַרְאֶךָּ **EL HA-ERETZ ASHER AREKA.** Show me the land. Teach me how to scale its heights so that I might see its beauty more clearly. The climb will surely be slow and hard, but I will get there just as others have done before me. As I have learned from Rav Kook's teachings, the journey is narrow and twisting. It does not follow a straight path, but neither do our lives. Like Abraham, I have taken years to begin to figure out what You were trying to tell me in the first place. My years on this earth are limited, yet I have much to learn. I accept that as the condition of the human reality, and, undaunted, I am willing to continue on the journey nonetheless. Will You continue to lead me and show me the way. **Dr. Kerry M. Olitzky, Hebrew Union College <Olitzky@huc.edu>**

דָּבָר אַחֵר **DAVAR AHER. AND I WILL MAKE OF YOU A GREAT NATION; I WILL BLESS YOU, AND MAKE YOUR NAME GREAT, AND YOU SHALL BE A BLESSING** [Gen. 12.2]. Here is a slightly different

Lekh Lekha

interpretation then Rabbi Artson's insightful analysis of Abraham's character and actions in light of Rabbi Berekiah's comparing Abraham to a "closed vial of myrrh." Perhaps Rabbi Berekiah is saying that until Abraham leaves his home and wanders the land spreading the message of his faith in one God, his personal faith is as limited and confined as a beautiful fragrance stored in a sealed bottle. It benefits Abraham, and perhaps his family, but no one else, and this does not fulfill God's vision for Abraham.

This analysis might parallel the rabbi's discomfort with Noah, whose righteousness "IN HIS GENERATION" raises midrashic questions about the relative value of Noah's behavior. Noah does not plead with God for his generation, but rather shuts himself and his family in the ark, quietly allowing his peers to drown. It seems clear that God desires not only our personal righteousness, but also that we be concerned about our neighbors, society, and world. Noah should have tried to influence his generation to stop their violent, corrupt behavior. Instead, he was satisfied to take care only of himself and his immediate family.

Abraham, who ultimately pleads for the people of Sodom and Gomorrah, obviously went beyond Noah's limitations, and Abraham's "fragrance" was disseminated throughout his world. **Rabbi Allen Juda, Congregation Brith Sholom, Bethlehem, PA.**

דָּבָר אַחֵר DAVAR AHER. WHEN THE שָׂרֵי SARAI (PRINCES) OF PHARAOH SAW HER, THEY PRAISED HER TO PHARAOH, AND THE WOMAN WAS TAKEN TO PHARAOH'S HOUSE [Gen. 12.15]. When looking at a tikkun, there seem to be two word plays in the text. In the story of Abraham and Sarai in Egypt, it is the praise of Sarai's beauty by Pharaoh's princes that leads Pharaoh into trouble [Gen. 12.15]. In Hebrew, שָׂרֵי פַּרְעֹה *Sare Faroh* "PRINCES" and "SARAI" have the same root. Perhaps the message is that one needs to be discriminating in listening to the words of advisors.

A little later in the parashah [Gen. 13.6–7], the word for Abraham and Lot's great substance, רָב *rav,* is virtually identical with the word for conflict, רִיב *riv*. This message is obvious. Do not allow possessions to cause conflict within the family. **Rabbi Allen Juda, Congregation Brith Sholom, Bethlehem, PA.**

דָּבָר אַחֵר DAVAR AHER. AND THE ETERNAL TOOK ABRAHAM OUTSIDE AND SAID, "GAZE TOWARD THE HEAVENS AND COUNT THE STARS IF YOU ARE ABLE" [Gen. 15.5]. With those words the Torah tells us God's promise, "JEWS WILL BE AS NUMEROUS AS THE STARS."

Something is troubling. Why was it necessary for Ha-Shem to take a field trip with Abraham in order to impress upon him the vastness of the universe? At the time, Abraham was 100 years old. Surely he knew that one cannot count the stars! Rashi, therefore, explains the verse on a deeper level. Abraham had been told by soothsayers and astrologers that he and Sarah would never bear children. Ha-Shem, however, took him outside. "Go outside of your preordained destiny," He exclaimed. "You are no longer governed by conventional predictions. I am taking you outside that realm."

It's quite interesting to note that Abraham's great-grandson, Yosef, followed literally in Abraham's footsteps. He too ran outside. Yosef was about to be seduced by the licentious wife of his master, Potiphar. She claimed she had a vision that a union with Yosef would produce prestigious offspring. (She did not know that Yosef would legitimately marry her daughter.) In Genesis 39.12 the Torah tells us that "YOSEF DROPPED HIS COAT AND RAN OUTSIDE." Perhaps he was saying "I am not governed by your visions and predictions. I must do what my faith and morality teach me. Like my forebears Abraham and Sarah, I go outside your visions."

The Jewish people are not controlled by the soothsayers of conventional wisdom. Predictions of defeat abounded when Israel's army was outnumbered ten to one and yet we survived. The dire predictions of mass assimilation amidst despair after World War II faded with the rebirth of a Jewish community and renewed Torah education on unparalleled levels. Conventional wisdom had lost hope for our Russian brothers and sisters, yet new embers of Torah Judaism are beginning to glow out of the former bastion of atheism. We are not ruled by conventional wisdom. Like our forefather, Abraham, we Jews are just outsiders. Good *Shabbes*! **Rabbi Mordechai Kamenetzky, <Ateres@aol.com>.**

Every American Jewish tourist who goes to Jordan returns raving about Petra. How could they not? That glorious ancient Nabatean city, carved into the rock by seemingly invisible hands, is truly on the runner-up list of the wonders of the ancient world. This past summer we visited Petra on our congregational trip to Israel and Jordan. As glorious as the scenery was at the final destination, it was the journey to that destination that taught me the most.

To get into Petra one must ride on horseback into the gorge and then begin a long walk to the ancient city. A Bedouin boy no older than ten led me on his trusty Arabian stallion. Like a New York City cab driver, he had become adept at the art of small talk.

"So, what do you do?" he asked me. (Why shouldn't Bedouin children know how to network?)

"I'm a rabbi," I answered.

"What's that?" he asked, with a confused look on his face.

"A rabbi?" I cast about for something that he might understand. "A rabbi is like an imam for the Jews."

"That's a good job," he countered, and I laughed.

"What do you do in your job?" he pushed on.

"Well, I do a lot of things. I tell a lot of stories."

"What kind of stories?"

Parashat Va-Yera

Genesis 18.1–22.24

Rabbi Jeffrey K. Salkin

RABBI JEFFREY SALKIN IS THE RABBI OF COMMUNITY SYNAGOGUE IN PORT WASHINGTON, NEW YORK. HE IS THE AUTHOR OF *PUTTING GOD ON THE GUEST LIST: HOW TO RECLAIM THE SPIRITUAL MEANING OF YOUR CHILD'S BAR/BAT MITZVAH* AND *BEING GOD'S PARTNER: HOW TO FIND THE HIDDEN LINK BETWEEN SPIRITUALITY AND YOUR WORK*, BOTH PUBLISHED BY JEWISH LIGHTS, WOODSTOCK, VT.

דָּבָר אַחֵר DAVAR AHER. AND THE ETERNAL APPEARED UNTO HIM BY THE TEREBINTHS (TREES) OF MAMRE, AS HE SAT IN THE TENT DOOR IN THE HEAT OF THE DAY. [Gen. 18.1]. This verse refers to visiting the sick—בִּקּוּר חוֹלִים *bikkur holim*. It may not seem like it, but both Rashi and Rambam say that it refers to God's visit to Abraham during the third day after his circumcision. The Talmud says, "The Holy Blessed One visited the sick, as it is written, ADONAI APPEARED TO HIM BY THE TEREBINTHS OF MAMRE, and so *you* must also visit the sick." This is an example of *imitateo dei* or imitating God. Though we fear God, we must be שֻׁתָּפֵי הַקָּדוֹשׁ בָּרוּךְ הוּא *Shtfi ha-Kadosh Baruch Hu*, partners with God.

The Talmud says that when Rabbi Yohanan was ill, Rabbi Hanina came and took Yohanan's hand and lifted him up. This story shows that everybody needs someone else to heal

וירא אליו יהוה באלני ממ

"What kind of stories?" The answer came to me. "I tell stories about Ibrahim and Yakub, about Musa and Daoud." I rattled off the Islamic equivalents of every biblical character that I could remember. He nodded.

"And I tell stories about Ishmael. Do you know those stories?"

Suddenly a faraway look came upon his face. He was looking somewhere far off in the distance, way beyond the canyons of Petra. He was looking far off in the desert, to a place perhaps with no name, to a place of memory or of legend. "Yes," he murmured, tugging on the reins of the horse, "yes, I know these stories."

Where was he looking? I wondered. Perhaps he was looking into the wilderness of Paran, way to the south. And his sudden silence? Perhaps he was straining his ears to hear the cries of a mother and child whose story was his story, whose tale was his tale, whose life was somehow implicated in his own life.

It was precisely at that moment that I came to understand Torah in a way that was hitherto closed to me. It was precisely at that moment that I realized that we liberal Jews have lost a story that is ours, a story we must reclaim. If we are in traditional synagogues on Rosh ha-Shanah, then we observe two days of the holiday. The Torah reading for the first day is the story of Hagar and Ishmael. The reading for the second day is *Akedat Yitzhak*. But if we only observe one day, then there is only one story, and it is the Akedah. The Reform *mahzor*, *Gates of Repentance*, assigns *Bereshit* as the alternate Torah reading. I believe this to be incorrect. Even though Rosh ha-Shanah is יוֹם הֲרַת עוֹלָם *Yom Harat Olam* (the day the world

---

them. Yohanan was an expert healer, but it is said "A prisoner cannot free himself."

The mitzvah of visiting the sick is not an easy one to observe. There are many guidelines created to assist in performing the mitzvah correctly. It is said that at the sick person's bedside you should defend neither religion nor God because when in physical anguish it is extremely difficult to hold back curses. In *Nedarim* 40a it is explained that a visit can cause pain or a large amount of annoyance. For example, there is a tale of a rabbi who talked and talked to a lady for so long that she fell asleep. My dad actually ran into a similar problem when he was an assistant rabbi. A sick old lady had to ask him to leave because she was getting tired of him visiting.

SYNOPSIS: *Three angels visit and announce the birth of Isaac. Abraham and God debate Sodom's future. The city is destroyed. Another wife–sister story, this time concerning Abimelekh. Isaac is born. Hagar and Ishmael are exiled. The binding of Isaac.*

RASHI OF THE WEEK:

Just before the Sodom debate begins, the Torah says, "AND ABRAHAM DREW NEAR (to God) [Gen. 18.23]. *We want to know what it means to "*DRAW NEAR TO GOD*" if God is everywhere. Obviously, "drawing near" suggests an emotional or spiritual place, not a physical one. Here are some examples:* DRAWING NEAR can mean preparing for battle: AND JOAB DREW NEAR [II Sam. 10.13] *and then went out and defeated the Syrians.* DRAWING NEAR can mean pleading: "AND JUDAH DREW NEAR [Gen. 44.18] *and then begged for Benjamin's life.* And DRAWING NEAR can mean praying: ELIJAH DREW NEAR [I Kings 18.21] *just before he out-prayed the priest of Baal on Mt. Carmel. Which of these kinds of* DRAWING NEAR *was Abraham trying to do? He did all three of these; he was prepared to do whatever it took,* to speak harshly *as if preparing for war,* to plead, *and* to pray. *There are indeed many ways of reaching God.*

was created), the real action takes place not in the opening moments of creation, but in the tugs and pulls of real families. Nothing could be more real than the story of Hagar and Ishmael.

The story begins in Genesis 16. Abram and Sarai are childless; Sarai gives her Egyptian servant girl, Hagar, to Abraham so that he might have children through her. Hagar becomes pregnant, and, as a result Sarai becomes threatened by her presence in the household. In a moment of apparent moral silence Abram shrugs his shoulders: Your maid is in your hands; deal with her as you think right. Sarai abuses the handmaiden, who runs away into the wilderness. There an angel finds her by a fountain of water, and the angel asks her the crucial questions of life: Hagar, slave of Sarai, where have you come from, and where are you going? Hagar says, "I AM FLEEING FROM MY MISTRESS SARAI." The angel convinces her to return to Sarai, comforting her with the knowledge that she will bear a son whose name will be Ishmael (God hears). HE WILL BE A WILD ASS OF A MAN; HIS HAND AGAINST EVERYONE, AND EVERYONE'S HAND AGAINST HIM, AND HE SHALL DWELL ALONGSIDE ALL HIS KINSMEN. Hagar then names the God Who spoke to her El-Roi, the God Who sees, and the place is therefore called Beer-Lehairoi.

Act II in the drama occurs chapters later in Genesis 21. The covenant has been sealed; Abram and Sarai are now Abraham and Sarah. Abraham has already bargained with God in the matter of Sodom and Gomorrah. Sarah has been promised a child, and God comes through on the promise. Isaac is born, and Hagar and Ishmael stand on the sidelines at his weaning ceremony, with Ishmael *metzahek* (The Midrash goes wild: Was he playing? Fooling around? Mocking the ceremony? Engaged in some kind of sexual play? Shooting arrows at Isaac?). The tension that has been lying dormant in the fam-

---

Va-Yera

Another rule concerns when not to visit the patient. You should not visit immediately after the patient has fallen ill. They might believe the problem to be more than it truly is because you have come so fast, maybe in response to hearing that they were going to die soon. This is from *Peah* 1 8b of the Jerusalem Talmud.

Personally I think that this mitzvah is one of the most important mitzvot. The mitzvah of *bikkur holim* is a vital part of a good Jewish community. **Ben Glaser, grade 8, Solomon Schecter Day School, West Hartford, CT.**

דָּבָר אַחֵר DAVAR AHER. **AS SOON AS HE SAW THEM, HE RAN FROM THE ENTRANCE OF THE TENT TO GREET THEM, BOWING TO THE GROUND.** [Gen. 18.2–3]. Abraham's behavior is quite different when he is dealing with

ily erupts. Sarah becomes angry and jealous of her handmaiden, Hagar. She is, after all, only the "help." How Sarah must have despised the presence of this young, healthy, fertile woman in her camp! And so the matriarch begs Abraham to cast Hagar and her son out into the desert, which means certain death. Abraham does so, giving them only a skin of water for the journey.

Hagar stumbles through the desert with her son. She carries the parched lad on her back. "LET ME NOT LOOK ON AS THE CHILD DIES!" she pleads, and so she casts the lad under a thorn bush. At that precise moment her eyes are opened to the presence of a gushing well of water. Ishmael drinks from the well and he survives to become the ancestor of the Ishmaelites, the Arab nation—and of the Bedouin boy at Petra.

At that moment in Petra I saw the gaze of the Bedouin boy. In my imagination he was staring into the wilderness looking for Hagar and Ishmael, his ancestors. His gaze reminded me that when we reclaim the story of Hagar and Ishmael, we reclaim something essentially human in ourselves as well.

What does it mean to be Hagar?

We rarely stop and realize that Hagar is a pivotal figure in biblical theology. She is the first woman to be told that she would have a child, the first woman to hear a Divine promise of descendants. She is the first woman to weep for a dying child. She is the first person visited by an angel. Not only this, she is the only person in the Hebrew Bible who has the gentle <u>h</u>utzpah to name God—אֵל רֳאִי *El-Roi*, THE GOD WHO SEES. She is, therefore, a new and radical Adam, taking over the power of naming and applying this power even to the Name.

When we look at Hagar we see our own image, but slightly distorted. She goes into forced exile back to Egypt. Her footsteps in the sands of the Negev and the Sinai were there for us to see on our way out (and my private midrash is that on the way out of Egypt our ancestors saw her footsteps still intact in the sands of the Sinai). As Phyliss Trible notes in *Texts of Terror*, Hagar experiences an Exodus without liberation. She experiences a wilderness, but with no covenantal moment of Sinai awaiting her. She wanders, but with no "land" in the distance. She knows unmerited exile, but with no hope of return.

Finally, her story is, in the best sense, multicultural. I once challenged my Torah students in the synagogue to name the custodians, the men who set up the chairs and make the coffee and clean up after us. They stumbled on the names.

So, too, with Hagar. Here comes the irony. She names God, but she is herself mostly unnamed. The only character in the story who calls her by name is the angel. To Sarah she is the *amah*, the help, the slave girl. You don't have to be totally politically correct to see what Phyliss Trible saw—her story represents

---

strangers than when he deals with his own family. He is quick to welcome strangers to his home; he argues with God about the destruction of Sodom and Gomorrah; he bargains and makes peace with Abimelekh. Yet he deals with his own family differently. He does not protect Sarah; he does not protest when he is told to send Hagar and Ishmael away; he does not argue with God when he is commanded to sacrifice Isaac. Is this symbolic of God's relationship to the Jewish people? **Randelle Landman, <rlandman@mciunix.mciu.k12.pa.us>**

דָּבָר אַחֵר DAVAR A<u>H</u>ER. AND HE (ABRAHAM) SAID, "MY MASTER, IF I FIND FAVOR IN YOUR EYES, DO NOT PASS OVER YOUR SERVANT " [Gen. 18.3]. *Mixmaster*: It's not often that one receives such diverse company on a single day, but if you're Abraham, anything can happen. The Torah begins this week as Abraham is sitting outside his tent, three days after his circumcision, on a boiling hot day. He is visited by none other than the Divine Presence. In the middle of the conversation Abraham looks up. He spots three Arab nomads meandering in his direction in the intense heat. Imagine yourself: You are recuperating from an operation that most males receive

three causes of oppression: nationality, class, and gender. She is the poor woman, the homeless woman, the bag lady, the resident alien, the single mother. She is all that is cast out. She is not only Hagar, but Hagar the stranger. She is the piece of ourselves that we deny, that embarrasses us.

What does it mean to be Ishmael? Ishmael is that piece of us that remains on the sidelines, the piece of us that cannot understand what is going on in the ritual moment, the piece of us that is alienated and therefore alienating.

But in the midst of the wilderness, when the lad is dying, we read that God heard his cries בַּאֲשֶׁר הוּא שָׁם-*ba-asher hu sham*—WHERE HE IS. The Midrash relates that the angels cried out to God, "Oh Master of the Universe! Let him die! Don't you see that in days to come it will be the sons of Ishmael who will wage wars in the Holy Land and ravage its cities? (And bomb its buses?)" "No," says God, "I hear the cries of the child where he is now, at this moment, in crisis." The truth of the midrash is that God sees us in our present state, judging us only on our merits at the moment.

Finally, what does it mean to be Abraham and Sarah? For Abraham, this incident was a test—the final test before the Akedah (the Binding of Isaac). Rabbi David Polish, ז"ל *Zikhrono liVrakhah*, suggests that the Akedah was necessary precisely because of the incident with Hagar and Ishmael. God saw that Abraham was all too willing to sacrifice them. Therefore, it was after these things that God tested Abraham: "You were willing to sacrifice the unloved (the poor, the cast-off, the unattractive ones). Let us see how you do with the sacrifice of the loved, with Isaac."

Moreover, that Abraham and Sarah are so wrong in this story, so flawed, is a powerful message to us about our own parents and our own stories. It is impossible to

---

Va-Yera

ninety-nine years earlier; you are in the middle of a conversation with God Almighty; and three Arabs happen to pass within shouting distance of your tent. We all know what we would and would not do. Let us analyze what Abraham does and how he does it.

The Torah tell us, AND HE (ABRAHAM) SAID, "MY MASTER, IF I FIND FAVOR IN YOUR EYES, DO NOT PASS OVER YOUR SERVANT" [Gen. 18.3]. The Torah is unclear. Who was Abraham referring to when he said "My Master?" Is he telling God not to withdraw as he welcomes some nomads, or was he respectfully interrupting his conversation with God as he shouts to the wayfarers, "Don't leave me, I'll be with you as soon as I finish this conversation with God?"

A story can explain: Rabbi Isser Zalman Melzer[1] was once sitting with a group of students when suddenly

enter adulthood without having been wounded, betrayed, or in some way disappointed by our parents. It is impossible to enter adulthood without saying, "I will not do it the way my parents did." That is what Isaac said. That is what Jacob said. And yet, the Genesis parenting style—choose one child over another, cast the leftover kid into the wilderness—endured. It endured until the time of Ephraim and Menasseh, the two brothers who share the same blessing.

Is there redemption here? Do we leave these two hapless souls in the wilderness?

No. Ishmael will go on and father a nation. He will have twelve sons long before Jacob has twelve sons, meaning that his nationhood precedes our own. When Abraham dies, Isaac and Ishmael together bury their father [Gen. 25.9]. There is awkward silence at Machpelah. It is like the brothers Mort and Irving, sitting in the waiting room at the local funeral home. It is five minutes away from the funeral service for their mother. Mort and Irving have not spoken for twenty years because of a long forgotten family fight. But finally, Mort goes up and hugs Irving and says: "Let's cut it out already. It's time to bury Mom." And Torah lives again, even and especially in our lives.

A generation later Esau will go to Ishmael and marry his daughter, Machalat. It is a natural for Esau. I imagine him and his father-in-law sitting around the fire in the desert, talking about what it means to be cast out.

A story cast out of our memory? It took a Bedouin boy at Petra to teach me to reclaim it. Now I realize that Hagar and Ishmael, Abraham and Sarah are more real than I had once thought, more present than I had been willing to imagine. Like Hagar, I might also find a well of water in the wilderness of life that had been there all along.■

---

one of them looked out the window and announced that one of Israel's leading Torah scholars was coming toward the home. Rav Melzer quickly prepared his modest Jerusalem apartment to greet the honored guest. The table was bedecked with a freshly laundered tablecloth and adorned with a bowl of fruit in honor of the distinguished visitor. Rabbi Melzer changed into his *Shabbes* attire so as to show his respect.

Suddenly there was a knock. Reb Isser Zalman rushed to the door to greet the honored guest. However there was no rav at the door. In his stead stood a simple poor Jew who needed a letter of approbation in order to raise funds. From the distance he appeared like the scholar, but obviously the student had been grossly mistaken. To the surprise of his wife, and even more so the visitor himself, Rav Melzer ushered the poor man into his dining room. He proceeded to seat him at the head of the table and converse with him. He then offered him a glass of hot tea and gave him the respect he would have afforded a revered guest. After discussing the man's needs, he wrote a beautiful letter full of complimentary descriptions regarding the man and his situation.

After the man had left, Reb Isser Zalman commented, "Who really knows how to evaluate and differentiate the value of people? Perhaps this is the way one must treat every Jew. I was happy to channel my enthusiastic expectations of the rabbi's visit toward this simple Jew."

Abraham knew that there is a mitzvah to love Ha-Shem, but he also knew that God created man in God's image. Was he addressing the actual Master-of-the-Universe, or the master that was created in the image of the ultimate Master? Perhaps one of the ways that Abraham manifested his great love for Ha-Shem was through his actions toward his fellow human beings. And believe it or not, the Master waited. Good *Shabbes*. **Rabbi Mordechai Kamenetzky, <Ateres@aol.com>**

Footnote:

1. Rabbi I. Z. Melzer (1870–1953) was the Chief Rabbi of Slutzk, Poland. He founded the yeshiva in Kletzk, Poland, and in 1925 was appointed to head the illustrious Eitz Chaim Yeshiva in Eretz Yisrael

Va-Yera

Nahum Waldman

"MOREOVER, SHE IS INDEED MY SISTER, MY FATHER'S DAUGHTER, THOUGH NOT MY MOTHER'S DAUGHTER; AND SHE BECAME MY WIFE" [Gen. 20.12].

A multidimensional look at this text.

ABRAHAM AND JACOB IN BIBLICAL EXEGESIS: The wife–sister motif in Genesis where Abraham has Sarah declare that she is his sister and not his wife [Gen. 12.13], or where he spreads that message himself [Gen. 20.23], has long been an embarrassment to Bible readers and commentators. There are several possibilities:

(1) The patriarch is telling a total lie, for she is not his sister at all; (2) His story is partially true, as she is his sister in a limited sense, i.e., through the father but not the mother [Gen. 20.12]; (3) She had been his kinswoman ("sister") before he married her; or (4) She has the legal privileges of wives and sisters available to women in Hurrian society.

None of these interpretations of sisterhood removes the moral problems of Sarah's defilement in the bed of the ruler or Abraham's telling an untruth. Many have justified Abraham's questionable ethical behavior in terms of human nature, i.e., his natural fear of mortal danger. It is reasonable to expect that as a human being he would do whatever he must to save his life. On the other hand, it has been argued that Abraham deserves not excuses but censure; he is no ordinary ma,n and we expect from him a greater faith in God and readiness for martyrdom.

RABBINIC MIDRASH: The midrash interpreting Genesis 12 attributes no fault to Abraham. It emphasizes Sarah's beauty and the impetuousness of the

---

(Palestine). He was instrumental in the founding of a network of Torah-true day schools in Israel and was a beloved teacher to literally thousands of students.

דָּבָר אַחֵר DAVAR AHER. SHALL NOT THE JUDGE OF ALL THE EARTH ACT WITH JUSTICE? [Gen. 18.25]. One lesson that seemed apparent to me in light of the assassination of Prime Minister Rabin by a self-proclaimed religious extremist during the week of *Parashat Va-Yera* is that we are shown how we are permitted to question God, even to argue with God. In fact, I believe that this questioning maintains for us a healthy and sane relationship with God. An unquestioning belief in God leads to religious fanaticism, the results of which we saw firsthand the previous week.

This is illustrated in two ways for us in *Parashat Va-Yera*. First we are given a positive example, a way we should

ancient Egyptians, both motifs heightening the danger facing Abraham and justifying what he did. The midrash also sees in Abraham's adventure a historical-determinative force, a foreshadowing of the entrance of the Israelites into Egypt in the time of Joseph because of famine, and their exit, laden with wealth [*Genesis Rabbah* 40.4–6].

The parallel biblical story in Genesis 20, however, indicates some discomfort with Abraham's actions and makes an effort to justify them. Abraham lamely says, "SHE IS IN TRUTH MY SISTER, MY FATHER'S DAUGHTER, THOUGH NOT MY MOTHER'S." He also depicts his action as a response to the cruel policy of the king, who freely takes to his palace any woman who appeals to him. Abraham rebukes the king: "I THOUGHT SURELY THERE IS NO FEAR OF GOD IN THIS PLACE."

However, the midrash criticizes Abraham more severely for his saying that Sarah was his sister, as he did this without her consent. Sarah protests vehemently that Abraham escaped what she has been suffering, namely the fear of being defiled: "Abraham is outside the boat but I am inside it," she says. Abimelekh gives Abraham a thousand pieces of silver to be for Sarah "A COVERING OF THE EYES," that is, vindication. The midrash, however, offers a different interpretation. Abimelekh says, "you covered my eyes and the child who will be born to you will have his eyes covered" (i.e., you deceived me, and Isaac will become blind) [*Genesis Rabbah* 52.4, 12, 13].

ISLAMIC INTERPRETATIONS: Abraham occupies a place of great importance in Islam. God showed him the kingdom of heaven and earth so that he might be of those who had certainty of faith [*Koran*, vi, 75ff]. He was neither a Jew nor a Christian, but he was ever inclined to God and obedient to Him [*ibid.*, iii, 68]. Abraham was tried with certain commands, which he fulfilled, and God said to him, "I will make you a leader of men." Abraham and Ishmael built the Kaaba, the spiritual and ritual center of Islam, and purified it for those who perform the circuit [*ibid.*, ii, 125–6]. For Jewish commentators living in an Islamic milieu, to present Abraham as telling a lie or violating a standard of appropriate behavior would create great difficulties. Moslems would be likely either to condemn the Bible itself or to categorize its Jewish scholars as willful distorters. Moslems indeed did accuse the Jews of "falsification," "alteration," "abrogation," and "lack of reliable transmission."

Post-Koranic commentators disagreed about Abraham's conduct as presented in the Bible, as well as about other stories. The Spanish Moslem writer Ali ibn Ahmad Ibn Hazam (died 1046) criticized what he maintained to be outrageous behavior, such as the story of Lot and his daughters or Abraham's marriage to his half-sister, Sarah.

---

model. Abraham argues with God to save the righteous people of Sodom and Gemorrah: "SHALL NOT THE JUDGE OF ALL THE EARTH ACT WITH JUSTICE?" Abraham challenges God to "ACT" with the best judgment, to search for the right way, not necessarily the easy way. We should use this as a role model for ourselves—to learn to speak out against injustices, no matter how powerful or influential the offending party might be. And to enter into dialogue with God, to act with the gift of reason with which we are each endowed.

The second example is one we should not model but is a lesson from God. In rereading the binding of Isaac this year, I read it as God telling Abraham (and us) that it is not blind faith that is required of us. Rather, God says, "No! I do not want you to sacrifice your son—that is crazy." God's intervention before the sacrifice of Isaac is to tell us that Abraham should have spoken up, should have questioned. It is our lesson to learn that we should not blindly follow any teaching or idea—a lesson sadly brought home again and again in our post-Holocaust world.

As we fear for one Yitzhak and mourn another, let us remember that it is our obligation as Jews to question and to argue with God so

He also considered the latter story to be one of the passages the Jews had altered. Other interpreters accepted the "kinship" idea and asserted that Abraham and Sarah really were cousins. Some believed that Abraham's relationship to Sarah was even closer than cousinhood. The historian Al-Tabari (839923) sought to defend Abraham from charges of falsehood by citing several extraKoranic traditions that impute to Sarah spiritual sisterhood, saying she was Abraham's "sister to God," meaning that he and she were at that time the only Islamic believers on earth. One Islamic school argued that a prophet is immune to sin, while another contended the opposite—that a prophet can sin, and that Abraham is proof of this.

MEDIEVAL JEWISH INTERPRETATION: Saadiah Gaon (Egypt and Iraq, 882–942), in his long commentary on Genesis, felt compelled to respond to critics (Jewish or Moslem) who said: "Why did Abraham not tell the truth, demonstrating by this that he had faith in God, for is it not better that the Egyptian should sin through knowledge (that she is his wife) than that he should lie?"

In his response Saadiah defends Abraham's integrity and accepts his human fear, setting a pattern of exegesis many others followed. Abraham, he says, was one of the wise believers, and if he feared death, it was because he had established the truth—that the people of Egypt did kill men just to get their wives. He was therefore justified in employing an evasion in saying that Sarah was his sister, in the sense of "kinswoman." Abraham did not act hysterically but had a detailed plan. In claiming that Sarah was his sister he was avoiding death, and the Egyptians would be spared the sin of killing him. If they insisted on taking Sarah, they would deal with Abraham either peacefully or violently. In the first case, he would

---

Va-Yera

that we keep our feet firmly and sanely planted in this world, and yet in doing so, remain connected to God for eternity. **Cantor Susan C. Dropkin, Temple Shalom, Aberdeen, NJ.**

דָּבָר אַחֵר DAVAR AHER.

ABRAHAM SAID OF SARAH HIS WIFE, "SHE IS MY SISTER." SO ABIMELEKH, KING OF GERAR, SENT AND TOOK SARAH [Gen. 20.2]. *Sarah's Test-A Midrash.* The incident with Abimelekh? Sooner or later, I knew you'd inquire about that. I'll try to explain. It was a most difficult period in our lives. Can you imagine an elderly couple traveling by camel across the desert to avoid starvation? We took not only our flocks and other worldly possessions with us, but also the memory of the destruction of Sodom.

How proud I was when Abraham pleaded with the Judge of all the

calmly describe the real situation to them; in the second, he would give Sarah a divorce.

Another possibility Saadiah considers is that it was already a custom in biblical times for those entering a dangerous set of circumstances to give their wives a conditional divorce. Abraham may have already done this, or he may have given Sarah an unconditional divorce. This would explain why he says of her "She is my kinswoman" and not "my wife." Moreover, this story motif is narrated twice for Abraham and once for Isaac. If there were any feeling in the Torah that such behavior was reprehensible, it would not have been repeated.

Later Jewish commentators are also uncritical of Abraham. They seek to defend him by enlarging upon the vice and immorality of the Egyptians. Rashi (1090–1105), following the midrash, gives further support for Abraham's fear of the Egyptians by demonizing them, saying that they are lustful and are not used to seeing a pretty woman.

Hezekiah bar Manoah (France, thirteenth century), in his *Hizkuni,* reflects upon the level of civilization and morality accepted and actually practiced by the sons of Noah (including the Egyptians) after the flood. They were commanded to respect the dignity of the wife of another man; but though they were also commanded not to murder, their desire was so great that they could not control their impulses. Ovadiah Seforno (Italy, 1470–1550) cites Ezekiel 23.20 to demonstrate that Egypt was the home of lust.

David Kimchi (Provence, 1090–1165), renowned for his rationalistic approach to the Bible, offers a fuller treatment. He both denigrates the Egyptians and justifies Abraham's fear. Softening only somewhat the harsh opinions of the midrash and Rashi, Kimchi states that the Egyptians were not as attractive as the Canaanites because they were southerners, and therefore ugly and lustful. Abraham did not fear repeated raping of Sarah; that kind of behavior would not have been condoned by the Egyptians. What he feared was the one-time act of his being killed, which would leave Sarah alone and helpless. Of this Abraham was greatly afraid, despite God's promise that it would not happen; but his fear is transformed by Kimchi into a positive religious value. Abraham is concerned that his own sinfulness would negate God's promise, and he goes on to cite the Talmudic teaching that when in danger one must not depend upon a miracle [*TB Pesahim* 64b]. King Solomon praised this kind of legitimate fear: "HAPPY IS THE MAN WHO IS ALWAYS AFRAID" [Prov. 28.14].

However, a real change in exegetical approach is brought about by Moses ben Nahman (Ramban) (Spain, 1124–1200). He does not hesitate to criticize the behavior of Abraham and Sarah and to say that

---

earth to save the city for the sake of the righteous ones. How devastated we both were when ten righteous souls could not be found to avert the catastrophe. Gloom continuously pervaded our thoughts as the caravan traveled south. Our anxiety increased tenfold as we approached the region of the Negev and settled between Kadesh and Shur. Would this region also be an unholy place, inhospitable to strangers?

At Gerar Abraham haltingly announced that I would be introduced as his sister, for he feared that Abimelekh, the powerful king there, would see me and want to bring me to his chamber. If we were married, I would be forbidden to him, and so Abraham would first have to be eliminated. It was momentarily flattering to think that Abraham still found me so beautiful that he imagined others would desire me. This thought passed, quickly, though as the full meaning of Abraham's request made its impact.

No, Abraham was not insistent. The trope, the sound of his request, was more a statement than a question. "What about the covenant?" he whispered. "If I am murdered, how will the covenant be perpetuated?"

My husband felt humiliated by the sacrifice requested of me. He could

they sinned. Ramban also sees the biblical story as a foreshadowing of things to come. Thus he draws in detail the parallels between the experiences of Abraham in Egypt and those of the people of Israel, saying that nothing happened to the patriarch that did not also happen to his offspring. We shall see examples of the interconnection of the events of history, the former determining the latter.

Ramban makes the following amazing statement: "Know that our father Abraham sinned a great sin unintentionally by bringing this righteous wife before a stumbling block of sin because of his fear that he would be killed, for he should have trusted that God would protect him, his wife, and all that he possessed, for God has the power to help and save; also his leaving the Land...because of the famine was a real sin, for God would have redeemed him from death in the famine, and for this act exile under Pharaoh in Egypt was decreed against his offspring." Again, Ramban makes use of the foreshadowing exegesis: An earlier event in history determines a future one. Ramban continues and states that Sarah sinned in tormenting Hagar, and so did Abraham for allowing her to do so.

Ramban does not deny that Abraham feared a real danger. He asks why Abraham became afraid of the implications of Sarah's beauty just at the entry to Egypt, and he answers that Abraham was always aware of them. He had this fear whenever he approached a royal city, for it was the custom for the king to take the wife and kill the husband. Ramban notes that Sarah did not accept calling herself Abraham's sister, but the Egyptians were "very evil and sinful" and took her to the pharaoh's palace. However, Ramban softens his harsh judgment by stating that Abraham sinned "unintentionally" (בִּשְׁגָגָה *bish'gagah*); he was correct in recognizing the objective danger.

Va-Yera

barely allow his eyes to meet mine. The man who smashed his father's chief idol and argued with the Judge of all the earth stood before me with no vision for our salvation except a plan that would shame us both.

You say you condemn him for his cowardice? You must instead be merciful, for you can't imagine his desperation. Truth be told, I think you are viewing the story only from Abraham's perspective and see me as just a victim. But perhaps this story is about my test, not his. I was promised God's blessing, too. I was to bear a son, Isaac, and God would maintain the covenant through him. From my womb nations would rise, rulers of peoples would issue. Would all this be lost in the chamber of Abimelekh?

My agreement to pose as Abraham's sister was my own statement

Ramban, then, does not minimize the danger to Abraham, but he differs from Saadiah in his expectations of him.

Underlying Ramban's criticism of Abraham is his lofty estimation of the patriarch's spiritual power and responsibility. Precisely because Abraham is not an ordinary man he is criticized for his sin, and no allowance is made for his natural fear and weakness.

In various places in his commentary Ramban points out the spiritual excellencies of Abraham, such as his attainment of the higher level of daytime prophecy as against night visions, and his being named "lover of God" because he was ready to face martyrdom in Ur.

We have discussed so far the concrete, historical Abraham of the *peshat*, the literal. However, we must remember that Ramban was also a mystic. In numerous places in his commentary on the Torah he alludes to kabbalistic doctrine with the formula *al Derech ha-Emet*, according to the way the truth, or *Sitrei ha-Torah*, the mysteries of the Torah.

In kabbalistic thought, the Divine flow (*shefa*) makes its way to the lower world through the *sefirot* (vessels), which are the expression of God's attributes. The goal is to achieve a Divine flow that balances love and judgment, correcting the imbalance caused by a primordial sin that has flawed the system. The patriarchs, while real historical beings, can simultaneously be seen in kabbalistic terms. They are identified with certain *sefirot*, channels for Divine influence, and are connected with a higher cosmic reality. Ramban interpreted the Bible simultaneously on the two parallel tracks, the literal and the "way of truth." I suggest, therefore, that the interplay of *peshat* and mysticism is also operating in Ramban's elevation of the status of Abraham and, later, of Jacob. The literal interpretation of Abraham by Ramban has already revealed a man of heroic proportions. Add to this the enhanced Abraham of the cosmic *sefirot*, and there is simply no way to excuse the human fears of the patriarch. His sin must be criticized.

Finally, another question must be raised. Why does Ramban not criticize Jacob, who lied to his blind father, Isaac, pretending to be Esau [Gen. 27.19]? There is no lack of defenders for Jacob. For example, Rashi twists Genesis 27.19, "I AM ESAU, YOUR FIRST BORN" into "I AM [the one who brings this food to you]; ESAU IS YOUR FIRST BORN." Ibn Ezra on Genesis 27.12, however, maintains that Jacob is mouthing a legitimate lie.

If Abraham, with all his spiritual excellence, is to be criticized for moral weakness, then Jacob, also a man of formidable attainments, should also be held to high standards. Yet Ramban does not single out Genesis 27.19 for any critical evaluations of Jacob. On the contrary, he notes in several places Jacob's excellences.

---

of faith that surely God would not allow the covenant to be broken. Though I did not know what lay ahead, I believed that the Shekhinah, God's presence, would be with me, and I was not afraid. Abimelekh and I were never intimate. God came to Abimelekh in a dream, informing him that I was a married woman and must be returned to Abraham. Abimelekh pleaded with God to spare his life, for he was indeed blameless. Then he confronted Abraham as to the reason for the ruse.

Abimelekh seemed both stunned and saddened. Did sojourners in his land perceive that he would kill a husband for the pleasure of the wife? This was not the kind of ruler he wished to be. His longing to change was noted by Abraham, who then wondered if he had judged Abimelekh incorrectly in the first place. The veil of skepticism that had covered our lives since Sodom was lifted, and so was the curse on Abimelekh's household. Through Abraham's prayerful intervention, Abimelekh's wife and concubines became fertile again. And it was soon after, as God had promised, that I conceived and bore a son to Abraham.

I see by your expression that you have another question—one you are

Let us note, however, that criticism of Jacob is found in the midrash. It is told that Jacob was furious with Leah, calling her "a deceiver, the daughter of a deceiver (Laban)," for answering him during the wedding night as if she were the Rachel he thought he was addressing. Leah's answer to him was "Is there a teacher without disciples? Did not your father call you 'Esau' and you responded to him (as if you were he")?

The answer to our question lies in Ramban's conception of the nature of Esau, against whom Jacob is fighting for dominance. Esau is a supremely dangerous opponent, on both the literal and the kabbalistic levels. This situation is quite different from the earlier ones—Abraham's fear of Pharaoh or Abimelekh, who were not all so mighty, or Sarah's harshness against the powerless Hagar.

The problem began with Isaac, says Ramban, who failed to perceive any flaws in Esau's character. Rebekah was more realistic. She told Jacob that if Esau received the blessing, given through the Holy Spirit, it would belong to his offspring forever, and Jacob would never be able to stand up against his brother. Important also is the widespread Rabbinic and medieval identification of Esau and Rome, the Empire and the Church. Jacob foresaw the tragedy of his children's relationship with Esau on several levels. Here Ramban cites the medieval historical book *Yossipon*, which describes wars between Joseph and Esau's grandson.

Also operating is the principle of prophecy establishing a future reality. Isaac's blessing to Esau of "By the sword you shall live" determined, according to Ramban, the warlike and fearsome character of Esau and his offspring. Another prophecy was uttered by Jacob when he divided his camp into two parts, anticipating Esau's onslaught: "Now all of Israel will

---

Va-Yera

reluctant to pose. It is about my age? Ah, you want to know how old I was when Abimelekh desired me and how old I was at the birth of Isaac. The only answer is that it's not really important. One can be beautiful at any age if the *neshamah*, the inner beauty, dominates. And about Isaac? When one waits for a child, it is an eternity. The birth of a child, though, gives one new life. **Shoshana Silberman, Princeton, NJ.**

דָּבָר אַחֵר DAVAR AHER. AND IT HAPPENED AFTER THESE THINGS THAT GOD TESTED ABRAHAM AND SAID TO HIM, "ABRAHAM," AND HE REPLIED, "HERE I AM" [Gen. 22.1]. Much has been written, spoken, and thought about the Akedah—the binding of Isaac, or, what some Jewish and most non-Jewish writers call the Sacrifice of Isaac. It is, on the simplest level, depicted as the symbol of complete, unquestioning obedience to God by

fall into the hands of Esau." To paraphrase Ramban's words, Esau will not wipe out our names but will do harm to some of us in various lands. When one king decrees against our property or persons, another will show compassion and save the refugees.

Finally, we must reiterate that in the thought of Ramban, realistic and mystical motifs operate side by side. This is seen in Ramban's interpretation of the Yom Kippur ritual in Leviticus 16. On this day the scapegoat is sent to the wilderness as an offering to Azazel, the being who presides over desolate places and who is the guiding angel of the destructive maker of war, Esau. Indeed, Esau and Azazel are both identified with the prince of evil, Sama'el. This seems to be a risky movement toward dualism, where God must contend against the powers of evil. It is clear, then, that Esau has been elevated in the mystical thought of Ramban and others far beyond the historical, concrete level. He is seen as a dominant force for evil in the universe, which limits the reign of God, though he is not equal to God.

We may conclude that Ramban does not consider the situations of Abraham and Jacob to be equal. Abraham and Sarah dealt with helpless Hagar and with two kingdoms of limited strength. In Ramban's thinking, Jacob had to deal with Esau as a cosmic principle. The danger from Esau's possibly receiving the Divine blessing was so serious on a cosmic level that it had to be dealt with by Rebekah and Jacob on the human level by whatever means were available, including deceiving the old and blind Isaac.■

---

orthodox Jews, fundamentalist Christians, and pious Moslems.

In fact, the simple reading of the text (what in Jewish studies is referred to as the *peshat*, the seemingly obvious surface meaning of the material) would indicate such understanding: God wishes to test Abraham by asking him to sacrifice his son, and Abraham proves his submission to the Divine verdict. However, there are problems. First of all, our modern sensibilities, as well as our sense of Jewish ethics, stand aghast at such a Divine request, as well as at Abraham's acquiescence. Second, Isaac is the son promised Abraham by God, and if Isaac dies before producing sons, the Divine promise of future generations of descendants cannot be fulfilled.

So how can we, Jewishly and humanly, make sense of the binding of Isaac story? Perhaps a close reading of some of the original text will help.

"It was after these events (the peace treaty with Abimelekh, king of the Philistines) that God tested Abraham and called to him, 'Abraham!' and he answered, 'Here I am!' [Gen. 22.1]. How did such Divine communication take place? Was it God speaking to Abraham face to face? We know that only one human being spoke with God face to face, namely Moses [Deut. 34.10]. The only ways in which such Divine encounter is possible to other persons is through dreams or visions.

Then God said, "Take, please, your son, your only son, whom you love, Isaac, and go to the land of Moriah and sacrifice him there as a burnt offering at the place which I will show you" [Gen. 22.2]. There are a great number of Divine communications in the Bible—to Moses, to other prophets, also to Abraham himself. But this is the only instance when God does not simply command. "And Abraham got up early in the morning" [Gen. 22.3]. The key in this sentence is "got up," *va-Yashkem* in biblical Hebrew. This simply means to wake up early from sleep. And so, suddenly, we see a different picture! Abraham slept; he had a dream—and in this dream God appeared and asked him: Please, sacrifice your beloved only son to Me!

What do dreams mean? One is inclined to think that in ancient civilizations they had tremendous weight: predictions, premonitions, revelations of hidden truths, as in the story of Joseph interpreting the dreams of Pharaoh. But, in fact, there was no sophistication or skepticism. It was obvious that most dreams did not come true, and our ancestors were well aware of it. Take, for example, Rabbi Samuel

Va-Yera

ben Nachmani (early third century), who said: "A man in a dream only dreams what is in his own thoughts" [*Talmud Bavli, Brakhot* 55hb).

Abraham was surrounded by cultures in which child sacrifice was commonly practiced as a way to pacify the wrath of gods, show one's gratitude to them, or influence them in one's favor. He had done nothing to thank God for His many blessings, and, swayed by the practice of his neighbors, he would have felt remiss if he did not sacrifice Isaac. But by the same token, Isaac himself was part of this Divine favor bestowed on Abraham and was therefore not to be sacrificed. And so there is the solution in Abraham's dream: God appears in a dream, and both God and Abraham know that Isaac cannot be sacrificed. So God pleads with Abraham, and Abraham agrees, trusting that the sacrifice will not take place. He is willing to go along because he knows that God will substitute another victim. And his trust and submission to God are precisely in this knowledge.

So he sees no need to tell Sarah why he takes Isaac and two servants on a week-long trip—he knows they will be back. When, while walking up the slope of Mount Moriah, Isaac asks, "Where is the ram for the sacrifice?" he replies, "God will provide it." And before that, at the foot of the mountain, he says to the two servants: "STAY HERE WITH THE DONKEY. I AND THE BOY WILL GO UP AND WORSHIP AND THEN WE WILL RETURN TO YOU." Notice the verb is "worship," נִשְׁתַּחֲוֶה *nishtahaveh*, not sacrifice; and נָשׁוּבָה *nashuvah* "WE WILL RETURN"—in the first person *plural*!

So it seems the dream is the mirror image of Abraham's inner conflict between indebtedness to God and the desire to protect Isaac. And it is, in a larger sense, the separation and differentiation of Abraham and his descendants (including us today) from the pagan practices of his day—and perhaps of our day as well. **David Jordan, Temple Beth El, Haworth, NJ.**

דָּבָר אַחֵר DAVAR AHER. "TAKE YOUR SON, YOUR ONLY SON, THE ONE YOU LOVE, ISAAC" [Gen. 22.2].

If I Could Turn You Out Like A Light:

Bis a hundert un tzvansig, we say in Yiddish:
May you live to see a hundred and twenty years.
When I use that phrase
you wince, and sag, and mutter,
"No. Oh no. Not that."
Thus I learn the danger of mercy killing.
(THE WORD OF THE ETERNAL CAME TO ABRAHAM AND HE SAID
ABRAHAM ABRAHAM
AND HE SAID HERE I AM
AND HE SAID TAKE YOUR SON
YOUR ONLY SON
THE ONE YOU LOVE
ISAAC
AND OFFER HIM UP AS A SACRIFICE ON ONE OF THE MOUNTAINS I WILL SHOW YOU.)
How easy would it be now, right now, to suggest
that you're tired, that it's all gone on too long.
To imply gently, without words, that the old are a burden,

the sick and crippled a misery.
Our fathers would be better and
happier dead,
and of course the money has
nothing to do with it.
(In the morning he saddled his donkey
and set out for the mountain.)
"You look tired these days, Dad," I
could say with an understanding
smile,
and we'd go and see the doctor
and talk,
and attend the mandatory
counseling sessions and fill in all
the forms,
and I would explain the legal and
ethical details
dispassionately, careful not to
influence you,
careful to let you come to the right
decision yourself,
a fair trial and all that first, and hang
him afterwards.
(Isaac said Father
and he said Yes Son
and he said Here is the fire and the
knife but where is the sacrifice?
and he said God will provide the lamb
for the sacrifice
and they walked on together.)
Then would come a sad day in the
rain
and a needle or something in a
quiet room
with that Beethoven quartet you like
so well
playing on the stereo,
your life ending before the cut on
the record.
(He stretched out his hand with the
knife ready to kill his son and the
angel said
Abraham Abraham
and he said Here I am
and the angel said Do not kill the lad
or do anything to harm him)
The wonder is
not that Abraham ever dreamed of
stabbing Isaac
but that he heard the angel's voice
before it was too late.
We kill each other so
conscientiously these days.
Parents gas and starve their
children,
children smother and poison their
parents,
all in the name of love.
As if I could shrug you off like a
coat;
As if I could turn you out like a light.

Stephen Aberle

דָּבָר אַחֵר DAVAR AHER. "Take...Isaac, whom you love, and go to the land of Moriah, and offer him there as a burnt offering" [Gen. 22.1–2]. Throughout the middle ages the assumption was that God's test of Abraham was one of obedience or loyalty. Our great Jewish philosophers struggled with the Akedah story because it raised the problem of theodicy, God's sense of justice. How could it be that Abraham is commanded to do something not only cruel in itself but contrary to the repudiation of human sacrifice, which is part of the bedrock of our ethics? Maimonides agreed that this was a test case of the extreme limits of the love and fear God demands. Nachmanides saw it as the first instance of the compatibility of Divine foreknowledge and human free will. Others attempted to justify it with typical medieval gyrations.

What if Abraham failed the test? Consider the scene portrayed. Not only is Abraham compelled to lie to his son as they walk up the mountain, but he is humiliated at the very end. With knife in hand he hears a voice say (to paraphrase), "Hold on there, Abe. Do you know what you are doing? This is your one and only son. After all this contracting and all these commitments from you and promises from God, you're prepared to crash it all? What will the sense of your entire life have been if you end it all here? You should tell God that the deal is off. Better to put the knife to your own throat. Then at least your heritage—all that you began—will live on, and your life will have made good sense."

The scene does humiliate Abraham. The intention was never for Isaac to be the sacrifice. The ram was there all the time. Further, Abe names the place בְּהַר יהוה יֵרָאֶה *Behar Adonai yireh*. Even JPS translated "On the mount of the Lord, there is vision." There was great vision and understanding. Abraham grasped at that moment that God was challenging him vis-à-vis his own blood and flesh as he had vis-à-vis the wicked and evil people of Sodom and Gomorrah. Did Abe care about his work but not his home and family? Could Abe apply the ethics that he grasped from God to a personal situation?

Where was the moral outrage, which surely God expected from him? After all the struggling with a newfound relationship with this new God, Abe is put to a final test. How seriously will you consider this life-

Va-Yera

long struggle to comprehend your Adonai? So God puts him to the test, and he fails. But the failure gives Abe the greatest lesson of all: namely, that this is not like the pagan gods who created man only to serve their whims with sacrifices. This is the God-of-the-Universe who demands that man be partners in *tikkun olam*—not unquestioning order-takers of a supreme being. Often we learn the most when we fail. Abraham learned the most when he failed God's final test, *Behar Adonai yireh*.

Postscript: Why didn't the rabbinic commentaries pick up on this point? Why was there the propensity to view the test as one of strict obedience to God? First of all, we know that the only text that was well preserved was the *Tanakh*. Rabbinic commentaries (until the printing press) relied on transcribers to get the products to Jews desperate for knowledge and understanding. We can imagine that an Ibn Ezra may have raised the question of whether Abe passed or failed the test. But who will ever know what the copiers excluded? After all, they were out to sell their products. And when Jews needed to believe that obedience to God was their only hope in a dismal world, they needed Abraham as a model of obedience. *Kiddush ha-Shem* was desperate comfort when life was tenuous. And if you think that our medieval ancestors would have accepted any other view, consider their resistance to the Zionist movement or the ghetto uprisings in the Nazi era. The strong belief throughout the middle ages of suffering being our fault (see the musaf prayer, וּמִפְּנֵי חֲטָאֵנוּ *u'miPnei Hatah-eynu*) would never have allowed for the consideration that Abraham had failed the test.

What then are the implications if Abraham serves as our model for challenging and questioning God? There are abundant essays on the Jews' role of challenging and questioning. Isn't that why we are called עִבְרִים *Ivrim*—"one who is over there," and not part of the crowd? Looking in from the outside and doubting and questioning has been our historic role. It is so ordained by *Adonai, Eloheinu*. **Rabbi Morris A. Kipper, Coral Gables, FL.**

דָּבָר אַחֵר DAVAR AHER. ABRAHAM STRETCHED OUT HIS HAND, AND TOOK THE KNIFE TO SLAUGHTER HIS SON [Gen. 22.10]. What makes us think that Abraham did not fail the test? From the time Abraham accepted God's instruction (even if he prayed in his heart that God might avert the act), the fate of Abraham and Isaac – parent and child – was sealed. Freeze the frame for a second. Look into Isaac's eyes as they meet those of Abraham on Mt. Moriah. At the moment Abraham raises the knife against his son, Abraham destroys their relationship. Isaac may have descended Mt. Moriah without any bodily harm, but he was maimed, even destroyed, forever. Would that Abraham had gathered the moral courage to stand up to God when God called out to him and had simply said "No!" **Rabbi Kerry Olitzky, <Olitzky@huc.edu>**

דָּבָר אַחֵר DAVAR AHER. *Yiftah as a parallel to the Akedah:* This reading is about promises, deals, and facing the consequences. Unfortunately for him, Yiftah has to face the consequences after he makes a promise to God that results in his having to sacrifice someone very important to him.

Yiftah is a judge and is soon to fight the Ammonites. He asks God to ensure that he beats them, and he promises in return to sacrifice the first thing that comes out of his house to greet him when he returns.

God keeps his part of the deal, and Yiftah returns home safely, having beaten the Ammonites. As he arrives at his home in Mizpah his daughter (and only child) comes out of the house to meet him. He loves his daughter very much and feels a great sadness at the very thought of giving her to the Lord as a burnt offering. She tells him to keep his promise to God but to give her two months to go to the hills and think about things. He agrees. After the two months Yiftah sacrifices his only daughter.

I think Yiftah was too eager to win and would go to any lengths to ensure this, but he should have thought of the consequences before making such a dangerous promise. This story is very easy for me to understand because, like Yiftah, I have the desire to win at everything, and I very rarely stop to think about the consequences when I make promises; I find it very hard to think about what may be in the future when concentrating on present activities.

I think that Yiftah was wrong to try to beat the Ammonites with the aid of God. In my opinion he should have fought them fair and square. It was a very bad move to make a promise that he couldn't definitely keep, but it was a mistake that could have been made by anyone very easily. I wonder if maybe Yiftah could have asked that God excuse him from his promise, bearing in mind the circumstances, though I think it was very brave and honest of both him and his daughter to stick to the original deal without arguing.

This story is related to my Torah portion by many things. For example, in both of these stories someone has to make a choice about whether they will sacrifice a very important person in their life in order to do what is right by someone else. Abraham has to choose whether he will send his child away for the sake of his wife, and Yiftah has to decide whether he will literally sacrifice his daughter in order to keep his promise with God.

Also, I have noticed that in both of these stories God makes a promise to someone. God promises Abraham to make a nation out of both Ishmael and Isaac. And God promises Yiftah to help him defeat the Ammonites. Both of these stories involve tough decisions regarding personal choices.

This story has taught me not to make promises I can't keep, to think about what consequences a decision will have, and in general to think about my actions before I make a mistake that could affect the rest of my life.

דָּבָר אַחֵר DAVAR AHER. ON YIFTAH. ***A theological Q&A:*** If you have heard the news, you will know of the assassination of Yitzhak Rabin. Many people will mourn for a long time over the passing of a great man they did not personally know. This assassination sets a bad example for more than one reason. Why, from now on, should people be willing to do the right thing? When Rabin fought for peace, all it brought was more war, and his death. No one wanted to believe that history would repeat itself. Why, when Israelis wanted peace, did one of the leaders of a nation have to die?

This also sets a bad example of how Jews act. Why did a JEW kill Rabin, of all people? I know people are against the peace process, but killing isn't the answer. Why? ***C. J. Glass***

Dear C. J.: Here is what I know: My friend Andrew Gilbert, who lives in London, wrote to me with a Torah question. He is a silk merchant, but he also does bar/bat mitzvah tutoring because he thinks it is important. (He is a kind of hero of mine that way.) His rabbi shifted haftorot and matched the Akedah, this week's sidrah, with the story in Judges of Yiftah. His job was to help a bat mitzvah girl write her Davar Torah, and he asked for my help in making sense of the text.

Here is the story. Yiftah is the soldier son of a prostitute. We know the story: fatherless son from the gutter rises to power. Personal strength is

Va-Yera

his thing. Israel calls on him to lead them in a fight against Ammon. God's spirit visits him—because he is doing holy work. He knows he is on God's side. He makes an oath with God: "If I win, if I get back safe, the first thing I see when I get into town, the first thing out of the door of my house, I will offer to God." He goes and wins. He comes home, and his daughter dances through the doorway. The text goes: "AND HE DID AS HE HAD VOWED...AND SO IT BECAME A CUSTOM TO SAY DIRGES FOR THE DAUGHTER OF YIFTAH" [Judges 11.28].

This story seems like a worse version of the Akedah, not with God asking for a sacrifice, but rather with a man, just because he felt close to God, thinking that God wants him to sacrifice his daughter.... Cut to *Tanhuma* (a midrash collection) (see page 109 of *The Book of Legends*): Yiftah was as learned as a block of sycamore wood. He lost his daughter because he was stupid....

The Qadosh Barukh Hu said, "His vow was stupid. If a pig came out of his door first, would he have sacrificed that to me?" (*And I add in God's voice, "Did he want to make it like with the Nazis, and have me choose which of my creatures were to lose their lives?"*)

Phineas the high priest could have stopped it, but he was too proud to talk to a lowlife thug like Yiftah, even though he was in power. Yiftah could have gotten Phineas to stop it because priests can annul vows [cf: Lev. 27.8], but he was too proud a "leader" to ask anyone to help him. Both died in shame and pain.

Yiftah's daughter said to him: "You don't have to do this. Jacob [Gen. 28.22] promised to give 10% to God, and yet he didn't offer 1.3 of his 13 sons. Hannah vowed to give her son to God [1 Sam. 1.11], but she didn't kill him on the altar. Death isn't what God wants." Yiftah sacrificed her anyway!

Then the Qadosh Barukh Hu screamed in pain: "Did I ever ask people to sacrifice human life to me? I HAVE NOT COMMANDED IT. I HAVE NOT SAID IT. I NEVER EVEN CONCEIVED OF IT" [Jeremiah 19.5]. Yiftah's daughter died because though he thought he knew what God wanted, he was as stupid as a block of sycamore wood.

The lesson is simple. Yigal Amir wants to be a good Jew. He is passionate and dedicated. He read in the Torah that it is a mitzvah to protect Jewish lives and believed that Rabin was putting many lives at risk with a peace process that would end in a bloodbath. He was a Jew who read in the Torah that it is a mitzvah to conquer and occupy the entire Land of Israel. He believed that Rabin was trying to keep good Jews from fulfilling that command from God. He was well-meaning. His mother runs a preschool. His father is a *sofer*. And he is as ignorant as a block of sycamore wood.

The lesson of the Akedah and of Yiftah, and, unfortunately, the lesson of Barukh Goldstein and Yigal Amir, is that like other faiths, Judaism can be dangerous—if you don't read the whole Torah. When you set one vow over all the other commitments Torah asks you to make, when you forget that Jews have to live lots of values—then we make sacrifices on vain altars to a God who is made into an idol. The scary thing here is that a man who wanted to be good, who believed that he was faithful and religious in a tradition we share, could be the source of evil. It leaves us with only two choices: (1) to study and teach less Torah; (2) to study and teach more Torah—and foster real Torah thought. You know which one I will choose. **Joel Lurie Grishaver, <Gris@TorahAura.Com>**

ועשרים שנה ושבע שנים

Parashat Hayyei Sarah

Genesis 23.1–25.18

Savina J. Teubal

SAVINA J. TEUBAL IS THE AUTHOR OF *SARAH THE PRIESTESS: THE FIRST MATRIARCH OF GENESIS*, *HAGAR THE EGYPTIAN: THE LOST TRADITIONS OF THE MATRIARCHS*, *SIMCHAT HOCHMAH* (*JOY OF WISDOM, A CRONE RITUAL*) WITH DRORAH SETEL, AND THE WORDS TO ITS THEME SONG *L'KHI LAKH* WITH DEBBIE FRIEDMAN.

SARAH'S LIFETIME—THE SPAN OF SARAH'S LIFE—CAME TO ONE HUNDRED AND TWENTY-SEVEN YEARS. SARAH DIED IN KIRIATH-ARBA—NOW HEBRON—IN THE LAND OF CANAAN; AND ABRAHAM PROCEEDED TO MOURN FOR SARAH AND TO BEWAIL HER [Gen. 23].

Proper internment of the dead was a matter of importance to the peoples of the ancient Near East, but the Bible gives us little information about ancestral burial rites or ceremonies.

Was ancestor worship customary among the early Hebrews? The importance given to burial places suggests some belief in survival after death. The survival of the spirit or the soul of venerated persons would be particularly important to the community. Consequently, burial rites and gravesites came to reflect the status of the deceased; members of society honored and respected during their lifetimes were deserving of like consideration in death. Stories would circulate that enhanced their reputation and perpetuated their memory. It is striking, considering the scant attention given their lives, that burial places of women in the Bible were so carefully selected and recorded. Do the records of burials tell us something about biblical women that the texts fail to do?

The most detailed information about any biblical burial places concerns Makhpelah, the site chosen by

---

דָּבָר אַחֵר DAVAR AHER. SARAH'S LIFETIME WAS ONE HUNDRED YEARS [Gen. 23.1]. *Sarah's Story.* Long ago there was a young girl whose name was Sarai. She was growing up to be a priestess, just like her mother and her mother before her and her mother before her. Sarai's mother was the most respected member of her society, and Sarai was looking forward to being just like her one day.

Sarai was becoming a young woman and had learned much about her role as a priestess—how to solve problems and resolve disputes; how to make people feel better when they were sick; and how to talk to the gods. The people she called mother and father came to her and told her that she would be married to a man of the tribe of Terah. This would be good for her people, who wanted to live in peace

ויהיו **חיי שרה** מאה שנה

Abraham for Sarah. Much has been written about the price of the plot, the ethnic origin of the sellers, the source of the contract negotiations, and so on. Nevertheless, today's portion is about the death of the matriarch Sarah and the future of her descendants.

The report of Sarah's death significantly links the notice of the birth of Rebekah (which comes before it) with the narrative of Rebekah's betrothal to Isaac at the end of the Parashat: ISAAC THEN BROUGHT HER [REBEKAH] INTO THE TENT OF HIS MOTHER, SARAH, AND HE TOOK REBEKAH AS HIS WIFE. ISAAC LOVED HER, AND THUS FOUND COMFORT AFTER HIS MOTHER'S DEATH [Gen. 24.67].

That Isaac needed consoling after his mother's death makes us wonder why he was not there to mourn and bewail his mother's loss with Abraham. No mention is made of Isaac during Abraham's detailed negotiations for Sarah's resting place. According to the text, Isaac's last words to his father were "BUT WHERE IS THE SHEEP FOR THE BURNT OFFERING?" spoken as he and his father ascended the mountain to offer the sacrifice [Gen. 22.7]. Isaac never speaks to his father again in the text. In fact, Isaac does not appear on the scene again until Rebekah comes to Haran to marry him. The narrative that so dramatically centered on father and son now turns to Sarah and Rebekah.

Abraham is alone as he addresses the people of Hebron at the town gate. He asks them to intercede with Ephron, the owner of the Cave of Mekhpelah, to sell him the plot. The burial site is described in detail: the field with its double cave and all the trees within the confines of that field, Mekhpelah, facing Mamre. That the proceedings occur at the town

SYNOPSIS: *Sarah dies and is buried in the cave of the Mekhpelah. A servant finds Rebekah for Isaac. Abraham remarries and then later dies.*

RASHI OF THE WEEK:

In verse 24.3 Abraham makes his servant swear by "THE GOD OF HEAVEN AND THE GOD OF THE EARTH/LAND." *In verse 24.6 Abraham talks about* "THE GOD OF HEAVEN WHO TOOK ME FROM MY FATHER'S HOUSE." *Rashi asks:* What happened to "THE GOD OF THE LAND?" When I left my father's house, God was only the "GOD OF HEAVEN," but now, because I have taught all kinds of people about the One God, GOD is also known all over THE EARTH. GOD STARTED OUT AS THE GOD OF HEAVEN, but after I spread the word, the peoples of THE EARTH knew about GOD. *(And your editor thinks that in Haran the SKY GOD was a universal inspiration. In the LAND of Israel GOD became part of history.)*

---

with Terah's people. Sarai was excited to be able to help her people—and besides, she heard that Avram was a handsome and strong young man.

After they were married, Avram explained to Sarai that his God spoke to him and that they must leave Ur to go to the land of Canaan. Although Sarai did not hear the voice of God at that time, she understood what it meant to be commanded to do something for the good of your people—and she willingly went along. She would be the priestess to the people in the new land.

Sarai, like her mother before her, did not plan to bear her own child. She understood that the woman who actually gave birth to her was her mother's handmaid, whose name she had forgotten. Sarai hoped that one day she would have a handmaid who would have a baby, hopefully a girl who would become a priestess like Sarai and her mother.

After Sarai and Avram left Ur they went to the land of Canaan, but there was a famine there, so they went to the land of the great river Nile. There Sarai said that she was Avram's sister—which was true. Avram and Sarai had the same father but not the same mother.

gate implies that this transaction concerns more than just the seller and buyer of a plot of land. Despite belonging to one individual, the site concerns the whole community. Abraham, then, is not seeking to buy any old cave, but one that was a venerated site for the locals.

Does Abraham's choice of Mekhpelah as Sarah's resting place reflect her standing in the community? If Abraham was purchasing a family vault, as most scholars contend, Sarah's status is not an issue. Yet throughout the negotiations Abraham specifies that the cave he wants to purchase is to bury Sarah. The constant theme throughout the passage, BURY MY DEAD/BURY YOUR DEAD, repeated over and over (seven times in twenty verses), reads like a slow drumbeat. The "dead" they are referring to is, of course, Sarah.

Individual graves were not common in ancient times, and Mekhpelah did become the communal sepulcher of Sarah's extended family. However, double caves were often regarded as sacred resting places for exceptional people. Abraham may very well have initially purchased a particular sepulcher that conformed to Sarah's standing in the community, and it may very well have been hallowed ground. This is not an unreasonable interpretation because, as we shall see, all the graves allocated to the matriarchs were, or became, sacred sites.

Though the account of Rebekah's life is quite extensive the time of her death is not recorded and her burial in the Cave of Mekhpelah is only cursorily included with those of the rest of the extended family [Gen. 49]. On the other hand, a notice is given of the death and burial place of Deborah, Rebekah's nurse [Gen. 35.8], about whom we have no other information at all! She is presumably the unnamed nurse who left Paddam-Aram with Rebekah [Gen. 24.59]. At any rate, Deborah was buried under an oak below Bethel, and the tree was

---

Hayyei Sarah

They each came from a different handmaiden-mother. Saying she was Avram's sister was her way of telling Pharaoh that she was not a woman of the flesh but a priestess. Pharaoh wanted to violate her priestly code, but the God of Avram intervened. Sarai saw that the God who spoke to Avram in the land of Ur cared for her as well. When they left Egypt Pharaoh gave her many riches, including a handmaiden of her own named Hagar.

Sarai was pleased to have Hagar as a companion. Life was difficult traveling from Egypt back to Canaan. Sarai was well trained as a priestess, but traveling and preparing meals on the road were not really part of her education. Hagar helped her to understand what needed to be done and how to help the servants to do their work. Sarai soon saw

named Allon-Bacuth, the Oak of Weeping (or Tears). Deborah must have been an important figure in Hebrew legend, not only because her death was recorded but because the sacred tree under which she was buried acquired a name on account of her death. Nurse Deborah's Oak is often identified with the oracular palm tree under which Judge Deborah presided [Judges 4.5]. However, it seems to me that a sacred oak is not to be confused with an oracular palm, particularly since the former acquired a specific designation. It might be questionable that a palm tree grew in the hill country of Ephraim, but if it did, that would make it all the more exceptional. The only similarity between the trees of the two Deborahs is that both were located south of Bethel, a sacred area. That both women bore the same name is not exceptional either, given the era. (Deborah, meaning honeybee, was a title given to certain priestesses.)

Rachel died on a road close to Bethlehem some 3,500 years ago, giving birth to her youngest son, Benjamin. Jacob, her husband, placed a pillar over her grave. The pillar did not survive. The extant shrine was built by the Crusaders. The matriarch's impact on countless generations is quite amazing.

Rachel is a venerated ancestor to Arabs as well as Jews. I visited Rachel's tomb after the Six Day War, in which Israel captured the Sinai peninsula, Jerusalem, and the Golan Heights. The shrine was filled with people, mostly Arab women wailing and praying and beating their breasts. I asked my taxi driver what was going on. "They are pleading with Rachel to return Jerusalem to them," he replied.

All the matriarchs mentioned so far belonged to the generations that first settled in Canaan. All were buried in hallowed ground. As we turn to the next episodes in Israelite history, told in Exodus and in the wilderness narratives (Numbers), we find that Miriam, the most prominent woman in the stories, was no less exceptional than her foremothers.

It was Miriam who led the women in song and dance after the crossing of the Red Sea [Ex. 15.20] and who, together with Moses and Aaron, led the Israelites through the wilderness [Micha 6.4]. To her merit was due the well, which, according to legend, accompanied the children of Israel as long as she lived. Miriam died in Kadesh, and it was after Miriam's death that the people complained to Moses that there was no water to drink! This is really remarkable because Kadesh was an oasis. Obviously it had dried up when Miriam died. Kadesh and Kedesh were names used for cities in Canaan that were ancient water sanctuaries. Miriam was buried on this hallowed ground.

Miriam's story follows the pattern of accounts about women in the Bible; little is said about them that

---

that life in the new land with her new husband Avram was going to be different from her life back home. She was eager to have a daughter whom she could teach about the old ways so that her mother's way of life could be preserved. She asked Hagar to fill the sacred role of handmaiden, to mother a child with Avram so that Sarai's priestess line could be preserved.

Avram, of course, agreed to Sarai's plan, as he knew that both he and Sarai had been conceived in this way. Sarai was also pleased but not surprised when Hagar told her the very next day that she was sure that she was pregnant. What did surprise Sarai was that Hagar no longer treated her like her best friend. Instead, she acted meanly toward Sarai, teasing her for not being able to have children and sharing with her secrets that Avram had told her while they were together in his tent.

Sarai was very angry with Avram for this [Gen. 16.5]. This was not the way of her people. Hagar was Sarai's *shifha*, and Avram was not supposed to have a personal relationship with her. Why was he doing this?

"It is your fault," she said to Avram, "that Hagar is no longer treating me

explains their burial in sacred ground. We are left with the uneasy feeling that many of their experiences have been dropped from the records.

Hayyei Sarah, the account of Sarah's death and burial, must be viewed as the beginning of a long line of female successors to that matriarch. The stories of their lives have not survived in great detail, but the records of the matriarchs' deaths and places of burial supplement some of the silences.■

Hayyei Sarah

like a priestess and a friend. You are changing the rules, and God must decide which way is right."

At that moment Sarai's life changed forever. She opened her heart to the words of the God who had spoken to Avram—and she saw that the old ways must go forever. The God who had commanded them to go to the land of Canaan saw all people—Hagar, Sarai, and Avram—as created in God's image. Sarai saw that Avram was right when he treated Hagar as a wife—she was a person in God's eyes as well. No more could Sarai treat her as merely an instrument of her own will—no matter how righteous she thought she was being.

So Hagar was freed from her role as Sarai's *shifha*. She wanted and needed to leave the family of Avram and Sarai to find her own home. But God had other plans for her. God spoke to her and asked her to stay with Avram and Sarai, at least until her son was born. Hagar, too, was part of God's plan—so important a part that he spoke to her twice. Hagar was allowed to name God, and she called God "The God Whom I Have Seen."

God also spoke twice to Sarah. One time, when Avraham was being visited by messengers of God, Sarah feared that they were earthly men who were going to force her to break her priestly vows. She laughed when they said they had come to bring the news that she would become pregnant, because she thought they were trying to trick Avraham into asking her to sleep with them—or, worse, that they were planning to force themselves on her. She was afraid. But when she saw that they were messengers of God and that she really was going to bear her own child, she realized that there was no turning back to the old ways [Gen. 18.15].

But still she was afraid. So much was changing. In the old life she would have been an honored priestess. Her mother and her mother's mother had not had to work in the tent or raise their children or be wives to their husbands. In the new way, Sarah would have to do all of these things. Even her children would belong as much to her husband as to herself and would even carry his name. Was she really willing to give up the old ways?

As she was pondering this question she and Avraham came to the land of Abimelekh. Again she and Avraham said that she was Avraham's sister. Abimelekh treated her with the respect that was due her [Gen. 20.16]. Sarah reflected on all that was happening. She did not know when she left the Land of Ur that this God who wanted them to go to Canaan would so change their lives. Did she want to go back to Ur and to the old ways? This God who spoke and who saw demanded much of her—to be a woman of this world, yet still to be all the things she had been as a priestess; a woman who was created in God's image and who could be holy within this world and with the people, not above them.

Sarah was ready to accept the new life and the new God. And God was ready for her, as God visited her and she became pregnant, as promised, with the son Isaac, the laughter and the hope for the new ways.

After Isaac was born it was even clearer than before that Hagar did not have a place in the tribe of Sarah and Avraham. She and Ishmael were a reminder of the old ways. Hagar had changed. She no longer acted as a junior priestess to Sarah, but neither could she take the role as Avraham's partner. That was Sarah's job. Because he didn't fit in, Hagar's son Ishmael was always getting into trouble. Sarah saw that in order for them to find their place in the new order, as well as for the sake of peace in her own tribe, Hagar had to leave—as she had tried to do even before Ishmael was born.

God supported Sarah in the decision to have Hagar leave. And God supported Hagar when she was near death in the desert. God spoke to Hagar again and showed her the well of life. She knew that she and Ishmael were to bring the new God and the new order to the people who were not part of Sarah and Avraham's tribe.

Avraham was a good man. He did what Sarah told him when it came to Hagar. He followed his instincts and saw that, with a God who cared about all the people, no one could be less than equal. But still he was not sure where he fit into the scheme of things. He had seen the ways of Abimelekh and of Pharaoh. He knew that his covenant with God made him and his people different, but what were they to do? God had shown the way to Hagar and to Sarah. They had been tested and had chosen to accept the new ways and be leaders in the new order. Avraham had been commanded and had followed, but he had not seen the old order of his life shaken. He had not been changed to the core, as had Sarah and Hagar. Sarah and Hagar had sacrificed a way of life that was holy to them and that gave them great respect for the ways of God. Was Avraham willing to do the same? Did he really understand how much had changed from the old ways? He, too, needed to be tested.

Avraham's testing came with his sons, Ishmael and Isaac. Perhaps he failed the first test, when he was asked by Sarah to cast out Ishmael. Should he have considered other solutions? Avraham came now to believe that God wanted him to sacrifice his son Isaac at Mt. Moriah. When God intervened, God knew that Avraham also got the message. All of the old values had to go. Only personal responsibility and faith would do—but with these, Avraham, like Sarah and Hagar, would be guided onto the right path. But that's another story for another time.

Isaac witnessed what his parents did. He saw the courage of Sarah: She stood up to Avraham and forced the casting out of Hagar and Ishmael because she knew it was the right thing to do. He saw his father's growth: Avraham went along with the commandments of God from the very beginning. Of course, it felt right to him, but it never really challenged him to choose or to give up anything important. Only when he was tested with having to sacrifice Isaac did Avraham learn that he, too, had to be willing to give up important parts of himself—and to have faith that he would never be asked to do more than he could or more than was right.

Sarah knew that Isaac had seen these things. She was very old, she died content, and even in her death she was treated by Avraham with the respect that a priestess of God deserves. **Nancy Adel, Los Angeles, CA.**

דָּבָר אַחֵר DAVAR A<u>H</u>ER: *ON SARAH'S STORY.* I loved Nancy Adel's beautiful midrash about Sarah and

H̲ayyei Sarah

was only disappointed that Abraham's two great tests, the expulsion of Hagar and Ishmael and the near-sacrifice of Isaac, are "another story for another time." Perhaps she can offer an interpretation of why Sarah, who is the dominant figure in the first of these events, is silent in the second. (Or did it happen after her death, as some interpretations have it?) I very much look forward to the next installment. **Robert Chodos, <leischod@nic.wat.hookup.net>**

דָּבָר אַחֵר DAVAR AH̲ER: *ON SARAH'S STORY.* I think that Sarah knew something was up. My wife certainly would have. And my mother definitely would have. I think we don't hear from her because she followed along secretly. Maybe she was worried about having convinced Abraham to cast out Hagar and Ishmael. Maybe she was worried about what might happen to her own son. She knew she couldn't dissuade Abraham, so she crept along silently. When she saw what was about to happen, either she placed the ram (which she would have had to have brought with her) in the thicket or she became the ram herself, sacrificing herself for Isaac's sake, and perhaps explaining her death right after this episode. **David Parker, <Parques@aol.com>**

דָּבָר אַחֵר DAVAR AH̲ER. And Abraham said to his servant, the elder of his household, "To my land and to my kindred shall you go and take a wife for my son for Isaac." [Gen. 24.2–4]. I have two questions on the Torah portion. Why does Abraham send away for a wife for Yitzh̲ak? And why isn't it Yitzh̲ak who goes? **Shaye Horwitz**

(1) WHY SEND FOR A WIFE? The "official answer" is that Abraham was worried that if Isaac took a local girl, he might become involved with her family and do all their idol stuff and forget about this new religious thing—THE ONE GOD DREAM—that his father was messing with. But if we send back to the old country, get a girl "just like the one who married dear old dad," while she won't understand THE ONE GOD DREAM immediately, she will feel closer to Abe's family (who speak her language and follow most of her customs) than to the locals, so she will learn THE ONE GOD DREAM from them and not lead Isaac astray.

(2) WHY DIDN'T ISAAC GO? What I remember from some lesson long ago (but cannot find today) is the reason that Abraham says in verse 24.8, "If the woman will come—good—but under no conditions let my son Isaac go back there" is that it may have something to do with either not trusting Isaac to come back to the father who almost killed him, or that in order to make sure that they kept their title to the land of Israel they needed to be around. I don't remember. **Joel Lurie Grishaver, <Gris@TorahAura.com>**

דָּבָר אַחֵר DAVAR AH̲ER. "To my land and to my kindred shall you go and take a wife for my son for Isaac." [Gen. 24.2–4]. I had the same question, but from this perspective.

Why, if Abraham had followers who believed in this one God idea (he had at least 318 that fought for Lot's release), did he need to send away for a mail-order bride? I think this is a great topic about going out of one's tribe to marry. I am also not sure why Abraham did not send out Eliezer to just bring back Rebekah if he had already been told by God that she would be Yitzhak's wife. One more thing is if Rebekah came to the self-realization about one God at the age of three and she was surrounded by bad guys, then why is she not given any of the credit that Abraham gets for this monotheistic idea? **Arye Berk, <lberk@freenet.columbus.oh.us>**

דָּבָר אַחֵר DAVAR AHER. "TO MY LAND AND TO MY KINDRED SHALL YOU GO AND TAKE A WIFE FOR MY SON FOR ISAAC" [Gen. 24.2–4]. On the question of why send away for a wife, we had a *mahloket* about this at our congregational Torah discussion last weekend. One side saw it as simply an early version of "I don't want my son to marry a *shiksa*," but there was another, subtler interpretation that I think your reply points to. If Isaac married a local woman, he would assimilate into local society, whereas by sending to his birthplace for a wife Abraham ensured that his family would remain apart—retain their otherness—so that THE ONE GOD DREAM, as you say, would survive. As for Isaac's staying home, and, in fact, not being consulted about any of this, I think it fits into a larger picture.

AND THEY SAID, "LET US CALL THE MAIDEN AND ASK HER DECISION" [Gen. 24.57]. Note that Rebekah, by contrast, is consulted and freely gives her consent. As we move on it is Rebekah whom God tells that the older of the twins she is to bear will serve the younger; Isaac is kept in the dark. And it is Rebekah who ensures that God's instructions are carried out by masterminding the switched-blessing caper; again, Isaac has to be manipulated for this to happen. In other words, the effective transmitter of the covenant in her generation is Rebekah. For whatever reason, Isaac simply does not have what it takes to be entrusted with the decisions on which the whole future of the Jewish people depends. The first step is to ensure that there is a woman of great strength, wisdom, and resourcefulness around to make up for Isaac's deficiencies, and this is what we get with Rebekah. **Robert Chodos, <leischod@nic.wat.hookup.net>**

דָּבָר אַחֵר DAVAR AHER. "TO MY LAND AND TO MY KINDRED SHALL YOU GO AND TAKE A WIFE FOR MY SON FOR ISAAC" [Gen. 24.2–4]. In the general scheme of Jewish history, Isaac seems to play an insignificant part. He has the status of neither Abraham nor Jacob. In fact, in almost every episode of his life someone is doing something for him or to him. Yet with all that happens to him, he emerges with dignity.

One of the events in which Isaac seems to be almost irrelevant is when Abraham, on his deathbed, sends his servant to find a wife for Isaac. The servant is nameless, unlike the named servant "Damesek Eliezer" in Genesis 15.2. It is unclear whether this servant is the same Eliezer. And to add more anonymity to this parashah, it is unclear whether Rebekah even knows anything about her future husband, since the Torah records nothing about her asking about him until they are actually within sight of each other!

Rebekah seems to be silent. The servant has no name. Rebekah's father Bethuel does not play a part in the betrothal, and in fact, the Torah is not sure if he is even alive! Even the angel who is supposed to lead the servant doesn't seem to be doing much. To top it all off, Isaac is back at home wandering about and meditating [Gen. 24.63]. In fact, the only ones who really seem to play an active part are Laban and the unnamed servant—and we all know what Laban is really after. All in all this parashah is a skit with very odd actors whose names are unknown, whose motivations are unclear, and whose parts don't really have much character development!

Yet in spite of it all, this story is essential to the development of the Jewish people. Without each of the players doing what they did at that precise moment in history, there would be a very different Jewish people today. Isaac is a precious link between Abraham and us; Rebekah is the mother of Jacob, the primary progenitor of the Jewish people; greedy Laban agreed to the terms with the servant who permitted Rebekah to leave, thus giving Isaac a wife; and the unnamed servant was the catalyst that made it all happen.

<u>H</u>ayyei Sarah

This parashah, despite its oddness, is really an acknowledgment of some of the most important players in Jewish history. Our history is not just filled with super-prophets who speak to God on mountaintops, who challenge or inspire kings, or who destroy idol worshippers with God's fire and earthquakes. Rather, the great majority of Jews, then and now, are nameless ones. They have no power of prophecy. They do not have revelations. Their lives are lived in the service of their families, God, and the Jewish people. They are much like you and me.

Like you and me, these ordinary people doing ordinary things are the ones who perpetuate what is best about Judaism and the Jewish people and are the *"Am"* in *"Am Yisrael."* To be the common person in Israel is to be part of the infinitely precious chain that passes Torah from generation to generation. Most of us will never be famous, but that does not mean that our tradition sees us as anything less than precious. **Rabbi Cy Stanway, Temple Beth El, Las Cruces, NM.**

דָּבָר אַחֵר DAVAR A<u>H</u>ER. SHE WAS A VIRGIN, NO MAN HAD KNOWN HER [Gen. 24.16]. The story's riddles are just beneath the surface. Near the end of his life the patriarch Abraham solicits his trusted servant Eliezer to return to his ancestral family home to seek a wife for his son Isaac. Eliezer must find a woman whose values match the high standards of the founder of ethical monotheism. He devises a personality test: He will position himself at the city's well and ask the city's maidens for water. The one who both provides him with water and offers to draw water for ten thirsty camels is the appropriate match for Isaac. And indeed, Rebekah, the daughter of Bethuel – identified as the king of Na<u>h</u>or by the midrash in *Pirkei d'Rabbi Elazar* – appears and fulfills the requirements exactly and graciously. In Jewish tradition she becomes the model of *<u>h</u>esed*, compassion.

Yet why was the princess drawing water at the well like some common girl? Also, the sages say in *Bereshit Rabbah* that hers was a wicked family. Where did she learn compassion? A clue lies in the biblical overemphasis on her chastity: "SHE WAS A VIRGIN, NO MAN HAD KNOWN HER" [Gen. 24.16]. Commentators explain the double phrase as meaning that in her society young girls technically protected their virginity but were expected to engage in other sexual practices. Rebekah's beauty—"SHE WAS VERY FAIR TO LOOK UPON"—made her all the more vulnerable.

Rebekah is able to fend off strangers, but the real danger is at home. When first petitioning the family Eliezer speaks to both her brother Laban and her father Bethuel. Yet the next morning only her brother and mother are present. *Bereshit Rabbah* explains that her father died that night. Rabbi Meir of Rotenberg, the 13th-century Talmudist, ties together this midrash and the Talmud's discussion in *Tractate Ketubot* of the *droit du seigneur*, the "lord's right" of the first night, and posits that Bethuel is a word-play on *betulot*, virgins. As king of his city, he argues, Bethuel was the forceful deflowerer of young brides. Betrothed that night, Rebekah waits in terror for this act of forced intercourse from which only Bethuel's death can free her. "NO MAN KNEW HER" gains the additional meaning that her father did not have the opportunity to rape her. Nonetheless, she may have been molested previously—not willingly engaging in the immoral practices of her community but a victim for whom status offered no protection.

Rebekah was raised in a family where sexual assault on young women was taken as the norm. In modern parlance, her family is dysfunctional. Susan Forward, an authority on sexual abuse of women, uses the stronger term "toxic parents" for those "whose negative patterns of behavior are consistent and dominant in a child's life." Toxic parents can be verbal, physical, or sexual abusers of their children, alcoholics or substance abusers, or inadequate parental figures. Children raised by them, Forward argues, can develop low self-esteem, feelings of inadequacy, guilt, rage, or self-destructive behavior.

Rebekah, while bearing scars from her upbringing, makes decisions that take her life in a different direction, making her the victor over her upbringing rather than its victim. Her time at the well was an opportunity for contemplation; she realizes that another way of life is possible. Compassion becomes her response to being raised in cruelty. When given the chance for a different life, Rebekah seizes it. She leaves the next day with Eliezer, though her family wants her to remain to prepare for the marriage and to mourn her father. In Isaac Rebekah finds "the safe male" who loves her for her compassion.

Rebekah, like many children raised in abusive atmospheres, is vigilant and aware. She knows that her son Esau, Isaac's favorite, who exhibits her family's propensity for momentary pleasures, cruelty, and self-involvement, is not the right choice to lead the Jewish people. Jacob possesses the steadiness of purpose and purity of nature for that role. Yet, scarred by her past, Rebekah is unable to confide in Isaac. Instead she resorts to subterfuge both to secure the blessing for Jacob and to save him from Esau's anger. Still, the continuation of family and of ethical monotheism results from her ability to see past appearances.

Before aiding the stranger Eliezer Rebekah has courageously decided not to succumb to the wickedness of her surroundings. And she is at the well. She is there waiting for a different and better reality. She is there in hope and as the model for others that the abuse of one's youth can be overcome and that a life can be built instead on ethical values. Daniel Landes & Sheryl Robbin. **Rabbi Daniel Landes is director of Pardes Institute of Jewish Studies. Sheryl Robbin is a writer and a psychologist. They live in Jerusalem. This piece originally appeared in *The Jerusalem Report*, November 14, 1996. Reprinted with permission of the authors.**

Parashat Toldot

Genesis 25.19–28.9

Dr. Neil Gillman

NEIL GILLMAN IS THE AARON RABINOWITZ AND SIMON H. RIFKIND ASSOCIATE PROFESSOR AND DEPARTMENT CHAIR IN JEWISH PHILOSOPHY AT THE JEWISH THEOLOGICAL SEMINARY OF AMERICA. HE IS THE AUTHOR OF *SACRED FRAGMENTS: RECOVERING THEOLOGY FOR THE MODERN JEW* (JPS, 1992), AND OF *CONSERVATIVE JUDAISM: THE NEW CENTURY* (BEHRMAN, 1996). HE IS CURRENTLY AT WORK ON A STUDY OF JEWISH ESCHATOLOGY.

Blindness and deception. These are the twin themes that run through this week's Torah portion. In fact, the second—deception—is central to the rest of the Genesis narratives.

What is striking about the tone of this narrative is the total absence of any judgmental attitude toward the behavior of the protagonists, doubtless because the editorial assumption of the text is that it is God's hand guiding the proceedings.

Though God's involvement remains well hidden, the narrator is freed from having to pass judgment on what is transpiring.

Instead, the protagonists are portrayed as acting in a thoroughly natural way. They do what people typically do in similar circumstances. What remains striking is the richness of the character portrayals that are evoked.

First Isaac. The conventional wisdom is that of the three patriarchs, Isaac is the most shadowy (as a reaction to the trauma of the Akedah?). It has even been suggested that Isaac never existed at all, that he represents simply a bridge between his monumental father and his complex son Jacob. But this assumes, among other things, that Abraham and Jacob are indeed historic personalities, which, of course, is equally open to question.

דָּבָר אַחֵר DAVAR AHER. AND REBEKAH TOOK THE CHOICEST GARMENTS OF ESAU, HER ELDER SON, WHICH WERE WITH HER IN THE HOUSE AND PUT THEM UPON JACOB, HER YOUNGER SON [Gen. 27.15]. It is a well-known fact that history repeats itself, but nowhere is it more apparent than in our Bible. It seems that one of the most common themes that links generation to generation is deceit. Instead of the word "**begat**" we could easily insert the word "**deceit**" or another word with the same meaning to paint a picture of our family tree: The Serpent **beguiled** Eve. Eve **deceived** Adam. Abraham **hustled** Sarah. Abraham **ensnared** Isaac. Isaac **hustled** Rebekah (like father, like son), Rebekah, in turn, **manipulated** Isaac. Jacob **bamboozled** Esau, and then Jacob **duped** Isaac. Laban and Leah **tricked** Jacob, and Joseph's brothers **shafted** everyone. If we took out the

ואלה תולדות יצחק בן

But the shadowy quality of Isaac's depiction was confirmed when I consulted Louis Ginzberg's *Legends of the Jews*. I noted that Part V of Ginzberg's first volume is devoted to Abraham, and Part VI to Jacob. Where is Isaac? He is portrayed in the last chapters of the Abraham material and the first chapters of the Jacob material. In other words, Isaac seems to have no independent identity beyond his relationships with his father and his son.

Nothing revolutionary happens in Isaac's time. All of his accomplishments repeat those of his father. His is an age of stability, of consolidation, a plateau between the towering experiences of his father and his son. But we should be grateful for periods of consolidation. They enable us to integrate what we have learned, internalize it, and prepare to transmit it to those who follow us.

Isaac was blind. Or was he? The text contains sufficient hints that Isaac knew perfectly well that it was Jacob who stood before him for the blessing, not his beloved Esau. Neither was Isaac's failure an intellectual blindness, but rather the intuitive reaction of a mild-mannered man who could not confront his son or his wife and deal openly with their trickery. Isaac was blind to the fact that failure to deal with conflict simply perpetuates the conflict, never resolves it.

Rebekah emerges as the most rounded of the matriarchs. Her behavior reminds us again that these biblical women are strong-willed, self-assured, and competent human beings. Rebekah clearly loves her husband, but because she also understands her sons she is determined to protect Isaac against himself. She knows what has to be done and pro-

---

deceit and the schemes from these stories, we wouldn't have been expelled from the garden, we wouldn't have ended up in Egypt, and therefore we wouldn't have made it to Israel.

But of all these events, there are only two that are not a simple question of deceit. These are the stories of Abraham and Rebekah. They demand a closer look, because unlike the other characters who are involved with plotting and scheming, Rebekah and Abraham deceive members of their family in order to fulfill God's prophecy.

Our parashah begins with the usual lineage:

וְאֵלֶּה תּוֹלְדֹת יִצְחָק בֶּן-אַבְרָהָם
אַבְרָהָם הוֹלִיד אֶת-יִצְחָק,

v'Eyleh toldot Yitzhak ben-Avraham, Avraham holid et-Yitzhak AND THESE ARE THE GENERATIONS OF ISAAC,

SYNOPSIS: *Jacob and Esau struggle in the womb over a birthright and over the family blessing. Isaac has a wife-sister story and then redigs Abraham's wells. Both sons are blessed and Jacob leaves home.*

RASHI OF THE WEEK:

At the end of the blessing of Esau (who is actually Jacob), Isaac says: THE SMELL OF MY SON IS LIKE THE AROMA OF FIELD WHICH יהוה THE ETERNAL HAS BLESSED—THEREFORE MAY הָאֱלֹהִים GOD GIVE YOU OF THE DEW OF THE LAND [Gen. 27.27–8]. *Why does Isaac first call the Deity "The Yud-Name" and then call the Deity "God"? Rashi answers that* the Midrash says, God uses The "E-Name" to conjure the Midat ha-Din *(the aspect of Judgment)* saying may God be just—If you are worthy may the Judge grant you these blessings, but if you are not worthy may the Judge not grant you anything. But when he actually blessed Esau (as Esau) he said, "THE FAT PLACES OF THE EARTH SHOULD BE YOUR HOME." *Because as your father, I love you unconditionally, I want things to be good for you. Showing his parental mercy. God is never mentioned in the actual blessing given to the real Esau, because if judged, Esau (like most of us) would never be blessed.* This is why Solomon built the temple *(in a fat place)*, according to this lesson [1 Kings 8.43].

ceeds to do it in whatever way is available to her.

Jacob is the deceiver. That is his name and that is his role, a role that clings to him throughout his career. For the message of the Jacob story is that deception begets deception. Jacob will suffer many times because of people who deceive him—Laban, his sons, and ultimately his beloved Joseph.

The full irony of the story emerges only in the later tradition, when Esau, identified first as the father of Amalek and later with Rome, still later becomes identified with Christianity. The theme of Christian supersessionism (the idea that God's covenant through Jesus of Nazareth was designed to supersede or supplant God's earlier covenant with Israel), which is commonly understood to be central in Paul and later becomes normative Christianity, is an ironic commentary on Jacob's supplanting of Esau. That is Esau's ultimate revenge on Jacob/Israel, and only within the past few years, in the writings of Christian theologians such as Paul van Buren, has that reading of Paul begun to be questioned.

Finally, there is Esau. There are precious few hints of sympathy for Esau in the Rabbinic Midrash, but the biblical narrative itself captures the full measure of pathos that he evokes. His "WILD AND BITTER SOBBING" [Gen. 27.34] when he hears of Jacob's trickery is one of the most powerful emotional outbursts in the Bible. His anger at his family is palpable and clearly justified. Rebekah is terrified of the potential destructiveness of that anger, which is why she orders Jacob to flee.

Part of our discomfort with Esau is surely cultural and sociological. Esau is the blue-collar worker, rough-hewn, gruff, tanned, and hairy, a man who works with his hands—an outdoorsman. For most of our history we Jews have been more identified as Isaacs; we are indoorsmen, we dwell in tents, we

---

Toldot

ABRAHAM'S SON; ABRAHAM FATHERED ISAAC.

While the men in the Bible never seem to have any problems begetting, the women never seem to be able to have children without God's help. So after Rebekah and Isaac were married, Isaac entreated the Lord for her because she was barren. And when Rebekah finally does conceive, she feels the children struggling inside her. So much so that instead of relying on her husband again SHE GOES TO INQUIRE OF GOD directly וַתֵּלֶךְ לִדְרֹשׁ אֶת-יהוה, *vataleh̲ lidrosh et-Adonai.*

For the first and only time in the Bible, the text says the following words: וַיֹּאמֶר יהוה לָהּ, *va Omer Adonai la,* "AND GOD SPOKE TO HER." To Rebekah. An unmediated encounter with God.

study and teach, we hold white-collar jobs in management and the professions.

We also know that at critical moments in our life experience we need Esaus to repair our cars, to move our furniture, to till the fields, to build our homes. Despite that dependency, or more probably because of it, we tend to view our Esaus with a modicum of contempt, and they are surely aware of that reaction on our part. They may not be as articulate as we are in expressing their feelings, but the feelings are there.

The paradox is that Israel's history is much more that of Esau, the supplanted one, than of Jacob, the supplanter. Jacob/Israel's triumph was short-lived. The voice may well be the voice of Jacob, and the hands, the hands of Esau. Yet it is Esau's sobs that echo throughout the generations of Jewish existence.

For further study. We are blessed with three outstanding books on these Genesis stories, all published within the past year: Norman J. Cohen's *Self, Struggle and Change: Family Conflict Stories in Genesis and Their Healing Insights for Our Lives* (Jewish Lights); Avivah Gottlieb Zorenberg's *The Beginnings of Desire* (JPS); and Peter Pitzele's *Our Fathers' Wells* (HarperCollins). Also helpful throughout is *The Torah: A Modern Commentary*, edited by W. Gunther Plaut (UAHC). ■

Midrash Rabbah states, "Rabbi Judah and R. Simeon and R. Johanan, in the name of R. Eleazar b. R. Simeon, said, 'The Holy-One-Who-is-to-Be-Blessed never engaged in speech with a woman save with that righteous woman, Sarah, and that, too, was due to a special cause.'" So, the rabbis note that this, too, is a special cause. The prophecy that God gives her reveals that two nations are in her womb, and that the older shall serve the younger.

These prophecies are reminiscent of another biblical character's journey: Abraham, the father of the Jewish faith, received a similar prophecy. In fact, he received command after command until at last he was tested by God to sacrifice his own son, Isaac. When Abraham, the ever-ready servant of God, received this command from God he hastened to perform the task.

Rebekah, on the other hand, did not sit around and wait to receive a command from God. Instead she seized the moment, searching for God's prophecy for her. When she heard Isaac telling Esau to prepare food so that he could bless him, she was finally faced with the situation that she had assumed God had planned out already. There it was in front of her—Isaac had called upon Esau to receive the blessing. How was she going to insure God's words —that Jacob, and not Esau, would receive Isaac's blessing before his death?

Just as Abraham neglected to include his wife, Sarah, and his elder son, Ishmael, in the fulfillment of God's command, Rebekah left her husband, Isaac, and her elder son, Esau, out of her plans to implement God's prophetic words.

As we look back to the events in Genesis 22, when Abraham is preparing Isaac for the sacrifice, laying the wood in order and binding his son, the ram that is used in place of Isaac has parallels to Rebekah's commands to Jacob: "GO NOW TO THE FLOCK, AND FETCH ME FROM THERE TWO GOOD KIDS OF THE GOATS." In order to prepare her son Jacob to receive the blessing, Rebekah, like Abraham, goes through careful ministrations and preparation: AND REBEKAH TOOK THE CHOICEST GARMENTS OF ESAU, HER ELDER SON, WHICH WERE WITH HER IN THE HOUSE AND PUT THEM UPON JACOB, HER YOUNGER SON. AND SHE PUT THE SKINS OF THE KIDS OF THE GOATS UPON HIS HANDS, AND UPON THE SMOOTH OF HIS NECK. AND SHE GAVE HIM THE SAVORY FOOD AND THE BREAD, WHICH SHE HAD PREPARED, INTO THE HAND OF HER SON JACOB.

Midrash Rabbah again depicts Rebekah as one who is directly involved with God. What the Midrash states regarding the verse AND SHE GAVE HIM THE SAVORY FOOD is that "She accompanied him as far as the door and then said to him: 'Thus far I owed thee (my aid); from here onward thy Creator will assist thee.'"

Hazan Ira Rohde

Hazan Ira Rohde is the cantor/educator at Congregation Shearith Israel in New York City.

Toldot

Everyone is familiar with the custom of eating an egg or something round at the mourners' meal; the source of this custom is in Rashi on Genesis 25.30. Jacob had originally cooked the "Pottage of lentils" he served Esau as a meal of mourning upon the death of Abraham. Lentils, like eggs, are round, symbolizing the cyclical recurrence of mourning (and, we might add, that of rebirth as well). Another explanation is given in an old version of Rashi:

Something round has no indentation or opening, like the mourner who has no "mouth" to speak or to answer. I've felt a lot of this lately—it's been a rough week for writing.

Our forefather Yitzhak was the first sabra among the patriarchs and of the first generation born in the Land. Indeed, he was prevented from ever leaving the Land. He has always struck me as the most rooted of the patriarchs, the closest to the soil, the one most in harmony with nature, with the earth. About no other patriarch are we told of the agricultural productivity of their land, only Isaac. Isaac went to meditate in the field; he loved the taste of wild game. He sought God in and through nature; the scent of the field upon his son's clothing reminded him of God and put him in the proper frame of mind for pronouncing the blessing. His inner harmony with God and the earth is what enables him to find sources of physical and spiritual water wherever he goes. He is the most passive of the patriarchs; he can simply walk away from a confrontation with the

---

The description in the text of Jacob as he approaches his father disguised as Esau begins: And he came unto his father and said: "My father," and he said, "Here I am; who are you, my son?"

וַיָּבֹא אֶל-אָבִיו וַיֹּאמֶר אָבִי,
וַיֹּאמֶר הִנֶּנִּי מִי אַתָּה בְּנִי

va-Yavo el-Aviv va-Yomer Avi va-Yomer Hineini Mi Ata B'nai? This echoes Isaac's own brush with death on Mount Moriah: And Isaac spoke to Abraham his father, and said, "My father," and he said, "Here am I, my son."

וַיֹּאמֶר יִצְחָק אֶל-אַבְרָהָם אָבִיו,
וַיֹּאמֶר אָבִי וַיֹּאמֶר הִנֶּנִּי מִי אַתָּה בְּנִי

va-Yomer Yitzhak el-Avraham Aviv va-Yomer Avi va-Yomer Hineini v-Nai. But the echo that stands out most clearly is the similarity of sound and sight between the word יַעֲקֹד, *yakod*, to tie hand to foot, and יַעֲקֹב, *ya'akov*, named so because "his hand had hold on Esau's

וְאֵלֶּה **תּוֹלְדוֹת** יִצְחָק בֶּן אַבְרָהָם

Philistines, and yet his deep sense of rootedness and tenacious persistence earn him his enemies' respect and fear, if we are to judge from the epithet given to Isaac's God, the "FEAR OF ISAAC."

It is no wonder that Isaac, the man of "natural religion," loves Esau, the MAN OF THE FIELD. Physical appearances, however, can deceive, and one who always demands that the outward expression match and be in harmony with the inner spiritual content is likely to be led astray.

Yaakov comes from a root meaning "the crook of the heel." It is at the heel and ankle that the leg bends into the foot and becomes "crooked." The story of Yaakov's life is that of his transformation into Yisrael, of the "crooked being made straight." As I mentioned last year,

Rabbi Ovadiah, Maimonides' grandson, contrasts the spirituality of Isaac, the hermit of the fields, with that of Jacob, the hermit in his own tent, the spirituality of nature versus the spirituality of civilization. But what is this "spirituality of civilization?"

In Genesis 25.26 it says, "AND HE CALLED HIS NAME JACOB," and doesn't mention the subject. Rashi gives two interpretations. "The Holy-One-Who-is-to-be-Blessed [thus named him]; another explanation: his father called him Yaakov because he was grasping the heel." What is the difference between God calling him Yaakov and Isaac doing so? Another version of Rashi adds to the first explanation "you have given your firstborn a name, I, too, will give my son, my firstborn, a

name." But Rashi does not say the reason that God calls him Yaakov. Why not?

It seems to me that God calls him Yaakov based on a meaning of the name that Rashi mentions earlier. The root *kv* has the derivative meanings "following upon the heels of" or "consequent to." "Following upon" or "consequent to" are the meanings the term *ekev* has in Genesis 22.18, as well as in Deuteronomy. The spirituality of civilization is not as concerned with communion and harmony with nature as it is with following the mitzvot and bearing responsibility for the consequences of one's actions. It is for this reason that the firstborn of The Holy-One-Who-is-to-be-Blessed proudly called him Yaakov. ∎

HEEL." Not only is Jacob sent to bring the savory meal to Isaac, but the skins of the goat disguise him as the sacrificial animal itself, recreating the role Isaac played to his father in the Akedah. The plan that enabled Rebekah to secure Jacob's place as the son who received the blessing from Isaac is the same plan that later caused Jacob to be confronted with his own death when he met up with Esau, the brother he deceived, and the 400 men with him. Another near-sacrifice.

All of the details that suggest Rebekah's active involvement in this parashah lead me to conclude that Rebekah, like Abraham, is portrayed

as a model of faith for us to consider. Her forthrightness, her willingness to see God's prophecy fulfilled rivals that of other God-fearing characters in the Bible. And just as we struggle with the story of יִצְחָק-עֲקֵדַת, *Akedat Yitzhak*, we must also wrestle with the choices that Rebekah made. All of the Genesis tales provide us with endless moral dilemmas. In order to understand each character's motive, we must first contend with the fundamental question of why the writer or writers of the Bible wove tales of deceit into the fabric of our text— linking generation to generation in such an intriguing way. Only then may we begin to understand the significance

of Rebekah's actions and how they relate to our history, the generations of the Jewish people. **Rachel Smookler, Hebrew Union College, New York, NY.**

דָּבָר אַחֵר **DAVAR AHER. AND THE ETERNAL SAID TO HER: "TWO NATIONS ARE IN YOUR WOMB"** [Gen. 19.23]. This week's Torah portion is *Toldot*, from the book of *Bereshit*. When reading through my Torah portion I discovered several extremely interesting subjects.

First of all, the struggles between Yaakov and Esav. What did it mean when God told Rebekah that she had two great nations in her womb? Abarbanel says that the two sons

Toldot

would be different even in race. He gives the example of being German and Indian. Also he says that they will be different mentally, as if Esav would represent materialism, but Yaakov spiritualism. I think that I agree with Abarbanel. Also, Esav could have been the "father" of the Arabs we know today. I base my opinion on the fact that later on in Jewish history we find out about a group called the Edomites. Esav was also called Edom. At first I thought that this was my original idea, but after doing some research I discovered that many famous scholars also hold this opinion.

Another thing that really caught my eye was all the rights of the firstborn son. Ramban ponders the real rights of the firstborn in ancient times. He says that the main benefits were the inheritance of the father's prestige and authority, and greater distinction and respect within the family unit.

Also, many Biblical scholars (and I) have noted that the Torah rarely issues its own verdict on actions committed by the characters. Usually the Torah just states the facts without evaluating. In my opinion, God wants us to draw our own conclusions about events. Our ancestors had problems that we have now. There is still sibling rivalry. In some cases it is more severe and in some cases less, but it still exists. There is still fighting over "birthright." These days it is more about wills and inheritances. Sometimes families split up and long-lasting feuds begin, just because of a few extra dollars.

Most people think of the Torah as happening "way back when," but the Torah can and should be used as an everyday guide to life even in the 1990s. If you ever have any doubts about Judaism or anything else in the world, the Torah will usually have a very satisfying answer. Abraham, Isaac, Jacob, Sarah, Rebekah, Rachel, Leah, and all the other biblical characters made mistakes and were not perfect. God had a purpose in writing the Torah as it is. All Jews are supposed to learn from the mistakes of our ancestors. Doing so will make us all better Jews and better human beings. **Vicki Levin, grade 7, Solomon Schecter Day School, West Hartford, CT.**

ויצא יעקב מבאר שבע וילך

Dreams have always been an important part of my life. I always have tried to remember my dreams and make sense of them. One of my most vivid childhood memories is standing under my father's *tallit* and, while the *kohanim* were blessing the congregation, reciting the prayer that states, "Master-of-the-Universe, I am Yours and my dreams are Yours. I have dreamed a dream and I know not what it means. If my dreams are for good, strengthen them, and may they be fulfilled for me and for others as were the dreams of Joseph, the righteous; and if they need healing, heal them as You healed Hezekiah, King of Judah, from his illness, Miriam the prophetess from her leprosy, and Naaman from his leprosy." For me this prayer meant a number of things. First, it meant that dreams were to be taken seriously. Second, it meant that dreams both reveal and conceal. Unlike Moses, to whom God spoke PLAINLY AND NOT IN RIDDLES [Num. 17.7], dreams speak to us ambiguously—teasingly, if you will. Somewhere among all the images we dream, many of them simultaneously seductive and repulsive, lie deep truths about ourselves and the world in which we live.

Because of my love for dreams, the story of Jacob's dream at the beginning of *Parashat Va-Yetze* has always been a poignant one for me. Jacob is the first true dreamer in the Torah. Certainly, God appears previously to Abimelekh in

Parashat Va-Yetze

Genesis 28.10–32.3

Rabbi Eliezer Diamond

ELIEZER DIAMOND IS ASSISTANT PROFESSOR OF TALMUD AND RABBINICS AT THE JEWISH THEOLOGICAL SEMINARY OF AMERICA. HE IS CURRENTLY COMPLETING A BOOK ON FASTING AND ASCETICISM IN THE RABBINIC PERIOD.

דָּבָר אַחֵר DAVAR AHER. JACOB AWOKE FROM HIS SLEEP AND SAID, "SURELY THE ETERNAL IS IN THIS PLACE AND I DID NOT KNOW!" [Gen. 28.16]. *"Ayinization,"* when the most that can be said about something is nothing (from the Hebrew *ayin* meaning "nothing"). What did Jacob take from this dream? Jacob said, "GOD IS IN THIS PLACE AND I DON'T KNOW A DARN THING" [Gen. 28.16].

Jacob's words are a way of describing the paradox of God everywhere, all the time, yet a child dying, a war happening, an earthquake, a disease, a famine, a curse. It's a way of authenticating the whole grand scheme—it is what it is, and it is still full of God. Not either/or but both. All of the above. Don't I know this about life? I do know it, but I don't have words for it. Neither did Jacob, so he said, "God is in this place, and I don't know a darn thing," a feeling so expansive it drives everything else out, all the contradictions, gone.

a dream [Gen. 20.3], but Jacob is the first to have a dream that contains symbols that need to be deciphered as well as unambiguous Divine communication. Of course, part of Jacob's dream is an explicit message: God's promises that the land upon which Jacob lies will be given to him and to his descendants, and that God will protect Jacob in his wanderings and eventually return him to the land that God has promised him [Gen. 28.14]. However, Jacob's dream also contains the imagery of angels of God ascending and descending a ladder that reaches from the earth to the heavens [Gen. 28.12]. Jacob interprets this to mean that the place in which he finds himself is THE GATEWAY TO HEAVEN [Gen. 28.17].

It is worth asking why the nature of Divine messages changes at this point in the Torah. Why does God speak in riddles when it is possible for God's will to be known clearly? Perhaps this shift coincides with the first time the people of Israel, as represented by its eponymous founder, go into exile. Indeed, when those bringing the first fruits recount our enslavement in Egypt they begin by recalling that MY FATHER WAS A WANDERING ARAMEAN [Deut. 26.5]. Exile means estrangement. It means the link between God and Israel is attenuated. It means that it is difficult to sense God's presence and to hear God's word. It means that we hear and see God speaking in riddles and symbols.

An important consequence to symbolic dreams is that they require interpretation unlike explicit communications. In other words, I cannot interpret God's visions unless I have the ability and the willingness to create visions of my own. Such a process places a great deal of responsibility on the dreamer's shoulders; one can never be sure that one's interpretation is what God actually intends. On the other hand, such involvement in understanding God's message forces one

Va-Yetze

God is in this place, this moment God, the rocks God, the ground God, too, you me God, the light the darkness God. The dream? God. The night terror God, too. No place empty of God. When Jacob felt that, all the illusions collapsed into one long affirmative embrace that pushed all his prior notions out of him. Jacob said, "Surely God is in this place, and I don't know a thing." This is the beginning of wisdom: "I don't know," the *ayinization* of Jacob. Now he is free to be taught the truth of the world. **James Stone Goodman, <Stavisker@aol.com>**

דָּבָר אַחֵר DAVAR AHER. **LABAN HAD TWO DAUGHTERS. THE NAME OF THE OLDER WAS LEAH AND THE NAME OF THE YOUNGER WAS RACHEL. LEAH'S EYES WERE TENDER, WHILE RACHEL WAS BEAUTIFUL OF FORM AND BEAUTIFUL OF**

to use one's imagination, and imagination, I believe, is an important component of faith. Faith, after all, involves a willingness to accept as real a Being who cannot be truly known if we use only the tools we generally employ to obtain knowledge, namely, our five senses and our rational capabilities. Only if we are willing to imagine can we hear, see, and feel God's presence. Let it be clear that I am not describing faith as a game of make-believe; rather, I mean to say that the deepest truths so far transcend our own limitedness that only the generosity of mind and spirit called imagination can allow us to go beyond the narrowness of self and embrace the reality of God, God's universe, and God's Torah.

The imaginative nature of Jacob's response to his dream is evident in that the vision he creates goes far beyond the specifics of the dream itself. He understands the dream not merely as information (that he finds himself in a holy place) or promise (that God will be with him wherever he goes), but challenge. Jacob's is a vision that builds on God's; his dream tells him that the place in which he finds himself is God's abode. While this may be clear to dreamers like Jacob, there is no material manifestation of the fact. Jacob therefore erects a pillar on the spot, makes an offering upon it and vows that, if God allows it, he will return at some time in the future to construct an abode in God's honor on the very same spot. In other words, Jacob's religious imagination functions on two planes. It allows to him to imagine how the spiritual character of the place should be expressed materially, and it allows him to commit himself by means of a vow (another act of religious imagination) to a significant physical and financial undertaking at a time when he

APPEARANCE. [Gen. 29.16]. *Dear Joel Grishaver:* I have two questions. (1) Why doesn't Laban tell Jacob the truth before he marries Leah? (2) Why is Rachel mad at Jacob about not having children? (And isn't it strange that she says: *v'im ayin, met anokhi*...but *davka* the opposite, is what kills her. **DH**) Bye. **Shaye Horowitz.**

Dear Shaye: The answers to your questions are very simple, too simple, and therefore I am looking for something deeper. (1) **Why doesn't Laban tell Jacob the truth before he marries Leah?** Laban tells the truth in the end. It is the custom to marry off the elder daughter first. We also know that she has bad eyes (we don't know if she is ugly or almost blind) and we know that Rachel is gorgeous. Therefore he figures (coz he is that kind of guy) that it is easier to

SYNOPSIS: *Jacob leaves Canaan. On the way out he has a dream of angels at Beth El and then meets Rachel in his father's homeland. He is tricked into marrying both Leah and Rachel, and, with them and their handmaidens, produces twelve of his thirteen children. In the end he leaves for home, and there is some parting conflict between him and Laban.*

RASHI OF THE WEEK: On the way out of Canaan Jacob has the dream of angels going up and down a ladder. ON THE WAY BACK INTO CANAAN THE TORAH SAYS: "JACOB WALKED ON HIS WAY—AND ANGELS OF GOD MET HIM" [Gen. 32.1]. RASHI COMMENTS: "These are the ministering angels who guard the Land of Israel. They met him to escort him into the Holy Land." *It is from this verse that Rashi explains why angels are going first "up" and then "down" back in 28.12: There he says,* "Those angels who escorted him in the Land of Israel were not permitted to leave the Land. They ascended to heaven, and the angels who were to guard him outside the boundaries of the Land descended to be with him." *Angels bracket this journey.*

seems not to have a shekel he can call his own.

The same is true of his response to God's promise not to abandon him and to return him eventually to the land. Jacob ups the ante and speaks not merely of returning to the land but of returning to his father's house [Gen. 28.21], a point on which the vision was silent. For Jacob, there can be no return without seeing his father and mother once again; and indeed, many years later, JACOB CAME TO HIS FATHER ISAAC AT MAMRE [Gen. 35.27]. Moreover, the return is to be IN PEACE [Gen. 27.21], an allusion to the cessation of the hatred and hostility of Jacob's brother Esau toward him. This, too, comes to pass; together, Jacob and Esau bury their father [Gen. 35.29]. Thus Jacob takes God's promise and molds it in accordance with his own inner vision, a vision of peace and reconciliation between father and son and between brother and brother.

Jacob's vow to give a tenth of all he has is equally breathtaking in its faith—one could almost say *hutzpah*. As noted above, Jacob appears at this time to be penniless; nowhere do we read of camels laden with gold, silver, and finery as we do in the case of Abraham's servant's mission to Aram to find a wife for Isaac. Given his present state, Jacob is offering 10% of nothing. Yet to Jacob such a vow is not ludicrous. He is confident that if God merely supplies him with enough to eat and a shirt on his back, he will use these gifts to prosper so that he can, in turn, give of that prosperity to God.

Jacob is not a passive dreamer, he is an active one. Dreams for him are pieces of the puzzle that is his existence, but Jacob never confuses the part with the whole. He knows that his destiny is to be shaped by fusing the visions that come in dreams with the dreams shaped by human vision. At this moment of estrangement from his birthplace

---

Va-Yetze

"trick" Jacob and get rid of Leah (the klutz) by using Rachel as the bait. That is the obvious answer. But there are three other answers.

(a) God was teaching Jacob a lesson—letting him know how Esau felt—by playing "whatever-goes-around-comes-around." Jacob was a younger kid who "tricked" his older brother (and got the birthright) and "tricked" his father (and got the blessing). Now he was in love with a younger daughter. Laban, an older brother and a father, tricks him back, and Jacob gets stuck with Leah as well as Rachel.

(b) Leah was a big blessing. Even though Jacob didn't recognize her strength and her importance, half of the Jewish people—six tribes (including Judah and King David)—came from her. Laban knew what he was doing. Rachel gives us Joseph and the tribes that become the nation of

and his family Jacob keeps alive his memory of both and joins them with the promise God has made to him.

Jews have often been called dreamers. Often enough this is meant derisively and suggests we have not the faith and imagination to act. In this century we have been privileged to rebuild the State of Israel. Does anyone imagine that we could have done this if our ancestors had not the faith to say at the end of each seder, no matter how preposterous the words seemed, "Next year in Jerusalem"? Yes, we are dreamers. May we dream for good, and may we have the vision and courage to make our dreams a reality.■

Israel. But Leah gave us Judah and the family that became the kings of Israel. Either Laban or God was smart enough to know that without Leah, the Jewish people would not grow.

(c) Laban was a big crook. Everyone knew that. Haran was a town of crooks (sort of the Las Vegas of Aram), and Laban was the biggest crook in town. When Jacob came to town, blessings came with him. Crops grew better. Sheep had more wool, more meat, and more little lambs than ever before. People thought he did something good to the well. No one wanted Jacob to leave. So they paid Laban big bucks to trick him into staying. The wife switch-a-roo got him an extra seven years of blessing [*Genesis Rabbah* 70.17].

(2) Why is Rachel mad at Jacob about not having children? This one is simple, too. Leah was picking on Rachel because she was the "good wife" and Rachel was useless—because they were both stupid enough to believe the lie that women are only as good as the children they birth. And Jacob seemed to be going along with it because he wanted sons—and he forgot to make Rachel feel good, too.

But here are some deeper answers.

(a) There is a story about Lamekh, one of the descendants of Cain who was around just before Noah. He had two wives. The midrash says, "One he used for having children—and she became fat, and tired, but was a great mother." The other he gave a medicine so she could not have children—she was kept for enjoyment and loving. She was a painted woman. It was always her job to look beautiful and be happy. She became like a doll. She was something for enjoyment, She couldn't be herself. She couldn't eat what she wanted. She always had to exercise and work out. (Maybe she even ate things and threw them up so she could have the taste, but not the fat). She couldn't just wear jeans and a T-shirt. She became a thing—what we now call a "sex object." I think Rachel may have felt that way. "Leah gets to be the real woman—Jacob just wants me to paint my nails and stay in the tent until he is ready to enjoy my beauty. He doesn't love me for who I am—just for what I can look like."

(b) When Rachel says, "Without kids I will die," Jacob says, "You will not!" Rachel says, "I am not talking about death in this world, I am talking about spiritual death. If I don't have children, then I lose my spiritual future. If I don't help to build the Jewish people (and without me there will be no Elijah), I will lose my place in the Olam ha-Bah. Besides, there will be no one to say kaddish for me and remember me" [*Midrash ha-Gadol* 30.22].

That's what I know. Which answers do you like? Which other answers do you have? **Joel Lurie Grishaver, <Gris@TorahAura.com>**

דָּבָר אַחֵר DAVAR AḤER. **Jacob left Beer-sheba, and set out for Haran** [Gen. 28.10]. Va-Yetze is a story of continuing deceit. It is a story of accomplishment. It is a fantastic love story. It is a "just so" story like the ones Kipling wrote. It could also be called a journey into faith. Let's look at each of these concepts, preceded by a review of the parashah.

Jacob is on the run from his brother Esau as Esau is mad at him for stealing both his birthright and the blessing for the firstborn. According to a

Navah Kelman

Navah Kelman is currently the Assistant Director of Camp Ramah in California, as well as an MBA student at the University of Judaism.

Va-Yetze

A Mother's Thoughts—A Family's Legacy

My Dearest Dina:

For an instant, when your grandfather, Lavan, kissed me good-bye this morning, I felt like the child he paid so little attention to when your Aunt Rachel and I were growing up. We were so innocent then, so unprepared for the women we were to become. But that kiss...something about that kiss took me back to the years before womanhood, before the jealousy, before the pain.

Perhaps because it was with a kiss that my own journey through womanhood began so many years ago.

I remember the day Jacob came into our lives as if it were yesterday. It was the shepherds he met at the well that morning who first told me about the stranger who rolled the stone off the well and greeted your Aunt Rachel with a kiss. To this day I wonder if things would have been different had I been the one at the well that day. If I had been the one he kissed.

It was your grandfather's idea to have us switch places on what should have been their wedding night. From that moment on your father, your aunt, and I were drawn into a cruel circle of wanting what we could never have and having what we didn't necessarily want. I had Jacob's children, but not his love or attention. Jacob had children, but not the concentrated love of the one person he most desired. And Rachel had Jacob's undying love, but her passions were diverted by her inability to bear children.

---

midrash, Esau sends his son after Jacob to kill him. After Jacob pleads with him, the son literally strips him naked, taking everything he has. This is why he arrives in Haran without anything. In order to get him there clothed, the rabbis said that as Jacob journeyed he came to a stream where a rider had drowned. So he took the clothing and the horse that were there. (An aside: if there was any animal that Jacob would have ridden, it would have been a camel. According to the best evidence, the horse was unknown in the Middle East at the time of the patriarchs. Of course, the rabbis of 2000 years ago wouldn't have known that. They rode horses, so Jacob would have ridden a horse!)

As we all know, Jacob lay down at night and dreamed a dream about angels ascending and descending a ladder going from earth to heaven. The rabbis said that those ascending were those

We fought a war, your aunt and I, through your brothers. Their very names are the remnants of the passion, hatred, and jealousy that consumed those early years. Sometimes I fear they will internalize the jealousy they were born into and let it run their lives as it did mine. I worry that they will carry on the legacy Rachel and I left behind of sibling rivalry, possessiveness, and frustration.

You, Dina, were my last child. I felt such a sense of calm after you were born. You were the first daughter in a house of sons, the first female in the next generation of women, and a sign to myself to end the struggle with my sister. Nobody asked, but it was because you were that sign that I named you Dina. You were the sign that God had judged us all. We had all suffered enough, and it was time to lay our differences and fighting aside. If there was any proof that you were that sign, it was that your Aunt Rachel finally became pregnant with Joseph soon after you were born.

I put those turbulent years to a quiet rest so long ago, yet they speak volumes about my life's journey as a child, as a wife, as a lover, and as a woman. I have learned so much on that journey.

Love can be intense or humble, found in the most common of places or waiting where you least expect it. I always felt I had to go out looking for love. Even after being married for quite a few years I still used to go out to the fields to find Jacob at the end of the day. For that I earned a reputation as a "loose woman." Know your boundaries, my daughter, and be careful where you wander. Wait for the love that will speak to your heart—for the kiss that will spark your journey as it did mine so many years ago.■

---

who accompanied Jacob in Canaan; those descending were those who would accompany him outside of Canaan. He arrives in Haran, meets Rachel, with whom he falls instantly in love, and is invited to his uncle's house, for Laban is his mother's brother. He works for seven years to marry Rachel, is tricked into marrying Leah by Laban, marries Rachel a week later, and works another seven years for the privilege of having married Rachel. In the meantime, twelve of his thirteen children are born. At the end of this time he wants to get paid for his work and go back to his father's house. We'll talk about his wages in a moment. He sneaks off with his household while Laban is away shearing sheep, a major celebratory time for shepherds. Laban pursues him. Before Laban overtakes Jacob he is told by God not to harm his son-in-law. So they make a pact never to approach each other in hostility. Jacob continues on into next week's parashah, where he meets his brother Esau.

I started by saying this is a story of continuing deceit. How so? Recall that last week Jacob deceived his blind father into thinking that he was Esau, tricking Isaac into giving Jacob the blessing meant for the firstborn. This week we deal with another firstborn, Leah. Jacob worked for Laban for seven years so he could marry Rachel. On his wedding night a woman was brought to the nuptial chamber. In the dark Jacob, like his father, was blind. He thought he had one daughter when he actually had the other. The rabbis taught that Jacob was wary of Laban's treachery and had arranged for Rachel to touch the big toe of his right foot, his right thumb, and his right ear so he would know it was she. Though Rachel loved Jacob, she also loved her sister and did not want to see her disgraced. So she told Leah the signs. And whenever Jacob called Rachel, Leah would answer him, as Jacob had answered his father. So the deceit he had perpetrated on his father came back to him in the same fashion.

Laban is portrayed as a wealthy man who would do anything to increase his wealth, all the while being very civil. When Jacob asks for wages he says he wants all the striped and spotted goats and the dark sheep. Laban agrees, then takes all those animals from his herds and hides them away. Jacob uses a trick with striped pieces of wood to cause the goats to be striped and spotted and the sheep to be dark. Thus he grows rich.

Va-Yetze

Trickery answered with trickery. The rabbis asked how such a pious man as Jacob could do such things. After all, he was well versed in Torah and studied and prayed all the time! They answered that a pious man had the right to answer trickery with trickery.

Frankly, I think Jacob was a scoundrel, but a lovable one. The Torah seems to think so, too, as he didn't have an easy life. His favorite wife died in childbirth. His favorite son was thought to be dead for many years. He suffered through famine. His daughter was raped. Two of his sons destroyed a town. His oldest son lay with one of his wives. He paid for his crimes.

How is this a story of accomplishment? Think about it. Jacob arrives at Laban's penniless and leaves a rich man with four wives, eleven sons, and one daughter. I would call that an accomplishment. And a love story? How many of you men would have worked seven years for your future father-in-law so you could marry your wife? And then another seven because he cheated you? The Torah says Jacob's love was so great that the first seven years seemed to him as days. Now that's love!

You remember Kipling's "just so" stories? Like how the elephant got its trunk? Well, this is one of our "just so" stories. Earlier in Genesis we learned how the world was created, how life, especially humans, came to be, how we learned right from wrong, and how we came to speak so many different languages. When we read about Abraham we learned how Israel came to be our land and how God came to be our God. In this parashah we learn how Bethel came to be such a sacred place. Bethel, it must be remembered, was the holiest site in Israel after the split between Israel and Judah. The writer is justifying Bethel use as the site by having Jacob name it and declare it God's abode after his dream of the ladder. We also get the origin of tithing, as Jacob says he will set aside a tithe for God if He brings him back safely to his father's house. We also learn the origins of the tribes, how most of the tribes received their names and what is the origin of the name. For example, Yehudah comes from Odeh, which means praise, for in Genesis 29.35 it says: LEAH SAID "THIS TIME I WILL PRAISE THE LORD" THEREFORE SHE NAMED HIM JUDAH.

We also have answers to how two customs associated with a wedding came to be. In orthodox Judaism, after a couple is wed they go to friends' and relatives' houses for a week of partying. The origin of this week comes from Jacob having to wait out Leah's bridal week before he can marry Rachel. The second custom is *bedeken*, when the groom goes to the bride before the wedding ceremony and veils her face. This custom originated to prevent the man from marrying the wrong woman, as Jacob had done.

According to midrash, another "how" is also answered in this portion. That is, how come Rachel died while she was young, on the road to Bethlehem giving birth to Benjamin? When Laban asked

Jacob about his missing gods (which Jacob did not know Rachel had stolen), Jacob said, "ANYONE WITH WHOM YOU FIND YOUR GODS SHALL NOT REMAIN ALIVE!" [Gen. 31.32]. The rabbis said God let Rachel live long enough to give birth to Benjamin so he could father his tribe, and then God carried out Jacob's vow. We can learn from this, too. What you say may come back to haunt you at a later time.

This parashah is a journey into faith. At the beginning of the parashah, after his dream with the ladder, Jacob vows, "IF GOD REMAINS WITH ME, IF HE PROTECTS ME ON THIS JOURNEY THAT I AM MAKING, AND GIVES ME BREAD TO EAT AND CLOTHING TO WEAR, AND IF I RETURN SAFE TO MY FATHER'S HOUSE—THE LORD SHALL BE MY GOD" [Gen. 28.20–21]. The rabbis took this last part, "THE LORD SHALL BE MY GOD," to mean that Jacob would dedicate himself to God. I look at it another way. I take the statement at face value. Jacob is saying, "Hey, God, if you keep me safe and let me prosper, then I will worship you." What is not here is the "otherwise": otherwise, you *won't* be my God. He's making a *brit* of his own with God. We actually have to peek into next week's portion to see that Jacob does put his faith in God. When he is about to meet Esau, he prays to God to help him survive the encounter. At no time in dealing with the wily Laban does he ask for any help from God. Knowing he has prospered, Jacob fulfills his part of the *brit* by praying to God for the first time.

Treachery, accomplishment, love, faith. This parashah deals with the gamut of human deeds and emotions. As I tell my sixth grade students, what is most important is what we can learn from these stories. Treachery and deceit don't pay; they may come back and haunt you. Work hard, and you may be rewarded. To truly love another is something beautiful and to be desired. To have faith in God, one must test that faith. God will not be found wanting. **Charles Flum, <cflum@juno.com>**

לפניו אל עשו אחיו

Our Ancestor Jacob, the One with the Bad Leg, and Other Tales

Parashah Va-Yishlah
Genesis 32.4–36.43

Danny Siegel

Danny Siegel is a well-known author, lecturer, and poet who has spoken in more than 200 North American Jewish communities on topics of tzedakah and Jewish values, besides reading from his own poetry. He is the author of 23 1/2 books on such topics as mitzvah heroes and practical and personalized tzedakah. His most recent books are *Heroes and Miracle Workers* and *Good People*, collections of essays about everyday people who are mitzvah heroes.

By Way of Introduction, a Personal Note:

As the old Yiddish saying goes (in translation), "Before I begin to speak, I wish to say a few words." People wonder why I, with a perfectly good Hebrew name—Daniel—have the Hebrew name Yaakov, Jacob.

The explanation is simple: my grandmother, (צירל דבורה בת בנימין), wanted an Avraham, a Yitzhak and a Yaakov in the family (my father is Yitzhak, and my older brother, Stan, is Avraham).

All my life I have followed the story of Jacob, worried about him, and reviewed two passages again and again—the dreams with the ladder and with those angels going up and down [Gen. 28.10–22], and his wrestling match with the angel [Gen. 32.25–33]. I have tried to make sense of them in the broadest sense, in the overall context of his life, but with little success. All I come up with are pieces here and there, fragments of some ancient piece of pottery, but not quite enough to see whether it is a simple water jug, a container for the winter grain, or one of those marvelous jars found decades ago in the Judaean desert containing scrolls that will help make ultimate

---

דָּבָר אַחֵר **DAVAR AHER.** "No longer will it be said that your name is Jacob, but Israel" [Gen. 32.29]. Further thought on the meaning of the names Jacob and Israel: In Va-Yishlah God tells Jacob that he shall no more be called Jacob, but rather Israel. The classic question is: Why, unlike the Abraham and Sarah, who are never again referred to by their former names, does the Bible continue to refer to Jacob/Israel by both names? Rashi on *Parashat Toldot* writes that Jacob was not merely the name given by Isaac, but the name chosen by God Himself. Indeed, if ever a baby's name was determined from the very moment he was born, Jacob's position at birth determined it—it was almost as though he was born with name tag attached. This could explain why the name Jacob doesn't just disappear: A name given by man might, in time, be

וישלח יעקב מלאכים

sense of God's world and what we, the People, must do to make it "The Best of All Possible Worlds."

The Wrestling Match vs. the Dream

Jacob wrestles with the angel, is told he has struggled with a Divine Being and a human being, emerges triumphant, is injured, has his name changed from Yaakov to Yisrael, and then gets on with his life.

This commentary is not about how all of life is a struggle, how if you take on the mighty ones—corrupt corporations, evil forces, governments and councils who care not for their citizens and wards, classic family dysfunctionalities—you will have to fight mightily and will emerge exhausted and scarred for life. I never liked that approach, though it is certainly true some of the time. The message is too discouraging: Take on God's and humanity's injustices and you will be covered with dirt and grime, perhaps never to recover from the contest. Look elsewhere for a fleshing out of that theme.

I prefer Jacob's earlier, more gentle, and more soothing encounter with the Divine, the silent dream. In this dream he followed the angels up the stairway to heaven, saw God's plan, returned to earth with the vision firmly implanted in his imagination, awoke, and set out to live his life as a Jew.

וַיֹּאמַר מַה-נּוֹרָא הַמָּקוֹם הַזֶּה
אֵין זֶה כִּי אִם-בֵּית אֱלֹהִים
וְזֶה שַׁעַר הַשָּׁמָיִם

He calls the place AWESOME [Gen. 28.17], GOD'S HOUSE, THE GATE OF HEAVEN, and wherever he will go until his last day will be awesome, God's House, and the Gate of Heaven. He then takes an oath about tzedakah [Gen. 28–22]:

וְכֹל אֲשֶׁר תִּתֶּן עַשֵּׂר אֲעַשְּׂרֶנּוּ לָךְ

---

superseded; a name given by God will not be obliterated. On a deeper level, I proposed in *Toldot* that God calls him Jacob not because he is crooked or deceitful, but because he is destined to become a true "follower," one who "follows upon the heels of" or "brings himself to heel to" the Divine command, alluding to עֵקֶב אֲשֶׁר-שָׁמַע אַבְרָהָם בְּקֹלִי *'ekev asher shama' Avraham b'Koli* [Gen. 26.5]. But if Jacob is already a good God-given name, why does he get another, and in what sense is his name "no more said to be Jacob" [Gen. 32.29]?

Here is the lesson I derive: To be a true follower one must struggle. One must struggle to straighten the עָקֹב הַלֵּב *akov ha-lev* "the crookedness of one's heart." One must struggle not merely to follow, but to follow with all one's

SYNOPSIS: *Jacob divides his camp, prepares to meet Esau, prays, then wrestles with a stranger who changes his name to Israel. The reunion of the brothers takes place. Dinah becomes involved with a man from Shekhem. God reaffirms the name Israel, and then Rachel dies giving birth to son number twelve, Benjamin.*

RASHI OF THE WEEK:

Close reading is a wonderful skill. Watch Rashi work. The text says [33.6–7] THE HANDMAIDENS CAME CLOSE [TO ESAU]. THEY AND THEIR CHILDREN. AND THEY BOWED. AND LEAH, TOO, CAME CLOSE, WITH HER CHILDREN, AND THEY BOWED. AND AFTERWARDS, JOSEPH AND RACHEL CAME NEAR AND BOWED [Gen. 33.6–7]. *Rashi notes:* In every other case the mother preceded the children, but when it came to Rachel, Joseph went first. Why? *From a simple shift in word order, Rashi reveals the true nature of Joseph.* Joseph said, "My mother is a beautiful woman. Esau is a wicked man. I will protect her by placing myself between him and her and preventing him from gazing at her." It is for this reason that Jacob was blessed with many positive associations with the eye [*Gen. R.* 78]. *From a simple list comes a heroic moment—and a foreshadowing of Joseph's literary motif.*

Va-Yishlah

"I will give away a tenth of everything you give me."

I would be a dreamer rather than a wrestler. Indeed I would. In my imagination I can feel the smooth glide of the angels going up and down the stairway to heaven, the angels extending their hands, beckoning me to follow.

Our Ancestor Jacob, the One with the Bad Leg

[*N.B. I would wish the reader to remember that I have a learning disability, and though it is mild, it is real; I am one of those people that some refer to erroneously as "them."*]

It is summertime in Jerusalem. I am making my annual rounds with my interns and the hundreds of USY pilgrims who will visit tzedakah projects and meet mitzvah heroes here and throughout the country. We must wonder if our ancestor Jacob, visiting our synagogues in 1995 for the bar or bat mitzvah of a grandchild, would be able to get up to the *bimah* for an *aliyah*. If there were no ramp, how would he do it?

וְהוּא צֹלֵעַ עַל-יְרֵכוֹ

All night he struggles with the angel, and as dawn breaks by the Yabbok [Gen. 32.32] he limps, the consequence of a nasty all-night struggle. Either he injured his sciatic nerve, or he dislocated his hip, or he tore ligaments and joint-connectors and limped in pain for a day or a few days or for the rest of his life. Whatever the simple meaning of the text, he was not the man he had been the evening before.

For that matter, we might wonder if his father, Yitzhak, would be able to follow along in our siddurim—Yitzhak, with severely impaired vision in his old age [Gen. 27.1] and no large-print siddur to use.

וַיְהִי כִּי-זָקֵן יִצְחָק וַתִּכְהֶיןָ עֵינָיו מֵרְאֹת

Would we have left two of our ancestors out of the life of the congregations (and other communal activities) for lack of access? Indeed, at least three out of seven

---

heart. One cannot merely follow a tradition; one must make it one's own. Jacob left his father's house a "follower" in the footsteps of his fathers; he returns a leader in his own right, his own man. There will always be Esaus in the world (and Esau's guardian angels) to accuse us of hypocrisy and self-deception in our "following." But the struggle to follow as well as lead, to lead as well as follow, to integrate one's personality so that one can follow with wholeness, straightness, and honesty of heart—these are the eternal struggles of Jacob/Israel.

Hazan Ira Rohde, <75610.1722@compuserve.com>

of our direct ancestors might be on the fringes of Jewish life: וְעֵינֵי לֵאָה רַכּוֹת Leah's eyes were weak [Gen. 29.17].

It is summertime in Jerusalem, and I am making my rounds. Just last night my friends and I visited Yoel Sharon and Nachum Prital, founders of Etgarim/Challenge. Etgarim provides sports, athletics, and wilderness survival opportunities throughout Israel for individuals with physical disabilities. We saw videos of people going down rocky hills, backwards, tied to a cable, rocking in their wheelchairs, tilting at serious angles, sometimes tipping over, emerging triumphant. We saw clips of a man doing his thing on water skis (it seemed irrelevant whether he had lost a leg by accident, disease, or genetic mishap) and another man, blind (by accident, disease, or genetic mishap), doing the same, and we saw groups of Israelis on sit-down, single-ski contraptions enjoying their thrills in the Austrian Alps, wind-and sunburned at day's end, triumphant. One would hope that the descendants of Jacob and Isaac and Leah would meet the Etgarim people (who consider themselves neither tzaddikim nor heroes) and—though perhaps discouraged at first, distraught at disability in the abstract and in their real lives—would have some fun, some sublime fun.

Just three weeks ago we met Yosef Lev, the master who teaches martial arts to many individuals with disabilities, physical and otherwise. He knows how to teach people the joys of karate, judo, and the other classical modes of self-defense. It is a wonder to behold, and according to my assistants (some of whom wound up on the floor after trying to attack individuals in wheelchairs), a greater wonder to experience. One would hope that the descendants of Jacob and Isaac and Leah would meet Yosef Lev (who considers himself neither a tzaddik nor a hero) and—though perhaps discouraged at first, distraught at disability in the abstract and in their real lives—would have some fun, some sublime fun, and more peace of mind.

And, of course, me and my *hevrah* and students have been to see the Mighty Mitzvah Horses many times, in Bet Yehoshua near Netanya and now in Jerusalem, the glorious equine angels used for therapeutic horseback riding under the trainers' gentle hands, miracle workers.

A Re-examination of My Grandma Tzirel's Wish

יעקב Yaakov: It is a very uncomfortable name to have, to carry with you all your life. Everyone tells you it comes from the root עקב, which means that Yaakov is the Tricky One, the Sly One, the One-Who-Is-Willing-to-Take-Advantage—which is the point of the wrestling match with the angel. His life as trickster is finished. His new name is to be ישראל Jew, Yid, a person with *e Yiddishe neshoma*, a Jewish soul.

I am stuck with יעקב Yaakov. No one ever renamed me ישראל. Am I forever condemned to struggle, to overcome my name, to resist the urge to walk over people to get to things, to ideas, to goals that are phony gods?

When I was a student about twenty-five years ago, one of my *Tanakh* rebbis, the late Moshe Held, מנוחתו שלום, taught me that one of the meanings of the root [עקב] is "to guard, to watch," as in Jeremiah 17.9: עָקֹב הַלֵּב מִכֹּל Keep watch, guard your heart, protect it from all bad things.

So the struggle is over: I, יעקב Yaakov, and all others bearing the name are assured God's protection, as the verse states in Jeremiah 30.10.

וְאַתָּה אַל-תִּירָא עַבְדִּי
יַעֲקֹב נְאֻם-יהוה
כִּי הִנְנִי מוֹשִׁיעֲךָ מֵרָחוֹק

"Be not afraid, my servant, Jacob," declares God. "I will save you, even at times when I appear to be so far away you cannot sense My Presence."

As long as we can feel the touch of the angels, keep a clear vision of what they showed us at the very top of the stairway to heaven, all of us will most assuredly be safe, תַּחַת כַּנְפֵי הַשְּׁכִינָה, under the glorious wings of the Shekhinah.■

אביו בארץ כנען

Parashat Va-Yeshev
Genesis 37.1–40.23

Rabbi Herbert Bronstein

RABBI HERBERT BRONSTEIN IS THE AUTHOR OF THE BEST SELLING CCAR (REFORM) *HAGGADAH* AND OTHER LITURGICAL TEXTS. HE IS A WELL-KNOWN LECTURER ON SUBJECTS RANGING FROM LITURGY AND MODERN HEBREW POETRY TO SHAKESPEARE. HIS WRITINGS HAVE BEEN WIDELY PUBLISHED.

"INSIGNIFICANCe" and Significance

Recently, on the London stage, I saw a powerful drama entitled "INSIGNIFICANCe" by Terry Johnson (the small "e" is deliberate). It was based on an imaginary confrontation, with tragic overtones, between four characters modeled on well-known figures: Albert Einstein, Joseph McCarthy of the House Un-American Activities Committee, Marilyn Monroe, and the professional athlete Joe DiMaggio.

Undoubtedly the playwright chose these personae because they are, or at least were, such celebrities on many levels of consciousness that they became mental and even mythical icons to multitudes.

The drama ranged over a series of issues from the Holocaust to nuclear and neutron bombs that destroy people and leave buildings intact, to the limitations on our capacities to love due to emotional trauma, to personal guilt and responsibility, and even to issues of the relationship between truth, knowledge, and understanding. All of these issues somehow touch on questions of power and integrity. All touch in some way on the obsession in our time with fame or celebrity as the measure of personal significance, or the absence of celebrity (God forbid) as, therefore, insignificance.

For those who passed on and recorded the stories preserved in the Torah, all the persons specifi-

---

דָּבָר אַחֵר DAVAR A<u>H</u>ER. A MAN DISCOVERED HIM, AND BEHOLD, HE WAS BLUNDERING IN THE FIELD; THE MAN ASKED HIM, SAYING, "WHAT DO YOU SEEK?" [Gen. 37.15]. One could argue that the most significant character in the second half of the book of Genesis is the anonymous man הָאִישׁ *ha-Ish* who gives Joseph directions to his brother's encampment [Gen. 37.15–17]. His brief conversation with Joseph sets in motion a series of events that lead to the sale of Joseph into slavery, his imprisonment, and his eventual rise to power. Indeed, the anonymous *Ish* can be said to be responsible for Israel's sojourn in Egypt and their ultimate salvation! Yet he has no name or identity in the text. Despite the efforts of the Midrash, Rashi, and others, הָאִישׁ *ha-Ish*, the man, remains a mysterious, nameless figure who changes history. Maybe the

וישב יעקב בארץ מגרי

cally mentioned in the Bible must have been significant. But whom in all the narratives of *Bereshit*, the book of Genesis, might we consider the most significant? Surely Abraham, one might say, the father, the founder with whom the first covenant is made, the pleader for the possibly innocent of Sodom and Gomorrah, called to the supreme test of the binding of Isaac? Or would it be Joseph, whom the great novelist Thomas Mann called "Joseph the Provider" because he sustained an empire and its people?

If we were to measure significance in terms of the sheer amount of space, sheer text devoted to each of the biblical personages in the book of Genesis, the answer would have to be Jacob. Yes, more text is allotted to Jacob than to any other significant figure in the Genesis!

An argument could be made that from the beginning of this week's portion it is the powerful Joseph who seems to dominate, even to the last verse, which describes Joseph's passing. But the greater comparative significance of Jacob, even in relation to his son, the prime minister of Egypt, is signaled in the text in many ways. Not the least of these is the way the Torah introduces Joseph to the stage of our great drama. How? Even in the process of introducing Joseph, Jacob is mentioned first: NOW THIS CONTINUES THE STORY OF JACOB: JOSEPH BEING SEVENTEEN YEARS OLD... [Gen. 37.2]. The mention of Jacob here is only apparently gratuitous. Surely it is meant to establish precedence. Though according to Rabbi Joseph Hertz, in his edition of the Pentateuch, Joseph becomes the center of what I call the "great narrative," in the meantime we

---

real message of his presence in the text is that even the most insignificant person can be significant and change the world. *Ha-Ish* is no less important in the biblical narrative than Abraham, Isaac, or Jacob. Could it be that the Torah reminds us through the presence of הָאִישׁ *ha-Ish* not to dismiss the presence of even the most insignificant person with whom we have contact in our daily lives? Who knows how a chance encounter with a stranger on a street corner, in a store, or on a bus can change our lives! **Rabbi Mark B. Greenspan, Beth El Temple, Harrisburg, PA.**

דָּבָר אַחֵר DAVAR AHER. "THE DAYS OF MY LIFE HAVE BEEN FEW AND BITTER" [Gen. 47.9]. With the deaths of Jacob and Joseph, we have reached the end of Genesis.

SYNOPSIS: *Enter Joseph: the coat of many colors, dreams, and sibling rivalry. Break for Judah, Tamar, and Onan. Return to Joseph: the pit, slavery in Potiphar's house, conflict with Potiphar's wife, jail, jail success, the baker's and butler's dreams. Cliffhanger!*

RASHI OF THE WEEK:

Just enjoy this one. After the sons report that Joseph is dead, this is Jacob's response. AND JACOB TORE HIS CLOTHES, AND DRESSED IN SACK CLOTH, AND MOURNED FOR HIS SON MANY DAYS [Gen. 37.34]. *How many days?* Twenty-two years! From the time he left him *to see his brothers in the field* until Jacob went down to Egypt. We know this from the Torah itself, which first teaches us [Gen. 37.2] that JOSEPH WAS SEVENTEEN YEARS OLD at the beginning of the story and thirty years old when he stood before Pharaoh (two years into the famine) [*Meg.* 17a]. This is exactly parallel to the twenty-two years that Jacob did not honor his father, but rather pursued his own ends in Laban's house. This is the meaning of Genesis 31.41: I HAVE NOW BEEN—on my own account—TWENTY YEARS IN YOUR HOUSE. I chose to be here, and later I will merit equal punishment for that choice.

are not allowed to forget Jacob. Jacob's presence thereafter, in thought or in person, is repeatedly made known.

In the stories that ensue Jacob appears as the most powerful figure. This may sound astounding or even ridiculous. Is the elderly Jacob, sometimes irascible, given in his later years to reminiscence, more powerful than the king Pharaoh, cosmocrator of the ancient Near East? Is he more powerful than Joseph, who is second only to Pharaoh and in whose hands are the state systems, the control over the life and death of untold numbers of people, before whom the multitudes cower in abject terror?

Thomas Mann, no mean figure, seems to think so. In his reading of the portions of the Joseph saga that describe the meeting between Jacob and Pharaoh, Mann senses an ill-at-ease Pharaoh whose discomfort rises out of a sense of inferiority to Jacob! Perhaps, muses Mann, Pharaoh recognizes in Jacob a leading-edge world outlook that will someday supplant his own. It is sufficient to note that at the end of the interview it is Jacob who blesses Pharaoh [Gen. 47.50].

As to Jacob's power over Joseph, the text contains many indications. We see not only Joseph's continuous care for his father, but his deference to him; and how in the world, ask the rabbis, was Joseph able to resist the formidable temptation of Potiphar's wife? She was beautiful, rich, and forceful and had considerable authority as mistress of the household in which Joseph worked. An *aggadah* tells us that at the instant Joseph was about to succumb to her seductions, an image of the face of his father appeared in Joseph's mentality so starkly that is seemed to Joseph as if Jacob were peering at Joseph through a window [*Bereshit Rabbah* 87.7 and *Tanhumah* "Va-Yeshev"].

Va-Yeshev

Jacob is the first modern man in the biblical story. He is multi-dimensional, very unlike saintly Abraham or quiescent Isaac. He is torn by inner conflicts, and nothing comes easily to him. His decisive hour arrives at the shore of the Yabbok when he faces his own past in a night-long struggle. He survives but will limp for the rest of his life. In short, he can be any one of us.
David Jordan, Haworth, NJ.

Further, when Joseph's two sons are brought to the ailing Jacob to be blessed, he not only does it his way, and not Joseph's, but he has his own words to say about the influence that the force of his own character will have on his grandchildren. He tells Joseph: "AND NOW YOUR TWO SONS, WHO WERE BORN UNTO YOU IN THE LAND OF EGYPT BEFORE I CAME UNTO THEE IN EGYPT, ARE MINE; EPHRAIM, AND MENASSEH EVEN AS REUBEN AND SIMON SHALL BE MINE [Gen. 48.5]. THE GOD BEFORE WHOM MY FATHER ABRAHAM AND ISAAC WALKED BLESS THE LADS; AND LET MY NAME BE NAMED IN THEM AND THE NAME OF MY FATHER ABRAHAM AND ISAAC; AND LET THEM GROW INTO A MULTITUDE IN THE MIDST OF THE EARTH....BY THESE SHALL ISRAEL BLESS SAYING: GOD MAKE THEE AS EPHRAIM AND MENASSEH" [Gen. 48.16-20].

And this proved to be the case. Although Egyptian-bred amidst the highest aristocracy and refinements of Egyptian culture, Ephraim and Menasseh became Israelites and lived on in the name of their ancestor Israel, as well as in the blessing that is invoked at the Shabbat table of the people of Israel to this day. Is there such a "Pharaoh blessing" today?

And the text of the blessing itself explains at least two sources of Jacob's power. First there are the repeated overtones of a strong sense of identity rooted in Jacob's awareness of his past and his ancestry, his rootedness in a strong heritage. Generations of commentators have perceived in the opening words of the portion a hint of that heritage rootedness: AND JACOB SETTLED IN THE LAND OF HIS FATHER'S SOJOURNING [Gen. 37.1]. His intent to pass on that grounding to his grandchildren appears in his blessing of them as he invokes the God of his fathers: "THE GOD BEFORE WHOM MY FATHERS WALKED BLESS THE LADS; AND LET MY NAME BE NAMED IN THEM, AND THE NAME OF MY FATHERS."

Second, just as Jacob passes on to the next generation a sense of covenant-purpose grounded in the past, he also focuses on the future: "BY THEE SHALL ISRAEL BLESS SAYING...." For every individual a sense of identity empowers, while a purpose for the future is life itself. Surely there is a lesson here for us. We ask, what is our strength and our power? The answer is a sense of identity rooted in the past and a sense of spiritual purpose for the future.

Jacob's strength has other sources, which explains the amount of text devoted to him in the Torah. Everything about Jacob is double: his two names, the blessings he receives and gives, his visions. He is two people because he is transformed in the course of the narrative from one person to another. He changes from the self-seeking, on-the-go, upwardly mobile, aggressive and, yes, grasping Jacob (Yaakov means "he will take over") to the self-transcending patriarch, serving a purpose beyond himself (Yisrael: "God will rule").

It takes time to tell such a story, and a lot can be said about it, but "sufficient to the day is the burden thereof." On this occasion it remains only to say that in the modern Western view power has to do with physical might, material control, monetary influence. "How many troops does the Pope command?" asks Napoleon. Jacob's power had nothing to do with a nuclear bomb or the clout of a United States senator, or the influence of fame or sexual allure, or the commercial value of the photographs of a star baseball player on millions of bubble gum cards, or even the power implied in the phrase "the keys to the kingdom." Jacob's power, far more enduring, of far more significance, is that of his spiritual consciousness. ■

ופרעה חלם

Parashat Miketz
Genesis 41.1–44.17

Dr. Jo Milgrom

Jo Milgrom received her Ph.D. in Theology and the Arts from the Graduate Theological Union, Berkeley, where her teaching has focused on Jewish Life and Art, and on Art, Midrash, and Symbolism in the Narratives of the Hebrew Bible. She is the author of *The Akedah: The Binding of Isaac, A Primary Symbol in Jewish Thought and Art* (1988), and *Handmade Midrash* (1991).

Was Joseph really the eleventh son born into that family? A quick reread of Genesis 30 confirms that Leah had borne her half dozen; the two surrogate wives, Bilah and Zilpah, had each borne two sons; finally Leah gave birth to a daughter, briskly named Dinah without the naming fanfare that ornamented each son's birth, accenting the irrelevance of the circumstances of a daughter's birth and her mother's emotional state. And finally God opened Rachel's womb. Joseph's name was given a double language play: "God has gathered up my shame," said Rachel, reflecting on her barren past (the root is [אסף] *asaf*), and then she added, looking to the future, "God will add another son for me" (root, [יסף] *yasaf*).

Four wives/mothers, twelve sons, and a daughter, all orbiting around a single stud. (Forget the complex relationships for a moment; just think of the laundry.)

Joseph's brothers were practically grown men when this brat came on the scene and took all. Years later, when he told the stranger in Sheckem that he was looking for his brothers, he was indeed in search of a fraternal relationship, frustrated from the outset by the unconscious cultivation of envy and hate fostered by his father Jacob, himself a "victim" of parental favoritism. (The role of the chance meeting with the stranger is skillfully developed by Peter Pitzele in *Our Fathers' Wells* (1994), an excellent read using psychodrama as modern midrash.) The very fact of being "all" to his father made him "not at all" to his brothers, non-existent in relationship. Ironically, the root of brother in Hebrew, אָח *a<u>h</u>*, is [אחה] *a<u>h</u>o*, "to stitch together, mend, heal the breach." Though he had eleven brothers, there was no fabric of "fraternity" in this family. Yet the absence and presence of relationship is the motif that governs the Joseph narrative.

Joseph's nonexistence to his brothers, and his misery as favored isolated son, becomes poignantly clear when he rises to power, marries, and himself becomes a father. He names his two sons Menasseh ("God has enabled me to forget all

וַיְהִי מִקֵּץ שְׁנָתַיִם יָמִים

my misery and everything in my father's house") and Ephraim ("God has made me fruitful in the land of my affliction"). He couldn't even send a postcard home to let his mourning father know he was alive and flourishing. Did he think he was also nonexistent in the memory of the old patriarch?

Nonexistence recurs in the echoing of the word אֵינֶנּוּ *Einenu*, "he is not." We hear it for the first time in Genesis 37.30 when Reuben returns to the pit to rescue Joseph after he has already been removed and sold to the Ishmaelite caravaneers.

הַיֶּלֶד אֵינֶנּוּ וַאֲנִי אָנָה אֲנִי-בָא

"HE IS GONE, NOW WHAT DO I DO?" *Einenu* occurs again when Joseph accuses the brothers of spying and they attempt to clarify their identity and mission,

וַיֹּאמְרוּ שְׁנֵים עָשָׂר עֲבָדֶיךָ אַחִים
אֲנַחְנוּ בְּנֵי אִישׁ בְּאֶרֶץ כְּנָעַן
וְהִנֵּה הַקָּטֹן אֶת-אָבִינוּ הַיּוֹם
וְהָאֶחָד אֵינֶנּוּ.

"WE ARE TWELVE BROTHERS; THE YOUNGEST IS WITH OUR FATHER, AND ONE IS GONE" (*einenu*). When the youngest one is finally presented on the next descent to Egypt, Joseph falls apart even before Benjamin speaks. Rashi fills in the lacuna to Genesis 43.30 with a midrash cited by Aviva Zornberg. I am indebted to her for much enrichment, even beyond her sensitive exploration of the psychological implications of Joseph's nonexistence in *Genesis, The Beginning of Desire* (JPS, 1995).

It seems that Joseph asks Benjamin, "Do you have another brother by the same mother as you? And do you have sons? What are their names?" Benjamin responds that he had a brother whose whereabouts he doesn't know. And he responds further with the names of his ten sons (the entire inventory of sixty-six souls, eleven brothers and their sons, is listed separately in Genesis 46.8 to 27). The difference between the inventory of Genesis 46, which is just a list like a population census, and the inventory in the midrash is that in the midrash each name acquires a midrashic meaning to keep the memory of Joseph alive in Benjamin's family. Joseph asks, "What are the ideas underlying those names?" Benjamin replies with the most extensive example of creative midrashic linguistics I have yet encountered. Midrashic linguistics is often tongue-in-cheek (by definition), but when there's a string of pearls, ten in a row, that is a tour de force. Benjamin continues, "They all have some reference to my brother and the troubles that have befallen him. I called them בֶּלַע *Bela*, because he was swallowed up among foreign nations בְּלַע (*bl'a*); בֶּכֶר *Bekher*, because he was firstborn of his mother בְּכוֹר (*bekhor*); אַשְׁבֵּל *Ashbel*,

SYNOPSIS: *Joseph is taken from jail to interpret Pharaoh's two dreams. Ten of Jacob's sons come to Egypt. Jacob tricks them. Benjamin is brought to Egypt and thrown in jail. Cliffhanger!*

RASHI OF THE WEEK:

Deep into the famine in Canaan we are told: AND JACOB SAW THAT THEY WERE SELLING CORN IN EGYPT [Gen. 42.1]. How did he see? He could not have seen Egypt, but he might have heard about it. In the *next verse he tells his sons*, BEHOLD I HAVE HEARD! Then why did the Torah begin by saying, "AND JACOB SAW?" To show us that Jacob had a faint holy vision that there was hope for him in Egypt—but he did not have a true prophetic prophecy telling him that it was Joseph *in whom his hope rested* [Gen. Rabbah 91]. *The word "saw" teaches us that Jacob had holy hunches.*

Miketz

because God sent him into captivity שְׁבוֹא-אֶל (*shevo-el*); גֵּרָא *Gera*, because he had to live in a foreign country גֵּר (*ger*); נַעֲמָן *Naaman*, because he was so pleasant נָעִים (*na'im*); אָחִי *Ahi* and רֹאשׁ *Rosh*, because he was my brother and first אָח (*akh*) רֹאשׁ (*rosh*); מוּפִּים *Mupim*, because he learned from my father's mouth פֶּה (*pe*); חוּפִּין Huppin, because he could not be present at my marriage חוּפָּה (*hup-pah*: wedding canopy); nor was I present at his; and אָרְד *Ard*, because he went down יָרַד (*yarad*) among the nations."

Now it dawns on Joseph, perhaps to his relief and wonderment, that he was not "אֵינֶנּוּ *einenu*" to Benjamin. That every year for at least the ten years it takes to birth ten children he has been uppermost in Benjamin's mind. It is at this point that Joseph overflows with emotion and leaves the room to compose himself. He has really been present for someone for all the years he was absent.

That being the case, this midrash really sets up the atmosphere for Judah's plea, which follows in the middle of Genesis 44, the beginning of Va-Yigash. Try this: start with Genesis 43.19 and read to the end of the chapter, 15 verses. Count the number of times any close family relationship is mentioned. I count thirty-four incidents of father, son, lad, brother, child, wife, mother, including *love* "him," verse 20, and the phrase HIS SOUL WAS BOUND UP WITH HIS SOUL, verse 30.

In this manner, averaging twice in a verse, and with that key motif *ein, einenu*, HE IS GONE occurring four times, Judah hammers away, repeating the anguished tale of a rent family fabric yearning to be mended, healed, made even better than it was in the beginning.

I am writing this just a few days before Rosh ha-Shanah in Jerusalem, remembering a Davar Torah of Zalman Schacter-Shalomi. He translated the three titles of the Rosh ha-Shanah musaf into a *tshuvah* activity. *Malkhuyot* (kingship) meant ordering your priorities. *Zikhronot* (remembrance) meant deciding what needs to be remembered and what needs to be let go of, forgotten. *Shofarot* (playing also on the root לְשַׁפֵּר *l'shapper*), to listen carefully to what needs to be improved, repaired. This insight works well with the lesson of Miketz. What Joseph needed to do was to place the mending [אחה] (*aho*) of the family fabric high on his priorities; then to remember the abundant love and nourishment sometimes submerged beneath hurts inflicted on both sides knowingly and unknowingly. That was his shofar call, and ours.■

Rabbi Rami M. Shapiro

Rabbi Rami M. Shapiro trained in mysticisms both Eastern and Jewish, holds Masters degrees in Judaism and world religion, a Ph.D. in Contemporary Jewish Thought, and is a graduate of the rabbinical program of the Hebrew Union College—Jewish Institute for Religion, NY. Rami founded Temple Beth Or in 1981 and the Rasheit Institute for Jewish Spirituality in 1994.

An award-winning poet and author of over a dozen works in Jewish spirituality, Rami's most recent book is *The Wisdom of the Jewish Sages* (Bell Tower, 1995). A world-respected teacher of Jewish spirituality, Rami lectures extensively across North America as well as in Israel and India.

Torah is a map of the human quest for holiness (or rather "wholiness"); her characters and images are aspects of our own psyches. In this sidrah Pharaoh is the ruling mind, the ego, and Yosef is the intuitive mind, the soul. Separated from each other, the one is haunted and the other wrongly imprisoned; united with each other, they hold the key to personal and planetary transformation.

Pharaoh has a dream. He stood by the river and saw seven healthy cows rising out of the river only to be eaten by seven ill cows; seven ears of healthy grain swallowed up by seven lean ears. Pharaoh dreams of the impermanence of all things; he is haunted by the inevitability of old age, sickness, and death.

Pharaoh's whole world is death-denying. He is a god-king who will live forever. Ego posits this illusion in each of us.

Ego, like Pharaoh, seeks to control the world, to ward off personal suffering and deny the reality of its own mortality.

Yet Pharaoh cannot control his dreams. The *Zohar* tells us that to dream of a river is to long for peace, for it is written: "Behold I will extend peace to her like a river" [Isaiah 66.12]. In Hebrew, "peace" and "wholeness" share a common linguistic root. Peace comes only when we are whole. Being whole means embracing the flow of life from birth to death and accepting the ego's own transience in the process. Only when ego sees its own impermanence as part of the eternal flow of life can it relinquish its mad quest for control and enjoy the wondrous, albeit temporary, blessings of life.

On its own, ego cannot grasp this. Yet all of Egypt's magicians and sages fail to satisfy Pharaoh. The ego cannot learn what it must learn by going outside the self. It must go deeper into the self. In our story Pharaoh does this by summoning Yosef from the dungeon. Yosef is intuitive mind, the soul. The soul knows the impermanence of all things. It is imprisoned in ego's dungeon in order to keep its wisdom from spoiling ego's illusion of immortality. But the illusion fails to bring peace, and Pharaoh is forced to turn to the prisoner for help.

Yosef is brought out of the dungeon, cleaned up, made presentable so Pharaoh can converse with him. In other words, the insights of intuition have to be voiced in a way that ego can understand. Pharaoh does not go into the dungeon. The ego has its place, and it must be honored. Instead, intuition is elevated to share the throne with ego. Reason without intuition is lifeless scientism; intuition without reason is mindless spiritualism. Intuition is to be "added" (Hebrew yosayf/yosef) to reason, for only the two together can know the meaning of life. And the knowing is immediate: FOR YOU TO HEAR A DREAM IS TO TELL ITS MEANING [Gen. 41.15]. There is no need for intermediaries. Each of us must call up the soul for ourselves.

Yosef then reveals his real source: NOT I BUT GOD [Gen. 41.16]. When ego and intuition work in consort the greater reality of God is revealed, and with that revelation come the peace and wholeness each of us seeks. Torah urges us to achieve this wholeness within ourselves and then reach out to a starving world and offer it the way to wholeness as well.■

Miketz

ויגש אליו יהודה ויאמר

SERAH̲ BAT ASHER

THUS JACOB AND ALL HIS OFFSPRING WITH HIM CAME TO EGYPT. HE BROUGHT WITH HIM TO EGYPT HIS SONS AND GRANDSONS, HIS DAUGHTERS AND GRANDDAUGHTERS—ALL HIS OFFSPRING [Gen. 46.6–7].

The sages of the Talmud and the Midrash were masters at weaving straw into gold. Drawing on the Oral Law that Moses was said to have received at Mount Sinai along with the Torah, they developed a system of reading between the lines of the Torah to discover the answer to all of their unanswered questions. The method they evolved, what we might call the midrashic method, enabled them to fill in the gaps in the biblical narrative, as well as to resolve apparent contradictions in the text. Using this method they were able to distinguish between the light of the first day, when God said, "LET THERE BE LIGHT", and the light of the fourth day, when God created the sun and the moon and the stars. Using this method, they provided an appropriate death for Cain, the first murderer, and described what the childhood of Abraham was like—information that is missing in the text of the Torah.

Using this midrashic method, they were able to create a full identity for a figure whose name appears only twice in the Torah, in two lists. Nothing else is said about her. Yet the rabbis were able to bring her to life and make her play an essential role in many biblical episodes, including the identification of Moses as

Parashat Va-Yigash
Genesis 44.18–47.27

Howard Schwartz

HOWARD SCHWARTZ HAS EDITED A FOUR-VOLUME SET OF JEWISH FOLKTALES, INCLUDING *GABRIEL'S PALACE: JEWISH MYSTICAL TALES*, PUBLISHED BY OXFORD UNIVERSITY PRESS.

דָּבָר אַחֵר DAVAR AH̲ER. "I AM JOSEPH YOUR BROTHER WHOM YOU SOLD INTO EGYPT" [Gen. 45.4]. Freedom begins with the tale told truthfully: "I AM JOSEPH YOUR BROTHER WHOM YOU **SOLD** INTO EGYPT." In the telling of his own tale Joseph rises above the events, above his own anger and hurt; as he is speaking he begins to float above the lowly *peshat*, and he says, "DO NOT BE DISTRESSED OR REPROACH YOURSELVES BECAUSE YOU SOLD ME, IT WAS TO SAVE LIFE THAT GOD SENT ME AHEAD OF YOU" [Gen. 45.5]. The verb changes from "SOLD" to "SENT," and the entire series of events is reconstrued for a higher purpose of which none of the participants had been aware until that moment of transformation, when the surfaces give way, when what was once opaque is now transparent; and within the events Joseph sees a higher wisdom. Until he told his own story and squeezed it for all its hidden Godliness, the truth of his own life had eluded him, and he hears him-

the Redeemer, Moses searching for the coffin of Joseph, the crossing of the Red Sea, and other important episodes.

This figure, Serah bat Asher, about whom nothing is said in the Torah, springs into existence in the Talmud and the Midrash and becomes one of the favorite figures of the rabbis, whom they draw into the narrative as often as possible. How they did this is an object lesson in the midrashic method.

The story of Serah bat Asher, who, according to midrash, lived longer than anyone else, even Methuselah, starts as a name in the list of the sixty-nine relatives of Jacob who traveled with him into Egypt, as recounted in Genesis 46.17, including Asher's sons: Imnah, Ishvi, and Beriah, and their sister Serah. Serah might have remained as one of the unimportant names in this list if not for a strange coincidence. In another list, in Numbers 26.46, that of the census taken by Moses in the wilderness, the name Serah bat Asher pops up again: The name of Asher's daughter was Serah.

Now what are we to make of the fact that the same name appears in two lists separated by at least two hundred years? From our perspective it might be discounted as a coincidence. After all, Asher was a respectable name, and it is certainly possible that more than one person named Asher might name his daughter Serah. But from the point of view of the ancient rabbis, the fact that these two lists had this one name in common cried out for explanation. And so they arrived at what was for them the logical conclusion: They were the same person.

That resolves the problem of the identity of the two Serahs, but it doesn't explain how she lived so long. However, Rabbinic ingenuity found a solution for this problem as well. Using the midrashic method, the rabbis searched for the "right place." This is the place in the text

---

Va-Yigash

self saying, "SO NOW IT WAS NOT YOU THAT SENT ME HERE, BUT GOD" [45.8]. Joseph is known in the Kabbalah as "the harvester," he is the one who harvests events to reveal truth. It is a surprise even to him. **James Stone Goodman, <Stavisker@aol.com>**

דָּבָר אַחֵר DAVAR AHER. **ALL THE PEOPLE OF JACOB'S HOUSEHOLD WHO CAME TO EGYPT—SEVENTY** [Gen. 46.27]. In this past week's parashah, *Va-Yigash*, Yaakov is said to bring seventy souls into Egypt—Mitzraim. The Plaut, Hertz, Rashi, and JPS offer no answer as to WHY the Torah states that it is exactly seventy. The individuals listed in the Torah do not exactly amount to seventy and (as the JPS points out) we cannot be certain who is actually being counted anyway. We can be reasonably sure that seventy carries

that gives the necessary clue, which makes it possible to read between the lines. And in this case the clue involved another matter that is missing in the biblical narrative: how the sons of Jacob finally informed him that his beloved son, Joseph, was not dead after all.

It all goes back to the brothers' discovery that Joseph was still alive. Indeed, he was none other than the prince of Egypt. Once Joseph had revealed his true identity, he commanded his brothers to bring their father and the rest of the family to Egypt, for there was a famine in the land. This must have presented a dilemma for Joseph's brothers, since they had cast him naked into a pit and then sold him into slavery and had then told their father that he had been slain by a wild beast. Now they had to go back to their father, Jacob, a frail old man, and tell him that Joseph was alive after all.

Reading between the lines, the rabbis intuited that the brothers were filled with guilt and remorse, as well as with fear that Jacob might die of the shock when he heard the news. They needed a way to break it to him gently. So one of them came up with the idea of letting little Serah, who was then a child, play the harp for her grandfather and sing him a little song with the words "Joseph is alive, Joseph is alive." Serah, of course, was glad to sing a song for her grandfather, and when Jacob realized what she was saying, he jumped up and asked, "Is it true?" When she told him it was true, well, he blessed her with such a great blessing that she lived as long as she did [*Sefer Yashar* 109b-110a]!

Let me note here that I once gave a talk about Serah bat Asher in Indianapolis, and afterward a little old lady with an ill-fitting wig came up to me and said: "That's

SYNOPSIS: *Judah pleads for Benjamin. Joseph reveals himself to his brothers. Then Pharaoh welcomes Joseph's family. Jacob moves the family to Egypt and they settle in the Land of Goshen.*

RASHI OF THE WEEK:
Sometimes Rashi just gives us access to some really fun midrashim. THESE ARE THE DESCENDANTS OF LEAH, WHOM SHE DID (START TO) BIRTH WITH JACOB IN TWIN PEAKS (*PADAM-ARAM*)..ALL HIS SONS AND DAUGHTERS TOTALED THIRTY-THREE [Gen. 46.7]. *But if you count the list in the Torah*, there are only thirty-two. *Who is missing? The answer,* Yokheved, *Moses' mother.* She was born "between the walls" just as they crossed the border *of Egypt.* We learn this in Numbers 26.59: Yokheved, the daughter of Levi, was born to her mother in Egypt. She was born in Egypt, but not conceived there [*Sotah* 12a]. *And this spiritual truth of being born in Egypt but not conceived there was passed on to her son.*

---

primarily a symbolic message; so what then is that message in our tradition?

We know of (1) the seventy *Panim* faces of Torah; (2) the seventy original nations of the world according to the seventy descendants of Noah; (3) the seventy archetypal languages; (4) the seventy scholars who translated Torah into Greek (*Septuaginta*); (5) the seventy Elders of Yisrael who accompanied Moses to Mt. Sinai; and (6) the seventy members of the great Sanhedrin.

Seventy seems to have significance not only in regard to numeric quantity, but also in regard to time, such as (1) the seventy years of Babylonian exile; (2) the age of Avram's father, Terah, when Avram was born (seventy); (3) the seventy days of mourning for the death of Yaakov; and (4) the mention in Psalm 90.10 that "THE DAYS OF OUR YEARS ARE SEVENTY."

Here we have seventy souls who enter Mitzraim to grow ultimately into a nation of 600,000 plus. (Of course, this number has its own symbolic content and should not be understood as an actual count at all.)

Let us consider several *gematriot* (numeric values, equivalences, and

not how I heard it at all!" I said, "Okay, how did you hear it?" She said,: "I heard that Jacob was furious that Serah was tampering with this most painful episode in his life, and he jumped up and said, 'You should live so long!' And she did." Afterwards I wondered if I had just heard the truth from none other than Serah herself.

In either case, this midrash brought Serah to life and explained how she lived for so long. That might have been enough, if all that the rabbis wanted to do was to identify Serah and explain how Jacob learned that Joseph was alive. But the rabbis found Serah very handy to call on in several other cases as well. One of these involved the identity of the Redeemer. There was an understanding that there would be a kind of code that would identify the Redeemer, a secret sign that God had communicated to Jacob, who in turn revealed it to his sons, and in this way Serah learned it from her father, Asher. The sign of the true Redeemer is that he would say: "I will surely visit you." Thus when Moses said these words, Serah identified him as the Redeemer [*Exodus Rabbah* 5.13].

Then we arrive at what is perhaps Serah's most important role. For it was she who informed Moses where the coffin of Joseph could be found. This midrash fills in a major gap in the biblical narrative between the vow that Joseph made the sons of Israel swear on his deathbed that "YOU SHALL CARRY MY BONES FROM HERE" [Gen. 50.25] and the report that Moses took the bones of Joseph with him [Ex. 14.19].

Here again we have a classic example of the workings of the Rabbinic imagination. On the day before they took their leave from Egypt, while the Israelis were despoiling the Egyptians, Moses searched everywhere for the coffin of Joseph, but he could not find it, since several hundred years had passed, and no one remembered where Joseph was buried.

Va-Yigash

correspondences) that may point to a meaningful perspective of seventy:

אָדָם וְחַוָּה *ADaM V'CHaVaH* "Adam and Eve" = 70

אָבִי וְאִמִּי *AVI V'IMI* "my father and my mother" = 70

סוֹד *SOD* "secret" = 70

Momentarily, we shall understand the nature of this secret because

נְקֵבָה *NeKeVaH* "female" = 157

זָכָר *ZaCHaR* "male" = 227

therefore "male" and "female" are separated by 70. This gap between opposites is defined by 70, by the סוֹד *SOD*.

Similarly,

עִבְרִית *IVRIT* "Hebrew" = 682

בְּרִית *BRIT* "Covenant" = 612.

The gap between עִבְרִית *IVRIT* and the בְּרִית *BRIT* with God must be bridged by עִבְרִית *IVRIT*'s ability to

Returning empty-handed, Moses encountered a little old lady who asked, "Why so downcast, Moses?" And when Moses told her, she said, "I can lead you to the coffin of Joseph." "Who are you?" Moses asked, "and how do you know where Joseph is buried?" "I'm Serah bat Asher," she replied, "and I know because I was present at the funeral of Joseph, and his coffin was sunk into the Nile!"

Serah then leads Moses to the very spot where the coffin was sunk into the Nile. Now Moses knows where it is, but he has a new problem: how to raise a heavy coffin from the Nile. So Moses leans over the shore and says, "Joseph, Joseph, we're leaving. If you want to come with us, come now. If not, we did our best." At that moment a miracle takes place, and the coffin of Joseph floats to the surface where Moses is able to pick it up and bring it with him [*Mekilta de-Rabbi Ishmael, Beshallah* 24a-24b].

Nor does the legendary history of Serah end there. She is identified as the one Israelite crossing the Red Sea who saw things that none of the others saw. In her vision she saw the multitude of angels who had gathered to watch the children of Israel cross the Red Sea. So, too, did she see the Divine Presence, which descended among them when Miriam played the tambourine and sang the Song of the Sea. In that vision Serah even saw the Holy One commanding the waters of the Red Sea to part. For other than Moses, Serah was the only one alive in that generation who could look upon the Holy One and live.

There are many other brief appearances that Serah makes in her long life. She even shows up at the house of study of Rabban Yohanan ben Zakkai. Rabban Yohanan once asked his students to describe the appearance of the walls of the Red Sea when the waters parted for the children of Israel to cross. When none could do so, Rabban Yohanan described them as resembling a lattice. Then, all at once, they heard a voice say: "No, it wasn't like that at all!" They looked up and saw the face of a very old woman peering in the window of the house of study. "Who are you?" demanded Rabban Yohanan. "I am Serah bat Asher," came the reply, "and I know what the walls of the Red Sea looked like, because I crossed the Red Sea, and they resembled shining mirrors." When she finished speaking Serah took her leave and disappeared once again [*Pesikta de-Rab Kanana* 11.13].

There are two legendary accounts of the ultimate fate of Serah. One reports that she met her death in a fire in a synagogue in Isfahan, Persia, in the ninth century. That synagogue was rebuilt and named after her, and it is still the holiest Jewish site in Iran, to which Persian Jews used to make pilgrimages when they were still permitted to do so. There is another legend that Serah never died—that

---

unify the paradox of the SOD. Separation and reunification arguably form a principal theme in Torah cosmology. In Genesis 1.1 we read six times וַיְהִי-כֵן *VaYeHI CHeN* "and it was so". Since כ *Khaf* 20 + נ *Nun* 50 = כֵּן *KHeN* 70, this phrase could and should be simultaneously understood as "and it was 70."

It was כֵּן *KHeN* 70 that separated and unified light and darkness, evening and morning, the upper waters and the lower waters, etc. The same idea is expressed in the manifestation of this *brit* (covenant), תּוֹרָה *TORaH* 611 and יִשְׂרָאֵל *YiSRaEL* 541 [611-541=70]. Once again, the gap reverberates with the same סוֹד *SOD* 70. Only when we understand the momentous mystical function of 70 will we ever understand why דִּינָה *DINaH* 70 (*kolel* value) had to be recaptured and why her rape was ultimately avenged with such incredible fury. On a mystical level, the *B'nei Yisrael* recognized that without Dinah they had lost their link to the covenant with God.

Only a few parashot ago, יַעֲקֹב *YaAKoV* 182 was given the name Yisrael after a mystic battle with the stranger as he readied himself to finally cross the יַבֹּק *YaBoK* 112. It was יַעֲקֹב *YaAKoV*'s ע *Ayin* 70 that emerged after crossing over to the

she was one of nine who were taken into heaven alive [*Sefer Yashar* 110a and *The Alphabet of Ben Sira* 28a]. As this rich legend of Serah bat Asher makes abundantly clear, it is the latter version that is the right one. Serah never died. She was created out of the imagination of the rabbis, and she lives on in our own imaginations, a sharp-tongued female Elijah wandering around the world, setting things straight.■

Va-Yigash

other side of the יַבֹּק *YaBoK* (182 - 112 = 70, or subtract the letters contained in יַבֹּק *YaBoK* from those of יַעֲקֹב *YaAKoV* and the letter ע *Ayin* remains). In recognizing the existence of his ע *Ayin* 70, Yaakov attained the fortitude to reunite with his brother Esav. Here we have yet another instance of 70 bridging the gap. Though Yaakov doesn't know it yet, it is at this moment that Yaakov liberates/frees his ע *Ayin* 70 and thus he enables himself to take his ע *Ayin* 70 down to Mitzraim.

In connection with the preceding example, it seems reasonable to suspect that the letter ע *Ayin* itself may contain some clues as to the meaning of 70, since this is the numeric value of the ע *Ayin*. Indeed, ע *Ayin* 70 represents not only "eye" but it may also refer to "source/well/spring/fountain/origin." This association endows many words beginning with the ע *Ayin* with a particular resonance. Furthermore, 70 plays a significant role with 26 (the gematria of the *Tetragrammaton*) as in 70 x 26 = 1820. According to the scribes, the *Tetragrammaton* is mentioned in all of Torah exactly 1820 times. As such, 70 is elevated to a most auspicious status along with the *Tetragrammaton* value.

It appears that 70 alludes to three interconnected principles: (1) origin/source/foundation; (2) hidden/secret—that which separates and connects opposites; and (3) critical mass/collective consciousness. These aspects interconnect inasmuch as the origin (birth) of our own existence stems from the sacred ability of male and female to overcome the gap that separates them and in doing so to fuse in one creative moment, thereby providing the foundation for the principle that will eventually generate a critical mass.

"Adam and Eve" as well as "my father and my mother" speak clearly of our ORIGIN. We therefore recognize that the סוֹד *SOD* secret lies in what separates male and female. The fusion of these two is, after all, the origin of all subsequent *hayot* "living beings".

סוֹד *SOD* 70 can also mean "assembly" and is therefore a direct allusion to the secret of "group power" [Psalm 111.1]. It required the presence of seventy members of the Sanhedrin to provide the diaspora with the collective awareness to guide and maintain their Jewish identity and integrity. We already learned how Yaakov attained the ability to bring ע *Ayin* 70 to

Rabbi Kerry M. Olitzky

Rabbi Kerry M. Olitzky is the Director of the School of Education at Hebrew Union College—Jewish Institute of Religion, NY. He is author of numerous books and articles, including (with Lawrence S. Kushner) *Sparks Beneath the Surface: A Spiritual Commentary on the Torah* (Jason Aronson, 1993).

The climax of the Joseph saga erupts in this parashah when Joseph, unable to maintain the ruse any longer, finally utters the simple phrase "I am Joseph" [Gen. 45.3]. As he says these three words the recorded history of our people suddenly seems to stand still. We are overwhelmed by the moment, having relived it so many times in our own lives. Estranged family members finally back in the fold. Former friends in contact with one another. Next-door neighbors talking once again.

My friend Abe Peck, himself born in a D.P. camp and with few surviving relatives, boils with anger when he learns of families whose members *choose* not to speak with one another. He was never given the choice!

As a result of Joseph's self-revelation, his estrangement from his family is eclipsed by the long-awaited reunion. We learn why he had not attempted to contact his father after all these years, why he had waited so long to reveal himself. Joseph was not ready to confront his family. He had much to learn about himself before he could make contact with his father and brothers once again. The Torah wants us to believe that Joseph's brothers do not recognize him. True, they only remember him as a young boy—and certainly do not expect him to have achieved a place of prominence in Egypt. They have not seen Joseph in many years, but it is puzzling that his brothers detect no family resemblance, see no common gestures. Nothing at all appears familiar to them. I sometimes wonder if I would be able to recognize my own brothers

---

Va-Yigash

Mitzraim. The secret meaning of Yaakov's seventy seeds/souls is that they represent the critical mass necessary to ensure the survival of *B'nei Yisrael* in a foreign land and their development as an eternal well-pring of Jewish life.

Ha-Shem already promised Avraham immediately following the Akedah (Binding of Isaac) that his seeds would be as numerous as the stars in the heavens and as the sand וְכחוֹל *V'KHaHOL* 70 upon the sea shore. The implication seems to be that Avraham's seeds would gain the critical mass to endure forever. And indeed, Yaakov did his part to fulfill Ha-Shem's promise. Bearing in mind that similar to the letter *Alef*, the ע *Ayin* 70 is not vocalized by itself; the ע *Ayin* 70 is the "eye" that beholds the secret…leaving us speechless. **C. Moshe Harlan, <CMosheH@aol.com>**

Va-Yigash

after similarly long separations. When we were younger, my oldest brother and I were often mistaken for twins. Even my wife, seeing us approaching from a long way off, was עִבְרִי (hebrew) unsure who was who.

And the Torah insists Joseph's brothers had no sense whatsoever that the man who stood in front of them was their brother. Perhaps it is because they remembered Joseph as he was: presumptuous, pretentious, precocious. But Joseph had changed, grown, matured. Here in this portion, by proclaiming "I AM JOSEPH," he is not merely identifying himself. He is implying that he can't be defined any longer by the way others perceive him. As a result of his inner struggle he has come to understand the full depth of self and is ready to share that insight with others. In that moment, for the first time in his life, Joseph reveals his essential self to his brothers. Hence, one verse later he repeats the phrase "I AM JOSEPH," and this time says "I AM JOSEPH *YOUR BROTHER*" [Gen. 45.4]. Some verses later, Joseph is able to tell his brothers the real Torah that he has learned in his life's journey that took him down to Egypt: "GOD SENT ME HERE, NOT YOU" [Gen. 45.8]. Joseph learned—as we must—that until we come face to face with our essential self, we are blocked from such spiritual learning. Or perhaps it is through intimacy with God, an understanding of God's direction in our life, that we are able to come to know our essential self. Rabbi Isaac Ben Moses Aroma, known as the Akedat Yitzhak, put it best when he interpreted Joseph's words by saying, "I arrived to this place through God."

The Joseph saga seems to be a human story about one man and the relationship he develops with his brothers. It is also about each of us as we struggle to come closer to the members of our families and to our inner selves. But the Joseph story is much more, for with Joseph and his brothers the Torah offers us a foreshadowing of what all Israel will learn in the parshiot that follow: The possibility of deliverance from slavery only comes from the self-awareness that emerges through intimate contact with the Divine. The Hofetz Hayyim even sees the messianic here, for when Joseph utters the words of self-disclosure, "I AM JOSEPH," it is actually God (speaking through the mouth of the Messiah) saying, "I am God doing my work in the world through Joseph." We, too, embody God's presence in the world as we grow, mature, and reach our higher selves—and commit to doing God's work in the world, struggling to bring forward the messianic.■

ויחי יעקב בארץ מצרים

The book of Genesis ends as it begins—with birth and blessing. But as Genesis begins with separation (of the various parts of Creation) and exile (from Eden), Genesis ends with the promise of return from where the first family has migrated, back to the land of promise.

And the blessing is different, too. In Genesis 1 it is God who blesses the creatures of the sea and the air and human beings; in Va-Ye<u>h</u>i it is human beings who bless Jacob and Joseph.

For in Genesis 12, God conveyed the power of blessing upon Abraham; and Jacob, whose own blessing from his father was so contested, restores paternal blessing to its rightful place with the deathbed ethical wills he bestows on his twelve sons.

Where is birth in this portion? Despite its title "AND (JACOB) LIVED" [Gen. 47.28], most of the portion seems to deal with death. There is birth, but a kind of messianic birth. When Jacob asks Joseph to bring him Menasseh and Ephraim, "JOSEPH BROUGHT THEM OUT FROM BETWEEN HIS KNEES." [Gen. 48.12]. While the phrase is ambiguous, tradition understands the "knees" to mean Jacob. In Genesis 30.3 Rachel uses the phrase to indicate that children born to her handmaid Bilhah will be reckoned (or adopted) as Rachel's children, but in our text we see that the ritual is a symbolic birth—as though Jacob himself had

Parashat Va-Ye<u>h</u>i

Genesis 47.28–50.26

Rabbi Richard N. Levy

RABBI RICHARD N. LEVY IS THE EXECUTIVE DIRECTOR OF LOS ANGELES HILLEL COUNCIL, THE PRESIDENT OF THE CENTRAL CONFERENCE OF AMERICAN RABBIS AND THE EDITOR OF *ON WINGS OF AWE*, *ON WINGS OF FREEDOM* AND THE FORTHCOMING *ON WINGS OF LIGHT*.

דָּבָר אַחֵר DAVAR A<u>H</u>ER. JACOB LIVED IN THE LAND OF EGYPT SEVENTEEN YEARS; AND THE DAYS OF JACOB —THE YEARS OF HIS LIFE—WERE ONE HUNDRED AND FORTY-SEVEN YEARS [Gen. 47.28]. We arrive at the seam that serves as an end to several stories: the seam of the death of Jacob, the seam of the death of Joseph, the seam of the end of the book of Genesis, the seam of the narratives of our mothers and fathers, the seam of the beginning of Serious Exile. Yet the parashah is "closed"—there is no space in the scroll between the end of Va-Yigash and the beginning of Va-Ye<u>h</u>i.

There are no ends, no beginnings, just seams, the delusion of all endings, all beginnings, all arrivals, all starts—there is only process and journey and movement and motion and the inevitable ebb and flow of existence, not its starts and stops. It's

given birth to his grandsons. Recall Moses' later plaint, "HAVE I BEEN PREGNANT WITH THIS PEOPLE, DID I GIVE BIRTH TO THEM, SHALL I CARRY THEM IN MY BOSOM AS A NURSING FATHER אֹמֵן (*Omen*) CARRIES A SUCKLING CHILD?" [Num. 11.12]. We may hear some expressions of a man's longing to bear children as well as father them. In Jacob's case, it is also an expression of the grandparent's role of intervention when children are being raised in a foreign (in our time read non–Jewish) environment. If the birth parents are not raising children in a way that will lead them to the God of Israel, Jacob teaches us that it is the proper role of the grandparents to step in and, as it were, give birth to them all over again in their true heritage.

Did Jacob know about Max Weber, the theoretician who would one day write about the routinization of charisma? Jacob is aware that, with his eyes dim [Gen. 48.10], he is in the same situation as was his father when Isaac blessed him [Gen. 27.1], and what Isaac seemed to do by accident, Jacob now does intentionally: Blessing is an act of will, not chance; birth order shall no longer determine destiny. And by declaring, "THROUGH YOU SHALL ISRAEL CONFER BLESSING" [Gen. 48.20], Jacob is saying something very important to the sons of Israel who would be blessed by invocations of Ephraim and Menasseh.

What did Ephraim and Menasseh ever do to deserve this honor? Just as Ephraim and Menasseh received their merit not through any acts of their own, but only because they were alive and were descendants of Jacob (as are we all), so Jewish boys need not feel that their parents' love is dependent upon their accomplishments, but that they are beloved just because they are children. For Jewish girls, however, who might be inclined by society's prejudices to think that because they are girls they need not set their sights very high, the blessing

---

Va-Yehi

the Great Stew, existence; it doesn't begin and end, it just is. It's the great Is, the river that flows out of itself into itself.

It's the Sea, and we would like the delusion that we can swim it. This is not a sea that we can swim; this is a sea that we float. The portion is closed, no beginning, no end, just the gentle rise and fall of the sea. We are left here floating on our backs on the great sea, up and down the gentle cadence of the ineffable sea, reliable, infallible, no beginning, no end, the beautiful rhythm of life's ebb and flow. This is a sea you cannot swim in; you only float. When you learn to float, it is so beautiful you wonder how you ever did anything else. **James Stone Goodman, <Stavisker@aol.com>**

holds up to them the highest models: May you be like the greatest women the Torah knows—Sarah, Rebekah, Rachel, and Leah.

The blessing of Ephraim and Menasseh serves as the overture to the great symphony of blessings that is the main section of this parashah. For it is blessing that gives meaning to the title of this portion. The portion announcing the death of Sarah is called *Hayyei Sarah,* the Lives of Sarah, and continues with the finding of a wife for Isaac. The rabbis arranged this week's parashah to begin with the phrase "AND JACOB LIVED" to suggest that Jacob's death, like all deaths, was a prelude to eternal life. Sarah lives on in the lessons Isaac and Rebekah learned from her life, and Jacob will survive his physical departure through the teachings he passes down into the subsequent generations, who become the tribes founded by his sons.

His sons—Where is a blessing for Dinah? The beginning of Exodus does not include Dinah among those of Jacob's children who entered Egypt, suggesting that she died in Canaan. Did Jacob bless her before she died? Was his blessing not recorded because it was private, intended for her alone? Is Jacob suggesting that not all ethical wills should be published?

In the case of his sons, perhaps not all of them *should* have been published. He describes his first-born, Reuben, as "ROLLING LIKE WATER"; of Shimon and Levi he says, "LET ME NOT ENTER THEIR COUNSEL." On the other hand, perhaps he made such comments public to demonstrate that: (1) parents need to have some objectivity about their children; (2) love and criticism are not mutually exclusive; and (3) it is never too late to

דָּבָר אַחֵר DAVAR AHER. **THEN ISRAEL SAW JOSEPH'S SONS AND HE SAID, "WHO ARE THESE?" AND JOSEPH SAID TO HIS FATHER, "THEY ARE MY SONS WHOM GOD HAS GIVEN ME HERE." HE SAID, "BRING THEM TO ME, AND I WILL BLESS THEM"** [Gen. 48.8-9]. Adoptive parents might find some guidance for developing a Jewish adoption ceremony from the story of Ephraim and Menasseh in Genesis 48.8–16. Joseph brings his sons to his father for a blessing but receives something more. Jacob chooses to adopt his two grandsons so that "Ephraim and Menasseh shall be as Reuben and Shimon." What follows is a ceremony of adoption that consists of several different acts:

Jacob asks Joseph to identify his sons [verse 8-9]. It's not that Jacob's dimming eyesight does not allow him to recognize his

SYNOPSIS: *This is the end of the family history. Joseph promises to bury Jacob in Egypt. Jacob blesses the family, dies, and is buried in the cave of Machpelah. Joseph dies and is buried in Egypt. The children of Israel promise that one day his bones will return home.*

RASHI OF THE WEEK:

Right after Jacob dies, Joseph tells his brothers [Gen. 50.19–21]: *"FEAR NOT." He is saying, "Even though Jacob is dead, you have no reason to be afraid." The Torah ends his speech by telling us* "HE SPOKE INTO THEIR HEARTS"[Gen. 50.20]. Rashi, of course, asks, *"What does it mean that HE SPOKE INTO THEIR HEARTS?" It means* he spoke in a way they could understand: Joseph said to his brothers, "Listen, before you came here, everyone said 'Joseph is lying about his past, he is actually a slave kid who made it lucky.' If I kill you, then what would people say? That he used these fine young men to establish a lineage and then killed them so they could not tell the truth? No man kills his real brothers. Keeping you alive is in my own best interest." *Joseph lied, which was the only way his brothers could understand the truth!*

דָּבָר אַחֵר DAVAR AHER: He said to them: "If ten lights could not extinguish one light, how can one light extinguish ten?" [*Megillah* 16b].

encourage those you love to do *tshuvah.*

The most arresting aspect of Jacob's blessing, of course, is its metaphors. He learned from his father's blessing that the essence of blessing is the hope for fruitfulness—this is also the substance of God's blessing to the creatures of earth, sky, and heaven. Isaac blessed Jacob with evocations of the fragrance of a field blessed by God, the dew of heaven, fat places of the earth, corn and wine—these are meant both literally and metaphorically. Jacob, however, moves totally to metaphor (and simile as well): water, lions, scepter, young horses and donkeys, milk, wine, serpents, deer, a fruitful vine by a fountain, a ravenous wolf. Long before Chagall's windows, these images became part of our associations with the tribes that flowed from the loins of his sons.

What are we to make of such an outpouring of images? On one level they make us uncomfortable—they are so close to the natural objects worshipped by the Canaanites and the animal god-images of the Egyptians; how does metaphor distinguish itself from idolatry? Are the sons to be rewarded with tribes because they partake of the qualities of these animals? Or are these attempts to demythologize these creatures by making them "only" metaphors, suggesting that if human beings share the qualities of animals, the animals are in no way divine?

Consider the roles that animals have played in Jacob's life—goats whose skin turned his arms into Esau and whose flesh turned Esau's blessing into his; the goats in Laban's flock who saw the mottled branches and conceived mottled offspring to benefit the fortunes of Jacob, with his mottled character. From Joseph's life Jacob learned that some images are portentous: the sheaves, the sun, moon, and stars of the youthful

---

Va-Yehi

grandsons; rather this act of identification is ritualistic.

Jacob embraces and kisses the boys as an expression of love.

Joseph places the boys between Jacob's legs as a sign that it is as if he personally gives birth to them. Note that the word בִּרְכָּיִם *birkaim,* his knees, is from the same root as the word בְּרָכָה *brakhah*—blessing.

The statement that precedes this act of adoption now takes on a new meaning: קָחֶם-נָא אֵלַי וַאֲבָרְכֵם *Kahem-na eili va-avarakheim*—not "Bring them to me that I may bless them" but "Bring them to me that I may adopt (place between my legs) them." Could this passage serve as the basis for developing an authentically Jewish adoption ceremony?

Adoption is a sacred act, and those who choose adoption should be

dream. Does Jacob, in blessing his children, intend these animal images as portents of the fate of tribes his sons will found? Could it be that Jacob, the creator of metaphor, is merely describing his sons' natures or their tribes', with no attempt at prophecy? As God conferred on Abraham the power of blessing humans, so here Jacob takes the portentous power of dreams (with all the destructive force he has seen them possess during the life of his son Joseph) and transforms them into a safer, merely human blessing. A blessing is now just a prayer that God might grant to each son's progeny, wishing for the qualities each animal represents. God and humans were controlled by the dreams that God sent; Jacob's metaphoric blessings restore free will.

Unlike Joseph's dreams, Jacob's blessings inspire no negative responses on the part of his sons. Indeed, they even inspire a peacefulness. The rabbis argue that the brothers concocted a deathbed message from Jacob that Joseph should forgive his brothers' sin, justifying this apparent lie (it does not appear as a direct quotation from Jacob) in the interests of family peacemaking. Even truth, they argue, is subordinate to peace.

So the book of Genesis ends where it began, with blessing but also with birth. For the last word of the portion is Mitzraim, Egypt—but also, literally, the constricted place, the straits, the womb, as it were, not of an individual but of the Jewish people, separated from the loins of Jacob into twelve tribes, born at the parting of the birth waters of the Sea of Reeds, the subject of a new book of Torah. Israel lives indeed.■

---

honored and supported by the Jewish community. The Talmud even says that one who adopts is considered as if, he/she has given birth. Along with Batyah bat Paraoh, adoptive parents can now find a new role model in our tradition. **Rabbi Mark M. Greenspan, Beth El Temple, Harrisburg, PA**

דָּבָר אַחֵר DAVAR AHER. MAY YOU BE LIKE EFRAIM AND MANASSEH [Gen. 48.20]. A transcendent moment: each Friday evening, as I sit at the head of the shabbos table, regardless of the noise that surronds us, my boys come to me for blessing. (Even if I am away for Shabbat—the only time they articulate any real resentment of my absence—they ask me to bless them over the telephone before they sit for dinner.) It is a brief moment, a few carefully selected words that Jewish tradition takes from Jacob's final blessing to his own children, augmented by the familiar priestly benediction. Then finally a kiss—something particularly special for a father of adolescent boys who eschew such public displays of emotion, particularly when it takes place in full view of their peers. "DAD!" they usually shriek as they wriggle out from my lingering embrace, "you're embarrassing me." Secretly, I enjoy the scene they make for their friends.

But somehow Shabbat is different for them. It offers us permission. The rules of their youthful culture, which intrude on most demonstrative emotional behavior between father and son, can be set aside. Whatever may have taken place during the week, even moments before we sit for a Sabbath meal, is eclipsed. The fights, the arguments and disagreements, the exchange of ill-considered and often hurtful words. All for the sake of this one moment that defies time. It is only in these few seconds that I am able to even approximate the intense physical relationship of bonding that God gives to mothers who are able to issue forth children from their own body. I still remember standing as somewhat of an outsider throughout pregnancy and birth—even as a devoted and attentive Lamaaze coach. And so on Shabbat I set my principles of equality aside; they come to me for blessing alone. **Rabbi Kerry Olitzky, <olitzky@huc.org>**

דָּבָר אַחֵר DAVAR AHER. SO HE BLESSED THEM THAT DAY, SAYING, "BY YOU SHALL ISRAEL BLESS SAYING, 'MAY GOD MAKE YOU LIKE EPHRAIM AND LIKE MANASSEH...'" [Gen. 48.20]. We would like to expand on Richard Levy's interpretation of the parental blessing by noting that Ephraim and Manasseh, Sarah, Rebekah, Rachel,

Nechama Tamler

NECHAMA TAMLER IS MARRIED TO HOWARD TAMLER AND IS THE MOTHER OF DOV, TAMAR, AND YONI. SHE SPENT A YEAR AS A JERUSALEM FELLOW IN 1992–93 STUDYING TORAH WITH NECHAMA LEIBOWITZ, AVIVA ZORNBERG, AND NOAM ZION. SHE NOW STUDIES TORAH IN PALO ALTO WITH THE PALO ALTO EGALITARIAN MINYAN, AND WORKS IN JEWISH EDUCATIONAL PLANNING AT THE JEWISH COMMUNITY FEDERATION OF SAN FRANCISCO. SHE HOLDS A MASTERS DEGREE IN FAMILY AND CHILD COUNSELING PSYCHOLOGY.

My understanding of Va-Yehi is informed and inspired by Dr. Aviva Zornberg's chapter on this parashah in her book *Genesis, The Beginning of Desire* (Image Books, 1996).

Paradoxically, while וַיְחִי *Va-Yehi* means "and he lived," this parashah deals with the deaths of both Yaakov and Rahel. According to Dr. Zornberg, this is a פָּרָשָׁה סְתוּמָה *"parashah s'toomah"*—that is, a closed or blocked portion, referring to the physical layout of the actual letters on the parchment.

In a "closed" portion, which is quite rare, the words of one parashah begin on the same line as the preceding week's sidrah, with no space between them to mark the separation. With an "open" portion, in contrast, there are usually at least nine blank spaces to separate one week's reading from the next.

Regarding Va-Yehi, Rashi gives two explanations of this blockage, one of which describes the last message. Before he dies, Yaakov wants to deliver a message to his sons about the ultimate meaning of life. Although Yaakov wants mightily to convey what will befall his family in the end of days [Gen. 49.1], he instead conveys blessings full of metaphors and is unable to share an integrative vision about the end of time, the end of exile and redemption. What accounts for this blockage?

Zornberg suggests that the key to Yaakov's blockage can be traced to the powerful memories he has evoked in recalling his beloved wife, Rahel. Indeed, the parashah begins with

---

Va-Yehi

and Leah were all outsiders to the Jewish people who chose to be affiliated with the community. This reminds us that the children of Israel actively chose to accept the Torah at Sinai. As we bless our children on Shabbat, we hope they will follow in the footsteps of those cited in the parental blessing by actively choosing to become involved in Jewish life. We hope they recognize that this choice will lead to a life of many blessings. **Regina and Steven Silver, Ann and Elliot Sturman, <70771.2337@compuserve.com>**

דָּבָר אַחֵר DAVAR AHER. **WHEN JACOB FINISHED INSTRUCTING HIS SONS, HE DREW HIS FEET ONTO THE BED; HE EXPIRED AND WAS GATHERED TO HIS PEOPLE** [Gen. 49.33]. *FOR JACOB MARCUS* ז"ל: Parashat Va-Yehi details the end of the Biblical patriarch Jacob's life—unlike other portions, it begins in the middle of a paragraph. According to the Sefas Emes, a wise and

Yaakov eliciting a solemn promise from Yosef (Rahel's firstborn) to carry his remains out of Egypt and to bury him with his father in the cave of Machpelah [Gen. 47.29–30]. The irony of this request is that Yaakov asks Yosef to do exactly what he (Yaakov) didn't do for his own wife, who died in childbirth after a painful labor to produce a son whom she names בֶּן-אוֹנִי *Ben-oni* (the son of my affliction) and whom Yaakov renames בִּנְיָמִין *Benyamin* (the son of my right hand). He buries Rahel בְּדֶרֶךְ *be-Derekh* (on the way, on the road) to Efrat, somehow implying a place that is not quite the place of proper burial, which for this family is the cave of Makhpelah.

In the next scene, in chapter 48, Yaakov is dying and ready to bestow his final blessings. He is about to formally adopt his two grandsons, Ephraim and Menasseh, when he begins to talk about Rahel. The words that call out to me are in verse 7, following a startling change of direction between verses 6 and 7. One minute Yaakov is talking about the inheritance of his two grandsons, who are to be considered his own sons, and in the next moment he says, "And I, when I came back from Padan, Rahel died on me in the land of Canaan, on the way, with still a stretch of land left to come to Efrat, and I buried her there, on the way to Efrat, that is Bet Lehem." In the very next sentence he looks at his grandsons and asks "Who are these?"—no longer recognizing them, as though his vision itself is blocked.

What is it about this powerful recollection of memories surrounding Rahel's death and unceremonious burial that evokes such pain as to block him both from recognizing present company and from making sense of life? Does he finally realize that his own behavior is at the nexus of the rivalry, jealousy, and suffering that he, his wives, and his children have experienced? Does he see the common thread running through his life that any reader of Genesis can perceive? What does he understand about the connection between cheating Esau and being cheated himself on his wedding night? Does he connect being favored by Rivka with his own favoring of Yosef? Does he realize that his (perhaps) careless curse on the stealer of the terafim (the household gods, which Rahel steals from her father) might have caused her premature death? Does he associate his favoring Yosef when he was a child with the pain of losing Yosef—believing he was dead, torn apart by a wild beast—and not seeing him for twenty-two years, indeed, remaining in a state of unconsoled grief? What overwhelming associations occur in the mind of our father, Yaakov, as he digresses from blessing Ephraim and Menasseh?

Whatever he experiences at this moment is to be so intense that he seems transported to another

---

insightful spiritual teacher, this intentional graphic layout of the text suggests that Jacob sought to reveal the end of days to his children before he died, a time when Israel's exile would finally end. His vision—like the Torah text—was closed to him. No matter how hard he tried, he could not bring an end to the exile of his people. Like his biblical namesake, our teacher, Jacob Rader Marcus, tried to teach all of us—the numerous generations of rabbis who sat at his feet during the seventy years he taught at HUC in Cincinnati—that Israel's exile finally came to an end when we reached the shores of this golden land and ushered in the golden age of American Jewry. He once thought he had found the messianic in Germany, only to learn that he had been deceived. So he turned to America and singlehandedly created the field of American Jewish history. For all of those who were blessed to know Jacob Rader Marcus and loved him as I did, we understood that he dedicated his life to documenting the experience of our people on these shores, particularly because of the devastation and destruction of European Jewry. He vowed that he would not allow the record of our experience here to slip through the hands of the Jewish

consciousness. He is metaphorically blinded, or blocked, at the end of his life—from truths that may be slightly beyond his grasp, and from a full reintegration of his experience. There is, however, someone else in Yaakov's life who is able to hold conflicting truths simultaneously and who can live with ambiguity, and that is Rahel. Therefore, she has become our consummate intercessor, standing up to God to ask that we be forgiven and redeemed from exile.

Rashi's comments on verse 7 ("RAHEL DIED ON ME") let us know that it was not an accident that Rahel was buried ON THE WAY, for it is precisely here that the children of Israel passed during their exile from the Land, and she came out of her grave and wept and entreated God for mercy for them, as it is said, A VOICE IS HEARD IN RAMAH—WAILING, BITTER WEEPING—RAHEL IS WEEPING FOR HER CHILDREN. SHE REFUSES TO BE COMFORTED FOR HER CHILDREN, WHO ARE GONE. THUS SAID THE LORD: "RESTRAIN YOUR VOICE FROM WEEPING, YOUR EYES FROM SHEDDING TEARS; FOR THERE IS A REWARD FOR YOUR LABOR, SAYS THE LORD" [Jeremiah 31.15–16].

And just why does God take Rahel seriously? What qualifies her to intercede successfully? Because she has been there—she has been a favorite wife who, despite her husband's love, had to share him with a rival. She was able to cope with that reality, able to tolerate not having everything just the way she wanted it. She reflects this back to God and asks, "If I, a mere mortal, could live with ambiguity and incompleteness, can't You find it in Your power to do the same, to forgive the Jewish people, to tolerate their sins, to redeem them and to end their exile?"

Yaakov's life ends amidst great fanfare, with blessings aplenty to bestow on his sons. He has a deathbed scene rivaled by none, yet he is blinded to the ultimate unity behind all the disintegration in his life and therefore is blocked

---

Va-Yehi

community. So he zealously collected, traveling from city to city—and lovingly placed everything one item at a time in the American Jewish Archives that he created and nurtured from the 1940s onward.

Marcus was a historian par excellence. He wrote incessantly. Never mastering the computer and using the typewriter rather infrequently, he wrote everything out by hand. He was always working on a new book project—some projects he worked on for years by collecting materials and filing them away until he was ready to sit and write. Then he would sit for hours, stooped over his desk, surrounded by hundreds of books and documents, scraps and scribbles of paper that he carefully shaped into meaning. His bibliography lists over 250 items. Ironically, his latest book appeared on the day of his death. This volume,

from foretelling the end of days. Rahel, on the other hand, who dies in childbirth, on the road, with no deathbed speeches, lives on in the Midrash as one who can reflect back to God how fragmented this world appears, how fraught with separation, and she is therefore ever-present in Jewish folklore as arguing for our ultimate redemption, the end of our exile.■

For a complete treatment of these ideas, please see "Genesis, The Beginning of Desire," *by Dr. Aviva Zornberg* (Image Books, 1996).

Maunderings, reflects the wit and wisdom of a man whose life neared 100 years. Like his other students, I learned from him every moment when we were together. Wherever we were, whatever we were doing, regardless of the topic. He always had Torah to teach. His laboratory was life itself and the people who formed the American Jewish community.

From the first day I set foot on the Cincinnati campus of Hebrew Union College I learned that HUC and all it stood for was synonymous with his name, for Marcus came to the college at the age of fifteen and, except for the time he spent studying for his Ph.D. in Germany, never left. But Dr. Marcus was more than just a scholar; he was a gentle, human soul bridled with a fierce passion, who loved strongly. When you became one of Marcus' boys, as he used to call us, you were his for life, and so were your spouse and children. All became part of the growing Marcus family with Jacob Rader Marcus at its core.

Again referring to the patriarch Jacob, the Torah records that at the end of his life HE (namely Jacob) GATHERED HIS LAST AND WAS GATHERED INTO HIS PEOPLE. In commenting on this verse, Tzena U'renah suggests that the reason that the Torah never mentions Jacob's death is that when those who came after him cited a teaching in his name, his lips actually moved in the grave. In that way, he never really died. Many things that Jacob Rader Marcus taught his students are now repeated in classrooms throughout the world. I know that whenever we teach, Dr. Marcus stands alongside each one of us—continually teaching us even as we teach students of our own. Perhaps Jacob Rader Marcus may no longer be counted among the living, but he will never be gone from our midst. **Rabbi Kerry Olitzky, Hebrew Union College, NY, <olitzky@huc.edu>**

דָּבָר אַחֵר DAVAR AHER. BUT JOSEPH SAID TO THEM, "FEAR NOT, FOR IS IT ABOUT ME INSTEAD OF GOD?" [Gen. 50.19-21]. So they all go to bury Jacob in the homeland, as he had instructed. When they return to Egypt the brothers of Joseph fear that now Joseph will let loose with all his hidden resentment and take his revenge for what they had done to them. They really don't believe, in their heart of hearts, that he has transformed, though he clearly told them in the last parashah "DO NOT BE DISTRESSED OR REPROACH YOURSELVES BECAUSE YOU SOLD ME OUT, IT WAS TO SAVE LIFE THAT GOD SENT ME AHEAD OF YOU" [Gen. 45.5]. "SO NOW IT WAS NOT YOU THAT SENT ME HERE, BUT GOD" [Gen. 45.8]. Naaah, they thought, nobody is that transformed.

They send a message to Joseph. Joseph weeps when he hears it. He weeps because of the distance he feels from his brothers; he feels even more distance than he would if he still considered them his victimizers. They didn't hear him the first time; they didn't believe him. He has moved to a different place; they haven't. He is no longer that boy who left Israel in a caravan, but a whole human being weathered and stripped of self. This was Joseph who meant it when he said to his brothers, "SO NOW IT WAS NOT YOU THAT SENT ME HERE, BUT GOD..." [45.8].

Joseph always leads with the truth, with the *peshat,* with what happened, the Great What It Is, "AS FOR YOU, YOU MEANT EVIL AGAINST ME..." [Gen. 50.20], but he moves to the interior, "FEAR NOT, FOR IS IT ABOUT ME INSTEAD OF GOD? AS FOR YOU, YOU MEANT EVIL AGAINST ME, BUT GOD MEANT IT FOR GOOD, TO BRING TO PASS AS IT IS THIS DAY TO SAVE MANY PEOPLE ALIVE. NOW THEREFORE, FEAR NOT, I WILL SUSTAIN YOU, AND YOUR LITTLE ONES" [50.19-21]. Joseph has moved to the inside of events, where the secret advantage of every descent, the hidden ascent, clarifies; where the problems of a few people don't amount to a hill of beans; the *peshat* gives way, releases its opacity, the tyranny of events, of surfaces, of facts, of self dissipates. Is it about me instead of God? Naaah, it's about God.

Joseph knows this now. The first time he said it he may have been the most surprised person in the room [Gen. 45.1–15], but this time he knows it in his heart, and this time he speaks it into the hearts of his brothers so that they will know it as he does.

Hidden within, deep within the events, never evading the truth, never wandering too far from the *peshat*, Joseph dies in the place where he has come to live, beneath the *peshat*, below the plot, tutored by nothing loftier than the poetry of his own life. For Joseph, it's all in the *peshat* because the *peshat* is the All. **James Stone Goodman, <Stavisker@aol.com>**

Va-Ye<u>h</u>i

שמות

Shemot

The Cry of Moshe

Shemot is not only the beginning of the great biblical drama of liberation, but our introduction to the Bible's premier human personality, Moshe. To borrow Shakespeare's words about Caesar, Moshe bestrides the world like a colossus. He is the towering embodiment of a man of God.

When we first encounter this colossus today, he is an abandoned baby, lying in a makeshift cradle, alone, under a decree of death, left by a riverbank.

Not only is he apparently helpless, but, to detract even more from the dignity of this presumed giant, Moshe is crying. The Bible informs us of this in an awkward and uncharacteristic way; we read THE DAUGHTER OF PHARAOH CAME DOWN TO BATHE IN THE NILE, WHILE HER MAIDENS WALKED ALONG THE NILE. SHE SPIED THE BASKET AMONG THE REEDS AND SENT HER SLAVE GIRL TO FETCH IT. **WHEN SHE OPENED IT, SHE SAW THAT IT WAS A CHILD—וְהִנֵּה-נַעַר בֹּכֶה *V'HINEH NA'AR BOKHEH*—AND BEHOLD, A BOY CRYING. SHE TOOK PITY ON IT AND SAID "THIS MUST BE A HEBREW CHILD."** [Ex. 2.6]

Why does the text resort to that strange, synoptic phrase, "AND BEHOLD, A BOY (*NA'AR*) CRYING?" Why is the word נַעַר *na'ar*, usually taken to mean a young lad, applied to

Parashat Shemot

Exodus 1.1–6.1

Rabbi David Wolpe

RABBI DAVID WOLPE IS THE SENIOR RABBI AT TEMPLE SINAI IN LOS ANGELES. HIS MOST RECENT BOOK IS *"WHY BE JEWISH?"*

דָּבָר אַחֵר **DAVAR AHER.** WHEN **MOSES WAS GROWN UP, THAT HE WENT OUT TO HIS BROTHERS, AND SAW THEIR BURDENS** [Ex. 2.11].

The Midrash asks, what does "HE SAW" [Ex. 2.11] mean? It answers that it means that Moses saw their suffering and he cried and he said, "Woe is me, would that I could die instead of them." Then God said to Moses, "Just as you have put aside (turned aside) your business/your life/your complacency and have shared the suffering of Israel, and have behaved 'IN THE MANNER OF BROTHERS,' so I will leave the ones on high and the ones below and will speak with you." Thus, in Exodus 3.4: AND GOD SAW THAT MOSES HAD TURNED ASIDE (from his business/ his life/his complacency) TO SEE, SO GOD CALLED TO MOSES FROM THE BUSH AND SAID, MOSES, MOSES....

S. R. Hirsch makes the point that before Exodus 2.24–25 (GOD HEARD

Moshe, who is an infant? How does this crying, its nature, quality, resonance, have anything to do with Pharaoh's daughter's certainty that this is a Hebrew child?

Numerous suggestions have been advanced to answer these questions. Why the use of the word *na'ar*? One Rabbinic response is that Moshe was acting old beyond his years, more a young lad than an infant. For he was restraining his tears, refusing to cry, when the angel Gabriel descended from heaven and struck him so that he would weep, evoke the compassion of Pharaoh's daughter, and be saved.

Another explanation of *na'ar* is that, although a child, Moshe cried with the *kol* of a *na'ar*, the voice of a young man. There was something unnatural, overripe, different about the cry that came from Moshe's basket, and it was clear he was an extraordinary child.

A final explanation of the use of *na'ar* is that the verse is quite literal. Pharaoh's daughter saw a *na'ar*, a young lad, cry. The *na'ar* was not Moshe, but Moses's older brother Aaron, who, standing far off and watching his brother being taken, was certain he would never see Moshe alive again and began to weep. Witnessing this familial love, Pharaoh's daughter knew this must be a Hebrew child, a Hebrew family.

Lastly there is an explanation that turns upon the curious fact that the Bible speaks of Pharaoh's daughter seeing, never hearing, Moshe. That is because, we are told, Moshe did not cry aloud. His cry was silent. It was עָצוּר מִמַּעֲמוֹק הַלֵּב *Atzur mi-Ma'amoke ha-Lev*—STOPPED UP IN THE DEPTHS OF HIS HEART, and all the

SYNOPSIS: *The family becomes a whole people. Pharaoh turns them into slaves. Moses is born, hidden, and found, grows, turns outlaw, and marries. God talks to him at the burning bush.*

RASHI OF THE WEEK:

In Exodus 2.10 the Torah says: "AND THE CHILD **GREW**, AND SHE BROUGHT HIM TO PHARAOH'S DAUGHTER." In the next verse it says: "AND IT CAME TO PASS, LATER WHEN HE HAD **GROWN**, THAT MOSES WENT OUT TO TALK TO HIS BROTHERS." *Rashi quotes Tanhuma*, Rabbi Judah the son of Eloai asked, "How come it says that the child grew twice?" Rabbi Judah answered: "The first growth was a physical growth—he became larger in size. The second growth was spiritual—he became a man to respect, and so Pharaoh gave him authority over his palace." *We learn that growth comes in many sizes and spirits.*

THEIR CRY AND GOD SAW), God was not personally involved with Israel, as it were, but allowed events to take their natural course. Now God is moved to act by Moses' model. Moses, IN THE MANNER OF BROTHERS, turns away from his life, from his standard, from his complacency, and does not a great thing, just the right thing. Moses gives himself away. מְסִירַת-נֶפֶשׁ *Mesirat Nefesh*. He turns away from self. He becomes בִּטּוּל *bittul*. He gives himself to the suffering of his brothers. Only then God hears their cry and is moved to act. God enters the communal drama inspired by the action of Moses. In the same manner God enters the personal drama of Moses when Moses turns away from the burden of self, when Moses has given himself away. **James Stone Goodman <Stavisker@aol.com>**

דָּבָר אַחֵר **DAVAR AHER. GOD HEARD THEIR MOANING** [Ex. 2.23-24]. At the end of chapter 2 [Ex. 2.23] we are groaning from our bondage, and our cry rises to God, and God hears our moaning and remembers the covenant with Abraham, Isaac, and Jacob. Is this the moment when God is called, so to speak, out of complacency and enters the liberation drama in a personal way? Is that what the text is saying? The

sadness and terror he felt was reflected on his face. This kind of face, the eloquence of its agony, the refusal to cry aloud, is uniquely Jewish, and so it was clear that Moshe was a Hebrew.

Obviously the midrash and commentators are casting about to explain the peculiarity of this cry. We can understand this impulse, for the biblical introduction of this historical hero cannot simply be as a tearful and bewildered child: Our collective image of the mien and motivation of Moshe is too sharp and distinct; that which impels the Moshe we know is not tears, but power, courage, prophetic vision, near-Divine force. In the midrash, in the supple storytelling hands of the rabbis, Moshe dissolves in tears before the prospect of his death. However, in the Bible he is power, anger, and strength.

Yet Moshe is so deeply mourned in the Torah, in the tradition, that we ought to ask, could anyone be worthy of so many tears, if they had never cried themselves? What is the deeper significance of Moshe's very first utterance being a cry? When the Torah relates that Moses died at age 120 and his eye was undimmed, could it be that it was not dimmed because his eyes had once, a century before, been clouded by curative tears?

All of these interpretations of Moshe's cry, all the struggles with its significance, are vital. For Moshe's cry is not the simple cry of a child. It is a paradigm; it stands for all manner of tears and mourning and grief. It is like the Yiddish play where an actor appears upon a blackened stage, is illuminated by a single spotlight, looks out into the audience, screams *gevalt*, and leaves. A Jewish audience instinctively understands. *Gevalt.* The quintessential cry. Its unadorned and powerful simplicity stands for all the screams that echo through all the darkened corridors of our history. *Gevalt.*

Shemot

midrash, however, takes us back to the moment of decision when Moses moves out of his complacency and defends his brother Hebrew [2.12], and it cites that moment as the moment when God, so to speak, moves out of God's complacency, precisely because of Moses' example. But there is something more subtle here that is given in the name of R. Levi Yitzhak of Berditchev, who asked the *koan*/question: when does our freedom saga begin? Like all *koans*, the question is designed to move us out of complacent ways of thinking. Freedom is infinitely regressible; that's what the midrash is reaching for by taking us back to Moses' action, because when he goes out to his brothers we ask the same question of our lives—what preceded this action?

Within Moshe's cry is something for each of us. There are those among us who weep according to the first understanding of the rabbis. We shout only when struck. We struggle through life restraining our tears, refusing to cry, maintaining the equanimity of perfect balance until life deals us an unendurable blow, when all the pent-up anger and anguish and sorrow of a lifetime come pouring forth. The angel Gabriel struck Moshe on behalf of all who cannot cry until life leaves them no choice.

Others can cry, but not in the conventional sense. Like the קוֹל *kol* of a נַעַר *na'ar*, a young lad, coming from a mere baby, some can cry only in a strange voice. Perhaps not with tears, but in charity, in poetry, with acts of compassion. Perhaps they cry only in songs, in sermons, or in prayer.

Some, among the most tragic, are too young or stricken too severely to cry for themselves. Tears enter their lives because they evoke the cries of others. This is the Moshe who did not cry himself, being too young to understand his fate, but who coaxed terrible tears of grief from his brother Aaron. The cry is no less bitter for belonging to someone else.

There are those whose cries are silent. They are עָצוּר מִמַּעֲמוֹק הַלֵּב *Atzur mi-Ma'amoke ha-Lev* stopped up in the depths of the heart. They cannot be heard, although they can be seen in a glance, a gesture—with the vague sense that somewhere inside is weeping. Neither the blows of an angel nor the compassion of another human being will bring the tears to the surface, for they lie too deep.

The seemingly natural cry of a sacred child is freighted with significance for us and for our understanding of Moshe. The Torah begins the chronicle of Moshe with a cry because it is the pivot of his character. Anyone who aspires to greatness, to goodness, must have a cry at the center of the soul. "The world," said the novelist Horace Walpole, "is a comedy to those who think, and a tragedy to those who feel." The Jews have always felt and have always known that in the midst of the goodness of this world is great tragedy. That is the message of the poignant and wrenching legend that a giant vat stands in heaven, into which flow all the tears of all the generations of Jews, and until that seemingly bottomless vat is filled we will not be redeemed. Because although there is Jewish humor, song, dance, and art, we recognize that the world is ever part tragedy, and so the fundamental Jewish expression is the cry.

Perhaps the deepest cry comes from a particular kind of Jew, a cry that we, in our incomparably savage century, know all too well. For Pharaoh's decree was to kill all the sons of Israel. As Jews have noted throughout the ages, it was the first attempted genocide of our people. What we can now appreciate is

---

What did Moses learn at his mother's breast to bring him out of his complacency at that moment? What had his mother received from her people to have transmitted this to Moses? Who said what to you, when, that slipped the message past your psyche, snuck it by the guardians of your equanimity? Who taught you to resist, who led you to believe that you could transform, that you could be free? Who was it? What teacher? What voice?

When we are sitting in our leather living rooms in the science fiction of the late twentieth century, and the courage erupts in us to change our lives in ways our ancestors could not have imagined, who made it possible for us to be free? Who known, who unknown? You made it possible for me to get free, you, unknown, who passed through silent streets hugging your books to your chest, teaching your children in rooms warmed by fireplaces with the darkness swirling about, teaching a wisdom strong enough to survive even its own breakdown, because there was certain to be a generation or two somewhere who would not receive it, and who could not pass it on. You made it possible for me to be free. But it is more subtle than that. Freedom is infinitely

that if this was the first attempt to destroy Jewry, then when we listen to the cry of Moshe we are hearing the cry of the first survivor. Moses was the first one to grow up with the guilt and the pain of inexplicably having lived when so many of his contemporaries must have died.

It explains so much about Moshe: his sense of personal unworthiness of God's mission; his unshakable insistence upon carrying out that mission once he had been chosen; his refusal to abandon the people—his people—to vengeance, even if it is the vengeance of the Lord. For at Moshe's core, beyond even his indestructible sense of self as a prophet of God, is an unexpected softness, the knowledge from youth that the world can be unrelentingly cruel, and that those who make their way through it intact, with whatever pain or difficulty, owe a perpetual debt to those who do not make it, those who are no longer here. Jeremiah knew that pain when he said: "OH THAT MY HEAD WERE WATERS AND MY EYES A FOUNT OF TEARS! THEN WOULD I WEEP DAY AND NIGHT FOR THE SLAIN OF MY POOR PEOPLE" [Jer. 8.23].

Moshe, in the Bible, does not weep day and night. He gives this solitary, symbolic cry, וְהִנֵּה-נַעַר בֹּכֶה *v'Hineh Na'ar Bokheh*—behold, look, see a child crying. Know its significance. Understand its centrality. Learn from this weeping.

Years later, when Moshe walked out of the palace and saw the burdens of his people, he understood the import of the cry he had given as a child. It was for all who were gone, and for all whose lives he now beheld, for the oppression, the סֵבֶל *sevel*, the suffering. Moses' cry was the cry of both a survivor and a contemporary; he cried for those whose lives were cut short and for those who lived but were empty, ignoble, and sad.

The philosopher Santayana taught: "The young man who will not cry is a savage; the old man who cannot

---

Shemot

regressible. Each act in the chain of behavior that leads to freedom is built on a previous act.

Every act contributes in some partial way to freedom. No deed is done, no thought is thought, no dream is dreamed for nothing. Everything contributes in some inscrutable way to freedom. When does freedom begin? It may begin today, with this thought. This thought was preceded by the dream the day before. Back beyond today. Every act, every thought may be a gesture for freedom. Every act has a liberating potential of which we may be unaware. No deed wasted, no thought for nothing. When did we get free? When we paused, when we resisted, when we dreamed it, back beyond, way beyond, before it came to be.

But it is more subtle than that. All time is redeemable not as future or

laugh is a fool." We are now a very old people, and we have not forgotten how to laugh. In this parashah we are a nascent people, a people being born, the youngest of nations, and we are already learning how to cry. It is yet another lesson from Moshe Rabbenu, Moses our Teacher. And the midrash contains the seeds of this teaching when it tells of Moses' death. After his death, the rabbis relate, not only did the children of Israel cry, but his disciple Joshua, unable to find his teacher and realizing that he was gone forever, began to cry, and then the heavens cried, and the earth cried. Finally, having taken Moses' soul away with a kiss, God wept.■

---

past but all as eternally present. There is no earlier or later in the Torah. It is all the Holy Now, the Completely Present. "Time present and time past are both perhaps present in time future, and time future contained in time past. If all time is eternally present all time is unredeemable" (*Burnt Norton, Four Quartets*, T.S. Eliot). Except in Torah time, all time is redeemable.

It is more subtle than that, for there is the companion question: When does freedom end? When can I claim freedom, jump off a truck, and run hollering down the street cheered on by the faithful who are showering me with the confetti of victory? I want it and I want it now! I want the whole thing, not the temporary freedom, the incremental freedoms, but the durable freedom.

But that's not what I get; I get the רָצֹא וָשׁוֹב *ratzo va-shov* [Ezekiel 1.14], THE RUN AND RETURN of freedom, the systole and the diastole, the moving toward and the moving away, the wonder and terror of the journey, of the dirt work, the work inside and the work outside, that precedes durable freedom. I get to celebrate the cycle that necessitates the wilderness before Sinai, that necessitates Mitzraim before the wilderness, that necessitates עֲבְדוּת *avdut* (servitude) before יְצִיאַת *yetziat* (exit). Mitzraim, that necessitates the first act of defiance before עֲבְדוּת *avdut*, that necessitates the first stirrings of freedom way back, way beyond thought, when we dreamed it, or when it was dreamed for us by those whose names are unknown. **James Stone Goodman, <Stavisker@aol.com>**

דָּבָר אַחֵר DAVAR AHER. AND THE BUSH WAS UNCONSUMED. [Ex. 3.2–4]. Moses was available to see the bush burning, but he was present in a transcendent way to see that the bush was not consumed. The burning bush was and is a metaphor for the Jewish people: Despite assimilation or enslavement our people were not consumed. Why was Moshe available to "see"? Because Moshe had started to see and feel injustice. His actions with the taskmaster and the shepherds at the well in Midian proved to Ha-Shem that Moshe was now a man of his people and of action. He railed against injustice as a man of action. We also must be ready to speak out and act against injustice. Coincidentally and ironically, the birthday of Martin Luther King falls around the time of this parashah. To add another dimension, Abraham Joshua Heschel, a leading theologian and civil rights leader, died around this time; he also added a strong voice and actions against injustice. The late Rabbi Marshall Meyer, a student of Heschel, whose Hebrew name was Moshe, died during this parashah. Rabbi Meyer is well known for his courageous stand against the Argentine government in support of freedom. I remember all these men at this time, and the parashah comes alive in new ways each year. **Joel Friedman, <JFried0920@aol.com>**

דָּבָר אַחֵר DAVAR AHER. MOSES SAID, "I WILL TURN AWAY AND SEE THIS GREAT SIGHT, WHY THE BUSH IS NOT CONSUMED." [Ex. 3.3]. It is said that the Baal Shem Tov derived a lesson in *tshuvah* from the episode of the burning bush. In Exodus 3.3 MOSES SAID אָסֻרָה-נָּא *Asurah-nah.* "I WILL TURN AWAY AND SEE THIS GREAT SIGHT, WHY THE BUSH IS NOT CONSUMED." Why would Moses have an audience with God and then turn away?

אָסֻרָה *Asurah* is an unusual word: Rashi writes "to go away from here

Rabbi Eliezer Finkelman

ELIEZER FINKELMAN IS RABBI OF CONGREGATION BETH ISRAEL IN BERKELEY, CALIFORNIA. HE RECEIVED SEMIḤAH FROM YESHIVA UNIVERSITY IN 1973, AND HIS PH.D. IN COMPARATIVE LITERATURE FROM CITY UNIVERSITY OF NEW YORK, 1992.

Words of Torah for *Parashat Shemot*

In this week's parashah the family of Jacob goes down from the Promised Land to Egypt. Their status changes over the course of the years from honored guests of the Pharaoh to his hated and despised slaves.

Modern people have become accustomed to see history as contingent: Things happen because they happen to happen.

This descent from freedom and independence in our destined homeland to slavery in a foreign land does not just happen. It was foretold to Abraham [Gen. 15.13–14]. The Divine plan included a descent into foreign slavery. Why?

Perhaps, the conventional wisdom goes, so that Jews could ultimately look back on our years as slaves. The Bible repeats this warning many times: YOU SHALL NOT OPPRESS THE STRANGER, SINCE YOU KNOW THE HEART OF THE STRANGER, FOR YOU WERE STRANGERS IN THE LAND OF EGYPT [Ex. 23.9]. Knowing the feelings of the powerless should help us behave compassionately even when we exercise power.

Note, however, that this conventional wisdom assumes that we ought, at some time, to have power. It does not allow us the ideal of powerlessness. Lord Acton observed, famously, that "power tends to corrupt." Hans Morgenthau went further: "The political act is inevitably evil." I once heard an interreligious colloquy in which the spokespersons for various faiths fought

Shemot

and to come close there." This is what *tshuvah* is, said the Baal Shem Tov, "getting unstuck." It's about movement and change and transformation. It's not about arriving but about approaching. It's not about destinations, but about journeys; not about arrivals at all, but about roads; not about achieving, but about being; not about performance, but about effort, to move from here and come close to there. It's not even about sin; it's about change.

We celebrate the journey when we make *tshuvah*. And when we lose our way we are taught that the right path calls us back; when we lose our way the roads go into mourning. This is especially true of the hard case scenario, of every difficult transformation. From one moment to the next the transformation that is possible for everyone might be concealed. This means you never give up on anyone. This means that the possibilities for repair and reconciliation,

for the high ground, each claiming that his or her faith endorsed the purest pacifism. Only the rabbi on the panel, an honest man, did not join in denouncing political authority.

Indeed, political authority seems an unavoidable condition of the world in which we live. If our morality were to insist that we avoid political authority in order to remain pure, it would thereby belong on some nicer planet. Morality would apply beautifully in Mr. Rogers' Neighborhood and would make no claims on actual political leaders. Torah demands that we behave well even when we have the power to do otherwise.

Consider that the Torah expects us to imagine slavery and become compassionate. Identifying with past weakness may make people kind, but it is not inevitable. In the United States today we witness the unedifying spectacle of various ethnic groups competing in the comparative victimization sweepstakes, with the winner entitled to extra rights. All over the world individuals imagine the past weakness of their people and seek bloody revenge.

The Torah calls upon us to remember our years of slavery, and our long years of exile, and to behave with compassion at all times, but especially when we live in our own state. ■

---

transformation and reclamation, *tshuvah*, are always present. You never give up on anyone. Especially the hard case stories. I consider myself such a story. If I could get it, anybody could get it. **James Stone Goodman, <Stavisker@aol.com>**

דָּבָר אַחֵר DAVAR AHER. The midwives, fearing God, did not do as the king of Egypt told them; they let the boys live. [Ex. 1.17]

Parashat Shemot tells of the birth of Moses until his first rejection by Pharaoh. A lot of you probably have an idea of how Moses lived though the Pharaoh had decreed that all male babies born to the Hebrews were to be killed. A lot of you may think it was his mother who alone saved him—but it was actually several women: the midwives, Siphrah and Puah; the princess, Pharaoh's daughter; and Moses' older sister, Miriam. You might ask how all these people saved him. Let me tell you.

The midwives saved Moses because they went against Pharaoh's evil decree to murder all Hebrew male babies. The Torah says, "The midwives, fearing God, did not do as the king of Egypt told them; they let the boys live." When the Torah speaks of "fearing God," it refers to that part which "humanizes" our dealings with other people—our compassion, our conscience.

The midwives show that people have free choice and are free to *not* follow evil decrees. God rewarded the midwives by making their families prosper. The midwives were honored for choosing to do good by having their names remembered in the Torah.

The princess saved Moses by not following her father's decree to murder all Hebrew male infants. She unquestionably knew Moses was a Hebrew child because he had been placed in the river—an act unnecessary for a child not at risk—and she commented to her attendants, "This must be a Hebrew child." Her immediate choice is between killing the child and keeping it. She chose to keep it—she chose life. Again Moses is saved by someone with a conscience and with compassion—someone who exercised free will to choose to do the compassionate thing, the humane thing, in the face of an evil decree.

Moses' sister, Miriam, was very clever and smart. She watched Moses, and when the princess found him she risked going up to the princess to ask if she wanted a Hebrew nursemaid for the child. This way Moses was reunited with his mother. His mother was then able to teach him about God and that he was an Israelite. As a result Moses always identified with the Israelites. Thus Miriam proved herself devoted to her brother.

Jews often say that "if you save one life, it is as if you have saved the whole world." Here these women saved one life and saved a people—for Moses was God's tool for delivering the Israelites from slavery. Pharaoh's plans to annihilate the Jews were defeated by women: the

Names

We begin the second book of Torah learning about the importance of names. Instead of being individuals we are considered a nation for possibly the first time. The actions of one become attributed to all. After we get our lineage in the first few verses we are known by another name, "SLAVES." This is the name that stays with us for the rest of Torah. We who came out of Mitzraim are never able to live as free people in the Promised Land.

This first parashah sets the stage for our wanderings and for the key to our deliverance. According to the midrash, we are supposed to imagine that we were slaves in Mitzraim each year at Pesah. When we tell the story of Pesah, are we telling about the slavery we are in now? Do we feel the yoke of our own slavery? Are we willing to cry out loud enough so that Ha-Shem will hear us? Many of us Jews are not even wandering yet because we are still in denial of our own slaveries.

Are we ready to read Shemot with an eye to finding how we enslave ourselves? I think that we are given the strength to do this here. GOD HEARD THEIR GROANING AND REMEMBERED HIS COVENANT WITH ABRAHAM, WITH ISAAC, AND WITH JACOB [Ex. 2.24]. This is the antidote to our suffering, our enslavement.

We are in slavery now, we are in Mitzraim, narrow places! The only hope we have is to groan loud enough and with our entire *neshamah* (soul) to get Ha-Shem's attention.

At the end of this parashah Pharaoh makes it harder for us Jews to do our

Mark Borowitz

MARK BOROWITZ IS THE DIRECTOR OF OUTREACH, *BEIT T'SHUVAH*, LOS ANGELES.

Shemot

human feelings of the midwives; the tender sympathies of a woman of royal birth; and a sister's watchfulness and resourcefulness in the time of extreme distress. The Rabbis say, "**It was to the merit of pious women that Israel owed its redemption from destruction in Egypt.**"

This parashah has taught me several things. One is that we should treat all people with dignity and respect, even if they appear different from us. Another is that everyone has free choice—and can choose to do evil or to do good, can choose to not do what everyone else is doing. Free choice is about both choice and responsiblilty for your choice. This parashah also taught me that you cannot be a good leader without compassion and a sense of injustice. But leaders are not just presidents and people in government; each of us has leadership potential in our own communities. One cannot effect change in one's commu-

daily work by not giving us straw, but he expects us to make our quotas anyway. This is how our internal Pharaohs make it harder for us to realize the potential of our souls/spirits. We lie to ourselves and we cover up our inner truths so that it is harder for us to reach Ha-Shem. The response by the children of Israel is to blame Moses and Aaron. We blame the people that bring us the message if it is not instant and exactly what we want to hear.

God tells Moses to use I WILL BE WHAT I WILL BE as God's name so *B'nai Yisrael* will know that (יהוה) Adonai has sent him. This is not enough for us when it seems as if we don't get instant results. We forget Ha-Shem if we don't get the answers that we think we should, and we become more enslaved. Just as our ancestors did, we have to be taught exactly how much bondage we are in. This is what is happening all around us in both the Jewish world and the larger world. We are continually looking to enhance ourselves, not Ha-Shem. We are not grateful and/or aware of the talents we have and where they have come from. We are too wrapped up in our own needs and wants to hear and see what our souls are yearning for. The levels of our ritual practices do not ensure the rising of our spiritual connection with Ha-Shem. We are a nation of priests, a nation that supposedly has learned what slavery is like and has tasted the bitterness of our enslavement, yet we continually go back to our own Egypts, our own narrow places.

When will we groan loud enough to hear our own suffering and do something to change it? When will we be able to call ourselves free by choosing God as our authority, by getting rid of the many false gods we use now, and by starting to know our true names and souls? With the help of God, let it be now. ■

---

nity or our own society without a sense of injustice and compassion. As Moses always identified with his people, regardless of how educated he became, so I, too, have learned to identify with my people and heritage. **Jessica Reina Amado, on her Bat Mitzvah, Los Angeles, CA, December 24, 1994.**

יצחק ואל יעקב באל שדי

Parashat Va-Era

Exodus 6.2–9.35

Rabbi Malka Drucker

MALKA DRUCKER IS THE AUTHOR OF MANY FINE JEWISH BOOKS, INCLUDING *JACOB'S RESCUE* AND *THE FAMILY TREASURE OF JEWISH HOLIDAYS*. SHE IS THE CO-AUTHOR OF *RESCUERS, PORTRAITS OF MORAL COURAGE IN THE HOLOCAUST*. MALKA RECENTLY RECEIVED SEMIHAH AT THE ACADEMY FOR JEWISH RELIGION IN NEW YORK.

Fire and Ice

The title of the second book of Moses, *Shemot*, means names, and it is in this book that the children of Israel will acquire a new name to reflect their transformation from a large, hungry family into a nation. After this group emerges from the broken waters of the Sea of Reeds they will be called the Jewish people. In Parashat Va-Era, God, already known by two names, אֱלֹהִים Elohim and יהוה Adonai, will reveal the meaning of the name Adonai. This name will be a balm, a reassurance to a people and a leader in despair.

Until this moment God has appeared, *Va-Era*, only as אֵל שַׁדַּי *El Shaddai*, the God who said דַּי *Dai*, "enough," at the time of creation. Despite the knowledge of both names, the patriarchs only knew the *Elohim* part of the Divine, the God who is revealed through nature. The sun, the moon, and the stars assured our ancestors that God's hand was in all. But for the Israelites, numb from slavery, the reality of things as they are seems unbearable; they no longer hope, and they question a God who allows them to suffer.

Just before the portion begins, Moses challenges God: "WHY DO YOU MISTREAT YOUR PEOPLE? WHY DID YOU SEND ME? AS SOON AS I CAME TO PHARAOH TO SPEAK IN YOUR NAME, HE MADE THINGS WORSE FOR THESE PEOPLE. YOU HAVE DONE NOTHING TO HELP YOUR PEOPLE" [Ex.

דָּבָר אַחֵר DAVAR AHER. MOSES SPOKE BEFORE GOD, SAYING, "BEHOLD, THE CHILDREN OF ISRAEL HAVE NOT LISTENED TO ME, SO HOW WILL PHARAOH LISTEN TO ME? AND I HAVE SEALED LIPS!" [Ex. 6.12]. **Who was Moses, and what can we learn from him?** Our tradition teaches us that Moses is the greatest of the prophets, the one who spoke to God face to face, the most faithful and greatest of the human nation. But Moses was very human. He made mistakes; he did not start his career like a leader. His life's story began with what most people would take to be extraordinarily good luck. While the Hebrews were being killed, Moses was living in the lap of Pharaonic luxury. He had it all. And Moses decided, in an act of conscience, to give it all up. He gave up the wealth, power, luxury, and safety of the house of Pharoah.

וארא אל אברהם אל

5.22]. God's promise to Abraham, Isaac, and Jacob is no longer enough for the Israelites; they need more than a promise to lift them from their disillusionment and lack of faith. God will no longer simply appear; now God will be known.

Va-Era opens with God answering Moses, "אֲנִי יהוה I AM *ADONAI*." Not *Elohim*, the God of reality, the God of isness. *Adonai*, the Keeper of Promises, is speaking. The name *Adonai* first appears in the Torah on the seventh day of creation, when God creates humanity and we become joined with nature: THESE ARE THE CHRONICLES OF HEAVEN AND EARTH WHEN THEY WERE CREATED, ON THE DAY *ADONAI ELOHIM* COMPLETED EARTH AND HEAVEN [Gen. 2.4]. These are names we will call the Eternal, but we still only understand the God of nature until Moses, the stammerer, confronts God and says, "What You have shown us is not enough."

A deeper intimacy must be established for Moses' generation to believe again in their Creator and in creation. All relationships require trust. Friends and lovers must know that they can speak their truth, their discontent, and their desires to one another, and that their words matter to the listener. The safer we feel, the more we allow all of ourselves to be seen, and so it is with Moses and God.

Moses trusts God when he speaks for his people; they must know more than their ancestors, because they are lost in their suffering. My teacher, Rabbi Harold M. Schulweis, says, "We discover meaning not in calamities assigned as 'acts of God' but in the course of nature understood through the exercise of our divinely given intelligence,

***Synopsis:** Moses and Aaron visit Pharaoh and say, "GOD SAYS, 'LET MY PEOPLE GO.'" Then we have the first seven plagues: blood, frogs, lice, insect swarms, cattle, blight, boils, and hail.*

RASHI OF THE WEEK: AARON STRETCHED OUT HIS HAND (*Why Aaron? Rashi has already told us* [Ex. 7.19] *that "what goes around comes around;" the river protected Moses when he was in the basket.*) AND THE FROG CLIMBED AND COVERED EGYPT [Ex. 8.2]. *Isn't "frog" a typo? Shouldn't it be frogs? No; see Shemot Rabbah* 10.6. Only one frog came out of the Nile. Then, when the Egyptians, believing they could stop this plague, beat it, the frog broke into streams and streams of frogs. *There are definitely times when human ego and naïve technological solutions make things worse.*

By killing the Egyptian who was striking the Israelite, Moses was biting the hand that fed him, even saved him, and he was revolting against the regime whose rules made Israelites into slaves and himself into a prince. **How many of us would make the choice and sacrifice made by Moses?**

In last week's portion, Shemot, Moses said "No" to Pharaoh and to oppression; in *Va-Era*, Moses tries to say "No" to God. Moses tells God, and through God the reader/learner, that he is כְּבַד פֶּה *Kevad Peh* and כְּבַד לָשׁוֹן *Kevad Lashon*, HEAVY TONGUED, apparently slow and uncomfortable with the spoken word. When Moses claimed he was עֲרַל-שְׂפָתָיִם *Aral-Sefatayim*, OF UNCIRCUMCISED LIP, he meant that the flesh of his mouth was too thick for him to move his mouth with ease. This Moses, this do-gooder, who is all conscience and no sense, who is all principle yet no practicality, with strong mind but no mouth, is also the most modest of all men.

And this Moses was chosen to be the redeemer and *rabbenu*/teacher of Israel. This choice on the part of God makes sense when we understand what the Torah is teaching us: [1] **The Torah is concerned with *what*, not *who* we are**. Moses

courage, hope, and faith." If we learn nothing from our pain, if it does not lead us to greater clarity and insight, then we cannot endure our lives. Moses questions Divine judgment, and through this risk the world changes. The first humans may have known the name יהוה *Adonai*, but until they yearn for its meaning, they do not yet have a moral world.

Behavior is contagious. When Moses speaks from his heart he opens the heart of God. Through Moses, meeting face to face with the presence of the clear light of morning, God learns more about the nature of human beings. Now the Eternal knows that humanity is ready to understand an evolving universe in which God is more than the laws of nature; God is also wonder and possibility. This is the dawn of another step human beings will take in being partners with God in perfecting the world.

Just as God drew Adam, Noah, and Abraham close to reveal the holy through the laws of nature, now God will defy the laws of nature to demonstrate that the laws of nature are simply part of creation. We not only learn about God through this exercise—because we are made in the Divine image—but the more we see of God, the more we gain a knowledge of ourselves. Through deeds rather than words, with Moses as the vessel, the laws of nature will be turned upside down through ghastly, unnatural phenomena inflicted upon the Egyptians.

God will tell Moses not to go to Pharaoh, but to come to him, because Moses must join with him, influence him, to free the Jews. Moses fails because Pharaoh's hard heart makes him blind and deaf to the cries of the people and their leader. *Shemot Rabbah* (7.13-14) describes a hardened heart as angry. כָּבֵד *Kaved* not only means hard or heavy, it is also the name of the liver, which, according to the ancient world, was the seat of

---

Va-Era

was chosen because he was a man of courage and conscience. Being right is more important than looking right. Moses taught us to be individualists of conscience, not conformists of convenience. [2] **Moses was not a good speaker**. Moses began his speaking career haltingly. This *rabbenu* would have a difficult time being hired by a shul. His first three acts, stopping the bullying Egyptian, the bullying Hebrew, and the men bullying the Midianite women, did not involve eloquent speech, but these acts embodied eloquent ethics. Moses' career reminds us not to style or profile, but to say the truth with simplicity, honesty and clarity. [3] **Moses is the most modest of all humans.** The one human being who speaks to the Creator of All directly, פָּנִים אֶל פָּנִים *panim el panim*, face to face, would not

anger. God has hardened Pharaoh's heart not by casting a spell, but by creating human beings to choose their steps: Good deeds lead to good deeds and vice versa. Once a heart habituates itself to one path or the other, God does not stop the direction, because all is not in the hands of God, but in the fear of God. If *Adonai* brings possibility, anything, good or bad, can happen. Each time Pharaoh responds to Moses' plea with anger and stubbornness, he steps further away from his ability to act with compassion, and so his choice enslaves him.

Only through human beings can *Adonai* participate in earthly transformation. So the plagues begin, not so much as punishment but as moral education; they will instill the knowledge of God in all who witness them. Because of his connection to earth and heaven Moses will deliver the aerial plagues of fiery hail, locusts, and darkness. R. Tanhuma explains that Moses does not participate in two of the plagues—he does not contaminate the Nile with blood because he was saved in that river; he does not bring lice that began with dust because it was with dust that Moses covered the Egyptian taskmaster that he had slain.

Despite their cosmic surprise, the first six plagues flow logically through nature (Abarbanel). The first plague is the bloody Nile, life source of the Egyptians. The second plague, frogs, fills the river and brings the third plague, gnats. These insects attract the fourth plague, wild animals, who die of the fifth plague, pestilence, which leads to the sixth plague, boils.

The seventh plague, however, is the ultimate defiance of nature. Here hail the size of snowballs envelops fire and crashes upon the earth. "It was like [the light in] the glass in which water and oil are mixed together, and the light burns within. Imagine two fierce legions who were always at war with one another, but when the king needed their service for his own battle, he made peace between them, so that both should carry out the orders of the king" (Rabbi Nehemiah).

Va-Era describes only the first seven plagues, which the Maharal sees as a correspondence to creation: seven steps to creation, seven steps to destruction, all from the same Source.

Pharaoh's recognition of God after the seventh plague—HAIL AND FIRE FLASHING UP AMIDST THE HAIL [Ex. 9.24]—makes clear that the plagues have done their job; God has been revealed to the world. Pharaoh admits, "I HAVE SINNED THIS TIME; *ADONAI* IS RIGHTEOUS AND MY PEOPLE ARE WICKED" [Ex. 9.27].

Pharaoh, however, will not be convinced for long, because he is like the part of us that demands to be free, the part that rules others but refuses to surrender to anything or anyone. This is the part that relies on no one, has no teacher, and believes that we have no equal in

---

likely be the most modest of all people, but this man of charismaless courage is most modest. He gave respect to all, but deference only to God. For Moses, only God is God; no human being is God. Moses speaks to God "face to face," as an equal.

Moses taught us to be free by teaching us that character really counts; what we are is more important than who we are. Moses taught us that *what* we say is more important that *how* we say what we say. He taught us to talk with integrity. Our words are important only when they are true. Moses taught us to be modest. But he taught us that by talking to God face to face we do not give false flattery to any other human being, for to do so makes one human the master of the other. **Rabbi Alan J. Yuter, Congregation Israel of Springfield, NJ.**

דָּבָר אַחֵר DAVAR AHER. On **עֵצִים וּבָאֲבָנִים** ***Etzim uva-Avanim***: **THERE SHALL BE BLOOD THROUGHOUT THE LAND OF EGYPT, EVEN IN THE WOODEN AND STONE VESSELS** [Ex. 7.19]. There is a curious link between the first (according to Jewish tradition) murder in human history and our sidrah. We are told that there was blood everywhere—in every pool of water, throughout the land, and **עֵצִים וּבָאֲבָנִים** *Etzim uva-Avanim*,

knowledge. One midrash imagines that Pharaoh was the sole survivor at the Sea of Reeds because he was destined not to die but to be transformed. So it is with us. We cannot kill the darkness within us, but with the help of *Adonai* our flaws can become teachers. When we choose to learn from our mistakes and wrongdoings, i.e., we do *tshuvah*, we find ourselves in the presence of God.■

---

literally 'IN WOOD AND IN STONE,' generally understood as meaning in vessels of wood and stone, but perhaps also referring to trees or wood and stones. After Abel has been murdered God says to Cain: "THE VOICE OF YOUR BROTHER'S BLOOD CRIES TO ME FROM THE GROUND." But the Hebrew says "bloods" in the plural. In the mishnah, one explanation given for this is that Abel's blood was scattered *al ha-Etzim ve-al ha-Avanim*! "ON THE TREES AND ON THE STONES!"

This reference to trees and stones may be taken from our sidrah, for the phrase occurs only here and in a few other places, which we will come to. The Tiferet Yisrael, a 19th-century commentator, explains the mishnah as telling us: "Cain did not know how to kill, so first he tried using wood and then using stone." Wood and stone then bore the imprint of Abel's blood. These two fundamental substances, the basis of primeval tools and other aspects of primeval life, became tainted with the blood of the first murder victim. That wood and stone were filled with blood during the first plague then takes on greater significance. It suggests that even the fundamental materials of life, wood and stone, became tainted with blood. Just as the soil around Auschwitz and the other extermination camps is full of the ashes of the victims, so in Egypt blood was ubiquitous. We have ample evidence of the cruelty of the regime: the killing of all the baby boys, the harsh servitude, and the ruthless beatings of slaves. Perhaps bloodshed was so widespread the Egyptians had become accustomed to it and were no longer even shocked by the sight of it.

In our time, too, we have become accustomed to murder and violence. Yet as Jews we cannot give up hope. We continue to look toward the time of redemption, the time when human beings will beat their swords into ploughshares and will no longer learn war. That time of redemption may be symbolized by the transformation of wood and stone, ordinary materials, which yet bear the imprint of what goes on in the world. Before the Exodus wood and stone were soaked with blood.

The phrase עֵצִים וּבָאֲבָנִים *Etzim uva-Avanim* is also found in connection with the building of the Temple, for which wood and stone were used. Of course, the Temple was in reality far from ideal, but it

Rabbi Alan Kay

Dr. Alan Kay is a rabbi and Professor of English at New York City Technical College, The City University of New York. He is the author of *A Jewish Book of Comfort* (Jason Aronson, Inc., 1994).

Moses was eighty and Aaron was eighty-three when they made their demand on Pharaoh to let the Israelites depart from his land [Ex. 7.7]. My mother is eighty and my mother-in-law is eighty-three. Rose is no Moses, and Agnes is no Aaron. But they were not meant to be. Rabbi Zusya of Hanipoli, the Hasidic rabbi, reminds us that on the day of judgment God will not ask Rose why she had not been Moses, or Agnes why she had not been Aaron; rather, God will ask whether Rose had been Rose and Agnes had been Agnes.

They have been and they are. Rose is Rose. Agnes is Agnes.

I am grateful they have been true to themselves. Like the team of Moses and Aaron, the team of Rose and Agnes has shown effective leadership. Where Agnes did not have the word, Rose did. Where Rose did not have the stamina, Agnes did. They recreated themselves as teammates after their first mates, Milton and Maty, could no longer lead. They were effective because we—their family—let them lead. They never let us down. After the Israelites let them, the team of Moses and Aaron demonstrated effective leadership. Where Moses did not have the word, Aaron did [Ex. 7.1-2]. Where Aaron could not summon the thunder and hail, Moses did [Ex. 9.23], And in the end the sons of Amram never let the Israelites down.

I am reminded of Rose and Agnes and of the increasing number of eighty- and eighty-three-year-olds who will inhabit our nation in the next decade and beyond. I muse on the leadership they will provide to a younger generation crossing the wilderness of the end of

---

symbolized a vision of peace. The stones that were to be used for the construction of the Temple were אֲבָנִים שְׁלֵמוֹת *Avanim Shelemot*—complete stones. The word *shalem* is related to the word for peace. So is the name of the king who built the first Temple, Solomon or *Shelomo*. In the building of the Temple wood and stone were to be transformed. Once soaked with blood, they were used to construct a building that would symbolize that greatest of all blessings, the blessing of peace. The basic materials used by human beings would be used for peace and not for war. Just as in the prophetic vision, swords would be transformed into ploughshares; so wood and stone, which according to *aggadah* Cain had used to try to kill Abel, and which in Egypt had been soaked with blood, would be transformed and incorporated into a vision of peace. In the time of redemption there will be such a sense

the twentieth century C.E. and the beginning of the twenty-first.

In the hands of an eighty-year-old and an eighty-three-year-old *Adonai* entrusted the Jews and Judaism. Into their hands *Adonai* placed the past, the present, and the future of Judaism. I can only ask myself now if I will be such a trustworthy leader when I am eighty or eighty-three, if I can answer that I let Rose and Agnes lead today.

I am reminded of Rose and Agnes and of the increasing number of eighty-and eighty-three-year-olds (and older) who will inhabit our nation during the next forty years. Today the American Association of Retired Persons reports 3.5 million Americans are over eighty-five. In forty years the number will be 5.8 million. Through whom will *Adonai* speak to call upon them to lead the younger generations across the wilderness of the new millennium? If called upon, will they lead? I think they will. If they accept leadership, will we listen? Here I am uncertain.

Has our own spirit, like that of the Israelites, been so crushed by cruel bondage that we will turn away from that leadership and seek it elsewhere, even in bondage itself, because it is at least what we know?

Adonai tells Moses to say to the Israelites: "I AM THE LORD. I WILL FREE YOU FROM THE LABORS OF THE EGYPTIANS AND DELIVER YOU FROM THEIR BONDAGE" [Ex. 6.6]. But WHEN MOSES TOLD THIS TO THE ISRAELITES, THEY WOULD NOT LISTEN TO MOSES, THEIR SPIRITS CRUSHED BY CRUEL BONDAGE [Ex. 6.9].

There is much that keeps me in bondage today: mortgage and home equity loans, car payments and college tuition, a long commute to work and a long commute home; I am bound to my computer and to my desk and to my *New York Times* and to my news radio; I am bound to Israel and to Bosnia, to Northern Ireland and to Rwanda, to guns and drugs in my city; I am

---

Va-Era

of peace that even the material world will seem to be imbued with it. **Rabbi Dr. Margaret Jacobi, Birmingham Progressive Synagogue, Birmingham, UK.**

even bound to study. In all of this, where is God?

"Where is God?" asks Rabbi Menachem Mendel of Kotzk: "Wherever human beings let God in." Adonai told Moses to say to Pharaoh, "The Lord, the God of the Hebrews, sent me to you to say 'Let My People go that they may worship Me in the wilderness'" [Ex. 7.16]. I do not ask Rose or Agnes or any octogenarian to lead me to God. I only ask them to do what they have always done: to point me in the right direction. As long as I value their leadership, they will always point me in the right direction.

I do not ask Rose or Agnes to pay my loans. They have lived longer than I, and they know there is more to living than paying loans and reading *The New York Times*. There is God. Adonai is somewhere out there in the wilderness, and if I will only let Rose and Agnes lead, I know I will find God because I will have opened myself to let God in. ■

Rabbi Marc Gellman

MARC GELLMAN IS THE RABBI OF TEMPLE BETH TORAH, MELVILLE, NEW YORK. HE IS THE AUTHOR OF *DOES GOD HAVE A BIG TOE?*, *WHERE DOES GOD LIVE?* AND *HOW DO YOU SPELL GOD? ANSWERS TO BIG QUESTIONS FROM AROUND THE WORLD* WITH MONSIGNOR THOMAS HARTMAN. THIS MIDRASH, *THE PHARAOH AND THE FROG*, IS FROM HIS COLLECTION OF STORIES, *GOD'S MAILBOX: MORE STORIES ABOUT STORIES IN THE BIBLE*.

Va-Era

The Pharaoh and the Frog

When Moses told the Pharaoh of Egypt to let all his slaves go free, the Pharaoh of Egypt said to Moses, "What are you, nuts? Let my slaves go free? My slaves are the reason I am rich. My slaves build my pyramids and my palaces, they harvest my crops, they dig for my gold, they make my bed, they cook my food, they go shopping for me, they get the mail, and they walk my dogs. I'm not going to let them go ANYWHERE! What I am going to do, Moses, is throw you out of my palace. Go tend your sheep or whatever it is you do now."

So Moses said to God, "Thanks a lot! Boy, do I feel like a jerk. I walked into Pharaoh's palace, asked him to let my people go, just like You told me, and the Pharaoh threw me out.

God, I can't go back there without some heavy ammunition." God agreed, and the next day Moses appeared again before the Pharaoh.

This time Moses did not say a word; he just put his big walking stick into the pool in the throne room, and THWACK! the water in the pool turned to blood. Pharaoh was amazed and said, "I hate blood!" He was about to let the Israelites go when his chief magician said, "Turning water into blood is a cinch. Just watch!" Then he turned the water in Pharaoh's cup into blood. So Pharaoh said, "Nice try, Moses, but no cigar! Get out of here right now!" Moses left the Pharaoh's palace to tell God that turning water into blood was good, but not good enough.

The next day Moses returned, and this time God had showed him how to make frogs fall from the sky. The Pharaoh was amazed and again was about to let all the slaves go free when suddenly his magicians plunked their magic twangers, and *they* made frogs fall from the sky, too. "You almost tricked me this time," Pharaoh said as he had Moses and all the frogs thrown out of his throne room.

When everyone had left the palace and the Pharaoh was left alone he went out onto his balcony to see if the frog rain had stopped. The Pharaoh looked up into the sky, and suddenly, SPLAT! a frog fell on his face.

The frog jumped off the Pharaoh's face onto his shoulder and croaked in his ear, "Could you please tell me what is going on here? I was just sleeping on my lily pad in my pond, not bothering anybody, and this big wind sucks me up into the air, and the next thing I know I am sitting on your face looking up your nose. No offense to your face, but I would like directions back to my pond if you don't mind."

The Pharaoh screamed, "THERE'S A FROG ON MY FACE!" as he rushed out of the throne room. After he washed the frog slime off his face he looked in the mirror and said, "I hate blood! And I hate frogs!"

The next day Moses returned to the Pharaoh's palace, but he could not enter the throne room. Pharaoh had put up posters everywhere in the palace. Each poster had a picture of Moses and a picture of a frog with this message: "If this guy or this frog shows up, kick him out!" Moses called up to Pharaoh from the courtyard, "Hey, Pharaoh, watch this!" Pharaoh peeked out from behind a curtain and saw Moses banging his big walking stick on the ground. With each bang a cloud of fleas rose from the dust and flew everywhere.

The fleas swarmed everywhere in Egypt and got onto everyone. Even the Pharaoh started to itch all over from the fleas that landed on him. He ripped off his clothes and threw them into the pool in his throne room. His clothes landed on the frog, who was sleeping on a lily pad in the pool. The frog woke up with a start and croaked, "Get these stinky Pharaoh clothes off me!" The Pharaoh was surprised to hear his clothes talking to him but soon realized that it was not his underwear talking but the frog who had fallen from the sky and landed on his face. The naked Pharaoh ran from the throne room mumbling, "I hate blood, I hate frogs, and I hate fleas!" His servants tried not to look or laugh, but it was real hard because they just didn't see naked mumbling Pharaohs running away from fleas that often.

The next day the Pharaoh was bathing in the river to get rid of his fleas when suddenly there was Moses standing in front of him and blowing as hard as he could. Out of Moses' mouth came flies, millions of flies, billions of flies, *gozillions* of flies.

"That's disgusting!" said the Pharaoh as the flies flew out of Moses' mouth and filled the skies all over Egypt. The Pharaoh ran as fast as he could into his throne room and dived into his pool to get away from the flies. When the Pharaoh poked his nose and eyes above the water to see if the bugs had gone away, the frog was snatching flies out of the air with his tongue.

"Want one?" the frog croaked. "Flies are very tasty this time of the year." The Pharaoh ran from the pool waving his hands and whining, "I hate blood. I hate fleas. I hate flies. But mostly I hate frogs!"

The next day Pharaoh woke up and all his cattle were dead. The Pharaoh slumped down in his throne and cried, "Oh, me! Oh, my! Why are my cows dead?" Then the Pharaoh heard the frog laughing, "Oh, me! Oh, my! Why are you such a jerk? Your cows are dead because you were too stubborn to let Moses and his people go free."

The Pharaoh growled, "I am not going to sit here and talk to a frog. Get out of my pool! Get out of my house! Get out of my life!" The Pharaoh ran into his bedroom, slammed the door, and moaned, "I hate blood. I hate frogs. I hate fleas. I hate flies. I hate dead cows! And if that frog says one more word to me, there is going to be one dead frog in Egypt to go along with all my dead cows."

The next day Pharaoh looked out of his window and saw Moses and his brother Aaron picking up ashes from the campfires and throwing them into the air. The Pharaoh laughed. "Oh, Moses, I'm really scared now! Please don't throw dirt into the air." Pharaoh was laughing and all his servants were laughing when suddenly a big wind blew the ashes high into the sky. Every little speck of ash that came down and landed on a person turned into a big ugly zit, and the Egyptians ran all over complaining about the plague of zits, especially the teenagers.

Pharaoh sat down on the edge of his pool, and the frog hopped up on his shoulder and croaked into his ear, "You may just be the dumbest man in the whole wide world. You are wrecking your country, killing your cattle, spoiling your people's complexions, and all because you won't let Moses and his people get

Va-Era

out of here." The Pharaoh stood up, grabbed his hair, and yowled, "I AM THE PHARAOH! I AM THE BOSS OF EVERYBODY! I AM A GOD! NOBODY TELLS ME WHAT TO DO—NOT MOSES, NOT MOSES' GOD, AND DEFINITELY NOT SOME SMELLY OLD FROG! IF ANYBODY THINKS I'M GONNA LET MY SLAVES GO FREE BECAUSE SOME OF MY PEOPLE HAVE ZITS, THEY HAVE ANOTHER THINK COMING!" Then the Pharaoh stomped off into another room. His servants heard him say, "Blood, frogs, fleas, flies, dead cows, and now zits. I hate them all, but mostly I HATE THAT FROG!"

The next day the Pharaoh woke up, peeked over his blankets, looked out the window, and said just one word: "YIKES!" What he saw was ice balls falling from the sky. This was strange enough because Egypt is a very warm country and there is hardly ever snow, much less ice balls, but what was even stranger was that mixed in with the ice balls were balls of fire. When the fireballs hit people they screamed "OOCH!" and when the ice balls hit them they yelled "OUCH!" Pharaoh just pulled the blankets over his head and covered his ears so he wouldn't hear the sounds of "OOCH! OUCH! OOCH! OUCH!" that were coming from all over Egypt.

While he was under the covers he heard a frog voice counting. "Let's see now, plague number one was blood, then there were frogs (that's how I got here), then fleas, then flies, then dead cows, then zits, and now we have this charming plague of ice balls with fire mixed in, and STILL you won't let the people go? What a dope!"

The next day, while Pharaoh was eating his cereal, a bug flew into his bowl. "Yuck, what was that?" he asked. Then he saw that the floor was filled with locusts. The frog was happily hopping around gobbling some of them up. The frog smiled, burped, rubbed his fat tummy, and said, "I love the plagues I can eat! The fleas and flies were good, but these locusts are just delicious—keep it up, Einstein!"

"Who's Einstein?" asked the Pharaoh.

"Never mind," said the frog.

The next day the Pharaoh woke up at his usual time, but he looked outside and saw that it was still dark, so he went back to bed. He woke up again a little later, but it was still dark outside, so he went back to sleep again. Later on he sat up in bed, saw that it was still dark, and screamed, "WHERE'S THE SUN? IT'S DAYTIME ,BUT THERE'S NO DAY! WHAT'S GOING ON HERE?"

Then the Pharaoh went to the window and saw a really strange thing. Everywhere in Egypt it was dark *except* over the houses of Moses and his people. Over their houses the sun was shining. This went on for three days, and by then all the Egyptians had gathered around the Israelite homes to tie their shoes, thread their needles, wash their clothes, and do everything else that needed to be done in the daylight.

The Pharaoh was also going crazy from having no daytime. One day he put on some shepherd clothes so nobody would recognize him and joined the crowd in the sun around Moses' house. The people were talking about him. "That stupid Pharaoh. When is he going to learn that it's wrong to have slaves, it's wrong to go against God, and it's wrong to wreck your country just because you're stubborn? Because of that dumb Pharaoh our country has been filled with blood, frogs, fleas, flies, dead cows, zits, ice balls with fireballs mixed in, locusts, and now darkness in the daytime! It's just not fair!"

Then the Pharaoh, who was hiding in the crowd, threw off his robe and shouted, "I AM THE PHARAOH. I DON'T CARE WHAT ANYBODY THINKS. I COMMAND THE SUN AND THE MOON AND THE STARS. EVERYONE AND EVERYTHING HAS TO DO WHAT I SAY!"

Moses walked forward, looked the Pharaoh in the eye, and said, "Why don't you just command the sun to come out again, then?"

The Pharaoh squirmed and said, "I'm getting around to it."

Then Moses put his arm around the Pharaoh and said to him quietly, "Listen to me, and listen well. This is the last time we will see each other. If you do not let my people go by this time tomorrow, the last plague will come, and it will be so horrible you will never forget it. Don't make God punish you and your people this way. You can't win. You can't stand against freedom, and you can't stand against God."

The Pharaoh screamed, "God has nothing to do with all this stuff. We've just hit a run of bad luck, REAL bad luck! I am going home now, and I am going to sleep. When I wake up everything will be all right again. I will have good luck again. And one more thing. Moses, if you are in Egypt tomorrow, I will have my soldiers find you and kill you, along with that frog!"

But that's not what happened.

The next day the tenth plague happened. After the blood and after the frogs, after the fleas and after the flies, after the dead cows and after the zits, after the ice balls with the fireballs mixed in, after the locusts and after the darkness, every first-born person and animal died in all the land of Egypt. That day the Pharaoh cried a cry so loud that people all over Egypt heard him. That day the Pharaoh let the people go.

As Moses and his people walked out of Egypt with all their stuff and with all their animals they did not cheer and they did not laugh and they did not sing. They saw how the plagues had ruined Egypt, and they were sad for the Egyptians, so they just left quietly.

The Pharaoh was alone. Between his tears he heard a frog voice disappearing into the distance. The frog was croaking over and over, "You can't stand against freedom, and *you can't stand against God!"*

From Exodus 7.14–12.36. ■

הכבדתי את לבו

Tefillin: Bound For Greatness

Ask most members of a Jewish audience to conjure up a mental image of a "pious Jew" and chances are good that that vision will be of a bearded male garbed in a black kippah and large tallit. Chances are also good that he'll be wearing *tefillin,* the leather boxes containing four biblical passages (including the Shema) that are worn on the forehead and wrapped around the arm.

The first reference to those holy items is found in today's Torah portion. Speaking about the miraculous liberation of the Israelite slaves, the Torah recounts God's instruction to EXPLAIN TO YOUR CHILD ON THAT DAY, "IT IS BECAUSE OF WHAT ADONAI DID FOR ME WHEN I WENT FREE FROM EGYPT" [Ex. 13.8]. Each of us is to view this act of freedom as a personal gift from the Creator-of-the-Universe directly to us.

Immediately following this instruction the Torah relates, AND THIS SHALL SERVE YOU AS A SIGN ON YOUR HAND AND AS A REMINDER ON YOUR FOREHEAD—IN ORDER THAT THE TEACHING OF ADONAI MAY BE IN YOUR MOUTH—THAT WITH A MIGHTY HAND ADONAI FREED YOU FROM EGYPT. YOU SHALL KEEP THIS INSTITUTION AT ITS SET TIMES FROM YEAR TO YEAR [Ex. 13.9]. The simple reading of this verse doesn't sound like it is referring to *tefillin* at all. Instead, it seems the Torah is instituting the observance of Pesah and instructing us that teaching our

Parashat Bo
Exodus 10.1–13.16

Rabbi Bradley Shavit Artson

RABBI BRADLEY SHAVIT ARTSON IS THE EXECUTIVE VICE PRESIDENT OF THE BOARD OF RABBIS OF SOUTHERN CALIFORNIA AND IS THE AUTHOR OF *IT'S A MITZVAH! STEP-BY-STEP TO JEWISH LIVING*, BEHRMAN HOUSE AND THE RABBINICAL ASSEMBLY. HE IS RESEARCHING A BOOK ON JEWISH ENVIRONMENTAL ETHICS FOR THE JEWISH PUBLICATION SOCIETY.

דָּבָר אַחֵר DAVAR AHER. "YOU WILL THEN BE ABLE TO CONFIDE TO YOUR CHILDREN AND GRANDCHILDREN HOW I DID FEARSOME ACTS WITH THE EGYPTIANS AND HOW I PERFORMED MIRACULOUS SIGNS AMONG THEM—YOU WILL THEN FULLY REALIZE THAT I AM GOD" [Ex. 10.1–2]. Up to now I have found *Learn Torah With...* full of fascinating ideas. However, I feel I must take issue with your second essay (page 144) on *Parashat Bo*, which has disturbing theological implications. It is claimed that, according to Rashi, millions of Jews died in Egypt because they were too assimilated. The parallels with Nazi Germany and other times in Jewish history are obvious. The implication is one that has been stated by others: that the victims of the Holocaust brought their fate on themselves because they were so assimilated into German society. I do not know whether the author

בא אל פרעה כי אני

children about the miracle of Passover is to be a permanent part of the festival's celebration.

In fact, the Torah continues by insisting that the celebration of Pesah̲ continue after the wandering in the wilderness has concluded with the successful conquest of the Land of Israel and then reiterates, AND SO IT SHALL BE A SIGN UPON YOUR HAND AND AS A SYMBOL ON YOUR FOREHEAD THAT WITH A MIGHTY HAND ADONAI FREED US FROM EGYPT [Ex. 13.16]. However as it might seem that the Torah is merely using metaphorical language to say that the Pesah̲ story is fundamental to Jewish identity (in fact, Rashbam insisted that was the "deep, straightforward meaning"), preponderant rabbinic tradition expanded its meaning in a rather concrete direction. Thus *Targum Onkelos*, the ancient Aramaic translation of the Torah, renders the Hebrew word for symbol (*totafot*) as "*tefillin*." Similarly, the Talmud (*Massekhet Menahot*) quotes Mar as saying that the first reference to a sign refers to the *tefillin* placed on the head and the second refers to the *tefillin* worn on the arm. Hizkuni, a great medieval rabbi, specifies that the *tefillin* of the head "memorializes the signs and wonders that the Holy Blessing One did in our sight" and the *tefillin* of the arm "memorializes God's strength." Others have understood that wearing *tefillin* on the forehead and arm represents our pledge to use both mind and strength in the service of God.

Why have *tefillin* remained as such lasting symbols of Jewish piety, of Jewish identity itself? To answer that question moves us beyond the words of Torah, directing us to look at what the practice creates. Each morning (other than a Shabbat or festival)

---

intended to say this, but he/she comes close to doing so.

I would find it unnecessary to spell out the problem with this theory, except that in describing the piece as wonderful you seem oblivious to its implications. To suggest that millions of innocent people, who—although assimilated—may have been, and often were, good human beings, died as a result of the Divine plan seems to me tantamount *to* a חִלּוּל-הַשֵּׁם *H̲illul-Ha-Shem*, and I hope that you will distance yourselves from this idea. B'Shalom, **Rabbi Dr. Margaret Jacobi, Birmingham Progressive Synagogue, Birmingham, UK.**

דָּבָר אַחֵר DAVAR AH̲ER. GOD GUIDED AN EAST WIND THROUGH THE LAND ALL THAT DAY AND ALL THAT NIGHT [Ex. 10.13]. GOD TURNED BACK A VERY POWERFUL WEST WIND AND IT

SYNOPSIS: Plagues eight, nine, and ten: locusts, darkness, and the death of the firstborn. Plus the mitzvah of the New Month and the celebration of Pesah̲ Mitzraim—Passover in Egypt.

RASHI OF THE WEEK:

This week we get Passover's name verse [Ex. 12.23]: HA-SHEM WILL CROSS (AVAR) TO KILL THE EGYPTIANS AND WILL SEE THE BLOOD ON THE LINTEL AND ON THE DOORPOSTS—AND THEN HA-SHEM WILL PESAH̲ THAT OPENING, AND WILL NOT GIVE THE SLAUGHTERER THE OPPORTUNITY TO COME INTO YOUR HOUSES TO SLAUGHTER. *What is the meaning of* **PESAH̲**? *There are two possible meanings:* One is "God will have Mercy" (*see Rashi on verse 13*). The other possible meaning is "God will pass over." *What is the meaning of* **AND WILL NOT GIVE?** *God will not give the forces of destruction the opportunity to come into the Israelite houses. This is parallel to the usage in the passage about Laban* [Gen. 31.7]: AND GOD DID NOT GIVE HIM THE OPPORTUNITY TO DEAL EVILLY WITH ME. *Now we see (1) the way the rabbis connected Laban and Egypt (An Aramean tried to destroy my father…) and (2) that once the forces of destruction are put into motion they have a life of their own and know no boundaries, and it takes God's intervention to protect us.*

after waking, dressing, and washing, I go downstairs and wrap myself in my *tallit* and bind myself with my *tefillin*. As I perform these mitzvot I recite the ancient words that have regularly accompanied them: I speak of God also being wrapped in a *tallit* of light, and I close with the passionate words by our prophet Hosea: I WILL BETROTH YOU TO ME FOREVER. I WILL BETROTH YOU WITH RIGHTEOUSNESS, WITH JUSTICE, WITH LOVE, AND WITH COMPASSION. I WILL BETROTH YOU TO ME WITH FAITHFULNESS, AND YOU SHALL LOVE ADONAI. The combination of the words and the deed creates a sacred space, physically, by carving out the space within the *tallit* and bound by the *tefillin* that is now devoted to prayer, and mentally, by focusing my mind and soul on God's loving betrothal of the Jewish people, of which I am both a part and an embodiment. There is an awe and a strangeness about the *tefillin*. I can see that by the way my young twins look at the *tefillin* and ask to touch them, by the way they like to be in the room watching as I *daven*, by the way they call out "Bye-bye, *tefillin*," as I pack them away. In fact, the power of that sign is one that links the generations across time.

Congregants whose fathers put on *tefillin* speak about their childhood sense that the sun came up with the same constancy and regularity with which the *tefillin* went on. Both were part and parcel of a proper morning. And my little Shira, who announced (at age 2) that she is going to be a rabbi, likes to help her Abba *daven* by taking the box coverings off the *tefillin* and then handing them to me. As I wrap my *tefillin* she takes colored yarn and wraps one thread around her head and two around each arm (she's *frummer* than I am!). What a gift she brings to my morning prayers. We greet God and the dawn together, and I know that those *tefillin* will be etched into her young mind (and that of her

---

Bo

CARRIED THE LOCUST-SWARM AND HURLED IT TOWARD THE SEA OF REEDS [Ex.10.19]. *Parashat Bo* begins with the eighth plague, locusts, which were brought in by an east wind [Ex.10.13] and carried away by a west wind [10.19]. The wind blows from both east and west for the Children of Israel.

The east wind brings the silent, unself-conscious heart of wisdom, unreflective and undifferentiated, the long seamless embrace of existence before language; it is חָכְמָה *Hokhmah*, the heart's deep wisdom.

The west wind is the exceedingly self-conscious spirit of inquiry and ideation, identification, conceptualization, language; it is בִּינָה *Binah*.

The west wind is conscious, linear, practical, rational. The east wind is intuitive, lateral, mystical, accepting. חָכְמָה *Hokhmah* and בִּינָה *Binah*, the right and the left sides, one of the

brother) as a powerful symbol of Jewish wholeness.

Morning, in their experience, is *tefillin* time. The rising of the sun and its setting are linked, inextricably, to the rhythms of Jewish ritual, to our faithful response to a mitzvah. For thousands of years we Jews have worn *tefillin* to testify to our liberation from slavery and our betrothal to God. Generations of Jewish children have learned to love their heritage and to revere their God by watching their fathers wearing those *tefillin* to start out the new day. In our own time the privilege of wearing *tefillin* has been embraced by a growing number of women as well as men.

As innovative as this practice appears, it may well have some ancient precedent. According to an ancient midrash, Michal, the daughter of King Saul, took upon herself the obligation to wear *tefillin*, and the sages did not object. A medieval legal code, the *Or ha-Hayim*, authorizes women to say the *brakhah* while putting on *tefillin*, and this ruling is supported by Rabbenu Tam, the medieval giant of Jewish law. Binding ourselves in love to God, standing in the place where generations of pious Jews have stood, we ensure that our children's image of a "pious Jew" will be diverse, inclusive, faithful, and passionate. In creating their memories we will fashion our own reality. Do we owe our children any less? Don't we also deserve as much? ■

---

thirty-two paths of wisdom that the hidden God engraved during the Emanation. Both winds blow through our camp, then as now. We are an east/west people, perched on our western branches, recovering our eastern roots, sometimes unaccustomed to the tree itself. Our goal: always integration, union, *shalem, shalom*, the perfect expression of which is Shabbat, the ceremony of sacred union, cosmic union, when all the terrible twos of existence fold into One. Integration, union, *shalem, shalom* always the goal. The nemesis: Pharaoh, the disintegrator, the one who insists on separation, from פרע *Peh Resh Ayin*, separated, rent, split. פַּרְעֹה *Par'oh* is the great separator.

On Shabbat we celebrate integration, union, wholeness, *shalem*; we separate from the other side, the side of separation, the rent in the seam of existence, and that's why we had to leave Pharaoh, to become one with ourselves. Shabbat Shalem/Shalom. **James Stone Goodman, <Stavisker@aol.com>**

Somehow, in an electronic universe, the authorship of this wonderful piece of Torah got separated from its file. We don't yet know whom to credit, and we are sorry that the redemption will have to wait. Please help us make t'shuvah.

Bo

A Second Essay

"You will then be able to confide to your children and grandchildren how I did fearsome acts with the Egyptians and how I performed miraculous signs among them—you will then fully realize that I am God" [Ex. 10.1-2].

It took ten plagues to teach Pharaoh a lesson. But the last three taught us something as well. A lot of things. But this week we will look at two lessons in particular.

Both begin in a midrash, later taught to us by the greatest biblical commentator, Rashi. It was during the ninth plague, the plague of darkness, that the Egyptians finally began to understand the power of God. The darkness was palpable so much so that people were afraid even to move. They were literally paralyzed by fear—no one moved for three days.

Yet as terrible as this plague was for the Egyptians, it was far worse for the Jews. For the darkness that was created was part of a Divine plan to conceal the deaths of four out of five of all the Jews in Egypt. Or to put it more bluntly—and to use a little bit of math—if two to three million Jews survived this plague and ultimately left Egypt, then during the plague of darkness eight to ten million Jews died! More Jews died during the plague of darkness than in the Holocaust!

And why did they die? It was a punishment from God, explained the midrash. Because four out of five Jews refused to leave Egypt. They had become too assimilated, too comfortable, too unwilling to accept or participate in the reality and responsibility of Jewish life. That's lesson number one.

And lesson number two? Well, let's start with Cecil B. DeMille. Why Cecil B. DeMille? Because for most people, and maybe even most Jews, most of what they know about the ten plagues and the Exodus from Egypt goes back to him and his movie *The Ten Commandments*. Before the tenth and final plague (the death of the firstborn) God told Moses to tell the Jews to take the blood of the paschal lamb and smear it on the doorways of their homes. Why? As a protection from the plague. But where exactly should they smear the blood? According to DeMille, on the outside. According to our rabbis, on the inside. And what's the proof? It's a verse in this week's Torah portion—The blood will be a sign for you on the houses where you are staying [Ex. 12.13]. Not a sign for anybody else—but for you! (Sorry, Cecil.) That's lesson number two.

What's the connection between these two lessons? Simple. It's an article by Professor Steven M. Cohen in the December 1996 issue of *Moment* magazine. It's in an article that asserts that many of the statistics of the 1991 National Jewish Population Survey are wrong. Not that our Jewish community is growing—it's not. Intermarriage, while not 52%, is still, according to Cohen, 41%. But "what we are really witnessing is a transformation, using the current argot, to a leaner and meaner American Jewish community, a somewhat pared down version that is, in many ways, stronger, more committed and more observant."

Why? Well, the Jews who are intermarrying tend to be more assimilated to begin with. While the Jews who remain are studying more (day school enrollment continues to climb); observing more (Jews in their mid-thirties to fourties are 50% more likely to observe Shabbat and six times more likely to fast on the Fast of Esther than Jews in the 55-64 age group); and having more children (about 6% of American Jews in their fifties are orthodox, while 12% of children under ten years old are orthodox). So what happened during the exile in Egypt? Basically the same thing that is happening in the exile of America today. Millions of Jews disappeared in the dark. Vanished because they were too assimilated, too uncommitted to survive.

But those who did remain—the strong and committed minority, the "leaner and meaner Jews"—were the ones who took the lessons of Judaism into their homes. They marked the doorposts of their homes not from the outside, but from the inside. To them, and to us, Judaism was something that one lives and does not just observe. Judaism was family, children, and teaching and learning. So they survived the plagues, and they were redeemed. They survived the plagues, and we are their descendants.

Those are two of the lessons of this portion. Lessons that we would do well to learn ourselves.■

ולא נחם אלהים

Parashat Beshallah
Exodus 13.7–17.16

Professor Carol Meyers

CAROL MEYERS, AUTHOR OF *DISCOVERING EVE: ANCIENT ISRAELITE WOMEN IN CONTEXT*, IS PROFESSOR OF BIBLICAL STUDIES AND ARCHAEOLOGY AT DUKE UNIVERSITY. SHE CO-DIRECTS DUKE'S SEPPHORIS REGIONAL PROJECT, A DIG IN ISRAEL NEAR NAZARETH; AND SHE IS ASSOCIATE DIRECTOR OF THE WOMEN'S STUDIES PROGRAM AT DUKE.

This Torah portion contains an account of perhaps the most important moment in Israel's long history. In recounting the flight from Egypt and the miraculous parting of the Reed Sea the biblical narrative presents what can be called a prototypal event—an event that took place in historical time, in the long-distant past, but that continues to this very day to affect people's lives. The magnitude of the experience for those who departed Egypt made it a formative event, so profound in its impact that it not only changed the destiny of our ancestors who escaped from Pharaoh's armies, but has also influenced subsequent generations ever since. In reenacting some of the Exodus events at Passover, and in retelling the dramatic story, the actions involved in the original moment of redemption are reexperienced and made effective and true for the inheritors of the Exodus tradition.

In thinking about this seminal event, two significant issues should be considered. The first is the nature of the religious meaning that was perceived in the raw fact of human experience. How did the Children of Israel understand the apparent miracle of their redemption from bondage, of their being saved from disaster by the drowning of Pharaoh's chariots? The second question concerns the way the meaning was ascertained. How was

---

דָּבָר אַחֵר DAVAR AHER. ON CAROL MEYERS: Although we cannot all afford to meet Carol Meyers, we cannot afford not to marvel at the picture she has painted of other heroic women and the courage and compassion that they expound throughout the Bible. Her analysis of Miriam and the "Song at the Sea" reads like an eyewitness account laced with imagery of humanness. Carol Meyers asks us to consider two significant issues, basically (1) how was the miracle of being saved from disaster originally understood, and (2) how was this meaning ascertained at that historical time. Her answers enlighten, but I am left to ponder a third significant issue (in my historical times). If this is how it actually felt then, how can we possibly feel similar today? Are today's modern day Miriams too busy, too inaccessible to be heard aloud by

the message of the Exodus event first expressed? Who first declaimed what the Israelites felt about their participation in the Exodus? The very status of the Exodus as a prototypal, formative event means that we take its message for granted; that is, we assume the profound significance that can be seen in the liberation of the Israelites has always been known. But it took one point in time for the meaning to be first proclaimed; it involved one or more humans first giving it voice.

Both these issues, and the questions surrounding them, can be addressed by looking at the centerpiece of *Beshallah*: the poetic accounts of the Exodus in chapter 15, the so-called *Shirat ha-Yam,* the "Song at the Sea." Because of its archaic language the Song is generally understood to be one of the oldest pieces of literature in the Hebrew Bible. Although it comes immediately after a prose narrative [Ex. 13.17-14.31] that describes the departure of the Israelites from Egypt and the subsequent parting of the sea, the poetic version in Exodus 15 is generally understood to be older. In its glorious poetic language the "Song at the Sea" captures the intensity of what the Israelites felt at being rescued from doom. Even though it has some elements of narrative, it is a response to events that are already known to its audience. It brings us back, as closely as possible, from the distance of some three millennia, to the euphoria of escape rather than the fact of redemption. It is not a recapitulation of the Exodus event but rather a lyrical outpouring of emotion that celebrates that event.

In examining the song that is the centerpiece of *Beshallah*, it is

---

more than a select few who know the tune or have to pay a price to learn it? When will the "Song at the Sea" be heard by my daughters? And who will be the Miriam to sing it? **Professor Thomas Michael Kowalick, Sandhills Community College, Pinehurst, NC.**

דָּבָר אַחֵר DAVAR AHER. **THEN MOSES AND THE SONS OF ISRAEL SANG THIS SONG TO ADONAI. THEY SAID, SAYING: "I WILL SING TO ADONAI BECAUSE HE SCORED TOTAL VICTORY. THE HORSE AND ITS RIDER HE HAS THROWN INTO THE SEA"** [Ex. 15.1]. Chapter 15 of Exodus describes in parallel scenes the separate reactions of men and women to this miracle. It consists of two sequential closeups. First we get the

SYNOPSIS: *This is a week of action adventures. The Israelites flee from Egypt. They are trapped by Pharaoh and troops at the Reed Sea. Then, thanks to a miracle, they escape, performing the "Song at the Sea" on the opposite shore. Then, as desert life continues, we complain about water, and Moses hits the rock. Then we win a battle against Amalek.*

RASHI OF THE WEEK:

[Ex. 15.20] MIRIAM, THE PROPHETESS, THE SISTER OF AARON. When did Miriam become a prophetess? *And isn't she both Aaron and Moses's sister? What is the Torah trying to tell us? The Torah is cueing a story that is expanded in the Talmud, Sotah 12b.* She became a prophetess *(as we are told there)* before Moses is born *(when she was just Aaron's sister) by predicting* "My mother will give birth to a son." *The theme of women as prophets continues later in the verse* AND ALL THE WOMEN WENT OUT WITH HER WITH TAMBOURINES AND DANCES. *Where did the tambourines come from? Why were they brought? The righteous women brought them from Egypt because they knew for sure that the Qadosh Barukh Hu would perform miracles in order to enable their escape, and songs and dances of praise would be their proper response.*

clear that the military context is a major feature. The imagery and the momentum of the poem are suffused with the language of combat. The mighty chariots, officers, and army of the Pharaoh are the antagonists. Their demise is what frees the Israelites and gives rise to the poetic accounting of a prototypal victory over the enemy. Ancient literature is replete with this kind of expression—songs that celebrate victory, that give voice to the exultation of survival against great odds. What is different about this song is that the protagonist is not a human general, monarch, or army. Rather than a panegyric hymn praising a human hero, Exodus 15 is a sublime proclamation that Israel's God is responsible, through Divine might and fury, for redeeming and rescuing the Israelites. What most people would construe as a military victory fought on the battlefield is here construed as an act of God, carried out by the weapons of a Divine warrior. The poem celebrates the triumphal intervention of God in the arena of human affairs.

This foundational interpretation of events happening in history becomes, in essence, a central religious theme of Israelite and Jewish tradition: God has the power and the will to affect the course of history in order to bring about the redemption of the downtrodden. In giving voice to what they felt about the Exodus, the poet or poets responsible for the "Song at the Sea" expressed a core element of biblical faith.

The issue of the identity of the poet or poets who first sang of this victory as Divine triumph is more complicated than it might seem. After all, the text tells us that MOSES AND THE ISRAELITES SANG THIS SONG [Ex. 15.1]. Were this the only information about authorship, we would attribute the composition of the Song to the poetic skill and theological acumen of Moses, even though the bulk of the

---

Beshallah

men's version: THEN MOSES AND THE SONS OF ISRAEL SANG THIS SONG TO ADONAI. THEY SAID, SAYING: "**I WILL SING** TO ADONAI BECAUSE HE SCORED TOTAL VICTORY. THE HORSE AND ITS RIDER HE HAS THROWN INTO THE SEA" [Ex. 15.1]. This then leads into a long song of praise, a description of God as a "Man of War" who utterly defeated and dispersed the Egyptians. At the end of this chapter we find the parallel women's experience: AND MIRIAM THE PROPHETESS, AARON'S SISTER, TOOK IN HER HAND A DRUM, AND ALL THE WOMEN WENT OUT AFTER HER DRUMMING AND DANCING. AND MIRIAM ANSWERED THEM (masculine, meaning "the sons of Israel"): "**You** (masculine plural) **SING** TO ADONAI BECAUSE HE SCORED TOTAL VICTORY. THE HORSE AND ITS RIDER HE HAS THROWN INTO THE SEA" [Ex. 15.20]. This biblical scene then fades to black. One would expect Rashi and his crew to make a big

Pentateuchal tradition has Moses as an expositor in prose. But another tidbit of authorial information appears at the end of chapter 15, in verses 20-21, where it is reported that MIRIAM...TOOK A HAND-DRUM [not "tambourine" or "timbrel," instruments not yet in use in biblical times] IN HER HAND, AND ALL THE WOMEN WENT OUT AFTER HER IN DANCE WITH HAND-DRUMS. AND MIRIAM SANG TO THEM: 'SING TO THE LORD...' Miriam's song, which follows a brief prose summary of the Exodus (in verse 19), has been recognized by literary historians for many decades as the initial "Song at the Sea." That is, Miriam, with her chorus of female dancers and drummers, first uttered this *shirah* (song) proclaiming God's redemptive might. When Moses and the people recited the *shirah*, the full text of which appears in verses 1-18, they did so in response to Miriam's exhortation "SING TO THE LORD."

The report of Miriam's composition of the Song appears in the biblical sequence after the account of the singing of it by Moses and the Israelites. This reversal of expected chronological order is perhaps the result of what is called "analepsis"—the intentional but temporary withholding of information until a later point, apparently out of sequence. In this case, the performance by Miriam and her female colleagues serves as an end to the Exodus story, for the next verse begins the account of the wilderness period. It is fitting for women to end the Exodus story because women began it: The first Hebrews we encounter in Exodus 1 are the Hebrew midwives who delivered Hebrew babies, including, presumably, Moses, born in Egypt, into the world.

The primacy of Miriam as composer/performer is borne out by information other than literary considerations. Women in many periods and places have been the traditional singers of poetry of various kinds. In particular, women often compose and sing love songs, lullabies, and laments, and in addition, they sing songs of victory to welcome home triumphal armies. That tradition of women celebrating military victory was clearly part of Israelite culture. When King Saul vanquished the Philistines women came out with songs, dance, and drums to celebrate his victory [I Sam. 15.6-7]. When Jeremiah anticipates Israel's restoration he proclaims that women will once again sing out with drums and dance [Jer. 31.4]. One can call this composition/performance tradition a victory song genre, one that is specifically within the domain of female musicians. Archaeological evidence bears out this connection in that ceramic statuettes of women (and not men) playing the hand-drum are a significant part of the repertoire of votive figurines found at sites of the biblical period. Furthermore, the sages recognized the association of women with the victory song genre by selecting the

---

deal out of the men singing, "**I WILL SING** TO ADONAI..." and the women singing "**YOU GUYS SING** TO ADONAI...." I thought there would be great wisdom revealed in explanations of why men were first person praise and women were second person praise. But when I opened up the commentaries and collections of midrash I got nothing. Silence. Having been through all the official Rabbinic answers in my quest to find the essence of "male" and "female" worship, I was awestruck by the tradition's silence on this passage. When the tradition was silent I did what I often do: I brought the problem into the classroom. I turned it over to day school students with whom I was doing a "guest shot." I introduced the passage and gave them (because I am pro-choice) the opportunity to invent midrashim on one of two questions. One was our question, "Why do the men sing one thing and the women sing another?" The second was a question I borrowed from Rashi, who borrowed it from the *Mekhilta* (an ancient collection of midrashic sermons): "Where did the women get the timbrals?" (Because if most of us played the "What would you take from your house if you only had five minutes?" values clarification game, very few of us would have our tambourines

"Song of Deborah," recounting victory over the Canaanites, as the Haftorah for *Beshallah*. Thus Miriam, following the deliverance from the Egyptians, and later Deborah, after rescue from the Canaanites, are said to have formulated the texts that celebrate victory. They announce that survival in the face of the enemy is not a matter of human triumph over adversaries but rather a result of God's glory and power. They give voice to two of the earliest messages in the Bible about God's redemptive might.

The *shirah* of Miriam, as sung out by Moses and the rest of the people, has had a special place in the liturgy since late biblical times. The recital of the poem as a whole, or the verse announcing God's incomparability, is part of sabbath and daily services. Indeed, the sabbath when *Beshallah* is read is called *Shabbat Shirah*, "Sabbath of the Song." When Moses accepted the call to sing out the song composed and performed by Miriam he initiated perhaps the oldest hymnic tradition in religious liturgy and acknowledged the validity of Miriam's understanding of the Exodus as a momentous act of divine deliverance.■

Beshallah

on the list.) As usually happens, the kids added a third question. Rhey wanted to know: "What did the Egyptian horses do wrong, that they deserved to die along with the Egyptian soldiers in the Reed Sea?" None of the fifth graders wrote midrashim that could answer my question. Still, they taught me my answer!

One group of three girls presented a well-worked, carefully rehearsed, and re-edited collective story that answered the question: **"Where did they get the drums?"** These girls answered with a rehearsed performance, each reading her assigned part. They said: **"They didn't actually have drums with them. It was such an emotional experience, and their hearts were beating so loudly, that their heartbeats sounded like drums. When they sang, they sang with their hearts."** It was really a beautiful answer; it sent a shiver through me.

One of the boys stood up and said, **"Wrong. I wrote about why the horses had to die, but this is the right answer—I think they were Egyptian (war) drums that floated to the surface."** This boy's midrash taught a powerful truth, too. **Joel Lurie Grishaver from *The Bonding of Isaac*, Torah Aura Productions, 1997.**

Cantor Jeff Klepper

JEFF KLEPPER IS A CANTOR AND COMPOSER SERVING BETH EMET THE FREE SYNAGOGUE, EVANSTON, IL. HE IS ONE HALF OF THE MUSICAL DUO KOL B'SEDER.

Beshallah

I am beginning to know how Nahshon felt. Nahshon ben Aminidav, midrashic hero, leapt into the Sea of Reeds while the others said, "Please, after you..." Like Nahshon, I have stood on the sidelines thinking and waiting without committing my thoughts to Macintosh. Looking back over my shoulder, I can see the Torah Aura chariots gaining ground. I must leap...

From out of *Beshallah* the *Shirah* calls to us. Ancient, bold, majestic, it leaps off the Torah parchment; it cannot be ignored. Like an oasis in the desert it says, "Come here, look at me, listen to me." This brick-like ladder of poem-song (for the Hebrew language makes no distinction between "poem" and "song") is revered in our tradition. It tells in poetry the climactic episode of our deliverance from slavery, a story as vivid and dramatic as that of Sinai, as mystical and mysterious as creation itself.

The *Shirah* earned an important place in the Temple's liturgy, and later in the siddur's daily worship. In synagogue, during *p'sukei d'zimrah*, the Sephardim chant it to a supposedly ancient, bitter-sweet tune. We rise to hear it chanted to another old melody each year on *Shabbat Shirah*, named in its honor. In it is contained one of our oldest liturgical fragments, מִי כָמֹכָה *Mi Khamocha*, and its response, יהוה יִמְלֹךְ לְעוֹלָם וָעֶד *Adonai Yimlokh l'Olam va'Ed.*

The siblings Moses and Miriam loom large here. They play the leading roles in this grand opera of history, fantasy, and faith. It is Moses' voice that begins the song, and it is Miriam's that ends it, yet it is also their finest moment as a duo. Miriam is more than a cheerleader after Moses' song. Just as she helped save his life at another body of water when Moses was a baby, again she supports her brother as only a sibling can. Yes, Moses writes and presents the script, words and music, but it is Miriam who adds movement, rhythm, and color to the work of art. Ever the free spirit, it is she who takes the liturgical text to the next level as her right brain creativity offers a perfect counterpoint to Moses' left-brain logic.

Her contribution is underappreciated in the text. (Today, Debbie Friedman has captured the essence of Miriam beautifully in her joyous *Miriam's Song*.)

"A poem is a naked person," Bob Dylan once said. What we say (or do not say) reveals much about who we are, what we think, and how we feel. The *Shirah* is essentially a song of faith in God's power, a war song that, while opening with violent language of retribution against the enemy, clearly shows by its end the developing relationship between God and Israel that was soon to bring us together again at Sinai.

A cantata of clashing images, at once warlike, and loving, this great song serves as a prism through which to gaze at the shifting colors of meaning and interpretation within our tradition. The rabbis found the *Shirah* to be deserving of its own commentary in the *Mekhilta* (Tractate *Shirata*), for hidden between

the notes, embedded in the archaic Hebrew, are secret codes that bring together past, present, and future. Are the opening words, אָז יָשִׁיר מֹשֶׁה Az Yashir Moshe (understood to mean "Then sang Moses"), in the past or future? Isn't *yashir* the future tense of "to sing"? The sages jump upon this ambiguity in order to make a compelling argument that the *Shirah* is a statement of faith in the coming of the Messiah.

What the sages discover in their *pil-pul* is nothing less than the power of song. It is this notion that engages me, for I have come to believe in the power of the words אָשִׁירָה לַיהוה *Ashirah L'Adonai*—I will sing to God. For some, opening one's mouth to sing takes as much hutzpah as Nahshon's legendary leap of faith. But it is essential that we dive into the songs with our voices.

Like a good hazan, Moses knew well the importance of including the community in song. THEN SANG MOSES AND THE ISRAELITES begins the *Shirah*. According to the *Mekhilta*, Moses taught the song line by line to his congregation using the ancient responsorial song form. Another midrash again likens the scene to a teacher and his students. Forty years later, the midrash tells us, a grown-up Israel was able to sing the "Song of the Well" [Num. 21.17] quite nicely without Moses' help. It begins THEN ISRAEL SANG THIS SONG...

But I see another meaning here, with thanks to my colleague, Menahem Kohl, for his suggestion that we look at yet a third biblical song, *Ha'azinu*, for a beautiful insight into liturgical music. Moses' final song begins [Deut. 31.30]: THEN MOSES RECITED THE WORDS OF THIS POEM, leaving no doubt that hazan Moses is about to take a solo turn at the microphone.

When we compare the three songs' introductions we learn the formula for a successful cantorial–congregational partnership. While the balance may differ from place to place and time to time, it is upon three things that healthy worship stands: the hazan needs the opportunity to sing his song, the congregation needs to sing their song, and together we need to sing our song.

Varied are the sounds that resonate out of our many different and beautiful traditions. The sacred music of our people is one of our most enduring legacies, for the song we sang with Moses and Miriam at the Sea of Reeds continues to this day. When each of us sings, אָשִׁירָה לַיהוה *Ashirah L'Adonai*, when we leap like Nahshon into the sea of holy sound, when our voices join together and our hearts beat in synchronous rhythm, it reminds us that the song of the heart is nothing less than the pathway to the presence of God. ■

"The Sounds of Silence"

The mystery and awesome power of the revelation overwhelmed the Israelites at Sinai.

ON THE THIRD DAY...THERE WAS THUNDER AND LIGHTNING....NOW MOUNT SINAI WAS ALL IN SMOKE, FOR THE LORD HAD COME DOWN UPON IT IN FIRE; THE SMOKE ROSE LIKE THE SMOKE OF A KILN, AND THE WHOLE MOUNTAIN TREMBLED VIOLENTLY. THE BLARE OF THE HORN GREW LOUDER AND LOUDER. AS MOSES SPOKE, GOD ANSWERED HIM IN THUNDER [Ex. 19.16-19].

THE LORD SPOKE THESE WORDS...TO YOUR WHOLE CONGREGATION AT THE MOUNTAIN, WITH A MIGHTY VOICE OUT OF THE FIRE AND THE DENSE CLOUDS [Deut. 5.19].

So terrifying was the experience that the people who stood at Sinai appealed to Moses to intercede: "YOU SPEAK TO US...AND WE WILL OBEY; BUT LET NOT GOD SPEAK TO US, LEST WE DIE" [Ex. 20.16]. God had made God's presence manifest in such a way as to strike fear and trembling in the hearts of the faithful. They witnessed the greatest sound and light show ever. They were obviously impressed by God's display of power. And they were convinced that God was Almighty. Or were they?

Curiously enough, when the smoking mountain once again provides the setting for a revelation—to Elijah this time—the supernatural elements are vigorously deemphasized. The event occurs following Elijah's resounding defeat of the prophets of Ba'al on Mount Carmel when he is compelled to flee for his life [I Kings 19]. Passing into the

Parashat Yitro
Exodus 18.1–20.26

Rabbi Chaim Seidler-Feller

CHAIM SEIDLER-FELLER IS HILLEL RABBI AND LECTURER IN SOCIOLOGY AT UCLA.

דָּבָר אַחֵר DAVAR AHER. I AM GOD, YOUR GOD, WHO HAS TAKEN YOU OUT OF THE LAND OF EGYPT, FROM THE HOUSE OF SLAVERY [Ex. 20.2]. Last week, we were discussing that age-old question, "Is the first commandment of the Ten Commandments a commandment or not?" (See *Torah Toons II*, the Rambam/Abravanel debate in *Parashat Yitro*.) In the class discussion Jared Tron, age twelve, who was playing Rambam, stated that the line "I AM YHVH..." is a commandment for us to call God by that name, just as when we meet someone and tell them what our name is, we are in effect telling them to call us by that name. **Michael Cohen, <75607.3672@compuserve.com>**

דָּבָר אַחֵר DAVAR AHER. I AM GOD, YOUR GOD [Ex. 20.2]. One of my childhood treasures, which, I am sad to say, has been lost through the years and half a dozen moves from one city to another, was a tiny enamel pin in the shape of

wilderness, he walked FORTY DAYS AND FORTY NIGHTS AS FAR AS THE MOUNTAIN OF GOD AT HOREB. THERE HE WENT INTO A CAVE AND THERE HE SPENT THE NIGHT [I Kings 19.8-9].

Elijah is drawn in the image of Moses. Not only is the sacred period of time duplicated, but so is the location; none other than Horeb-Sinai (in Exodus the mountain of the Lord bears the name Sinai; in Deuteronomy it is referred to as Horeb). Moreover, the midrash perceptively notes that the cave in which Elijah lodged when God was revealed to him at Horeb was the same as the one in which Moses concealed himself while God passed in review before him.

But it is at this juncture that the similarity is moderated and that Elijah's confrontation with God assumes its own singular character.

> AND LO, THE LORD PASSED BY. THERE WAS A GREAT AND MIGHTY WIND, SPLITTING MOUNTAINS AND SHATTERING ROCKS BY THE POWER OF THE LORD, BUT THE LORD WAS NOT IN THE WIND. AFTER THE WIND AN EARTHQUAKE; BUT THE LORD WAS NOT IN THE EARTHQUAKE. AFTER THE EARTHQUAKE FIRE; BUT THE LORD WAS NOT IN THE FIRE. AND AFTER THE FIRE—קוֹל דְּמָמָה דַקָּה *KOL DEMAMAH DAKAH* (A STILL SMALL VOICE) [I Kings 19.11-12].

There was indeed a thunderous wind [cf. Ex. 19.16] and a shuddering earthquake [cf. Ex. 19.16, 18] and a blazing fire [cf. Deut. 5.20]. Yet with a touch of irony the text poignantly and repeatedly proclaims, BUT THE LORD WAS *NOT IN* THE WIND,...*NOT IN* THE EARTHQUAKE,...*NOT IN* THE FIRE. It is as if I Kings 19 serves as a commentary—perhaps even a critique—on Exodus 19 and Deuteronomy 5, in an effort to impart a grand lesson. God's desire is that Elijah realize that the era of magic is coming to a close and that it is no longer necessary for God to "show off" in order to persuade people that there is a spiritual essence to their being. Elijah is herein reproached for having forced God's hand at Mount Carmel

---

Yitro

the Ten Commandments. I received it, to the best of my memory, as part of a consecration service in religious school. I am happy to report that some traditions never fade away; the same pin was presented to our religious school children in our own consecration service this year. I was tempted to appropriate an extra one for myself, but I know it just wouldn't be the same as the one I lost so many years ago.

In reading this week's parashah, *Yitro,* the portion that describes in such powerful language the revelation on Mt. Sinai and the giving of the Torah, I paused to ask myself why that little enamel pin, that representation of the Ten Commandments, had such an impact on me in my childhood. Surely at the age of five or six I wasn't able to grasp the ethical implications of the Ten Commandments. And although I may

[I Kings 18]. What hutzpah it was calling forth such a spectacular miracle (fire descending from God to burn the offerings that were set on an altar drenched with water). Henceforward, however, the prophet is not to teach by causing a cataclysmic eruption, but by using the word, by educating his listeners.

In fact, Rabbi Meir Leibush Malbim [on I Kings 19.11] suggests that קוֹל דְּמָמָה דַקָּה *Kol Demamah Dakah* alludes to the fine (דַק *Dak*) brightness in Ezekiel I from whose midst there was a "GLOW AS AMBER" חַשְׁמַל *Hashmal*, i.e., חַשׁ *hash*: silent, מְמַלֵּל *memalel*: speech. In other words, Malbim says, "Speaking in silent whispers and not with noisy diatribes is the only course that will bring true illumination."

Not only is the old "wow 'em" mode adjudged to be religiously offensive, but it is viewed as harmful to one's spiritual development and an ineffective means of nurturing a deep relationship with God. Rabbi Menahem Mendel of Kotzk was aware that already at Sinai the people were seduced by material attractions. Commenting on the phrase ALL THE PEOPLE SAW THE SOUNDS [Ex. 20.15], he writes: "The people were looking at the external manifestations: the thunder, the lightning, etc." The possibility of worshipping a golden calf is thus implicit in the Sinaitic experience. Indeed, it was not too far into the future before it became a reality.

There will always be children who require absolute proof of God's presence, who demand certainty and who are galvanized by outpourings of fire and brimstone. There will always be religious idolaters. But the mature individual, exhibiting insight and a refined spiritual sensibility, understands that a storming wind, a crashing earthquake, and a flashing fire are only partitions that mask the holy. For God sends

---

have been given over to murderous rages when I didn't get my way, I daresay I was never in serious danger of violating the more explicit commandments. What was it, then, that made such an impression on me? No doubt the impression was formed cumulatively; the Bible stories, Charlton Heston's portrayal of Moses, the ever-present tablets in every synagogue I'd ever been in. All of these elements combined to convey the impression that the Ten Commandments lay at the very core of what it means to be Jewish. Imagine my surprise, years later, to discover that the Ten Commandments are just as precious to non-Jews. It was a piece of information I had to reconcile with my unique relationship to my little blue Ten Commandments pin, my emblem of my Jewishness.

SYNOPSIS: *This is Yitro, the biblical epic and epoch of the Ten Utterances. Both Yitro and Moses' family show up. Moses follows Yitro's advice and appoints judges. Then the fireworks and real special effects begin.*

RASHI OF THE WEEK: *In this Torah portion Yitro, Tziporah, and the two kids show up. Rashi uses this verse:* YITRO, MOSES' FATHER-IN-LAW, TOOK TZIPORAH, MOSES' WIFE, AFTER HER HAVING BEEN SENT AWAY [Ex. 18.2] *to ask the question, "Didn't they come to Egypt with Moses? When were they sent away?" Rashi provides this midrashic answer:* Earlier in the book the Qadosh Barukh Hu told Moses in Egypt, "GO AND RETURN TO EGYPT," and the Torah tells us, AND HE TOOK HIS WIFE AND HIS CHILDREN AND HE RETURNED TO THE LAND OF EGYPT [Ex. 4.19-20]. *Next we learn* AND MOSES MET AARON AT THE MOUNTAIN OF GOD [Ex. 4.27], where Aaron said to him, "Who are these folks?" To which Moses said to him: "This is my wife who I married in Midian, and these are my sons." Next Aaron asked, "Where are you taking them?" Moses answered, "To Egypt." And then Aaron said, "What, are you crazy? We're already worried about all the Jews who are stuck in Egypt. Do you want to add to the refugee list?" So Moses sent them back home to wait for his word. This is the meaning of "AFTER HER HAVING BEEN SENT AWAY." Sometimes hearts aren't hardened enough.

the prophets to approach the people with the *sounds of silence* and thus attract them with bonds of love and gentle words. It is not through the harsh sounds of authoritarianism, but rather through the soft tones of reason, through modeling, through patience and relationship, through all the processes and silences that punctuate the religious dialogue that genuine learning unfolds.

UNTO YOU SILENCE IS PRAISE [Ps. 65.2], the sounds of silence—קוֹל דְּמָמָה דַקָּה *Kol Demamah Dakah.*■

Yitro

As the years passed and my Jewish knowledge grew I came to understand more and more about the role played within the Jewish tradition by the *Aseret ha-Dibrot*, the Ten Commandments. I learned of the subtleties of interpretation our Bible commentators have brought to bear on the Commandments throughout the centuries; I was exposed to various methods of subgrouping the Commandments so as to reveal special affinities that certain of the Commandments have for each other; I learned of covenant treaties from other ancient civilizations that closely parallel the form of the Ten Commandments. I learned how much there is to learn.

And I learned something that I had not expected to learn: that there exists within our tradition a voice that suggests that we, the people Israel, accepted the Torah only after God exerted coercive force against us. Consider the following midrash found in the Talmud (*Shabbat* 88A, 129B). It was not indeed quite of their own free will that the children of Israel declared themselves ready to accept the Torah, for when the whole nation, in two divisions, men and women, approached Sinai, God lifted the mountain and held it over the heads of the people like a basket, saying to them, "If you accept the Torah, it is well, otherwise you will find your grave under this mountain." They all burst into tears and poured out their heart in contrition before God and then said: "ALL THAT THE LORD HATH SAID, WILL WE DO, AND BE OBEDIENT."

What impulse led to such a midrash; why such a disparaging view of both our unwillingness to accept the Torah without threats or promises of rewards and God's need to dangle a mountain over our heads? I suspect it emerges from a very pragmatic understanding of human nature. Picturing our ancestors in the Sinai wilderness, fresh out of slavery and still grumbling over lack of water and decent food, the midrashists recognized them for what they were—people, just people, like yourselves and myself. It was hard for them to accept the notion that an entire people might willingly bind themselves to a God they could not see and a moral and ethical code whose implications they could not

Rabbi Morris J. Allen

Rabbi Morris Allen is the rabbi of Beth Jacob Congregation in Mendota Heights, Minnesota.

My first memorable encounter with Moshe Rabbeinu occurred on my first day of kindergarten in Denver, Colorado. In my class at Hillel Academy each of us was to give our teacher, Morah Toby, our Hebrew names. By the time the name circle came to me I was undoubtedly misbehaving when I proudly proclaimed that my name was Moshe. Morah Toby proceeded to tell me that Moshe was a very bad man who didn't listen to God and therefore didn't get to enter the Promised Land.

Amazed and angered that my parents would have given me the name of a *Rasha*, I burst into tears and became the only child in my class who went only by his English name and refused to answer to *Moshe* or *Moish* or whatever other diminutive one could make from our rabbi's name.

What Morah Toby was attempting to teach me at that moment was that in order to become a passionate Jew one needed to identify with the master narrative of our people and measure how well our personal narrative matched the master narrative. To be religious, to be observant, one made the assumption that the master narrative of our tradition was the vehicle by which one's personal life was defined. So, for example, while it was always possible to ask questions about Moshe's leadership of the community, always possible to seek answers to Abraham's call or Sarah's laughter, we never asked in those days: "What kind of person was this Moshe, anyway? Was he a good father, a loving husband?"

---

fully understand unless those elements of coercion and reward were operative.

And you know something? Not much has really changed. Jewish life still operates on a system of coercion and rewards. The threat dangling over our heads? Assimilation and the disappearance of the Jewish people. The reward? The life-enhancing richness of our tradition, Shabbat, the prophetic message, Jewish grandchildren.

One thing, at least, has definitely not changed. Our Torah tells us that at Mt. Sinai our entire people heard the voice of God. Some were scared out of their wits, others were awestruck, and others simply denied the importance of what they heard and set out to fashion a golden calf. But the voice *still* is there to be heard, an echoless voice that speaks in the laws of nature, in the beating of our hearts, in the beauty of a Mozart string quartet (after all, *Amadeus* means 'lover

Questions of that sort were considered extraneous to the learning process. They seemed to do little to aid the understanding of our tradition's master narrative. Today, failure to ask such questions is tantamount to sinking into irrelevance. For the tables have turned, and people in contemporary times begin their search for religious meaning by attempting to tailor a faith to their personal lives rather than by fitting their lives within the context of a faith's master narrative. Currently, unlike the day when I was in kindergarten, one's religious quest does not begin by affirming the type of life that Moshe lived, the familial relationships he shared, and the scope of his concerns.

Interestingly, Parashat Yitro provides me with a glimpse of this personal side of Moshe, which can perhaps remind us that within Torah itself both our personal and master narratives are to be found. What fascinates me about this parashah is the family dynamics in what we read. Imagine, after leading the people out of Egypt, experiencing the religious moment of crossing the sea, and singing God's praises as a community for the first time, what the encounter between Moshe and his wife and children would be like. Shouldn't we see a man who is overwhelmed by the events of the past few months eagerly embracing his wife and children? We would love to read of this, but unfortunately it is not there.

In fact, what is there, sadly, is the realization that Moshe and Zipporah are likely divorced or divorcing and that the picture of Moshe as a father is less than appealing. Finally, we may understand Yitro's pleas with Moshe as the plaintive pleas of an enraged father who is amazed that his son-in-law is unable to set realistic priorities in life. Notice the second verse of our parashah. After hearing all that has happened with the

---

Yitro

of God'), in the mores of decency and compassion that lie at the very core of our identity as Jews. It is the voice that eternally speaks the first commandment: "I AM ADONAI, YOUR GOD." It is the voice that gives ultimate authority to the other nine commandments.

I harbor an unrealistic hope that one day I'll be cleaning out some drawer, or an old box of personal effects, and there, at the very bottom, will be my blue enamel Ten Commandments pin. But even in if I never recover that potent symbol from my childhood, the impact of that symbol will remain with me. To be a Jew is to constantly hear the voice of God...and to respond.

Rabbi Elias J. Lieberman, Falmouth Jewish Congregation, East Falmouth, MA.

Israelites, Yitro grabs his daughter to attempt a reconciliation. What is so interesting is that the language of this verse is nearly identical with the language found in *Ki Tetze* [Deut. 24] that details the means by which biblical divorce is effected: The man sends the woman away from his house. Note that Yitro grabs Zipporah to accompany him to greet Moshe AFTER SHE HAS BEEN SENT AWAY. Here is the moment for reconciliation, for a renewal of his marital relationship as well as a resumption of his parental role. Instead, Moshe is able to engage his father-in-law only on "master narrative" issues, unable to address either his (ex-)wife or children. An exasperated Yitro must have been thrown completely off guard. And in the attempt to offer one final opportunity for Moshe to reorient his life he offers suggestions as to how Moshe can reposition himself within his role as leader. Yitro tells Moshe: "YOU TAKE ON TOO MANY OF THEIR PROBLEMS, YOU CAN'T SURVIVE THIS WAY." Meaning, of course, that you can't live a life that is going to be full and blessed if you choose to live it in isolation from the rest of the world.

Unlike Aaron, who maintains a relationship with his children throughout his life, Moshe has no more contact with his children after this moment. The beautiful midrash that is found detailing how God was the responsible party for handling Moshe's funeral arrangements is made necessary by the fact that after his brother and sister have died, he is sadly left with little family to attend to such matters. Luckily for Moshe, he has God.

We learn much from Moshe Rabbeinu. In many ways he is a model of a religious giant. Yet, perhaps unbeknownst to her some thirty-five years ago, Morah Toby taught me something powerful about why Moshe didn't enter the Promised Land: He never learned to set his priorities in order and accept the responsibilities nearest and dearest to him—creating a loving family with a beloved partner. ■

תשים לפניהם

We have just been at Sinai. Amid thunder and lightning God has revealed the Decalogue, which includes some major theological and moral principles by which one should live.

By contrast, this week's Torah portion includes many detailed *mishpatim*—judicial rulings. We hear about slaves and homicide, personal injuries and property damage, bailments and theft, the bride price and sacrifices to other gods, ill treatment of strangers, widows, orphans, and the poor, giving testimony in court—indeed, a whole potpourri of subjects. This is not the world of establishing fundamental relationships with God and the broad principles that should govern them; it is rather the world of the nitty-gritty rules necessary to make society run well.

In the *Mekhilta*, one of the earliest Rabbinic commentaries, though, the rabbis note that this week's Torah reading begins, AND THESE ARE THE JUDICIAL RULINGS THAT YOU SHALL SET BEFORE THEM. The "AND," according to the rabbis, means that just as the Decalogue was revealed at Sinai to the people Israel with the full authority of God, so, too, all of the specific rulings that appear in this week's portion were so revealed. That means that God's authority is as much behind the prohibition of cursing one's parents [Ex. 21.17] as it is in the Decalogue's demand to honor them; it is as much behind the rules about accidental homicide

Parashat Mishpatim

Exodus 21.1–24.18

Rabbi Elliot N. Dorff

RABBI ELLIOT N. DORFF IS RECTOR AND PROFESSOR OF PHILOSOPHY AT THE UNIVERSITY OF JUDAISM IN LOS ANGELES.

דָּבָר אַחֵר DAVAR AHER. THESE ARE THE RULES THAT YOU SHALL SET BEFORE THEM [Ex. 21.1]. My favorite professor at Brandeis who taught Bible, Professor Nahum Sarna, wrote a book, *Exploring Exodus,* that was published about ten years ago as a follow-up to his book *Understanding Genesis,* which contains an excellent review of ancient Near Eastern laws and their development as they relate to the "Book of the Covenant."

What becomes obvious from the review is that written laws were mostly exceptions, amendments, and reforms of customary law. Sarna offers a number of observations about the nature of the other law collections and the nature of the Torah's law collections. They were not complete compilations, nor were they regarded as "sacrosanct authoritative legislation that served as a source for judicial decisions." He

[Ex. 21.13] and assault [Ex. 21.18–25] as it is behind the Decalogue's prohibition of murder; and it is as much behind this week's rules about property damage and bailments as it is behind the Decalogue's prohibition of theft. The many laws in this week's portion may seem almost prosaic compared to the majestic and magisterial principles of the Decalogue, but God's authority undergirds this week's laws no less.

This has had an immense effect on our tradition. It has meant that as Jews we are to understand what God wants of us in legal terms. Authority does not rest in our individual conscience, as it does for most Protestant denominations; it is not found in the decrees of a specific group of persons, as it is, for example, for Catholics; and it is not a function of the rule of the majority, as it is for democratic cultures such as that of the United States. For Judaism, instead, authority rests in the laws, and we are to use legal methods to apply them to new situations and generations.

Indeed, as the rabbis understood the Torah, God may be the creator of the law and its ultimate judge and enforcer, but after the Torah had been given, determining the substance of its rules was now out of God's hands. "THE LAW IS NOT IN HEAVEN" [Deut. 30.12], the rabbis remind a heavenly voice that attempts to intrude on their decision-making, and God laughs in acquiescence and agreement [*Bava Metzia* 59b]. Authority, then, rests not in individual conscience, a person or group of persons, or even God, but rather in the law itself. That bespeaks a remarkable sense of trust in the law as a source for human direction.

SYNOPSIS: *God teaches Moses a basic law code including rules of slaves, a list of capital crimes, rules of damages, and basic rules for courts. The families of Israel accept these laws.*

RASHI OF THE WEEK:

Mishpatim: *The last verse of Parashat Yitro is:* YOU SHALL NOT ASCEND THE RAMP UP TO MY ALTAR SUCH THAT YOU EXPOSE YOUR NAKEDNESS ON THE WAY UP [Ex. 20.23]. *This week's sidrah begins:* AND THESE ARE THE MISHPATIM (JUDGMENTS). *Rashi asks:* Why does the Torah juxtapose these two verses? What are we supposed to learn by going from altars to courtrooms? This is to teach us that the Sanhedrin needs to be placed next to the altar, the Beit Din near a Beit Knesset, because a courtroom must be as much of a place to meet God as is the sanctuary (*Mekhilta*).

---

suggested that they generally do not delineate when new laws replace old ones and remain silent on important spheres of legal practice. Sarna also cites court documents that deal with many topics omitted from written laws and offer decisions that do not conform with the written ten laws, and there is no reference to these written laws in the court documents. Sarna concludes that there was a tremendous body of unwritten customary and common law that governed everyday life, and that the written laws were mainly religious in nature. He basically concludes the same thing regarding Torah laws as well and suggests that oral laws circulated in ancient Israel, many of which developed as laws shared in a common legal culture by many western Semitic tribes in the ancient Near East.

What is unique about *Mishpatim* is the commingling of secular laws with *Devarim,* the ethical, moral, and religious precepts that cannot be legislated by man or enforced by the courts. It is probably stating the obvious, but our Torah does not separate secular and religious aspects of law, but rather attributes all to Divine will as an integrated whole. It is also clear that the narrative woven together with the laws

Using the law to determine what is right and wrong, what is required, forbidden, or optional, has some distinct advantages and disadvantages when compared to other possible methods of making such decisions. On the minus side, employing legal methods can, and sometimes does, lead to legalism, where people become too concerned with the details of the law to see its underlying goals. It can also freeze practices much too firmly such that needed changes are not made. For those who value autonomy, the legal method removes the authority to choose from the individual and places it in the hands of those empowered to interpret the law.

On the other hand, there are many benefits to deciding moral issues or, put theologically, to discerning what God wants of us through legal methods. For one, the law defines the scope of our moral duties. To take a simple example, it may seem obvious that one has a moral duty to return a lost object, but exactly how far does that duty go? If you announce the find and nobody comes forward to claim it, do you need to take it home and store it? Do you need to advertise it in the newspaper? If it is an animal, do you need to feed it? If so, at whose expense? What if you are allergic to this kind of animal in the first place? You, after all, innocently were in the wrong place at the wrong time, and so when and where does your obligation cease? It is precisely this kind of specificity that the Jewish legal structure provides—in this case, in the second chapter of *Bava Metzia*. Without it moral norms would be absolute and insatiable, making it impossible to fulfill them while still having a life.

Second, if everyone decides on his or her own, there are no barriers against totally outrageous decisions; each person's sovereignty is often tantamount to each person's foolishness. The legal method, in

---

Mishpatim

and commands is unique to Judaism, as is the Divine nature of the covenant and the process of oral revelation followed by the written confirmation followed by a rereading of the written version. Moshe's public teaching of the law becomes an example for all future generations to study the law. The Torah also displays many distinctive legal differences in terms of language; the nature of punishment versus revenge as seen in an eye for an eye; the sacredness of human life; protection of the downtrodden; and the treatment of slaves and strangers.

Nehama Leibowitz in her *Studies in Shemot* provides an excellent explication of the topic. She points out that we are instructed not only here not to *vex* or *oppress strangers*, but in thirty-five other points in the Torah, more times than any other

contrast, requires rabbis to justify their decisions in terms of the precedents and methods of the law before the public, who can read such justifications and argue with them. The whole community may be wrong, of course, but at least this way we each provide a check for each other's poor judgments and outright errors.

Third, if everyone decides matters on his or her own, there is little chance to form shared norms. If those who know the law are entrusted to interpret and apply it, however, there can be a sense of community standards. Judges, of course, may differ with one another, but historically the Jewish tradition has devised methods—as has every living legal system—to determine which of several conflicting judicial opinions will be recognized as the law. Sometimes different communities follow different rulings, so that there is no universal Jewish practice; but at least portions of the Jewish people can be united into a group through common practices shaped by the law.

Fourth, the law acts to counter fads, for it takes some doing to change the received precedent. This is the opposite side of the point made earlier against the use of legal methods—namely, that sometimes the law does not change rapidly enough. That is true. The converse, however, is also true—namely, that moral rules should not be subject to instantaneous change. If moral rules are not simply going to condone whatever we want to do now, if they are indeed going to be normative, they must have some staying power. The legal method of handling moral issues, when used properly, provides for change, but by insisting that changes be justified legally, it protects us from changing standards too hastily. In so doing it preserves not only the normativity of norms, but also their—and the community's—continuity.

Finally, while treating moral issues in legal terms entails the risk of legalism, it also provides the opportunity for love. Children who grow up in households with no rules do not experience that as love; they see it—correctly—as apathy on the part of the parents. Laying down rules—reasonable ones, of course, and reasonably enforced—is no less than the way in which parents express love for their children. Christian sources wrongly ignore this when they depict the Jewish commitment to law as a preference for law over love. Quite the contrary; the law is the very vehicle of God's love, as the paragraph before the Shema in the siddur, the traditional prayerbook, indicates: "With everlasting love You have loved the House of Israel, You have taught us Torah and commandments, statutes and judicial rulings."

As good as the law is, though, it is not, and cannot be, sufficient. Judaism put more trust in the law than perhaps any other religion or

---

injunction. She recounts the interpretations of a number of texts and commentators including the *Mekhilta*, the Talmud, *Sefer haHinukh*, Ibn Ezra, Rashi, and the Ramban, including on the significance of saying both *vex* and *oppress the stranger*, the importance that we were strangers in Egypt, and the usage of the word *lahaz* for oppression.

The reason that I mention this in particular is that I viewed the significance of the treatment of strangers slightly differently than the commentators as I looked at it in the context of discussing legal systems. It occurred to me that Jewish law was developed in different periods and under varying circumstances. Much of the customary, common law developed before and after the Jews were a sovereign nation. The written law is geared toward the Jewish people as we were making a transition to sovereignty and was intended for application to a Jewish nation. That, in a sense, makes treatment of strangers an extremely important tenet in Judaism in providing guidance to treat strangers/foreigners fairly in our sovereign nation. There is also some sense of anticipation that we were not always governing our own destiny, and therefore we should be careful about judging strangers

culture. Even American ideology, which also manifests a much larger degree of trust in law than the thought and practice of most other groups, finds it reprehensible, if not impossible, to legislate morality. Jewish law had no such qualms. Most of the norms that contemporary Americans would consider the realm of the moral as distinct from the legal, Jewish law has no difficulty putting into law even to the point of defining how much charity one must give and in what manner (see Maimonides, *Mishneh Torah, Laws of Gifts to the Poor*, Chapter 10) and how often a man must offer to have conjugal relations with his wife [*Mishnah Ketubbot* 5.6].

And yet even Jewish tradition recognizes that there is a realm of moral norms beyond the letter of the law. Indeed, the Mishnah maintains that to say that what is mine is mine and what is yours is yours, while just and even a fulfillment of the commandment of loving your neighbor as yourself [Lev. 19.18], is "the trait of Sodom" [*Avot* 5.10]; and according to the Talmud, we force Jews not to act that way [*Eruvin* 49a; *Ketubbot* 103a; *Bava Batra* 59a, 168a]. The law may define a good deal of what we mean by the moral, and it may articulate even what we understood God to want of us in our own day, but there are still moral norms beyond its scope, a state that must be recognized and obeyed.

While we must recognize the limits of the law and the need to do the moral thing even beyond its demands, we must also understand and appreciate the important contributions it makes to our moral sensitivity and our knowledge of God's will. We read the laws of this week's portion, then, with the awe of Sinai and the authority that that setting invokes as well as the gratitude appropriate to God for the Divine gift of these laws of love. ■

Mishpatim

because we might once again live in exile without control of our own governance. Indeed that is the case even today and certainly was the case for most of the past two thousand years.

That for me is part of the importance of what this parashah represents. First and foremost Judaism is dedicated to a rule of law. While we may disagree with some of the laws included in this portion, that seems trivial in comparison to the importance of what we have contributed to the world as a religion and culture of the ancient Near East developing a living legal system that contributed to the development of rule of law. For Jews of the Diaspora this is not only a great contribution to society, but it offers us, as a minority, our greatest protection. Yet there is a certain paradox that our Jewish legal system was designed

Dr. Steven Fine

DR. STEVEN FINE IS ASSISTANT PROFESSOR OF RABBINIC LITERATURE AND HISTORY AT THE BALTIMORE HEBREW UNIVERSITY. HE WAS CURATOR OF *SACRED REALM: THE EMERGENCE OF THE SYNAGOGUE IN THE ANCIENT WORLD* AT YESHIVA UNIVERSITY (FEBRUARY, 1995), EDITOR OF THE CATALOG (OXFORD UNIVERSITY PRESS), AND AUTHOR OF *THIS HOLY PLACE: ON THE SANCTITY OF SYNAGOGUES IN THE GRECO-ROMAN WORLD* (SCHOLARS PRESS, 1996).

"I will bless you" [Ex. 20.21]. Finding God in Our Local Synagogues

The destruction of the Jerusalem Temple in 70 C.E. created a religious crisis of cataclysmic proportions for our Sages. How were God's people to procure Divine blessings when the Divinely ordained Temple was in ruins? The Mekhilta of Rabbi Ishmael, a late Tannaitic midrash, offers us an entrée into the early Rabbinic discussion that leads to the synagogue as we know it: IN EVERY PLACE [WHERE I CAUSE MY NAME TO BE REMEMBERED I WILL COME TO YOU AND I WILL BLESS YOU] [Ex. 20.21], WHERE I REVEAL MYSELF TO YOU—IN THE TEMPLE. From here they said: "The Tetragrammaton may not be pronounced in the outlying areas" (*Ba-Hodesh* 11, ed. J.Z. Lauterbauch, 2.287).

This text sharply restricts the openness of Exodus 20.21, which allows for the recitation of God's name, Y-H-W-H, "IN EVERY PLACE" to the Temple alone. The awesome name of the Lord may not be pronounced outside the Temple. Beginning with Rabban Yohanan ben Zakkai, during the seventies or eighties of the Common Era, certain Temple behaviors were integrated into synagogue life. The shaking of the lulav during the entire week of Sukkot and prayer, recited at the times when sacrifices had been offered in the Temple became synagogue rituals. At the same time Temple rituals like the pronunciation of the Tetragrammaton were forbidden within the synagogue. Local synagogues were not to become

---

as a theocracy, an issue that is clearly being played out in Israel today. For the majority of Jews in the world the notion of living in a theocracy is, to say the least, difficult, yet that is where the roots of our legal heritage come from. While we are beholden to democracy and the protections offered by the rule of law, that puts us somewhat in conflict with our heritage. It also leaves open the question of where Israel will head in the future as she confronts a growing polarization of society between those favoring democracy and those supporting theocracy. **Nate Geller, Congregation Beth Shalom, Teaneck, NJ.**

DAVAR AHER. WHEREVER I PERMIT MY NAME TO BE MENTIONED I SHALL COME TO YOU AND BLESS YOU [Ex. 20.21]. *Commentary on "Finding God in our local synagogues" by Dr. Steven Fine*: Sadly, it is often a challenge to find God and spirituality in the modern American synagogue. In addition to Rabbi Eliezer B. Jacob's citation,

replacements for the Temple in Jerusalem.

Our *Mekhilta* tradition goes on to explain that, despite the limitations set on its development, the synagogue should be a place where Jews can intimately experience the Divine Presence. Rabbi Eliezer b. Jacob says: "If you will come to my house, I will come to yours. To the place that my heart loves, my feet will lead me. From here they said: Whenever ten people congregate in the synagogue the Divine presence is with them, for it is written, אֱלֹהִים GOD (*ELOHIM*) STANDS IN THE CONGREGATION OF אֵל God (*EL*)" [Ps. 82.1].

In the centuries that followed the synagogue became a truly sacred realm, an institution where God could be found, experienced and reexperienced. Encountering God's intimate presence is not a simple task, especially for modern Jews. It requires that our synagogues become, for each of us, what they are for God: "the place that my heart loves, (the place to which) my feet will lead me." ■

Mishpatim

we can fortunately look to the Kotzke Rebbe, who teaches us that "God dwells wherever we let Him in," and Alice Walker in *The Color Purple*: "Have you ever found God in church?...any God I have felt in church I brought in with me...other folks too...they came to share God, not find God." Some changes are desperately needed. **Dr. Lawrence J. Deutsch, Flushing, NY.**

דָּבָר אַחֵר DAVAR AHER. THEY SAW THE GOD OF ISRAEL...AND THEY BEHELD GOD [Ex. 24.9–11]. We saw, then we "BEHELD" God, according to Rashi (quoting *Tanhuma*), in the heart. A deep vision. And what did we do? We had lunch. We feel the proximity of God everywhere. Is it irreverent that we behold God in our hearts, in our chest, and have lunch? That is always the point, God everywhere, on the mountain, at the diner, in the Torah, at lunch, waiting for the light to change, at the Brownie meeting, God everywhere. The place is irrelevant, the reverent truth of God in our hearts, here, there, everywhere.

The last line of *Parashat Mishpatim*, Exodus 24.18, is **AND MOSES CAME INTO THE CLOUD AND WENT UP THE MOUNTAIN AND MOSES WAS ON THE MOUNTAIN FORTY DAYS AND FORTY NIGHTS.** What did Moses see? In the Zohar Moses ascends wearing the garment of colors draped over his shoulders; he saw what he saw, enjoyed "the All" up at that place. What place? The place where language meets its limit, beyond which there is nothing to say, or the most that we can say is: nothing. Is there such a place? Here is the impenetrable edge of the forest; now that we have mentioned it, follow me into its depths. What did Moses experience? Everything. The All. *Ha-kol*. What place? The place where only Everything is everything. What did Moses see there? Everything. It's like this…and it's like this…and this….Now do you understand? An old man like me doesn't offer a single version like a word rattling around an empty bottle. First you understand the obvious, then you are introduced to the less obvious, even the secret, to emerge again at the obvious, the plain sense, the opacity of the text released now, and everything appears through the obvious. It's all in the *peshat*, the plain sense, now transparent and revealing: Everything.

So you see there are no limitations and no secrets. There is only Everything, and when you perceive that, said the old man, all the surfaces give way, everything is perceived through the *peshat*, through the story, the plain sense of it all, just as the One contains the many, just as the garment of colors is the refraction of the One, just as the rainbow is many and it is One, it is the multiplicity of colors, it is the unity of light, the One, the many, the same, Everything. **James Stone Goodman, <Stavisker@aol.com>**

Mishkin: Making a Dwelling Place for God

Parashat Terumah
Exodus 25.1–27.19

Rabbi Mordecai Finley

Mordecai Finley is rabbi of Ohr HaTorah congregation and co-rabbi of Makom Ohr Shalom. He thanks all his study partners in both shuls and his former study partners at the Shabbat Minyan at Stephen S. Wise Temple for all the insights they have given him concerning this portion over the years. Special thanks to Rabbi William (Wild Bill) Kramer.

A retelling of a Ba'al Shem Tov story: The Besh't is speaking at a large synagogue, filled, relative to the locale, with the upper crust. After the davening he says, "This synagogue is so filled with prayer." The chests of those there begin to swell. "Yes, so full. I've never been to a shul so filled with prayer."

They can barely stand it. They hadn't expected such salute! "Not one prayer in this room rises to heaven," he continues. "All are stuck here in this room."

Our hearts are often so full of ourselves. How are we to make space for God? We must empty ourselves, we must turn our hearts, the core of our being, into מִשְׁכָּן Mishkan, a dwelling place for the שְׁכִינָה Shekhinah, the presence of God.

In contemplating this portion the Sages say: הִקְדִים תְּרוּפָה לְמַכָּה *"Hikdeem Terufah la-Makkah."* "God provided the antidote before people got the disease." In last week's Torah portion God provided a well-set table of moral, civil, criminal, and religious law. In this week's Torah portion Moshe is still on Mt. Sinai receiving revelation, but the nature of the revelation changes dramatically. Now he is receiving the architectural plans for the Mishkan, the tabernacle the

דָּבָר אַחֵר **DAVAR AHER.** They shall make a Sanctuary for Me—so that I may dwell among them [Ex. 25.8]. A happy addendum to Rabbi Mordecai Finley's wonderful essay on the *Mishkan*. He astutely observes that the root [שכן] usually means to dwell and "hardly ever is used to mean 'to place'". The root has a semantic range, a field of meanings, and the Akkadian primary meaning of the root is to place and God places God, as an act of Divine will, among the faithful Israelites. Congratulations on a reading that is scientific and anthropological on one hand, and religiously inspiring on the other. **Rabbi Alan J. Yuter, Congregation Israel, Springfield, NJ.**

דָּבָר אַחֵר **DAVAR AHER.** They shall make a Sanctuary for Me—so that I may dwell among them [Ex. 25.8]. Like so many, I have won-

Israelites will build in the desert, and designs and instructions for all of its machinery.

Meanwhile, back at the foot of the mountain, the Israelites are already longing for Egypt, in their own way. They seem to say, "That Moses chap—quite the fellow! Ten plagues and all—not to mention the Lord—parting the sea like that! Still and all, we wish we had something we could touch, feel, something heavy, something not just symbolic but *emblematic*, yes, indeed, something like a massive, three-dimensional *hieroglyph* wouldn't be bad at all...." As the addict who has not quite given it over to God longs for that substance or experience that will lie to the body or ego and say that everything is all right, the Israelites brood in that emptiness resulting from the absence of God in their hearts. They hunger. The entelechy of that thick brooding is the Molten Calf, already taking shape just beyond the spiritual horizon.

God would prefer, of course, that we remember that the only image of God we need is the one we see in the face of our neighbor or in the mirror. God would prefer that the only structure we need is the one we are to build in time, the Sabbath. But God knows, of course, that taking the Israelite out of Egypt is one thing, and that taking Egypt out of the Israelite is quite another. We need some reminder in space.

And so the Mishkan. The Torah tells us [Ex. 25.1] that a תְּרוּמָה *Terumah* is to be taken from every person אֲשֶׁר יִדְּבֶנּוּ לִבּוֹ *Asher Tidvenu Libo* WHOSE HEART INCLINES HIM TOWARD NOBILITY. תְּרוּמָה *Terumah* means a donation or offering but is rooted in the Hebrew word רום "room"

---

dered about the text "MAKE ME A SANCTUARY." Thus, I like to translate it as "MAKE ME A SANCTUARY BUT I WILL DWELL IN YOUR MIDST." **Rabbi Kerry M. Olitzky, Hebrew Union College, NY.**

דָּבָר אַחֵר DAVAR AH̲ER. YOU SHALL MAKE... [Ex. 25.17]. If we were to count the number of occurrences of various phrases in the entire Torah, the winner would undoubtedly be וַיְדַבֵּר *Va-Yiddaber Adonai el-Moshe*, "AND THE LORD SAID TO MOSES." If we were to count the number of occurrences of various phrases in this week's *Parashat Terumah*, the winner would undoubtedly be וְעָשִׂיתָ *v'Asitah* AND YOU SHALL MAKE, for thus begins each specific commandment in this tale of the construction of the *Aron Kodesh* and the Mishkan, the holy ark and the tabernacle in

SYNOPSIS: *Moses asks the families of Israel to donate gifts and materials for the Mishkan. Thirteen specific kinds of materials are specified. The* aron, *the* shulh̲an, *and the* menorah *are each detailed.*

RASHI OF THE WEEK:

Terumah: *Here is a Rashi that gives me comfort. Exodus 25.16 reads,* YOU SHALL PUT INTO THE ARK הָעֵדוּת HA-AYDUT (the Testimony), WHICH I SHALL GIVE YOU. *Rashi asks, "What is* הָעֵדוּת *ha-Aydut (the Testimony)?"* He then gives a straightforward answer: הָעֵדוּת *Ha-Aydut* is the Torah, which is the Testimony to the covenant between Me and you. The mitzvot I have commanded you are written there. *Then in verse 21 it reads:* AND INTO THE ARK YOU SHALL PUT הָעֵדוּת HA-AYDUT. *Rashi then asks: "Why is this idea repeated? What are we supposed to learn this time?" His answer:* I do not know why this has been repeated, for it has already been stated above. Perhaps this is to teach us that while the Ark is uncovered, we should put the Torah in it, and then afterwards put the lid on it. This is suggested by a later verse. When Moses sets up the Mishkan, the Torah says, AND HE PUT הָעֵדוּת HA-AYDUT INTO THE ARK and then HE PUT THE LID ON THE ARON ON TOP [Ex. 40.20]. *It is comforting to know that there are some things that Rashi hasn't figured out.*

meaning "high, exalted." *Terumah* is a superbly heuristic term; the word referring to that which we give refers back to the inner state, elevation, ta accompanies the giving. The Mishkan is built, then, out of the stuff of noble purpose.

Our portion starts with the description of the Mishkan just as you would imagine—from the inside out. By the time you finish the portion (and a bit of next week's), here is (roughly) what you end up with: a large rectangular structure divided about in half. When you walk in the gate (heading west) into the front half you encounter a copper altar upon which the sacrifices are made. Behind that is a copper laver. Halfway into the Mishkan courtyard, just behind the copper laver, you come to the entrance of a structure that stands in the second half of the Mishkan, the אֹהֶל מֹאֵד *Ohel Mo'ed* (the tent of meeting). At the entrance to the אֹהֶל *ohel* is a מָסָךְ *masakh*, a screen that separates the tent from the courtyard of the Mishkan. When you go into the אֹהֶל מֹאֵד *ohel mo'ed* ("you go" meant figuratively, of course; see next week's Torah portion) you see in front of you the golden altar upon which the incense is offered. On your right is the table where the bread offering is made. On your left is the מְנוֹרָה *menorah* where the light offering is made. Behind all that is a פָּרוֹכֶת *parokhet*, a partition. Behind the *parokhet* is the space called the קֹדֶשׁ הַקְּדוֹשִׁים *Kodesh ha-Kidashim* Holy of Holies, where the אֲרוֹן קוֹדֶשׁ *Aron Kodesh* (ark of Holiness) stands. The tablets with the Ten Commandments are in there. But that is not all that is in there. It's a gate.

Now, I want to share something with you that to me is just astounding. Maybe you know it already. I've known this for several years, but every year when I make my journey into the Mishkan I am astounded all over again.

Terumah

which the Israelites would worship during their forty years in the wilderness. An ark of acacia wood; rings and poles to support it; a cover of pure gold; two cherubim; a table of acacia wood; a gold rim for the table; rings and poles to support it; a tabernacle of cloth with very specific lengths and loops and hooks and clasps and sockets. The instructions take up the entire text of the parashah; there is not a word of narrative, nor is there a commandment whose literal significance reaches beyond the work at hand. There is no point of perspective in *Terumah* (or in the whole second half of the book of Exodus, for that matter) to which we could step back and take a look at the finished product. It is very difficult to imagine anyone able to keep all the details sufficiently clear in mind to form even a "mind's-eye" view of

You walk into this structure, made of boards and curtains, and you are impressed that it feels light and spacious. You see the copper altar, certainly, but that is not the center of the action. Animal sacrifice is not the core of service in the Mishkan. First clue: The laver for washing is behind the copper altar [see Ex. 30.17-21]. If the only function of the laver was to purify the כֹּהֲנִים *Kohanim,* the priests, before they performed animal sacrifices, or to wash up afterwards, you would expect it to be in front of the copper altar. The Torah tells us that to enter the tent of meeting/אֹהֶל מֹאֶד *ohel mo'ed* the priests had to be cleansed of any impurity, including the bloody work of the sacrifices. (Maybe it also means that you can't get to the Holy without some messy, bloody work beforehand—and you need to cleanse yourself of it to proceed.)

When you push past the מָסָךְ *masakh* into the אֹהֶל *ohel* you have entered the inner precinct, close to the core of the action. You have a light offering on your left (south), representing the purely ethereal, the mystical, the primordial light of creation. On your right (north), you have the table with the bread offering, representing the worldly, the bodily, the corporeal and tangible context of the Holy. And in front of you is the incense altar (see Ex. 30:1-10), mediating between the two. Incense is neither radiance nor body—it remains suspended between the two, the interstices between light and matter. We ingest its insubstantial presence into the deepest recesses of human sensation. In sensing/seeing it we see the רוּחַ *Ruah* wind/spirit of God wafting through. We are drunk in the staggering metaphoric beauty. We know that one step beyond is the ark, and within the ark the tablets. The tablets are given their meaning by the spaces created within them. The letters engraved through and through make the מָקוֹם *Makom/* Space for הַמָּקוֹם *HaMakom*, the Omnipresent One, to be present.

Dare we? We push aside the פָּרוֹכֶת *parokhet* to gaze upon the Ark, and our eyes cannot believe what we see. For above the כַּפֹּרֶת *kaporet,* the cover of the tablets into which, by the way, is inscribed the commandment not to make graven images, are two of the gravenest images you will ever encounter. The כְּרוּבִים *K'ruvim* [Ex. 25.17-22] are winged creatures, made of pure gold, facing each other. And between their faces is where God will condense God's presence and become present to Moses. We step back, startled, כְּרוּבִים. And we look about and see and recall that woven into the fabric of the curtains housing all the elements of the Mishkan and the Holy of Holies are representations of כְּרוּבִים *k'ruvim.* At the center of this diaphanous and layered structure are these dense beings; representations of what? I was startled years ago when I finally paid attention

---

the ark and tabernacle. Details catch our attention: the cherubim with wings spread; the golden lampstands; the blue, purple, and crimson embroidery on the linen screen at the entrance of the tabernacle. But the whole is forever out of our sight, too much to imagine all at once.

In fact, the entire drama of the construction of the ark and tabernacle is a drama of doing, not of seeing. Our hands are busy with this most sacred task, occupied by one detail after another. And in this drama of doing, I think, is a great lesson.

Our ancestors in the desert had in their time the most sacred task of building the tabernacle. We in our day have as our most sacred task the building of homes and families, the raising of our children and care of our aging parents. And like the work of the tabernacle, it is a drama of doing. Life is a seemingly endless series of minor tasks, everything from "changing the diaper" to "driving to soccer" to "picking up the arthritis medicine." There is precious little time to step back to enjoy the scenery. Perhaps at a graduation or wedding we are granted an opportunity to enjoy the work of our hands, but then the caterer needs to be paid, a fuse blows in the basement,

and read this portion carefully and saw them. But not yet astounded.

What astounded me the first time I really saw those *k'ruvim* was when I remembered, seconds later (still startled), when I had seen them last. Remember?

AND GOD SENT HIM (ADAM) OUT FROM THE GARDEN OF EDEN TO WORK THE SOIL FROM WHICH HE WAS TAKEN. IN EXPELLING HIM, HE PLACED וַיַּשְׁכֵּן-*VA-YASHKEN* EAST OF EDEN THE כְּרוּבִים *K'RUVIM* AND THE FLAME OF THE EVER-TURNING SWORD TO GUARD THE WAY TO THE TREE OF LIFE [Gen. 3.23-24].

The Torah uses the same root as Miskhan and Shekhina to describe the positioning of the *k'ruvim* east of Eden! Now, the root [שכן] is virtually always used to mean "dwell" and hardly ever used to mean "to place." This is a very unusual usage of the word, so the Torah must be telling us what by now is obvious: Wherever you find כְּרוּבִים *k'ruvim* you have found the way to the tree of life, the gate back to Eden. The Mishkan, which leads us into this exquisite journey into God's presence, houses the Edenic כְּרוּבִים *k'ruvim* as well. If they are above the Ark, then the Torah, the Word of God, is the עֵץ חַיִּים Etz Hayyim, the tree of life from which we were separated back in our origins in Eden. Those כְּרוּבִים *k'ruvim* are the proverbial קֶרֶשׁ *Keresh* board whacking us over the head. "Here is what they are doing here," God seems to be saying. "They are right where I placed them—guarding the way to the tree of life!"

And here we have it. God says, "MAKE ME A SANCTUARY—THAT I MAY DWELL (שָׁכַנְתִּי *SHAKHANTI*) AMONG THEM" [Ex. 25.8]. This מִקְדָּשׁ *Mikdash/* מִשְׁכָּן Mishkan, sanctuary/dwelling place is filled with symbols of the inner life, an architectural poem that we have only begun to interpret here. At its center are the tablets, guarded by the כְּרוּבִים *k'ruvim*, and at the core of the tablets are the spaces that make up the letters. As we live those spaces, engrave those spaces in our hearts,

---

Terumah

or Grandma is confused again, and we are thrown right back to work.

But we cannot allow ourselves to be discouraged or depressed by the press of circumstance. We create holiness in our lives one detail at a time, task after task after task, just as our ancestors created the tabernacle.

Holiness is in the doing, in the doing of everyday things with attention and love. We must simply pay attention to each task as it comes to us, for it is through faithful engagement with the tasks of each day that we earn our share of eternity. **Rabbi Michael Joseph, Kingston, PA, <michjose@cris.com>**

דָּבָר אַחֵר DAVAR AHER. THE CHERUBIM SHALL BE WITH WINGS SPREAD UPWARD, SHELTERING THE COVER WITH THEIR WINGS WITH THEIR FACES TOWARD

we are taken back to primordial union with God in Eden. As we make room for God, the Presence dwells within. Our yearning is met with encounter. Our prayers rise to heaven. We eat of the tree of life.

If, as Joni Mitchell and Crosby, Stills, Nash and Young would have it, "We've got to get ourselves back to the garden," then the כְּרוּבִים *k'ruvim* will show us the way. We turn our hearts into a Mishkan—at our center, a space that is the gate of God. ■

ONE ANOTHER; TOWARD THE COVER SHALL BE THE FACES OF THE CHERUBIM [Ex. 25.20]. In *Parashat Terumah* God requests an offering from the Israelites, saying, "THEY SHALL MAKE ME A SANCTUARY, AND I SHALL DWELL AMONG THEM." All the details of the construction of the ark of the covenant—the table, the menorah, the beams, the partitions, the altar, and the hangings of linen that enclosed the tabernacle in the desert—comprise this parashah. What got my attention was that among all the color, cloth, and precious metal there were angels. God designed a sanctuary where the Israelites would be surrounded by representations of angels. Golden כְּרוּבִים *k'ruvim* face each other, their wings lifted on high, shielding the Ark of the Covenant, while all around more כְּרוּבִים *k'ruvim* are woven into the tapestries of the enclosure. Why? Before I try to answer this puzzling question, let's talk about angels.

The כְּרוּבִים *k'ruvim* mentioned in *Terumah* are not the only kind of angels. מַלְאָכִים *Malakhim*, שְׂרָפִים *seraphim*, אֳפַנִּים *ofanim*, חַיּוֹת *hayyot*, בְּנֵי אֱלֹהִים *benei elohim*, עֶרְלִים *arelim*, and חַשְׁמַלִּים *hashmallim* are also noted in the liturgy. כְּרוּבִים *K'ruvim*, however, are the first angelic presence in the Torah, for after the expulsion of Adam and Eve from the Garden of Eden God placed כְּרוּבִים *k'ruvim* at the east of Eden to guard the entrance. Our rabbis have had differing opinions on what כְּרוּבִים *k'ruvim* looked like. Rashbam thought they were birdlike creatures. Ralbag thought they had faces like human infants. In Ezekiel's vision כְּרוּבִים *k'ruvim* were fantastic creatures with wheels, wings, and hands. Ezekiel's כְּרוּבִים *k'ruvim* had four faces. One was the face of an eagle, one a lion, one a man, and one an ox. All this still leaves us wondering, what do כְּרוּבִים *k'ruvim* look like? Some angels have looked like men—like the angel that wrestled Jacob or the angels that announced Isaac's impending birth to Sarah.

Some angels have been invisible. Balaam, a renowned mystic and prophet, was famous for his deadly curses. Balak, king of Moab, commanded him to curse the people of Israel. An angel, sword in hand, barred Balaam's way. Balaam's donkey would go no further. Why was the angel invisible to Balaam when his donkey could see it clearly? Maybe Balaam didn't want to see the angel because he knew what he was doing was wrong. Sometimes we don't see what we don't want to see. The Bible says that finally God uncovered Balaam's eyes and he saw the angel. The donkey's eyes were already open.

Some angels have appeared in flames. An angel spoke to Moses from the burning bush, which makes me think, what's an angel got to do to get a guy's attention? When Shadrach, Meshach, and Abednego were in the fiery furnace, an angel was there to protect them.

Very few angels have names. Name magic was, to ancient Jews, a very powerful force. To know an angel's name was to command it. When Jacob was wrestling with the angel he asked its name. The angel would not answer. From infancy Jewish children learn the names of the angels in the bedtime Shema: Raphael, Gabriel, Michael, and Uriel. Some say there are more names for Satan, a fallen angel, than there are for God.

In the story of Job, Satan is portrayed as a law-abiding member of the angel community, doing God's bidding, which is to roam the earth

Ari Kelman

ARI KELMAN IS A GRADUATE STUDENT AT NEW YORK UNIVERSITY IN THE AMERICAN STUDIES PROGRAM AND A JEWISH STUDIES TEACHER AT RODEPH SHOLOM DAY SCHOOL IN NEW YORK CITY.

The commandment that opens *Parashat Terumah* is not a commandment to give, but a commandment to receive. It reads, "TELL THE ISRAELITE PEOPLE TO BRING ME GIFTS; YOU SHALL ACCEPT GIFTS FOR ME FROM EVERY PERSON WHOSE HEART SO MOVES HIM *(sic)*" [Ex. 25.2]. Despite the discrepancy in the English translation between "bring" and "accept," the Hebrew text employs one verb in both expressions of the act of giving—קָח, which translates as "to take." Thus, taking or receiving the gift is the obligatory action, not giving it.

This formulation of tzedakah suggests a radical understanding of the relationship between giver, recipient, and gift.

In our parashah the giver and the gift are specified, yet the role of the recipient is unclear. The giver can be anyone "WHOSE HEART SO MOVES HIM *(sic)*," and the gift can be any number of objects from God's wish list [Ex. 25.3-7], which will then be used in the construction of the *mikdash*. The recipient is given no prescription for behavior or identity beyond accepting the gifts. So a relationship develops between a giver, who cannot be solicited and must therefore be self-initiating; a gift, which can only be one of fifteen specific objects; and a recipient whose acceptance of the gift is mandatory, but whose ownership of the gift is deferred, as the gifts ultimately constitute the building materials of the *mikdash*.

The gift occupies a critical role as the mediator between giver and recipient, and as such requires some investigation. A gift always carries with it a set of social meanings, values, and expectations, which constitute an aura

Terumah

observing the behavior of God's people. This is strange to think about when Satan is believed to be the essence of evil and the antagonist of God.

Hagar, heavily pregnant, flees her mistress Sarah, who treats her horribly. An angel tells her to return to Sarah, that she will be granted many descendants, and tells her to name her child Ishmael, which means "God has heard" (her prayers). In this celestial encounter the angel performs no miracle but encourages Hagar to help herself. Many people believe that an angel is the voice within that urges us to do the right thing.

In the story of the sacrificing of Isaac God commands Abraham to slay his son. As Abraham is about to kill Isaac an angel stops him. The story of *Akedat Yitzhak*, the binding of Isaac, demonstrates that while only God can pronounce a death sentence, an angel is sufficient to revoke it.

around the object itself, which, in turn, reflects back onto the giver–recipient relationship, complicating and transforming it. Often an initial act of giving necessitates a reciprocal act of giving in which the roles of giver and recipient are reversed. Yet with each exchange the relationship between giver, gift, and recipient is renegotiated, redefined, and reestablished in light of the exchange. In this way the object exchange is merely a vehicle through which two or more individuals negotiate their relationship. Thus configured, giving and receiving are actions that help us to mediate a private relationship while situating it within a much broader social context.

The recipient of the gift in our parashah, however, never quite owns the gift given, nor is the gift ever repaid to the initial giver. Instead the gift is used according to God's request, "LET THEM MAKE ME A SANCTUARY THAT I MAY DWELL AMONG THEM" [Ex. 25.8]. The sanctuary is not intended as a house for God, but a medium for the divine presence to DWELL AMONG the people. In other words, the sanctuary is a social construction providing holy space within the social world. In the selfless act of giving a gift to a willing recipient a relationship is established that both honors and transcends all participants and makes space for Divine presence. God does not dwell in the lampstand, the ark, the altar, or any other of the utensils described in the parashah, but in the selfless giving and gracious acceptance of a gift. Individual people and objects do not, in their sheer existence, create a dwelling for God but, through relationships of equality, mutuality, and selflessness, create holy space. ■

In medieval Jewish mystic poetry Sandalfon, a fiery angel, bears the prayers of humans before God.

In the passage that precedes the Shema, the prayer that declares God's oneness, God is praised as the Creator of holy beings, beings who accept the yoke of heavenly sovereignty. Another prayer, taken from the Zohar, says: "Not in man do I put my trust, nor do I rely on any angel, but only in the God of heaven, who is the God of truth." What can we learn from this? The rabbis who assembled the prayerbook wanted to make it clear that angels are not mini-gods and that there is only one God. Angels are only God's creations. Still, references to angels are numerous in the prayerbook. On Friday evenings we sing Shalom Aleihem to greet the angels of peace. In the vision of Isaiah the fiery seraphim call out to each other: "Holy, Holy, Holy is the Lord of Hosts."

The bedtime Shema is a wish to be surrounded and protected by the Shekhinah, the feminine aspect of God, and four special angels. Each of these four angels has his own unique attributes: the angel Michael is known as the protector of Israel and as a warrior angel. Gabriel is the messenger angel. He is a master of courage; his gift of courage helped Enoch, in the book of Genesis, stand before God. It was Gabriel who wrestled with Jacob and gave him the courage to face Esau. Gabriel is noted in the writings of other religions for appearing to the Virgin Mary and to Mohammed. Raphael's name means "God heals." Raphael is the protector of the young, the innocent, of pilgrims and other travelers. Raphael is the angel of prayer, love, joy, and especially healing. In the story of Tobit, Raphael cures Tobit's cataracts and exorcises a demon from his daughter-in-law's head. Uriel means "God is my light." As with the other angels, the name suits its function. Uriel is placed at the east of Eden to guard the tree of life. Uriel is associated with light and is the angel of illumination.

Rambam writes that angels, unlike humans, are pure creatures. They can do only one job, whereas humans can do many things. The task of the three angels sent to Abraham's tent was to inform Sarah that she was to have a child. What happened to this angel after it completed its mission? Maybe the angel was assigned a new job, or maybe the angel just ceased to exist.

ויקחו אליך

Terumah

So now back to my original question: Why are angels used in the tabernacle?

There are many possibilities. Rashi believes that כְּרוּבִים *k'ruvim* are angels of destruction that guard the garden of Eden. They remind humans that before they are allowed into paradise they must pass the angels of purgatory. This could be the significance of the angels used to decorate the tabernacle.

I think that since angels are God's messengers, they remind people of the nearness of God.

I saw an angel on the December 1996 cover of *Life* magazine. Sixty-nine percent of Americans say that they believe in angels. One hundred new nonfiction books were published last spring on the subject. The Brown family wore angel pins at the O. J. Simpson trial. The post office has angel stamps. Angel images are everywhere, from your local supermarket to the 140 new angel boutiques that have opened nationwide. The world has not been so hungry for angels since the Renaissance.

God wanted the Israelites to be surrounded by images of angels in the tabernacle, and now Americans are experiencing the same thing. I believe the key may be in Psalm 91.11: FOR HE WILL GIVE HIS ANGELS CHARGE OVER THEE IN ALL THE WAYS. THEY SHALL BEAR THEE UPON THEIR HANDS, LEST THOU DASH THY FOOT AGAINST A STONE. In times of high stress and mass disillusionment the message that God will send a personal, caring, ever-vigilant guardian in times of need is very comforting. Where now is the tabernacle in the desert with its hangings of blue, purple, and scarlet, the table of acacia wood, sweet incense, spiced oil for anointing accoutrements of pure gold, silver, brass, and onyx? Where especially are the tablets of stone on which Moses engraved the law? Nothing is left—but two things. The Torah, the word of God that outlived the mere stone it was written upon, and the angels who, whether we believe in them or not, still surround us.

If angels are beings that provide comfort and protection, then we only have to look as far as our own family, friends, and community to find our angels. So here I stand today, as in the tabernacle, surrounded by angels. **Rachel Frank, 13, Congregation Netivot Shalom, Berkeley, CA.**

ואתה תצוה את בני ישראל

Parashat Tetzaveh

Exodus 27.20–30.10

Rabbi Harold Kushner

RABBI HAROLD S. KUSHNER IS RABBI LAUREATE OF TEMPLE ISRAEL OF NATICK, MA, AND THE AUTHOR OF *WHEN BAD THINGS HAPPEN TO GOOD PEOPLE*, *WHEN CHILDREN ASK ABOUT GOD*, AND *WHEN EVERYTHING YOU'VE ALWAYS WANTED ISN'T ENOUGH*.

We know that the Kotel, the Western Wall, is one of the holiest sites in Judaism. It links us to the second Temple, where our ancestors experienced the presence of God until it was destroyed by the Romans in the year 70 C.E. For centuries it was thought to be all that remained of Herod's temple, though in recent years extensive portions of the western and southern walls have been unearthed. We know, too, that nothing remains of Solomon's temple, destroyed by the Babylonians in 586 B.C.E.

But does anything remain of the Mishkan, the tabernacle where our ancestors first worshipped in the wilderness in the days of Moses? I would suggest that something does.

Although the details of the tabernacle are started in last week's reading, *Parashat Terumah*, and completed this week in *Tetzaveh*, and although the story of the Golden Calf comes next week in *Ki Tissa*, many scholars believe that the events are not given in their chronological order, and that the tabernacle was a response to the sin of making the Golden Calf. The ark housing the tablets of the Ten Commandments, the central feature of the tabernacle, was known as *Aron ha-Edut*, the ark of witness, because it testified to the fact that God was still found in Israel's midst even after the incident of the Golden Calf. The instructions to build the tabernacle were placed before the account of the Calf perhaps to assure us as we read

---

דָּבָר אַחֵר DAVAR AHER. THEY SHALL TAKE FOR YOU PURE, PRESSED OLIVE FOR ILLUMINATION, TO KINDLE THE LAMP CONTINUALLY [Ex. 27.20]. Rabbi Harold Kushner reminds us of the eternal light burning ever so brightly in the synagogue. Perhaps that's where our parents got the idea to leave the light on the front porch when we were adolescents, reminding us that however far we travel into the night, the light will always be on guiding us home. "The Torah of God is a lamp. In God's light do we see light." **Rabbi Kerry M. Olitzky, HUC-JIR, New York, NY, <olitzky@huc.edu>**

דָּבָר אַחֵר DAVAR AHER. THEY SHALL TAKE FOR YOU PURE OLIVE OIL, PRESSED, FOR LIGHTING, TO FIRE UP THE LAMP CONTINUALLY (NER TAMID) [Ex. 27.20]. The first mitzvah of the concretization of the spirit (the Mishkan) is to make sure that a light rises within it. Light is one of the images of choice for the spirit, and for the intellect,

the latter that the story would not end disastrously.

According to that view, the making and worshipping of the Golden Calf led God to understand how hard it was for the Israelites, newly freed from Egypt, to comprehend a totally abstract God, a God with no form or visible presence. At first they fastened on Moses as an incarnation of God. Then, when Moses disappeared up the mountain for almost six weeks, they fashioned the Calf to represent the Divine presence (not surprising for people who had grown up in Egypt). To satisfy their need for a visible reassurance of God's invisible presence without resorting to idols or images, God called on them to fashion a tabernacle "THAT I MIGHT DWELL IN THEIR MIDST." It was a tentlike structure that contained, in addition to the ark, a table and lamp to simulate God's dwelling place and a *ner tamid*, an eternal light, hanging in front of the tent to indicate that the Divine resident of the tabernacle was at home.

The ark of the covenant no longer exists, despite what movie makers might tell us. There is no portable shrine, no table, no gold menorah. What remains of the tabernacle? The eternal light, burning in front of the ark that houses the Torah scrolls in every synagogue in the world. While the other symbols have disappeared and even the temple with its sacrificial altar has been consigned to ancient history, the eternal light continues to symbolize the real presence of an invisible, intangible God.

What is it about light and fire that have made them such compellingly effective symbols of God for three thousand years? For one thing, light itself is invisible, but it makes other things visible. We cannot see light, but light enables us to see each other. I am a graduate of Columbia University, whose

---

Tetzaveh

but this will have to be a place of fire as well as light.

נֵר *Ner* (lamp) is also an acronym for נְשָׁמָה *Neshamah* and רוּחַ *Ruah*, two complementary qualities of soulfulness. All the terrible twos of existence are harmonized in the lamp, נְשָׁמָה *Neshamah* and רוּחַ *Ruah*, feminine and masculine, human and godly, left and right, intuitive and rational, me and you, spiritual and material, light and dark, reconciled in the spiritual purity of raising the lamp of *neshamah* and *ruach* continually, that is, daily. AARON AND HIS SONS SHALL ARRANGE IT FROM EVENING UNTIL MORNING [Ex. 27.21]. Renewed every day, the life of the spirit is a daily notion, a few twenty-four hours strung together in the life of the spirit, embodied in the lamp, fired up in the sanctuary. How do you live such a life of the spirit? Stay in the day. If not today, tomorrow. **James Stone Goodman, Stavisker@aol.com**

motto is a verse from Psalms, BY YOUR LIGHT DO WE SEE LIGHT [36.10]. Just as light enables us to see the beauty of the world and the other people in it, God enables us not to see God but to see God's world and to see the people in it as bearers of God's image.

Furthermore, light is one of the constants of the world we live in. Einstein's theory of relativity taught us that the speed of light was the one unchanging standard against which all relative standards of movement could be measured. In a similar way, God is the constant against which relative and evolving standards of morality can be measured.

We cannot understand light. Quantum physicists are baffled, telling us that sometimes light acts like a wave and sometimes like a set of particles. It is *sui generis*, defying conventional laws of physics. But we can all benefit from the light even without understanding it. So too we can benefit from what God does without understanding what God is. Jewish theology, when not compelled to articulate itself in Christian or Muslim terminology, has never been about the nature of God. Jewish theology has been about the will of God; not what God is, but what God demands of us.

When Moses brings about the reconciliation between God and Israel in next week's reading, he goes on to ask of God, "LET ME SEE YOUR FACE THAT I MAY KNOW YOU." God replies "NO MAN CAN SEE MY FACE AND LIVE. BUT HIDE HERE IN THE CLEFT OF THIS ROCK AS I PASS BY, AND YOU WILL SEE MY BACK" [Ex. 33.18–23]. It is perhaps the most perplexing verse in the Torah. After so strenuously insisting that God has no shape, no form, no body, how can the Torah speak of God's face and God's

---

דָּבָר אַחֵר DAVAR AHER. YOU SHALL MAKE VESTMENTS OF SANCTITY FOR AARON YOUR BROTHER, FOR GLORY AND SPLENDOR [Ex. 28.2]. In last week's Torah discussion using *Torah Toons II* it was asked: "Why did God want Moshe to make Aaron's garments personally?" Michael Katz answered: "We know that Moshe had a speech impediment and that Aaron would often do the talking for him. As a way of showing thanks for his brother's help, Moshe wanted to make Aaron's priestly garments." We sing,

הִנֵּה מַה טּוֹב וּמַה נָּעִים
שֶׁבֶת אַחִים גַּם יָחַד

Hine Ma-Tov uMah Nayim Shevet Ahim Gam Yahad, BEHOLD, HOW GOOD AND PLEASANT IT IS WHEN BRETHREN DWELL TOGETHER IN UNITY, which the Midrash says is about Moshe and Aaron. **Rabbi Michael M. Cohen, Israel Congregation, Manchester Center, VT, <75607.3672@compuserve.com>**

SYNOPSIS: *We learn about pure, beaten olive oil. The Cohen family becomes the* kohanim. *We make all their special garments. We describe their installation sacrifices, too.*

RASHI OF THE WEEK:

Near the end of this sidrah, *we find this statement about the* Mishkan (tabernacle) [Ex. 29.43]: I WILL MEET THERE WITH THE FAMILIES OF ISRAEL, AND IT WILL BECOME HOLY THROUGH MY HONOR. "I will meet there": *How does God meet with people, when God can never show up face to face? God means,* I will meet them with words—like a king who sets aside a special place to meet with his servants. "And it will become holy": *To what does the "it" refer? It means the* Mishkan. "Through My Honor": *How does God's honor (which is everywhere) make one place especially holy? The obvious meaning is that the Miskhan becomes the place where the* Shekhinah *resides. But there is a midrash that teaches: Do not read the word as "My Honor" but rather as "my honored ones." God is foreshadowing the death of Aaron's two sons on the day of the* Mishkan's *dedication. Later, Moses finally understands this hint and says, "This is what was meant when God said: "I will become Holy through those near to me" [Lev. 10.3]. That moment is Moses recalling that God had told him: "And it will become holy through My Honored ones." Their sacrifice will set My place apart, more than anything I can do.*

back? I take the verse to mean "You cannot see Me face to face, but you can see My aftereffects, the difference I make as I have an impact on people's lives." Like light, God is real but not visible. We don't see God; we see things differently because of God.

What is true of light is equally true of fire as a symbol of God. Fire is not an object. Fire is a process, the process of liberating the energy concealed in a lump of coal, in a log of wood. And God is not an object, a physical being that can be located in a specific place. God is the process of liberating the potential energy, the potential compassion, the potential goodness in every one of us. When my teacher Mordecai Kaplan defined God as "the power that makes for salvation," the power that impels us to be more human, I suspect that this is what he had in mind.

Three thousand years after the Golden Calf was destroyed and the tabernacle constructed, we still struggle with the idea of an abstract, formless Deity. Our prayers still speak of "the sight of God," "the hands of God." Christians offer us God incarnated in human form because a totally abstract God is so hard to relate to, to pray to, despite the problems caused by God being incarnated as a man, not a woman; a Caucasian, not an Asian or African, a young man, not an older one. But the eternal light, the oldest surviving symbol in all of Judaism, would remind us that it is our limitations, not God's reality, that lead to those images and those metaphors. God has no eyes, no hands, no sexual organs. But God is real, just as light and fire are real, and our world is very different because of that reality. ■

Broken Pieces

Parashat Ki Tissa
Exodus 30.11–34.35

Vicky Kelman

VICKY KELMAN IS THE DIRECTOR OF THE JEWISH FAMILY EDUCATION PROJECT, A COLLABORATION OF THE JEWISH COMMUNITY FEDERATION AND THE BUREAU OF JEWISH EDUCATION OF THE SAN FRANCISCO BAY AREA. HER MOST RECENT PUBLICATIONS ARE *JEWISH FAMILY RETREATS: A HANDBOOK*, CO-PUBLISHED BY THE MELTON RESEARCH CENTER AND THE WHIZIN INSTITUTE FOR JEWISH FAMILY LIFE AT THE UNIVERSITY OF JUDAISM (WHERE VICKY ALSO IS SERVES ON THE FACULTY) AND *FAMILY ROOM: LINKING FAMILIES INTO A JEWISH LEARNING COMMUNITY*, PUBLISHED IN JUNE 1996 BY WHIZIN.

This parashah contains among the most dramatic and pivotal events in the history of the Jewish people: the story of the Golden Calf. The people, struggling to maintain their faith in an abstract God during Moses' long absence, collaborate to create the Golden Calf. When God tells Moses what has happened at the foot of the mountain, Moses is able to soothe God's anger [Ex. 32.7-10], but when he descends and sees with his own eyes what the people have done in his absence, Moses smashes the tablets that he is bringing back to the people from God [Ex. 32. 15-18].

There is an interesting juxtaposition here: The people create something expressly forbidden by God while Moses destroys something that is a direct creation of God.

In the commentaries of the rabbis Moses escapes unscathed from any criticism for smashing the tablets in the heat of his anger. This seems puzzling in light of the fact that we also know that later Moses is punished—and for something that seems like a far smaller infraction. This kind of anger is a familiar human experience. The rabbis recognize strong emotions at play here and the potential for the whole Jewish people enterprise to be shipwrecked at this point. They have tremendous empathy for Moses' pain.

As I read this I always find myself wondering: What happened to the broken pieces? They are never mentioned again in the Torah. It would seem that

---

דָּבָר אַחֵר **DAVAR AHER. ON VICKY KELMAN'S BROKEN PIECES.** Vicky Kelman's thought-provoking message on *Ki Tissa* was both enlightening and inspirational. Why, after all, was it written that Moses broke the first set of tablets? And why was the story preserved that way? Wouldn't it have been enough for Moses or God to have destroyed the Golden Calf? Perhaps the message is that it wasn't the tablets themselves that were holy and in need of preservation, but rather the thoughts and ideas that were summarized on them. It's a good thing this all took place before they invented Krazy Glue! **David Parker, <Parques@aol.com>**

דָּבָר אַחֵר **DAVAR AHER. ON VICKY KELMAN'S BROKEN PIECES.** In a column in today's *Plain Dealer* (Cleveland's paper), Elizabeth Auster eloquently commented on the care with which "rabbis wearing latex gloves were methodically combing

these broken shards would be valuable souvenirs of a critical moment in history. Wouldn't people want to collect the pieces of this direct message from God? Don't we treasure the artifacts that link us to history (pieces of the Berlin wall) or to personal events (seashells labeled with date and place, arrowheads, pottery shards, pressed flowers). It seems a basic human inclination. If you had been there, wouldn't you have wanted to pick up and save a piece of those tablets?

Although the Torah makes no further mention of the pieces, the rabbis do think further about it, and from their reflections we have several possibilities from which to choose:

TEXT ONE: Rabbi Judah bar Ilai taught: Two arks journeyed with Israel in the wilderness, one in which the Torah was kept and one in which the tablets broken by Moses were kept. The one in which the Torah was placed was kept in the Tent of Meeting; the other, containing the broken tablets, would come and go with them [p. *Shek*, 1.1; 49c; *Yalkut Sam* par. 101; *Sefer Ha Aggadah*, par. 83].

This text supports the idea that the pieces were important enough to be kept safe.

Answer one: They were kept in a separate ark. An addendum to this text adds that the sages said, "There is only one ark."

TEXT TWO: To everything there is a season and a time to every purpose under heaven...a time to be born and a time to die...a time to cast away stones and a time to gather stones [Ecc. 3.1]. A time to cast away (the verb is identical to the verb our text uses to describe Moses' action in casting the tablets onto the ground) stones—that is what Moses did when he cast away the tablets. A time to gather stones—that is when God says to Moses, "Hew/carve yourself פְּסָל-לְךָ *P'sol-lekha* new ones like the first" [Ex. 34.1]. We can also understand פְּסָל *p'sol* (hew) as standing for the word

---

Ki Tissa

the area...looking for pieces of human flesh," as reported by a CNN reporter. An explanation of Jewish law followed three reporters' comments, continued Auster. She then talked about the gruesomeness of the rabbis' job and confessed that she "questioned CNN's taste in repeatedly mentioning those rabbis and their gloves and plastic bags. But the network was right," said Auster.

"Each bit matters," they seemed to insist as they picked up another piece. Each shred of life will be handled with care.

"While the rabbis," said Auster, "have no solutions to the bombings, in their own quiet way those rabbis demonstrated yesterday that it is still possible, even in the most grisly scenes of death, to show respect for life." From this, for Auster, came hope.

pesolet (chips or trash) and לְךָ *lekha* (to thee) as meaning for you; i.e., God says to Moses, "The chips (broken pieces) are yours, Moses."

To this the midrash adds: From this did Moses become rich—for what were the tablets made of? They were made of the sapphire stones of which the throne of glory was made [*Ex. Rabba* 46.2]. **Answer two:** Moses kept the chips (the broken pieces).

TEXT THREE:
לוּחוֹת וְשִׁבְרֵי לוּחוֹת מֻנָּחִים בָּאָרוֹן *Luhot v'Shivrei ha-Luhot Munahin ba-Aron*. The (whole) tablets and the broken pieces of the tablets were kept in the ark. [*Menahot* 99a (also *Berakhot* 8b)]. And the text goes on to say that this shared occupancy represents the requirement to respect an old man who through the unavoidable circumstances of aging has forgotten what he once knew.

Answer three: The broken pieces of the tablets and the whole new tablets rested side by side in the ark.

So although the Torah itself makes no further mention of the broken pieces, Rabbinic sources provide us with three answers to the question of what happened to the pieces of the tablets of the law that Moses smashed on the ground.

Answer #1: There were two arks, one for the whole tablets and one for the broken tablets. **Answer #2:** Moses kept the pieces. **Answer #3:** The broken pieces and the whole pieces were kept side by side in the ark.

Which answer do you prefer? The minute I read text three I knew it as "right." The minute I read it I knew that there was one ark that held both—but it meant something entirely different to me. That is, I think the rabbis came to the right conclusion but had the wrong reason; I liked the *Mashal,* not the *Nimshal*. It isn't about respecting a scholar. I think the

SYNOPSIS: *We have rules for the census, the handwashing basin, the incense, and the anointing oil. We have rules for Shabbat. Finally, our plot continues with the physical reception of the Ten Commandments and the Golden Calf. Moses then reprises the reception of the Ten Commandments.*

RASHI OF THE WEEK:

In this sidrah we meet Betzalel: "SEE I HAVE CALLED BY NAME BETZALEL, SON OF URI, SON OF HUR, OF THE TRIBE OF JUDAH. I FILLED HIM WITH A GODLIKE SPIRIT, HAKHMAH (WISDOM), WITH BINAH (UNDERSTANDING), AND WITH DA'AT (KNOWLEDGE) OF EVERY KIND OF CRAFT." *Rashi reads and asks:* "What is the difference between HAKHMAH, BINAH, *and* DA'AT? *His answer:* HAKHMAH (wisdom) is what one person can learn from another. BINAH (understanding) is something that someone comes to understand on his own using intelligence and experience. DA'AT (knowledge) is that which comes from Divine inspiration and is gained by a visit from the Shekhinah.

Auster's column threw me back to Vicky Kelman's comments last week on this week's Torah portion in *Learn Torah With...* for even the broken pieces were put in the ark with the two whole tablets of stone. Careful, respectful people that we can be, we bury the pieces with the whole. Each little sliver is holy, sanctified, worthy. **Julie Auerbach.**

דָּבָר אַחֵר DAVAR AHER. **"WHEN YOU TAKE A CENSUS, LIFT UP THE HEADS OF THE FAMILIES OF ISRAEL ACCORDING TO THEIR NUMBER"** [Ex. 30.11]. This week the Torah opens, GOD SPOKE TO MOSES SAYING: "WHEN YOU TAKE A CENSUS, LIFT UP THE HEADS OF THE FAMILIES OF ISRAEL ACCORDING TO THEIR NUMBER—EVERY PERSON WILL ATONE FOR HIS/HER SOUL WHEN YOU ARE COUNTING THEM" [Ex. 30.11–12]. It evokes two questions. (1) Why does the literal phrase תִּשָּׂא אֶת-רֹאשׁ *Tisa et-Rosh* "LIFT UP A HEAD" come to mean "TAKE A CENSUS?" And (2) Why does a counted soul need to atone? Is demography really a sin? A story and a Hasidic insight: Last night we had a **C.Ha** editorial meeting in a private room in an Italian restaurant. The waiter was big on entertaining us. Each "service" brought an interruption in a conversation. He was being friendly. We were being patient. Nine kids and

right place for the broken pieces of the tablets was beside the new, whole set of tablets of the ark. The reality of one ark containing both strikes me as reflective of a deep human truth: Everyone carries broken pieces along with whole pieces in their ark, which is the human soul (or heart or psyche).

The broken pieces can't be left behind, thrown out, forgotten or atomized. They have to be taken along and kept beside the new and the whole. It is true on a national level, as in the story of this week's parashah, and it is true on a personal level in our individual lives.

The pieces are part of who we are. They go where we go. I think that the difference between people (individuals and nations) who can go on and those who can't is the difference in ability to keep each in its place. People who fall by the wayside are those who are so busy with the broken pieces that they are constantly being rewounded by the sharp edges, losing awareness that there is a new whole. People who go on are those who are able to hold onto the broken pieces and yet maintain concentration on the whole. Those broken pieces never loose their power to bruise, sometimes at the oddest, least expected times, but they never have the power to deny or overshadow the existence of the new whole. Each has its place.

The Jewish people got past the shattering experience of the Golden Calf. They were able to repair the ruptured relationships, but what had happened could never be wished away, undone, or forgotten. They had to carry the broken pieces of the first set of tablets, symbols of that rupture, into their new life. And for each of us as individuals, the broken pieces remain within us, in their place beside the whole, as we journey.

לוּחוֹת וְשִׁבְרֵי לוּחוֹת מֻנָּחִים בָּאָרוֹן *Luhot v'Shivrei ha-Luhot Munahin ba-Aron*. The tablets and the broken pieces of the tablets rest side by side in the Ark. ■

Ki Tissa

two adults is a strange gathering. He was trying to figure us out. When he came in during our talk about the Passover issue, he shouted: *"Landsmen! I'm half Jewish and half Italian."* Within thirty seconds the word *schvartzeh* had been thrown in to "prove our connection." That got rewarded—the shared look of embarrassment from nine kids (fourteen to eighteen) was the privilege, as was the conversation that followed.

The Avnei Ezel taught: "When one counts and organizes Jews into a community, they are raised up and exalted. They no longer have to hang their heads in shame. When an individual joins the community, their head is lifted up." It is a lovely

Rabbi Ed Feinstein

Rabbi Ed Feinstein is a rabbi at Congregation Valley Beth Shalom in Encino, California and teaches at the University of Judaism, Los Angeles, CA.

The elegant architecture of the Book of Exodus: Four weekly Torah portions tell the story of the Exodus from Egypt. Two portions relate the revelation at Mt. Sinai. Four portions describe the building of the *Miskhan*—God's dwelling place among the people Israel. A perfect symmetry, both literary and theological. In four portions of Torah God enters history to redeem His people. As He did at the beginning of Genesis, He brings order out of chaos by dividing the waters.

There in Genesis He separated the physical/metaphysical waters to create an inhabitable world. Here in Exodus He divides the turbulent waters of human events to create moral history. Two portions form the book's fulcrum. Two portions in which God shares His dream—a holy people, a kingdom of priests. And in the four closing portions, Israel responds, building the *Mishkan*—our own act of creation, fashioning a world of rite and of right. Again, with perfect symmetry two portions lay out the instructions, two portions describe their precise fulfillment. Exodus is order, precision, symmetry, balance. Ten weekly Torah portions. Ten Commandments; ten words of creation. It is good.

Ah, but wait, there's an eleventh portion. Jammed between the instructions of *Terumah/Tetzaveh* and the constructions of *Va-Yak-hel/Pekudei* there's an extra Torah portion. *Ki Tissa* clearly doesn't belong. It breaks the narrative flow, brutally interrupting the construction of the *Mishkan*. The surrounding portions are distinguished by the pious,

---

little piece of *musar*—half the truth. (Not a half-truth.) The other half of the truth is that when you see only your community, you will have something to repent for. We seem to be losing our ability to balance universalism and particularism. Evidently sound bites only have time for half the truth. And half the truth only rushes toward a half-truth. So hold your head up high and then repent! The penne was very good. **Joel Lurie Grishaver, <joel@torahaura.com>**

דָּבָר אַחֵר DAVAR AHER. And God spoke to Moses and said: "When you take a census of the children of Israel, every man shall give a ransom for his soul...every one half a shekel...as an offering to God, every one who is twenty years old or older shall give this offering...The rich shall not give more, nor the poor less...as an expiation for their persons [Ex. 30.11–16]. ***The Sin of War.*** A seemingly banal statement, an order to collect money for the sanctuary. However,

methodical, determined fulfillment of God's word. (For the only time in history, Jews are actually commanded to stop giving contributions!) *Ki Tissa* is anything but. *Ki Tissa's* temper is hotter—filled with fear, anger, envy, despair, and at the end, healing. A frightened, faithless people conclude that "that man Moses" isn't returning from atop the quaking Sinai, and they gather against Aaron and force him (or did he cooperate? After all, how long can a man be expected to play second fiddle to his younger brother?) to create the Golden Calf. God's wrathful intention to annihilate the untrusting people is turned by Moses. Moses descends the mountain, drops the holy tablets, and punishes his people.

For what? What, exactly, was the sin of the Golden Calf? What, after all, is the difference between the idolatrous Golden Calf and the sanctified *Mishkan*? Was the Calf any more a pagan image than the cherubim that sat on the cover of the holy Ark? At least in Aaron's mind, the Golden Calf was not itself a god any more than the cherubim of the Ark. Like the cherubim, the Calf was understood as a "footstool"—a place above which God's presence dwelt. That's how Aaron, having completed the Calf, could announce that "TOMORROW SHALL BE A FESTIVAL OF THE LORD" [32.5]. So what was the sin?

In real estate they say that the three most important facts are location, location, location. Look again at the location of this story. Jammed into the narrative of *Mishkan*-building, *Ki Tissa* is offered as a midrash on the building of the Mishkan—a warning about the construction of all sacred symbols. Jammed into the exquisite architecture of Exodus, *Ki Tissa* is a warning about the construction of history.

Any symbol can become an idol. Perhaps Aaron envisioned the Calf as the Lord's footstool, but the people declared, "This is your god,

---

Ki Tissa

there are some disturbing questions. Why only men over the age of twenty? And why exactly half a shekel (about the value of a quarter ounce of silver) even from those who could give more?

We know that in biblical terms twenty was the age when a man was considered able and obligated to take up arms in war. In other words, a census of able-bodied men over twenty could only be seen as preparation for armed conflict.

And consider the time. The Israelites are in the Sinai desert, having been recently freed from Egyptian bondage, not by their own fighting efforts, but by the hand of God. They now receive at Sinai the commandments and instructions that will turn their tribes into a single people; from now on they will have to fight their own wars, with

O Israel, who brought you out of the land of Egypt!" Mixing up the symbol for its referent—confusing the sanctity of the symbol for the holiness of its object—embracing the part and forsaking the Whole—is the clinical definition of idolatry. And humanity has a nasty readiness to sacrifice life in defense of its idols.

But the most powerful and vicious idols are made not of gold or stone or wood. They are made of history. *Ki Tissa*, the eleventh portion, the portion that doesn't fit, is a scream of protest against constructions of history promising certainty, simplicity and control—constructions that deny the complexity of human existence, the freedom of the human imagination, and the sanctity of the human being. So neat, so elegant, so simple, so tyrannical, so cruel, so murderous. National socialism. Dialectical materialism. Social Darwinism. *Ki Tissa* is a warning about the deadly idolatries of historical construction. And we have the experience of the twentieth century, humanity's ugliest and bloodiest, to testify to *Ki Tissa's* truth. ■

---

the blessing of God, it is hoped, but with their own bodies, welding their own arms, and risking their own lives.

But why expiation? Other peoples—the Egyptians themselves, the ancient Greeks and Romans, and others—paid their soldiers for taking up arms. (And of course, all modern nations including the United States do so today.) The word "soldier" is itself derived from the ancient Latin name of this payment, the *solidus*. Then why were our ancestors required to pay half a shekel as an *atonement for becoming soldiers*?

This leads us to the question of war itself. What is war in the frame of Jewish ethics? How did our ancestors relate to the shedding of blood in battle? Basing itself on biblical sources, the Talmud distinguishes two kinds of war: obligatory war (*Milhemet Hovah*) and discretionary war (*Milhemet Reshut*). The first includes basically all defensive wars, the second wars of conquest. Thus, for example, King David's war against the invading Philistines was considered an obligatory war. Years later, when he set out to enlarge his kingdom, it was considered discretionary. And there are, as usual in discussions of Jewish subjects, a number of open questions. What about pre-emptive wars? (Maimondies has one opinion; others differ.) And how about the original conquest of the Promised Land (the war against the seven nations—Hivites, Jebusites, etc.)? And how about the command to destroy the tribe of Amalek who attacked the poorly protected rear of the Israelites in the desert?

But in both types of wars blood is shed, and the Torah forbids the shedding of human blood. And so the soldier does his atonement not after having killed, but before. Joining an army, one does not know if one will, or will not kill. And even those who do not directly participate in the killing help in it indirectly by being part of the military organization. It makes no difference whether this is obligatory or discretionary war. And another indicative point—the Hebrew word used for expiation in Exodus 30 is כֹּפֶר *kofer*, the same word used for expiation in cases of the unintended, accidental killing of another person. And so all men over twenty, the potential soldiers, pay the half shekel in expiation for the potential sin of killing a human, even an enemy, even if causing that death indirectly.

Thus a seemingly unimportant detail in Torah can take on important ethical dimensions upon further study. War is still with us in many parts of the world; perhaps it is part of the human condition. And if so, we as Jews have to learn from the teachings of our tradition that the shedding of human blood cannot be mitigated by political aims. That is not pacifism; our history has taught us that we must fight when attacked—not as an ennobling and praiseworthy experience, but as a necessary evil, a *Milhemet Hovah*. And our sorrow, as Jews, at having to kill and hurt in self-defense will serve as some sort of expiation, our half-shekel כֹּפֶר *kofer*, if you will. **David Jordan, Haworth, NJ.**

Ki Tissa

דָּבָר אַחֵר DAVAR AHER. THE ENTIRE PEOPLE REMOVED THE GOLD RINGS THAT WERE IN THEIR EARS, AND BROUGHT THEM TO AARON. HE TOOK IT FROM THEIR HANDS AND BOUND IT UP IN A CLOTH, AND FASHIONED IT INTO A MOLTEN CALF. THEY SAID, "THIS IS YOUR GOD, O ISRAEL, WHICH BROUGHT YOU UP FROM THE LAND OF EGYPT." [Ex. 23.3]. One way to understand the relationship between the Mishkan and the Golden Calf is that from seeing the Calf, God ruefully accepts that the people need a physical focus for their experience of God—and gives them the Mishkan in place of a calf. In this approach, the story as we have it in the Torah is "out of order," chronologically reversed.

But try turning this around, accepting the chronology as it appears in Torah: Mishkan first, Calf second. Why do the people need a calf anyway? Because Moshe's long absence frightens them. And why is Moshe away so long? Look at the text of what Moshe hears upon the mountain, and we see that perhaps three-fourths of it is God's description of the Mishkan! If the description had been briefer, perhaps as sketchy as the rules of *Mishpatim* about how to shape a sacred society, Moshe could have come down after perhaps 20 days, not 40! The people might never have become so frightened.

Why does the Torah describe God as taking so much time and space to describe the Divine Indwelling Place?

Perhaps the Mishkan was, כִּבְיָכוֹל *k'v'yahol* (if we dared to be able to say it), God's own golden calf, God's own triumphalist idol. Even the God Who has all earth and heaven for a dwelling place can swell with pride at imagining the place where one small people will come to worship with the Presence. And the people? Dimly, from the foot of the mountain, they hear the overtones, a blur: "Plenty of gold? Uh-huh. And something about horns? Must be a golden bull-calf!"

So they build it. For God as well as us, the truth is firm: what you sow, that you shall reap. Or to put it in another way, certainly earth is spirit, but there needs to be a physical context for the spiritual path. (A "path" is very earthy.)

But do not get addicted to the physicality, do not turn the earthen altar into golden splendor, do not become a "spiritual materialist" who piles up the golden moments of spiritual experiences as if they were gold, to be held tight, possessed, sought for their own sake.

Do not spend all your time imagining God's house instead of making society a home for human beings! For if you do, the addiction, no matter how spiritual it may have been at the beginning, no matter how inspired by God, will degenerate into an atavistic idol. **Rabbi Arthur Waskow, <Awaskow@aol.com>**

דָּבָר אַחֵר DAVAR AHER. "AND I HAVE ALSO GRANTED WISDOM TO ALL WHO HAVE A HEART OF WISDOM, THAT THEY MAY MAKE EVERYTHING I HAVE COMMANDED YOU." [Ex. 31.6]. The rabbis said, God grants wisdom to those in whom wisdom is already present. New paradigm rising. Wisdom is present within, make room for your God-given wisdom to rise. Clear out the space. The Shekhinah rests in the prepared space. New paradigm rising. Not vertical, hierarchical, professional, but horizontal, collaborative, shared. The shared truth, lurking within us all. Clear out the space quietly, make room for the wisdom to rise. God says, whatever you seek, you already have. I place it within you, I have granted wisdom to all who have a heart of wisdom, I breathed it into you. Be silent and allow your wisdom to rise. There is only the silence and the knowledge that what you seek, you are. New paradigm rising, God says, be still and be found. **James Stone Goodman, <Stavisker@aol.com>**

דָּבָר אַחֵר DAVAR AHER. Between Me and the Children of Israel it is a sign forever that in a six-day period God made heaven and earth, and on the seventh day He rested and was refreshed." [Ex. 31.17]. "What is Shabbat?" asked Bar Yochai. The suspension of work, or the attention to holy matters? Or something even more holy? IT IS A SIGN FOREVER...[Ex. 31.17]. After years of hiding from the Romans in a cave, Bar Yochai emerged into the hot, narcotic Palestinian night. "What needs to be done?" he asked. There was a cemetery that was not carefully bordered. There was danger of ritual contamination. Bar Yochai went to work and marked the borders of the cemetery. "What else?" he asked. The Romans were still in the land. He returned to his home. There, with his son and a devoted assistant, he worked the ancient manuscripts. He wrote small commentaries on the texts, took lunch in the sunshine, tended a garden and watched his son grow. When he died, it was said that he had spent his better days observing the Shabbat, believing that if he could only observe two Sabbaths properly, the world would be redeemed. "The Shabbat is a celebration of sacred marriage," said Bar Yochai. He taught that the Shabbat said before the Holy One, "Master-of-the-Universe, everyone has a mate, except me. The Holy One said, "Israel shall be your mate," as it is said, "Remember the Shabbat, to betroth it." "Every human union recapitulates the divine union, the celebration of sacred marriage," said Bar Yochai "In your prayers, when you say בָּרוּךְ אֶת הַשֵּׁם *Barkhu Et Ha-Shem* you bless first אֶת *Et* which is Shekhinah, then you bless Ha-Shem which is *Ha-Kadosh Barukh Hu*, the She and the He of Godliness. When you pray Barkhu, when you say it, you initiate union there, as it is here. This is the secret connection: every human union recapitulates Divine union." Sometimes initiates it. **James Stone Goodman, <Stavisker@aol.com>**

דָּבָר אַחֵר DAVAR AHER. They were tablets written on both their sides. [Ex. 32.15]. The Ten Commandments were weird. That was the whole idea. Mystical commentaries abound with the deep "meanings" of their being written by God's hand—of their being written on both sides. Rashi quotes the Talmud, saying, "THEY WERE CARVED IN SUCH A WAY THAT THE SAME CARVING COULD BE READ ON BOTH SIDES." That is some weird topography. Just imagine the twists and turns that takes. These are mobius letters. Or they twist into n-space. Or something. Personally, I just don't know. (Mysticism is not my thing, but mystical special effects are fun—they give Industrial Light and Magic something to aim for.) I can dig the fact that, like the Commandments, people are written on both sides, three-dimensional, etched by God's hands. I can also see the real mitzvot (not the words, but the commanded actions, attitudes, and realities) being written on both sides, too. Fasting on Yom Kippur can be good, or it can go over to the dark side. Keeping Shabbat can be a liberation from the workday week, or it can be a kind of solitary confinement. Context and meaning can change a mitzvah. Giving tzedakah can "save a person from death," or it can be an obscene manipulation which destroys self-esteem and imposes your manipulative will on others—all in the name of goodness. Fasting on Yom Kippur can make you humble, can let you really live your inner-life, can be all light. Or fasting can become an Olympic event, an excuse for competition, pride, hurt, and darkness.

Everything has two sides: the holy, and the other side. Mystics call it the *sitra aharah*—but that is just Aramaic for "the other side." The Zohar teaches that "The Torah was written in black fire on white fire." In my life, I have felt Torah twinkle like the evening star (and I have wished on it). I have warmed myself in Torah light, like sunbathing at high noon. I have felt the Torah go super nova and threaten to destroy all human life. I have definitely been scorched by Torah. I have also seen Torah as a cold red orb, sinking away from me. I have had my Torah sunset moments. And I have felt the tug of the dark black hole of Torah, the vortex of Torah into which one can disappear. I can understand a two-sided, double-edged Torah, which twists in its inner life to allow itself to be read on each side. I understand a Torah engineered to allow us to always have a way in—though almost never a way out. My question, though, is which side of the tablets was Moses showing to the rest of the world? **Joel Lurie Grishaver, <gris@torahaura.com>**

דָּבָר אַחֵר DAVAR AHER. **You cannot see My face, for man may not see Me and live.** [Ex. 33.20]. *Shabbat Hol Ha-Moed Pesah*: It is only once our Seder celebrations are concluded that many people begin to experience the true liberation of Passover. After all, it was not an easy project to make our homes ready for the holiday, to prepare our Seder meals, and, of equal importance, to plan the content and conversations of our Sedarim. So now it is Shabbat and Pesah. A time to refresh ourselves, reflect on the joys and meanings of our festival and share in the dream of redeeming our world.

As we acknowledged at our Seder table, redeeming the world requires our effort everyday in partnership with God. It also means that we have to understand something about religious faith. The Torah portrays God as the author of each plague, but it is Moses who has to challenge the Pharaoh. The Torah describes to us how God parted the Red Sea, but it is Israel who has to have the courage to walk through to their future.

In the Haggadah we read that "in every generation a person must feel as though he or she had been redeemed from Egypt." Our retelling of the Exodus story is not for memory alone, but for the inspiration we need to understand our opportunities and accept our responsibilities today. In the Torah portion we read on this Shabbat Hol Ha-Moed Pesah, Moses too seeks to confirm his relationship with God in order to continue his task.

In Exodus 33.2–23, Moses asks to see God's ways, to be shown God's glory. In support of Moses' request God offers to let him and Israel experience the journey of their lives with the Divine Presence. But God's face we cannot see, "for man shall not see Me and live," Moses is told.

I have always learned from this vignette in the Torah the abstract and spiritual nature of my Jewish faith. For all of the Torah's anthropomorphic descriptions of God, it is the metaphor of the text and the Torah's religious imagination that touches me. Faith is not fact, I always declare. What I believe is that which I know in my life and the life of my people to be true. True to my experience, true to my instincts and common sense, true to the ideals of my dreams and desires for God's presence in our world.

Ki Tissa

Today we seek nothing less than Moses. We want to confirm our relationship with God in the work that we each do, in the struggles and achievements we know everyday, on our family and social relationships and in the covenant of the Jewish heritage we share. To do this requires that we recapture a sense of the religious imagination that our ancestors used in telling us the truths—but not necessarily the facts—of their lives, their experiences, and their religious faith.

I'll tell you a story that I made up. It's based on something incredible that took place not so long ago.

Some years ago there lived in Ethiopia an impoverished group of Jews who believed that they were the final and only remnant of the Jewish people. They lived in the worst conditions of suffering through famine, political oppression, isolation, and disease. They didn't know about the comforts of life we take for granted, such as plumbing, electricity, and every other modern convenience. They also didn't know that there were other Jews, many of whom were prosperous and well, spread throughout the larger world.

This group of Ethiopian Jews knew the Torah, but not the Talmud or later Jewish traditions. For the most part, they had been cut off from the history of our people. They spoke their own language and organized their own religious lives, and yet they lived a Jewish lifestyle fully recognizable to other Jews who came to know them.

These people also dreamt of their redemption. They believed there was a Promised Land, an Israel, to which God would one day deliver them. Their Exodus from poverty, famine, and oppression would be to a land flowing with milk and honey, freedom, and a better future.

One day, messengers of God began appearing in their village. These messengers spoke of other Jews in the world. They told stories of a real place called Israel. They held out the promise of redemption—if only they could organize the people to prepare for what would be a hasty departure.

Then, one night in the darkness, God made large birds appear in the sky. The birds swooped down into the village and swallowed the Jews of Ethiopia into their bellies. These birds then flew away and carried the Jews of Ethiopia from their oppression.

Passover's meaning does not lie in the facts of how the Exodus occurred. Passover's purpose is found in the faith it teaches us to express. To confirm God's presence in our experiences means using our own religious imaginations to describe the truths we believe in, and by which we ought to live.

At our Sedarim we spoke of freedom and equality. We discussed the imperatives of social justice and human dignity. We retold to our children and to ourselves the most compelling story we know in order to teach these very lessons.

Now, during the rest of our Passover holiday, it is time to tell the stories of our lives and the lives of our families, communities, people, and society. In our stories we will discover our values. In our narratives we will explore our dreams. In our tales we will find the truths of our won circumstances. Our values, our dreams, and our truths—each of us can contribute to these in a religious partnership with God, can contribute to the redemption of our world. *Shabbat Shalom. Hag Sameah.* **Rabbi Ronald Shulman, Los Angeles, CA.**

דָּבָר אַחֵר DAVAR AHER. "**Then I will take my hand away and you will see my back; but My face must not be seen.**" [Ex. 33.23]. God's back: While reading the Passover parashah about Moses' encounter with God, the following thoughts occurred to me regarding Exodus 33.23.

I wondered why, of all the ways God could have shown himself to Moses, does He choose to show him his back?

The answer came to me while recapping the major events that transpired just prior to this portion of Exodus.

The impatient Israelites had just been caught dancing around the Golden Calf, thus enraging God to the point of God wanting to destroy them all. Moses learns that his own brother, Aaron, not only allowed it to happen, but even fabricated the idol. Then there's the slaying of the 3000 who would not rally to God. As if that were not enough, Moses, as their leader, had to endure the knowledge that it would be only a future generation, not this generation, that would finally enter the Promised Land. All of this, for Moses,

Ki Tissa

must have been seriously disheartening.

Moses enters the Tent of Meeting to commune with God. In his despair and probable aggravation with the situation Moses asks God for clarification. He asks, "What is Your plan? What is it that You want me to do so that I may fulfill Your plan and continue in Your favor? You say that You have singled me out by name to lead these people and that I have gained Your favor. Help me understand what it is that You want."

God, sensing Moses' feelings, said, "I WILL GO IN THE LEAD AND LIGHTEN YOUR BURDEN" [Ex. 33.14]. And in an effort to revive the spirit of Moses, God says that God will make all of God's goodness pass before him. But the apprehension of God is a powerful and overwhelming experience, and even Moses cannot comprehend looking directly at the face of God and living.

To protect Moses, God covers Moses' eyes instead of having Moses close his own eyes to ensure that he does not accidentally look God in the face and die. God even puts him in the cleft of a rock as a safe place, a sort of cradle, to protect Moses from looking left or right so that he doesn't inadvertently see more of God than he can grasp. If even the profile of God should be seen, it could be too much, and serious harm could befall Moses. Finally, when the protecting hand of God is removed from the eyes of Moses, Moses sees the back of God. A strong back, a back that is a symbol of the strength of God. Shown to Moses so that he too could share in God's strength and be revitalized. A powerful back, the back that will help lead and lighten the burden of the future journey.

Even though the days of Moses crossing the desert have long passed, it is comforting to believe that God's influence and strength are still somehow up in front of us, leading the way. The "back of God," the strength of God that God shares with us is seen every time we pull together as a community to overcome the modern trials of Jewish life. Each time we pull together we take another step to strengthen our own collective future. **Randolph Rothschild, Congregant of Temple Beth El, Las Cruces, New Mexico.**

דָּבָר אַחֵר DAVAR AHER. **THE LORD PASSED BEFORE HIM AND PROCLAIMED: "THE LORD, THE LORD, A GOD COMPASSIONATE AND GRACIOUS, SLOW TO ANGER, ABOUNDING IN KINDNESS AND FAITHFULNESS; EXTENDING KINDNESS TO THE THOUSANDTH GENERATION, FORGIVING INIQUITY, TRANSGRESSION, AND SIN; YET HE DOES NOT REMIT ALL PUNISHMENT, BUT VISITS THE INIQUITY OF FATHERS UPON CHILDREN AND CHILDREN'S CHILDREN, UPON THE THIRD AND FOURTH GENERATIONS"** [Ex. 34.6-7]. *ADULT BAT MITZVAH DRASH*: I chose this week's parashah for my bat mitzvah because it contained a subject that has intrigued me for some time. The topic is actually in the fifth aliyah. The action takes place just after the Golden Calf debacle, when Moses goes back up on Mt. Sinai to get the second set of commandments and begs to behold God's presence. Moses is not permitted to see God's face, but Moses is allowed to view God's back, or God's presence, as it passes by him.

What Moses then sees, or experiences, is what has come to be known as "God's divine attributes" or the nature of God. After naming God three times, יהוה, יהוה, אֵל *Adonai, Adonai, El*, the Torah specifies that God is רַחוּם *Rahum*, compassionate; חַנּוּן *Hanun*, gracious; אֶרֶךְ אַפַּיִם *Erekh Apayin*, slow to anger, giving people an opportunity to repent; רַב-חֶסֶד *Rav-Hesed*, abounding in kindness; אֱמֶת *Emet*, truth, נֹצֵר חֶסֶד לָאֲלָפִים *Notzer Hesed la-Alafim*, extending kindness to the thousandth generation; נֹשֵׂא עָוֺן וָפֶשַׁע וְחַטָּאָה *Nosei Avon va-Fesha ve-Hata-ah*, forgiving iniquity, transgression, and sin; and וְנַקֵּה לֹא יְנַקֶּה *ve-Nakeh Lo Yenakeh*, yet does not remit all punishment, i.e., there are limits to God's mercy.

Jewish tradition has distinguished thirteen different divine attributes from this verse, but the exact number and nature of these have been a matter of intense discussion among Jewish scholars starting with Philo almost two thousand years ago. In the twelfth century Maimonides devoted ten pages to deliberating the attributes in his *Guide to the Perplexed*, then claimed that they only showed that God was ultimately unknowable; that is, human beings cannot really know what God is. The thirteen attributes interpret only God's actions, not God's being. Others have agreed with the view, interpreting God's face to mean God's essence and God's back to mean God's deeds.

In the eighteenth century Moses Sofer, the Hatam Sofer, took this interpretation even further, asserting that God's back is God's actions in history, and that we cannot know God from current events, only from a long historical view. Sofer believed that we will only be able to see the truth of God's ways in retrospect and at the end of days, in the messianic time, when we will have the full perspective of history behind us. Moses Sofer was the leader of Orthodox Jewry at this time and an ardent opponent of Reform Judaism and innovation of any kind. What I see as his interpretation of these verses is, in other words, "If the great Moses couldn't see God's face, don't you get any bright ideas that you're likely to either, or at least not until the Messiah comes."

Nachmanides, in his thirteenth-century commentary on the Torah, sees the three names of God listed first in the verse as synonymous with God's *midot* (attributes)—that is, God of Goodness, God of Mercy, and God of Repentance.

However, Nachmanides was a Kabbalist, and he wrote that this section of scripture cannot possibly be grasped by one who has not heard the secrets of the Torah—in other words, by one who has not studied the mystic traditions of the Kabbalah.

Actually, I wasn't inspired by any of the traditional interpretations of these verses. To go back to the text in Exodus 34.7, God visits the iniquity of the parents on their children, upon the third and fourth generations. This is obviously a difficulty; how can God be compassionate, merciful, forgiving, etc., yet punish children for their parents' sins? As the Talmudic Rabbis say, "*La Kasha*," "No problem!" In the Book of Ezekiel, chapter 18, the prophet addresses this contradiction directly. God tells Ezekiel that a son who sees the sins his father has committed but takes heed and does not imitate them obeys God's rules, and he does not die for the iniquity of his father but shall live. Then Ezekiel even asks God, "WHY HAS NOT THE SON SHARED THE BURDEN OF HIS FATHER'S GUILT?" And God answers, "BUT THE SON HAS DONE WHAT IS RIGHT, HE SHALL LIVE."

Several books later, in Jonah, chapter 4, Jonah recounts the Divine attributes from our parashah, but he ends with "renouncing punishment" instead of "visiting the sins of the fathers on their descendants." In fact, the rabbis who compiled our liturgy reinforced this theology that each of us is responsible for our own sins and not those of our ancestors in the High Holiday prayerbook. On Rosh ha-Shanah, between the Avinu Malkeinu and the Torah reading, we pray the thirteen attributes, starting out with the wording of Exodus 34, but ending as amended by Jonah.

This is all interesting stuff, but the question that engaged my mind on this subject is, "Why are these particular thirteen attributes shown to Moses out of all the many and varied Divine attributes that are found in the whole *Tanakh*?"

And by extension, why are they shown to us? The Torah is a

Ki Tissa

summary of God's attributes, some of them virtues, but some of them ones we'd rather see less of in the world. We read that God is, at times, impassioned, jealous, angry, wrathful, vengeful, provoked, fierce, and even cruel. It seems that God in the *Tanakh* spends a lot more time being wrathful than slow to anger and can appear to be more vengeful than gracious. But my purpose here was not to judge God's behavior. God only knows why God does what God does or doesn't do. I wanted to understand what is so unique about the attributes in this verse. I found some clues in verses from other books of the Torah.

In the first chapter of Genesis we read that we are created in God's image. The commentaries have put in a lot of discussion on this subject, since it's obvious that God doesn't have a body, or even a mind that is anything like a human being's. The Kabbalists draw a comparison between man's body and the various *sefirot*, and this metaphor may be useful for meditation. But for me, God tells us that we are made in God's image for a purpose, and that purpose is revealed when God's presence passes before Moses. The way I see it, the image of God is those attributes. When we are compassionate, gracious, and abounding in kindness, it is because of God's image in us. When we recognize, speak, and respect the truth, it is because of God's image in us. We must judge and punish evildoers, but more so, we must forgive.

In Numbers 6.24, in the priestly benediction, we ask for the blessing of God's presence (literally God's face) to shine עָלֶיךָ *Alekha*, usually translated as upon us. But my concordance shows that עַל *Al* could be translated as "concerning," "on account of," or even "because of." With this interpretation we find that we have the capacity to make God's presence shine not only upon us, but because of us. Most of us want to experience God's presence, and for many of us God's presence passes before us only occasionally and fleetingly, if at all. But God has told us how to accomplish this in our parashah. When we are slow to anger rather than provoked, gracious instead of wrathful, kind not cruel, and, most importantly, when we are forgiving instead of vengeful, then God's image in us shines through us upon others. And when another person has been compassionate, truthful, and merciful towards us, particularly when they could easily have treated us otherwise, we have seen God's presence pass before us.

Have you ever been daydreaming while driving on the freeway when suddenly you realize that you're going to need to cut across several lanes of traffic rather quickly to get to your off-ramp? And when you attempt this maneuver, the drivers in the other lanes let you through rather than honking at you or perhaps making a rude gesture? Okay, maybe you're a great driver, and you were one of the guys in the other lanes who got cut off. You see, we yearn to see God's face, or even God's back, yet we do not recognize it when these kinds of things happen. To paraphrase our ancestor Jacob, surely God's presence is in many places, maybe even on the L.A. freeways, and we do not know it.

In summary, I think that this parashah shows us how to see God's presence in other people's actions and to make God's presence apparent to others through our own behavior. We don't need to wait for the Messiah to come first. **Maggie Parkhurst, <MagPrkrst@aol.com>**

דָּבָר אַחֵר DAVAR AHER. And it came to pass, when Moses came down from mount Sinai with the two tables of the testimony in Moses' hand, when he came down from the mount, that Moses knew not that the skin of his face sent forth beams while God talked with him [Ex. 34.29]. Sometimes the most obvious thing passes our notice. For instance, as I was perusing the section of Torah where Moses comes down from the mountain after receiving instruction to re-carve the Tablets of the Law, I saw something that was always there but never registered.

It says that when Moses came down BEARING THE TWO TABLETS OF THE LAW, MOSES WAS NOT AWARE THAT HE HAD קֶרֶן אוֹר *KAREN OR*. The JPS translation has this as "radiant skin," but this does not quite capture the dramatic picture the Hebrew paints. *Karen or* is, of course, a ray or beam of light. It never occurred to me that he was unaware of what he possessed! I now wonder how it is possible for Moses to have had this unique physical feature and not know! So pronounced was it that when he came down from the mountain AARON AND ALL THE CHIEFTAINS SHRANK FROM COMING NEAR HIM [Ex. 34.30].

Tradition holds that Moses brought back the second set of tablets on Yom Kippur (see Rashi). As I studied this passage one day after Yom Kippur, a familiar chord was struck. The Yom Kippur liturgy exhorts us to be less selfish and more humble. How illustrative of this idea is Moses' ignorance of the light that shone forth from his face. He came down from Sinai with a mission to his people after a lengthy second absence (Ramban says that he was up at Sinai for so long because he did not learn the whole Torah on the first round!). His focus was outward, not inward. On the holiest day of the year Moses was oblivious to his own appearance and focused on bringing Torah to the Jewish people.

We sometimes spend too much time worrying about the blemish on our face or whether or not we are wearing the right clothes or driving the right car and less about the blemish of our vanity. And if we excel, how often we make sure that everyone knows about our own beams of goodness and insight. Moses did not know about the beams because of his humility. But even more than this, he was so preoccupied with bringing Torah to his people that his shocking appearance meant little. And even when he was made aware of it by Aaron and the chieftains, his response was that HE SPOKE TO THEM AND INSTRUCTED THEM CONCERNING WHAT THE LORD HAD IMPARTED TO HIM ON MT. SINAI [Ex. 34.32]. **Rabbi Cy Stanway, Temple Beth El, Las Cruces, NM.**

בני ישראל ויאמר אלהם

Parashat Va-Yak-hel

Exodus 35.1–38.20

David Kraemer

DAVID KRAEMER IS ASSOCIATE PROFESSOR OF TALMUD AND RABBINICS AT THE JEWISH THEOLOGICAL SEMINARY AND A SENIOR PROGRAM ASSOCIATE AT CLAL. HE IS THE AUTHOR OF *THE MIND OF THE TALMUD: AN INTELLECTUAL HISTORY OF THE BAVLI* AND OF THE RECENTLY PUBLISHED *RESPONSES TO SUFFERING IN CLASSICAL RABBINIC LITERATURE* (BOTH OXFORD UNIVERSITY PRESS).

Perhaps the best known feature of *Parashat Va-Yak-hel*—though many may not realize that it appears in this parashah—is the juxtaposition of the prohibition of Shabbat labor with the directions concerning the erection of the tabernacle. This juxtaposition, it is widely repeated, lies at the origin of the categories of work prohibited on Shabbat: If such labor was performed in connection to the tabernacle, that same sort of labor is prohibited on Shabbat.

To be sure, if you compare the Mishnah's list of categories of prohibited Shabbat labor with the directions articulated in this parashah, you will have a very difficult time finding such a correspondence. But the rabbis saw what we may not (some will claim), so we may rest assured that the system is a coherent one.

Actually, the story is considerably more complex than just suggested. The Torah, you may well know, does not elaborate on what it means when it prohibits *melakhah* (work or labor) on Shabbat. Nor may such an elaboration be found elsewhere in the *Tanakh*. The first complete listing of labors prohibited on Shabbat is found in the Mishnah [*Shabbat* 7.2], and, though some of its categories are in evidence in earlier documents (the *Tanakh*, the Dead Sea Scrolls), the Mishnah's systematic presentation is apparently original to the rabbis. We may

---

דָּבָר אַחֵר DAVAR A<u>H</u>ER. "EVERY WISE-HEARTED PERSON AMONG YOU SHALL COME AND MAKE EVERYTHING THAT GOD HAS COMMANDED" [Ex. 35.10]. The word חָכְמָה <u>H</u>okhma, wisdom, is applied to the artisans who are charged with putting together the Mishkan—the portable sanctuary that accompanied the Israelites through the wilderness on their way to the Promised Land. The sense is that wisdom and artistic skills go hand in hand. In general, wisdom is applied to intellectual capability, not art.

In the Talmud (*Tamid* 32a) the Rabbis ask, "Who is the wise person? The one who sees what is yet to be." I do not believe they were linking wisdom with fortune-telling, but rather with seeing future consequences of present action. An artist generally sees the portrait or project as it will turn out if she or he uses

thus read this mishnah as a sort of Rabbinic commentary on the Torah's term, *melakhah*.

The problem is, the mishnah merely offers us a list of categories of prohibited labor without any rule or general principle to explain what is prohibited and what is not. In other words, the rabbis of the mishnah do not comment on their own commentary, and it is therefore left to later generations—including our own—to make sense of the mishnah's system. What, then, is the principle that is manifest in the system of prohibited acts? Is the mishnah's list truly derived from the work of the tabernacle? Or does the Shabbat, as symbolized by its prohibited labors, perhaps articulate some other principle or set of values?

The Mishnah, on a few occasions, does indeed hint at the connection of its prohibitions with the labor of the tabernacle. But the mishnah that elaborates the categories of prohibited labor makes no mention of such an association, and some of its categories actually seem to contradict the claim that the Tabernacle is the source. We shall return to this later. But first, how do the rabbis themselves understand the origin of the "thirty-nine categories of labor" that the mishnah lists?

The *Talmud Yerushalmi* [*Shabbat* 7.2] suggests three possible sources: (1) the number of times the word *melakhah* appears in the Torah; (2) the number of times the words *melakhah* or *avodah* (also "work") appear in connection with the tabernacle; or (3) a *gematria* (=counting of the numerical value of letters) relating to the word "these" in verse 1 of chapter 35 in this parashah. What is crucial in these suggested sources is not the

---

certain colors or certain materials in certain ways.

It is said that each of us paints a portrait of life with the details of daily activity. The wise person is thus anyone who thinks not so much about the details of life as about the way those details come together to form a portrait of life, a work of art that we enhance each and every day by what we choose to do.

As we study and learn we must keep the overall picture of life in mind; it is the wise thing to do.

Rabbi Rick Sherwin,
<rbirick@aztec.asu.edu>

SYNOPSIS: *Va-Yak-hel: More Shabbat review. The actual work of constructing the Mishkan. The limitation of donations.*

RASHI OF THE WEEK: *In Exodus 35.30 the Torah reintroduces Betzalel by telling us* HE WAS THE SON OF URI WHO WAS THE SON OF HUR FROM THE TRIBE OF JUDAH. *Usually, we are only given a single generation when we identify a person—Rashi asks—who was Hur and why are we told about him. He answers it very simply*—Hur was Miriam's son. *But, that is not the end of the answer. At verse 34 we meet Oholiav. We are told:* OHOLIAV, THE SON OF AHISAMAKH OF THE TRIBE OF DAN (35) WAS ALSO WISE OF HEART AND SKILLED TO DO EVERY CRAFT...*In describing Oholiav, we learn about Hur and about Betzalel. Rashi says,* "The Eternal put Oholiav as the equal to Betzalel to share in all the work of the Mishkan." Betzalel came from Judah, the most noble of tribes, Oholiav came from Dan, a lowly tribe. This teaches the lesson found in Job 34:19: "THE NOBLEMAN IS NOT RECOGNIZED AHEAD OF THE PAUPER.". *But, there is more to the Hur story. Hur was Aaron's equal. He held up the other one of Moses' hand when Aaron held up the other—when Israel defeated Amalek. Later, when Aaron makes compromises with the Golden Calf—Hur is killed trying to prevent it. The story here is simple, Hur was famous; Ahisamakh was an unknown. For Israel to meet God—all must be involved: famous and ordinary, nobleman and layperson. That is the point of the Mishkan project.*

Va-Yak-hel

details, which are generally what we would consider fanciful, but the fact that the connection with the tabernacle is so tenuous. Only the second suggested source makes mention of the purported association, and none (not even the second) proposes that we may actually examine the sorts of labor performed in the tabernacle to derive those labors prohibited on Shabbat.

The situation is slightly different in the *Talmud Bavli*. There, on page 49b of Tractate *Shabbat*, the *gemara* also asks of the source of the "thirty-nine categories," and it quotes a source that makes the connection with the labor of the tabernacle explicit. Still, this is only one of two proposed sources in the present Talmud text, and, more importantly, when the Talmud tries to support this connection, it recognizes that the correspondence is sometimes difficult or impossible to support. So on page 74b of the same tractate R. Pappa asks why the mishnah lists among its categories of labor "kneading and baking" instead of cooking spices for incense, the latter of which—*but not the former*—was present in the tabernacle. The answer, suggested simply and without apology, is that "our mishnah teaches the order of [baking] bread." The Talmud here detects another interpretation of the labors listed in the mishnah, an interpretation that we would do well to pursue.

If you were to read the list of prohibited labors recorded in the mishnah and ask yourself what kinds of labor are represented, you would probably answer, "Oh, these are the kinds of work necessary for the preparation of food, clothing, writing (the writing of sacred scrolls? More probably for business and personal matters), and shelter." The precise delineation of the labors and the order of their presentation supports this interpretation powerfully: Plowing is followed by sowing, then (not including all steps) harvesting, threshing, winnowing, grinding, kneading, and baking—all for the preparation of bread (see Irving Greenberg's *The Jewish Way*, pp. 159-60, for a full listing and clarification). We would have no difficulty recognizing the preparation of food, clothing, and shelter as acts essential to human life on the most basic level. If writing is for business, then the same will be true of these labors. In any case, it seems likely that what is prohibited on Shabbat, for the rabbis of the Mishnah, is attention to fundamental life support.

Further support for this interpretation is found in the lesser-known Talmudic teaching, which remarks: "'Do not perform any *melakhah*.' This excludes blowing the shofar and separating the loaf from the wall of the oven, for these are special skills and not *melakhah*" [*Shabbat* 131b and parallels]. In other words, as the rabbis understand the Torah, special skills, such as playing musical instruments, are not prohibited on Shabbat because they are not *melakhah*—not labors necessary for basic sustenance. If the labor is not basic to human survival, it is not forbidden (according to the Torah, at least) on Shabbat.

What is the meaning of all this? Remember: The prohibited labors articulate in practice a rabbinic interpretation of the message of Shabbat. As we have now understood it, Shabbat is meant to be a time when basic human labors are unnecessary. It is a time when all needs are already provided (hence the requirement to prepare all of your food before Shabbat). It is, in other words, a reenactment of the human experience in the Garden of Eden, when God provided all and we could live in complete harmony with the world and with each other. Alternatively, it is a reenactment of the Exodus from Egypt, when God provided all our needs. According to this interpretation, Shabbat is a garden in time, or a contemporary Exodus liberation, when struggling for basic needs ceases, along with the worry and heartbreak such struggling often causes.

But this is only one interpretation of an interpretation. It is also true that there are interpretations that see the prohibited labors of Shabbat as those that were necessary in the work of the tabernacle. We must, therefore, interpret Shabbat according to this system as well: Shabbat is a time when the work of the tabernacle is unnecessary. The structure is built, the altar ready, the incense prepared. We are perfectly ready, on this day, to serve God perfectly. According to this interpretation, Shabbat is a tabernacle in time, a day on which we are all priests in God's service.

A garden in time, an Exodus-liberation in time, a tabernacle in time—take your pick or, better, choose them all. We need them all, desperately. Or elaborate your own interpretation, founded on your own juxtaposition.

My interpretation: I am writing in Wellfleet, Cape Cod, a place of beauty and peace. On one side the ocean, on the other the bay. In between dunes, forests, ponds. Not too many people but, relatively speaking, many Jews. But here they are not visible. I do not know who is a gentile, who is a secular Jew (certainly most of the Jews here are), who is more observant. Yet come Friday the local bakery shelves are filled with hallot. For people who do not observe, this must be their way of observing. A juxtaposition: hallah with waves, knotted together, and dunes. An interpretation: Shabbat is a day when flowing, wavy loaves and flowing, wavy earth are God-provided—in glorious, harmonious partnership. ■

Rabbi Gordon M. Freeman

Rabbi Gordon Freeman, Ph.D., is the rabbi of B'nai Shalom, Walnut Creek, CA. His special interest is Jewish political tradition. Author of *Heavenly Kingdom* (UPA: Latham, Maryland), *Proverbs and People* (Judah Magnes Press), co-editor of *Morh Derekh Rabbinical Assembly Rabbis' Manual* (Rabbinical Assembly). He is on the editorial board of the *Political Studies Review* (Jerusalem Center for Public Affairs).

Va-Yak-hel

The proper name of the synagogue always begins with the two Hebrew letters, ק״ק, the abbreviation for the words, קְהִילָה קְדוֹשָׁה, sacred community. This week's Torah portion begins with the word וַיַּקְהֵל, And Moshe congregated the entire community of Israel. Our word for congregation is found in its dynamic verb form. Moshe activated a community that had been formed because they all witnessed the redemption from Egypt and the revelation at Sinai (the word used for community, עֵדָה, is related to the word for witness, testimony).

Here was a group of people that had been brought together and remained rather passive (except when it came to complaining). Moshe succeeded in activating the sense of congregation amongst them in ways that have marked the meaning of synagogue life and Jewish community since that time.

Jewish community is dynamic and actively engages its individual members when it follows the directive of Moshe.

The first way, which begins our Torah portion, is contained in the mitzvah of Shabbat observance. Shabbat sanctifies time and establishes an island of time in a sea of survival anxiety. One commentary suggests that Moshe began his congregation activation program with Shabbat so that the people could find the peace in their relationships with one another. A community is made up of individuals, after all, who need to find the opportunity to accommodate one another's differences, to appreciate the special quality of each. Shabbat is a time when we cease trying to manipulate the chaos of the world. Shabbat is the day when we can enjoy a sense of community. Whether within our family or our congregation, meaning and strength are gained through the interaction of individuals in a positive setting.

The second way that Moshe creates the congregation of Israel is through the construction of the sanctuary. Everyone is invited to participate in this project. The Torah explains that each person willingly participated using his or her own unique talents and abilities. The Mishkan, the sanctuary, was to be the place of the *Shekhinah*, God's indwelling presence. The place to establish peace between the human and Divine realms of existence.

Just as Shabbat was the time to establish peace within the human community, the Mishkan was the place to establish cosmic peace. The Shabbat emphasizes that in order to find our spiritual peace we must first find reconciliation with one another. Our congregation gathers its individuals to discover a sense of mutual *oneg*, pleasure from being together. Only in that context do we establish a spiritual peace.

Spirituality is not an individual moment of fulfillment. Rather, it is a communal enterprise of cosmic proportions.

Without Shabbat the Mishkan makes no sense. Why spend the time, energy, and resources to construct a beautiful building if it will remain empty for Shabbat and other holy communal moments? The sanctuary is constructed so that the sacred communal times can be celebrated and observed as a community. Hence the command regarding the Shabbat precedes the command regarding the construction of the sanctuary.

However, it is the construction of the sanctuary that captures the imagination and enthusiasm of the people of Israel. It was, without a doubt, the most successful building project in Jewish history. The Torah explains [Ex. 36.5-7], AND THEY SPOKE TO MOSHE SAYING: "THE PEOPLE HAVE BROUGHT MORE SERVICE FOR THE CONSTRUCTION WORK THAT THE ETERNAL HAS COMMANDED TO DO." AND MOSHE COMMANDED AND THE VOICE WAS COMMUNICATED THROUGHOUT THE CAMP SAYING: "MEN AND WOMEN, DON'T DO ANY MORE WORK IN REGARD TO THE SACRED OFFERING." AND THE PEOPLE CEASED FROM BRINGING, AND THE WORK WAS SUFFICIENT...TO ACCOMPLISH THIS TASK, AND THERE REMAINED (A SURPLUS).

Moshe had to call a halt to the donations. Amazing! Can you imagine a building appeal that needs to be stopped because the people responded so well that there is a surplus? (It would be great if we could figure out the secret of Moshe's success and apply it to the constant fund-raising that takes place in the Jewish community!)

First we must remember that this story immediately follows the story of the Golden Calf, the greatest theological scandal in Jewish history. Imagine the people of Israel, having experienced the miraculous redemption from Egyptian bondage, and having consented to accepting the exclusive authority of the One God, having been the recipients of God's direct communication, throwing it all away by worshipping an idol they created. It is difficult to believe that any people could be so profoundly ungrateful, rebellious, and just plain theologically silly as to create their own image and attribute power to it. Moshe responds by smashing the stone tablets, a testimony to their broken promise.

The depth of guilt must have been pervasive, since they pursued the opportunity to find a means of reconciliation with an uncommon energy and passion. We learn that one of the basic foundations of successful fund-raising is guilt. If the fund-raiser can tap into the inevitable fountain of personal guilt and somehow connect it to the project, people will respond.

Obviously, the Torah does not contain this story merely to teach us about how to run a successful synagogue building campaign.

The construction of the sanctuary contains a much more profound message, which informs the quality of Jewish community. In their commentaries the rabbis demonstrate how each aspect of the sanctuary needs to be understood as an instrument for the transmission of values.

For example, we learn that the reason God commands the building of the sanctuary is so God can DWELL IN THEIR MIDST [Ex. 25.8]. The Kotzker Rebbe asked: "Where is this sanctuary, where is God to be found?" And he responded: "Where we let God in, into our lives and hearts. We build that sanctuary in our hearts by the way we choose to live."

The command to collect the donations begins with the word "to take" rather than "to give." Our sages explain: The giving of *tzedakah* should be in the spirit of receiving it, and through our giving to others we receive a greater gift.

The measurements of the ark of the testimony, the center of the sanctuary, are stated in halves, demonstrating that none is complete in and of itself: we are completed only through our relationship with others. The ark was to be covered inside and out with gold. Why the inside, where no one would see it?

Va-Yak-hel

To teach us the lesson of integrity, that each of us should be like the Ark; our actions and intentions should be in concert for good.

The cherubim on top of the Ark have the faces of babies so that we understand that guarding this ark, this Torah, this Divine teaching, are not powerful soldiers or frightening gargoyles, but babies. As a community we must dedicate ourselves by providing and supporting Jewish education for the next generation. Only in that way can we ensure its continuity.

Finally, in implementing the actual construction the Torah repeats the word וַיַּעַשׂ, And it was done. This word is part of the creation vocabulary. In ancient days sanctuaries were built to celebrate the divine act of creation. The message here is that God's creation of the world is bound to the reciprocal human task of constructing the sanctuary. Humankind, our tradition teaches, is God's partner in the continual process of creation. So the Torah portion begins with congregating and goes on to record the creative efforts on behalf of the community. The Shabbat command reminds us that we must take one day each week to cease our own acts of creation in order to acknowledge and appreciate God's gift of creation.

The Mishkan symbolizes the human–Divine partnership. The Zohar's commentary on this week's Torah portion contains the prayer that we recite as the Ark is opened, בְּרִיךְ שְׁמֵיהּ. The act of revelation that we are about to experience in reading the Torah is connected to the act of creation, as symbolized by our continual construction of the מִשְׁכָּן, the location in time and space of God's presence. The very words of this prayer point to the redemptive promise that is mediated through our observance of the Torah, that we "open our hearts to God's word...for good, life, and peace." Let us hope that the world can be transformed to the holy sanctuary of our construction so that we can fulfill our task as God's creative partner. ■

אלה פקודי המשכן משכן

"Torah is life. All the rest is just details." And that's what comprises the majority of this week's parashah, *Pekudei*: details. A summary of the building materials used in the construction of the Tabernacle. Details. Guidelines for the production of the priestly garments. Details. More and more details until we reach the part of the portion that recounts Moses' blessing the people following the erection of the Tabernacle.

The priests are then anointed, and the Torah describes the significance of the cloud filling the Tent of Meeting: a symbol of God's presence in the midst of the people. Israel is to understand the movement of the cloud as God's instruction when to make camp and rest on their desert journey. Then, when it is time to continue the journey, suggests the text, God will provide the Divine light of guidance by raising the cloud above the Tabernacle. During the day the cloud will be lifted, but the journey at night will be illuminated by fire. The commentary of *Tzenah U'renah* offers us a hint of the messianic here. Presently—as was the case during the travel of the Israelites in the Sinai desert—we can only see God's presence diffused by the radiant light of the fire, but in messianic time (*mashiachzeit*) we will be able to see it more clearly. This comment echoes the words of the prophet Isaiah: FOR EYE TO EYE SHALL THEY SEE WHEN GOD RETURNS US TO ZION [Isaiah 52.8].

Parashat Pekudei

Exodus 38.21–40.38

Rabbi Kerry M. Olitzky

RABBI KERRY M. OLITZKY, D.H.L. IS VICE PRESIDENT OF THE WEXNER HERITAGE FOUNDATION. HE IS THE AUTHOR OF OVER 30 BOOKS AND HUNDREDS OF ARTICLES. LOOK FOR HIS NEWEST BOOKS OUT THIS YEAR *FROM YOUR FATHER'S HOUSE...REFLECTIONS ON BEING A JEWISH MAN* (JEWISH PUBLICATION SOCIETY) AND *THE BOOK OF BLESSINGS*" (JEWISH LIGHTS PUBLISHING).

דָּבָר אַחֵר DAVAR AHER. **AND MOSES SAW ALL THE WORK, AND BEHOLD, THEY HAD DONE IT, AS GOD HAD COMMANDED, SO HAD THEY DONE IT. AND MOSES BLESSED THEM** [EX. 39.43]. Everything about the sanctuary has a symbolic character. Everything in it means something more than it appears. The objects, the ark, the art, the table, the menorah, the hangings, the curtains, the tapestries, the garments, the colors—everything has a symbolic value. So if we missed the point the first time or the second time, this time, in chapters 36 through 39, we are reminded. The repetitions remind us that the artists, Bezalel, Oholiav, Moses were aware themselves of the deep sense of each object. What a bonus not only to build the sacred, but to be aware of it. The repetitions also remind us that no ordinary, much less extraordinary, object can be perceived in all its magnificent multiplicity, its deep holiness, with just one exposure. I picked up a piece of music today, Sor Study #2,

While the book of Exodus begins with the seeming absence of God as the Israelites are forced to endure the cruelties of their Egyptian enslavement, the portion ends, as does the entire book of Exodus at the conclusion of Pekudei, with an overwhelming sense of the presence of God made manifest. According to Nachmanides, it is the end of the first exile for the Jewish people. This is the one that prefigures all other exiles in the life of the Jewish people and, as a matter of experience, the life of the individual Jew. It signals the ultimate redemption, the one for which we struggle our entire lives, personally and collectively.

It's easy for any reader of the Torah text—particularly during this week's reading—to get lost in the summary details of the materials used in the making of this somewhat mysterious Tabernacle and the requisite priestly garb for those who will render service in that portable structure. The material is familiar to us. It is not the first time we have reviewed much of it. We previously read it as part of the detailed blueprint for the actual construction of the Tabernacle. So why repeat it here? The sidrah seems to offer no obvious reason and the tent of meeting certainly bears little resemblance to our contemporary models for worship and synagogue. So it is easy to get bewildered by the Hebrew text, which lists item after item. Likewise, it is easy to get lost in the details of the world and the particulars of routine life. As a result some people actually focus on the minutiae and, in doing so, forget the essential nature of the holy work we are instructed to do in this world. Liberal Jews, in particular, sometimes get "hung up" on the endless details of living a disciplined Jewish life and reject many of them out of hand because of a seeming complexity. But the details offer us a sense of the whole and of the holy. Thus the

---

Pekudei

transcribed by Segovia, and I played it for the umpteenth time. On this morning, when I most needed the instruction, I noticed for the first time Segovia's little directive in the corner of the sheet, *con gracia*, with grace.

When the Mishkan was finished Moses saw "THAT THEY HAD DONE IT" [Ex. 39.43]; it was they who had done it, every part, every detail, their mark on it, their heart in it, "AS GOD COMMANDED, SO HAD THEY DONE IT" [Ex. 39.43].

I played the Sor Study #2 for my teacher. After a moment of silence he said to me, his eyes soft and luminous, "The musician needs three things: technical skill, soul, and blessings. Bravo." Blessings. I never thought of that, with music, before. AND MOSES SAW ALL THE WORK, AND BEHOLD, THEY HAD DONE IT, AS GOD HAD COMMANDED, SO HAD THEY DONE IT.

recording of the specific materials used in the construction of the desert tabernacle shows that the Israelites—in this case—did what they were specifically instructed to do, something, we must realize, that was not always typical of the behavior of our biblical ancestors. Such Torah (that is, the building of the Mishkan) can only be fulfilled, said the *Or ha-Hayim*, when the Jewish people work together to bring such holiness and beauty to our midst. The details are given again in this Torah portion to teach us quite explicitly that we should not take the profound beauty of the desert tabernacle's construction for granted. *Parashah Pekudei* thus begins by suggesting that it takes a lot of parts to make the holy whole. In the midst of their journey, freed from the shackles of Egyptian slavery, inspired by the revelation of the Sinai and the encounter with the Divine, the ancient Israelites followed God's instructions as they understood them, with one basic goal in mind: to achieve holiness. And the portable sanctuary that they built afforded them the opportunity to take that Sinai experience with them wherever they went on their journey. In continually engaging the text we can do the same.

But what is it about the erection of the ancient tabernacle that continues to intrigue us, we who have built beautiful synagogues, often empty of people to affirm the very foundation on which these magnificent edifices were built? Perhaps it is the dedication of our ancient ancestors who, in the midst of their desert journey, responded to the word of God as they heard it. They were eager to create a visible means to demonstrate their commitment to an ongoing relationship only recently established with God. They took all that they had, whatever resources they brought

---

AND MOSES BLESSED THEM [Ex. 39.43]. **James Stone Goodman, <Stavisker@aol.com>**

דָּבָר אַחֵר DAVAR AHER. AND MOSES SAW ALL THE WORK, AND BEHOLD, THEY HAD DONE IT, AS GOD HAD COMMANDED, SO HAD THEY DONE IT. AND MOSES BLESSED THEM [Ex. 39.43]. *Stavisker wrote: "Blessings. I never thought of that, with music, before."* Stavisker has once again struck a chord (no pun intended). This one reminds me of a different magical musical moment.

It was at CAJE 20 summers ago in Indiana. I was doing my usual photo-popping shtik. Getting pictures of Debbie Friedman was its usual frustrating task, because flashes really bother her, and there's never enough light.

SYNOPSIS: *Pekudei: Moses' annual report on the use of donations. The actual Mishkan dedication. A farewell image of the cloud by day and the pillar of fire by night.*

RASHI OF THE WEEK:

The book of Exodus ends, FOR THE ETERNAL'S CLOUD WAS THE MISHKAN BY DAY AND THE FIRE WAS ON IT AT NIGHT—BEFORE THE EYES OF ALL THE FAMILIES OF ISRAEL, IN ALL THEIR *MAS-AYHEH* (JOURNEYS). Earlier we learned: AND THE ETERNAL WENT BEFORE THEM BY DAY IN A PILLAR OF CLOUD TO LEAD THEM ALONG THE WAY, AND BY NIGHT IN A PILLAR OF FIRE TO GIVE THEM LIGHT, THAT THEY MIGHT TRAVEL BY DAY AND BY NIGHT [Ex. 13.21]. *Rashi asks,* "When they had the Mishkan, did God stop leading them? No! *Mas-Ayheh* (journeys) actually means the stages of their journeys, the camps." *As they journeyed the cloud would stop and rest at the place where they were supposed to set up camp. This use of* Mas-Ayheh *as "camp" and not "journey" is similar to Numbers 33.1,* THESE ARE THE JOURNEYS OF THE FAMILIES OF ISRAEL, *which actually goes ahead and lists the campsites. A "resting place" is actually a "journey" because it is a place from which you start out again. This is why a campsite is called a journey. Our lives often seem to have many resting places and not so many settlements. In many ways we are always on our journeys.*

out of Egypt or accumulated during their sojourn in Sinai, and transformed them by incorporating them in this wondrous structure. Simple cosmetic mirrors, for example, became bronze basins for consecration. Each item took on profound religious significance in its new form. Here the *Kol Dodi*, David Feinstein, can instruct us. He wrote, "*Kedushah* has the potential to elevate us and at the same time, when we show significant devotion to achieving *kedushah*, we can actually elevate *kedusha* itself to a higher level." In other words, *kedushah* is not an end in itself, but rather a product of our deeds. The nobler our deeds, the higher the level of our sanctity and the sanctity of the One-Whom-We-Serve.

Thus we learn that we can achieve a state of holiness—the appropriate goal of the current interest in spirituality that is sweeping our community—only when we are in a dynamic relationship with it. This is spiritual logic at its finest. When we are in pursuit of holiness by means of the life we live and the acts we perform, our lives can become holy (wholly?) other. When we do holy work we elevate the holiness, and the holy act elevates us even higher.

In a sense, the human construction of the tabernacle reflects the divine creation of the world. Even the Hebrew syntax is built the same way in this section of Exodus and in the account of the creation of the world in Genesis. If we suggest, as one midrash on *Parashat Bereshit* does state, that the world was intentionally left unfinished by God so that we humans may join in its completion, then we may be bold enough to propose that the construction of the Tabernacle was not finished by the Israelites. Instead God כִּבְיָכוֹל *kiv'yakhol* completed its construction. But how is that possible? The text certainly does not express it that way. If the tabernacle is evidence of our com-

---

Pekudei

Anyway, it was Wednesday afternoon, Debbie's Chorale was that night, the final rehearsal was at dinnertime, and Miriam Van Raalte told me the group was going to present Debbie with a gift of a hand-painted *tallit*. I had had some pretty good luck with the light at the Chorale rehearsal the year before in San Antonio, so I thought I'd give it a try.

At some point Miriam surprised Debbie with the *tallit*. And I took my shots. They started practicing "A Blessing for the Ones You Love," which is based on the Priestly Blessing.

Frankly, it was kind of flat—not the off-key kind of flat, just the hungry, hot, dirty, tired, blah kind of flat. Debbie stopped the music. Told them to do it again with feeling. It

mitment to the Sinaitic covenant, then we must work to make sure that the presence of God is always made manifest in the tabernacle designed for that purpose. When we do holy work, God's presence abides. This alone is what makes the construction of the Tabernacle complete. As this portion has suggested, even as it lists the details for construction, there is more to building a place for God's presence than just bricks and mortar, or gold and bronze and precious stones. Empty of God, the tabernacle is unfinished. Listen to the words of the text: EVERYONE WHOSE HEART WAS STIRRED...EVERYONE FOR WHOM HIS [OR HER] SPIRIT WAS WILLING. When we do God's work in the world and bring the word of God to others through comfort and healing and inspiration, then our synagogues, like the ancient portable sanctuary, will be complete. And then so are we! ■

---

was louder, but still no oomph. Debbie stopped the music again.

And then it happened. Debbie asked how many of those present had ever been blessed. Several hands went up. Then she asked how many had ever blessed someone else. Fewer hands. So she had everyone pair up. She helped one person bless the other. "יְבָרֶכְךָ יְיָ וְיִשְׁמְרֶיךָ. *Yi-va-re-khi-kha A-do-shem ve-yish-me-re-kha...*" Then she helped the other bless the first. Everyone in the room had been blessed and had blessed someone. Debbie told everyone to try to capture how it felt to be blessed and to bless someone, to remember the feeling and to put it into the song.

Well, I can't figure out how to put it into graphical form. So I'll just tell you. That all of the souls of all of the people infused their voices, came together as one, and filled the room. The music, the sound, really had a presence all its own. The experience lifted us all to a place we hadn't been a moment before and carried us all the way through the evening. It was a moment I won't soon forget. **David Parker, <Parques@aol.com>**

ויקרא
Va-Yikra

אליו מאהל מועד לאמר

. . . AND GOD CALLED AND SPOKE TO MOSHE! In an act of calling-naming-speaking God introduces a subject that is most fundamental and most esoteric at the same time: the *korbanot* קָרְבָּנוֹת, "offerings" or "sacrifices" by which we are to be brought near to God.**

It is not enough just to speak, continuing the discourse of previous encounters, but Moshe is called to attention: "MOSHE!" This was the first revelation "FROM OUT OF THE TENT OF MEETING," the newly built tabernacle.

The word *Va-Yikra* here echoes the *va-yikras* of the time of creation: "AND HE CALLED THE LIGHT 'DAY,'...THE DARKNESS 'NIGHT.'" Moshe, the Midrash tells us, answers, "*Hineni*, here I am."

Now there is a new realm of work—not God's work of creation, but rather the work of human beings. In the services of the מִשְׁכָּן Mishkan Moshe is the new Adam who brings forth this possibility. The Jewish people follow in his pathway, as the text emphasizes by calling the person who brings an offering *adam* rather than אִישׁ *ish*. "IF A PERSON BRINGS AN OFFERING..." We are to remake the world as it was in Eden.

The most wondrous characteristic of that world was that in Eden human beings and God walked together. They were close. Human beings were the image of God. Now we're far apart—the separation caused by our sins—and it is our job to recreate the way it was when we could be with God. This isn't a mat-

Parashat Va-Yikra

Leviticus 1.1–5.26

Tamar Frankiel

TAMAR FRANKIEL IS AUTHOR OF *THE VOICE OF SARAH: FEMININE SPIRITUALITY AND TRADITIONAL JUDAISM* AND CO-AUTHOR OF *MINDING THE TEMPLE OF THE SOUL*. SHE AND HER HUSBAND HERSHEL WORK AT RAISING FIVE CHILDREN IN LOS ANGELES.

דָּבָר אַחֵר DAVAR AHER. SPEAK TO THE ISRAELITE PEOPLE, AND SAY TO THEM: "WHEN ANY OF YOU PRESENTS AN OFFERING OF CATTLE TO THE LORD..."[Lev. 1.2]. Welcome to the wide world of sacrifices. *Leviticus Rabbah* teaches: "The *minhag* is to teach small children Leviticus as their first book of the Torah." We ask, "Why?" They answer, "The little children are pure and the sacrifices are pure. Let the pure ones deal with the pure ones."

When we see "sacrifices" we think "*Joe and the Volcano*." We don't see pure—especially not the vegetarians among us. Likewise, in her weekly summary for **C. Ha** this week, seventeen-year-old Hilary Bienstock wrote, "This week is also *Shabbat Parah*. We read a special haftarah called (appropriately enough) *Haftarah Parah. It's a group of laws about bodily purification and other important, although uninteresting, topics*" (empha-

ter of changing God—we don't hold that God should become man! So it must be that we should become Divine.

The first type of offering is the voluntary offering, the עֹלָה *Olah* or ELEVATION-OFFERING, as the Artscroll translation has it: an offering to elevate the soul. We may recall the first offerings of Cain and Abel soon after the expulsion from *Gan Eden*, offerings that led to jealousy and disaster. But here all types of offerings can be made—carefully, with great attention and concentrated energy—to bring about קָרְבָּן *Korban*, a drawing near to God by elevating ourselves. We have animal offerings of four-legged animals and birds, meal offerings of flour from the vegetable world, cakes and loaves—the work of human farmers and bakers—representing, in effect, the range of creation. (As R. Samson Rafael Hirsch points out in his commentary on *Parashat Terumah*, all these levels were represented in the materials of the מִשְׁכָּן Mishkan itself.)

The only thing omitted is offerings from the sea. But, the Midrash explains, this is included too, in the salt that had to accompany all offerings. The sea had complained about its status from day two, when the lower waters were separated from the upper waters. God had promised that as a compensation it would have a part in the Mishkan, the effort to recreate the world. Since its water ultimately rejoined the upper waters through evaporation, only the salt was condemned, so to speak, to stay earthbound. Now, through the offerings, it too would be elevated. We take the world and all its kingdoms and return them to God through offering and eating, and we go along, too.

---

sis added). If I were still teaching Hilary, her wonderful sarcasm would have been the opening for a great lesson.

Here is what I know. Sacrifices are like taking a bath. They show us that we can get clean again. Basically, in Jewish law two things "slime" us—sin and death. We can be "haunted" (see God's speech to Cain) by sin. We know that at least in our dreams and our reflections ghosts haunt us for a long time. I picked up the phone to call my father for years after I buried him—before I stopped needing to catch myself. The lesson we need to teach children—the lesson we can often learn from teaching children—is that falling down is not always that bad. Picking one's self up is a possible and desirable act. Likewise, baths do work. What is

SYNOPSIS: *We are now into the Torah of the Kohanim. We begin with five kinds of sacrifices:* Olah—*the regular daily offering;* Minhah—*the flour offering;* Shelamim—*peace offerings:* Hatat—*sin offerings;* Asham—*guilt offerings.*

RASHI OF THE WEEK:

The Book of Leviticus begins: AND GOD CALLED TO MOSES. *God usually "speaks"* TO MOSES, *so Rashi notes the difference. He asks:* Why did God choose "call"? What are we supposed to learn from calling rather than "speaking"? *Calling actually means calling by name. God did this before every commandment. Calling is an indication of affection. It says: I am talking specifically to you—not just in general. It is the tone that the ministering angels use. We know this from the story where Isaiah sees them flying around in the Temple. He says:* "AND THEY CALLED ONE TO THE OTHER AND SAID: "HOLY HOLY HOLY..."*God didn't use this tone with non-Jewish prophets. In Numbers 23.4 we see:* AND GOD VA-Y'KAR (HAPPENED) TO BALAAM. VA-Y'KAR *is* VA-YIKRA *(called) without a final alef. Here God's speech is secular.* The VA-YIKRA *that starts Leviticus tells us that God started this book, speaking to a colleague and saying, "We've got holy work to do together."*

Yet still the process is opaque. The parashah begs us to ask and keep asking, How does this work? How does this draw God close? Bringing animals, birds, flour, cakes, salt to this blazing fire—this recreates the world? The continual cycle of life to death, the products of our hands to a column of smoke—this is what elevates us and brings God and us near to each other? What is God trying to tell us here?

The imagery is too condensed and the reality too far from our lives for us to understand. We are obsessed with words and concepts, and the power of ceremony is taken too lightly. The sages of Talmudic times also faced this symbolic density, this light too bright to be seen, and began to unpack it for us. The sacrificial service, they said, should be replaced in the post-Temple era by three things: *tzedakah*, our table, and prayer.

1. *Tzedakah*: We give money—simple enough. But we do not often think of it as a holy act. When we write a check or give a coin to a homeless person we should let part of our mind fly to Jerusalem—"lest I forget you...my highest joy."

2. *Our table*: We eat food that is pure, ritually and healthfully. As Rabbi Avigdor Miller has observed, we are **all** part of the "nation of *kohanim*" and may consume sacrifices. After washing hands and donning garments like the *kohanim*, after relieving oneself (on "the model of removing the ash from the *mizbeah*<u>h</u> before bringing offerings upon it"), after praying, "the kosher food (or even the sacred meat of the offering) is then consumed on the holy altar of the Israelite body."[1]

Eating the offering was a way of sharing a meal with God. Certain parts, like the fat and the blood, belonged to the Divine realm; others were for the *kohanim*, as God's surrogates (WHEN THE KOHANIM ATE THE OFFERING, THE SINNER GAINED ATONEMENT); other parts were for us in our most purified state. Today eating is still a central, indeed an enormous feature of our holy days and

---

Va-Yikra

true for our bodies is equally true for our spirits. Teaching *Va-Yikra* is a privilege, both in what you can share and in what you can relearn. **Joel Lurie Grishaver on Va-Yikra, from the Torah Aura Bulletin Board.**

דָּבָר אַחֵר DAVAR A<u>H</u>ER. AND GOD CALLED TO MOSES... "WHEN A MAN AMONG YOU BRINGS AN OFFERING TO GOD, FROM ANIMALS—FROM THE CATTLE OR FROM THE FLOCK SHALL YOU BRING YOUR OFFERING" [Lev. 1.1]. In the town where I grew up the city fathers passed an ordinance forbidding slaughtering and roasting livestock in the backyard. There were many immigrants from a small community in Iraq whose culinary practices had led to the ordinance. I don't know what it feels like to slice up a goat, roast its meat, and invite God to sit down and enjoy the meal with me, but they did. So did my

celebrations, from the Pesah seder to the bar/bat mitzvah *seudah*, but we often forget the extraordinary holiness of the act. If we are praying at *shaharit* and *minhah*, we usually come to the act of eating after intense prayer. How does that affect our eating?

3. *Prayer*: The Zohar says that since the loss of the Temple we have nothing but prayer. Rabbi Eli Munk explains that the priestly ceremony of going around the altar throwing the blood on the corners so that it will drip onto all four sides is paralleled by the thirteen **middle** blessings of the daily Shmoneh Esrei (blessings 4 through 16). They represent the formation of the Israelite camp and the formation around the Mishkan, in four groups of three tribes:

East: Judah, Issachar, and Zebulun, corresponding to the blessings for individual spiritual well-being—knowledge, *tshuvah*, forgiveness.

North: Asher, Naftali, and Dan, corresponding to the blessings for individual material well-being—liberation from our struggles, healing, sustenance. The middle (tenth) blessing connects the individual to the collective.

West: Ephraim, Menasheh, and Benyamin, corresponding to blessings for national spiritual well-being—restoration of justice, destruction of evil, and the rise of the *tzaddikim*, the beings of excellence.

South: Reuven, Shimon, and Gad: corresponding to blessings for national material well-being—rebuilding, Jerusalem, anointing of a Messiah, and the fulfillment of all our prayers.[2]

We must continue to unravel this mystery in our own lives. As Rabbi Miller observes, we have to use "the imagination of our emotional minds" to make the offerings real to us.[3] The care with which these ceremonies were performed, step by step, hints to us of the awareness of process and meaning that we can develop in our daily actions. When we write a check for *tzedakah* we can think: This is to remake the world by helping our fellow and to connect with God. When we dress, wash, or exercise we can imagine being *kohanim* preparing our bodies for service. When we cook or eat a meal we can imagine it going through the fire of the altar within, to nourish ourselves in a refined way. We can invite God to our meal more sincerely. When we address God we can try, at least some of the time, to pour out our hearts on the altar. Rabbi Nahman of Breslov says that the "outpouring of the soul," הִשְׁתַּפְּכוּת-הַנֶּפֶשׁ *Hishtap'kut-ha-Nefesh*, in meditative seclusion (הִתְבּוֹדְדוּת) is the key to prayer. This practice means a set time of talking to God in our own words, as well as through the formal prayers. This is to be like the outpouring of blood on the altar. It has the potential to dissolve our egos—at least once in a while.

This is only the beginning of reflection. We can also contemplate the *kavanah* of offering. The person making an offering had to place his hands on the head of the animal,

---

ancestors, I presume. But the Rambam didn't, nor did many of the commentators. The classic disagreement about the whole sacrificial system is over whether it was a concession to more primitive practices, designed to wean us out of our primitivism (Rambam), or whether concealed within the practices is a secret spiritual sensibility not available to the post-sacrificial mind (Ramban).

Asks R. Assi, "Why do children begin their studies from *Torat Kohanim* (*Va-Yikra*) and not from *Bereshit*? Because children are pure and the sacrifices are pure. Let the pure come and occupy themselves with the pure." Here is another approach, a mythic sensibility that affirms there is something pure and beautiful, primary and symmetrical about the Levitical practices.

The artist has another angle. All the great *darshanim* loved Leviticus precisely because the imagination has to supply so much to retrieve sense, meaning, beauty from the mysteries sealed in the past. We have clues, of course. *Korban* we translate inappropriately as "sacrifice" from the root that means "to come close." It was a way of coming close, and the "burnt offering" we use for עֹלָה *olah*, which comes from the root meaning "to

identifying with it and leaning into it with all his strength! Can we lean with all our strength into prayer?

The animal was cut into pieces and carried to the fire limb by limb, each piece placed on the fire one after the other. This is an echo of the ecstatic vision of the apprentice shaman, where she saw her own body being dismembered. From this she learned the nature of each limb and organ, its placement and its energy—and became a healer. We too can learn to meditate, with awe and gratitude, on each limb and organ of the body and on how it functions in our lives. We can imagine each limb singing its own song of praise and gratitude to the Creator: "ALL MY PARTS SAY: HASHEM, WHO IS LIKE UNTO YOU?" [Psalms 35.10].

The 248 limbs and organs and the 365 sinews and nerves are also, symbolically, the 613 mitzvot. The mitzvot are acts of connection, the little acts every day as well as the big acts on holidays, where we dramatize with great fanfare the continuous spiral of recreation. We can become healers of the world by concentrating, leaning into, loving all these bits and pieces of the reality we are remaking. Then we can imagine every piece going up in smoke like the limbs of the animal, always a straight column of smoke, its essence rejoining its Creator. For THE SPIRIT RETURNS TO GOD THAT GAVE IT [Eccl. 3.21,12.7]. We imagine letting go, not being attached, turning it over, returning it to its source.

The *olah* is what elevates. *Vidui*, the confession, can also mean to "raise up," in the sense of singling oneself out. The commandment to wash our hands is *netilat yadaim*, lift up the hands. "I LIFT MY EYES TO THE MOUNTAINS, FROM WHENCE DOES MY HELP COME?" Prayer is called a ladder, like Jacob's ladder. We keep going up...up...up! Eventually there is God. To say it is one thing. To do it—that was what the *korbanot* were for. Now we have to re-imagine it. But not only imagine.

Va-Yikra

rise up." Come close and rise up. Clues.

Still we interpret the past in our own terms. We tend to forget that we are creatures of our own present just as surely as those we are reading about were once creatures of theirs. We tend to forget that the past, even the distant past, was once a present, and that our present will someday be a past to those who may sit in wonder or confusion about us. What odd spiritual practices they had, they might say about us.

Someday thoroughly contemporary people may sit in their astro-seats and wonder what kind of people would build theaters to worship God. They stood up, sat down, stood up, sat down, listened to choirs sing, put organs in their places of worship (organs belonged in baseball parks, they might say,

We must turn it around and around until we can put it into our bodies, into physical action, to recreate the world.■

Notes

[1] Rabbi Avigdor Miller, *A Kingdom of Cohanim* (Brooklyn, NY: Avigdor Miller, 1995) on Va-Yikra 6:4, p. 73

[2] Rabbi Dr. Eli Munk, *The World of Prayer*, Vol. 1: Daily Prayers (New York: Feldheim, 1987), pp. 124-127.

3 Miller, op. cit., p. 38.

---

remembering baseball parks); they built edifices that looked like Caesar's Palace to pray in, they might say. Let us forgive them right now for misunderstanding us, as we may misunderstand our ancestors in *Va-Yikra*.

Let us forgive them in advance for forgetting that we once sat together in these big rooms and understood what we were doing. **James Stone Goodman, <Stavisker@aol.com>**

דָּבָר אַחֵר DAVAR AHER. And He called to Moses, and God spoke to him from the tent of meeting, saying: "Speak to the Children of Israel and say to them: 'When a man among you brings an offering to God: from animals—from the cattle or from the flock shall you bring your offering'" [Lev. 1.1]. My first instinct is to ignore the sacrifices, to say "I don't understand why," to look for a more "humane" verse or two. But then I thought perhaps there is mileage in at least finding out what others have to say about *Va-Yikra*—sacrifices and all.

So what approaches can be taken to understand this detailed description of the temple sacrifices? Professor Jacob Milgrom distinguishes four possible purposes for a sacrificial system: (a) to provide food for the god; (b) to assimilate the life force of the sacrificial animal; (c) to effect a union with the deity; and (d) to induce the aid of the deity by means of a gift. He then proceeds to exclude the first three as being inapplicable to Israel and points out that the gift must be of value to the giver and hence the prohibition of the use of wild animals as sacrifices. He says much more—of course—but we can say approach one is the anthropological approach—Why did that civilization do that then?

The next approach is to treat the sacrifices as a prototype to ethical behavior or maybe a step along that path. (a) The animal sacrifices replaced human sacrifice or idol worship; (b) the sacrifices gave us kashrut; (c) kashrut gave birth to the humane society; and (d) ultimately, everyone on earth will be vegetarian again.

To make the situation even more problematical, we find the prophets emphasizing that sacrifices are no replacement for atonement and that sacrifices without real atonement are worse than nothing at all. We read in Amos, "I hate, I despise your feasts, and I take no delight in your solemn assemblies. Yea, though you offer Me burnt offerings, I will not accept them...But let justice well up as waters, and righteousness a mighty stream" [Amos 5.21–24].

Some may say the prophets are not condemning sacrifice itself, but only condemning it when morality and atonement do not accompany it—but (perhaps because it is what I want to see) I hear them saying, Don't worry about the sacrifices—just do the rest.

Flipping through the references to sacrifices in my copy of *Everyman's Talmud,* I found the story of Rabbi Yohanan ben Zakkai and his disciple R. Yehoshua. On one occasion, when they were leaving Jerusalem, the latter gazed upon the destroyed Temple and cried out, "Woe to us! The place where Israel obtained atonement for sins is in ruins!" R. Yohanan said to him, "My son, be not distressed. We still have an atonement equally efficacious, and that is the practice of benevolence."

Certainly the prophets and the rabbis of the Talmud were more than happy to reassure us that the loss of the sacrifices did not detract from Judaism as an effective religion. I will let the last word go to **Rabbi Keith Stern, <Jazzman900@aol.com>**. He writes: "I hold my breath

Va-Yikra

Rabbi Peter S. Knobel

Rabbi Peter S. Knobel of Beth Emet the Free Synagogue, Evanston, Illinois, is Chair of CCAR Liturgy Committee.

***Va-Yikra* describes in detail worship as animal sacrifice and offerings of grain. They are collectively called קָרְבָּנוֹת *korbanot,* which is derived from the root קרב *kof resh bet*—to draw near. Sacrifice and, therefore, worship is the means by which humankind approaches God. For us moderns and post-moderns the notion of animal sacrifice is almost instinctively repelling. It seems primitive and cruel. Even the offering of grain has little appeal. In fact, for many, Leviticus as a whole drives us away.**

Our worship is neatly structured recitation of words and engagement with texts. It does not involve risk. Nothing is lost because the words can be repeated *ad infinitum,* but the animal and the grain must be constantly replaced with a new living entity. Only once in our lives (and only with male children) do we perform a rite with the inherent tension of animal sacrifice. Even *brit milah* (the covenant of circumcision) is under attack as child abuse. A number of families have their sons circumcised in the hospital without prayers or family and community participation. The blood and the cries of the child do not fit the sanitized and sterilized religion that demands little from us in the way of deed or personal involvement. Our religion has been intellectualized.

In contrast, the Judaism of Leviticus is embodied religion. It is about eating, making love, coping with illness, and guilt and forgiveness. It is a messy religion—a hands-on religion. Our hands must get dirty, and we must wash them. The noise, the odors, and the red blood spattered on the white priestly

---

as *Va-Yikra* comes rolling out over the Torah table. All this talk of suet and guts and entrails and buckets of blood. *Gevalt*! Do I dare ask where God is in all of this/ Perhaps objectively I can relate to sacrifices in anthropological terms. Otherwise it seems to me vaguely ironic that the destruction of the Temple wiped out the sacrificial cult and thus saved Judaism. **Adam Bernard, <it06@bcs.org.uk>**

דָּבָר אַחֵר DAVAR AHER. When a man among you brings an offering to God [Lev. 1.1]. Two thoughts on the etymology of the Hebrew word for sacrifices, which the always marvelous Peter Knobel offers in his discussion of *Parashat Va-Yikra.*

1. Because its root [קרב] *K-R-V* denotes proximity and nearness, the best translation of קָרְבָּן *Korban* in our spiritual setting might be "communion." That term captures the majesty and sanctity and

tunics leave an indelible impression on the heart, mind, and soul.

Our Torah portion is directed to the whole Israelite community. It is a manual not for the priests but for the people. It is about not elite religion but popular religion. The passage presents us with a challenge to turn our own worship *(avodah,* sacred work) into a series of offerings that correspond to those described in the text. There is a danger in trivializing the concept of offering. Ultimately, in the case of each category, we are called upon to give of the best that we have.

The עֹלָה *olah* is a lifting up of self, with a sense of dedication to achieving the highest degree of spirituality available to us. This requires engagement with the world and understanding that if we do not raise ourselves to God, the world is at risk; and in raising ourselves we put ourselves at risk. The offering is both elevated and transformed in the act. The מִנְחָה *minhah* is a gift of nourishing bread. It provides sustenance to the priests who minister at the altar. This requires our sustaining, materially and spiritually, the institutions that preserve our unique connection to God as a covenanted people. Moreover, we must help sustain all who are hungry. The זֶבַח שְׁלָמִים *zevah shelamim* (the שְׁלִים *shlim* sacrifice) aims at the creation of שְׁלֵימוּת *shleimut,* wholeness, first for ourselves and then for the world around us. Ironically, the offering must be broken to make the individual whole. It is actions and words that repair damage and help us experience our full potential as beings created בְּצֶלֶם אֱלֹהִים *b'tselm elohim* (in God's image).

The חַטָּאת *hatat,* the sin offering, and the אָשָׁם *asham,* the guilt offering, are in recognition of inadvertently transgressing a negative commandment. Acts of inadvertence can often be traced to indifference and lack of attention. They are serious because they can frequently cause great damage. They must be expiated. But these offerings are not limited to inadvertent acts. Deliberate transgressions must be confronted, and compensation must be paid to restore the relationship.

Renewing and restoring our relationship with God is a combination of words and acts. It is to stand before the altar and present ourselves. It is to view our relationship with God as being at risk because we have not been adequate in our offerings of thanksgiving, because we have not contributed to making the world whole, and because we have not appreciated that the produce of the earth must be shared. Finally, sin, remaining unacknowledged and without acts of atonement, produces a distancing from God, which ultimately distances us from one another. Worship is the sacred work of offering our best to God. It is a drawing near to God, to others, and to ourselves.■

---

mystery of the altar as the point of tangency between heaven and earth, between the transcendent and the temporal, and as the site where the mortal worshipper has the privilege of meeting with the Eternal One to share a gift of covenantal faithfulness. It is likely that English speakers immediately connect "communion" with the rituals of the church, but that is all to the good; our association of the term with sacred ceremony serves to corroborate—rather than preclude—its usage in the Jewish spiritual milieu. No other theological term so aptly and meaningfully captures the truest nuance of the Hebrew.

2. On a different level, the root [קרב] is also the basis for the noun *k'rav,* meaning "battle." With tongue firmly in cheek we note that this validates Peter's central point: Both our personal spirituality and the communal rituals that enact and express it often involve a struggle. **Rabbi Mark Win. Gross, Temple Beth Orr, Coral Springs, FL.**

דָּבָר אַחֵר DAVAR AHER. WHEN A MAN AMONG YOU BRINGS AN OFFERING TO GOD: FROM ANIMALS—FROM THE CATTLE OR FROM THE FLOCK SHALL YOU BRING YOUR OFFERING [Lev. 1.1]. I learned that a sacrifice is called a קָרְבָּן *korban,* which is like קָרוֹב *karov,* mean-

Va-Yikra

ing "to approach". So maybe God is happy because we want to approach Him. My question is—why some animals and not others? **Shaye Horwitz, <Rabbidanny@aol.com>**

Dear Shaye, I know two answers from the midrash,and I want to create a third. In *Pesikta d'Rav Kahana* God tells Moses: "There are lots of animals, and only ten are kosher. There are ten kosher animals and I will allow only the ox, the sheep, and the goat to be my sacrifices. I don't want you hunting. I want you to learn that just because it is alive, it doesn't mean you can eat it. Just as I asked you to take only some animals, I, too, will take only some animals." So the first answer is to teach humans to respect life.

The better answer is in *Sifre* (another midrash collection). God teaches that each animal was chosen to remind us of a blessing. Abraham served an ox to his three visitors who told him that Sarah would have a child. That was a blessing. A lamb was sacrificed instead of Isaac—and Abraham was blessed. Two goats were served to Isaac when Jacob fooled him and stole Esau's blessing. Each kind of animal reminds us of a time that God gave Israel an important blessing.

I would like to write a midrash about the animals choosing to be sacrificed (like at the end of a war movie). Which of us get to/have to give up their lives so that Israel can be blessed? The winner of the contest would be the Jewish cow, Jewish sheep, and Jewish goat, who each had the best story of why they should be chosen. If you were writing this midrash, what would be the winning (or losing) reasons to be chosen? **Joel Lurie Grishaver, <GRIS@torahaura.com>**

דָּבָר אַחֵר DAVAR AHER. HE SHALL BRING THEM TO THE KOHEN, WHO SHALL OFFER FIRST THE ONE THAT IS FOR A SIN-OFFERING; HE SHALL NIP ITS HEAD AT ITS NAPE, BUT NOT SEPARATE IT [Lev. 5.8]. In *Zakhor*, Deuteronomy 25.19, we are told to BLOT OUT THE MEMORY OF AMALEK, AND TO NOT FORGET. How can we do both? In last week's Torah portion, in Leviticus 5.8, in describing how the priest sacrifices turtledoves and pigeons, we may have a suggestion. The priest is to PINCH THE BIRD'S NECK, WITHOUT SEVERING IT. The word for pinching the bird's neck without severing it in this case is וּמָלַק *u'Malak*. Perhaps this is how we should treat the memory of Amalek: pinch it off, shun it, take the life out of it without its being completely severed or ever quite forgotten. **David Parkhurst, <Parques@aol.com>**

צו את אהרן ואת בניו

Parashat Tzav

Leviticus 6.1–8.36

Professor Arnold Eisen

Arnold Eisen is Professor of Religious Studies at Stanford University and author of *Rethinking Modern Judaism: Ritual, Commandment, Community*, published by the University of Chicago Press.

Ritual has not often received good press in the modern West. It has been denigrated as rigid, formalized, stereotyped; even today one often finds it contrasted unfavorably—by scholars and lay people alike—with such good things as spirit, intention, or creativity. The prevalence of anti-ritual sentiment probably stems from enlightenment attitudes that grew out of Protestant polemics against the Catholic church.

I mention this bias at the outset of a d'var Torah on *Tzav* because we are all the heirs of that bias to a certain extent, and it affects the way we approach the Book of Leviticus—or, in many cases, refuse to approach Leviticus, resolved to keep a safe distance from the endless details of blood and sacrifice.

That aloofness toward *Va-Yikra* is a great mistake. To miss out on the ritual practice at the heart of the book, to turn our backs on its sacred formalities, is to miss one of the most powerful teachings our tradition has to offer: the connection between properly understood and performed ritual, and the sanctification of everyday life. Leviticus takes us as we are—people who eat and make love, who desire and die, who do much good in this world and much harm—and tries to force us to reflect on how we are living, to send us on a different path. That path, in its lexicon, is called mitzvah. The state of affairs that characterizes it is called *kedushah*, holiness.

דָּבָר אַחֵר DAVAR AHER. THEN HE BROUGHT NEAR THE SECOND RAM, THE INAUGURATION RAM, AND AARON AND HIS SONS LEANED THEIR HANDS UPON THE HEAD OF THE RAM. HE SLAUGHTERED IT, AND MOSES TOOK SOME OF ITS BLOOD AND PLACED IT UPON THE MIDDLE PART OF AARON'S RIGHT EAR, UPON THE THUMB OF THEIR RIGHT HAND AND UPON THE BIG TOE OF THEIR RIGHT FOOT. [Lev. 8.22–24]. The Torah is filled with odd ceremonies, especially in the book of Leviticus. One of the oddest, at least to the Western mind, is the one described on the day of the ordination of Aaron and his sons. The "ram of ordination" is sacrificed and its blood smeared on the new priest's right earlobe, right thumb, and right big toe. What is the meaning of this?

There is abundant evidence that dabbing the blood of a sacrifice on something to give it a different status was a common Near Eastern practice. The best known would be the use of the blood of the paschal sacrifice on the doorposts on the

At first glance, of course, Leviticus presents far more obvious reasons for contemporary repugnance at its instructions than generic objections to ritual. For one thing, more than any other book of the Torah or the rest of the Bible, it seems directed to a particular group of which we are not and cannot be members. The priesthood is no more. Temple and tabernacle no longer function. Reading this week's parashah, we seem to be eavesdropping on a conversation intended for someone else. The details are arcane. We quickly lose interest in what we are overhearing and tend to skip over the repetitions. The relevance of the endless detail escapes us.

If we continue reading, we are likely to encounter further occasion for alienation. Much of what the priests were supposed to do all day, according to Moses' instructions, was involved with the slaughter of animals. Our heads spin with the calculation of how many tens of thousands of deaths must have been inflicted on living creatures each year upon the altar of Israel's wilderness tabernacle. Vegetarian or not, we tend to be disturbed by this. Our unease persists despite the realization that many of the animals offered up to God became food for human beings (priests and ordinary Israelites) who would have killed animals in order to eat anyway. They are sharing a meal with the Creator-of-All-Flesh. No wanton or useless slaughter here, then, but a powerful means of expiation and communion. Yet still, as likely as not, we want no part of it.

Our unease is not entirely bad as long as we stick with the attempt to comprehend what Leviticus wants to teach us. Indeed the book *wants* to disturb u, as honest talk about basic things generally does. The subjects of Leviticus could not

Va-Yikra

evening that the Israelites were to leave Egypt, so as to protect the inhabitants from the Angel of Death. But other civilizations and cultures of the ancient world used to do the same thing. In such cultures they smeared the *vulnerable* parts of an object to protect it from outside forces. Sometimes it would be a corner of a house or a doorpost. Sometimes it would be the corner of an altar. But in any case, the outside edges, the corners and all the vulnerable places would be covered with the blood of the sacrifice to protect the object. This apotropaic protection would guard against demonic forces and would keep the object pure. When Moses daubed Aaron and his sons he was doing essentially the same thing. Midrashically, Moses was keeping them pure to keep the demons of corruption and hubris far, far away. His choice of ceremony

be more basic: life and death; sex and desire; the relation of human beings to the world, a relationship never more direct than when, several times each day, we take the world into our bodies as food. Reflection on these things is all the more disturbing when—as always in the Torah—it comes to us performatively. Attentiveness is not couched in philosophy that we can study, objectify, render abstract. Instead it hits us bodily, in actions that we are commanded to perform. We cannot but perform these actions in one way or another. We have to eat, will inevitably fall short of the ethical mark some of the time, will face death, and will die. The question is how we will live. Leviticus aims at holiness.

To appreciate its method, consider the earlier chapter's detailed description of the offenses that can be atoned for through the various sorts of sacrifice set forth in this week's parashah. Almost all involve infractions of the ritual system of purity and impurity, not of the ethical system of right and wrong. One is not wrong to become impure by burying a relative who has passed away, but the act renders one impure. Conversely, it is not a horrible thing to commit petty theft, or to tell the truth but not the whole truth on the witness stand. But these ethical infractions are about the most serious acts covered by the offerings that Leviticus describes. More serious crimes demand remedies that sacrifice cannot provide. By contrast, ritual infractions stain us and the holy tabernacle.

Their realm is symbolic. The ethical and ritual systems must be distinct because impurity does not mean evil. Yet the two must be

SYNOPSIS: *We have got rules for the* kohanim's *Mishkan practices, the rules of how to offer sacrifices, and rules for eating meat.*

RASHI OF THE WEEK:

The sidrah ends: AND AARON AND HIS SONS DID EVERY THING WHICH THE ETERNAL COMMANDED MOSES [Lev. 8.36]. *Rashi looks at this verse and wonders: Why is it necessary (1) to tell us that they did it and (2) to specifically list Aaron and his sons. The Maskil Le'David restates the question: "Why didn't the Torah just say: 'They did so'? Why the specifics?" Rashi answers:* To give them merit for precisely following God's instructions and not improvising at all; they did not swerve to the right or to the left. *Often, not being creative is hard. The Gur Areyeh adds: "In worship—getting it right is as important as feeling." We can imagine the Baal Shem's response.*

---

makes a lasting impression upon the new priests much as the moment of ordination for a new rabbi is something never forgotten.

You see, Aaron and his sons were chosen for a unique service to both God and the Jewish people. It was a service rooted in God's direct word to Mose,s and every Jew knew it. Since God knows that we are only human and subject to human faults and shortcomings, how better to remind the new priests of their responsibilities than with a hands-on ceremony of daubing blood on the most vulnerable parts of their bodies? The ceremony of putting blood on their earlobe, their thumb, and their big toe was God's way of saying, "These are your most vulnerable parts. Guard them well if you want to serve Me and My people."

The ear is very vulnerable to corruption. Whenever a Jew would come before the priest to offer a sin-offering he would confess his sin. Imagine the power that the priest had! Imagine if he went home to his wife and said, "By the way, dear, you'll never guess who I saw at the altar today and what he said he did!" The priest was to listen only so he would be able to help the Jew with the sacrifice. He was not there to offer judgment, atonement, or advice. That was God's department. The priest

related, since pure and impure are meant to stimulate reflection on right and wrong. Leviticus seeks to school us in performance of the good by having us see ourselves act out the pure time and time again. Ritual thus offers a precious experience rarely if ever available in life: the experience of getting things absolutely right. Playing Bach inventions time and again on the piano, entering heart and soul into the music after mastering the technique, I was occasionally able to know I had gotten the music right in a way I rarely get my child-raising exactly right, or my teaching, or my marriage.

This would be valuable enough, but Leviticus offers me something more. Its insistence on detail reminds me that there and there alone, daily life is lived. We shall be judged, as the Hasidic story goes, not by whether or not we were Moshe Rabbenu or Akiba, but by whether we were ourselves. As the saying goes, God is in the details. Good and evil and all the gradations in between are enacted in everyday relationships. We all know our capacity to hurt those closest to us. That is why Leviticus commands is to love the *re'a*, the one nearest, the neighbor. It demands that we sanctify things like eating and drinking and sex—the stuff of ordinary life—and insists that these can, through our attentiveness, be raised up to holiness. After Freud we all know that sex is the master passion, and the current attention to rape and harassment confirms that sex is also the area in which ordinary people have the capacity to do immense amounts of harm—or to repair harm and do good.

I find this powerful stuff. It says to me that valuing existence does not

---

Tzav

was there only to make sure the sacrifice was done correctly. In the parlance of today, what was said at that altar stayed at that altar.

The priest's thumb was daubed with blood, too. Why the thumb? Maybe because the human hand is the only one in nature that we know of that accepts bribes. How tempting it would be for a man in such power as the priest to accept a little *protectzia* from a wealthy patron. Priests were the politicians of the day, and their influence must have been enormous. Daubing the sacrificial blood on the thumb provided a powerful way of remembering that what the priest was to receive in his hand was not favor or bribe but only the sacrifices of the men and women who appeared before him.

And what of the toe? I think the toes are the most neglected parts of the human body. We pay no attention to them until someone steps on them or we stub them on something. Then we are very aware of them! And when those nasty things happen, what happens to us (after the cussing is over, that is!)? We limp. We can barely move. In fact, the

lie on the world's historical stage of mythic events and persons. It rests with us—you and me—every day. We sense this whenever we discover meaning to life in conversations with our kids at unexpected moments, or connect deeply with spouse or friends over a cup of coffee in the kitchen, or contemplate a sunset at a spot that we have visited countless times before. Ritual repetitions are satisfying because they take place again and again in the time and place we inhabit, bringing the experience of perfection to every day. They are all the more satisfying because we enter into them with all our bodies: move and dance, sing and eat. That power is increased by the fact that we perform rituals together, with those to whom our lives are connected. We enact, in countless inevitable variations, a common script.

I confess that I sometimes wish Leviticus could have conveyed this path in another way, rather than through details of priests and animal slaughter. I wish one did not have to strain to hear its message, block out so much, work so hard. But I know too that in its time Leviticus would have been inaccessible had its idiom been anything other than sacrifice—and that there is power, even now, in the image of people placing their hands on living creatures, feeling their dread, smelling their odor, as the animals meet the fate that awaits us all. The point of the book is not to enjoy the gore, and certainly not to encourage morbidness. It wants us to face death without repression so as to live; to sanctify desire rather than suppress it. Its way is to contain both within a life so rich, an order so profound, that one can say in good faith: I can be good, life can be good. And that way may be all the more valuable because it is not one which we can walk in precisely the fashion that Leviticus describes. Rigidity and rote are the occupational hazards of ritual. We must make them live—in and through our performances—as they enable us to live.

"AND YOU SHALL ABIDE AT THE DOOR OF THE TENT OF MEETING DAY AND NIGHT FOR SEVEN DAYS, AND KEEP THE CHARGE OF THE LORD, THAT YOU DIE NOT—BUT LIVE, EVERYDAY, IN THE PROXIMITY OF GOD." SO AARON AND HIS SONS DID ALL THE THINGS WHICH THE LORD HAD COMMANDED BY THE HAND OF MOSHE [Lev. 8.35-36]. An experience of perfection rarely available in life, and not even guaranteed in ritual, as we learn from the very first words of next week's parashah. But Leviticus helps. It points and puts us on the way. ■

---

toes are not for walking at all. They are for balancing. And therein lies the reason for daubing blood on the big toe.

The priest had, at all times, to hold his identity in balance. He was, after all, the center of the community and chosen by God. His job was ripe for accusations of corruption at worst and hubris at best. How each understood himself and his position would give rise in future generations to both the most glorious chapters in Jewish history and some of its most embarrassing moments.

What is true of those ancient priests is true of us as well. God said to the Jewish people, "You are a kingdom of priests, a holy people." Every Jew, whether descended from the priests or a brand-new member of the people, is a holy person and part of the kingdom. Though we do not daub our earlobes, thumbs, and big toes as part of any apotropaic rite, its lessons must never evade us.

We are Jews. The Torah calls us נִבְחַר *nivhar*—"chosen." But, like the priests, this hardly means "better." It means only that as Jews, our responsibilities far outweigh any privileges that come with the title. We do not use the name to lord over others or to set ourselves as somehow better than others. Our task is to live Torah and to sanctify all that we do. As Hillel summed it up more than 2200 years ago to the man who asked him to recite the whole Torah while standing on one foot, "All that is hateful to you do not do to your neighbor. All the rest is commentary; go and learn it."

Rabbi Cy Stanway, Temple Beth El, Las Cruces, NM.

משה לאהרן ולבניו

This sidrah contains one of the most difficult passages in the entire Torah—those three terse verses that describe the death of the sons of Aaron, Nadab and Abihu. It tells the story of how, on the day of the consecration of the tabernacle, these two young men, on their own initiative, made their own offering to God, a "STRANGE FIRE" that "GOD HAD NOT COMMANDED," and how a fire came out from before God and consumed them.

It is the story of premature death, of people who die young, before they have reached the fullness of years; it is also about how to deal with a sense of outrage when this happens.

This commentary is also an offering, mine, in memory of friends who died young. In the twenty-six years that I lived in Jerusalem many were killed in Israel's wars: Mena<u>h</u>em and Mikki in '67, Shimshon and Arieh and Yehudah and David in '73, and another David, and Moshe and Shmulik, in the intervening "minor" campaigns and incidents. It is also dedicated to those who died young following terrible diseases, cancer, AIDS, and accidents, both in Israel and here: Naomi and Ariella and Elizabeth and Richard and Rob, and baby Benjamin; and there were others, forgive me, I can't remember all their names. And there were those who died at their own hands, Mel and Sarah and Josh most recently.

Parashat Shemini

Leviticus 9.1–11.47

Rabbi Jonathan Omer-Man

RABBI JONATHAN OMER-MAN IS THE DIRECTOR OF METIVTA CENTER FOR JEWISH WISDOM IN LOS ANGELES, CALIFORNIA.

דָּבָר אַחֵר DAVAR A<u>H</u>ER. A FIRE CAME FORTH FROM BEFORE GOD AND CONSUMED THEM, AND THEY DIED BEFORE GOD [Lev. 10. 2]. Rabbi Omer-Man's thoughts on the tragic deaths of Nadab and Abihu cut close to home for me as I read the morning paper. Jessica Dubroff, the seven-year-old would-be pilot who died yesterday, was to have arrived in my community, Falmouth, today. I remember seeing her when she lived in this town, riding her bike with her mother and siblings. As *Shemini* teaches us, and Rabbi Omer-Man amplifies, there are too many times in our lives when we are forced to confront stories of "premature death, of people who die young, of those who pass on before they have reached the fullness of years."

And I hear the echoes of Aaron's silence in my own inability to put into words the complex mix of emotions I feel in the wake of this young girl's

ויהי ביום השמיני קרא

Each and every one of these deaths was an outrage against what we feel is right, the way the world should work.

"The good die young," they say. It's true, they were all good, these dead friends, the very best. We can psychologize and observe that they ended their lives before they encountered the complexities of existence that make necessary the compromises that we survivors must make in our relationships, our careers, our friendships, our artistic or our political visions, but that's not really the point. They died, all of them, with a simpler, purer life behind them. Now I am sixty-two, and I no longer fear a premature death. My prayers are for a passing with dignity, preferably with a clean desk behind me and my surviving loved ones close at hand. But I look at the world around me and I am fearful. I hope that this is the last time I speak or write about this Torah portion.

Our tradition relates to the story of the deaths of Nadab and Abihu in one of two ways: the "mainstream," majority interpretation and the mystical minority view. The first, which I find truly obnoxious, simply blames the victims. The second, to which I have always been drawn in the past, sees in it a profound redemptive mystery. Maybe there is a third path today, that which sees God working through chance and statistics, but I prefer not to look that way.

The rabbis of the Talmud noted that the short description of the two youngsters' deaths is followed by an injunction against priests drinking alcohol before entering to perform

---

death...inexpressible sorrow (as the parent of an almost-seven-year-old), anger at parents who burden children with inappropriate expectations, awe at the ability of Torah to reach out to me from the headlines of a newspaper. **Rabbi Elias Lieberman, Falmouth Jewish Congregation, Falmouth, MA.**

דָּבָר אַחֵר DAVAR AHER. **A FIRE CAME FORTH FROM BEFORE GOD AND CONSUMED THEM, AND THEY DIED BEFORE GOD** [Lev. 10.2]. Rabbi Jonathan Omer-Man's explanation of the deaths of Nadab and Abihu was stimulating and moving. The young priests did not sin, but rather reached spiritual fulfillment. To reach the conclusion that God killed them because of the harsh words of the

SYNOPSIS: *The Mishkan is dedicated. Nadab and Abihu, Aaron's sons, die in a work-related accident. God warns Aaron and the other priests about drinking. Rules are given about which animals, birds, fish, and insects can be eaten.*

RASHI OF THE WEEK: *This week we have a ceremony, listen to Rashi's color commentary, and learn.* [9.1] IT WAS ON THE EIGHTH DAY.. *The eighth day of what? The eighth day of the inauguration of Aaron & Sons into the* Kahunah *(priesthood). The date was actually the first of Nisan, for on that day the Mishkan was erected. And this took the ten crowns that are in taught in* Seder Olam Rabbah.

When you check out Rashi's reference, we find these ten crowns: These ten things happened for the first time on the first of Nisan: (1) first day of Creation; (2) first offerings of the tribal princes; (3) first day of Aaron & Son's installation; (4) first day of regular sacrifices; (5) first day fire from heaven landed on the altar; (6) first day that altar cooking had to be eaten on the grounds of the Mishkan; (7) first day of no outside altars; (8) first day of first month of the year; (9) first day that Shekhinah dwelled with Israel; and (10) first day that the *Kohanim* performed their blessing. *Here the Mishkan and the Creation are directly linked (Seder Olam 7).*

(9.2) HE SAID TO AARON: "TAKE FOR YOURSELF A CALF..." *Why a calf?* To let Aaron understand that the Holy One had forgiven him through this calf for the Golden Calf. *When Aaron learned that* tshuvah *worked he could then help others make* tshuvah *in the same way.* (9.4) FOR THE ETERNAL APPEARS TO YOU TODAY. *No one can see God and live. How can God appear?* God will land the Shekhinah through the work of your hands. *And why the word "today"?* To show that today, when the sacrifices and their process of *tshuvah* begin, God can be experienced.

the divine service and conclude that the two were drunk! Another, similar interpretation is that they were disrespectful of their elders. We find here no sense of outrage or even mystery, though attention is given later to Aaron's grief and his way of mourning, which is in silence. (Mrs. Aaron lurking, unnamed, somewhere in the background there.) Ultimately, according to this reading, the two brothers were just bad boys.

A first intimation that this interpretation may not be correct can be found in the selection made for the Haftorah for this week. It is from Samuel II, and it tells another story of sudden, early death. It happens while David is trying to transport the ark to Jerusalem on a new oxcart, with great ceremony and music. Suddenly one of the oxen stumbles, and as the ark starts to fall Uzzah, apparently someone who just happens to be there, puts out his hand to save it. God is angry at him for this, and he is struck dead. This parallel text makes it quite clear that Uzzah had done nothing intentionally wrong (despite Hertz's "act of undue familiarity"), and that perhaps we can derive that Nadab and Abihu were similarly blameless. And in fact the mystical rabbis, also following subtle textual leads, conclude that not only were they innocent, but they were souls who had reached the highest possible level of purity. One such hint lies in the language of the Bible: "THEY DID WHAT THE LORD HAD NOT COMMANDED." It does not say that they did something that God had forbidden, but rather that what they did was over and beyond what was demanded. They make their offering out of great, possibly excessive love of God, not insobriety or impudence. And so in a line that flows through the Ari and Chaim Vital, through the Menahem Nahum of Chernobyl (from whose *Ma'or Einayim* most of these insights are derived) through the late Lubavitcher Rebbe (in a remarkable piece in his *Likkutei Sikhot*), we learn that what Nadab and Abihu

---

Shemini

great rabbis (many years after the deaths occurred), we must assume that in Torah there is no beginning, no end, no time line. Some find this concept difficult to accept.

But whether we believe the "sin" or the "fulfillment" theory, or whether there is or is not a time line, there is a modern-day lesson in all of this. It's a lesson that we see in several succeeding portions of Leviticus. Words, and how we use them, are powerful. With words we have the power to kill, and with words we have the power to bring comfort and healing.

Rabbi Omer-Man's explanation becomes even more appealing when we read the very next chapter of this sidrah, on the dietary laws. If we are mindful of what goes into our mouths, perhaps we shall be mindful of what comes out. **Richard J. Molish, Amber, PA.**

did was a perfect act of worship; that they had reached a level of complete alignment with the Divine; that they had completed their souls' work and were joined in total union with the higher light; that they alone had the ability to approach God, and their souls cleaved to God; that their cleaving was so total that there was no way for them to return; that their work in this world was different from, and in no way inferior to, that of Moses and Aharon; that they were whole; that they knew God in total passivity and were filled by the Divine light; and that not only was their death not a punishment—it was a fulfillment.

But then we may well ask, if they were truly perfect, why does the story end the way it does, with their deaths? Is there no room on this earth for completed human beings? To this we receive an unexpected answer from the Chernobyler. The old rabbis of the Talmud, he wrote, said that Nadab and Abihu were drunk, that they were disrespectful, that they were flawed. And as God does not want to prove the rabbis of the Talmud wrong, the sons of Aaron had to die. They were perfect human beings, and their actions were perfect, and the rabbis of the Talmud caused their death.

May we not be among those who slay the sons of Aaron again and again.■

דָּבָר אַחֵר DAVAR AHER. **A FIRE CAME FORTH FROM BEFORE GOD AND CONSUMED THEM, AND THEY DIED BEFORE GOD** [Lev. 10.2]. Déjà vu all over again, said the great philosopher Yogi Berra. *Shemini* reminds me of Yogi—sounds farfetched, but wait. As a Liberal Jew I continuously struggle with this parashah—imagine being killed because you put your *tefillin* on wrong—imagine Nadab and Abihu's surprise when Ha-Shem punished them for bringing foreign fire. It's a mistake; didn't we just do sin offerings?

The Midrashim give reasons for their punishment; drunkenness is the favorite, or plotting insurrection, planning to replace their father and uncle. Does this all make sense? Maybe. While delivering a *drash* at our minyan about looking past the law and concentrating on worship, someone brought up an understandable point. Nadab and Abihu say "wow," and just like that, Ha-Shem comes down, and poof, everything is consumed. "Let's try that. We'll perform the same ritual and bring Ha-Shem into our midst." The moral—It's not only doing the act but doing the ritual in the prescribed way. The questions: Who interprets the "right way," and why doesn't the thought count?

How does all this help? For me, my mother used to say; "It's not what you say but how you say it." The teachers talk of *keva* and *kavanah*; and I struggle with the text because I don't know the right way but rather a way, and that makes all the difference. By study and turning the text meaning comes to me slowly. I still contend that the purpose is to approach Ha-Shem, and the method (law) is less important.
Yoel Friedman, <jfried@aol.com>

דָּבָר אַחֵר DAVAR AHER. **MOSES SAID TO AARON: OF THIS DID GOD SPEAK, SAYING: "I WILL BE SANCTIFIED THROUGH THOSE WHO ARE NEAREST ME, THUS I WILL BE HONORED BEFORE THE ENTIRE PEOPLE"; AND AARON WAS SILENT** [Lev. 10.3]. In addition, Aaron was silent after Abihu and Nadab were taken to Ha-Shem for offering "alien fire." How much more appropriate would silence have been after loosing a seven-year-old to a foolish publicity stunt, rather than compounding the action by speaking of a seven-year-old who died doing what she loved. How much richer a life can be is never known but Aaron's silence would be preferable to this mother's interviews.
Yoel Friedman, <jfried@aol.com>

Rabbi Laura Geller

Rabbi Laura Geller is the Senior Rabbi of Temple Emanuel in Beverly Hills, California.

Shemini

Like my friend and teacher Rabbi Jonathan Omer-Man, I mourn the death of friends who have died before their time. Like Rabbi Omer-Man, I am too often called upon to help grieving parents try to understand the death of their child, or to be present as people mourn the loss of loved ones who have died too soon. Often the tragedy overwhelms me, leaving me without any words. Just today I met with a family to plan the funeral of their son, murdered on the eve of his wedding. Where can there be comfort?

Is it in this week's Torah portion, in the painful story of the deaths of Aaron's sons, Nadab and Abihu? Rabbi Omer-Man outlines two paths to understand the story. The first, the mainstream view, suggests that Nadab and Abihu sinned and therefore deserved to die. The second, the mystical, teaches that Nadab and Abihu had achieved a higher level of spirituality and that their death was a fulfillment. Neither view satisfies me—the first leaves me angry and the second leaves me frightened of closeness with God. Neither view helps me deal with my sense of anguish or outrage when people die prematurely; neither view offers me comfort.

Even if one holds the traditional interpretation that Nadab and Abihu were drunk, or disrespectful to Moses and Aaron, or filled with unbridled ambition, or acting on their own without consulting their teachers or others, their punishment, sudden death by fire, seems outrageous. Imagine any young person you know.

דָּבָר אַחֵר DAVAR AHER. God spoke to Aaron saying: "Do not drink intoxicating wine, you and your sons with you, when you come to the tent of meeting, that you not die—this is an eternal decree for your generations" [Lev. 10.8–9]. The story of Nadab and Abihu has puzzled me since I first read it as a young child. I have never been satisfied with either the mainstream explanations of the brothers' drunken state nor the mystical explanations that reverberate with Sufi philosophy that the ultimate conjunction with the Holy One necessarily means death. To this day I struggle with the text and like Aaron, I am dumbstruck.

But there is an important lesson I derive from the text. Immediately after the death of his sons God speaks to Aaron alone, without Moses, and without the B'nai Israel listening in. This is the only time in the whole Torah when Aaron receives *dibbur* from God on his own. This means to me that even in one's darkest hour God can still be heard. Aaron, like any of us who have experienced tragedy, can still be attuned to the voice of God if he chooses to. To paraphrase the Hasidic master, "Where is God? Wherever and whenever we choose to let Him in." **Rabbi Cy Stanway, Las Cruces, NM, <Rabbicy@aol.com>**

Who among them is not occasionally drunk, often disrespectful to elders, filled with ambition, or inclined to act without consulting the advice of his teachers? If these are capital offenses, we are all in jeopardy.

Our tradition teaches us that we all sin, and we are all capable of תְּשׁוּבָה *tshuvah*—repentance. Earlier in the parashah [Lev. 9.7] Moses says to Aaron: "Go to the altar." Rashi explains that Aaron hesitated to approach, so Moses said to him: "Why are you hesitant? It is for this that you were chosen." A Hasidic commentary, *Minhah Belulah,* continues: "The midrash says that the sacrifice looked to him like a calf, and that was why he hesitated." As it is known, a person's imagination is a product of those matters that are on his mind. Aaron just could not forget the episode of the Golden Calf, and the sin kept haunting him. That is why what he saw on the altar looked to him to be a calf. Moses therefore said to him: "It is for this you were chosen—it is because you always remember your sin and are ashamed of it that you were chosen to be the high priest."

Aaron got a second chance. He lived to reflect on his sin, to be ashamed of it, to do תְּשׁוּבָה *tshuvah*. Why was it different for his sons? The view that they deserved to die makes no sense to me. It is, as Rabbi Omer-Man suggests, a version of blaming the victim.

Rabbi Omer-Man's second view, the mystical, leaves me unsettled. While some may find comfort imagining that their cleaving to God was so perfect that there was no way for them to return, I am left with grieving parents and loved ones who would chose instead an imperfect cleaving and a living child.

Perhaps there is a third way to understand the story. Several parshiot later in the book of Leviticus, the parashah that takes its name from the death of Aaron's sons begins: And the Lord spoke to Moses after the death of the two sons of Aaron when they drew near before the Lord and died. [Lev. 16.1].

Rabbi Stephen Wylen points to a midrash from Tanhuma (*d'fus Aharei Mot*). One sage comments on the text: "Nadab and Abihu turned their eyes away from the presence of the Shekhinah and would not enjoy its radiance. Thus, 'they died before the Lord.'"

Rabbi Yohanan objected: "Literally? Did they die in the actual presence of God, according to the Divine will? Rather, the Torah verse comes to teach how painful it is for God when the children of the righteous die in their lifetime."

The midrash turns on two different understandings of the word לִפְנֵי *lifne* before. The first interpretation, the traditional view described above, is that God chose to have them die because of their sins—they died in the presence of God's will. But the second interpretation, that of Rabbi Yohanan, is different. He does not comment on the issue of guilt or innocence, or of spiritual fulfillment. Instead he argues that the Torah teaches us that whenever the young of good parents die, their death is לִפְנֵי הַשֵּׁם *lifne Ha-Shem,* before God, because God shares in our sorrow.

A tragic death is, as it were, before God's consciousness, in God's mind and heart, just as it is on ours. We can never really know why innocent people suffer, but perhaps we can know that God suffers with us.

This week's parashah is the middle of the entire Torah. Perhaps there is a hint here of middle age. We are in the middle of the journey from slavery to the Promised Land, to a Promised Land that none of the generation of the desert will enter. Nadab and Abihu die, they are buried, and the people move on. Our people are middle-aged now, grown-up people who have experienced real life: joy and tragedy, birth and death, all the complex paradoxes of human existence.

They, like us, know from their own experience that life is sometimes full of pain, and there are no easy answers. Not for us, and not even, perhaps, for God.■

אשה כי **תזריע** וילדה זכר

Parashat Tazria
Leviticus 12.1–13.59

Rabbi Sheldon Zimmerman

Rabbi Sheldon Zimmerman is President of Hebrew Union College–Jewish Institute of Religion.

In last year's *dvar* Torah on *Tazria,* our teacher Rabbi Arthur Green reminded us of the many lessons that we learn from the role of the priest. Like many other teachers and rabbis, I have struggled with the portion. I have become more and more convinced of the centrality of the book of *Va-Yikra* and the role of the priest in our own self- and communal understanding. Permit me, then, to build on Rabbi Green's teaching and at the same time underscore the role of the priest.

The book of *Va-Yikra* helps us understand human weakness and frailty and the need for creating holy and healing communities. The need for rituals and support that enable us to transcend our alienation from God, transform our shame and guilt into wholeness again, and help us return to God (if you will, an at-oneness with God and ourselves). The rituals and sacrificial cult may be of another time and place, but the lessons are clear and profound. *Tazria,* in particular, is our teacher.

The Kohen is the watchperson, the guardian of the sanctity of the community and those who live in it. When a disease that was deemed to be dangerous to others struck, the Kohen examined the person and made the diagnosis. The illness was not always physical. It could be of the soul or spirit or both.

As rabbis, as Jewish leaders, we are required to be vigilant—both of the

---

דָּבָר אַחֵר DAVAR AHER. IF SHE GIVES BIRTH TO A FEMALE, SHE SHALL BE CONTAMINATED FOR TWO WEEKS, AS DURING HER SEPARATION…UPON THE COMPLETION OF THE DAYS OF HER PURITY FOR A SON OR FOR A DAUGHTER, SHE SHALL BRING A SHEEP WITHIN ITS FIRST YEAR FOR AN ELEVATION OFFERING, AND A YOUNG DOVE OR A TURTLEDOVE FOR A SIN OFFERING, TO THE ENTRANCE TO THE TENT OF MEETING, TO THE KOHEN [Lev. 12.5–6].

TAZRIA: THE WONDER OF BIRTH. *Tazria* teaches the proper ritual purification after childbirth. When we examine it in a larger Jewish and human context, the meaning of this often troubling passage becomes clearer. Indeed, Everett Fox notes that "ritual here reflects what is happening psychologically" (Everett Fox, trans. and ed.,*The Five Books of Moses*, Schocken, NY, 1995, p. 562. All biblical quotes are from Fox's

health of our community and of each individual in it. To guard the well-being of the community, persons may need to be singled out—quarantined—but at the same time, not ignored. The Kohen was required to care for them, even if it meant putting his own sanctity as a Kohen (because of potential impurity) and as a person on the line. For me this has meant intervention with alcoholics, with drug and substance abusers, to get them into recovery programs and, if need be, help remove them from the family or community that enabled their disease or was harmed by it. I acted not as a doctor but as rabbi. This involves putting our personness and dignity on the line with the person, the family, and the community. The same applies to such issues as domestic violence. People do not appreciate a diagnosis, calling attention to the illness. The Kohen required courage to call what was *tameh, tameh*!

We need to be on the alert for those whose behavior is dangerous to the sanctity of our community. Unethical or questionable business, legal, or professional behavior can result in a *hillul Ha-Shem* for the community. Too often we have honored men and women, given them leadership positions for their material generosity, and ignored the practices that might have produced the affluence. What are we modeling for ourselves, our children, and our community? The modern Kohen must lead in discerning *tameh* as *tameh*. At the same time these men and women need and deserve the message of potential healing and return that Torah offers, and that the teacher of Torah can help make real in their lives.

Often we cast out, leave out, or disregard the sick, the lonely, the unpopular, those with AIDS, those who no longer fit in (widows, the divorced, the dependent elderly, etc.). But they are not "dangerous"

translation). To see *Tazria* in a larger context we must see it in the context of other kinds of טֻמְאָה *tumah* (ritual stain), then in the context of the concern about blood. (Fox points out that the noun טֻמְאָה *tumah* and the adjective טָמֵא *tameh* refer to a ritual state and not to any uncleanliness in a physical sense. *Tameh* is better rendered either "ritually stained" or "polluted." See Fox, p. 497.) Finally, we can see *Tazria* as a ritual response to our great wonder at our body's ability to reproduce a new human being.

VARIETIES OF *TUMAH*. The *tumah* of childbirth is one of the three main forms of טֻמְאָה *tumah*: leprosy (צָרַעַת *tzara'at*), contact with the dead (human beings and some animals), and an issue from a sexual organ. There are a number of different issues from sex organs that cause טֻמְאָה *tumah*: emission of

SYNOPSIS: *Laws of impurity, skin disease, leprosy. Procedures for dealing with leprosy.*

RASHI OF THE WEEK:

In verses 13.12 and 13 the Torah teaches: THE *TZARA'AT* ERUPTS ON HIS SKIN, AND COVERS THE ENTIRE SKIN OF THE AFFLICTED FROM HIS HEAD TO HIS FEET—EVERYWHERE THE KOHEN CAN SEE. HE SHALL DECLARE THE AFFLICTION TO BE (NOW) PURE. *Then comes the surprising verse* [13.14]: AND ON THE DAY THAT THE HEALTHY FLESH APPEARS, HE SHALL BE IMPURE. *Rashi asks:* Why? Why is "the day" stated? *To teach us that there is a day when you need to look at afflictions to decide if they have become pure, and there is a day on which you do not look. From this verse we learn and the Sages taught that a bridegroom has seven days of celebration for him, his clothes, his robe, his garment, and even for his house, and even if he gets a tzara'at it is ignored until afterward. Likewise for any Jew during the week of a festival. Even though life slimes us with all kinds of spiritual afflictions and vortexes of depression, celebration has a spiritual force of its own.*

to the welfare of our community, and they must be brought back.

The image of the ark of the covenant described in *Berakhot* is a Torah imperative. What happened to the first set of tablets that Moses shattered? It was placed in the Ark with the second whole set: לוּחוֹת וְשִׁבְרֵי לוּחוֹת הָיוּ בָּאָרוֹן *Lukhot u'Shivray Lukhot hayu ba-Aron.* The ark is a metaphor for *shlemut*—the wholeness of our sacred communities. Both the broken and the whole have to be a part of it.

During the period of isolation the ill were tended to by the Kohen. Serving God was not limited to matters of the sanctuary but included, as a necessary component, caring for each individual created in God's image. The Kohen checked their condition and determined when they were healed. For us this means praying with, and for, the ill and their families, tending to their spiritual needs.

In a unique and caring way the priest enacted a ceremony of return so that the afflicted person could return home. Many men and women have complained about the difficulty of returning to their communities after an illness or after a change in their marital situation. Representing the religious institution, the Kohen created the venue for return through ritual and support, and his authority could not be questioned. What a dramatic and impelling mitzvah for us—God awaits the return, and we, as a holy community caring for each of its members, help make it happen by the support we offer—ritually, programmatically, and communally.

This act of bringing back the broken serves as a promise that from our brokenness can come healing. Our brokenness is paired with the unbroken set of tablets. *Shlemut* is not perfection. It is the wholeness born from the broken, the not-yet-broken, and the healed—for we are all broken at some time. The *Kohen* is our symbolic exemplar. ■

Tazria

semen, where the man acquires טֻמְאָה *tumah* [Lev. 15.16], emission of semen in sexual intercourse, where both the man and the woman become טָמֵא *tameh* [Lev. 15.18]; menstruation [Lev. 15.19]; and the blood of childbirth [Lev. 12.2]; which gives rise to the separation required in *Tazria.*

In Judaism blood is also connected to eating meat: "FLESH WITH ITS LIFE, ITS BLOOD, YOU ARE NOT TO EAT!" [Gen. 9.4].

We are warned, "AND ANY BLOOD YOU ARE NOT TO EAT THROUGHOUT ALL YOUR SETTLEMENTS, (EITHER) OF FOWL OR OF A DOMESTIC-ANIMAL. ANY PERSON THAT EATS ANY BLOOD—CUT OFF SHALL THAT PERSON BE FROM HIS KINSPEOPLE!" [Lev. 7.26–27]. (See also Lev. 17.10–14.) Blood represents life; we pour it during שְׁחִיטָה *she<u>h</u>itah* as a sign that we are not ultimately entitled to the life of the animal; all life comes from God.

Rabbi Margaret Holub

Margaret Holub is the Rabbi of the Mendocino Coast Jewish Community/Rural Alternative Shtetl. Rabbi Holub served as an advocate for the homeless in Los Angeles before coming to Mendocino Coast Jewish Community.

***Tazria* begins by saying that a woman who gives birth to a boy child is unclean for half as long as the woman who gives birth to a girl child. At the end of her period of uncleanliness she is required to make two sacrifices: a burnt offering and a sin offering. A sin offering? What is the problem here?**

Rashi asks why the verse אִשָּׁה כִּי תַזְרִיעַ וְיָלְדָה *Isha ki Tazria v'Yaldah,* A woman who spreads seed and gives birth, doesn't simply say, "A woman who gives birth".

As is sometimes the case, his question is better than his answer (that the "spreading seed" refers to the awful, and unlikely, possibility of birthing a dead fetus, which emerges pulpy like seed). So for now, hold that question.

Next we get a taxonomy for diagnosing skin diseases. When an Israelite comes to the priest with a skin affliction, the first question is whether the sore is deeper than the עוֹר-בְּשָׂרוֹ *or b'saro*, the skin of the flesh. If the sore has penetrated the epidermis, then it is considered to be leprous, and its bearer is unclean.

I have never been too happy with either of these uncleanlinesses, that of the mother or that of the leper. But this year I am struck by the detail of the spreading of seed and then that of the sore that penetrates the epidermis. In both cases what we have is a mixing of inner and outer reaches of the body, the inner flowing into the outer, the outer penetrating the inner.

Tazria is content with the presence of disease as long as the barrier of the epidermis is not violated. But if the skin is penetrated—unclean! I am trying to

---

Not only in the eating of meat in general but also in the sacrifices we are instructed, "any blood you are not to eat!" [Lev. 3.17] The presence of blood causes feelings of life and death within us. Blood symbolizes life, but bleeding may lead to death. When we return to our main concern we see that menstruation represents the ability to create life, while the flow of blood also connotes death. In birth there is the new life, but again the flow of blood connotes death. In a note on Leviticus 12.4, For thirty days and three days she is to stay in her period of blood purification, Fox explains: "That is, being 'decontaminated' from the state of danger between life and death that childbirth represents" (Fox, p. 565).

WONDER OF REPRODUCTION. Two very powerful human experiences come together here. One is the creation of life involving menstruation, sexual intercourse, semen, and childbirth, and the other is the blood of both life and death.

find some equivalency in the fact that childbirth, the ultimate example of inner coming outward (and also menstruation, though not in this chapter), likewise provokes the response of "unclean." But there is nothing unclean, nothing sinful about menstruation, about childbirth, or for that matter—except in terms of hygiene—about illness. Much pain is caused by these ascriptions of uncleanness and sinfulness.

There has been much debate about just what unclean and sinful mean. Maybe, say some authors, unclean doesn't mean unclean. Maybe a sin offering isn't for sin. But that's what the text says, and I can't find a way to undo it. What I can try to do is find a *nehemta*, a word of comfort, beyond this bad news.

And I find it in the protection of the barrier inner and outer. Sometimes I like to contemplate the useless and obvious point that I will never see most of my own body. I wonder if my heart has a freckle on it, if I really have two kidneys. In some ways our viscera are a little bit like God. They do countless miracles daily. We depend on them utterly. They are extraordinarily, but not entirely, forgiving. They operate most of the time without us ever thinking about them. And we don't really know all that much about them, even if we are scientists. It's nice to think that there is a precious, hidden inner world, that it is shielded by something itself as remarkable as skin, that it is protected from intrusion from without, and that we women—monthly and on the occasion of giving birth—flow outward, giving us a hint of what's in there, and that that flow from within scares the guys to death!■

Tazria

Why would a woman who experiences the miracle of birth be called טָמֵא *tameh* and placed ritually apart? Perhaps to remove the woman from the everyday stream of life, since what she experienced had such extraordinary power. Yet we would expect that a person would be told to make an offering or perform some act of drawing close to God as an expression of thankfulness or wonder rather than a separation, from the holiness of the Temple. One might remember that a woman does go into the Temple at the end of the separation after childbirth. Is it possible that she needs a time to fully recover both physically and existentially from "intimate contact with the life/death boundary during childbirth" rather than immediately going to the temple [Fox, p. 652]? Or is it possible that there were two kinds of holiness here that the tradition did not want to mingle?

CONTEMPORARY CONCERNS. One difficulty is that טֻמְאָה *tumah* is often understood as "uncleanness," connoting something dirty, when it really means ritually stained and requires a state of being apart.

טֻמְאָה *Tumah* and יְמֵי טָהֳרָה *y'may tahorah*, the days of blood purification may be considered as the time when a woman is removed from the daily routine after having been through an experience of life-death wonder. The new mother is set apart because she has been through a miraculous, numinous experience. From menstruation to sexual relations to childbirth—each one involves טֻמְאָה *tumah* to a greater or lesser extent and requires a drawing back. This is the picture of a person who has just experienced something very profound and needs time to work through and assimilate that experience with the rest of their lives. We do that with shivah after a death. Is birth any less profound?

Some have been troubled because the state of being apart is twice as long for a girl as for a boy, implying that a female child causes more "uncleanness" than a male. And yet if we see this being apart not as uncleanness but as a response to a profound experience, the double period of being apart acknowledges the mystery that this girl baby has the same potential to conceive, carry, give birth, and nurse a child as the mother.

THE CHALLENGE TO US. Torah not only confirms what we already believe, but it also confronts us, forcing us to examine our own ways of thinking. *Tazria* is one of those "difficult" passages that does just that. It challenges us with significant questions regarding our sexuality and the great wonder of our ability to reproduce: How are we to regain a sense of awe at our reproductive power? How are we to react to our awe? How are we to find a language to bring to mind and heart what we feel deep within us but which we may not know how to express? This is especially significant since we live in a time when sexuality is increasingly seen as recreational rather than reproductive. Perhaps in the appropriate understanding of sexuality as an important component in human intimacy we have lost sight of our reproductive power. This is especially true since we can now control so much of that reproductive power, whether thwarting it through birth control or enhancing it with treatments for infertility. **Rabbi Adam Fisher, Temple Isaiah, Stony Brook, NY.**

דָּבָר אַחֵר DAVAR AHER. IF SHE GIVES BIRTH TO A FEMALE, SHE SHALL BE CONTAMINATED FOR TWO WEEKS, AS DURING HER SEPARATION...UPON THE COMPLETION OF THE DAYS OF HER PURITY FOR A SON OR FOR A DAUGHTER, SHE SHALL BRING A SHEEP WITHIN ITS FIRST YEAR FOR AN ELEVATION-OFFERING, AND A YOUNG DOVE OR A TURTLEDOVE FOR A SIN-OFFERING, TO THE ENTRANCE TO THE TENT OF MEETING, TO THE KOHEN [Lev. 12.5–6]. **[1]** Why is a woman impure after the birth of a child? She didn't do anything wrong. She wasn't dealing with impure things. Is she impure so as to give her a time out? If you're impure, people will stay away from you. The mother would have a nice amount of time to relax before returning to the "real world." Why is she impure seven days for a son and fourteen days for a daughter? **[C.J.]**

[GRIS]: Here is a question I don't want to answer. I am not afraid of the answer; I am just not sure I really understand it. Here are the things I do know. *Tumah* is a tough concept. We translate it as "impure," but it is a spiritual category, not a question of dirt. It needs a spiritual change, not soap and water. Basically, two things make you impure—contact with death fluids and contact with sex fluids. You can get death-slimed and sex-slimed. Both things can wipe out your spiritual state. Here is the idea. If you come into contact with death, you are slimed. Your spiritual state collapses. A depression sets in, and you need to do some work in order to get your life back in balance. You are not bad. You are not dirty—rather your spirit is not טָהוֹר *tahor* (shining/pure) at that moment. Sex can do the same thing. It is not bad or dirty; it just draws your mind/soul to a different place. Birth is a combination of both—death-blood and sex-aftermath. And more than anything, birth wonderfully distracts a mother from her normal spiritual state. In her book *The Voice of Sarah*, Tamar Frankiel reaches the same conclusion you do—that the days of *tumah* following birth are a gift of spiritual isolation and bonding time between mother and child; just what a woman needs.

In *Leviticus Rabbah* 14.1 Rabbi Simlai asks the same question you did: "Why do daughters make a mother impure for twice as long as sons do?" (implying that there was something wrong with having girls). He answers his question by reading in context Leviticus 12.3, which addresses circumcision. He says: "It should have been fourteen days for both, but the circumcision needed to take place on the eighth day. Shortening the period of isolation allowed the mother to attend." **[GRIS]**

[2] Does the Kohen have to offer sacrifices in both circumstances, or does the *brit milah* automatically make her pure if she had a son? **[C.J.]**

The Torah makes it clear that the same sacrifice is offered in both cases—son or daughter. The fun part is that this is a sin offering. So you ask: "What is the sin in having a child? I thought this was a miracle." Rabbi Simeon says this in the Talmud on *Niddah* 31b: "She offers a sin offering not for the act of intercourse which produced the child, not for the act of giving birth, but to apologize for anything rude she might have said during labor." It is like the Bill Cosby routine where he says, "In the middle of labor my wife stood up in the stirrups and said that my father wasn't married to my mother." **Joel Lurie Grishaver, <joel@torahaura.com>**

Tazria

דָּבָר אַחֵר DAVAR AHER. THE KOHEN SHALL LOOK AT IT, AND BEHOLD!—THE AFFLICTION HAS CHANGED TO WHITE, THE KOHEN SHALL DECLARE THE AFFLICTION PURE; IT IS PURE [Lev. 13.17]. **צָרַעַת** *Tzara'at.* Leprosy. Rotting skin. Wounds that ooze endlessly with stagnant pus. Body odor that knows no cosmetic cover-up. Excruciating pain that tests the endurance of even the most faithful among us. A real disease that afflicts real people, causing real suffering, real disfigurement, and real death. It would be easier not to talk about it, to avoid it, to pretend that it does not exist—as did some of the early Reformers—and instead together probe the depths of meaning in other Torah text. But there is no point mincing words, no reason to try to turn the Torah into a kinder, gentler sort of document that radiates only Divine light and sheds no darkness, a sacred text that elevates the spirit while avoiding the existential realities of human existence. The Torah is as much of this world—the world of the physical body—as it is of the other world—the world of spirit and soul.

Parashat Tazria and *Parashat Metzora* may be about leprosy to the ancient folk, but they are not about sickness or disease of the body, not about folk medicine and healing, not even about ritual impurity and priestly cleansing. *Metzora* is merely a metaphor. It is about the disease of the soul, a disease to which we are all susceptible, a disease that is so powerful it can consume the body and the spirit in one fell swoop. Yes, our Torah portion is all about diseased and broken souls. But what is frightening about *Metzora* is not the wounds that require constant attention that are described in sickening detail here and elsewhere. No, what is frightening about our portion is the way *Metzora,* in its bleak and dismal darkness, finds a way to reflect the dark side of the self and make it even more so.

Through the genius of the biblical author—who points out through the body what she wants to teach us about the soul—we seem to learn just a little bit more about ourselves. Listen carefully to what she is teaching us. This week's Torah portion reminds us that with all the good we have to offer, everything commendable that we have discovered about ourselves, there remains a dark side, a defect, a misalignment of character. When we forget, that's when the disease erupts. Perhaps it is *davka* because of the haughtiness of self-aggrandizement, a belief that we have achieved a certain level of moral perfection; צָרַעַת *tzara'at* reminds us that we are human, imperfect, prone to moral error. Like so many other bodily diseases that live inside of us all the time, threatening to play havoc with our bodies when we least expect it, צָרַעַת *tzara'at* is always there, every ready to erupt and take control. And when the צָרַעַת *tzara'at* gushes forth, its lesions may adhere to our bodies, but it also casts a shadow over our souls. And only the bright light of Torah, which has the power to illuminate our lives, can diminish the darkness of our souls.

According to the Torah text, a white leprous swelling of the skin is a symptom of ritual impurity or uncleanness. However, when the skin on the entire body turns white, after the disease has run its course and the body has responded, this whiteness is then declared a mark of cleanness. And we learn from the text that the priest is the only one capable of healing a person of his or her leprosy. But what is taking place? The priest does not actually heal the person of leprosy. And the lesions do not disappear in their entirety; they leave their mark on the individual in the form of a white powder. And so by analyzing this unusual process of ritual cleansing we come to understand that through this process the priest takes on the leprosy himself. By transferring the burden from the one who is afflicted, he leaves only the trace reminder of the disease with the afflicted person. The priest—that's you and me in our particular understanding of the text—carries that burden and adds it to the burdens of others and of his own broken soul. By doing so, he is able to help people experience their lives as a blessing once again. At the same time we realize that although we, like the leper, are unclean and broken, through real healing we have the power to cleanse one another. When we recognize this profound spiritual truth, then we—as modern priests—can begin the process of healing our self and others. **Rabbi Kerry Olitzky, <olitzky@huc.org>**

דָּבָר אַחֵר DAVAR AHER. **As for the person with a leprous affection, his clothes shall be rent, his head shall be left bare, and he shall cover over his upper lip; and he shall call out, "Unclean! Unclean!"** [Lev. 13.45]. Why does the leper have to shave his head, and does that include shaving his beard? If the leper is a woman, do the same rules apply? What exactly does the leper cover his mouth with? And if they cover their lips with anything, doesn't that make it a lot harder to shout "Unclean, Unclean?" Just another reason to not take modern medicine for granted. **[C.J.]**

The head shaving is part of the cleansing ritual, not part of the cure. It is the transition from the end of the leprosy back to society. The Talmud asks the same sort of question you do: "All his hair?" And then answers, "Every bit of hair—everywhere (except for the eyebrows)." Sefer ha-Hinukh says, "All hair is shaved, so that the end of the disease feels like a rebirth, and he or she is now as naked as a newborn." The covering of the lip, the Talmud suggests, is clothing up to the lip. Imagine walking around with a turtle neck turned up and over your mouth. This is sort of a biblical surgical mask. **Joel Lurie Grishaver, Torah-Toons Gazette.**

דָּבָר אַחֵר DAVAR AHER. **As the cloud withdrew from the Tent, there was Miriam stricken with snow-white scales!** [Num.12.10]. "There is no longer צָרַעַת *tzara'at* (biblical leprosy) today because there is no קְדוּשָׁה *kedushah* (holiness) to cancel it. In the old days, when קְדוּשָׁה *kedushah* was strong enough to change things, צָרַעַת *tzara'at* came as a reminder that some actions needed to be curbed" [*Alshech*]. Biblical leprosy wasn't a medical condition; it was a spiritual one. (That's what the rabbis understood.) It was rooted in Miriam, the righteous lady who one time lost it with Moses' marriage and did some word-hurting. God got even. As a response she was zapped with צָרַעַת *tzara'at*—only because Miriam de l'Midrash is a holy enough lady "to change her evil ways," do תְּשׁוּבָה *t'shuvah*, and heal herself. When that kind of קְדוּשָׁה *kedushah* vanished from the

Tazria

world, God, the Teacher, pulled the plug on that kind of discipline. God's lesson was simple—if the utz doesn't teach, then pull the plug. The Talmud (*Brakhot*) discusses a strange concept called אִסּוּרִים שֶׁל אַהֲבָה *issurim shel ahavah* (wounds of love). The notion is that God picks on people whom God loves—just because they can take it and can grow from it. When God judges challenging words or the punishment, any kind of צָרַעַת *tzara'at* (spiritual blemishing) can't be self-healed; then God stops. We teachers need to be Godlike in the same way. Sometimes self-image needs to be pricked for growth—but only if there is enough קְדוּשָּׁה *kedushah* to put it back together. We are supposed to push as hard as we can when there is קְדוּשָּׁה *kedushah*, the holy power of change, and to back off when there isn't. This is a judgment line I miss all the time—I often err on the side of מָרוֹר *maror* (bitter herbs). Just ask some teachers I've tried to train recently. Knowing "when to hold them and when to fold them" is always hard. That is why teaching is an art. Today we are absent enough קְדוּשָּׁה *kedushah* and enough צָרַעַת *tzara'at* to ever really know the difference. Meanwhile, my own skin is itching. I guess God loves me. **Joel Lurie Grishaver, <joel@torahaura.com>**

זאת תהיה תורת המצורע

How Do You Free Yourself from That Which Isolates You?

P*arashat Metzora* outlines the way a person, once healed of scaled disease (not leprosy), was brought back to the community. The ritual recounted at the beginning of this parashah may, at first glance, seem bizarre: THE LORD SPOKE TO MOSES, SAYING: "THIS SHALL BE THE RITUAL FOR A SCALE-DISEASED PERSON AT THE TIME OF HIS PURIFICATION.

WHEN IT IS REPORTED TO THE PRIEST, THE PRIEST SHALL GO OUTSIDE THE CAMP. IF THE PRIEST SEES THAT THE SCALE-DISEASED PERSON HAS BEEN HEALED OF SCALE DISEASE, THE PRIEST SHALL ORDER TWO WILD PURE BIRDS, CEDAR WOOD, CRIMSON YARN, AND HYSSOP TO BE BROUGHT FOR THE ONE TO BE PURIFIED. THE PRIEST SHALL ORDER ONE BIRD SLAUGHTERED INTO AN EARTHEN VESSEL OVER SPRING WATER; AND HE SHALL TAKE THE LIVE BIRD, ALONG WITH THE CEDAR WOOD, THE CRIMSON YARN, AND THE HYSSOP, AND DIP THEM TOGETHER WITH THE LIVE BIRD IN THE BLOOD OF THE BIRD THAT WAS SLAUGHTERED OVER THE SPRING WATER. HE SHALL THEN SPRINKLE [THE BLOOD] SEVEN TIMES ON THE ONE TO BE PURIFIED OF THE SCALE DISEASE. WHEN HE HAS THUS PURIFIED THEM, HE SHALL RELEASE THE LIVE BIRD OVER THE OPEN COUNTRY" [Lev. 14.1–7].

Naturally, there are many ways of understanding this ritual. We will examine it from several points of view. As we do, it will be helpful to remember that the human need that generated this ritual—the need to be definitively rid of that which isolates a person from

Parashat Metzora
Leviticus 14.1–15.33

Rabbi Judith Z. Abrams, Ph.D.

RABBI JUDITH ABRAMS IS THE FOUNDER OF MAQOM, A SCHOOL FOR ADULT TALMUD STUDY IN HOUSTON, TX. IN ADDITION, RABBI ABRAMS TEACHES TALMUD ON THE INTERNET AT HTTP:\\WWW.COMPASSNET.COM\~MAQOM\.

דָּבָר אַחֵר DAVAR AHER. **IF, WHEN HE EXAMINES THE PLAGUE, THE PLAGUE IN THE WALLS OF THE HOUSE IS FOUND TO CONSIST OF GREENISH OR REDDISH STREAKS...THE PRIEST SHALL COME OUT OF THE HOUSE...AND CLOSE UP THE HOUSE FOR SEVEN DAYS** [Lev. 37–38]. Leprosy is described as "green or red stuff." Is leprosy then some sort of primitive fungus? What is the difference between skin leprosy and house leprosy? **[C.J.]**

We don't know what caused skin מְצֹרָע *metzora*—except that we know what isn't. Milgrom, in his amazing new Anchor Commentary on Leviticus, writes, "Biblical צָרַעַת *tzara'at* is difficult to identify. One thing, however, is certain, it is not leprosy." He then says, "The most recent, comprehensive medical analysis of צָרַעַת *tzara'at* reaches the following conclusion: psoriasis is the disease that fulfills most (but not all) of the characteristics except that נֶתֶק *netek* (Lev. 13.39)

other people and from God—is still present and functioning in our lives and informs two of the rituals that many of us practice today. We will use the four levels of Torah study—the simple level (פְּשָׁט *p'shat*), the allegorical level (רֶמֶז *remez*), the rabbinic level (דְּרָשׁ *drash*), and the mystical level (סוֹד *sod*)—to understand this text.

פְּשָׁט *P'shat:* Reinterpreting a Pagan Ritual

What in the world is this ritual all about? Let's unpack each symbol and practice outlined in the verses above, and it will become clear. Once a person who suffered from scale disease had been cured, he was considered pure. However, before he could rejoin the community he had to go through a three-step purification ritual. (The first step is outlined in the verses we are studying.)

Jacob Milgrom, in *The Anchor Bible Leviticus 1-16*, suggests that this whole ritual is designed to transfer the ritual impurity from the person through the first bird's blood, and the water, cedar, and hyssop to the live, wild bird that will then fly away and carry the impurity with it. In a new bowl (which is then broken because it, too, has absorbed the ritual impurity) the blood of one bird and "living" water (i.e., water drawn from a moving source such as a river) are mixed. Why do we need the water? For two reasons: (1) This mixture is intensely symbolic of life, since blood and water are the fluids without which life cannot be sustained; and (2) The blood of one bird would not suffice to conduct the ritual, so it must be diluted with water. Why *mayim hayim*, "living water"? First, the theme of life is, in itself, important to this ritual. In addition, the living water moves as a living person does, as opposed to lake water or ocean water, which is relatively stagnant and thus like a dead person.

Metzora

resembles *favus*, a fungus infection of the skin, and the pure skin condition called בֹּהַק *bohak* resembles vitiligo." Then, in a personal note, he adds that in checking with a dermatologist, while the symptoms match pretty well, the Torah's description of a two-week cure is out of context with anything we know.

Maimonides (also a doctor) writes, "This affliction is a Divine sign that God is displeased with one's behavior, and that God has withdrawn God's presence from the sinner, and that there is a need to examine one's actions and to see what needs to be improved" (Laws of Cleanliness, 16.10).

House leprosy seems to be a house with fungus growing. In ancient Mesopotamia black-colored wall fungus was seen to be a sign of health and prosperity, but white,

Why do we need the cedar wood (which can be red in color), red yarn, and hyssop (marjoram, which is like oregano)? The red components underscore the life-intensive nature of the ritual, as they are the color of blood, contrasting with the white color of the scale disease. The wood, spice, and yarn are bound together and dipped in the blood and water mixture; then the wild bird is touched with the liquid and is released, carrying the ritual impurity with it. Hyssop is often used as an "applicator" in purification rituals [e.g., Ex. 12.22, Num. 19.18].

These practices take place after the person has become healed from the scale disease. However, in the pagan world that surrounded the Jews at this time, similar rituals were conducted *before* the healing had taken place in order to exorcise the demon causing the disease. Thus the priestly practice of performing these rituals only *after* healing had taken place was a way of disconnecting ritual impurity and scale disease from the ideas of possession and paganism. The average person probably found this ritual highly effective and comforting and could not, or would not, do without it. Therefore the priests performed it but reinterpreted its meaning to distance it from its pagan sources.

רֶמֶז *Remez:* Reinterpreting the Reinterpretation

Our commentators saw the condition of the scale-diseased person and the ritual of purification as allegories regarding one's moral behavior. *Ba'al Haturim* suggests that the cured person is sprinkled with the bloody water seven times because it relates to the seven sins for which scale disease was thought to come upon a person (slander, the shedding of blood, vain oath, incest, arrogance, robbery, and envy; *B.*

---

red, and green fungus are signs of trouble. Fungal houses are known as real problems in all kinds of Middle Eastern literature. In the midrash *Pesikta Rabbatai* 17 we are given the relationship of clothes, house, and skin *metzora*. All are considered to be signs from God. The classical notion is that first God attacks the house with fungus, warning a person to repent. If that does no good, then his clothes become infested with fungus. And if that does no good, his or her own skin. **[GRIS]**

Just a point of information—the Spanish flag is red and yellow. The MEXICAN flag (and Italian and Bulgarian, I think) are red, white, and green. **Simon Goulden, London <aje@brijnet.org>**

[2] If the house a family is living in has leprosy, where do they live?

SYNOPSIS: *Leprosy II. How priests effect cures. Procedures for the cure. House leprosy. Other bodily discharges and their purification rituals.*

RASHI OF THE WEEK:

Inside Metzora is the strange case of House leprosy. Inside that case is this strange verse: THE KOHEN WILL COMMAND, AND BEFORE THE KOHEN COMES TO LOOK AT THE AFFLICTION, ONE SHOULD REMOVE EVERYTHING THAT IS IN THE HOUSE SO THAT IT SHOULD NOT BECOME IMPURE [Lev. 14.36]. *Here the* Kohen *is playing peek-a-boo with the leprosy. If he doesn't see it, it isn't impure. This is our first clue that we are dealing with a spiritual state, not an infection. Rashi asks:* What is the Torah trying to protect? If the Kohen comes and the house is declared unclean, little will happen to most things that are in it. Unclean utensils can be taken to the mikvah and rinsed. Food and drink can be consumed during his days of being impure. All that is left is the clay vessels, which cannot be purified by the mikvah. It was on these that the Torah took pity. *Learn from the language: for Rashi, God takes pity on vessels—we have a lot to learn.*

Arakhin 15b-16a). *Rabbeinu Bakhya* suggests that the two species, the tall cedar and the lowly hyssop that grows close to the ground, are used to suggest two stages of the person's development. He contracted the scale disease because he elevated himself as high as the cedar. Only when he belittles himself, like hyssop, will he be able to atone for his sins. Thus later sources reinterpret this powerful ritual in symbolic ways that make it refer to moral characteristics rather than a transfer of impurity from one entity to another.

דְּרָשׁ *Drash:* Returning to the Original Concept

Many Jews today engage yearly in two rituals strikingly similar to the purification ritual outlined in the verses we are studying. One is the ceremony called *tashli<u>h</u>*, which means "casting away" or "throwing away." On the afternoon of the first day of Rosh Ha-Shanah (unless it is Shabbat) Jews go to a body of water, "preferably one that contains living fish," and symbolically throw their sins away by casting bread into the water. We symbolically transfer our sins to the bread, and the fish eat our sins, as it were, and carry them away.

In a less direct parallel, but one that still has definite similarities to the ritual in Leviticus, before Pesa<u>h</u> one's whole house is cleaned to rid it of any leavened products. Finally, one symbolically searches out and collects leaven with the aid of a bird's feather (like the bird in our passage), a wooden spoon (like the cedar branch), and a candle. After it has been collected one "nullifies the leaven," declaring that any *<u>h</u>ametz* (leavened product) that has been overlooked is no longer considered part of one's property. Then one burns the *<u>h</u>ametz* the following day. This is the final preparation before the seder and is the symbolic ridding of oneself of leaven, which often symbolizes sin.

The same dynamic is at work in these ceremonies as the one under consideration from Leviticus. All are designed to symbolically rid a person of that which they have (presumably) cured—the healed skin disease, the repented sins, and the banished *<u>h</u>ametz*—and carry it away through flight, water, or fire.

Metzora

Are they allowed to take anything out of the house with them? **[C.J.]**

You can answer your own questions here. Just check out the Torah, Leviticus 14.33–57. It gives in detail the whole treatment, but yes, stuff can be taken out. Listen to a great Rashi: "House צָרַעַת *tzara'at* came from treasures that the Canaanites hid in the walls of their houses." God would make the walls of the house break out to show the Jews where to find these treasures. Rambam, of course, connects even fungal houses to speech crimes and similar sins. **Joel Lurie Grishaver, Torah-Toons Gazette.**

Obviously, we still need symbolic ways of ridding ourselves of those things that separate us from our communities, ourselves, and God.

סוֹד *Sod:* The Secret Code in *Tashlih*

According to the midrash (*Tanhuma, Vayeira 25*), when Abraham was on his way to sacrifice Isaac, Satan set a river before him to tempt him to turn back. Abraham waded into the river up to his neck and finally asked God to help him, whereupon the river disappeared. One explanation for the practice of *tashlih* is that we go to the river to recall this important moment in the *Akeidah*.

In the *tashlih* service we learn that "according to the *Zohar*, a deep river symbolizes *binah*, understanding, the ability to plumb the depths of knowledge—to expand, develop and draw conclusions." Abraham is portrayed as saying to God: "The waters of understanding are up to my neck. They threaten to drown my limited human intelligence. Nevertheless, I know that THE BEGINNING OF WISDOM IS FEAR OF GOD [Ps. 112.10]; the source of wisdom is not what my mortal mind conceives, nor the overwhelming compelling logic of Satan. I cannot refute his arguments nor cross his river, because my humanity limits me. But You, God—You are my Guide, and when all else fails me, I negate my wisdom to Your will."

On Rosh ha-Shanah, when we cast our sins into the water, we can almost imagine ourselves being utterly surrounded by the purifying water of deep understanding, much as one is totally immersed in the *mikvah*. This can be a frightening experience, as it must have been to Abraham, or an uplifting one, as the *mikvah* often is. In either case, when we truly immerse ourselves in learning and gain deep insight through mystical experience it quite often changes our lives forever, and we emerge on the shore more fully able to perceive God's will and perform it in our lives. ■

מות בני אהרן

Parashat A<u>h</u>arei Mot
Leviticus 16.1–18.30

Rabbi Harold M. Schulweis

Rabbi Harold Schulweis is the author of *For Those Who Can't Believe: Overcoming the Obstacles to Faith* (HarperCollins) and the spiritual leader of Congregation Valley Beth Shalom in Encino, California.

Living With Ambivalence

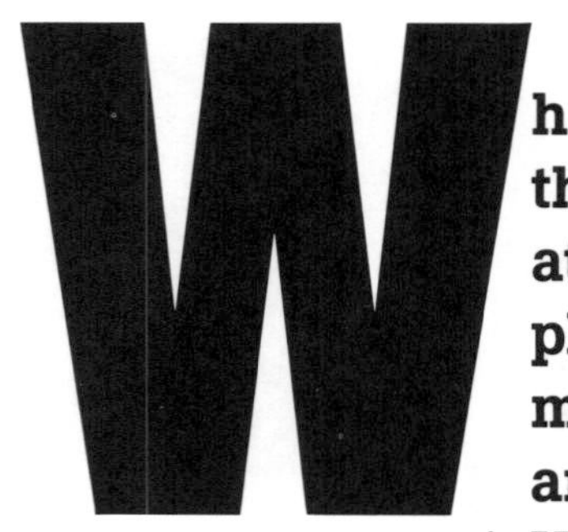

hat does it mean that the High Priest makes atonement for the holy places, for the tent of meeting and the altar, and for the Holy of Holies [Lev. 16.33]? Is there no sanctuary from sin and evil? Have we not rid ourselves of Azazel, the incarnation of evil, pushed over the precipice in the desert [Lev. 16.21–22]?

As if to address the anomaly of the atoning for the Holy, the Rabbinic imagination creates a strong and stunning insight recorded in the *Talmud Yoma* 69b.

The evil desire, the tempter of idolatry that has destroyed the sanctuary, burned the Temple, slain the righteous, driven Israel into exile is still dancing among us. It is discovered neither in the netherworld nor in the unholy places, but coming forth out of the Holy of Holies like a fiery lion. It is the last place one would think of finding Azazel.

The sages deliberate and propose to cast it into a leaden pot and to close the opening with lead because lead will absorb its terrifying voice. They would slay the evil tempter so that the world would be released from its sinister grip. But they soon learn that the suffocation of the *Yetzer* would simultaneously smother the libidinal energies indispensable for civilization (*<u>H</u>alya Olma*). There is then no recourse left but to release the *Yetzer*. Before doing so, some of the sages suggest that perhaps they can pray to the heavens for "half mercy" (*Ra<u>h</u>ame Apalga*). Let there be lust—but let it be restricted to one's own spouse. Let there be ambition and aggressiveness, but let it be restricted to noble and peaceful ends; let there be anger, but let it be limited to righteous indignation. In so praying they would extract the best of the impulse, the instinctive energies within us. But the plan is abandoned because of a profound reality of principle; "Halves are not granted from heaven" (*Palga Birkiah Lo Ya-have*). The world in which we live is not parceled out, neatly labeled good and bad. The world in which we live is not conveniently segregated. Therein lies the rabbinic recognition of ambivalence. The sacred and profane are intertwined. There is no place, no act, no person that is wholly evil or wholly good.

The *Zohar* explains that "when God came to create the world and to reveal what was hidden in the depths and disclose the light out of darkness, both were wrapped in one another. So it is that light emerged from darkness and from the impenetrable came forth the profound. So, too, it is that from good, evil issues, and from mercy, judgment issues. All are intertwined, the good and the evil impulse" [*Zohar* III, 80b]. In the ideal world, in God's essence, the left and the right hand are harmoniously ambidextrous. This is the unity that the prophet Zechariah envisions on that day when the Lord will be one and His name one. "I FORM THE LIGHT AND CREATE DARKNESS. I MAKE PEACE AND EVIL" [Isaiah 45.2]. In God and God alone all polarities are united. But on earth there is an ambiguity in all acts and events. Here what appears to emerge out of the pure, the sacred, the very temple is ambivalent. The High Priest is no exception, nor even the Holy of Holies, which is subject to contamination and must be purified and atoned for on Yom Kippur.

The world has many men and women of righteousness, but the deeper truth is that "THERE IS NO *TZADDIK* UPON EARTH THAT DOES GOOD AND DOES NOT SIN" [Eccl. 7.20]. The *Yalkut Shimoni* I, 44 explains that Azazel refers to the angels Shamhzi and Uzziah who fell from heaven pleading with God to let them live on earth so that the threatening flood against humankind [Gen. 6.4–5] may be averted. They, the angels, unlike mere human beings, would abide on earth without becoming corrupted by evil. But God predicted that the angels once on earth would be subject to the evil urge. Nevertheless they descended, and immediately THE SONS OF GOD TOOK THEM WIVES [Gen. 6.2], made swords and knives, wore ornaments. On earth even angels lose their halos. Possibly this is the reason for reading from the Torah at *minhah* the parashah on incestuous relations [Lev. 18.6-30].

The Rabbinic insight into the ambivalent character in human history is dramatically enacted in the section of the Torah in which two male goats are chosen on Yom Kippur. The first section of the sixth chapter of the Mishnah on Yoma explains that the two male goats of Yom Kippur should be alike in color, height, and price. And they should be

SYNOPSIS: *More laws for the kohanim. The Yom Kippur ritual. Laws about blood. Laws about eating meat. The "nakedness" (a list of sexual taboos).*

RASHI OF THE WEEK:

This week we learn about the rituals for Yom Kippur. Before Aaron begins the process we get this verse [Lev. 16.6]: AND AARON SHALL SACRIFICE A BULL FOR A SIN OFFERING OF HIS OWN, AND ATONE FOR HIMSELF, AND FOR HIS HOUSE. *Rashi notices the redundancy of HIS OWN and HIMSELF. In that repetition he finds this lesson: The repetition shows that his must bring his own bull, one that he himself purchased, and not the one bought with public funds. Even though this is a public, national rite, it only works when it is a personal, individual process.*

Aharei Mot

together in their purchase, both the one to be chosen by lottery as a sacrifice for Ha-Shem and the other as the goat to be destroyed for Azazel. They are initially indistinguishable, and only a mere lottery will differentiate them.

We can't rely upon such a lottery. It is the human task to distinguish good from evil in all human projects. No place or person is exempt from corruption; no place or person is devoid of the sparks of holiness. It requires wisdom to live with ambivalence. Alongside the insights of Jeremiah 17, THE HEART IS DECEITFUL ABOVE ALL THINGS, is the vision of Ezekiel 11 that promises the transformation of the stony heart into a heart of flesh.

This parashah, selected as the reading on Yom Kippur, begins starkly with the death of Nadab and Abihu, the priestly sons of the High Priest, Aaron. "*Intra ecclesia nulla salus.*" Even within the sanctuary no one is safe. Even those who, with pious zeal, bring fire and incense to the altar are not immune from the evil tempter, because of the charisma that wraps itself with pure and absolute holiness.

There is nothing original in sin; SIN RESTS AT THE DOOR [Gen. 4.2]. But that is a liberating awareness. Because we are aware of the ambivalence, we are cautious of anyone who claims to speak out of the sanctuary, without the stammer of fallibility, because we know that we are all human beings, and all our credos and acts are human projects. Conscious of the ambivalence in living, we may not forfeit critical discrimination or surrender moral judgment to another. We enter the sanctuary as fragile men and women seeking to sort the good from the evil, careful to extract the sparks of divinity lodged in the husks of existence. All are judged, all are atoned for, the pulpit and the pew, the laity and the priesthood, the vestibule and the Ark. And all may be cleansed. ■

דבר אל כל עדת בני ישראל

Parashat Kedoshim

Leviticus 19.1–20.27

Rabbi Daniel Pressman

DANIEL PRESSMAN IS THE RABBI OF CONGREGATION BETH DAVID, SARATOGA, CALIFORNIA. HE WRITES THE *TORAH SPARKS PARASHAT HASHAVUAH* SERIES FOR THE UNITED SYNAGOGUE OF CONSERVATIVE JUDAISM AND IS CO-AUTHOR WITH RONALD ISAACS OF *SIDDUR SHIR CHADASH FOR YOUTH AND FAMILY.*

With the first verse of this parashah, "YOU SHALL BE HOLY, FOR I THE LORD YOUR GOD AM HOLY!" we enter the holiness code, the priestly guide to the right action. Its most famous verse is probably Leviticus 19.18: LOVE YOUR NEIGHBOR AS YOURSELF. In last year's *Learn Torah With...,* Elliot Dorff pointed out that holiness is not left as "a pious platitude or an empty hope;" rather, the body of law tells us "in very concrete terms exactly how we are to achieve holiness." The same is true for LOVE YOUR NEIGHBOR.

It appears as a general statement of ethical principle, but our tradition insists on concrete applications.

We can see this clearly in two passages from Maimonides' *Mishnah Torah*. The first comes from *Sefer Hamada, Hilchot Dayot* 6.3:

"It is incumbent on every one to love each individual Israelite as himself, as it is said, YOU SHALL LOVE YOUR NEIGHBOR AS YOURSELF. Therefore, a person ought to speak in praise of his neighbor and be careful of his neighbor's property as he is careful of his own property and solicitous about his own honor. Whoever glorifies himself by humiliating another person will have no portion in the world to come."

The key word here is לְפִיכָךְ, *l'fikhakh,* hence/therefore. There has to be a therefore. Love as an internal feeling, even if we assume that it can be commanded, is not enough. As Rabbi Louis Jacobs writes, "The golden rule is not, in fact, an appeal to the emotions but a call to action."[1]

The first level of "LOVE YOUR NEIGHBOR" is much like the Hippocratic Oath: First, do no harm. It draws a protective fence around a person's core needs of property and honor (meaning both his reputation and his self-esteem). It follows Hillel's elaboration of this mitzvah: "That which is hateful to you, do not do to another."

However, this is not enough. In the Laws of Mourning [14.1] Maimonides codifies acts of חֶסֶד *hesed:* "The following positive commandments were ordained by the rabbis: visiting the sick; comforting the mourners; joining a funeral procession; dowering a bride; escorting departing guests; performing for the dead the last tender offices; acting as a pallbearer; going before the coffin; causing the bride and bridegroom to rejoice; providing them with

Kedoshim

all their needs (for the wedding). These constitute deeds of lovingkindness performed in person and for which no fixed measure is prescribed." Although all these commands are only on Rabbinic authority, they are implied in the precept YOU SHALL LOVE YOUR NEIGHBOR AS YOURSELF.

Imagine someone reading this commandment for the first time. This person wants to follow it, to do it, and so he meditates on it, asking himself over and over again, "And therefore? How can I act on this mitzvah in my daily life?" The result would probably look much like Maimonides' codification. Why? Because these commandments are all done with personal effort and presence, time and care. You can't delegate חֶסֶד *hesed* or pay someone else to do it for you. The love demanded is the commitment of the self. And the specifics address fundamental human needs that we all have, whatever our place on the ladders of wealth and age.

Russel Sanders writes, "Taking part in the common life means dwelling in a web of relationships, the many threads tugging at you while also holding you upright."[2]

What a powerful image. American popular culture glorifies the loner, who has no threads tugging at him, who fears being tied down, but he also has nothing to hold him up when the storm winds blow. What do we fear most? To be sick, to be bereft, or to die. But there is something worse than these inevitable losses: to be sick without visitors; to mourn in solitude; to die alone. To love your neighbors means to assure, with all your strength, skill, and passion, that you will be present at their moments of joy and loss. And it means that you will worry over the details of enactment and shun the perfunctory.

Sanders tells this story: "A woman who recently moved from Los Angeles to Bloomington told me that she would not be able to stay here long, because she was already beginning to recognize people in the grocery store, on the sidewalks, in the library. Being surrounded by familiar faces made her nervous, after years in a city where she could range about anonymously."

That woman understood something that many people are unwilling to acknowledge: If you want community—and we all say we do—you have to give up your radical freedom, be willing to tie yourself to a web of relationships. As Sanders says, "We [Americans] have understood freedom for the most part negatively rather than positively, as release from constraints rather than as *the condition for making a decent life in common."* It seems to me that the entire trajectory of the biblical narrative—from Egypt to Sinai, and then from Sinai through the rough breaking-in period of wilderness wandering, and beyond into the period of Judges, kingdoms, and prophets—is exactly about the struggle to make a decent life in common, as a covenant people, bound to a law of holiness and חֶסֶד *hesed.* That is the freedom that God gave us at the Red Sea: the freedom to love the neighbor and thereby build a covenant community.■

Footnotes

[1]*The Book of Jewish Values,* November, 1983, pp. 7-8.

[2]"The Common Life," *Georgia Quaterly,* Spring, 1994

SYNOPSIS: *The holiness code.*

RASHI OF THE WEEK:

"YOU SHALL RISE IN THE PRESENCE OF AN OLD PERSON AND YOU SHALL HONOR THE PRESENCE OF AN ELDER AND YOU SHALL HAVE FEAR OF YOUR GOD—I AM THE ETERNAL" [Lev. 19.32]. *This simple verse caused Rashi all kinds of problems. He wants to know: (1) What is the difference between an Elder (ZAKAYN) and an Old Person (SAY-VAH)? (2) What is involved in the Torah's selective usage—rising for one and honoring the other? (3) What is honor anyway? and (4) Why is the "Fear Your God" chorus tacked onto the end of this particular verse? He answers his own questions.* You shall rise in the presence of AN OLD PERSON. In case you might imagine that this commandment applies to even an evil old person, the verse also says Elder (ZAKAYN). An elder is only a person who has acquired wisdom [*Kiddushin* 32b/*Torat Kohanim* 7.12]. What is honor? One should not sit in an elder's place nor speak in her/his place, nor contradict his/her words. One might be able to close one's eyes and pretend not to see the elder—and thereby avoid rising before him and avoid honoring her. This is why the Torah adds, "AND YOU SHALL HAVE FEAR OF YOUR GOD—I AM THE ETERNAL," for this matter is a question of heart—one that no one can judge save for God, Who knows your true intentions—even matters of your heart.

Sweet Land and Liberty

A Dead Sea Scrolls conference brought me to the Annenberg Institute in Philadelphia, where for the first time (I am embarrassed to say) I saw the Liberty Bell. There I learned that the name "Liberty Bell" was not given to it by the American revolutionaries but by the abolitionist movement during the decades before the Civil War.

As all Americans know, the name stems from the quotation from Lev. 25.10 that borders the bell, "Proclaim liberty throughout all the land to all the inhabitants thereof" (Kings James Version). "Liberty" (Hebrew, דְּרוֹר *Dror*) in reality means "release," and it refers, as spelled out in the rest of the verse, to the jubilee year "when each of you shall return to his kin group." This verse implies that the indebted Israelite had lost his land and was separated from his family. In other words, he had become a slave. That process is described in Leviticus 25.25–55. Thus the abolitionists, perhaps unwittingly, intuited the correct interpretation of verse 10, applying it to release from slavery.

Here, however, the similarity ends. Three steps describe the descent into slavery of the Israelite who has possessed ancestral land. First, overwhelming debt requires him to sell his land [Lev. 25.25-28]; next,

Parashat Emor
Leviticus 21.1–24.23

Jacob Milgrom

Jacob Milgrom is Professor Emeritus of Biblical Studies, University of California at Berkeley. He is currently living in Jerusalem.

דָּבָר אַחֵר DAVAR AHER. FROM THE 15TH DAY OF THIS MONTH IS THE FESTIVAL OF MATZAH, YOU SHALL EAT MATZOT FOR A SEVEN DAY PERIOD [Lev. 23.7]. In our neighborhood the local grocery store puts out boxes of matzah before every Jewish holiday as a gesture of support for our celebrations. Sometimes, amongst ourselves, we joke about this sincere misunderstanding. But in truth, matzah is a significant symbol of many of the core values all Jewish holidays celebrate. (No, I am not recommending that we eat matzah on holidays other than Passover!)

As we read in the Torah this Shabbat, there are offerings that were to be brought by ancient Israel that could not be consumed or prepared with *hametz*, leaven. These commands to Israel and the Biblical priests to bring the various sacrifices were for occasions other than

he becomes a tenant farmer on land he once owned [Lev. 25.35-38]; and finally, debt forces him to sell himself as a slave [Lev. 25.39-43]. The jubilee (the etymology is unclear) occurs every fiftieth year and cancels his entire debt. He regains his land even earlier if it is redeemed (see below). He starts afresh and, with prudence, good weather, and a little luck, may avoid catastrophic debt next time. In effect the Israelite never really sells his landed patrimony; he only leases it until the jubilee.

By what authority does Leviticus restore his land? It stems from God: "THE LAND IS MINE; YOU ARE BUT RESIDENT ALIENS UNDER MY AUTHORITY" [Lev. 25.23]. Israelites have the status of "resident aliens" who do not own land. Terminology confirms this status. In Leviticus the land is never called נַחֲלָה *na<u>h</u>alah,* inherited land, implying permanent possession. It is called אֲחוּזָּה *a<u>h</u>uzzah,* literally "holding" land, which Israel merely holds in trust but does not actually own.

The owner of the land is God, who decrees: "YOU MUST PROVIDE FOR THE REDEMPTION (גְאֻלָּה *ge'ullah*) FOR THE LAND" [Lev. 25.24]. Redemption means the restoration of the status quo, a responsibility that rests on the next of kin, called the גוֹאֵל *go'el,* the redeemer. He is variously: (1) the levirate who, as in Ruth 3.13, provides his deceased kinsman with a survivor by marrying his childless widow; (2) the receiver of reparations due his deceased kinsman [Num.5.7]; (3) the "blood redeemer" who is required to put to death the (unlawful) slayer of his kinsman [Num. 35.16-34]; and (4) (the case dealt with here) the one obliged to buy back the inherited field of his indebted kinsman [Lev. 25.25-28] and to

Passover. Yet the instruction does remind us of Pesa<u>h</u>, when Moses and Israel were told to consume the lamb's meat only with unleavened bread—matzah.

It seems that there is a distinction between *<u>h</u>ametz* and matzah that exists in the Torah and in Jewish tradition separate from Passover. When I point this out I am often asked how this could be so. We eat Matzah on Passover because in Israel's haste to leave Egypt they did not have time to properly bake their bread and other provisions, right? Well, yes. Exodus 12.34 tells us that. But at the beginning of the Passover narrative in the Torah, Exodus 12.15-20, God tells Israel and the Jewish people something quite different.

Two full weeks before the Exodus our ancestors were told what would occur and how they were

SYNOPSIS: *Still more rules about kohanim. What to do when a Kohen comes in contact with the dead; wants to serve in the Mishkan; needs to celebrate the holidays? Holiday descriptions for Shabbat, Passover, Omer, Shavuot, Rosh ha-Shanah, Yom Kippur, and Sukkot. The story of a man who cursed God.*

AN EXTENDED RASHI OF THE WEEK

Joel Lurie Grishaver

At the beginning of parashat Emor the book of Leviticus is in the ritual mode. It is flowing on about holiday celebrations. This Rashi is the story of a narrative passage breaking out in the midst of a perfectly good run of ritual halakhah. We get Shabbat, Passover, the Omer, Shavuot, Rosh ha-Shanah, Yom Kippur, and Sukkot. We get the rules for lighting the menorah, rules for the show bread; then the Torah interrupts the ritual descriptions to tell this story.

AND THE SON OF AN ISRAELITE WOMAN WENT OUT—AND HE WAS THE SON OF AN EGYPTIAN MAN—INTO THE MIDST OF THE FAMILIES OF ISRAEL; AND HE FOUGHT IN THE CAMP WITH THE SON OF AN ISRAELITE WOMAN AND AN ISRAELITE MAN [Lev. 24.10 ff.].

The narrative has jumped. We are reading along in a ritual mode and then—click—the Torah continues as if someone else has just hit the remote and shifted channels on us. We are suddenly in a different place. The "AND" is bothersome. It says "connection" when there doesn't seem to be one. What follows is just as confused—like badly edited

EXTENDED RASHI, CONTINUED ON PAGE 243

free him from slavery to a non-Israelite [Lev. 25.47-55]. The jubilee year guarantees redemption in case the redeemer does not fulfill his responsibility. Early in Israelite history it seems (to judge by Jeremiah 32) that the redeemer retained the land permanently. In that way, at least, the property remained in the possession of the clan. The jubilee, however, constitutes a revolution in the laws of landed property in that the redeemer must return the land to its original owner at the jubilee. Individual ownership is thereby preserved.

To be sure, statewide cancellation of indebtedness and the right of redemption are known in the ancient Near East (especially in Mesopotamia). However, the former is not cyclically fixed as in Israel but dependent on the whim of the ruler. And redemption occurs only if the buyer decides to sell the property, whereas in Israel even if the buyer wants to hold on to the property he must always release it to the redeemer.

There is one more problem I would like to address: There is no redemption provision for an Israelite slave of an Israelite owner. This omission is all the more startling because redemption of slaves prevailed in Mesopotamia. Why is it missing in Israel? The answer again comes from a divine edict, "FOR THEY [THE ISRAELITES] ARE MY SLAVES, WHOM I FREED FROM THE LAND OF EGYPT; THEY MUST NOT SELL THEMSELVES AS SLAVES ARE SOLD" [Lev. 25.42]. Instead, "IF YOUR BROTHER, BEING [FURTHER] IMPOVERISHED MUST SELL HIMSELF TO YOU, DO NOT MAKE HIM WORK AS A SLAVE. HE SHALL REMAIN UNDER YOU AS A RESIDENT HIRELING; HE SHALL WORK UNDER YOU UNTIL THE JUBILEE YEAR" [Lev. 25.40].

An Israelite is a servant to God, not to another person. Therefore he works for a wage. Since he pays no interest on his debt [Lev. 25.36-37], his work amortizes the principal. He may eventually see the light at the end of the tunnel. This

---

Emor

expected to behave and mark this wondrous event. Two weeks before the angel of death would pass over Israel's homes in search of the first-born of Egypt, Moses learned that every household was to select its lamb in ten days and then slaughter the animals on the eve of the fourteenth day. This was the original observance of Passover. Pesah, matzah, and maror, too.

We could ask, if Israel had two full weeks to be prepared for the Exodus, why did they not prepare their food in advance of their journey? Why does the actual moment seem to catch them unprepared? The answer lies in our own nature. We procrastinate, we doubt, we often don't pay attention to what is really happening around us. But now as Passover approaches many of us are getting ready. We are focused

reverses the Mesopotamian practice by which labor pays only the interest, thus virtually guaranteeing lifelong slavery. Moreover, the Israelite as a hireling is a free person. Finding more favorable conditions elsewhere, he may work for someone other than his creditor. A family member may cover his debt with a grant or loan, but the land will revert immediately to the original owner. This is not "redemption." Finally, if all else fails to clear the credit cards, the jubilee year, the *levitica deus ex machina*, will free him.

The people of Israel and its land belong solely to God; neither may be owned in perpetuity. Absolute ownership of ancestral property and Israelite persons is abolished; persons and land may be leased, not sold. Whether real or utopian, the laws in Leviticus seem to be a more sensitive safeguard against pauperization that we, here and now, have been able to devise, with our dispossessed sleeping in doorways and over hot air grates—in the shadow of the Liberty Bell. ■

---

on our switch from *ḥametz* to matzah. We will be prepared to tell the story of the Exodus again this year.

We can also ask about the symbolism and characteristics of leavened and unleavened foods that we are so careful about during Passover. I always start with the following definition. Since matzah is made from five of the same grains that produce bread—wheat, barley, oats, rye, and spelt—matzah is anything that is potentially *ḥametz*. In an attempt to reenact the experience out of which our Jewish people and heritage emerged, we look to the simple and lowly fare of the slave. Slaves ate matzah. The slave's humbled position and lack of personal status required him to serve the will of his oppressing master. His behavior could not reflect a will of his own. The slave's is the most humble of lives. In contrast, the taskmaster exalted himself and believed that others must do his bidding. His was a lavish style of food and life. In his own arrogance he convinced himself that his rule was law, his wish command. His behavior reflected a will only his own.

The Jewish people were born a humble, subservient people: individuals and a community not free to live or express themselves according to their own desires or with regard to basic human dignities. Passover marks a transformation. Our ancestors experienced liberation. In freedom, fought for throughout our history, Jews have grown to proclaim that a moral purpose and ethic attaches to our unique identity. In order to do so

EXTENDED RASHI

CONTINUED FROM PAGE 241

tape—or like a kid who is so excited that the whole story emerges in a jumble. We should be told: (1) Two Jews fought; (2) One was the son of a Jewish woman and an Egyptian man; (3) One was the son of two Jewish parents. Instead we get a series of disconnected thoughts linked by "and."

Rashi believes that there is powerful Torah in this verbal chaos—that as we work it the non sequiturs will actually provide connection. He unpacks the text clue by clue.

First Rashi asks: "From where did this man go out?" Logically, two men who wanted to fight should leave the camp to have that fight. (I'll meet you by the big rock at dawn!) But this fight takes place in the camp. The leaving has to be from somewhere else. Rashi has learned two different answers to this question in the midrash. He brings them to us.

R. Levi says: He went out of this world—meaning he died—or he lost his portion in the world-to-come. The "HE WENT OUT" is a teaser, an advance warning that this story is a tragedy.

R. Berakhyah says: HE WENT OUT means HE SET FORTH, an interpretation of the previous verse (EACH AND EVERY SHABBAT HE SHALL ARRANGE IT (the shew bread) BEFORE THE ETERNAL [Lev. 24.8]). The man with the Egyptian father scoffed at this teaching of Moses and said, "This rule doesn't make any sense…ON THE SHABBAT HE SHALL ARRANGE IT. It makes more sense to place new bread in front of God every day—not just once a week on Shabbat. It is the

EXTENDED RASHI, CONTINUED ON PAGE 244

EXTENDED RASHI

CONTINUED FROM PAGE 243

practice of kings to eat warm, fresh bread every day. What king would want to eat cold, nine-day-old bread"? His tone was definitely sarcastic. This irreverent remark was the cause of the fight between him and the man with two Israelite parents who defended Moses' honor and Moses' halakhah [Midrash *Tanhuma* 23, *Va-Yikra Rabbah* 32.3]. This is the first story, but it is not the end of the matter. The fight started here, but it did not happen here.

A baraita teaches another story [*Tanhuma* 24, *Va-Yikra Rabbah* 32.3]: This is another story that can be unfolded from the word HE WENT OUT. It tells us that he went out of Moses' Beit Din as the loser in the following court case: Even though he was the son of an Egyptian man, he came to pitch his tent in the camp of the tribe of Dan. They said to him,

EXTENDED RASHI, CONTINUED ON PAGE 245

we have always brought along our original collective memory.

For Judaism, the freedom and equality that we seek for all people require that humility, not arrogance, remains our ideal way. We must never become like the haughty taskmaster who sought to control others. We cannot live as people who serve our own wills alone. Fermented grain implies personal excess. Unleavened bread suggests modesty. *Matzah is every good intention or simple truth. Hametz is every good intention exploited, every simple truth disguised.* For fifty-one weeks each year we don't attach these value judgments to our daily bread. On Passover we live the cliché—we are what we eat. Passover teaches us that human arrogance is held in check by awareness of existence beyond ourselves. The change from hametz to matzah symbolizes that our efforts in life are in service of God and the values of God's presence in our world. On Passover these are among the necessary ingredients for human progress, justice, equality, and freedom. Just as all matzah is potentially *hametz,* so are we, descendants of unpretentious slaves, potentially the hardened and conceited of heart and mind. One week each year we return to the core ideals and basic visions of the goodness, honesty, and dignity with which we could live our lives and toward which we should guide society.

On Passover we turn our basic need for food and nourishment into the symbolic agent through which we express our faith and personal values. This is the lesson we understand from the Torah in God's command to ancient Israel's priests about the people's offerings. Ritual without ethics is also ritual without meaning. The physical process of cleaning, preparing, and changing our homes and kitchens is intended to inform our spiritual identities.

Pesah embodies our highest aspirations in life: values that must become genuine and personal for each one of us. It is this Jewish religious perspective and sense of per-

EXTENDED RASHI
CONTINUED FROM PAGE 244

"What is your connection here? You don't have one. You don't belong here!" He said to them, "I am the son of the tribe of Dan through my mother." They said to him, "The Torah says: 'EACH MAN OF THE FAMILIES-OF-ISRAEL CAMPS BY THE BANNER OF HIS FATHER'S HOUSE' [Num. 2.2]. According to Torah, you don't belong here." He went to Moses' Beit Din to get things straightened out and WENT OUT of that court a loser. Then he got up and moved in the direction of blaspheming. From the blaspheming he will die. This is a harsh story, but it is just beginning to unfold.

We then run smack into the second AND. This second AND introduces a new non sequitur. The Torah interrupts the fight that is about to break out to tell us that he was THE SON OF AN EGYPTIAN MAN. Rashi knows enough to know that the inserted detail must be critical. If it is inserted, it must teach something important. So it is with clear purpose that the Torah freezes the dominant action—with fists frozen in the air, the deadly words about to be spoken—to go up close and personal with the combatants. Rashi asks: "Which Egyptian man?" Then he finds his answer. He is the Egyptian whom Moses killed [*Tanhuma* 24, *Va-Yikra Rabbah* 32.4.]. How do they know it? The answer is simple. That story [Ex. 2.12] is the only other time in the Torah where some individual is called "AN EGYPTIAN MAN."

But now the story is much richer. An Egyptian with a Jewish wife is a tough taskmaster (quite possibly because he is worried about looking too soft). We know that story; it is a Holocaust story, a concentration camp and ghetto story....Years later the fatherless son runs headlong into the authority of the man who murdered his father. It happens over and over. First Moses teaches a law that seems ridiculous to him. (And we get to ask: "Why davka to him?") He challenges that law and winds up in a fight. Then, not being able to stay in Egypt, and not really belonging to the people with whom he fled, he tries to fit in but runs headlong into more Torah that Moses taught in God's name. Quite possibly, this second fight is with the same Dannite as the first Torah argument. So he goes to Moses, the man who murdered his father and made him an orphan without a father's flag, and demands justice. Moses again denies him justice. The anger is building. Wronged as a student, wronged as a member of the community, he faces a villain who is regarded by all others as the holy leader. But the explosion has not yet taken place; it is still building. But be warned, this is not just an anti-intermarriage story. It starts out feeling very racist, but it is actually much more Shakespearean, much richer, and the plot is still thickening. The disconnected AND has brought new connection.

Next the Torah says INTO THE MIDST OF THE FAMILIES OF ISRAEL, and Rashi asks, "Why was this phrase inserted into the Torah here, again delaying the

EXTENDED RASHI CONTINUED ON PAGE 246

sonal ethics that brings meaning to the sacred tasks of our lives. **Rabbi Ronald Shulman, from *Parashat Hashavuah*, the Board of Rabbis of Southern California.**

דָּבָר אַחֵר DAVAR AHER. On Joel Grishaver's Extended Rashi of the Week. Victim condemnation of Sh'lomit Bat Dibri is tempered (but not eliminated completely) in the midrash cited by Rabbi Louis I. Rabinowitz. *The Egyptian taskmaster…conceived an illicit passion for the wife of one of the Hebrew slaves. Although she was completely innocent, she could not be absolved from responsibility. For her name is given as "Sh'lomit Bat Divri," and our rabbis interpret the name as meaning she was a "*דַּבְּרָנִית dabranit,*" one of those talkative, chattering women who used to greet every man with a "*שָׁלוֹם לְךָ Shalom l'kha*" or "Hello." She is therefore partly to blame for the attention she attracted. The Egyptian taskmaster determined to have his way with her, and ordered the husband to perform some night work which should take him away from home. Clandestinely entering the house during this enforced absence, he assaulted her. When the husband returned, he discovered the disgraceful act and was filled with anger and resentment. When the Egyptian taskmaster realized that the husband*

EXTENDED RASHI
CONTINUED FROM PAGE 245

action? Why was it put here to interrupt?" Rashi answers his own question—to teach us that he had converted. Wow! But the problem confounds itself. If he had a Jewish mother, why did he need to convert? Rashi (on Ex. 24.6) says: "Our Rabbis learned from this that our ancestors entered into the covenant though circumcision, immersion, and the sprinkling of blood." In other words, everyone who stood at Sinai became a Jew-by-choice. Ramban, however, notes that other French Torah scholars argue that matrilineal descent began only at Sinai, so he personally had to convert. Here is a man—Jewish by birth, Jewish by ritual action and by life experience—who is still kept by the Torah from settling in his tribe. And Moses, his father's murderer, has refused to "settle" the problem. He, too, has seemed to say, "You are not really a Jew."

Finally the Torah gets to the point with another non sequitur "AND."...AND THEY FOUGHT IN THE CAMP. Over what did they fight? Over the issue of camping, the claim to be allowed to pitch his tent in the camp of the tribe of Dan. No matter what else came first, discrimination or bad settlements, Torah arguments or whatever, in the end he went back to the tribe of Dan and caused trouble. The convolution in the text reveals the convolution in the psyche.

And then the Torah tells us "AND THE ISRAELITE MAN." The son of the Egyptian man fought with The Jewish Man. The "the" bothers Rashi. He asks, "Why not 'a Jewish man'?" Do we actually know who "The Israelite" is? The answer is "Yes!" He is the Israelite man, the man from Dan who opposed him, who objected to his pitching his tent in the camp of Dan in the first place. Having been in a Torah fight, having lost a camp battle, having lost a court fight, having no father, having nowhere to turn, and having been wronged by the man who robbed him of father and people, the son of the Egyptian returns to seek his own justice. It is very *High Noon*. He is angry. He has good reason to be—but he is also

EXTENDED RASHI, CONTINUED ON PAGE 247

knew the cruel trick that had been played on him, instead of feeling remorse, his guilty conscience drove him to ill-treat still further the man he had wronged, and he made him the victim of sadistic persecution.

If the Egyptian father is indeed a rapist, rather than Sh'lomit's husband, we gain a new level of understanding.

Revisiting the story of Dinah [Gen. 34], we can compare the two stories. (1) Dinah's rapist is killed; Sh'lomit's rapist is killed. (2) Both stories contain uncomfortable rabbinic condemnation of the victims. (In Dinah's case, see Rashi on 34.1, "Like mother, like daughter.") (3) In both cases, the victims never speak on their own behalf. Torah is uncomfortable with their plight. By

EXTENDED RASHI

CONTINUED FROM PAGE 246

clearly way out of control. But that is still not "the rest of the story."

The story continues in the next verse. After losing this fight, too—or perhaps as an act of desperation during this fight—THE SON OF THE ISRAELITE WOMAN PRONOUNCED (וַיִּקֹּב VA-YIKOV) THE NAME AND CURSED—SO THEY BROUGHT HIM TO MOSES; THE NAME OF HIS MOTHER WAS SH'LOMIT THE DAUGHTER OF DIBRI, OF THE TRIBE OF DAN.

Again Rashi uses small problems in the text to unfold a much larger story. First Rashi turns his attention to the word וַיִּקֹּב va-Yikov (PRONOUNCED). It's a rare word—a rare usage, so Rashi gives a reference. This word is to be understood as *Targum Onkelos* translates it, "and he said explicitly," for he pronounced the special name of God, and he was cursed by using the explicit name of God that he heard at Sinai. So here is what we know. The man was at Sinai. He heard God's voice directly. He heard God speak the Divine name in commandment number one. He learned that cursing with the Divine name was against God's law, a denial of Sinai, and he did it on purpose. This was not any curse, but a denial of the entire God experience at Sinai. In the Torah experience, cursing with God's name is a kind of murder of the spirit. It is a capital crime, and our guy was present when the law was voiced, not by Moses' testimony, but directly by God's mouth. This is not any taking of God's name in vain. This is no show trial; this is the ultimate verbal assault on the empire of Heaven.

Then the Torah takes another left turn and we move back to THE SON OF THE EGYPTIAN'S origins. We echo God's NAME with his mother's NAME (knowing in the back of our minds that parents are supposed to be God's agents to their children). Rashi again picks up on the fact that the discontinuity in the narrative is a prompt to a deeper story. THE NAME OF HIS MOTHER WAS SH'LOMIT, DAUGHTER OF DIBRI, OF THE TRIBE OF DAN. Why does the Torah mention her name? This is the Torah's discreet way of conveying that she alone at this time was a prostitute. How do they know this? Because her name is a euphemism. Each of the parts of her name is a clue. SH'LOMIT—she is called by this name for she would chatter "Shalom Aleihem" (peace unto you)—chattering with words, asking after everyone's health. DAUGHTER OF DIBRI—this name teaches that she was a chatterbox (because Dibri is built out of the root [דבר] D-V-R, which means "speak"). She would speak with everybody. Too much talking was how she came to behave immorally. In other words, his mother did not teach him שְׁמִירַת הַלָּשׁוֹן *Shmirat ha-Lashon* (to guard his tongue). Unfortunately, he inherits the family sin, "loose lips lose lives" (*Va-Yikra Rabbah* 23).

The story continues: THEY PLACED HIM UNDER GUARD TO HAVE THE MATTER CLARIFIED BY GOD'S MOUTH.

Here comes the partial redemption in this tragic story. Why didn't they just kill him? He had clearly broken the law. They had the power—why the pause? Perhaps Moses had finally learned enough to disqualify himself from judging because he was an "involved party." Perhaps their own guilt was in the way their mistreatment had exacerbated the situation. Perhaps his status as "victim" in a

EXTENDED RASHI, CONTINUED ON PAGE 248

---

naming the women as it has, it wishes to arouse our thoughtful compassion for rather than our moral condemnation of the victims.

דִּינָה *Dinah* = Judgment. The jury never came back with verdict. Where was the justice in Dinah's case? Yaakov was too complacent, her brothers too brutal. Torah suspends judgment.

שְׁלוֹמִית *Sh'lomit* = Peace, wholeness. Her relationship with her husband was strained by the rape. Her child has no physical space to call his own in the community. Where is the peacefulness in her life?

The moralizing of the rabbis notwithstanding, Torah leaves us with painful eternal questions concerning our treatment of broken, fragmented lives. The best end result is a nonjudgmental community in which rape victims and their families (and all victims of violence, for that matter) are given the space and the resources to become whole again. **Simcha Prombaum, La Crosse, WI.**

EXTENDED RASHI

CONTINUED FROM PAGE 247

show trial played as well in their media as in ours. But the pause in the action catches Rashi's attention, and he brings from the midrash this insight. They placed him—by himself. They did not confine him with the one who gathered the wood on Shabbat [Num. 15.34], for although both of the incidents happened at the same time, the Torah says "THEY PLACED HIM UNDER GUARD" and not "THEY PLACED THEM UNDER GUARD." The families-of-Israel already knew that the one who gathered wood was to receive the death penalty, as it says "THOSE WHO DESECRATE IT SHALL BE PUT TO DEATH" [Ex. 31.14], but it had not been made clear to them through which death penalty he should be put to death. This is why it says, "FOR WHAT WAS TO BE DONE TO HIM HAD NOT BEEN CLARIFIED" [Num. 15.34].

How did they know that the two incidents happened at once? Easy—the word bridge between them CLARIFIED, told them. But with regard to the one who cursed, it says in our verse "TO CLARIFY FOR THEM," for they did not know if he deserved the death penalty or not. Suddenly we know that this story is no *To Kill a Mockingbird*. There is no rush toward the necktie party. Instead, unsure and ill at ease, the people back off. If this is a story of Israel at its worst, then this is their finest moment. Then God speaks: TAKE THE ONE WHO CURSED OUT OF THE CAMP, LET ALL WHO HEARD THE CURSE PLACE THEIR HANDS ON HIS HEAD AND LET THE ENTIRE COMMUNITY STONE HIM. THEN SAY TO THE FAMILIES-OF-ISRAEL, TEACHING, ANY PERSON, ANYONE WHO CURSES GOD IS TO BE PUT TO DEATH—YES, DEATH. THE ENTIRE COMMUNITY IS TO STONE HIM—YES, STONE HIM: THE JEW-BY-CHOICE AS WELL AS THE JEW-BY-BIRTH....

Once again Rashi begins the textual postmortem. ALL WHO HEARD, these are the witnesses. Why does it say ALL? To include the judges as well as the witnesses. Why does it say THEIR HANDS? To teach us that all—judges and witness—have to place their hands on his head. They say to him, "Your blood is on your head, and you are responsible for your own death, and we do not suffer punishment—through your death, for you brought it upon yourself." Yet they have to touch the person, make a connection in order to deny a connection. Here they go "hands-on" at the execution—and say that they will not suffer any punishment. Either God has seen too few prison movies, or God has taken the long walk down death row alongside a lot of murders and knows the dreams that follow. I hear deep irony.

The passage goes on for a while, listing other capital crimes, then concludes: THERE SHALL BE ONE LAW FOR YOU, IT SHALL BE FOR THE JEW-BY-CHOICE AND FOR THE JEW-BY-BIRTH, FOR I AM THE ETERNAL, YOUR GOD. Rashi asks one last question. Why was the chorus line "I AM THE ETERNAL, YOUR GOD" added to this verse? Rashi explains (probably in his own words and not from an earlier source): To show that "I AM THE GOD of all of you. Just as I connect My Name uniquely to you, so do I connect My

EXTENDED RASHI, CONTINUED ON PAGE 249

EXTENDED RASHI
CONTINUED FROM PAGE 248

Name directly to each Jew-by-choice." There was a lot of sin to go around in this tragedy, but only the son of the Egyptian sought to murder the reality of God with his words. (Think of blasphemy as "murder" and not just repartee.) Tragically insensitive behavior had exacerbated a bad situation and ultimately manifested itself as violence. Their treatment of him was abhorrent—his response was a capital crime. One does not exonerate the other. Let us assume that everyone walked home that day quietly, with heads hung low. Let us assume, in an image lifted from Elie Wiesel, that the manna everyone ate that night tasted like corpses. I can't begin to imagine Moses' sleepless night terrors that week. I suspect he washed his hands more than once.

AUTHOR'S NOTE: The part of this story that deals with Sh'lomit Bat Dibri is problematic. It calls for new midrash. It calls for analysis. But the simple rabbinic implication that "a woman who says 'Hello' is a hooker" calls for additional work. This excursus was not the place to do it. I invite others to investigate this problem and share solutions. **Joel Lurie Grishaver, <gris@torahaura.com>**

בהר סיני לאמר

Just before Pesah I hiked through a beautiful valley in the Judean hills, just below the entrance to Jerusalem. A pair of step buzzards soared overhead; dazzling red nuriot dotted fields that were a lush green after the rains. Picking green almonds from trees, we said a *sheheheyanu* and discovered their crunchy, lemony taste. Foxes still live in these hills, and deer. This beautiful Valley of Cedars, the last open green space in west Jerusalem, will soon be paved and covered with apartment buildings. The city's master plan called for preservation of this space, a vital spot for weekend picnickers, school-aged explorers, morning walkers, and those who long for breathing space and a stunning view. But unless the Society for Protection of Nature in Israel wins this latest round in its endless battle to preserve the environment, the mayor of Jerusalem and the city council will override that plan. As we walked through this threatened spot I kept thinking, "But this is God's land. It is under siege from its people. Who speaks for the land? What is the voice of tradition here?"

So when I read this week's parashah I wondered if I had found that voice. In verses 23 and 24 God, speaking through Moses, says to the Israelites: "BUT THE LAND MUST NOT BE SOLD BEYOND RECLAIM, FOR THE LAND IS MINE; YOU ARE BUT STRANGERS RESIDENT WITH ME. THROUGHOUT THE LAND THAT YOU HOLD *(AHUZATCHEM)* YOU MUST PROVIDE FOR THE REDEMPTION OF THE LAND."

Parashat Be-Har

Leviticus 25.1–26.2

Rabbi Rachel Cowan

RABBI RACHEL COWAN IS THE DIRECTOR OF JEWISH LIFE PROGRAMS AT THE NATHAN CUMMINGS FOUNDATION IN NEW YORK.

דָּבָר אַחֵר DAVAR AHER. Do NOT LEND HIM MONEY AT ADVANCE INTEREST, OR GIVE HIM YOUR FOOD AT ACCRUED INTEREST [Lev. 25.37]. What's wrong with lending money for interest? It isn't always a nice thing to do, but if you know somebody has the money they owe you and they just don't give it back, it's something you should do. It's not fair that you should be taken! Are you not allowed to lend money BEGINNING with interest, or not allowed to add interest as well? **[C.J.]**

Dear C.J.: Think Willy Nelson, John Mellencamp, and Farm Aid. If farmers borrow money at interest, they always lose the farm. Farming isn't a steady thing. There are always bad years. Money at interest really hurts

וידבר יהוה אל משה

The context of this verse is not a treatise on the environment. Rather, the parashah deals with the conditions attached to the Israelite's ownership of the land. It is concerned that no system develop in Israel that permanently removes land from God's domain, the public trust, by granting inalienable rights of ownership to any individual or group. God sets a year of jubilee every fifty years in which all lands will revert to their former owners. No transfer of property can be for a longer term, and each sale of land must be valued according to the number of years left until the jubilee. Apparently this system was never really implemented, and apparently its origins were in a specific historic situation.

Baruch Levine, in a brilliant essay in the JPS Torah Commentary on Leviticus, posits that this particular chapter was inserted into the developing Torah in the late fifth century B.C.E., after the Israelites' return from Babylonia, when the land, now part of the Persian empire, was under the jurisdiction of Nehemiah, the Jewish Persian governor. The exiles, Levine thinks, returned and found their land claimed by non–Israelites. The Persians needed a decree to compel the restoration of the land; the priests needed a theological legitimization. This chapter provides that rationale. Levine writes (on p. 273), "God had granted the Land of Israel to His people as an everlasting אֲחֻזָּה *ahuzzah*, 'holding'." His people were His tenants and were granted the right usually considered a sine qua non of ownership, the right to alienate what one owns. Following this reasoning, the edict of Cyrus was translated into a divine land grant. In the prophecies of Deutero-Isaiah it is explicitly stated that the God of Israel commissioned Cyrus to restore His people. It was hoped that the returning exiles, some of whom were impoverished when they arrived, would be helped by

SYNOPSIS: *Rules for sabbatical years, jubilee years, owning property in the Land of Israel, not lending money at interest.*

RASHI OF THE WEEK:

[Lev. 25.55] "FOR THE FAMILIES-OF-ISRAEL ARE MY SLAVES, *their contract with Me comes first.* I AM THE ETERNAL YOUR GOD *and no matter who rules them on earth, they are still Mine, and that new master is My agent.' Here is a whole lot of interesting and problematic theology in just one sentence.*

farming families. It could cause them to lose their farm and then starve. Later, when Jews went into business, they needed to borrow money. You can't develop a trading business without investments and futures. (The Stock Exchange is all about betting against interest that business will grow.) The farming rule, no interest, didn't work anymore. Jews needed to borrow money in order to make money. Just like the Prozbul, they needed a work-around. They needed a way to get around the Torah without breaking it. This time the solution was called an *iska*. It was a fancy kind of partnership. While Jews couldn't lend money to another Jew at interest, they could pay themselves back at interest. The *iska* was a way that a partner could invest money in a partnership; the other partner could use it and then pay the partnership back with interest. To borrow money you became a partner and paid yourself interest that your partner could take. The *iska* was created with a kind of protection that said that some of the loan was always to be forgiven.

their co-religionists in Babylonia and that they would band together, clan by clan, to help one another. Relatives were to redeem threatened lands. The goal was to regain control over the land. Leaders, like Ne<u>h</u>emiah, were needed to restrain the usual greed for land and worth so that redemption could be achieved. This parashah sets out the Divine Law to guide this process of redeeming the land.

Whether the system was ever actually implemented is not important here. (Scholars doubt that it was.) What stands out is the theological idea that the land belongs to God, and that the Israelites are resident strangers. In thinking about how this verse might apply to the future of the Valley of Cedars, I connected it with verse 4 from the same chapter: "BUT IN THE SEVENTH YEAR THE LAND SHALL HAVE A SABBATH OF COMPLETE REST, A SABBATH OF THE LORD: YOU SHALL NOT SOW YOUR FIELD OR PRUNE YOUR VINEYARD." This chapter, then, is not only concerned with how men own the land; it also speaks of how they treat it.

There are historical ecological motivations for the commandment to let the land lie fallow every seven years. Ancient Near Eastern civilizations were destroyed when their lands became oversaturated with salts from excessive irrigation. But more importantly, the land here is seen not only as the vehicle for the enrichment of man; its own Shabbat, its own holiness, its own rhythms are recognized as inherent. The land is part of God's plan for the holiness of the Jewish people in Eretz Israel—it is one part of the equation that balances the life of the Israelite people in their land.

As such, this parashah presents a vision of sustainable development. The government of Israel would do well to remember God's words: "THE LAND IS MINE; YOU ARE BUT STRANGERS RESIDENT WITH ME." The city of Jerusalem must develop alternative plans that save the Valley of Cedars while also providing housing for

Be-Har

The laws of רִבִּית *ribbit* (interest) are intense. You were allowed no benefit from a loan. The person who borrowed money was prevented from saying a more intense "good morning" than usual to the loaner, from lending the loaner his or her car or doing any other favor or act that was considered "benefit" from giving the loan. **Joel Lurie Grishaver, Torah-Toons Gazette.**

new immigrants, newly prosperous middle class homeowners, and burgeoning religious families. The country desperately needs a national plan that preserves the open spaces that are currently disappearing at a rapid pace to developers, that are being covered by highways that will soon become as clogged as the roads they are replacing. Israel also needs a plan to protect precious water sources and guarantee clean air. If not, the concern expressed by Shimon Peres may become reality. "If we are not careful", he said,

תִּהְיֶה לָנוּ מְדִינָה,
אֲבָל לֹא תִּהְיֶה לָנוּ אֶרֶץ

"Tehiyeh-lanu Medina, Aval Lo Tehiyeh-lanu Aretz—we will have a nation, but we will not have a land." ■

מצותי תשמרו

Parashat Be-Hukkotai
Leviticus 26.3–27.34

Arthur Kurzweil

ARTHUR KURZWEIL IS VICE PRESIDENT OF JASON ARONSON, INC., AND EDITOR-IN-CHIEF OF THE JEWISH BOOK CLUB. HE TEACHES INTRODUCTORY COURSES IN TALMUD AND JEWISH MYSTICISM AT THE MIDRASHA OF THE JEWISH EDUCATION ASSOCIATION IN NEW JERSEY. HE IS THE AUTHOR OF *FROM GENERATION TO GENERATION: HOW TO TRACE YOUR JEWISH GENEALOGY AND FAMILY HISTORY* (HARPERCOLLINS).

Our Torah portion begins, "This is what will happen if you follow My laws and are careful to keep My commandments: I will provide you with rain at the right time...."

A few years ago I drove to my office every day. Often, in the morning, I would listen to a Jewish radio station whose disc jockey was clearly a traditional Jew. He played all the new Jewish music, announced the Torah portion and Shabbos candlelighting times; he had guests whom he interviewed on religious subjects, and generally he offered a wonderful radio show for the Jewish community.

Yet I was annoyed by his weather reports. He would say, "Sorry to announce that it'll be a terrible day today; the forecast calls for rain." He was serious. I was often inclined to call him and say, "Wait a moment. Didn't we pray for rain three times yesterday? Instead of saying, 'It's raining, so it's a terrible day,' why not say, 'Ha-Shem answered our prayers again. Blessed be the name of the Lord?'"

A quick reading of this week's Torah portion gives me the impression that my relationship with the Creator-of-the-Universe is one of cause and effect: If I do what God wants, good things will happen to me; if I do things contrary to what God wants, bad things will happen to me. This seems reasonable. Sounds like karma. Sounds like

---

דָּבָר אַחֵר DAVAR AHER. BUT IF YOU DO NOT OBEY ME AND DO NOT OBSERVE MY COMMANDMENTS, IF YOU REJECT MY LAWS AND SPURN MY RULES...I WILL WREAK MISERY UPON YOU...[Lev. 14-16]. When this parashah is read the *brakhot* are read normally. But when the curses are read they are whispered. The idea is that we want to focus on doing good things and getting rewards rather than bad things and their consequences. **[C.J.]**

Notice that Joel lists the five blessings, then he just mentions that there is a list of over thirty-two curses. That way he saves space, paper, and keeps you from dwelling on bad things. After all this it's funny that we see vows mentioned. These can act as blessings or curses.

Busted. Last year I was doing a workshop in Orange County when a teenager said, "In my Torah portion, this Torah portion, God tells Israel

אם בחקתי תלכו ואת

basic ecology. If I am in sync with the world, things will be pleasant; if I'm out of sync, the results will be otherwise.

Of course, life is not so simple, and the sages, over the centuries, seem to have a great deal to say about human life in general and the experience of suffering in particular. In other words, if I am experiencing something unpleasant, am I to assume that this is the hand of God punishing me for my sins? If things are going well, can I assume that this is God's intention, to reward Kurzweil for the good he has done?

A recent new volume of the Steinsaltz edition of the Talmud in English includes a remarkable discussion dealing directly with this topic. The section of the Talmud known as *Ta'anit*, translated as Fasts, is not generally about the official fast days on the Jewish calendar like Yom Kippur, Tisha b'Av, or the Fast of Esther. Rather, *Tractate Ta'anit* concerns itself with public fasts that are declared by the leadership of a community in response to a calamity. For example, if the crops need rain and yet the rain has not fallen, to the point where the situation is getting serious, a general fast is declared. It is in this same volume of the Talmud that we learn most of what we know about a Talmudic personality who has, since I met him, been my favorite. Of all the volumes of the Talmud and of all the thousands of Talmudic personalities in the text, it is Na<u>h</u>um of Gamzu who truly captures my imagination. It's strange about Na<u>h</u>um: Although he was the teacher of Rabbi Akiva for over two decades, he appears only a handful of times in the Talmud. So while Rabbi Akiva is one of the superstars in the Talmud, appearing regularly, it is ironic to observe

SYNOPSIS: *Five blessings for following the rules. Thirty curses for not following the rules. Laws of vows, tithes, things promised to God, and things that need to be redeemed.*

RASHI OF THE WEEK: *A political Rashi. I leave it to you to decide whose politics:* "YOU WILL EAT YOUR FILL OF BREAD AND YOU WILL SIT SECURELY IN THE LAND. I WILL PROVIDE PEACE IN THE LAND AND YOU WILL LIE DOWN WITH NONE TO MAKE YOU AFRAID" [Lev. 26.5-6]. *If God promised security, why does the Torah need to add the promise of peace?* Perhaps you will say, *"Here is food and here is drink, but if there is no peace there is nothing!" This verse solves that problem with the promise of peace that is as important as everything else combined. That is why the Torah teaches [Isaiah 45.7]* GOD MAKES PEACE... [*Brakhot* 11b].

---

that they will eat their own children." He asked, "Why would God ever do that to anyone?" The Ramban works overtime to make the curses not so bad. He looks in the Talmud, *Gittin* 55b, and finds the story of the destruction of Jerusalem under the Romans. The Talmud says that Jerusalem was destroyed because of "groundless hate." It starts with a Jew whose servant invites his enemy, Bar Kamza, to a party instead of his friend, Kamza. The Jew insults Kamza, who in turn goes to the emperor and causes the destruction of the Temple and of Jersualem. In the seige of Jerusalem hunger and craziness spread. Some families do turn cannibal in order to stay alive. Ramban (not Maimonides, but the N. guy) weaves this all together and says: "God won't make you eat your young as a punishment, but if you forget the Torah, and forget God by not doing the mitzvot, you will begin a cycle of craziness which will end (as it did with the story of Bar Kamza) in Jews eating their own children." The curse is not caused by God but happens when we take God out of the equation. I hate the curses section. They make me uncomfortable, too. Therefore, I go past them as quickly as possible. **Joel Lurie Grishaver, Torah-Toons Gazette.**

Be-Hukkotai

that his teacher of twenty years only appears a few times. This oddity is easier to grasp when we learn what the curriculum was when Rabbi Akiva sat with Nahum. The Talmud tells us that Rabbi Akiva learned two things from Nahum of Gamzu. Surely he learned more than two things; I imagine that he learned countless lessons from his opportunities to be with Nahum. But the Talmud itself tells us that there were two major lessons that Rabbi Akiva learned from Nahum of Gamzu. In fact, these two things are usually ideas we associate with Rabbi Akiva himself, yet the Talmud informs us that Rabbi Akiva received these ideas from Nahum. The first notion is that every letter of the Torah has meaning; there is nothing extra, nothing superfluous, nothing missing. Every letter has meaning.

The second lesson is actually reflected in Nahum's name. Known as Nahum of Gamzu, we learn that "Gamzu" has a double meaning. Nahum came from the town of Gimzo, and Nahum's favorite saying was "*Gam zu l'tova*," meaning "This, too, is for the best."

Perhaps the best-known "This, too, is for the best" story is about Rabbi Akiva himself. He looks for a place to spend the night; nobody in town gives him lodging, and he says, "This is for the best." At night, in the outskirts of town, Rabbi Akiva camps out. His candle blows out, and he says, "This is for the best." An animal kills his rooster, and Rabbi Akiva says, "This is for the best." Another wild animal kills his donkey, and Rabbi Akiva once again says, "This is for the best." The next morning he learns that during the night the town was under attack; had Rabbi Akiva been given lodging, he might have been harmed. Had the candle not gone out, had the rooster not been killed, had the donkey not been killed, Rabbi Akiva might have been detected by the attackers and been vulnerable to them.

This classic story is but one of many within Jewish traditional literature on this theme. The question of suffering is not so simple; what seems like punishment or hardship is actually a reward, truly "for the best."

Sometimes I try to shock Jewish audiences at lectures or classes by saying that Jews do not believe that God created the world. In fact, despite the opening lines of the Torah where it states that "In the beginning God created the heaven and the earth," you will not find a traditional Jewish theologian over the centuries who believes that God created the world. Instead we believe that God creates the world. Big difference. We see this notion reflected in the most popular *b'rakhah*: the *shehehheyanu*. The blessing does not refer to God as the One Who created the world, but rather the One Who "keeps us alive, sustains us, and permits us to reach this season." Rabbi Harold Kushner, in his popular book of comfort, *When Bad Things Happen to Good People*, represents, in a way, the classical heretical position: Since I can't accept that God would tolerate bad things happening to good people, I must conclude that God is not all-knowing and all-powerful; God is all-knowing but not all-powerful. In other words, God created the world; God made it and then left it alone. For centuries our greatest sages taught the contrary: Nothing happens without God allowing it to happen; the movement of a blade of grass occurs only because it is the will of the Creator.

I know that I do not want to be glib about suffering, not mine and not anyone else's. In fact, I was once taught an important ground rule regarding the use of that expression, "*Gam zu l'tova*," "This, too, is for the best." The ground rule is this: You can only say it about your own suffering, not someone else's suffering. So when I see you fall and hurt your knee, I don't say, "Karma." Instead, I try to help you to relieve your suffering. But when I fall and hurt my knee, I don't say, "Poor me." Instead I say, "*Gam zu l'tova*," and I try to use the suffering somehow in my spiritual work on myself, my inner work on my soul.

A story that I have heard in several variations concerns a student who learns that we have a special blessing we say upon hearing bad news. "*Barukh Dayan Emes*," Blessed is the True Judge. We say this blessing, for example, upon learning of someone's death. The student was confused and went to his rebbe, asking for an explanation. "I can understand reciting a blessing upon hearing good news, but how can we say such a blessing upon hearing bad news and suffering?" The rebbe directed him to a man in the town who was well known by all to have had a life filled with pain and difficult trials of all kinds, "Ask him," said the rebbe. "he will be able to explain this to you." The student went to the man and said, "The rebbe suggested I speak with you. I have a question about suffering, and the rebbe thought you could help." The man responded, "I don't know why the rebbe said such a thing. I have no experience with this. I have never really suffered."

Perhaps the best known story about Na<u>h</u>um of Gamzu (also appearing in *Tractate Ta'anit* and translated with commentary by Rabbi Steinsaltz) is about the time Na<u>h</u>um's students found that his house was about to collapse. Na<u>h</u>um was in the house. As Rabbi Steinsaltz translates it, "He was blind in both eyes, both his hands were cut off, both his legs were amputated, and his entire body was covered with boils. He was so completely helpless that the legs of his bed had to be placed in bowls of water so that ants could not climb up the legs of the bed and distress him." Na<u>h</u>um's students expressed their sorrow at seeing their teacher in such a terrible condition, but Na<u>h</u>um of Gamzu, true to his name, told his students that all this had happened to him because he was once so insensitive to a poor man's plight that he failed to help the needy man in time, and the person died. Rabbi Na<u>h</u>um said, "Alas for me, if you had *not* seen me like this." Rabbi Steinsaltz explains that Na<u>h</u>um said, "I am glad to be subjected to all this suffering, for in this way I may expiate the insensitivity I showed to a poor, hungry man."

In the Steinsaltz Talmud, in *Tractate Ta'anit,* we find right in the midst of all the discussion about fasts, suffering, Na<u>h</u>um of Gamzu, and related subjects a most remarkable passage where, as Rabbi Steinsaltz states, "Having cited Rab Yehudah's interpretation of what appears to be a blessing as in fact being a curse, the Gemara continues with four cases in which Rav Yehudah interprets Biblical verses in the opposite direction, taking a seeming curse and explaining it as, in fact, being a blessing."

How do we know what is a curse and what is a blessing? How can we be sure that the trial of today is not really the reward of tomorrow? Clearly, we cannot. The best we can do is to understand the paradox; to work to repair the world; and to deepen our faith that in some enigmatic way all of our trials, all of our joys, all of our successes, and all of our failures are steps toward the Infinite One, the True Judge. ■

חֲזַק, חֲזַק וְנִתְחַזֵּק

<u>H</u>azak, <u>H</u>azak v'nit-<u>H</u>azek

במדבר

Be-Midbar

במדבר סיני באהל מועד

Parashat Be-Midbar
Numbers 1.1–4.20

Rabbi Jack Riemer

Rabbi Jack Riemer of Congregation Beth Tikvah in Boca Raton is the editor of *Wrestling With The Angel*, published by Schocken, and the co-editor of *So that Your Values Live On*, published by Jewish Lights. He is the Chair of the National Rabbinic Network.

Let me show you one tiny detail in today's sidrah. It may mean nothing at all. I may be reading more into it than is really there, but let me share it with you; you can see what you think.

If you look at the names of the princes of the twelve tribes that are mentioned in this sidrah, you will notice something strange. Eleven out of the twelve have religious names, by which I mean names that have the name of God within them.

They have names like אֱלִיצוּר *ELI TZUR*, which means "God is my Rock," or נְתַנְאֵל *NITANEL*, which means "God has given," or אֱלִישָׁמָע *ELISHAMA*, which means "God has heard." Some have double names of God within their names, a few have triple names of God within their names, and one even has a quadruple form of the names of God within his name: שְׁלֻמִיאֵל בֶּן-צוּרִישַׁדָּי *SHLOMI EL BEN TZURI SHADAI*. *SHALOM* is a name of God, as is *TZUR*, as is *EL*, as is *SHADAI*, so this is surely the most religious name anyone could possibly have.

Yet strangely enough, for some reason, these eleven princes who had the name of God as part of their names turned out to be not such a great credit to God. They were cautious, even cowardly, when it came to the service of God. The one who had the quadruple name of God within his name ended up not amounting to much at all.

דָּבָר אַחֵר **DAVAR AHER.** ON THE FIRST DAY OF THE SECOND MONTH, IN THE SECOND YEAR FOLLOWING THE EXODUS FROM THE LAND OF EGYPT, THE LORD SPOKE TO MOSES IN THE WILDERNESS OF SINAI, IN THE TENT OF MEETING, SAYING....[Num. 1.1]. We begin the book בְּמִדְבַּר *Be-Midbar* by doing honor to the road, by respecting the journey and taking notice of the way. That is where we are in our Torah saga, the wilderness.

Every year we enter the *Be-Midbar*, the book, on the shabbes just before Shavuos, the giving of the Torah. We are given in a deep way to the wilderness, the wilderness within and the wilderness without, before we receive the durable freedom, promised when we became free from Egypt, the durable freedom of receiving Torah, something new and transforming.

וידבר יהוה אל משה

Among the twelve there was only one who turned out to be really noble and brave, and that was נַחְשׁוֹן בֶּן-עַמִּינָדָב *NAHSHON ben Aminadav,* which derives from נָחָשׁ *nahash,* which means snake. What kind of a name is that for a Jewish boy? Go figure it out—the eleven that had pious names turned out to be not such a credit to God, and the one with the worst name turned out to be the best. When the Israelites stood at the edge of the Red Sea, all the other princes suddenly became very polite. Each one said to the other, "After you," but Nahshon had the courage to jump into the sea—before it split—and he was the one who saved the Jewish people.

The lesson that I would have you learn from this is that you can't tell who is really religious by whether they claim to be or not. A person may flaunt his piety and not be religious at all. A man may claim to be not religious, even antireligious, and yet when he is tested he may turn out to be truly religious just the same. Perhaps what the Torah is telling us is that there ought to be a "truth in advertising" law, not just for products but also for people. We ought to be wary of those who advertise their piety, because if you go around boasting of how pious you are, you are probably not pious at all.

Let me give you two examples of what I mean. During the Second World War there were two men, one in

---

But it is in the wilderness that we bake, it is here in the wilderness that we spend most of this freedom journey; it is the wilderness that required forty years of wandering. There would be no generation of redemption (דוֹר גְּאוּלָה *Dor G'eulah*) without a generation that dies out in the desert (דוֹר הַמִּדְבָּר *Dor ha-Midbar*); something has to die for something new to emerge, and that is where we are this week. We are the דוֹר הַמִּדְבָּר *Dor ha-Midbar*, the generation of the wilderness, making our way through the desert. The lessons of the wilderness are not lost on us: There is always a way out, as in any journey we move through by stations, one step at a time, no short cuts, we

SYNOPSIS: *A census is taken of men over twenty. Then directions are given for the arrangement of the camp by tribes. Finally, Aaron's family and other clans are identified.*

RASHI OF THE WEEK: EACH MAN OF THE FAMILIES-OF-ISRAEL SHOULD CAMP BY HIS (FAMILY) FLAG WITH THE SIGN OF HIS FATHER'S HOUSE [Num. 2.2]. *Rashi looks at this verse and senses that the Torah seems to be giving us too much information. It tells us both to camp by the family flag and to camp by the family sign. Why do we have to be told about both? Should the flag imply the sign, or vice versa? Rashi brings down two answers.*

ANSWER I: Each banner should be made with a sign—a *strip* of colored cloth hanging on it, each flag with a different color, these colors being the same as the stone on the breastplate [cf. Ex. 28.21] so that everyone can find his own camp (*Tanhuma*). *In other words, the extra phrase "signs" is a clue that the configuration of Israel's campsite paralleled the sense of unity found on the breastplate.*

ANSWER II: Davar Aher: These are the signs that Jacob gave to each of his sons. They were first used when they carried his body out of Egypt to bury in Canaan: *AND HIS SONS DID FOR HIM EXACTLY WHAT HE HAD COMMANDED THEM* [Gen. 50.12]. (*For details, look at that Rashi, too.*) For he had commanded that Judah, Issachar, and Zevulun should carry his bier from the east, Reuben, Simeon, and Gad from the south, etc. *Tanhuma on Genesis 50.12 explains this in detail. In others words, the extra words are a clue that the flags come from Jacob, that his burial was a rehearsal for the Exodus, and the encampment of the Families-of-Israel nightly is designed to recall that sacred task—returning the bones to the Land of Israel.*

What both of these interpretations teach is that the mention of the flags is designed to evoke a deep truth through association.

France, the other in the Vatican. The one who lived in France was Jean-Paul Sartre, and if you had asked him, he would have said that he was an atheist. Yet all during the war he risked his life to fight the Nazis and to save lives. If saving lives and standing up to evil is an important part of what religion is all about, then he was religious, even though he denied it. At the same time there lived in the Vatican a man who prayed every day, who wore a *kippah* at all times, who was the epitome of piety to millions, and yet this man, for some reason, never spoke up even once against evil. He never made waves, never rocked the boat for fear that if he did, the church that he headed might be endangered. One man risked his life, the other played it safe; which one was really religious? You can't always tell without a program.

I would like to suggest that the same suspicion we ought to show toward those who exhibit their piety should be extended to others—to those who wrap themselves in the flag, to those who act as if they have a monopoly on morality, to those who take any value and use it for their own purposes.

Even modesty is a tricky concept. If you are really modest, then you don't realize that you are, and you certainly don't boast that you are. One of my favorite stories is the one that Rabbi Stephen Wise used to tell about his meeting with Sigmund Freud. He used to say that he got a free psychoanalysis when he met Freud. Freud asked him: "Tell me, Rabbi Wise, who are the three greatest Jews in the world today? Wise said: "Einstein, Weitsman, and you, Dr. Freud." Freud said, "And what about you?" to which Wise replied: "Oh, no, no, no." Freud said: "One 'no' would have been enough."

One "no" would have been enough and one name of God would have been enough. The princes didn't need to have double, triple, and

---

Be-Midbar

are taught to make ourselves like the wilderness, free and ownerless, in order to be ready for the durable freedom of Torah, when something will have to die for something new to be born.

We also have learned to respect the place, to respect the wilderness, knowing that if we do not conquer it, it will conquer us. So we live in this tender kind of balance with the wilderness, the wilderness without and the wilderness within, and we have worked out a living relation, a reciprocity. We have given and we take; we respect and we subdue; we are in that kind of balance with the wilderness, the wilderness within and the wilderness without.

We as a people come of age in the wilderness. We grow up there; we come of age in the wilderness within; we submit and reconcile and integrate and move through. This is

even quadruple names of God within their name. It is a bit too much, is it not?

Let us learn that the real love of God is quiet, gentle, modest. The real test of whether we love God or not is not how fervently we pray in public but how genuinely we follow God's teachings in private. ■

---

not an endurance, not a conquering, but a move-through, so that we may be ready for the more durable freedom, the gift we are soon to receive at Sinai.

The wilderness is a challenge; it is like a personality. It has a character of its own. The road, as it were, is a player in our personal drama and our drama as a people. The road plays a part in the drama, and it is as if we come to listen to the call of the road, its message, its draw, its meaning, its direction. The journey is a character, a player, in the drama.

Rabbi Nahman said that every person is called in her own way, at his own level. God answers one person with a shout, another with a song, a third with a whisper.

It is like the shepherd and the sheep. As long as the sheep do not wander too far, they can hear the shepherd's flute. As long as the shepherd is close, the shepherd can hear the bells of the sheep. But when the sheep stray too far they no longer hear or are heard. The shepherd and the sheep can stray too far away from one another, and then nothing will bring them back together, not the call, not the bell, not the journey.

We are also taught that whenever someone interrupts his journey, whenever someone loses her way, the roads go into mourning. Shouting, singing, whispering.

So let us celebrate *Be-Midbar*, the journey,
let us celebrate not arrivals but passages
let us celebrate not doing but being
let us celebrate not there but here
let us celebrate the road
the moving through
the being here
the journey,
the wilderness,
within and without.

James Stone Goodman, <Stavisker@aol.com>

דָּבָר אַחֵר DAVAR AHER. THE ISRAELITES SHALL CAMP EACH WITH HIS STANDARD, UNDER THE BANNERS OF THEIR ANCESTRAL HOUSE [Num. 2.2]. In *Learn Torah With... Volume 2, Number 34,* Jack Riemer offers a lesson on *Parashat Be-Midbar*, pointing out the spiritual inadequacies of the Israelite tribal chieftains. We don't want to single out the leaders alone, however, and in a left-handed sort of way the Zohar makes the same point about the entire Israelite nation encamped at Mount Sinai. At *Be-Midbar* 118-b, commenting on אִישׁ עַל-דִּגְלוֹ בְאֹתֹת לְבֵית אֲבֹתָם *Ish al-Daglo v'Otot l'Vat Avotam* [Num. 2.2], Zohar praises the twelve tribes with a beautiful midrash, declaring that the addition to their name of the definite article ה *hey* and the adjectival suffix י *yud* (e.g. הָרְאוּבֵנִי מִשְׁפְּחוֹת *mishpahot haruveni*, "the Reubenite families") serves to connect the tribes with the Ineffable Name, proclaiming their piety as what Psalm 122.4 calls שִׁבְטֵי-יָהּ *shivtai-ya* (literally, the *Yod-Hei* Tribes). But as lovely as that may be, the reality is that the Torah refers to the Reubenites (and all the other tribes) with the distinction of the extra *yud* and *hey* not in this parashah but rather in Numbers 26, a narrative nearly forty years later in time and referring to a completely new generation of Israelites. That is important, because the very lack in this chapter of what the Zohar trumpets in *that* chapter serves to highlight the deficiencies in the generation of the Exodus. Forty years hence the children of the liberated slaves will have grown up to be loyal to God and worthy of being associated with God's Name—but as yet the newly freed slaves themselves do not merit such a distinction. **Rabbi Mark Gross, Temple Beth Orr, Coral Springs, FL.**

A Lesson on the Haftarah

I read a wonderful story recently, a story that is for me the key to understanding the strange story of Hosea and Gomer, which is the haftarah for this week.

The story is that of a young rabbi traveling on the D train from Brooklyn to Manhattan. As the train rattles along towards its destination he sits quietly reading a book, as do most of the other travelers. Enter two six-foot young men in gang jackets with a big boom box blasting away.

Near the rabbi sits a little old woman who probably tips the scale at eighty pounds and who might be five feet if she stretches. This little old woman doesn't like the noise coming out of the boom box, so she yells out, "Who's going to make them turn it down?" Everyone hunkers down in his seat, takes a deeper interest in what he is reading, and pretends that he hasn't heard her—including the rabbi.

One of the young toughs says to the woman, "Lady, if you don't like this music, you can try to turn it off." She shuffles across the subway with her hand in front of her, ready to take his dare. The ruffian puts down the boom box and hauls back to deck her. Up jumps the rabbi and blocks the tough guy's punch.

The guy is puzzled, and he looks down at the rabbi, who is about a foot shorter than he is and who probably only weighs half as much, and says to him, "What's your problem, boy?" The rabbi replies with a timid smile, "I have no problem, but just don't hit the woman, please," and he returns to his seat and

Anonymous

We received this wonderful essay without its author's name. We would like to give credit to this unknown author.

Be-Midbar

דָּבָר אַחֵר DAVAR A<u>H</u>ER. ON THE BOOK OF NUMBERS. Here is what I know. Numbers is the Torah of demography. It tries to predict the future by counting heads. I've spent a lot of time in small-town Jewish America this year. I've been places where there are only thirteen players out of which the minyan must always be made—well-counted heads. Recently I was told by a rabbi, "Here there isn't enough life cycle traffic to mask the emptiness in daily Jewish living." In that town there are fewer than two handfuls of *sim<u>h</u>ahs* a year. In another town the rabbi's thirteen-year-old son turned to me with sadness, not arrogance, and said, "What would be so bad if I went out with a non-Jewish girl if I knew that I wasn't going to marry her?" That isn't the celebration of pluralism. It is the well-known problem of reduced odds. Given five Jewish girls in the reasonable age range, all of whom he had known since infancy, all of whom were

goes back to his reading. The woman shuffles back across the car. And the young tough flips the power switch on the boom box again and inundates the entire subway train in full-force, deep-bassed, woofer-and-tweeter enhanced, penetrating, unmitigated, raucous, deafening noise.

Once again the old woman screams, "Who's going to make them turn it off?" Everyone on the train rereads his previous sentences with increased concentration. The young tough grins and invites her over. The little old woman shuffles over and once again reaches to turn off the power switch on the boom box. The young tough hauls back to hit her, the rabbi jumps up to block; the young tough looks confused, and says, "Now you're getting on my nerves, boy." The rabbi smiles and says, "Sorry. Just don't hit the woman," and he returns to his seat. The little old woman shuffles toward the rabbi's seat and stands with her back to him. And the two young toughs get off at the next stop.

As the rabbi is settling back into his book he glances up at the back of the little old woman and thinks, "Gee, I just risked my life, not once but twice, to protect her...and she doesn't even thank me." Then, after two minutes of self-righteous indulgence, the rabbi stops in his tracks with an incredible realization: "God just performed not one miracle but two to save my life, and did I stop to thank God?"

That story is the key to understanding this week's haftarah. The prophet Hosea has a wife named Gomer who betrays him, who takes his gifts and gives them to her lovers. At first he is filled with a towering rage. Then he realizes that what she has done to him we all do to God! God gives us so many gifts—health, wealth, and harvests—and what do we do with them? Instead of thanking God we spend God's gifts on trivialities and give them to false gods—to pride, to vanity, and to war. If we don't appreciate the gifts that God gives us and the favors God does for us, how can we be angry at those who don't appreciate the favors we do for them?

Those two toughs on the subway probably did not know much of the Bible. I bet they didn't even know that the story of Hosea and Gomer is the haftarah for this week. Nevertheless, they and the old woman taught this rabbi a lesson that he tried to remember when he came to shul on Shabbat *Be-Midbar* and that he tries to remember all the time as well. ■

---

his sisters, in a sense, the only choices were "incest," "celibacy," or "What would be so bad if I went out with a non-Jewish girl once in a while?" These days, when we tell the story with numbers, we always hear sad violins.

In deep Bava Metzia (like around 103, but I don't have a *shas* on this airplane) they tell this story. Rabbis Hiyya and Hisda are arguing. Hiyya says, "If the Torah was forgotten, I would argue it back into existence." Hisda says, "When the Torah was forgotten, I planted and grew flax. I made a net out of the flax. I used the net to catch deer. I slaughtered the deer and fed the meat to orphans and used the skin to write a Torah. I taught Torah to fives and Mishnah to sixes—and told them: 'Teach each other.'" That is how the Torah was restored to Israel after the Hadrianic persecutions.

After Numbers comes Deuteronomy. Numbers looks like the end of the Torah. Moses even waves goodbye—but, like the ending of *Ferris Bueller's Day Off*, the Torah comes back with Deuteronomy. Deuteromony is the retelling of the story. There is a lot to learn from Numbers—but the question for teachers is *"Where will your Torah end?"* **Joel Lurie Grishaver, <joel@torahaura.com>**

THE LOST MEANING

Our parashah derives its name from the opening word of the second sentence, שְׂאוּ אֶת רֹאשׁ *Se'u et Rosh,* MAKE AN ACCOUNTING.

The very same expression has already been seen in Genesis 40, where we learn how Joseph interpreted the dreams of the Pharaoh's chief cup bearer and baker (verses 13 and 19). But there, נָשָׂא *nasa* has opposite meanings, even though the Hebrew is identical and says both times יִשָּׂא פַרְעֹה אֶת-רֹאשֶׁךָ *Yissa Par'o et-Roshekha.* In one case it means to lift the cup bearer out of his dismal state, while the other time the baker's head will be literally lifted off.

Clearly, the root נשה *nasa* has multiple meanings.

A similar linguistic oddity exists in English. The word *levy* is derived from the French *lever,* to lift, which in turn comes from the Latin, *levis,* light. But in general parlance, a levy is considered something burdensome; it is imposed and is not light at all.

In our parashah שְׂאוּ *se'u* denotes the taking of a census. Most of us today don't like such a governmental undertaking and, in fact, have an innate resistance to being counted. Most likely it wasn't much different in antiquity, for counting meant military service or taxes.

The biblical prohibition against counting people except upon express divine authorization is confirmed by the tragic consequence of David's census, which is recorded in II Samuel 24 and I Chronicles 21. However, the first source tells us that God incited (tested?) Israel, while in the second it was Satan. Whatever the background of this dark tale, counting persons became taboo in Jewish tradition. Says the midrash, when the children of Israel are numbered for proper purpose, their numbers are preserved (as in our parashah and in *Parashat Pin<u>h</u>as*), but when they are not, their numbers are diminished (*Be-Midbar Rabbah* 2.17).

Even in North America, where numbers circumscribe our existence, we rebel against a census that asks

Parashat Naso
Numbers 4.21–7.89

Rabbi W. Gunther Plaut

RABBI PLAUT, SENIOR SCHOLAR AT HOLY BLOSSOM TEMPLE IN TORONTO, IS THE AUTHOR OF 21 BOOKS, AMONG THEM *THE TORAH—A MODERN COMMENTARY* (OF WHICH HE WAS THE EDITOR AND CHIEF COMMENTATOR) AND THE RECENT *HAFTARAH COMMENTARY*. THE SECOND VOLUME OF HIS AUTOBIOGRAPHY, *MORE UNFINISHED BUSINESS*, IS SLATED FOR PUBLICATION IN FALL, 1997 BY UNIVERSITY OF TORONTO PRESS.

questions that are too personal. Enough that our finances are monitored by government and credit services; that we have to state (and sometimes prove) how old we are; that we have to cue in our Social Security (in Canada, Social Insurance) numbers in order to establish our identity—all of these strike a sour note in us. We recall how the Nazis numbered us and robbed us of our identity. But even before them, counting people was avoided at all costs.

To be sure, it was necessary to determine whether enough persons were present for a minyan, and this posed a challenge. It was met by circumlocution. One went around the room and counted "not one, not two, not three," and so forth, thereby pretending not to count at all, or one recited a phrase from Psalms that had ten words, and with each word one counted those present.

Since a Divine command underlay the census in Numbers chapters 1 and 26, the counting was of course valid, and great care was taken to preserve the numbers exactly. The number 603,550 in our parashah agrees precisely with that given in Exodus 38.26 and is fairly close to the census recorded in Numbers 26. (Tradition explains the difference by pointing out that the intervening years had wrought some changes.)

But these figures are incredibly large. When we add women and young people we arrive at a wandering people of some two million, whose sustenance would indeed have to be provided by daily miracles. Therefore, modern scholars have often assumed that we deal here with a legendary counting, not anything related to reality. Others suggest, anachronistically, that 603 [thousand] represents the numerical equivalent of *B'nai Yisrael* by way of *gematria*. In any case, two million men, women, and children wandering in the Sinai desert for forty years does stretch one's faith in the inerrancy of the text.

But there is no need to doubt the numbers. The problem is not that the figures seem large; rather, it is our misunderstanding of their meaning that is deficient. The key is the meaning of אֶלֶף *elef*. Commonly it is understood as "thousand," but that was not its only meaning. George E. Mendenhall, in his classic *The Tenth Generation* (John Hopkins University Press, 1973), pointed out that אֶלֶף *elef* at one time denoted small units of nine or ten armed men, so that in our census the word should be rendered as "contingents." Thus Reuben's numbers would amount to "forty-six אֶלֶף *elef* five hundred", which

SYNOPSIS: A collection of priestly odds and ends: more rules for kohanim, *the role of the Levites in moving the Mishkan, the rules for Sota, Nazir, and Birkat ha-Kohanim, the gifts of the chieftains—and God and Moses talk in the tent of meeting.*

RASHI OF THE WEEK:

MAY THE ETERNAL (1) BLESS YOU AND (2) GUARD YOU. MAY THE ETERNAL (3) SHINE GOD'S FACE ON TO YOU AND (4) BE NICE TO YOU. MAY THE ETERNAL (5) LIFT UP GOD'S FACE TOWARDS YOU AND (6) GIVE YOU PEACE [Num. 6.24–27].

In this blessing we ask God for six things. Rashi wants to know the difference between each of them. He answers his own unverbalized question by explaining the uniqueness of each clause: **BLESS YOU** means your wealth increases. **GUARD YOU** means that no thieves come and take your stuff. For a human who gives a gift to a servant cannot protect it fully, and if a band of robbers steals it, then the gift will not be fully enjoyed. But the Holy One both gives (blesses) and guards. **SHINE GOD'S FACE ON TO YOU** means be friendly, smile. BE NICE TO YOU means give you HEN (good favor). **LIFT UP GOD'S FACE TOWARDS YOU** means God will hold back God's anger. (*Sifre.*)

meant "forty-six contingents equal to five hundred men." This method of reading the text would give us a total of 5,500 fighting men, which corresponds to the armies usually put into the field in the ancient Middle East.

In later centuries this old meaning of אֶלֶף *elef* was lost, and the current understanding of "thousand" remained the sole understanding. This loss has occasioned unnecessary questions about the historical memory underlying our parashah. ■

Birkat Kohanim: The United Field of Being

Rabbi Stephen Robbins

Rabbi Stephen Robbins is the spiritual leader of Congregation Nvay Shalom in Los Angeles, CA.

And God spoke to Moses, saying, "Speak to Aaron and to his sons, saying, 'Thus (in this manner) shall you (all) bless the children of Israel; it must be said to them (in this way only): God bless you and keep you; God make His face shine light toward you and be gracious to you; God turn His face to you and set for you peace. And they shall set My Name upon all Israel, and I will bless them" [Num. 6.24-27].

God confers upon Aaron and his sons the duty to bless the whole nation of Israel according to this set formula. In doing so God establishes for us the nature, purpose, and result of bestowing blessings.

The priestly responsibility "to bless" using the Birkat Kohanim was an act of obligation on the priests, not an act of their authority; the blessing was bestowed not by the action of the priests, but only as a response to a request from the people to be blessed. The blessing could be given only in the three-part formula so that the purpose, force, and meaning of the blessing would remain unchanged. The force of koh—or In this manner only—in the introduction to blessing (v. 23) establishes a limitation on the priests so that the blessing comes from God directly, not from any human. The fixed pattern of the priestly blessing also ensured that the effect of the blessing did not depend on the unique talents or personal limitations of any individual priest. This follows the principle that when serving at the altar or before the ark the priest must be absent of his unique personality or ego so that his own personal issues do not become an impediment to the fulfillment of the spiritual purpose of the ceremony. The obligation to bless was set upon all the priests so that the power to bless was not invested in any individual. Indeed it had to be authorized by the children of Israel, who commissioned the priest, by their request, to serve as the connection between them and the Shekhinah. It is the people who motivate the blessing because of their need, which would always be met by an ever-present caring God. Though called the priestly blessing, it is truly "the peoples' blessing."

The threefold blessing has a clearly stated goal: to set the name of God upon the people, so they will become blessed by bearing it (v. 27). "And they (the priests) will set my name upon all Israel" means that in doing so "I shall bless them" verse 27 is automatic and unconditional. This unconditional blessing is the unique gift of a compassionate and involved Divine Presence who will bless upon request those who bear God's name (S. R. Hirsch, Numbers 98ff).

This principle is similar to the Kabbalistic concept of "awakening from below," which teaches that what we receive from God is activated by us through our effort to awaken the perception and acceptance of the Divine Presence in ourselves. Our living then is a receiver and container of God's Being. The purpose of living is to contain the presence of the Divine Being, so it can be revealed and brought into the world through our moral actions and religious practices.

The simple and elegant beauty of the threefold blessing belies the complex and mystic dynamics of the blessing's content and purpose. The content of the blessing moves in a developmental process from one stage of life to the next, unifying all levels of existence into a single "unified field of being" expressing the pervasive presence of the Divine in all. The operation of the dynamic is revealed in the structure, flow, and content of the text itself.

The most familiar of interpretations of the text, from a variety of Rabbinic sources, inform us that the three parts of the blessing each refer to one of the three basic elements of the person and his related needs. The first line refers to the physical needs of humans for protection of all material needs, including possessions and the body. The second line refers to the mind, comprising the intellectual and emotional faculties of humans and our need for enlightenment. So as the Divine Light of knowledge is shone into the person each one can experience God's grace by knowing the truth of the Divine Presence and purpose. The result is to ease anxiety and confusion. The last line refers to the spiritual needs of humanity. As God TURNS GOD'S FACE TO YOU so that there is an intimate experience of God's caring presence, all needs are met and one comes to shalom—wholeness.

On a more mystic level the three-part structure of the blessing, divided into physical, intellectual, and spiritual elements, is an analog to the three-dimensional soul: נֶפֶשׁ *nefesh,* רוּחַ *ruah,* נְשָׁמָה *neshamah;* body, mind, and spirit. Thus the first line of blessing is for the healing and safety of the נֶפֶשׁ *nefesh,* the life force of the physical body. The second line is for the healing and expanding of the רוּחַ *ruah,* mind/consciousness. The third line is a blessing for the healing and strengthening of the נְשָׁמָה *neshamah,* the spirit, which is the Divine Presence in each of us as reflected in the צֶלֶם *tzelem* (image) by which we were all created. The final goal of the blessing is for humanity to find shalom, synergy, when God TURNS TO FACE US in an intimate experience of our being in God and of God. The priestly bless-

Naso

ing as a whole, then, is to reflect the unification of our souls within us and within God.

This can be illustrated in the simple but beautiful *gematria* (spiritual math) of the blessing. The first line contains three words; the second five words, and the third seven words, totaling fifteen words. The number fifteen is equivalent to the Hebrew letters י *Yod* and ה *Hey*, which spell the name of God. Thus we are unified body, mind and spirit in God through the priestly blessing.

At another level the blessing is meant to take us deeper into the experience of unification by the merging of our being into the greater structure of all existence. We must be more than unified in shalom personally; the true blessing is our unification with the process of existence itself into a unified field of being. This can be understood by viewing the blessing as expressions of the עֵץ חַיִּים Etz Hayyim—the tree of life. In Kabbalah the tree of life is the representation of ten *sefirot*, the ten dimensions of existence, that enable the process of creation to flow from God's Being into the physical universe. The familiar diagram of these spheres joined by twenty-two lines of communication is structured into three pillars. The central one is called pillar of consciousness (כֶּתֶר *keter*—the crown of God's Presence) and represents the constant flow of God's Spirit through all existence and even each of us. The right-hand one, called the pillar of dynamic (חָכְמָה *hokhemah*—wisdom), represents the active principles of creation as it transforms the essence of being into the process that creates the physical world. The left=hand one is the pillar of structure (בִּינָה *binah*—understanding) and represents the containment of the process of creation in a structure that will be stable and hold creation on a functional form. The two side pillars represent the constant tension and balance between the active giving process of creation and the passive receiving structure of the physical world. In this schema all existence is a managed process of balance between giving and receiving of the Divine Presence. That which is given must be contained so that it can be functional in this world.

This three-pillar structure of consciousness, dynamic giving, and structural receiving is reflected in the form and syntax of the priestly blessing in the following manner. The name of God always appears in the middle of each line, balancing two verbs, one on each side, and so refers to the conscious presence of God. The three verbs that begin each line—MAY GOD BLESS, MAY GOD CAUSE LIGHT TO SHINE, MAY GOD TURN HIS FACE—are principles of action and process and represent the dynamic principles of God's Presence. The three verbs at the end of each line, GUARD YOU, BE GRACIOUS TO YOU, SET PEACE FOR YOU, are all receiving actions that establish stability and structure to contain the action of the blessing. So as God BLESSES, ENLIGHTENS, and TURNS GOD'S FACE these actions are transformed into structures that can contain that Divine Action, its results being kept safe, given grace, and establishing peace. The sum of all this is for us to experience and know that the full blessing of God as the Divine is always present in every aspect of our world and our lives. God gives the unified field of Being, and we are all part of the One.

Each of us, the people of Israel, the world, all time and space, are but finite containers of the limitless Presence of the Divine Being whose purpose we serve. By serving those purposes we have God's name SET UPON us (v. 26). That is our blessing—to receive the Name of God upon us.

The act of bestowing the blessing reflects the mystic character of the blessing. In the ceremony of *duchaning* the *kohanim* raises their hands shoulder high while their heads (and so their personal identities) are hidden. They place their hands in the traditional formation with the fingers of each hand spread into a fan, so when joined together at the thumbs they provide a structure with five openings. It is said that the שְׁכִינָה *shekhinah* (Divine Presence) is revealed through the fingers. This is how God's "Name" is set upon the people.

What does this mean for us today, we who are not priests but fathers, mothers, children, rabbis, cantors, educators; who are all obligated to bless our children on Shabbat, our congregation at prayer? When we are called to bless we come not to represent ourselves, but to represent in our living the Sacred Being of God, which is in all of us. Our hands upraised or on the heads of our children or students remind us of the synergy of all individual lives and the harmonious unity of God's Oneness, and how each one of us is an *olam katan* (Universe in miniature) that reflects the Image of Divine One. When we bless them we acknowledge and accept the sacred unity of being that offers us lives of blessing, safety, enlightenment, grace, intimacy of God's Presence, and wholeness—shalom—all stamped with the name of the Holy One. ■

בהעלתך את הנרת אל

Parashat Be-Ha'alotekha
Numbers 8.1–12.16

Dr. Rachel Adler

Dr. Rachel Adler is a visiting faculty member at Hebrew Union College, Los Angeles. She is the author of *Engendering Judaism* (Jewish Publication Society, September 1997).

In their book *Metaphors We Live By,* Lakoff and Johnson recount that an Iranian student was charmed by the English expression "the solution of my problems." He imagined a bubbling vat full of liquefied problems. The goal was to dissolve one problem without having other problems precipitate out. In this metaphor problems can't be made to disappear. At best they can be kept fluid rather than intractably solid.

I volunteered to write about *Parashat Be-Ha'alotekha* because it contains a story for which I can find no solutions. The story is in Numbers 12, where Aaron and Miriam criticize Moses, and Miriam is struck with the impure skin disease the Torah calls צָרַעַת *tzara'at.* What is frustrating about the story is that by solving one problem I cause another to precipitate out.

Problems appear in the very first words of the chapter. (I am going to use Everett Fox's translations here, because he captures the flavor of the Hebrew so well.) "Now Miryam spoke and Aharon, against Moshe, on account of the Cushite wife that he had taken-in marriage." The subjects of the first verb are Miriam and Aaron, but the verb is feminine singular. Moreover, who is this Cushite wife? Is this an otherwise unknown Ethiopian wife, or is Cushite synonymous with Midianite, in which case the wife is Tzipporah? If Moses' mystery wife is Ethiopian, are Miriam and Aaron racists, or do they, like Ezra, disapprove of marriage with foreigners? The text does not specify the content of the criticism. Oddly enough, the second verse drops the issue of Moses' wife completely and instead contests Moses' monopoly on leadership: "Is it only through Moshe that YHWH speaks? Is it not also through us?" It is the leadership issue that provokes YHWH's angry and lengthy defense of Moses and dominates the chapter.

Documentary and historical criticism can account for these problems. If the Torah is composed of various traditions that have been edited into a single document, verses 1 and 2 may represent two different stories. The first story originally involved only Miriam; hence the singular feminine verb. It places its criticism of Moses' wife in the mouth of another prominent woman. Miriam is punished for this criticism with *tzara'at.* The second story takes up one of the major themes of the book of Numbers: challenges to Moses' authority and questions about the distribution of lead-

Be-Ha'alotekha

ership. Behind the conflicts of Moses, Aaron, and Miriam the historian deduces different groups struggling for sacral authority. The voice of YHWH confirms the unique authority of Moses in the special poetic language of prophecy. "IF THERE SHOULD BE AMONG YOU A PROPHET OF YHWH, IN A VISION TO HIM I MAKE MYSELF KNOWN, IN A DREAM I SPEAK TO HIM, NOT SO MY SERVANT MOSHE: IN ALL MY HOUSE TRUSTED IS HE; MOUTH TO MOUTH I SPEAK TO HIM, IN PLAIN-SIGHT, NOT WITH RIDDLES, AND THE FORM OF YHWH (IS WHAT) HE BEHOLDS. SO WHY WERE YOU NOT TOO AWESTRUCK TO SPEAK AGAINST MY SERVANT, AGAINST MOSHE?" [Num. 12.6-8].

This critical approach creates as many questions as it solves. Why merge the two stories, and why merge them so poorly? If the editors took the trouble to add Aaron's name, why didn't they also make the verb agree? Miriam and Aaron speak no more than the truth when they assert that YHWH does not speak only to Moses. Why is it sinful for them to wish that leadership be shared, when in the previous chapter seventy-two elders acquire charismatic authority? If Miriam and Aaron are allied, why is only Miriam disgraced? Like the story of the Golden Calf, this is another puzzling situation in which Aaron is guilty but gets off scot-free.

Why, moreover, is Miriam punished so harshly? Not only is she afflicted with *tzara'at* and shut out of the camp for a week, but YHWH's explanation brutally underlines the shamefulness of the punishment: "IF HER FATHER SPAT, YES, SPAT IN HER FACE, WOULD SHE NOT BE PUT TO SHAME FOR SEVEN DAYS (AT LEAST)?" Face, in the Bible, is the location of personal dignity, the meeting place between self and other, the place where spirituality shines. God's face, and especially God's mouth, confers intimacy upon Moses: "MOUTH TO MOUTH I SPEAK TO HIM." From that same mouth Miriam receives the ultimate gesture of contempt: the de-face-ment of the face.

This story marks the defacement of Miriam's reputation. In Exodus Miriam is the savior of the infant Moses. She watches over his basket on the Nile and boldly offers her mother's services to Pharaoh's daughter. At the Reed Sea the text calls her a prophetess. She sings and leads a victory dance dedicated to the Divine Warrior. In fact, since victory songs in the Bible are a women's genre, most documentary critics believe that the original "Song at the Sea" was Miriam's and that later editors transferred it to Moses.

In Numbers, however, Miriam is associated principally with impurity, *tumah*. She is the archetypal case of *tzara'at*. It is from Aaron's plea on her behalf that we learn that the imagery of *tzara'at* is linked to death and decomposition, is the antithesis of creation: "DO NOT, PRAY, LET HER BE LIKE A DEAD CHILD WHO, WHEN IT COMES OUT OF ITS MOTHER'S WOMB IS EATEN UP IN HALF ITS FLESH!" *Tzara'at* reduces the mother of the people to a miscarried fetus, as if her accomplishments had never existed. We never hear her speak again. Even her death in Numbers 20, verse 1 is juxtaposed with an account of impurity and its contaminations. Feminist historical critics ask whether Miriam's discrediting marks a movement to oust women from communal leadership and from sacred activities.

The rabbis and classical commentators continue Miriam's defacement by using Numbers 12 to identify *tzara'at* as the punishment for gossip. They imagine the content of this gossip as sexual in nature: Miriam disapproves that Moses has separated sexually from his wife in order to be in a continual state of purity in readiness to receive God's word. In the view of some historians, ascribing celibacy to Moses reflects a deep ambivalence in Rabbinic thought about whether holiness is compatible with sexuality. Since the rabbis see women as demanding or requiring sex, they assign the criticism to Miriam. God's answer, then, emphasizes the connection between women and impurity but sustains the ambivalence with which sexual continence is regarded. On the basis of God's answer one could argue either that continence enhances holiness or that only in Moses' unique case is sustained continence permissible.

These historical explanations attempt to make a puzzling story and its commentaries intelligible by reading them as depictions or responses to specific social and political situations. They are interested in what Miriam's disgrace tells us about the construction of gender in ancient Israel or in Rabbinic thought. But historical solutions for this particular story cause theological problems to precipitate out. If what we have here is a cultic power struggle or a rationale for excluding women from leadership, how can we read this story as sacred text? What Torah does it teach us? Conversely, how can we defend reading this story as sacred text without raising any questions about why one of the few prominent women in the Bible is so profoundly disgraced while both her brothers emerge with undiminished power and authority? Will we not damage our own integrity and that of sacred text if we justify Miriam's disgrace by drawing upon midrashim that rely on gender stereotypes of women as gossips, encroachers, and sources of impurity? Can we preserve

SYNOPSIS: *Again, odds and ends. The menorah is described, the Levites become assistant priests, the rules of the firstborn and Passover, complaints over food, the establishment of the council of seventy elders, and the fuss over Moses' marriage to a Cushite woman. The climax of this story is Miriam's case of leprosy.*

RASHI OF THE WEEK: *This is the end of Naso.* AND WHEN MOSES HAD COME INTO THE APPOINTED TENT TO SPEAK WITH GOD, THEN HE HEARD GOD'S VOICE SPEAKING TO HIM FROM OVER THE COVER OF THE ARK OF THE COVENANT FROM BETWEEN THE TWO CHERUBIM, AND GOD SPOKE TO HIM [Num. 7.89]. *This is the beginning of Be-Ha'alotekha.* AND THE ETERNAL SPOKE TO MOSES SAYING, "SPEAK TO AARON AND SAY TO HIM, WHEN YOU SET UP THE LAMPS, THE FACE OF THE MENORAH SHOULD BE ILLUMINATED BY THE SEVEN LAMPS" [Num. 8.1–2]. *Two things bother Rashi. The first is the dittograph* AND GOD SPOKE TO HIM, *followed directly by* AND THE ETERNAL SPOKE TO MOSES SAYING... *(with nothing said in between). The second is the discontinuity between the previous chapter, which describes the dedication of the Mishkan and the sacrifices offered by each tribal prince, and this set of rules for Aaron.*

On Numbers 7.89 Rashi says: The first AND GOD SPOKE TO HIM *shows that Aaron was now excluded from direct Divine communication. This echoes Rashi's first comment on Leviticus, where he quotes Rabbi Judah, who taught that only thirteen things did God directly tell both Moses and Aaron together. On Numbers 8.1-2 Rashi asks:* Why is this section on the menorah placed "next to" the section that deals with the offerings brought by the tribal princes? To make Aaron feel better. Because when Aaron saw the dedication of the Mishkan by the princes he felt uncomfortable that his sons and tribe had been left out—and so the Holy One said to him, "On your life! You guys are more important. I set you aside *to deal with the light*. Your job is the menorah and the lamps." (*Tanḫuma.*) *Our vocabulary of examples of "how to be Godlike" has just grown by one. While limiting Aaron's role, Aaron's uniqueness is simultaneously celebrated.*

Be-Ha'alotekha

the Torah's holiness by pretending not to know what we really know, that constructions of gender and distributions of power are not eternal verities but dynamic elements within historical contexts?

There are two time-honored rules for reading sacred text with integrity: (1) Thou shalt not justify God at human expense (think of Job); (2) Thou shalt not protect the text from rigorous intellectual examination. In this situation historical and critical explanations seem to undermine the text's sacredness, and traditional answers seem both to disregard fundamental historical principles and to justify gender injustice. When I apply my two rules of interpretation I must conclude that (1) I do not have any satisfactory explanation for this text, and (2) I still hope to find one.

Is my conclusion a religious response or a religiously objectionable response? Eliezer Berkovits, *z"l*, an Orthodox scholar of uncompromising integrity, used to say, "I would rather have a good question than a bad answer." For most of us, any answer is better than no answer. Dissolve those indeterminacies, ambiguities, and contradictions—ASAP! Most of our standardized exams reward students for guessing and penalize them most for not answering at all. We regard "I don't know" as the ultimate confession of incompetence. It is almost irresistible to fill in that terrifying blank.

On the other hand, to despair of an answer is seductively easy. By throwing up our hands and renouncing the struggle on the grounds of insufficient information we can relieve ourselves of responsibility. One of these irresponsible non-answers we might call vulgar relativism—the belief that since answers are merely opinions, one is as good as or as inadequate as another. Another non-answer, intellectual nihilism, declares that there are no answers because there are no values. Because there are no values, there need be no commitments; there is nothing worth committing to. These are easy outs. What is difficult is to maintain intellectual integrity and critical rigor without abandoning faith and commitments. I will be in shul when Numbers 12 is read, and, if called to the Torah, I will bless that reading. ■

Be-Ha'alotekha

Rabbi Robert R. Golub

Rabbi Robert Golub is the Executive Director of Mercaz, USA, the Zionist organization of the Conservative movement.

One of the more annoying ads on television is that for "pre-owned" Cadillacs, with images of handsome men and beautiful women, all appropriately upper middle class and middle-aged, gazing smugly at their Cadillacs while in the background runs the song "Love is Lovelier the Second Time Around."

It's all so lovely, so enchanting that one is likely to pass over the fact that we are talking about used cars! When did secondhand automobiles move from being the province of greasy-looking used car dealers to something "lovelier the second time around"?

If we think about it a little more, the fact that an item is secondhand or used doesn't mean that it is less valuable or desirable. If there is any question in the matter, just check out the prices raised in the recent "Jackie O" auction.

The truth is that there is quite an established market for "pre-owned" luxury items. From couturier gowns to automobiles to bridal dresses for the second-time bride (same white, without the train), one can feel appropriately proud, without the slightest twinge of shame or embarrassment, of one's secondhand purchase.

These thoughts of "the second time around" come to mind as we come to our parashah, *Be-Ha'alotekha*. It's now one year after the Exodus from Egypt, and for the past ten months the children of Israel have been encamped at Mt. Sinai. There they received the Ten Commandments and all the laws. There they committed the sin of the Golden Calf. There they were given the instructions as to the Mishkan and the sacrificial cult. Now the time to embark on the second phase of the journey toward the land of Canaan has arrived. Before they set out they must prepare themselves to celebrate Passover, the celebration of their national freedom. And thus Moses reminds the people of the procedures for carrying out the sacrifice of the Paschal Lamb that is to be slaughtered on the fourteenth day of the first month, Nisan, at dusk.

As Moses and Aaron are overseeing the preparations on that day we are told that a group of men come before the two leaders, very distressed. They point out to Moses and Aaron that Passover is that essential national activity that marks the entire people's liberation from slavery. These men bewail the fact that this year, on the first anniversary of that liberation, they will be precluded from participating in this great celebration of freedom because they are all ritually unclean, having come in contact recently with a dead body. Because the Paschal offering must be made in a state of ritual purity, these people will not be able to join with their fellow Israelites in celebrating the national holiday. They cry out, "WHY MUST WE BE DEBARRED FROM PRESENTING THE LORD'S OFFERING AT ITS SET TIME WITH THE REST OF THE ISRAELITES?"

Not knowing how to answer them, since the law of the Paschal Lamb as described in Exodus chapter 11 has no remedy, Moses tells them to stand aside as he consults God. The Lord answers Moses, saying, "WHEN ANY ONE OF YOU OR YOUR POSTERITY WHO IS DEFILED BY A CORPSE OR IS ON A LONG JOURNEY WOULD OFFER A PASSOVER SACRIFICE TO THE LORD, HE SHALL OFFER IT IN THE SECOND MONTH, ON THE FOURTEENTH DAY OF THE MONTH AT TWILIGHT. HE SHALL EAT IT WITH UNLEAVENED BREAD AND BITTER HERB...HE SHALL OFFER IT IN STRICT ACCORD WITH THE LAW OF THE PASSOVER SACRIFICE" (Num. 9.10-14). In other words, a new law is proclaimed allowing a "rain check" for the fourteenth of Iyar for those unable to participate with the rest of the people on the fourteenth of Nisan.

Quite extraordinary! For no other holiday in the Jewish calendar was a second chance afforded. If one missed Rosh ha-Shanah, one could not celebrate the beginning of the year in Heshvan. If one forgot Sukkot, the sukkah could not be erected one month later. (There is, admittedly, scholarly debate as to whether the original Hanukkah celebration is merely Sukkot deferred two months, but that is for another discussion.) Shavuot could not be postponed until the 6th of Tammuz. Only with Passover was there provided this opportunity to present the Paschal offering at a later time if the person was legitimately precluded from offering it at its proper time.

Why this exception for Passover? Clearly, the experience of Passover is crucial to the essence of what it means to be a member of the Jewish people. We were literally formed in that act of liberation from Egypt. From a ragtag collection of slaves we were molded in that act of Exodus into a single national entity, a people. The celebration of that act of nation-forming is not simply a celebration of the past; it is a reenactment and reexperiencing of that event in the present:

בְּכָל-דּוֹר וָדוֹר חַיָּב אָדָם לִרְאוֹת
אֶת עַצְמוֹ כְּאִלּוּ הוּא יָצָא מִמִּצְרַיִם

Be-Khol Dor va-Dor, Hayav Adam Lir'ot Et Atzmo Ke'Ilu Hu Yatza mi-Mitzrayim. Not "They were slaves in Egypt," but "*We* were slaves in Egypt," and thus not only our ancestors were liberated, but all of us. The Lord brought us all out with a "MIGHTY HAND AND AN OUTSTRETCHED ARM"; for this reason the Jewish people is eternally in God's debt. We were not present at the creation of the world, nor do we claim that we ourselves wandered in the wilderness for forty years or were physically present (spiritually, yes, but not physically) at the giving of the Torah at Mt. Sinai. But we do say that each of us was present in Egypt and that each of us was personally liberated from slavery there. Hence it is fitting that every Jew have the opportunity to relive this experience of liberation and give thanks to God, through the Paschal sacrifice, for all that God had done for us.

Obviously, since the destruction of the Second Temple in 70 C.E. there has no longer been a need for the institution of the Second Passover. We can no longer offer the Paschal lamb at its appointed time on the evening of the Fourteenth of Nisan; hence, there is no need to provide a second date for its presentation. Since all that Passover entails today is the eating of matzah and *maror* and the putting away of all *hametz*, moreover, since all of us are in a state of ritual impurity, every Jew, wherever or however s/he be, may observe the holiday in its set time.

While we no longer require the "rain date" of the Second Passover, the lesson it teaches us is still applicable. Like the Paschal offering, the opportunity to get involved in Jewish tradition is never a closed book, a gate shut, a once and never again experience. Rather, at every stage in a person's life the tradition is open and accessible. Like the Second Passover instituted over three thousand years ago, even if one did not have the opportunity to study and observe as a youth, there is always a second chance to know more and do more, to learn again and observe for the first time. Far more precious than gold, and certainly than a Cadillac, Judaism is lovely at whatever time around—first, second, or hundredth. ■

ארץ כנען

Parashat Shelah-Lekha

Numbers 13.1–15.41

Dr. Barry W. Holtz

Dr. Barry W. Holtz is Associate Professor of Jewish Education at the Jewish Theological Seminary of America. His books include *Back to the Sources* (Simon and Schuster, 1984), *Finding Our Way* (Schocken Books, 1990), and (with Arthur Green) *Your Word is Fire,* recently reissued by Jewish Lights.

This is truly a fateful parashah, for it is in this week's Torah reading that the Israelites react to the message of the spies and by their lack of courage condemn themselves to wandering in the wilderness for forty years.

The details of the story are clear: Moses chooses twelve representatives, one from each of the tribes, to scout the land that the people are about to enter. The spies are given a very specific assignment:

Come back with facts—Is this a good land? Are the people who live there strong or weak? What is the product of this land like? The spies set out, scout the land, and return with their report: Indeed the land is good, but the people who live there are too powerful for us to conquer.

Only Joshua and Caleb dissent from the report. Caleb says, "Let us go up and...we shall surely overcome it" [Num. 14.30]. But the other ten disagree—the people who live there are "stronger than we." The Israelites break into cries and complaints and ask to return to Egypt. And these complaints lead to the punishment of forty years wandering.

When we think about this parashah a number of questions come immediately to mind. First, we wonder what was the purpose of the entire scouting mission. Why did God instruct Moses to send out the spies in the first place? It is unclear from the text and has puzzled scholars

---

דָּבָר אַחֵר DAVAR AHER. And God said to Moses: Send out men to go and reconnoiter the land Cana'an which I give to the Israelites [Num. 13.1–2]. And so Moses selects twelve men, one from each tribe, to spy out the Promised Land while the rest of the people are camped in the desert of Paran on the Sinai peninsula. Forty days later the spies return bearing samples of the fruit of the land—grapes, figs, pomegranates—enthusiastic about the land itself, but hopelessly pessimistic about any real chance to conquer it. Surely the land which you sent us is flowing with milk and honey and very fertile. But the inhabitants are fierce, the cities are great fortresses, and we have seen giants there...we cannot fight against them, they are stronger than we are...compared to them we are like grasshoppers, and so were we in their

שלח לך אנשים ויתרן את

long before the modern reader. Medieval Jewish commentators, in particular Ramban (Nahmanides), were troubled by this question as well. Indeed, Ramban points out that the first chapter of Deuteronomy tells us that the people came to Moses and asked him to "send men ahead to reconnoiter the land for us and bring back word on the route we shall follow and the cities we shall come to" [Deut. 1.22]. Ramban reconciles the two versions by saying that first the people came to Moses with their request, and even though God saw no need for the enterprise, God acceded to their wishes. (Interestingly, the Deuteronomy version gives us the bad news that the spies report, but it ignores the conflict within the group of twelve—we don't hear Caleb's message of encouragement at all.)

If we follow Ramban's interpretation, God's anger at the people after the spies return with their negative report makes even more sense—after all, it was not even God's idea to send the spies, and now they return to discourage all the people with their sense of despair and inadequacy. God ends up in the role of the parent whose teenage child talks him into borrowing the family car only to return later that night with a smashed-up vehicle!

The purpose of the mission is not the only question the reader confronts. What was it about the report of the spies that led to God's disapproval? Were the spies lying? Did they give a false reply to Moses' questions? And if they were telling the truth, why should they be punished for simply reporting what they saw?

My sense is that the failure of the spies was not in misreading the

EYES [Num. 13.27–33], they reported to Moses and the people.

And then the story proceeds to describe the despair of the Israelites. THEY COMPLAINED AGAINST MOSES AND AARON SAYING: "WHY DID WE NOT DIE IN EGYPT OR IN THE DESERT? WHY DID GOD BRING US INTO THAT LAND (CANAAN) TO DIE BY THE SWORD, AND OUR WOMEN AND CHILDREN TO BECOME HELPLESS SLAVES?...LET US SELECT A LEADER THAT WILL LEAD US BACK TO EGYPT" [NUM. 14.2–4].

And so, after Moses pleads with God not to destroy the Israelites, they are condemned to wander in the desert for forty years. "As I live," says God, "just as you have complained to me, so will I do to you. Your corpses shall fall in the desert, all of you aged twenty and above...you will not enter the promised land. But your children of

SYNOPSIS: *Now we are back into the action. Twelve spies are sent into Eretz Israel. We have a rebellion and a threat from God, countered by Moses' intercession. Israel is sentenced to the rest of fortyyears of wandering. This is followed by the laws of the tzitzit.*

RASHI OF THE WEEK:

Here is why Rashi is a great trail scout. At the end of the sidrah we find the laws of tzitzit: MAKE A TZITZIT IN THE CORNER OF YOUR GARMENTS [Num. 15.38]. *It seems to have no context. Rashi establishes a logic to its placement with a great textual echo. The Torah portion begins* [Num. 13.2] SEND FOR YOURSELF MEN *V'YA-TURU* [AND THEY WILL SPY OUT] THE LAND OF CANAAN. *Pages later, after rebellions and executions, a whole range of adventures, God introduces the mitzvah of tzitzit.* MAKE A TZITZIT IN THE CORNER OF YOUR GARMENTS...THAT YOU WILL NOT *TA-TURU* [go spying] AFTER YOUR HEART AND NOT GO WHORING AFTER YOUR EYES [Num. 15.38-9]. *Rashi hears the echoing of the Hebrew word TUR and says*: The heart and the eyes are the "spies" of the body—they act as its agents for sinning. The eyes see, the heart covets, and the body commits sin (*Talmud Yerusalmi Ber.* 1.8, *Tanhuma*). *The mitzvah of tzitzit is placed at the end of the portion as a device to help us avoid the sins of the earlier passages. God teaches, "Wear a tallit and learn how not to be like the spies."*

nature of the land, nor in misrepresenting what they had seen. Rather, they had failed in other and more subtle ways. First, the ten scouts of despair failed to understand the social impact of their words. Their report brought despair and a virtual rebellion into the Israelite camp. By misunderstanding the role of leadership—we are told after all that each of the spies was a "CHIEFTAIN AMONG THEM" [13.2]—they proved themselves unworthy of the trust Moses had placed in them.

And secondly, the spies' failure was not in misstating the truth about the land and the people who lived there; rather the self-perception of the scouts brought about their downfall. True, the nations of Canaan were powerful. But Caleb announced that they would succeed against the inhabitants; the others proclaimed that they would fail. Surely both Caleb and the ten doubters had scouted the same land, seen the same things. But the doubters stated, "ALL THE PEOPLE WE SAW...ARE MEN OF GREAT SIZE...AND WE LOOKED LIKE GRASSHOPPERS TO OURSELVES, AND SO WE MUST HAVE LOOKED TO THEM" [Num. 13.33]. This is the most telling line of all. In their own eyes ("TO OURSELVES") the Israelite spies were weak. It was a failure of their own self-understanding, not the reality of the situation that was the problem.

Interestingly enough, the Torah verses Numbers 13.21–24 never tell us what the spies actually saw. There is no "objective" narrator telling us the real truth. We only learn what happened from the participants themselves. Truth, the Torah suggests, is the perception of reality that each individual brings. If, as a midrash in *Pesikta d'Rav Kahana* tells us, each person at Sinai received the revelation in his or her own individual and appropriate way—that is to say, each grasped the "Ultimate Reality" in his or her own particularity—what we have in this week's parashah is

---

Shelah-Lekha

WHOM YOU SAID THEY WILL BE SLAVES, THEY WILL ENTER THE LAND AND POSSESS IT" [Num. 14.28–31]. And so it happens; a seemingly simple story proving that one must trust in God's purpose as revealed by people like Moses who speak in the name of God.

But put yourself in the sandals of these ancient Israelites. They have gone through slavery in Egypt, suffering and oppressed, but also fed and housed. Now, as they listen to the spies' report, can they react differently? Trust in Moses, who says he speaks in the name of God? Leave the familiar to face reportedly insurmountable obstacles? Wanting to return to Egypt must have seemed the rational and responsible thing to do.

Or was it? Following the biblical narrative, we know that after forty years, after the generation of slav-

the terrifying other side of that midrash. Each person can doubt God's power in his or her own individual way. Thus the story of *Parashat Shelah-Lekha* forms a kind of undoing of the revelation at Sinai celebrated so recently at Shavuot. The people were condemned to die in the desert because they had failed God's expectations—having experienced Sinai in the depth of the individual soul, ironically they fail God by those most human of weaknesses—fear, despair, and their inability to believe in the destiny that God had prepared for them. ■

---

ery had died, the Jewish tribes did indeed conquer and settle Canaan. In other words: How can one make rational decisions in irrational times, in times of upheaval and radical change?

One hundred years ago, in 1896, Theodore Herzl, a highly assimilated Jew, Paris correspondent for a respected Viennese daily, watched from his window as Parisian mobs marched through the streets shouting *"Mort aux Juifs!"* (Death to the Jews). He knew the immediate cause: the trial and conviction of the Jewish Captain Dreyfus for selling French military secrets to the Germans. Dreyfus was innocent, but for Herzl the sight of these mobs in the streets of the most enlightened and cultured city in the world was a revelation. He sat down that night and began feverishly to write a small book in his native German, called *Der Judenstaat* (The Jewish State), in which he called for the return of the Jews to Zion and the establishment of a Jewish commonwealth in the ancient homeland. When the book was published he was laughed at and publicly scorned; he became the butt of jokes and was in danger of losing his job. A year later, in 1897, he opened the first Zionist World Congress in Basel, Switzerland, saying, "Today most people laugh at us Zionists, but in a few years, fifty at the most, they will see that we were right." In November of 1947 the UN General Assembly voted to establish an independent Jewish state in part of Palestine. But even among the Jews in Palestine—after World War II and the Holocaust—there were some who hesitated and, based on what they considered a rational analysis of the situation, suggested perhaps a UN role for the country. But the ones who dared, led by David Ben Gurion, won the day—and we know the outcome.

Where now is the lesson? Both— the Israelites in the desert as well as the Jews in 1947 Palestine—faced seemingly insurmountable opponents with large armies, huge reserves, and great prestige. In both cases a prudent decision would have been to change course. Return to the safety of Egypt; renounce political independence. And in both cases, what really happened was very different from the cautious, responsible, and "rational" scenarios. Is God the answer to the dilemma? If so, there is a host of other questions waiting around the corner. But of this another time. **David Jordan, Temple Beth El, Haworth, NJ.**

דָּבָר אַחֵר DAVAR AHER. **THE LORD SAID TO MOSES AS FOLLOWS: "SPEAK TO THE ISRAELITE PEOPLE AND INSTRUCT THEM TO MAKE FOR THEMSELVES FRINGES ON THE CORNERS OF THEIR GARMENTS THROUGHOUT THE AGES; LET THEM ATTACH A CORD OF BLUE TO THE FRINGE AT EACH CORNER "** [Num. 15.37–38]. In reading about tzitzit at the end of the parashah I was reminded of my experience in the Army Reserves in 1969. (Yes, folks, during the Vietnam War—just like Dan Quayle.) Basic training was, shall we say, not a lot of fun. One of the few times we got any relief was on Friday night when the Jews could go to services. We got a few moments of peace (pun definitely intended)—and the salami sandwiches weren't bad either. It was my first (only?) experience when it was actually an advantage to be Jewish.

So back to tzitzit. Our platoon commander (Capt. Unterbrink—no fooling) was, to put it mildly, not happy about our escape on Friday nights. He could stop us from going to the Jewish Center, but not to services. So he made us dress in full battle gear—fatigues, combat boots, helmets, field packs—and march there. We went anyway. (Maybe it was the salami?) But we arrived tired, dirty, sweaty—and dressed for battle.

Rabbi David Bockman

David Bockman is rabbi of Congregation Chevra Thilim in New Orleans, Louisiana, and an adjunct faculty member at the University of New Orleans. He is currently winding his way to a doctorate in Jewish philosophy at Baltimore Hebrew University.

Shela<u>h</u>-Lekha

"We do exactly what God and Moses say, and we get this? Plague, death in the desert? An abrupt about-face for forty years? It hardly seems fair!" Indeed! A generation in the desert among the scorpions and snakes, the air dry as dust and the wind howling over rocky promontories. The desert: A LAND UNSOWN [Jer 2.2] where AN EMPTY WASTELAND MOANS [Deut. 32.10]. But a punishment? I could show you ten thousand Navajos who would disagree. Because the great spirit loved and respected them as a people, they were given the vast land between the four mountain ranges, the desert land of endless sky, as their home.

Looking back from the vantage point of the city-dwelling farmers biblical Israelites have become, the desert seems quite daunting. But it was there that the Israelites first heard the voice of God! The expanse of desert sky, so broad and azure, a royal blue *techelet* garment embracing the entire people, was the source of God's most direct demonstrations of care and compassion. Edible manna fell daily from the sky with the gentle dew. Food for the soul, as well, never ceased from the people as they traveled those forty years: God's presence in fire and cloud a constant companion, God's advice never distant. No sign of Divine favor could be clearer!

For forty years the Israelites' clothes never became threadworn; their sandals always had soles. Turned back into the desert, cocoon of their miraculous rebirth as a people (a covenanted and sacred people), they metamorphosed, bloomed like Topsy. It was here they formed a rudimentary government, here they established a priesthood. In the

---

Which was when the chaplain started passing out the *tallisim*. He said that if everyone would put them on, it wouldn't matter who was an officer and who was not or who outranked whom. Nor would it matter who was in dress uniform and who was in battle fatigues. We would all be just Jews, being together, praying to our God. A *tallit* has never been the same for me. **David Parker, <Parques@aol.com>**

דָּבָר אַחֵר DAVAR A<u>H</u>ER. THAT SHALL BE YOUR FRINGE; LOOK AT IT AND RECALL ALL THE COMMANDMENTS OF THE LORD. [Num. 15.39]. David: As *tallitot* are a great equalizer...so are shrouds. **Ed Cohen, Nassau County, NY, <COHANIM@aol.com>**

wilderness they learned the dos and don'ts of communal living, came into their own as the most civilized of ancient peoples. With God on their side and forty years of learning how to be themselves they finally return to the challenge-land, the land soon to be called Israel, "struggling against God." A LAND THAT DIGESTS IT INHABITANTS [Num. 13.32] or vomits them out should they do wrong.

"But what of God's test, summoning twelve representatives to tour the land? They didn't pass, they failed!" Strange, though, that the only mention of testing in the text is Israel "testing" God as a bigmouth bass might test a fishing line, ten times a testing [Num. 14.22]. Parallel with Abraham's ten tests? A test like the Akedah of Isaac? Did Abraham pass his test? Did he fail? Or do we misunderstand? Perhaps God does not set his favorite people up to fail, but rather tests their mettle, gives them numerous challenges so they can learn more about themselves. Testing is not always about passing and failing. The best tests are those that stimulate learning and growth and self-judgment, tests that lead to improvement.

If God is benevolent, the turning-back toward the desert is good, too. No punishment, the turning-back may be just a consequence, an unavoidable consequence of the people's development at that point. Clearly appreciative of Canaan's physical beauty and very accurate in their description of the land and its inhabitants [Num. 13.27-29], the Israelites are curiously unprepared to enter and conquer, to settle and govern. Not yet fully done, they return to the desert incubator for forty years of people-building. And as we see time and again in the book of Judges, forty years is considered the complete time span of a peaceful era, without terror or failure or Philistine war-threat. A peaceful desert sojourn (we know absolutely no details of the desert other than in the first and last year) for a people who had probably never seen their elders die of old age, but only through Egyptian policies of overwork and more direct genocide—this time is rightly called a "honeymoon."

After all, a desert is not a terrible or dead place. Deserts are open, untamed areas, free of the shackles of civilization. The people must leave Egypt to create a new civilization but certainly will have no greater luck should they try to establish themselves amidst the Canaanites. No, the desert is the only place whose dry air is crisp enough, whose open spaces are expansive enough, whose fauna are free enoug, for the voice of God to sweep an entire nation into existence! As the end of our portion insists, they need to look at God's mitzvot (represented for this fringe people as the fringes on their garments) and not be led astray by what their eyes see, as they had done at the parashah's outset. They had seen but reported only physical and agricultural beauty and military threat. The next forty years would train them to look for God's commanding presence between all these surface elements. Only then can they become Yisrael, struggling with Divinity in all their worldly endeavors. ■

קהת בן לוי

Korah̲'s Riddle

Another figure comes to me out of the dark of the Book. He does not even ask to be named. Let him be anonymous, a speaker from the wilderness, a witness of sorts. I have summoned him to help me understand the story of Korah̲, this Korah̲ who has been stuck in my craw for years. Perhaps I have traveled too much among the Protestants (Jewish and Christian), for there is something in this incorrigible Korah̲—his opposition to the priesthood, to the spiritual power of an inherited elite—that speaks to me. But I know that part of what it means to me to be a Jew is to find out why the tradition has branded him and why in the text he is unequivocally annihilated. I have had the same kind of struggle with Ishmael and Esau: how to balance my identification with the outcasts and underdogs with some sense of the Torah's hard truth about legacy and boundary. Now I have been looking for a way to put my finger on the irregular pulse of my own dilemma about this corrosive Korah̲. Finally something emerges: a voice, a fragment of a story, a point of view.

In those days I was one of those who walked with Miriam. Not everyone around her was a woman. Some of us had no tribe; she made a place for us. And work. In those days of plague and terror and death

Parashat Korah̲

Numbers 16.1–18.32

Peter Pitzele

Peter Pitzele is the Director of Psychodrama Services at Four Winds Hospital in Katonah, NY, and the author of *Our Fathers' Wells: A Personal Encounter with the Myths of Genesis* and *Scripture Windows: Toward a Practice of Bibliodrama.*

דָּבָר אַחֵר Davar Ah̲er. They combined against Moses and Aaron and said to them, "You have gone too far! For all the community is holy, all of them, and the Lord is in their midst" [Num. 16.3]. Martin Buber does some interesting work with this, which I'll expand. He starts: So what's wrong with Korah̲'s position? Don't we—indeed we!—want the whole people to be holy, and not have to depend on an elite? But then Buber says Korah̲ thought the whole people was holy regardless of how it acted. Kind of racist holiness. It could kill, or worship gold, or rape the earth—it could do anything, thought Korah̲, and still be holy. Moses understood that the people had to become holy, always and over and over—had to act to make holiness out of ordinary life. Now comes my own part. Why is it Korah̲'s destiny to be swallowed up

ויקח קרח בן יצהר בן

there was endless work for us to do.

It was a time of fire. Fire everywhere. Tongues of fire, acts of fire. A pillar of fire at night, fire that smelted for us a golden idol, sky fires that made the children shriek, fires that flashed in the fire-pans, fires that scorched us with the law. Too much fire in those days; never enough water.

And then there was Korah. They all thought of him as a firebrand. Some called him an opportunist, others a prophet; some said he was envious, others that he was a twister of words. Even now, after all these years, I cannot judge. He was a proud man and an angry man. There were rumors of his plots, stories told about him even before things came to a head. I was in no position to know what was true and what was not.

He came to me one night alone, not long before things broke out into the open. I suppose he saw me as a sort of priest. It was all about priests. I had nothing to give him, yet it seemed he needed something. For a while we spoke of trivial things. Then we grew quiet together. He began abruptly. "Can it be right that this entire enterprise, this great liberation, this journey toward a promised land should rest on the shoulders of one man? Can it be right that the entire responsibility for the worship of our God rests in the hands of one family?" He was not being rhetorical. He was not there to persuade me. But it seemed to me a certain fury burned in him, though I could not tell whether it was the fury of pique or of righteousness, or both in some strange way crudely smelted together. "Didn't Miriam herself question this speaking of God only through Moses?"

---

by the earth? Since the Torah and Prophets almost always see a "punishment" as springing intrinsically from the misdeed, *middah keneged middah*, "measure for measure," "reaping what you sow," what do we learn about his misdeed from its result? And—this is also my own—Korah was not entirely wrong, and neither was Buber/Moses. We want the whole people to BECOME holy, but it was not then ready to be holy. (Still isn't.) Yet that is what we want to strive toward: the day when Korah will be right, the day when the whole people will be holy. Aha!!!!!!!!!! When God has heard Korah out, God says: "Korah, you are right—but only in *potentia*, only as a seed. You think the holiness is already full grown, fully fruitful. It is not. It is a tiny seed, and it needs time to germinate and

SYNOPSIS: *More actions (Korah's rebellion) and more rules (detailing the duties of the Levites and Kohanim, the firstborn, and tithing).*

RASHI OF THE WEEK:
Korah's rebellion is a serious challenge. Korah seems to have a reasonable complaint when he says, "ARE NOT ALL OF THE COMMUNITY HOLY, EVERY ONE OF THEM?" *His populous appeal seems compelling, his punishment totalitarian. Rashi disarms our concerns with one word. The sidrah begins:* AND KORAH THE SON OF YIZHAR TOOK THE SON OF KOHAT, THE SON OF LEVI.... *Rashi reads and asks:* Why does the Torah say "TOOK" and not "went with"? *This section is beautifully taught by Rabbi Tanhuma.* KORAH TOOK teaches that he took himself to one side with the intention of separating himself from the community so that he might challenge the authority of the priesthood. This is how Onkelos (*the Aramaic translator*) understands it when he renders it "AND HE SEPARATED HIMSELF." *There is merit to the notion that Israel is supposed to be a kingdom of priests. There is no merit in causing social chaos. Korah's sin was "process," not "content."*

"And was she not rebuked?" I replied.

"Yes, she was ostracized, but she spoke a truth. I see them"—and here he leans forward, his voice low, but no hint of conspiracy in it, only something urgent as if he is trying to resolve something for himself—"Moses and Aaron are only men. Yet they have put themselves out of reach, and they set up a pattern for times to come, the priest who is beyond authority, the leader beyond scrutiny. This cannot be right. I have spoken to Moses. 'It is too much for you,' I told him, 'you go too far. This work you have undertaken cannot be seen as the work of the few.' But Moses only looked at me and turned away. In the end the God of Israel must be a God in our midst. Kings, prophets, judges, women of wisdom, men of inspiration will come from unlikely places to lead us to unlikelier places. The God of Abraham must be also the God of Sarah, and Moses' God must be Miriam's." (And yours, too? I wondered.) "Does such a God obey the laws of inheritance, insist on them? What of the men and women called to serve from the conviction of God that they feel in their hearts?"

"The heart is a poor vessel for God," I said.

"But what other vessel is there in the end?" And when he spoke I realized with a kind of fear where this conviction would take him. And I said—it was, I know, out of character—"Kora<u>h</u>, be careful." In that moment I saw that he understood nothing of the law, nothing of how it is law and not sentiment or passion that protects us against idolatry and tyrants. And it was priests—even those who might function in their positions without conviction, without God in their hearts or in their midst—who in some paradoxical way freed us to worship.

When I returned my attention to him again he was saying, "...know that what I stand for is being perverted. Men who are jealous of Aaron look to me to make a revolution. It cannot be." He shook his head. "It doesn't matter. This generation will never reach the land that has been promised. Not Miriam, not Aaron, not Moses himself. Not me and not you; none of us will live to reach the land. Our children may; we will not. Has not Moses just said as much? So we play our parts, willingly or unwillingly, that something might be born. I have a part to play. The God that is in my midst"—and here he tapped his chest—"prompts me to

---

grow, time in the womb of Mother Earth. Kora<u>h</u>, what you need to learn is what it means to become seed deep in the earth, waiting for the season of your sprouting. "Into the earth, Kora<u>h</u>. Learn to be seed."
Arthur Waskow

my own action. I too have a vision. We must someday become a nation of priests. If we do not learn to see one another as holy, from the greatest to the least, then holiness itself will disappear." He was quiet then, his head down, and he seemed the loneliest man I had ever known. "Pray for me," he said at last, and over his bowed head I whispered a few words. Then he left. In a few days "Korah's rebellion," as it came to be called, was burnt to ashes.

My witness withdraws. But there is something here that will not dissipate. God's judgment was clear enough; my own is murkier. Who is Korah? What part of me does he embody? What part of us? Is he my idealism or my vainglory? The deepest motion in myself toward the image of God in us all? Or my own secret desire to live in an anarchy of the spirit? With the destruction of the Temple and the loss of the hereditary priesthood, does Korah speak now as a prophet for our times? Or must we always be vigilant against that force that exalts the people—"the whole congregation"—before that congregation has done the hard work of self-reformation under the discipline of *halakhah*? If Korah had some part of the truth, it is deep and difficult and easily abused. In the end I think not of Korah's rebellion, but rather of Korah's riddle. ■

Rabbi Janet Marder

Rabbi Janet Marder is Director, UAHC, Pacific Southwest Council.

Kora<u>h</u>

A couple of years ago I cut out an advertisement for a seminar called "How to Deal with Difficult People." I won't tell you who was on my mind at the time, but I will say I was fascinated by the course's claim that it could teach me to cope successfully with such unpleasant characters as the know-it-all, the complainer, the nay-sayer, the yes-man, the dictator, and the passive aggressor.

"Dealing with Difficult People." That might make a good title for this week's parashah, which tells story of Kora<u>h</u>, a charismatic leader who incites the Israelites to rebel against Moses.

You have to sympathize with Moses. Only last week, in *Parashat Shela<u>h</u>-Lekha,* he had to put down another revolt, that one provoked by the scouts who brought back a gloomy report about the land of Canaan, thus demoralizing the people so completely that they begged to return to Egypt.

Punished by God for their lack of faith, condemned to wander the wilderness for the next forty years, to die without ever entering the Promised Land, the Israelites are, for understandable reasons, not feeling very upbeat these days. And so, as our parashah opens, the grumbling begins again and rises to a crescendo of clashing wills.

Kora<u>h</u>, a fellow Levite and Moses' first cousin, gathers a few cohorts—Datan, Aviram, and On, members of the tribe of Reuben—and together they raise a band of 250 dissenters—all of them prominent citizens, the text says, leaders of the people.

It's like a Jewish professional's nightmare: Your most upstanding *balebatim,* the heavy hitters among your lay leaders, gang up against you and demand that you resign. Their words to Moses and Aaron are simple and undeniably stirring: *Rav lakhem,* they say, You go too far. You ask too much. *Ki khol ha'eida kulam kedoshim.* For the whole congregation is holy, and God is among them. Why then do you lift yourselves up above the assembly of the Lord?

We know we're supposed to be on Moses' and Aaron's side in this story, but something in Kora<u>h</u>'s argument appeals to us. His is, after all, the more democratic voice, the voice that demands equality, power-sharing with the laity, "empowerment" of the people, to use a trendy term. And Moses is clearly the elitist, demanding an absolute separation between the people and the holy man, the one chosen to come close to God.

Their argument is constructed with balance and symmetry. *Rav lakhem,* says

Moses to his antagonists. You ask too much for yourselves, you Levites. *Ha me'at mi-kem,* is it a minor thing that you have been chosen to perform the sacrificial service in the tabernacle? Can't you be satisfied with what you've got?

But the heavy hitters will not be appeased. *Ha me'at* —is it a minor thing that you have taken us out of a land flowing with milk and honey (mind you, they mean Egypt) to die in this Godforsaken wilderness?

Moses has had enough. "Wait till tomorrow," he says. "Then we'll see whom God has chosen, and who is holy."

Morning brings a conclusion that is horrific but deeply gratifying, at least to the rabbis who read this story. Korah, Datan, and Aviram stand at the doors of their tents. (On is inexplicably absent; tradition says that his wife got him drunk and he overslept). Suddenly the earth splits apart and swallows them up, together with their wives and children, their nursing babies, and all of their property. Even their clothing that was at the laundry, says one whimsical commentator, came rolling back to join them as they plunged into the pit. And another commentator adds that as the earth closed over their heads the rebels could be heard screaming in anguish: "Moses is King. Aaron is High Priest. And the Torah is true!" [*Yalkut Reuveni,* Num. 16.31].

Horrific, I said, but gratifying nonetheless. Because Moses, God's chosen one, is vindicated, and generations of rabbis have drawn from this story the lesson that rabbinic authority must not be challenged. The ending is also gratifying on the somewhat base level of infantile wish-fulfillment. Imagine for a moment that *our* worst enemies, those difficult people we face at work, at school, even, perhaps, in our own families—the people who make us want to run screaming in the other direction—could suddenly and conveniently disappear, never to annoy us again.

Much as I enjoy these revenge fantasies, I'm not happy reading the story of Korah merely as a message that dissent must be squashed and rabbinical authority must reign supreme. What about that appealingly democratic argument of Korah? Are we supposed to forget all about that and rejoice that he got his just desserts?

In fact, the problem of Korah's compelling power is worse than that. If we look at the midrashic elaborations on this story we find that the rabbis have made Korah into a formidable antagonist indeed—far more threatening than he actually appears in the biblical text. Korah, they say, not only challenged Moses; he ridiculed the Torah, pointing out how illogical and absurdly arbitrary its laws were.

Dressing his followers in *tallisim* made entirely of blue cloth, Korah asked Moses: "Are these garments kosher?" "No," said Moses. "But if we attached fringes with one blue thread in each corner—would they be kosher then?" "Yes," Moses admitted. Korah, the Midrash says, exploded in spiteful laughter. "You're telling me a garment all of blue isn't kosher, but four little blue threads make any garment kosher?"

Worse yet, the Midrash tells us that Korah attacked the ethical foundations of the Torah, or at least charged that Moses and Aaron were enforcing its provisions in an unethical manner, exploiting the poor by constantly gouging them for tithes and sacrificial offerings of all kinds [*Num. R.* 18.3; *Tanhuma, Korah,* 2].

In Korah, that is, the rabbis construct their own worst enemy. They project onto Korah their most troubling doubts and anxieties, the rebellious impulses they feel toward the religious system that governs their lives, their most corrosive self-criticism.

The midrashim on this story thus give us a fascinating window into the Rabbinic psyche and, I would venture to say, into all of our psyches. Seeing Korah in this way—as a figure employed by the rabbis to wrestle with demons in their own soul—makes me want to suggest that we look at Moses and Korah not only as two separate individuals—biblical antagonists locked in combat for millennia—but as two opposing forces within the self. Each of us, then, contains a Moses: courageous, imaginative, full of faith and trust, ready to launch new ventures and explore the unknown. But

Korah

inside us we also carry our own worst enemy: Korah. The face looks different to each of us, but we know the voice; it is pure negative energy, destructive of self and others, the demon we wrestle in the privacy of our own soul.

One message in this story thus has nothing to do with rabbinic authority, dissent, and the nature of leadership. It is, instead, a *religious* message about burying the Korah within us so that Moses is free to continue on the journey.

The rabbis understood that despite all the unpleasant characters we contend with in the world, the most difficult person we ultimately have to face is ourselves. *Ezehu gibor?* asks *Pirke Avot.* Who is mighty? And it answers: *Hakovesh et yitzro,* those who subdue their impulses. We need our greatest strength for self-mastery, to do battle against the inner Korah who saps our enthusiasm, mocks our dreams, stunts our growth, poisons our relationships.

הֵעָלוּ מִסָּבִיב לְמִשְׁכַּן-קֹרַח *Hei'alu Misaviv Mishkan Korah,* says God at a decisive moment in our story. "RISE UP FROM THE DWELLING OF KORAH. REMOVE YOURSELF FROM HIM; TURN ASIDE UTTERLY AND REPUDIATE HIM" [Num. 16. 24]. We know that God is right: We must separate from Korah if we are not to be dragged down into the pit with him. For Moses, victory is quick and decisive. For us it may take a lifetime to conquer Korah.

And so once a year we take up this odd and poignant story to remind ourselves what lies between us and the Promised Land. ■

זאת חקת התורה אשר

y son, Alexander, coming off the Ramah day camp bus, asks, "What does the story of the red heifer have to do with Moses hitting the rock?"

I tell him he has asked a good question, temporizing, but he already knows that I don't really have a good answer. It's such a good midrashic question, the kind an ancient rabbi would ask. I tell him that the rabbis themselves were perplexed by the heifer. Alex wants to know, "While we're at it, what's a heifer?"

This, at least, I can answer, "A cow," I tell him, "a rare cow with reddish skin. The color of penny loafers."

It takes me a while to answer his original question. To do so I have to sit through the Torah reading in *shul*. I trust Alexander will allow me to share my answer to him with you.

The story of the red heifer is a complicated ritual meant to respond to the death of a loved one. Death is difficult, perplexing; it requires response. Often we are left speechless, without proper words, even without recognizable emotions in our responses to death. God gives Moses the laws of the heifer, an elaborate, difficult, and perplexing ritual, as a response to a difficult and perplexing event.

Now, in order to understand what this has to do with the story, later in the week's Torah reading, of Moses hitting the rock, it helps to fill in the gaps. The Torah not only records these two events but also speaks of some incredibly important moments in Moses' and the

Parashat Hukkat

Numbers 19.1–22.1

Rabbi Burton L. Visotzky

RABBI BURTON L. VISOTZKY HOLDS THE APPLEMAN CHAIR IN MIDRASH AND INTERRELIGIOUS STUDIES AT THE JEWISH THEOLOGICAL SEMINARY OF AMERICA. HE WAS ORDAINED AT JTS AND SERVED AS THE FIRST RABBI OF ITS EGALITARIAN SYNAGOGUE. BURT IS THE AUTHOR OF *READING THE BOOK: MAKING THE BIBLE A TIMELESS TEXT*, PUBLISHED BY ANCHOR/DOUBLEDAY AND *THE GENESIS OF ETHICS*, PUBLISHED IN HARDCOVER BY CROWN PUBLICATIONS AND IN PAPERBACK BY RANDOM HOUSE..

דָּבָר אַחֵר DAVAR AHER. THE COW SHALL BE BURNED IN HIS SIGHT—ITS HIDE, FLESH, AND BLOOD SHALL BE BURNED [Num. 19.5]. On Shabbat *Parah* we are building a sanctuary in the wilderness. We are huddled around our tents and fires, giving freely to the sanctuary we are carrying through the wilderness, the symbol of our reconciliation, of our forgiveness. The sanctuary is the symbol of God's forgiveness; it is a sign that we have been forgiven our slip with the Golden Calf; it is the symbol of God's free and inexhaustible measure of forgiveness. How did our healing come to us?

It came to us through the mitzvah of the red heifer, the little red cow, the mysterious rite that gives this Shabbat its name, Shabbat *Parah*. Let the cow come and atone for the sin of the Golden Calf, like to like, the mitzvah of the red cow one of the most mysterious in Torah, a *hukkat ha-Torah*, which means it is a mystery, and not given to humankind to

people Israel's lives. This week's parashah tells of the death of Moses' sister, the prophet Miriam. It also records the death of Moses' brother, his prophet Aaron. Imagine how difficult a week (so to speak) this was for Moses. He loses both his sister and his brother in the same parashah! It was his sister who stood on the banks of the Nile to watch over him. It was Miriam who saved his life, restored him to his family, jealously worried about whom he was marrying. Imagine, I tell Alex, that Miriam is like your big sister Leora. And now she is dead. How might you feel?

Oddly, her death is recorded in the Torah in only half a verse. It is almost as though Moses and Aaron utterly ignore the elaborate ritual God had laid out for them in the twenty-two preceding verses. No mention of purity, no heifer, no ashes, no water, no hyssop, no sprinkling. Moses and Aaron, so imbued with the burdens of leadership, all but ignore the death of Miriam, one of the most important people in their lives. They turn their mourning inward, allowing no ritual expression of their enormous loss. No red heifer, no shivah, no sheloshim, no kaddish, no tears. They return from her burial to face immediately the challenge of a community without water. "WHY," the people ask them, "HAVE YOU BROUGHT US INTO THIS WILDERNESS FOR US AND OUR BEASTS TO DIE?" Wholly insensitive to the death Moses and Aaron are mourning, the people Israel wonder about their own deaths. They thirst but do not understand that their thirst is a product of their unexpressed mourning for Miriam.

Nor does Moses understand the connection between Miriam's death and the loss of water. Our rabbis, blessed of memory, recall the connection between the two events. It was by Miriam's merit that the people Israel drank. By Miriam's merit a well followed them through the desert to slake their thirst. With

---

Hukkat

understand. We are not given to understand because understanding itself may be an idol for us.

This commandment is especially holy because it was given to us in the form of a "Divine kiss" (*Avodah Zara* 35a), intimate and secret. The mystery is how the ashes purify those who have become contaminated, yet those who take part in its preparation become contaminated. It is a *koan*. For isn't it true that something that seems so polluting, so contaminating, may ultimately be salvational, purifying, holy? Cannot the holy emerge out of the unholy? The good out of the bad, the glory out of defeat, joy out of despair—cannot all of us search our experience for that which has saved us emerging directly out of that which almost overcame us?

When you come to the table with great sadness, feel the possibility of

Miriam's death the well of miracle dried up and was no more.

Moses, who has not mourned his sister's death, fails to see the connection that the rabbis, his disciples, discerned so many generations later. Unaware that he has suppressed his anger at Miriam's death, suppressed his hurt, his rage, his mourning, he moves on to attend to the Israelites' thirst. Is it any wonder that he acts out? Is it any surprise that instead of talking to the rock he lashes out and hits it? Is it a mystery that he cannot bear to obey God when God has taken his sister, his Miriam, away? Moses smites the rock, and the water gushes forth—all the tears he and Aaron did not shed pour forth from the rock. Aaron and Moses, who made themselves into rocks by repressing their mourning, now find symbolic tears as the rock weeps water on their behalf. The people Israel drink and perhaps learn their lesson.

Before the chapter is over we read of Aaron's death. Because of the waters, because of the incident of the rock, Moses and Aaron cannot enter the land. They are doomed to die in the wilderness where they buried their sister Miriam. So Aaron's turn comes first. At God's command Moses readies his brother for death. He goes through the ritual of passing on Aaron's mantle to his sons. When Aaron dies the entire community mourns the loss; they weep for thirty days. All the ritual is observed; the mourning is satisfied; despite the enormous loss he has endured, Moses can go on.

One more story needs to be told before the parashah comes full circle. As they are leaving Aaron's burial place the Israelites again complain about God and Moses. "WHY DID YOU

---

joy rising out of your sadness, know the willingness of darkness to yield to light, remember the potential of success to erupt out of defeat. As R. Yo<u>h</u>anan said, "It is not the corpse that contaminates or the ashes that purify." These are the laws of God, and in the laws of God, often that which contaminates ultimately purifies, and out of great darkness comes light. This is the principle of the red heifer. It is the principle of possibility. It is written on the walls of your heart, do not despair. **James Stone Goodman, <Stavisker@aol.com>**

SYNOPSIS: *This time, more laws and then more action. The law: the red heifer. The actions: the deaths of Miriam and Aaron, Moses hits the rock, confrontations with Edom, Canaanites, Amorites, and Og, the King of Bashan.*

TAKE US UP TO DIE IN THE WILDERNESS, THERE IS NO BREAD NOR WATER?" [Num. 2.15]. Again they insensitively remind Moses of the proximity of death. Despite a month of tears, they bewail the lack of water for sustenance. God sends fiery serpents to plague them, so many people die. The cure, it seems, is for Moses to make a copper serpent and mount it on a pole. "THUS IF ONE WERE BITTEN BY A SERPENT AND LOOKED AT THE COPPER SERPENT, HE WOULD LIVE" [Num. 21.9].

The rabbis of the Mishnah (*Rosh Ha-Shanah* 3.8) greet this story with incredulity. "Since when," they ask, "does a serpent give death and life?" The implications of the question are clear: This verse is too magical for comfort. It should be God who gives life and death, not some copper statue. How can it be that this lifeless form of forged metal might provide access to salvation? Is this not an invitation to idolatry?

"Ritual," the rabbis answer. "It is all about the power of ritual." For, they explain, when the Israelites looked up at the serpent on the standard, they were reminded of their relationship with their Parent in Heaven. In the face of death it is essential to have ritual. Symbol. Hope in Heaven. Belief in some saving power greater than we are. We must mourn in community. But we must mourn in ways that remind us that we have relationships that extend beyond our loss, beyond our community. We have a sustaining relationship to God in Heaven, giver of death and life. Without that we fall apart.

And that, Alexander, is why the story of the red heifer and the story of Moses hitting the rock are in the same Torah reading. They remind us that rituals, especially rituals that bind us to God and to community, are very important. Without them we wind up like Moses, striking the rock for water instead of talking out and crying our own tears. Without Jewish ritual we cannot enter the Promised Land. ■

The Meaning of the Red Cow Law

Rabbi Alan J. Yuter

Rabbi Alan J. Yuter is the Rabbi of Congregation Israel in Springfield, New Jersey, and teaches at Touro College in Brooklyn, New York.

Hukkat

Rashi understands the rule of the red cow (which, when properly prepared, ritually cleanses the defiled while defiling those who are clean) to be a command to have faith in the rightness of God's law, for he teaches that "one has no right to question the law" of the red cow, which is prefaced by the idiom זֹאת חֻקַּת הַתּוֹרָה *Zot Hukkat ha-Torah,* "This is a legislation of the Torah." A close reading of the Torah, Rashi's comments, and the source of Rashi's comment (*Numbers Rabbah* 19.4) will demonstrate the Jewish concept of freedom as understood by Talmudic Judaism's earliest heirs.

The rule of the red cow was enigmatically strange to the Rabbinic sages, who, in *Numbers Rabbah,* explained "I (= God) legislated a law, I have decreed a decree, and you have no right to disobey me.' Now, Rashi conflates the phrase of two verbs into a formula of a noun and a verb, "I have legislated a decree," demonstrating his bond with as well as his independence from the midrash. The midrash supplied Rashi with an idea; i.e., obedience is important in Judaism. But by recasting the midrashic syntax, Rashi declares his independence from the midrash. While the midrash demands behavioral obedience, Rashi's Torah commentary employs the formula, "you have no right to question" (the Divine decree). It is Rashi's restatement of the midrash rather than the origami midrash that has become part of traditional Jewish folk consciousness.

What forces contributed to Rashi's restatement of the midrash, and what did the midrash and Rabbinic Judaism mean in historical, ideological context? Rashi's career began at the beginning of the thirteenth century's "little Renaissance." Professor Touito of Bar Ilan University has shown that the concern for פְּשָׁט *p'shat* of Rashi, which was more pronounced in his school of thought, as exemplified by Bechor Shor, R. Isaac Qara, and R. Shemuel B. Meir, finds its concern in the spirit of the time. Just as the Church was concerned with theological correctness, we understand that Rashi wanted to emphasize that the rule of the red cow requires not only correct action, but correct belief in God as the ultimate Commander. It is an idea that is implicit in the midrash, but not explicitly stated.

Moderns can learn from this commentary that Rashi was bound to the

<u>H</u>ukkat

midrashic tradition for his precedents, but he used, applied, and shaped the midrash of early Geonic antiquity (which is the time frame for the *Aggadic* or *Amoraic midrashim*) to meet the pedagogic needs of the Jews living with him in the orbit of medieval Christian France.

One of Rashi's main concerns was פְּשָׁט *p'shat,* the simple meaning of Hebrew scripture. Rashi's concept of פְּשָׁט *p'shat* is grammatical and contextual. Midrashim that fill in the narrative gaps are consistent with his vision of פְּשָׁט *p'shat,* but not with that of R. Abraham Ibn Ezra, on one hand, or that of R. Shemuel b. Meir on the other. For these latter two scholars פְּשָׁט *p'shat* must be distinguished from דְּרָשׁ *drash,* or the Rabbinic interpretation. For our purposes, פְּשָׁט *p'shat* is "reading out" or exegesis, what we read out of the passage. And because we live at a certain station of history with the mental baggage we carry, our פְּשָׁט *p'shat* is unique to our age. The deconstructionists have correctly shown that there is no fully "innocent" reading of any work, any more than the Kantian "thing in itself" can ever be known outside of its being located in space, time, and casual relationships. דְּרָשׁ *Drash,* or isogesis, is "reading in" it is our response to the unchanging words of God recorded in the Torah.

The words זֹאת חֻקַּת הַתּוֹרָה *zot <u>h</u>ukkat ha-Torah* teach three exegetic פְּשָׁט *p'shat* reading out lessons that have isogetic, or דְּרָשׁ *drash,* implications. זֹאת *Zot* means "this" it is a demonstrative pronoun. The Torah teaches specific laws with limits and definitions. There are, by the traditional count, 613 laws in the Torah. This means that there are not 750 laws in the Torah. Laws are legislated, from the legislator. The idiom of legislation in Akkadian law codes includes inscription on a clay tablet; and following Hammurami's famous epilogue, there are curses that will befall someone who defaces the law code stela in any way. Jeremiah 32.11 speaks of sealing the inscribed חֹק *<u>h</u>ok* in a document. Seals authorize the contents of documents. While the biblical idiom usually connects חֻקִּים *<u>h</u>ukkim* with *mishpatim,* or "sentences" of the Judge/Legislator (Lev. 26.4, Deut. 4.5, 8, 14, 1 Kings 11.33, and other places as well), the Rabbinic reflex of this metaphor occurs in *Avot* 6.2, where חֵרוּת *<u>h</u>erut* (freedom) is conditioned by the concept of חָרוּת *<u>h</u>arut,* laws being unchangably engraved and inscribed on stone. Freedom cannot be enjoyed in a situation of anarchy or unlimited autonomy; it is circumscribed by the laws that are inscribed and publicly accessible. The individual must know the extent of the community's claim upon his behavioral loyalty, and when his autonomy, his rights, begin. According to Ronald Dworkin, a right is a trump of the individual against society. The Torah's concept of freedom inscribes laws with limits, insuring a defining order on one hand and personal choice and self-definitional dignity on the other.

Reading as metaphor our verse Numbers 19.2, "THIS IS THE LAW OF THE TORAH," we understand how the law is the seed of freedom. "THIS" refers to the specific rulings of the law, to which one may not add and from which one may not subtract (Deut. 13.1). The חֻקָּה *hukkah* is the legislation of the Legislator. The Jew obeys God's commands; only through God's commands does one achieve a measure of sanctity, of holiness. The commandment blessing uses the formula אֲשֶׁר קִדְּשָׁנוּ בְּמִצְוֹתָיו *Asher Kiddeshanu be-Mitzvotav.* In Friday evening liturgy we find the idiom קַדְּשֵׁנוּ בְּמִצְוֹתֶיךָ *Kaddeshenu be-Mitzvotekha*; we ask God to sanctify us through the commandments. Customs, invented practices, and contrived doctrines are not, for Judaism's classical definition, sources of sanctity. This public law is not given to gratuitous addition, to pious, zealous manipulation, or to the anarchy of unchecked autonomy. The Torah law provides a frame expressed by the demonstrative pronoun "THIS." The Torah is a work of legislation, of rules, of applied values, a חֻקָּה *hukkah.* And the Torah's laws are Torah, the root of which is [ירה] [YRH], meaning oracle. And for Isaiah, Torah comes forth from Zion, which is the word of the Lord whose throne is in Jerusalem (Is. 2.3).

The Rabbinic understanding of the red cow rule focuses upon obedience to the public law, the law in which the purifying priest becomes defiled even as the defiled person becomes purified. The priest does not control magic formula. The Torah laws are public, giving each and every Jew information, power, and rights. The word of the Lord is open to any and all who will come and learn. The law does not change, not because it is not responsive, but because any change in the law de-authorizes the law and the access rights of the individual under the law. If a charismatic claims that no one comes to God except by her or him, that person is restating, reformulating, and reforming the law in his or her image, to the denigration of the dignity of all others. If Korah takes himself to replace Moses, he replaces God as well.

The dignity of each and every member of the Israelite community is insured by three words, three principles: (a) "THIS," which indicates that God's command is knowable, objective, and clear; (b) חֻקַּת *hukkat*, which indicates that it is law, it is legislated, and only if it is legislated is it [c] Torah, the command of the Greatest Commander, the Author of heaven and earth. This Commander is not the king of any country, but the King of the Universe who has sanctified Israel with those commandments, among them the enigmatic law of the red cow. ■

Friend or Foe? Reflections on *Parashat Balak*

The story is a screenwriter's delight, filled with drama, conflict, suspense, violence, humor, and irony, not to mention contemporary relevance. A Moabite king asks a heathen prophet to curse the Israelites in anticipation of battle. The prophet claims to listen for God's call, plainly hears God's will for him, then proceeds to ignore it.

God sends an invisible messenger whom only the beast can see. The master furiously beats the ass, who is the only one in the story with clarity of vision and communication. The ass shows the way, the angel browbeats the prophet into doing his calling, and the curse for the people of Israel turns into blessing.

Among the delightful twists and turns in this beautiful story of blessing is the moment at which the angel of God arrives.

WHEN HE AROSE IN THE MORNING, BALAAM SADDLED HIS ASS AND DEPARTED WITH THE MOABITE DIGNITARIES. BUT GOD WAS INCENSED AT HIS GOING; SO AN ANGEL OF THE LORD PLACED HIMSELF IN HIS WAY AS AN ADVERSARY לְשָׂטָן לוֹ *(le-Satan lo).* HE WAS RIDING ON HIS SHE-ASS, WITH HIS TWO SERVANTS ALONGSIDE, WHEN THE ASS CAUGHT SIGHT OF THE ANGEL OF THE LORD STANDING IN THE WAY, WITH HIS DRAWN SWORD IN HIS HAND וְחַרְבּוֹ שְׁלוּפָה בְּיָדוֹ *(ve-Harbo Shelufa be-Yado)* [Num. 22.21-23].

Parashat Balak
Numbers 22.2–25.9

Rabbi Amy Eilberg

RABBI AMY EILBERG WORKS LOCALLY AS A PASTORAL COUNSELOR IN PRIVATE PRACTICE IN PALO ALTO, CALIFORNIA. SHE SERVES NATIONALLY AS A CONSULTANT AND TEACHER OF JEWISH SPIRITUALITY AND HEALING. SHE IS MARRIED TO DR. LOUIS NEWMAN AND IS MOTHER TO PENINA AND STEPMOTHER TO ETAN AND JONAH.

דָּבָר אַחֵר DAVAR AHER. AND THE LORD PUT A WORD IN BALAAM'S MOUTH AND SAID, "RETURN TO BALAK AND SPEAK THUS" [Num. 23.5]. The Torah frequently teaches by juxtaposing two apparently unrelated narratives, and such is the case in *parashat Balak*. The parashah consists of two stories. In the first God forces the gentile prophet Balaam to bless the Hebrew people. As I see it, the compulsion is psychological, not supernatural. God simply opens Balaam's eyes to the virtues of the Israelites, and he is unable to speak what he knows to be false. In the second story the Israelite men take on Moabite and Midianite mistresses and forsake their own religion to partake in their lovers' pagan rituals. I believe that the juxtaposition of these two stories is meant to teach us that there are virtues in our tradition that we fail to appreciate even

וירא **בלק** בן צפור את כל

A peculiar picture: an angel of God with a drawn sword in hand. Even the ass must have wondered, in her own way, what sort of creature this was standing before her, blocking her way, imposing, yet somehow an ally. Was this friend or foe? A harbinger of danger or a source of comfort?

We have reason to expect an angel to present itself as a messenger of good news, comfort, or salvation, such as the angel who appeared to Hagar as she despaired of her son's life [Gen. 16], the angel who called out to Abraham to stay his hand as Isaac lay ready for slaughter [Gen. 22], or the angel that physically guided the Israelites out of Egypt [Ex. 14.19—despite the Haggadah's protestations that the work was entirely God's], to name a few. So how are we to understand a creature paradoxically described as an angel of God sent to be an adversary לְשָׂטָן לוֹ (*lesatan lo*)? Are these not mutually contradictory descriptions?

Rashi answers this question by describing the creature as a מַלְאָךְ שֶׁל רַחֲמִים *mal'ah shel rahamim*, yes, an angel of mercy, who knew that God had asked Balaam not to go on Balak's mission, that Bil'am had given in to temptation, and so the angel came on a mission of mercy to prevent Balaam from completing his sin.

Still, an angel of mercy? This expression seems hyperbolic, evocative for us of, *lehavdil*, Mother Theresa, of a healer doing God's healing work at great personal cost: a nurse bringing love and tenderness to the children in the ICU, a medical team volunteering their time to

---

though they are self-evident to others.

I think of this parashah frequently when I address church groups on Jewish subjects through my connection with the Jewish Community Relations Bureau. Many Christians have a great deal of respect and admiration for the Jewish people and our traditions. At the same time we find large numbers of Jews abandoning their faith either out of indifference or out of the same motivation that impelled the men in this week's parashah—interfaith sexual encounters coupled with a belief that the religion of the dominant culture must be more exciting than their own. I have frequently conducted model seders for church groups, and when I see how strongly the participants react to the ceremony I

SYNOPSIS: The story of Mah Tovu followed by the sins at Ba'al Peor.

RASHI OF THE WEEK: *This last part of this portion begins with chapter* 25. It starts: AND ISRAEL CAMPED AT SHITTIM, AND THE NATION WHORED WITH THE DAUGHTERS OF MOAV. AND THEY (THE WOMEN) CALLED TO THE NATION TO SACRIFICE TO THEIR GODS AND THE PEOPLE ATE AND BOWED TO THEIR GODS. AND ISRAEL WAS YOKED TO BA'AL PE'OR AND GOD'S ANGER BURNED AT ISRAEL [Num. 25.1-2]. *Where was Shittim? Rashi knows this passage in the Talmud. Rabbi Eliezer said, "Shittim was a real place." Rabbi Joshua said, "It was a nickname based on 'shetut,' nonsense over all the sexual perversion and idolatry that happened there" (Sanhedrin* 106). *Rashi answers,* "Shittim is the name of a real place." THE PEOPLE BOWED TO THEIR GODS. *What did they actually do? Was it sexual or idolatrous?* When a man's desires were too strong to contain he went to one of the women and said, "Lie with me." She then took her amulet idol of Peor from between her breasts and said to him, "First bow to this—and then I will bend to you." *Thus we now understand the connection between sex and idolatry, and we better understand why tzitzit were supposed to keep us from whoring after our eyes.* What does Peor mean? It comes from the root [פער] PAR (meaning "bare"), because they bared their buttocks and relieved themselves during the process—that was part of their rite—*and even to this, lust made Israel blind. The warning about eyes being seduced has now come true. We all have our Ba'al Pe'or moments.*

Balak

care for refugees in a Third World country wracked with famine and disease. But a humanoid creature blocking the way, wielding an unsheathed sword, commanding obedience with the threat of violence? Rashi succeeds in resolving the apparent contradiction of how this violent figure can be an angel of God (though one need hardly look far in Torah to find examples of God directly initiating horrendous acts of violence). Even so, one senses that he overstates the case. An angel of mercy?

Yet if we listen to the echoes beneath this story, we are led to another biblical tale in which an angel appears in threatening form. Think of Joshua 5, when, following the historic first celebration of Passover in Eretz Yisrael and the circumcision of all the males of the community, we read the following narrative:

IT CAME TO PASS, AS JOSHUA WAS BY JERICHO, THAT HE RAISED HIS EYES AND LOOKED, AND THERE STOOD A MAN OVER AGAINST HIM WITH HIS SWORD DRAWN IN HIS HAND וְחַרְבּוֹ שְׁלוּפָה בְּיָדוֹ *(Veharbo Shelufa be-Yado)*. JOSHUA WENT TO HIM AND SAID TO HIM, "ARE YOU FOR US, OR FOR OUR ENEMIES?" AND HE SAID, "NO, I AM CAPTAIN OF THE HOST OF THE LORD; I HAVE NOW COME." JOSHUA FELL ON HIS FACE TO THE EARTH AND BOWED DOWN AND SAID TO HIM, "WHAT HAS MY LORD TO SAY TO HIS SERVANT?" THE CAPTAIN OF THE LORD'S HOST SAID TO JOSHUA, "REMOVE YOUR SHOE FROM YOUR FOOT, FOR THE PLACE ON WHICH YOU STAND IS HOLY." AND JOSHUA DID SO [Joshua 5.13-15].

What a striking comparison. This is physically the same angel figure: a forbidding man with unsheathed sword in hand. Yet how different the responses. Balaam, in the midst of his journey contrary to God's will for him, is unable even to see the angel and persists in struggling against its presence even as the evidence mounts. He beats and curses the ass, battling against his own inability to make sense of his situation, as if he could remove the obstacle by brute force. Only gradually does Balaam come to recognize the purpose of the angel's mission, which is to stop him before he carries out Balak's plan.

Joshua, by contrast, immediately perceives what stands before him and recognizes its ambiguity. Joshua, following God's word for him closely, has unimpeded vision and quickly grasps that the apparently threatening figure may be a creature of awe rather than of violence. Joshua immediately engages the stranger, asking him directly, "Are you friend or foe?" and then opens himself to the message. The

---

am saddened by the thought that many Jews no longer consider the holiday important enough to take time out of their busy schedules for. Perhaps we need to pay more attention to the Balaams in our midst who remind us what a wonderful tradition has been passed down to us. **Stu Lewis, Prairie Village, KS.**

message is, for Joshua, a simple reminder of God's presence. Pay attention: The place where you stand is holy ground. Joshua receives the message with ease and moves on with his holy work.

What an extraordinarily rich portrait of the foe as friend in spiritual life. It is hard enough to learn to recognize the angels that cross our path in real life, in plain clothes, without haloes or white flowing robes. It is harder still to recognize the angel who shows up clothed in hostility, threat, and pain as being a messenger from God.

I remember distinctly the first time someone called me an angel and meant it. It was in my first hospital chaplaincy job many years ago. The slight, lonely old woman was a little crazy, so it made me smile when she went on and on about how God had sent me to her room at just the moment she needed me. It was quaint how fervently she regarded my presence as an angel. I didn't know how to understand her.

I have since learned more about the presence of real-life angels. I will never forget the casual friend who spoke to me the week before I was to make a terrifying move across the country, a move I knew would change my life profoundly. Suddenly speaking with the power and wisdom of a prophet, such that I knew that her words in that moment came from God, she told me that someone was waiting for me in California, in my new home. Her prophecy gave me enormous comfort and guidance as I went on my way. As it turned out, she was right.

The women friends who brought me through dark times in my life, the clients and students who showered me with kindness, my daughter, who brings unspeakable joy and wonder—all of these and more are as real and as blessed as the figures with haloes and robes. And my husband, a source of astounding blessing, is a proof of the existence of God far more persuasive than anything the philosophers could produce, a presence in my life fully as powerful and wondrous as the biblical encounters with divine beings.

These experiences have even taught me, among other things, something about how to understand those moments when I am sent to be an agent of God in someone else's path. Not because I am any more angelic than the next person, but because this is what God has sent me to do. I am learning to understand this.

Still, these are relatively easy to recognize—the benevolent real-life angels, even our own occasional cameo roles as angels in God's drama. But what of the strangers with unsheathed swords in the middle of the road? How are we to recognize them as angels of mercy? I believe that essential to the message of *Parashat Balak* is this teaching: Even the apparently hostile, strange, and threatening figure may be a messenger from God whom we ignore at our own spiritual peril.

The boss or work colleague who is a source of pain and indignity; the family member who returns us to the very worst of our childhood vulnerability; the friend who betrayed us; the lover who abandoned us, leaving us exposed, ashamed, and alone. Is there any way—not in Pollyana-ish denial, but in spiritual maturity—to recognize the God-given quality of these and other "foes" in our lives?

The key, of course, is in our ability to see. Balaam, trapped in his own fear-driven disobedience of God's work for him, could not see beyond his own beast of burden. Balaam could not consider the possibility that the roadblock was a friend, the obstacle a guide, the threatening figure really an angel sent to protect him from his own misguided plans and thoughts. Joshua, by contrast, his spiritual vision crystal clear even at a treacherous time of transition, knew just which question to ask: Could this dangerous being be a friend with something to give me, something to teach me, some message to convey about the path I am supposed to walk?

We can be Balaam or we can be Yehoshua. But we have to open our own eyes. ■

Dr. Jonathan Woocher

Dr. Jonathan Woocher is the Executive Vice-President of JESNA, The Jewish Education Service of North America, and he is the author of *Sacred Survival: The Civil Religion of American Jews.*

Balak

"Seeing is believing." Perhaps. But truly understanding what we "see" and therefore how we must respond to it, is not always so simple.

Parashat Balak **is at one level an engaging morality tale with some "fantastic" elements thrown in for good measure. A close reading of the sidrah suggests, however, that there is more going on here than simply a pagan king and a somewhat suspect prophet getting their "comeuppance" (Balak doesn't get his curse, and Balaam doesn't get his wealth). The central motif of the parashah is "seeing": Who truly sees (and sees truly), and who understands and acts accordingly?**

This theme is announced in the first verse: BALAK, SON OF ZIPPOR, *SAW* ALL THAT ISRAEL HAD DONE TO THE AMORITES [Num. 22. 2]. He sees, but he fails to understand the import of what he has witnessed.

He sees a people so numerous that it "HIDES THE EARTH FROM *VIEW*" [v. 5], and he responds by calling upon the visionary power of the prophet to curse this threatening apparition. When Balaam agrees (reluctantly? eagerly?) to Balak's request it would seem that he understands well the Divinely ordained constraints under which he must proceed. But apparently this is not the case, for he fails to *see* what his ass does: an angel preventing his passage. Only when HA-SHEM UNCOVERS HIS EYES [v. 31] does he *see* the angel and understand: He must give up any hope of acting as a free agent (and deriving some profit from his venture); his role is solely to expound *God's* vision for the children of Israel, not that of a Moabite king.

Balak, however, still has his hopes, if only he can get Balaam into just the right position to see what Balak wishes him to see. But even gazing at only a portion of the people is enough for Balaam to see Israel from God's perspective as A PEOPLE THAT DWELLS APART, NOT RECKONED AMONG THE NATIONS [v. 9]. This is not a people that can be cursed like any other nation, because it is subject only to God's power.

Balak is, if nothing else, persistent. Perhaps a change in Balaam's perspective (literally) will produce a different result. In fact, however, seeing-with-understanding is not a matter of one's "point of view." There is truth and there is falsehood, and the one cannot be transformed into the other. So Balak's effort is doomed to failure. Balaam is now one whose EYE IS TRUE [Num. 23.3], his sight UNVEILED [v. 4]. He can see that NO HARM IS IN SIGHT FOR JACOB, NO WOE FOR

Israel, because Ha-Shem their God is with them [Num. 22.21]. By this time Balak has heard enough, but Balaam's vision now penetrates even into the distant future. Eventually all of Israel's enemies will fall [Num. 23.17–24]. Our story is over; Balak and Balaam go their separate ways.

But not quite, for the parashah does not end here—though we might initially think that it should. We know how God sees Israel, but how does Israel see itself? Do the people encamped below understand what Balaam has seen? Do they know their own nature and destiny?

Sadly, they do not. Like the spies a few chapters earlier who looked like grasshoppers in [their] own eyes [Num. 13.33], the people fail to see themselves as Balaam does. They are enticed by the women of Moab and begin to worship Ba'al Pe'or (Pe'or, the very place from which Balaam saw Israel encamped tribe by tribe, and the spirit of G-d came upon him [Num. 24.2]!). In an ironic, tragic anticlimax, what Balaam could not do directly he is able to achieve by taking advantage of the people's own inability to see the truth he has seen [cf. Numbers 31.16]. The people, whose numbers Balak feared so greatly, are assaulted by a plague that kills 24,000. It is only through the bold intervention of Phineas, when he *sees* the whoring taking place in the sight of Moses and of the whole Israelite people, that the plague is checked [Num. 25.7-9]. He sees that the people's behavior is incompatible with the vision that God has for them. And he acts on that understanding.

We are left, then, not with a happy ending, but with questions. What do we see when we look at ourselves today? Do we still see a people who dwells apart, but whose God is with us? Do we still see ourselves as blessed in a way that no human enemy can overturn? Or have we lost that vision of what it means to be part of the Jewish people, and with it some of the will to resist the temptations of a society and culture that do not necessarily see the world as we do?

And are we prepared to act on our vision? Do we have the self-confidence to leave the assembly, as Phineas did [Num. 25.7], and act decisively to preserve the values of out tradition? Zealotry is not our way, but neither is moral relativism. Can we defend the distinction between blessing and curse, good and evil, insisting that these not be confused or transmuted into one another?

The rabbis credited Balaam with his own "book" of the Torah despite his problematic character. Perhaps this is because his story is indeed no simple folktale. The age of prophecy is behind us. But the challenge to see clearly, to understand what we are seeing, and to act on that understanding and in keeping with our vision remains. ■

Parashat Pin<u>h</u>as

Numbers 25.10–30.1

Rabbi Dr. Jonathan Magonet

Jonathan Magonet is principal (president) of Leo Baeck College, The U.K. Rabbinic Assembly. He has published books on *Tenakh* *(A Rabbi's Bible, A Rabbi Reads the Psalms)*, and on spirituality with his colleague Lionel Blue *(How to Get Up When Life Gets You Down)* and has edited the three prayerbooks of the Reform synagogues of Great Britain. He has edited *Jewish Explorations of Sexuality* and co-edits the journal *European Judaism.*

I do not like Pinhas. I do not like the fact that he assassinated two people in full public view, and I do not like the idea that not only did he get away with it unpunished, but he received a special kind of reward from God. This is not a comfortable starting point for a pious reading of a biblical passage. But if the Bible was that easy, why would we bother to read it?

So let us look at the context of this troubling story, which is contained within Numbers 25, though the parashah itself only begins with verse 10.

How far afield should we go in defining the context? In this case, the whole book of Numbers has to be considered.

The first ten chapters of the book offer an idealized picture of the Israelite encampment as it is about to set out on its journeying. In particular, the tasks of the priests and Levites are sketched out, as is their central role in the sanctuary. A very clear hierarchy is described—only the priests, Aaron and his sons, can enter the holiest part of the sanctuary and touch its furnishings. The next outward stratum consists of the Levites, who are to serve the priests but are not allowed to handle the holiest materials directly. One step further removed are the Israelites themselves, who can only stay in

---

A CALL FOR TORAH. On Shabbat *Pin<u>h</u>as* Rabbi Eliahu Bakshi Doron, the chief Sephardic Rabbi of the State of Israel, compared the biblical figure Zimri to Reform Jews and praised Pin<u>h</u>as, the man who murdered Zimri for having sexual relations with a non-Jewish woman. While the politics of this Davar Torah are being played out in the press, we think it is important to go back into the sources. I'd like to make sure that this confrontation drives us back into the Torah to look for God's will and Judaism's lesson. Therefore, both in *LTW* and in the *LTW* book, we want to emphasize a reconsideration of this story. Please send us your best Pin<u>h</u>as Torah. We all need it. **Joel Lurie Grishaver and Rabbi Stuart Kelman.**

פנחס בן אלעזר בן אהרן

the outermost courts. If anyone crosses over his particular boundary into a "holier" realm, then God's anger will blaze out and plague will engulf the people [Num. 8.19].

Having established the theoretical structure of the encampment for their march through the wilderness, chapter 11 onwards chronicles a series of leadership challenges and disasters that nearly destroy the whole enterprise. The most damaging, since it causes the Israelites to wander in the wilderness till an entire generation dies out, is the negative report of the spies. On a political level the rebellion of Korah [Num. 16 and 17] almost brings the entire structure of the new society created by Moses toppling down. One of the issues is this newly established distinction between Aaron's family and the Levites, with the latter wanting to take Aaron's place. When the matter is still not resolved, despite the destruction of the rebels, a plague does indeed break out as the sanctuary is under threat, only to be stopped by Aaron [Num. 17.13]. The danger to God's honor has been removed.

After the Korah episode chapters 18 and 19 reconfirm the respective roles of the priests and Levites. We return to the theme of the journey and the leadership challenges, including the episode of Moses striking the rock that prevents him from entering the Promised Land. Battles are fought with local kings so that Israel gains territory. Within this sequence come three chapters about Balaam, who is summoned by Balak, king of Moab, to curse Israel, but who ends up blessing them. Then comes the Pinhas episode—in this context of the

---

דָּבָר אַחֵר DAVAR AHER. The Lord spoke to Moses, saying, "Phinehas, son of Eleazar son of Aaron the priest, has turned back My wrath from the Israelites by displaying among them his passion for Me, so that I did not wipe out the Israelite people in My passion [Num. 25.10-11]. *Response to "A Call for Torah" regarding Pinhas.* I am in a very peculiar position. As an Israeli I respect the Chief Rabbis of the State. As an American I can do nothing but be outraged!

The story of Pinhas when taken out of context is a very powerful one. On the surface it simply implies that "sleeping with the enemy" has one answer—death.

SYNOPSIS: *As the time in the wilderness draws to a close we have a few more adventures. Pinhas ends the incident at Ba'al Peor. This is followed by a war with Midian, a census, the problem of the daughters of Zelophehad, the choosing of Joshua, and another list of sacrifices.*

RASHI OF THE WEEK:

Last week Pinhas killed Zimri when he was doing all kinds of unholy things at the doorway to the Mishkan. This week's Torah portion begins with a reintroduction of Pinhas. It begins: Pinhas, son of Aaron the Kohen.. *Rashi asks, why do we have to reintroduce Pinhas? We already know his story and know who He is? Rashi answers by telling us a Midrash. The people of the camp were not happy with Pinhas. They were outraged. They started insulting him by saying,* "How can a son of Putiel (*Elazar's wife*, who was a descendent of Jethro)—whose mother used to fatten calves for pagan sacrifice—*tell us about the right way of worship.* He *even* killed a prince of Israel. That is why the Torah reintroduces him as Aaron's descendent. *Remember that even though Pinhas had to use violence, he is the heir of the leading advocate of peace in the Jewish tradition. Sometimes violence is the right path to peace. Some things must be challenged.*

relations between Israel and other local peoples and the temptation to accept their gods.

The Israelite men are seduced by the Moabite women and are led into idolatry, so that Israel "yoked itself" to Ba'al Pe'or [Num. 25.1-3]. The brief description in the Bible hints at any number of religio-political factors that come into play here. The story is narrated in the context of the Israelites settling in the towns they have conquered and presumably reflects a desire on the part of some to stay there and come to terms with the local population, including acknowledging their gods, as was customary at that time. The Israelite leadership appears to have been split by this matter, so much so that God orders Moses to hang the leaders of the people [v. 4]. Moses seems to be unable to undertake such a drastic action and instead orders the judges to slay those who have joined the Ba'al Peor faction [v. 5].

An unnamed man, who will later be revealed as Zimri ben Salu, a prince of the tribe of Simeon, takes Cozbi bat Tzur, a Midianite princess, into his family. Such a public act, which joins leading figures of the two peoples through intercourse or marriage, symbolizes political union between them. The "assimilationist" party has made its play for leadership. Nothing is recorded of Moses' reaction, and he seems to be paralyzed, together with the whole of the governing assembly [v. 6]. At this crucial moment Pinhas "sees"—a term used of the younger Moses when taking an initiative no one else does (compare Exodus 2.12, Isaiah 59.15-17). Pinhas takes his spear and runs the couple through.

Quite how or where he does this is not clear because of the use of two unusual words, הַקֻּבָּה *kubah* and קֳבָתָהּ *kovatah,* in the same verse [Num. 25.8]. Stefan Reif (S. C. Reif, "What Enraged Phinehas? A Study of Numbers 25.8," *Journal of*

Pinhas

Taken a bit deeper it implies that mixed marriages are a curse of such magnitude that both the Israelite and his/her partner are such sinners that the only answer for them is death.

True, the most important question we face today is how to deal with the rampant rate of intermarriage in North America. True, it is a plague that afflicts all of us, Reform Jews as well as Orthodox and Conservative, but is "death" the only response?

To simplistically equate Reform Judaism to idolatry and to Zimri and Kazbi is completely and utterly wrong. Mr. Bakshi-Doron is actually שׁוֹפֵךְ דָּם *shofekh dam* (shedding blood) by his edict! I might not be the greatest biblical scholar, but my understanding based on Hillel is that life is more sacred than anything. Leaving the faith is a serious

Biblical Literature Vol, 90 (June, 1971), pp. 200–206) suggests the word refers to a Midianite tent-shrine that Zimri has installed as part of accepting the presence of Midianite gods. Hence the sentence would read: "Following the Israelite into the shrine, he ran them both through, the Israelite and the woman in her shrine."

By this reading it is not some sexual act, or at least not that alone, that has offended Pinhas, but this blatant introduction to a form of foreign worship in the heart of the Israelite encampment. With the apparent lack of leadership from Moses, he takes the law into his own hands and strikes. His action is effective, because we are now told that a plague that has ravaged the people is stopped; so, like the cases where the sanctuary is affected, this event does seem to imply an infringement of God's honor.

As a result Pinhas acquires a reputation as a troubleshooter—or at least as someone to encourage wavering spirits. So he is present as the Israelites attack Midian [Num. 31.6ff]; he heads a delegation that investigates an altar set up by the two and a half tribes on the east side of the Jordan [Joshua 22.13ff]; he encourages the Israelites at the onset of their civil war with the Benjaminites [Judges 20.28].

The rabbis, building on the frequent references to his "zeal" for God, identified him with Elijah, who is similarly passionate. But they were understandably concerned with his taking the law into his own hands and assassinating people. Since God appeared to approve his action—he is also praised for it again in Psalm 106.30-31—they had to find a solution and assumed the existence of an emergency law that covered such a situation.

But what of the reward God offers him? In a bizarre paradox he is given God's "covenant of peace" [Num. 25.12], and to his descendants is given the "covenant of eternal priesthood." This latter may mean simply the ratification of the priesthood given to Aaron and his descendants, or even the granting of the High Priesthood. But how can we reconcile both these gifts with his act and with a man of such violence?

The best explanation I have heard came from Rabbi Dr. Norman Solomon, who asked the question, "What do you do with fanatics?" Since there are always such "zealous" people around and they can do a lot of damage if they are not kept in check, how do you contain them? His answer: "Put them in charge of the priesthood." All their fanaticism can be directed to ensuring the correct organizing and ritual of the sacrificial cult, the maintenance of all the hierarchical boundaries within the sanctuary, and the appropriate dispatching and distribution of the animal offerings. If any task was designed for precision, detailed observation, and fanatical care, it was that. Truly such work

---

sin, sleeping with the enemy is a serious sin, but practicing Judaism with a different interpretation is not a sin.

Mr. Doron should attend synagogue services in North America to see the devotion, the true *kavanah* of the congregations. He should be part of the life cycles of these people who truly believe in their Judaism and who are doing it because they *want* to, not necessarily because they are told to. This takes us back to Isaiah and his problems regarding *kavanah*. Isn't Isaiah the one who said, "I am full of the burnt-offerings of rams, and the fat of fed beasts; and I delight not in the blood of bullocks, or of lambs, or of he-goats. When ye come to appear before Me, Who hath required this of your hand, to trample My courts?...And when ye spread forth your hands, I will hide Mine eyes from you; Yea, when ye make many prayers, I will not hear: your hands are full of blood" [Isaiah 1.11-15].

Isaiah continues with his lesson of the important items of God's wishes, "put away the evil of your doings from before Mine eyes, cease to do evil, learn to do well, seek justice, relieve the oppressed, judge the fatherless, plead for the widow...Zion shall be redeemed with justice, and they that return of her with righteousness" [Isaiah 1.16-27].

would keep even a Pinhas safely out of harm's way!

Perhaps that was Moses' ploy, but instead I am tempted to see a weakened and demoralized Moses. Having recently been told he will not enter the Promised Land, he simply yielded to the evident power of Pinhas. Moreover, his action seemed to serve the immediate needs of the people if their journey to the Promised Land was to continue.

That it sets a precedent for the violent resolution of conflicts and reinforces and justifies Israelite xenophobia is left for later generations, particularly our own, to address. ■

כְּלַל-יִשְׂרָאֵל עֲרֵבִים זֶה בָּזֶה *Klal Israel, Arevin Ze ba-zeh*, are not important to Mr. Doron. I will suggest to him to go back to the Torah and *Tanakh* and to learn his lessons. Our first and second temples were not destroyed by internal love and compassion among our brothers and sisters. We should keep the lessons of Torah alive by learning what is really important and not by simply disregarding a large, very large part of our people as idolaters. I will be happy to escort Mr. Doron to my synagogue to see for himself what kind of Judaism is being practiced at Main Line Reform Temple, where I am the proud Director of Education. **Itzik Eshel, Ph.D, Director of Education, Main Line Reform Temple, Wynnewood, PA.**

Pinhas

דָּבָר אַחֵר **DAVAR AHER.** You pose the important question: "How do we teach Pinhas the next time it recycles?" For starters, I would suggest going to the statement regarding Pinhas in the *Talmud Yerushalmi*. In *Yerushalmi Sanhedrin*, Chapter 9, *Halakhah* 7, the Talmud discusses what the halakhah is regarding one who has sexual relations with an *aramit* (presumably an "Aramean woman"). The Talmud quotes the following halakhah: "If one has sexual relations with an Aramean woman, zealots may harm him." This halakhah is based upon the precedent that Pinhas set by his actions. The term used for zealots is the Hebrew word *kanaim*. In regard to this legal ruling, the *Talmud Yerushalmi* says, "This (ruling) is against the will of our sages, and Pinhas (and his deeds) are against the will of our sages. Rabbi Yehudah ben Pazi states, 'The community (in the wilderness) desired to ostracize him (Pinhas, for his actions), were it not for the fact that the Divine Spirit had intervened and said that Pinhas and his descendants shall be rewarded with the priestly covenant forever.'" What we come away with, so far, is that the Rabbis are uncomfortable with the halakhic ruling permitting zealotry, and as a matter of fact, in regard to the Torah's prototypical zealot, the Rabbis did not approve of his actions. Rabbi Yehudah ben Pazi expresses this disapproval of Pinhas' actions by concluding that the Israelite community in the

When the plague was over, Adonai said to Moses and to Eleazar, son of Aaron the priest, "Take a census of the whole Israelite community...." When I read those words from this week's Torah portion I have to ask, "When will this plague be over?" and if and when it does end, what will the census of our people tell us? Who among us will be left standing, and who among us will be able to respond to the questions of what we did while the plague was happening? When will this plague of AIDS/HIV end?

For more than fifteen years we have lived with this nightmare, watching, virtually helpless, as young men and women in the prime of their lives die. More people have died in this plague than in the Korean, Vietnam, and Gulf Wars *combined*. And the dying of this plague continues. There have been medical advances: People living with AIDS/HIV live longer and die more horrible deaths from new opportunistic infections that no one had heard of just a few years ago. The medical community has prolonged life for some and has made death a welcome release from the medically prolonged suffering.

When will this plague end? In *Les Miserables* there's an incredible song:

> There's a grief that can't be spoken,
> There's a pain goes on and on,
> Empty chairs at empty tables,
> Now my friends are dead and gone...
> Empty chairs at empty tables,
> Where my friends will sing no more.

Everyone who is living with AIDS/HIV or who loves someone who is living with AIDS/HIV or already dead knows the pain of multiple loss, the unending

Rabbi H. Rafael Goldstein

Rabbi H(arris) Rafael Goldstein is author of *Being a Blessing: 54 Ways You Can Help People Living With AIDS*, published by the Alef Design Group.

Pinhas

wilderness also did not approve of Pinhas' actions and would have ostracized him from the community were it not for God's intervention. God's intervention makes the entire episode problematic for us because God rewards Pinhas and therefore seems to be a God who rewards acts of zealotry. The Torah Temimah (a Bible commentator) explains as follows: "The fact the sages are uncomfortable with acts of zealotry is because in order for something to be a true act of zealotry, it must be done within the spirit of true zealotry in honor of God, and, therefore, we cannot give permission and license to anybody to act in this fashion, because we cannot really know if the person is acting truly on behalf of God, or for some other ulterior motive. The only way we may know that a person is truly a zealot is if God Himself comes down and validates the act, as was done with Pinhas. Since we may not issue halakhic rulings hoping

grief of reading each day's obituaries. And the unrelenting dread of the next day's continuing losses. Old people remember family and friends who have predeceased them. At the time of this plague young people remember scores of dead friends and relatives who have predeceased them. Multiple loss is normal for old people; it's a disaster for the young. How many empty chairs are at my table? How many empty tables are there in our community now, and how many will there be when this plague is over?

Dear God, when will this plague be over? I used to think that on the day of The Cure there would be dancing in the streets. Now I doubt it. How will we dance when each street we walk down reminds us of people who have died, places they will never go again? How do you celebrate the end of a plague? How did Moses and Aaron acknowledge the end of the plague they experienced? They counted the dead; they counted the living. The entire generation that left Egypt was now dead (everyone who left Egypt aged twenty or older) with the exception of Moses, Aaron, Joshua, and Caleb. Four men from the generation that left Egypt survived. How did the survivors respond to all these deaths around them? The Torah doesn't tell us, unless we assume that Aaron's "SILENT SCREAM" heard after the sudden deaths of Nadab and Abihu is also screamed here. How should I respond? I hope to be here, weeping with the survivors, asking "Why them and not us?" asking "What do we do now, how do we pick up the pieces of our lives and go on?" But there's no time for tears now—in the absence of The Cure there is so much work to do. After today's funeral there will be someone else to bury tomorrow, another bereft family to comfort, another person struggling to live just one more day, another confused, angry, and scared newly

---

Pinhas

that God will come and validate the outcome of the ruling, then we may not issue rulings in regards to acts of zealotry. In the case of Pinhas, he acted against the will of the sages, and only God was able to salvage him." What the Torah Temimah is essentially saying is that the case of Pinhas is not meant to be used as a precedent, nor as a license to issue similar rulings. The Torah Temimah and the Talmud seem to be saying that the Rabbis themselves were uncomfortable with God's response to Pinhas' deeds, and the only way they could justify it without questioning God or being disrespectful to God was to say that we really cannot understand fully what Pinhas did, nor do we know all of the details, so this must have been a unique situation that we will never understand fully, and that is therefore suspended in history as a

diagnosed person trying to live with a death sentence.

When will there be an end to this plague? At the end of the plague that began in last week's Torah portion the census taken was to apportion the Promised Land and to prepare for the upcoming wars of conquest. Later in this week's Torah portion the daughters of Zelophehad come to Moses and the chieftains to state their claim on their deceased father's holdings. Perhaps the message of their appearance at this moment in history is that each human being is of value, each person has worth, each dead person is missed, and the loss of each person has a "ripple effect" on the lives of the survivors.

At the end of this plague what will a census of our people tell us? Certainly it will tell us who actually believes the words כָּל-יִשְׂרָאֵל עֲרֵבִים זֶה בָּזֶה *Kol Yisrael Arevim zeh Ba-zeh* and has acted accordingly. Our rabbis teach us that we are all responsible to help. The end of this plague will tell us how deeply it has reached into our communities; we'll count the true number of our dead, including the many whose deaths have been hidden because of stigma or homophobia. At the end of this plague there will be a count of the enormous toll AIDS/HIV has cost humanity. At the end of this plague, we will all have to answer the question, "What did you do while they were dying?" At the end of this plague the heroes, the "righteous well," will be honored for all they did to help. But who will be counted?

May it be Your will, Adonai our God, that there be an end to this plague—soon and in our days. May we all find comfort beneath the shelter of Your wings as we count our losses, as we participate in responding, as we bring strength and hope to one another. May we come to a fuller awareness of what all these deaths mean to us all, and may we all be counted among the survivors. Amen. ■

---

unique case, which is why we may not use it as a precedent for any of our own actions. Therefore, if we are teaching Parashat *Pinhas* in our schools, it is very important to stress that the rabbis in the Talmud were not in favor of Pinhas' deeds, and they were the first to point out to us that neither were Pinhas' contemporaries in the Israelite camp, and that God's rewarding of Pinhas, an inexplicable response, certainly does not serve as a precedent, but on the contrary is a unique, strange case suspended alone in history with no precedent or duplication. In God's eyes, for some reason unknown to us or to the rabbis in the Talmud, Pinhas was a hero. In the eyes of the sages Pinhas' deeds were unacceptable. **Daniel Bouskila, Rabbi of Sephardic Temple Tifereth Israel, Westwood, CA, <RABBIBOUSK@aol.com>.**

ANGER, VENGEANCE, AND RESH LAKISH

Parashat Mattot
Numbers 30.2–32.42

Rodger Kamenetz

RODGER KAMENETZ IS A POET AND WRITER, AUTHOR OF *THE MISSING JEW* (TIME BEING BOOKS) AND *THE JEW IN THE LOTUS* (HARPER). HE TEACHES AT LOUISIANA STATE UNIVERSITY IN BATON ROUGE AND LIVES IN NEW ORLEANS WITH HIS WIFE AND TWO DAUGHTERS.

Personally, I find anger a very difficult emotion to contend with. In recent years it has been a difficult emotion for the Jewish people. Our historical experience as Jews in the past fifty years has encouraged us to use anger, to live anger, to be anger. As Jews we are angry about the Holocaust, angry about the enemies of Israel, angry about our rivals on the domestic political front. For a short time anger can be good therapy. It can also be good politics. In the long run anger has a high spiritual cost, especially when we take the presumed rightness of our cause as a license to become permanently angry people.

This Torah portion, *Mattot*, teaches us something about that cost—personal, spiritual, and communal.

In Hebrew the book of Numbers is called *Be-Midbar*, "in the wilderness." Even today a wilderness is considered a good place for a proving ground. In a landscape of harshness and extremes the slave generation enters the "proving ground" and through a series of tests is found unworthy to enter the Promised Land. Only after forty years will a new generation, purified and mature, emerge. Moshe, Aaron, Miriam—the leaders of the Exodus—will die before completing the journey.

Anger in such trying circumstances seems natural, especially for the leader of unruly, grumbling people. The temptation to anger is Moses' greatest spiritual test: Moses is found to be unworthy to enter the land of Israel because of his public display of anger at the waters of contention/Meribah [Num. 20.10-12].

As the children of Israel approach the Promised Land they are in transition between slavery and freedom. As slaves they had no choices; as free men they are free to choose wrongly. The slave generation fails test after test from the grumbling over the manna to the Golden Calf.

In *Parashat Pinhas* they fall into idolatrous worship of the Ba'al of Pe'or. It is revealed to Moses that Balaam, having failed at cursing the tents of Jacob, went to the Midianites with a plan: use your women to lure the children of Israel into idolatry [Num. 25.16-18].

Some five chapters later the story is resumed in *Parashat Mattot*. In Everett Fox's strong X-ray of a translation, "YHWH SPOKE TO MOSHE, SAYING: "SEEK VENGEANCE, THE VENGEANCE OF THE CHILDREN OF ISRAEL FROM THE MIDYANITES; AFTERWARD YOU WILL BE GATHERED TO YOUR KINSPEOPLE" [Num. 31.1-2]. The conjunction of clauses implies that the order to avenge is linked to the end of Moses' life. This is a warning to those like Pinhas who would willingly seek to be instruments of Divine vengeance.

Rabbi Abraham Twerski, in his helpful anthology *Living Each Day*, tells us that "The Talmud relates that although the Torah requires capital punishment for certain heinous crimes, the justices of the Sanhedrin (supreme court) would pray that they should not have to condemn anyone to death. So many times in life there are incidents where we feel we have been wronged by others, and when the opportunity arises to retaliate, the urge to take revenge is intense. The Torah forbids vengeance [Lev. 19.18]."

The difficult test for Moses as a leader is to be an instrument of Divine vengeance without becoming personally angry. The battle is successful, and Balaam dies in the midst of it. The warriors, led by Pinhas, return from their attack on the Midianites loaded with booty. Moses and Eleazar, Pinhas' father, rush out to greet them. When Moses sees the Midianite women among their captives he grows angry: "AND MOSHE WAS FURIOUS WITH THE COMMANDERS OF THE MILITARY" [Num. 31.14].

Moses is angry for a reason that is scarcely palatable today: The fighters have spared the Midianite women and their small boys. He orders their death. He states that these women were the lures to idolatry in the first place. Moses fears that the men will be tempted again. As readers we cannot deny or gloss over what amounts to collective punishment of women and children. We ought to use this text as an opportunity to confront the meaning of anger in our spiritual tradition. What does it mean to have an angry Moses? What does it mean to have an avenging, angry Lord?

In our parashah we learn how Moses' anger damages him as a

SYNOPSIS: *The book of Numbers is winding down. We get a bunch of "pre-occupation" texts. A war with Midian sets the context for rules for dividing spoils of war and for purifying warriors. Included as well is the request of two tribes to set up homes on the "wrong side" of the Jordan.*

RASHI OF THE WEEK: AND THE ETERNAL SPOKE TO MOSES, SAYING "AVENGE THE CHILDREN OF ISRAEL OF THE MIDIANITES—AND THEN YOU CAN BE GATHERED TO YOUR PEOPLE" [Num. 31.1]. *Rashi looks at this verse and asks,* "Why take revenge on Midian and not Moab?" *Two events have preceded this moment. In the first Balaam, a Midianite, tries to wipe out Israel with a curse for the King of Moab. The second is an involvement with cult prostitutes at Ba'al Pe'or. While the majority of the women are Moabites, the key player seems to be Kozbi, a Midianite priestess. Rashi answers his own question by saying:* Moab attacked Israel because they were afraid of Israel's plundering of their land, not because of groundless hatred. *This is proved by the verse Deuteronomy 2.9, where God tells Israel,* "DO NOT CONTEND WITH THEM IN BATTLE. I WILL NOT GIVE YOU ANY OF THEIR LANDS." *Unfortunately, Moab panicked and didn't believe this. Midian, on the other hand, was vicious and got involved in a fight they had no real part in. They fought for the sake of fighting. In other words, not all non-Jews, even non-Jews who attack Jews, are the same. Some may be ignorant, some are pointlessly vicious.*

Davar Aher *(another thing):* God protected Moab because two virtuous women would descend from Moab. Ruth, the progenitor of David and Na'amah, Solomon's mother [*Bava Kamma* 38b].

Mattot

leader. Resh Lakish, a Talmudic authority of the third century, focuses on the moment when the warriors return victorious from battle. (Perhaps it is a moment he understood from his former life—before taking up sacred studies he'd been a gladiator.) Resh Lakish said: "When a man becomes angry—if he is a sage, his wisdom departs from him; if he is a prophet, his prophecy departs from him. That his wisdom departs from him if he is a sage we learn from Moses, for after saying, AND MOSHE WAS FURIOUS WITH THE COMMANDERS OF THE MILITARY [Num. 31.14] it is said, ELEAZAR THE PRIEST SAID UNTO THE MEN OF THE ARMED-FORCE THAT CAME BACK FROM THE WAR, 'THIS IS THE LEGAL INSTRUCTION THAT YHWH HAD COMMANDED MOSHE' [Num. 31.21]. From the above it follows that (since Moses was not the one who spoke) the statute escaped Moses' memory [*B. Pes.* 66b]." (My source is *The Book of Legends/Sefer Ha-Aggadah*, ed. Bialik and Ravnitzky, tr. William Braude. New York: Schocken Books, 1992, p. 706.)

In the atmosphere of war and violence, anger spreads and contaminates like a virus. Rashi tells us that Moshe is angry at the young men to begin with because he fears they will SNATCH THE SPOILS of war. That is why he hurries out to meet them. He grows FURIOUS when he sees that they have brought back with them the Midianite women. He issues a dreadful order to kill the women and their young sons. He is so angry, says Resh Lakish, that when he gives the law for purifying the warriors and their garments—"EVERYONE WHO KILLED A PERSON OR EVERYONE WHO TOUCHED A CORPSE"—he leaves out the instructions for purifying their swords and other metal that they touched. Eleazar fills in the gap, tactfully associating the commandment with Moses so as not to embarrass him.

Vengeance, even in a righteous cause, leaves a permanent stain, an impurity that cannot easily be washed out. Anger leads us to forget our deepest wisdom. It is symbolic that in the passage cited by Resh Lakish Moses forgets a law of purification so that Eleazar must speak it on his behalf. "ANYTHING THAT CAN COME THROUGH FIRE—YOU ARE TO PASS THROUGH FIRE, THEN IT WILL BE PURE" [Num. 31.23].

Fire is fine for purifying metal. But how does the human soul cleanse itself from anger? We no longer have the rituals such as our parashah describes to cleanse ourselves of the contamination of anger. Therefore, it is best to avoid anger even when pursuing a righteous cause. Perhaps especially then. For that is when the temptation to mix in a personal anger is greatest. When I hear angry voices among those who would lead me or an angry voice within myself, I become wary. If Resh Lakish is right, anger cannot be wise, and anger is certainly no prophet.

But if that is the case, what does it mean when the Torah speaks, as in our portion [Num. 31.2], of a Lord who demands vengeance, or, elsewhere, of an angry Lord? Maimonides saw this contradiction plainly. He explains in Chapter 54 of his *Guide to the Perplexed* how an expression like the anger of the Lord can be understood. "Whenever any one of His actions is perceived by us, we ascribe to God that emotion which is the source of the act when performed by ourselves." To ascribe a human emotion to God would imply a God who is out of control. But in fact, the Rambam writes, God's actions cannot be the "result of any emotion: for He is above all defect."

This argument is good philosophy but bad poetry. The Torah's language creates powerful images; and, as the Rambam knew, many readers have taken the metaphor of God's wrath and vengeance all too literally. Anger is one of the great tests of spiritual maturity. And especially in a situation when we are in conflict with others. If our greatest prophet, Moses, cannot pass the test, the rest of us should be careful. Anger comes in beguiling disguises. We angry people find noble names for our habit—some of them are God, Israel, Judaism, honor, justice. Our anger is always justified anger, our indignation, righteous indignation. In reading Torah and in life we must struggle against an easy literalism, and never more so than when we are tempted to believe that our indignation is righteous. Maimonides is right to insist that God does not have human emotions. Whatever an "angry God" means—and it requires serious study—we must remember that an angry person is no better than a fool. ■

Rabbi Mark S. Diamond

Mark S. Diamond is the rabbi of Temple Beth Abraham in Oakland, California. He coordinates a team of rabbis answering questions and writing articles for AOL's Jewish Community Online. Mark is married to Lois and is the father of Adina, Ariella, and Jeremy.

Mattot

Chapter 32 of the book of Numbers offers a profound insight into the psychological dimensions of the conquest of Eretz Israel. The tribes of Reuven and Gad appear before Moshe and the Israelite leadership with an unusual request. They seek to remain on the land to the east of the Jordan River, a region well suited to raising cattle.

Moshe responds to their request with a sharp rebuke. He compares this generation with the previous one, condemned to wander for forty years in the wilderness. "Are your brothers to go to war while you stay here?" he pointedly asks the Reubenites and Gadites.

What follows is a classic Torah narrative of *takhlis,* bargaining between Moshe and the tribal spokespersons. The tribes propose to build sheepfolds for their flocks and towns for their children east of the Jordan.

Then they will serve as shock troops in the fight to conquer the land west of the river.

Moshe's reply injects a spiritual note into the discussion. He reminds the tribes that the conquest is a sacred mission. If the Reubenites and Gadites fail to carry out their end of the bargain, they will have sinned against God.

There is one other subtle difference between the tribes' request and Moshe's counter-offer. They had asked to build sheepfolds for their flocks and towns for their children. Moshe inverts the order when he tells them to "build towns for your children and sheepfolds for your flocks" [Num. 32.24].

Commenting on this change, Rashi notes: They were more worried about their money than they were about their sons and daughters, since they mentioned their cattle first and their children afterward. Moshe admonished them, saying, "Don't do it that way. Put the most important things first and the less important things second. First build towns for your children and then sheepfolds for your cattle."

In the end the Gadites and Reubenites seem to learn their lesson. Their reply to Moshe [Num. 32.25-27] places their children and wives before their animals. And it mentions God as the driving force behind the conquest.

Initially the tribes of Reuven and Gad seem to have been motivated primarily by material gain. The region to the east of the Jordan was a land conducive to their livelihood. Who can blame them for asking to settle there and thus avoid the arduous conquest of the land to the west?

Moshe eventually accedes to their request, but not before he places their proposal in its proper context. These tribes came to realize that their priorities were *farblunget*, mixed up. Their spouses and their children were far more important than their material possessions.

How easy it is to lose sight of what really matters in our lives. So many of us have frenetic schedules, bustling about from meeting to meeting, appointment to appointment. There is precious little time for our families.

Whenever I meet with bereaved families prior to a funeral I ask them a series of questions about their deceased loved one. How sad it is when I learn that the deceased was totally wrapped up in his/her work or his/her communal responsibilities to the exclusion of family responsibilities. Too often I hear that so-and-so was always at work but never home. I have never heard a child or spouse complain that the deceased spent too much time with loved ones!

Mattot reminds us to reexamine our priorities from time to time. In so doing, may we lead lives that bring honor and meaning to ourselves, to our families, and to God. ■

יצאו מארץ מצרים

Parashat Mas'ei
Numbers 33.1-36.13

Rabbi Murray Ezring

RABBI MURRAY EZRING WAS BORN IN ROCK ISLAND, IL. HE IS CURRENTLY RABBI OF TEMPLE ISRAEL, CHARLOTTE, NC. RABBI EZRING HAS SERVED CONGREGATIONS IN BOCA RATON, FL, AND OCEAN TOWNSHIP, NJ, AND HAS SERVED AS CHAPLAIN FOR THE PALM BEACH COUNTY SHERIFF'S DEPARTMENT AND THE CHARLOTTE/MECKLENBURG POLICE DEPARTMENT.

M*as'ei* closes the book of *Be-Midbar* (Numbers). The parashah begins by recounting the route and encampments of our ancestors through the forty years of wandering in the wilderness of Sinai. On the steppes of Moav they are instructed to settle the land across the Jordan, dispossess all its inhabitants, destroy their idolatrous religions, and divide the land among the tribes by means of a lottery.

The borders of the Promised Land are described, and the Israelites are told to apportion part of the land for the Levites. Six of their cities are to be designated as places of refuge for those who unintentionally kill another human being.

The Torah then establishes the blood avenger, a family member who was designated to avenge the death of his kin. Suddenly the direction changes, and the issue of the inheritance rights of the daughters of Zelophe<u>h</u>ad are raised. The reading concludes: THESE ARE THE COMMANDMENTS AND STATUTES THAT THE LORD ISSUED TO THE ISRAELITES, THROUGH MOSES, ON THE STEPPES OF MOAV, AT THE JORDAN, NEAR JERICHO [Num. 36.13].

Every time I review this Torah reading I have the feeling that I have just concluded the Torah. It briefly describes the creation of the Jewish people and tells our ancestors how to physically conclude the process of becoming a nation. A few laws are enumerated or repeated, and then the entire revelation is concluded in the final sentence. If our tradition and many biblical researchers are correct, and the book of Deuteronomy was only discovered in the days of King Josiah, this may very well have been the conclusion of God's revelation. What better way to conclude the theological and historical creation of a nation than to briefly remind them of where they have been, what happened there, and what their mission was to be? Israel was about to confront her greatest threat: taking up residency among an alien culture that could lure her people away from God.

In many ways this parashah can be viewed as Israel's seatbelt. The

אלה **מסעי** בני ישראל אשר

safety belt in our automobiles gives us enough space to move and have forward and lateral motion, while at the same time preventing us from confronting the dangerous elements of the car with which we might have contact. That may well be the purpose of this week's parashah. It is similar to the cute story about little Yohanan, who comes home from religious school one day and asks his mother: "Mom, where did I come from?" Not believing her ears, the young mother begins to give her six-year-old a detailed explanation of the birds and the bees. When she finishes she asks Yohanan, "Do you understand everything I explained to you?" "Yes," he answered, "But Mom, David comes from Connecticut and Maurey comes from New York. I just wanted to know where I came from!"

As Israel began its conquest of the land promised to Abraham and entered, seemingly forever, an idolatrous community, she had to be reminded where she came from, what her mission was, and who her benefactor was if she was to remain a unique and identifiable entity. God's concern for Israel's identity parallels our fears regarding Jewish continuity in these United States.

SYNOPSIS: *Mas'ei is "the first ending" of the Torah. (The entire book of Deuteronomy is a coda.) We are on the eve of entering Eretz Israel. The journey is reviewed. The laws of settlement are taught. The boundaries of the Land as well as the allocation of priestly and refuge cities are clarified. In a related tangent, the distinction between murder and manslaughter is made clear. And a feminist coda is added with the laws of inheritance being bent for the daughters of Zelophehad.*

RASHI OF THE WEEK: This sidrah begins: THESE ARE THE JOURNEYS OF THE FAMILIES OF ISRAEL AS THEY WENT OUT FROM THE LAND OF EGYPT WITH THEIR TROOPS—UNDER THE HAND OF MOSES AND AARON. *Rashi asks:* Why do we need to know this? Why the "trip-tych"? Why are the stages of the journey elaborated? *His answer:* So that we can learn about the *hesed* (loving kindness) of The One-Who-is-Everywhere (God). *While God ordered them to spend forty years wandering in the wilderness, you should not think that this meant that they were traveling from place to place every day without rest. Rather, if you count, you can see that in forty years they had only forty-two campsites. But it is even less chaotic then that. In the first year after leaving Egypt they had fourteen campsites (leaving only twenty-eight "road trips" for the remaining thirty-nine years). These first fourteen were stops along the* way from Rameses to *Ritmah, where the first group of spies went out. It was a more or less direct route toward Israel until the spies changed the plan.*

We learn this from a series of verses. Numbers 12.16 says, AND AFTER THIS, THE PEOPLE JOURNEYED FROM HAZEROT (AND CAMPED IN THE WILDERNESS OF PARAN). *Then verse 13.2 says,* THEN THE ETERNAL SAID TO MOSES, "SEND MEN WHO WILL SPY OUT THE LAND." *Now in this sidrah it says,* AND THEY JOURNEYED FROM HAZEROT TO RITMAH. *By drawing the two verses together and sharing information we learn that Ritmah is in Paran and near Eretz Israel. Except for the spies, the journey would have been made in fourteen or fifteen steps, just like the Passover seder, the entrance to the Holy House in the Temple, and the way up to God's throne. The first spies' sins complicated the process, making it more like the flood and less like a direct ascent.*

Eight of the steps happened after Aaron's death at Mt. Hor (and took them to the plain of Moab) [Num. 33.38]. *These eight steps filled the last year, the fortieth. That left only twenty sub-journeys in thirty-eight years. This was not endless and pointless wandering. It was not torture but careful preparation.* This lesson I learned from Rabbi Moses *The Maggid*.

Rabbi Tanhuma had a different explanation of the lesson found in the listing of the stages of the journey. He used a parable. A king had an ill son whom he wanted to cure. He took him to a distant place to effect the cure. When they returned home he told his son the story of the journey. He said, "Here we slept. Here we caught cold. Here you had a headache." Even the failures are important stages in our spiritual journeys.

Mas'ei

The Siftei Tzadikim writes that this world is a world in which we are able to correct our errors. This is what differentiates us from the angels. Angels are referred to as standing. They only stand on a single step in the ladder of existence. They cannot improve or raise themselves. Human beings, on the other hand, can move from level to level by recognizing their inadequacies and trying to improve upon them. Each change we make that brings us closer to a life guided by Torah raises us closer to God. The Siftei Tzadikim believes that the travels and encampments of our ancestors in the wilderness are recorded in *Be-Midbar* to show how they changed during the forty years. Each stage of travel brought them a better understanding of what the Torah requests of us.

Nehama Leibowitz notes that Rashi's commentary the *Be'er Yitzhak* teaches us to see the recorded wanderings as the record of Israel's reward and punishment based on whether or not the people followed God's law. "This short listing of the stages of their wanderings was designed as reading material for them after they settled down in their homeland. Each stage that was noted...would enable them to recall what had befallen them at that place. They would accordingly take to heart the kindness shown to them by the Omnipresent and the sufferings they endured for their disobedience so that, in the future, they would act rightly and not sin."

Rabbi Tanhuma explained similarly: "These are the stages of the people of Israel." This may be compared to a king whose son was ill. They traveled to a distant place in search of a cure. When they returned home the father told the story of their wanderings. "This is where we slept. This is where we were sick. That was where your head hurt." So God said to Moses, List the places where they angered Me.

Imagine! Even after experiencing the splitting of the *Yam Suf*, the ten plagues, and the miracles in the desert, even after the Torah states THEN THEY BELIEVED IN GOD AND IN HIS SERVANT MOSES, our ancestors still strayed and needed to learn and relearn the lessons of faith and adherence to mitzvot.

Rashi quotes Rabbi Moses the Preacher to show how the stages of movement were divided. During the first year the children of Israel made fourteen journeys and camps. In the following thirty-eight years they moved only twenty times. In the course of the last year there were eight excursions. When the former slaves first received their freedom there were many lessons to learn, many places to experience. As they learned, the number of journeys required to build adherence to Torah lessened. They were able to stabilize their lives and stay in each place longer. Suddenly the new generation that was to enter the Promised Land assumed leadership. They had to relearn much of what their parents had learned through the difficult years in which the people's relationship to God was being formulated, and they therefore traveled eight times in the final year to rediscover the faith in God necessary to enter and conquer the Promised Land. Perhaps the great lesson in *Parashat Mas'ei* is one meant for all generations. Before we can make our mark in the world and add our *tikkunim,* our corrections, to the world, there are several stages of life through which we must travel.

In order to create a generation of Jews committed to God, Torah, and the betterment of the world we need to know "where we come from." We and our children must travel the life cycle of birth, education, bar/bat mitzvah, marriage, giving birth, and raising our children. We need these stages of life, complete with the trials and tribulations that accompany them, in order to raise ourselves closer to God as only human beings can. It is only at the end of the journey, as we, like our ancestors, are positioned on the border of the Promised Land, that we can really know how successful we have been. While we confront modernity and the siren's call of a secular and free American society, will we allow the seatbelt called Torah to pull us back into the safety zone of life as defined by God?

In Deuteronomy 27.9 we read, "ATTEND AND HEAR, O ISRAEL: THIS DAY YOU HAVE BECOME A PEOPLE TO THE LORD YOUR GOD." Was it on this day that the Torah was given to Israel? Was not this day in fact forty years after the Torah was given? The verse intends to teach that, to those who study Torah, it is as beloved every day as the day when it was given from Mount Sinai (*The Book of Legends*).

P.S. We are often reminded that "more than the Jewish People has kept the Shabbat, the Shabbat has kept the Jewish people." Referring to the opening words of this week's Torah reading, *Ahavat Torah* states that the letter *zayin* never appears in the listing of the encampments. He teaches us that this implies that the Israelites never traveled on Shabbat. ■

דברים

Devarim

משה אל כל ישראל

Open virtually any parashah in the Torah and you will find something that looks totally extraneous to the portion. Yet sometimes these extraneous diversions, usually ignored in sermons and *divrei torah*, concern some of the most important principles of Jewish life. Take *Devarim*, for example. The bulk of the portion is essentially the beginning of Moses' valedictory address in which he retells the history of Israel in the desert, explaining and adapting the details to his homiletical purposes.

Early in Moses' career he was confronted by his father-in-law, Jethro, with the fact that he could not possibly judge the entire people of Israel on his own. He was persuaded to establish a judiciary system to maintain public order and to provide judgment in matters of dispute. Jethro suggested the appointment of "CAPABLE MEN WHO FEAR GOD, TRUSTWORTHY MEN WHO SPURN ILL-GOTTEN GAIN" [Ex. 18.21]; that is, honest judges. The Torah then tells us [Ex. 18.25-26] that Moses set up these men as chiefs of thousands, hundreds, fifties, and tens and commanded them to judge all minor matters while bringing to Moses himself all difficult cases.

When we compare the parallel account in our parashah [Deut. 1.12-18] we see that many details are different. Here Jethro does not appear. Instead Moses commands the people to set up the judiciary because he cannot bear the burden

Parashat Devarim

Deuteronomy 1.1–3.22

Lawrence Schiffman

LAWRENCE H. SCHIFFMAN IS PROFESSOR OF HEBREW AND JUDAIC STUDIES AT NEW YORK UNIVERSITY. HIS LATEST BOOK, *RECLAIMING THE DEAD SEA SCROLLS*, IS PUBLISHED IN HARDBACK BY THE JEWISH PUBLICATION SOCIETY AND IN PAPERBACK BY DOUBLEDAY-ANCHOR.

דָּבָר אַחֵר DAVAR AHER. "**SO I TOOK YOUR TRIBAL LEADERS, WISE AND EXPERIENCED MEN, AND APPOINTED THEM HEADS OVER YOU**" [Deut. 1.15]. I have been trying to figure out how Moses went about choosing the judges. What criteria did he use? Was there a system of checks and balances? It made me think about how shofar blowers are chosen. There once was a boy who played trumpet in his high school band. Could he ever blow shofar! At that time the shofar blower in the main adult service was a man in perhaps his forties or fifties who was, frankly, not very good at it. The boy knew he could blow rings around the man. He was always asked to blow for the Hebrew school, for the children's services, and even for morning minyan during Elul. But never in the main services on Rosh ha-Shanah or Yom Kippur. You see, the man had been

alone. The judges are to be drawn from the heads of the tribes, who will serve as chiefs of thousands, hundreds, fifties, and tens as well as bailiffs for the tribes. The qualifications are here described not in terms of honesty but in terms of wisdom. These judges are to be "WISE, DISCERNING, AND EXPERIENCED" [Deut. 1.13]—certainly appropriate qualifications for judges.

But Deuteronomy now picks up on the motif of judicial honesty and adds material not found in Exodus. Moses tells us that he commanded the judges to listen to the cases and to judge honestly, whether between two Israelites or between an Israelite and a sojourner. Further, the judges are commanded to be impartial in judgment, whether to the lowly or to the exalted, and to "FEAR NO MAN, FOR JUDGMENT IS GOD'S." Moses again commands that difficult cases should be brought to him [Deut. 1.16-18].

A quick look at the two accounts will reveal the primary difference between them. Whereas in the Exodus account Moses chose only incorruptible men to serve on the judiciary, in Deuteronomy, after choosing men well versed in the law, Moses explicitly spells out for the newly appointed magistrates the requirements of honesty in terms of not granting favoritism to anyone, whether on the basis of social or of economic status.

What accounts for the difference between these two accounts? On the one hand it is possible to see this difference

---

active in the synagogue for years. Maybe once upon a time he had been better at it, and the job was still his. The boy thought that the best shofar blower should do it—maybe there should be annual auditions (which he was sure he would forever win). But it never came to pass. As a young adult he joined a new synagogue where the shofar blowing was, well, spotty. He knew he could do much better, but once again the honor went to others. But he became active in the congregation, worked on various committees, and contented himself with morning minyanim during Elul. Until one year one of the main blowers had a dental problem. At the last minute the now middle-aged man was pressed into service. And from then on, although he

SYNOPSIS: *Moses begins his farewell address. He reviews the journey from Sinai to Kadesh, the appointment of assistants, the journey to Horeb and to Kadesh-Barne'a, the people's refusal to enter the Land of Canaan, and then the allotment of land.*

RASHI OF THE WEEK: *Moses is reviewing. He is talking about the rebellions that followed the giving of the Torah at Sinai. He reminds the people that he had once said [Deut. 1.12], "HOW CAN I, ALONE, CARRY YOUR LOAD, YOUR BURDEN, AND YOUR FIGHTING?" Rashi notices the "triplet." He asks,* "Why did Moses say LOAD, BURDEN, and STRIFE? What does each one teach?"

YOUR LOAD refers to the Israelites' involvement in trials. Moses is telling us that the Israelites were difficult to have as litigants. When one of them saw that his opponent in a lawsuit was about to win the case, the soon-to-be loser would say: I have another witness to bring. I have more evidence to add. I want to add another judge to the court. And thereby convolute and distort the process of justice.

YOUR BURDEN teaches that the Israelites were disrespectful to judges. If Moses left his home early in the morning, they would gossip that perhaps something was wrong with his marriage. If he left his home late, they would say, "He has been sitting at home and devising evil plots against you, and schemes against you." These personal attacks came because he was a public official.

YOUR STRIFE: The families of Israel were always suing one another. They used litigation to solve personal feuds and clogged the courts.

These three nouns teach us that Moses was not complaining about the rejection of his personal leadership and authority, but rather the distortion of God's Torah through the denial of day-to-day justice.

as the result of interpretation. In many cases the book of Deuteronomy provides explanations for commandments found in the previous books of the Torah. So in this case we could say that the Deuteronomy account is simply an interpretation of file material in Exodus. The later account of Deuteronomy simply draws the logical conclusions. If Moses went out of his way to appoint honest and upright people to the bench, he must have instructed them in the need to maintain honest courts. So Deuteronomy fills in the nature of his charge to the new judges.

But this may not be the full story. What has apparently intervened is a confrontation with reality. Even following a simplistic reading of the Torah one can easily see that the Moses of Deuteronomy is a more seasoned and experienced leader who knows the challenges of reality. He himself has faced the constant rebellions of the Israelites against his authority and even against the word of God. We can assume that in the thirty-eight years that intervened between the setting up of the court system and his valedictory speech to Israel there have been instances of corruption, and that Moses is here strengthening the Torah's stand against it. Further, by the time of Deuteronomy Moses clearly understands that the system of justice he had established will be tested in an environment vastly different from that of the desert community of Israel. It will soon have to withstand the forces of urbanization and rapid population expansion expected after the Israelites' entry into the Promised Land and conquest of the cities of the Canaanites.

The importance to the Torah of strict legislation prohibiting judicial corruption is evident in a number of additional passages, only some of which can be mentioned here. Exodus 23.6–8 requires that false charges not be brought since they

---

Devarim

continues to blow at morning minyan, he has been one of the main blowers (who handle the various adult services). By now he's approaching fifty, an officer of the synagogue, still a darned good shofar blower, and very happy with that role (and the way shofar blowers are chosen). But come Rosh Hodesh Av, when he starts to practice to get his lip and wind in shape, he can't help wondering if there isn't some high school trumpet player out there who can blow rings around him. **David "Tekiah" Parker, <Parques@aol.com>**

would lead to the execution of innocent people. Further, the acceptance of bribes, so common throughout the ancient world and especially in ancient Mesopotamia, is expressly forbidden as a miscarriage of justice. Deuteronomy 16.19 repeats some of the very same rulings, emphasizing that bribery and favoritism are expressly forbidden.

But apparently these biblical laws were not considered strong enough for some Second Temple–period Jews. We can imagine that in Hellenistic times, especially in the years of Hellenization leading up to the Maccabean Revolt of 168-164 B.C.E., governmental and judicial corruption became a very serious problem. Even in the Hasmonean era, when Israel was led by the Maccabean kings [152-63 B.C.E.], corruption must have been quite common.

The author of the Temple Scroll, one of the Dead Sea Scrolls, took up this problem in detail [51.11-18]. Actually, this text is a compilation of some earlier legal and interpretive traditions that was edited and completed in the late second century B.C.E.

The author first repeats the basic biblical obligation to appoint judges and officers who will judge righteously and who are not to show favoritism or take bribes. Then the author begins to diverge from his biblical source. He tells us that corruption and perversion of justice "defile the temple with sinful transgression." Such transgression renders tenuous the rights of the people of Israel to possess their land, and the implication is that corruption will lead them to be exiled from the Land of Israel. In this respect the author is taking up an old prophetic notion that temple worship and sacrifice, and indeed the entire ritual system of Judaism, have no real meaning unless practiced in a climate of ethics and morality. This, in fact, is axiomatic to Judaism.

But the Temple Scroll goes much further. It rules that "the man who takes a bribe and perverts righteous judgment shall be put to death, and you shall not be afraid of putting him to death." This exceptional ruling, no doubt conditioned by the author's view that the Hasmonean judiciary was corrupt, was buttressed by biblical interpretations that were supposed to prove that the Bible itself mandated the death penalty for this violation of Jewish ethics and law. The scroll, we should note, also specifically included a law prohibiting the king from perverting justice or from confiscating the property of his subjects.

The Dead Sea sectarians were not the only Jews who had on the books a requirement of the death penalty for corrupt judges. This extremely strict ruling was also incorporated into the polemical work *Against Apion* by first century C.E. historian Josephus. This book is one of the first Jewish polemics against anti-Semitism and is a spirited defense of the Jews and Judaism against the false accusations of the anti-Semite Apion. Here Josephus says that the penalty for judicial corruption is death. This ruling must certainly have shocked his non-Jewish readers, for whom bribery was effectively the norm. In his retelling of the laws of the Bible in his historical work *Antiquities of the Jews* Josephus gives an explanation for the prohibition of bribery that is most interesting. He says that corruption makes God appear weaker than the litigant who gains favor by bribing the judge. After all, the judge sets aside the command of God in order to do the bidding of the one who paid him off.

With this heritage of prohibitions on bribery there was little for the rabbis of the Talmud to do but repeat these laws and spell out some of the specific details. But in the case of the death penalty for corruption, despite their disgust for judicial dishonesty and the many ways they sought to prohibit it, the rabbis had to admit the truth: The Torah never really imposed so severe a penalty on corrupt judges. While no effort could be spared to root out corrupt judges and to prevent bribery and dishonesty in the courts, the imposition of the death penalty was simply too extreme a measure. Instead the rabbis took steps to insure that judges would be universally drawn from the Rabbinic class, thus ensuring a specific training and moral sensitivity that they hoped to develop in their students. Thus one of the primary functions of the rabbi in pre-modern times became that of judge and arbitrator, a role that the traditional Bet Din continues to occupy for many Jews even today.

All Jewish interpreters throughout the ages would have agreed with the Rabbinic interpretation of Deuteronomy 16.20. This statement comes at the conclusion of a long discussion insisting on the highest standards of judicial honestly (*Sifre Devarim* 16-17). It was composed at a time when the Land of Israel was under foreign domination, the people of Israel were in part exiled from the land, and many Jews were threatened with physical destruction in the Diaspora. Yet this beautiful statement is equally true for us today, when once again there is a Jewish state and a Jewish judiciary:

"[RIGHTEOUSNESS, AND ONLY RIGHTEOUSNESS SHALL YOU PURSUE,] IN ORDER THAT YOU SHALL LIVE AND INHERIT THE LAND." This teaches that the appointment of (righteous) judges is sufficient to sustain Israel and to cause them to dwell on their land, and to prevent them from being destroyed by the sword. ■

Devarim

Devarim

Rabbi Elyse D. Frishman

Elyse D. Frishman is the Rabbi of Congregation B'nai Jeshurun, The Barnert Temple in Franklin Lakes, NJ. Additionally, Rabbi Frishman is a composer and editor of liturgy for the CCAR.

We live in the month of Av. I don't just mean that this is the month of Av; we live here. Much of Jewish culture, whether we accept it theologically or not, resonates from the destruction of the Temple. Themes of loss, mourning, and comfort reach as far as summer camp programs.

It is also a time of hope: We will survive. There's nothing that can be taken from us that will eradicate our people. The destruction of the Temple was horrific, the loss of our spiritual center. Yet we survive again and again.

Consider the month of Av as a time of beginning. Av: אב *alef, bet*...The letter א *alef* represents the beginning, certainly as the first letter of the אב *alef-bet*. Now consider its formation, composed of a ו *vav* and two יי *yods*. These, the pillar and wings of God's Name, hint that God is present. But that א *alef* also suggests the paradox of our relationship with God; it is a letter with no sound. God is here, but the silence is overwhelming.

Av: אב *alef, bet*...ב *Bet* is a בַּיִת *bayit*, a home, God's home. We push out our breath and make a sound in the silence, creating something out of nothing, and we become God's partners in creation. The vocalization of our breath is the sound of our souls. We invite God to dwell in our world.

Av: This is where we live. Aware of the possibility of God, overwhelmed by the silence. Yet, giving sound to our souls, God enters. Our world is filled. The destruction of the Temple leaves us in silence: where are You, God? Yet we learn to create many places for God to reside. So the paradox: God is here...Where? God is where?...here.

Devarim means "words." These *devarim* were spoken in the wilderness. As Moses spoke God's words the wilderness came alive; it was not an empty place, a barren site, not a place where we would wander without direction, aimless, lost, but a place where God would dwell. And in a place where God is, the wilderness is not overwhelming. Indeed, God revealed Torah to us there. Silence was transformed into word. א *alef* moved into ב *bet*. Torah.

Av: אב *alef, bet*. The beginning of sacred speech. From silence to sound; from emptiness to meaning; from singularity to community; from loss to renewal.

Even with Torah we continue to wander. We are not at our goal. What does it mean to wander for forty years? This is life! We live in the month of Av. We wander, we wonder, we grapple with God's expectations. God's words give meaning to the search, voice to the silence. Life challenges us with its great joys and deep pain. But we are not alone; we are a people on a journey, blending our voices to become a holy community. ■

Parashat Va-Ethannan

Deuteronomy 3.21–7.11

Rabbi Debra Orenstein

Rabbi Debra Orenstein, senior fellow of the Wilstein Institute of Jewish Policy Studies and instructor at the University of Judaism in Los Angeles, edited *Lifecycles 1: Jewish Women on Life Passages and Personal Milestones* (Jewish Lights Publishing, Woodstock, VT). She is a frequent guest lecturer and scholar-in-residence at synagogues, universities, and community centers throughout North

In this week's Torah portion we, along with the ancient Israelites, are reminded what it was like to be at Sinai, to hear God speak to us face to face, out of the midst of the fire [Deut. 5.4].

The dominant emotion, perhaps surprisingly, was fear. Throughout the Sinai experience the Israelites were overwhelmed and overawed, even terrified. Having had a taste of direct interaction with God, they wished to withdraw.

Later generations would seek lovingly to imagine and reenact this central event of Jewish history, but the people physically present at Sinai wanted dearly to escape:

"Behold, God has already shown us Divine glory and greatness, and we have heard God's voice out of the midst of the fire. This day, we have seen that it is possible for God to speak to a human being and yet for that person to live. But now, why should we die when this fire out of which God speaks may yet consume us? If we continue to hear the voice of *Adonai* our God any longer, we shall die...*You* go near [Moses,] and hear all that *Adonai* our God says and you speak to us all that *Adonai* our God speaks to you" [Deut. 5.21–24].

So Moses assumed the risk, acting as intercessor between God and the Israelites. The people thus quelled their all-consuming fear of a potentially consuming God. God, in turn, only wished that such awe would

---

דָּבָר אַחֵר DAVAR AHER. "Let me go over, I pray You, cross over and see the good land that is beyond the Jordan, that good hill country, and Lebanon [Deut. 3.25]. What the Torah doesn't tell us is that Moses was supposed to have died ten times in the wilderness already, but that he had beaten that fate, and at the end of forty years, as Moses stood on Mt. Nebo and gazed at the Promised Land in the distance, he argued his case with God. It was a private language, mostly hand signs and grunts. Moses distrusted spoken language; his brother Aaron would do his talking for him. Still, Moses was a natural storyteller. He could tell stories with few words, and everyone understood him. He talked with his hands a good deal, and his eyes. He could speak a whole story without words, and everyone would nod with understanding and delight. He was able to

be maintained [Deut. 5.26]! But the people's physical and emotional vulnerability at Sinai betrayed their moral and theological weakness: More than they craved God, they feared death.

The Midrash offers an interesting twist on this portrait of the fearful masses. "Why did everyone quake at Sinai?" the Rabbis ask. "Because God spoke words of life" [*Exodus Rabbah* 29.9]. It only *seems* that the Israelites feared death more than anything. What they really feared, according to this midrash, was life.

We think we are afraid of death—and we are. We are terrified to leave our loved ones, to face the unknown, to meet and be judged by God. But living, to paraphrase a Yiddish idiom, is not so easy either. Many of us are even more intimidated by living than by dying. At one time or another almost all of us have dwelt in a valley of the shadow of death, and often one of our own making. Dwelling in life, facing and embracing the world of the living, can be even

---

talk with few words because his soul was bound up with the people to whom he spoke; that was his power as a leader. The people would sit around the fire at night, and he would speak their inner life, he would describe how they felt, and he was almost always right.

His soul was so bound up with his people that when they were withheld from the Land it was only natural that he be withheld, too. Because they were Moses, and Moses was the children of Israel,

SYNOPSIS: *Moses prays to be able to enter this land. This is followed by a warning against idolatry, the cities of refuge, and then a review of the experience at Sinai, including the first paragraph of the Shema.*

RASHI OF THE WEEK: *Here is the most famous "triplet" in the Torah.* AND YOU SHALL LOVE THE ETERNAL, YOUR GOD, WITH ALL YOUR HEART, WITH ALL YOUR SOUL, AND WITH ALL YOUR STUFF [Deut. 6.5]. *Rashi wants to know:* What is the difference between HEART-love, SOUL-love, and STUFF-love?

WITH ALL YOUR HEART: Notice that word לֵב *Lev* (heart) is spelled with two *vavs* and not the usual one. (לְבָבְךָ *L'vav-kha* rather than לִבְּךָ *Lib-kha.*) This is to show us that we must love God with both sides of our heart—the *yetzer ha-tov* and the *yetzer ha-ra* (both the good and the evil inclination) [*Sifre Brakhot* 54a].

DAVAR AHER. WITH ALL YOUR HEART *teaches that the heart should not be divided from The-One-Who-is-Everywhere. One's passions should bind one close to God, not create separation or division. HEART-love is loving God through all of one's passions.*

WITH ALL YOUR SOUL: Evokes the story of the martyrdom of Rabbi Akiva. At his death he expressed joy at finally understanding SOUL-love. Even when God takes back our souls and our lives end we should still love God fully [*Sifre Brakhot* 54a. 61b].

AND WITH ALL YOUR STUFF: STUFF-love is about property. מְאֹדֶךָ *Me'odekha* means "your stuff." There are people who care more about what they own than they do about their lives.

DAVAR AHER. *The word* מְאֹדֶךָ me'odekea (STUFF) *may also be connected to the word* מִדָּה midah, *which means measure. STUFF-love may then teach us that whether God gifts us with a good* midah *or with a less fortunate* midah, *we should still love God. This is what King David was teaching in Psalm 116.13 and Psalm 116.3. First he says:* I WILL LIFT UP THE CUP OF SALVATION —*when things are good*—AND CALL UPON THE ETERNAL'S NAME. *And then he says:* IF I FIND TROUBLE AND SORROW—I WILL CALL UPON THE ETERNAL'S NAME.

CONCLUSION: And what kind of love is commanded in these three cases? The kind of love prescribed in the next verse: "THESE WORDS WHICH I COMMAND YOU THIS DAY SHALL BE ON YOUR HEART." Because through the mitzvot we come to know the Holy One and learn to cling to God's ways. *HEART-love, SOUL-love, and STUFF-love are all challenging and different ways of connecting to God—but all of them grow through Torah and the mitzvot.*

more challenging. To be so completely alive that you hear lightning and see thunder, as the Israelites were said to have done at Sinai, is both exciting and scary. To *know* by personal experience what it is to HEAR GOD'S OWN VOICE AND YET LIVE implies that you are vital and attuned—and that great things will be expected of you.

Life can be so frightening that we sometimes actually gravitate toward death. Most of us have known someone who chose to "deaden the pain" with a toxic addiction in order to avoid the frightening problems of living. Alcohol, other drugs, gambling, sex can all be used this way and, denial notwithstanding, can literally kill you.

There are people in the Middle East today who dread peace more than war, who fear cooperation with the wrong people more than killing the "right" ones. War is familiar. War they can handle. War has become, for some, an idol to worship. But the prospect of peace is frightening—so frightening that some terrorists have strapped bombs to their bodies and blown themselves up in a suicidal/homicidal frenzy rather than face peace. And even the people who desperately pray for peace and crave it and will be grateful when peace finally breaks out, unencumbered, in the Middle East are nevertheless scared of it. Israelis and their "enemies" alike will have to confront internal problems and divisiveness. They will have to redefine themselves affirmatively absent a common enemy. Israelis and Zionists know all too well who they are when confronted with the prospect of death and destruction. Who are we, once assured of survival? The blessing of peace is like the blessing of hearing God's voice. In the light of such gifts, who will we have to become? In the aftermath of such grace, what will take up our time and our thought?

Va-Ethannan

and what happened to them, happened to him. Still, he was never quite reconciled to his fate.

Moses said to God, "You called me as your servant, and I served."

God said, "No."

Moses said, "Let me sneak into the Land alone. No one has to know."

God said, "No."

Moses said, "Let someone carry my bones after my death into the Land, like Joseph."

God said, "No."

Moses said, "Adam disobeyed and you forgave him...."

God said, "No."

"Let me enter for two or three years, then I'll die...."

God said, "No. I have resolved that you should not go there."

We fear the unknown of death, and we fear the knowns and unknowns of life. Most of all, we have the *habit* of fear.

There is an existential double-bind around fear. We are afraid of failure and of success, of poverty and of plenty, of war and of peace, of enslavement and of freedom. Like the Israelites in the desert, we are afraid of not having God, so we build idols, golden calves, useless testaments to our own insecurity. Yet we are afraid of *having* God, so we avoid a direct relationship and assign someone else (Moses, a child we send to Hebrew school, a spouse, a rabbi) to deal with God in our stead.

What shall we do with all this fear? Nahman of Bratslav has an oft-quoted teaching: "Know! All the world is a very narrow bridge, and the main thing is not be afraid at all." We are not crazy for feeling scared. On the contrary, our existential situation, our humanity, our good judgment about the narrowness of the bridge on which we stand, all give us ample reason to be afraid. But if we are to succeed, we cannot give in to the habit, nor even the logic, of fear. We must ask instead: What would I do if the bridge were as wide as the water? What would I attempt if I were not afraid? What would I choose if I knew I could not fail?

"Choose" is the key word. By what criterion do you choose what to do? It is useless to decide on the basis of fear, because anything and everything may provoke fear. As noted, a thing and its opposite may both arouse fear. Choosing on the basis of what scares you will not usually clarify a decision. It will, however, reliably reenforce the inclination toward fear.

The Bible provides us with a very specific instruction on how to choose: *u-Vaharta ba-Hayyim:* "I HAVE SET BEFORE YOU LIFE AND DEATH, BLESSING AND CURSE, THEREFORE CHOOSE LIFE" [Deut. 30.19]. Faced with the choice between life and death, many of us wish for a third option! But, as the Talmud says in another connection, *palga berakia lo yahavey*—they do not grant halves in heaven.

Let's assume that we accept the truth of the opposition—we may choose life or death, not both, nor neither, nor something else entirely. How can this be applied as a guideline? What does *u-Vaharta ba-Hayyim* mean in practical terms?

It is a wonderful spiritual exercise to engage all the myriad decisions you make in terms of this Deuteronomic either/or. For a day or a week, act as if nothing is neutral. Make every decision—what you eat for breakfast, how you talk to strangers, what you do in your leisure time, how you vote in a board meeting—by choosing the option that most inclines you toward vitality, creativity, energy, life. Reject possibilities that tend toward depletion, destructiveness, death. (I once made this suggestion

---

So Moses appealed for help. He went to the earth. "O Earth, speak to God for me. Perhaps then God will have pity on me and allow me to enter the Land."

The earth said, "I have my own troubles, DUST YOU ARE AND TO DUST SHALL YOU RETURN—we're all in the same boat. I, too, grow old and pass away."

He went to the heavens. He went to the sun and moon. He went to the stars and planets. He went to the hills and mountains. He went to Mt. Sinai, who told him she was still sore from the fire and smoke during his last visit. He went to the rivers. He went to the deserts. He went to the great sea, who told him that she had been beaten up enough by Moses when he parted her waters for the people to pass.

Moses recalled all the wonderful things he had done in his youth. "In those days I was king of the world. Now I'm a beggar for my life." He began to cry. The angels came and snatched his tears and words away so that God wouldn't hear them, but God loved Moses like a mother and always knew when something was troubling him.

God said to Moses, "Don't be afraid. It is not written that you should enter the Land. It was decreed before I created the world, and

to a synagogue group, and a woman objected that we are commanded to choose life all the time, not just for a day, week, or month. She was perfectly right, but I am recommending an intense, single-minded focus on the life-versus-death paradigm for a discrete period of time. This can be immensely illuminating *and* can produce skewed results. Long-term decisions may differ from those of the short term. Over the course of a day the life-affirming decision for breakfast might be "chocolate chip cookie dough." Exercised over the course of a year, that same choice would be anything but.

Whether applied for a day or a lifetime, *u-Vaharta ba-Hayyim* excludes fear as a consideration. It is amazing how choices become clear, how we do things differently and nonetheless when life, not fear, is the decisive criterion. Gradually fear loses its power. In the choice between life and death, fear has no vote.

The rabbis do suppose, however, that love may have a vote. At Sinai the Israelites suffered from a fear of intimacy with the Divine, as it were. Under these conditions one can focus on the fear or on the intimacy. The ancient sages recommend the latter. Fear and love, they say, cannot occupy the same heart at once. On the verse YOU SHALL LOVE ADONAI, YOUR GOD [Deut. 6.5], found in the Shema prayer and in our Torah portion, the Sifrei comments: "You [should] perform the commandments out of love, for you cannot have love where there is fear, or fear where there is love." Though we are commanded more than once in *Va'Ethannan* to fear God [Deut. 6.2,13, 24], the Sifrei and, later, Rashi hold that fear is a poor motivation for making decisions or following commandments.

When we look carefully at the events of the Sinai experience as related in this portion, it becomes obvious that love is as prevalent, though not as clearly verbalized, as

---

Va-Ethannan

yours is not to ask why. It just is. Now quit feeling sorry for yourself. It doesn't suit you."

Moses said, "I'm their leader, I earned it."

God said, "It's time for Joshua to take over."

So Moses spent his last days on a mountaintop, gazing longingly into the Promised Land in the distance, only partially resolved to the hand that had been dealt to him, thinking, It should have been me. **James Stone Goodman, <Stavisker@aol.com>**

fear. Underneath all the dread at Sinai is the longing for life and connection. The primary fear is not of God but of losing God's love. Yet we are assured in Va'Et<u>h</u>anan that God's love is not based on our deeds nor on our (ha!) impressive numbers. God's love is based in our history, our covenant, our relationship. God loves us, like any good parent, simply because God raised us. Simply because we are God's children.

May all God's children find the love that lies beneath our fears. May we be guided by life and love in our many choices. And may we brave the radiance, adjust our eyes, and know: Fear will never steady us on a narrow bridge, but God will carry us across. ■

Ira J. Wise, R.J.E.

Ira J. Wise, R.J.E. is Director of Education of Congregation B'nai Israel in Bridgeport, CT.

Va-Ethannan

The Israelites are near the end of their forty years of wandering. They stand at the edge of the Promised Land. Where have they come from? A little over three books and four centuries earlier, the first Jewish family (although they weren't called Jews yet) came to Egypt as refugees seeking famine relief. They were welcomed by their long-lost brother Joseph, who had attained a very powerful position in the Pharaoh's government. As we all know, a few generations after Joseph and his brothers the Israelite people were no longer viewed as guests by the Egyptians. They had been made into slaves. What had been an extended vacation or study abroad had become a form of exile. They were no longer free.

Many trees have been felled over the past two decades to allow discussions of whether or not Jews outside the land of Israel are in a state of *galut*—exile. Are Diaspora and exile synonymous?

Is there a difference between our circumstance and what the Israelites enslaved in Egypt felt? Certainly our situation is less immediate, less filled with danger or hardship. Like the Israelites in Egypt, we do not live in the Land with a capital "L." We do, however, have two things they did not.

First, we have a choice. The land of Israel is ruled by Jews—for the first time in nearly two thousand years. Second, we have a longer historical view. We know what happened in Egypt, in Israel under King David: we know about all of the wars and kings, the destruction of two temples, exile by Babylonia and again by Rome, the Crusades, England, Spain, and Germany. We also have had the positive events in history: redemption from Egypt, receiving the Torah, rebuilding the Temple, the Maccabees, Rashi, Rambam, and Herzl, the revival of Hebrew and the modern State of Israel.

Exile happened a lot. First from Egypt. Then the Assyrians deported the ten northern tribes—who were lost to history. Then Babylonia. And Rome. Nineteen hundred years passed. Each year we said, "Next year in Jerusalem." In 1948 Jews made that hope a reality. For the past fifty years we have had the option of return open to us. At the same time we have lived in freedom as full citizens of North American democracies. It sure doesn't feel like exile.

But back to the text. Moshe is near the end of his life. In order to make certain the people have learned from their experiences, he is going over all of the instructions one more time. He also reviews what will happen if the people do not uphold the covenant.

In my religious school we don't have punishments. If you misbehave, neither the teacher nor I come up with some activity that is meant to correct your behavior. I believe that punishment is nothing more than creating a conditioned response, much like training an animal to respond to pain and pleasure by performing specific actions. Students are not animals—usually. Conditioned responses are not our goal. We want our students to learn how to do the right thing. We use consequences. There are specific things that happen if you behave inappropriately. Everyone knows what they are before the school year even begins—or at least we tell them in writing, if they choose to read it. If you do A, then B will happen. What Moshe is saying in our reading is if you do A—pray to idols instead of God—then B will happen—you will be exiled from the Land. And everything that has happened since Abraham first heard from God in chapter 12 of Bereshit has told us that if we do not maintain a connection with the Land, we are somehow incomplete as a people. Therefore being exiled is not unlike having a leg amputated because we didn't take good care of ourselves. Exile, therefore, is the worst of possible consequences.

This piece of the sidrah is also about leadership. And this provides us with a segue from the theme of exile, which we explored last week, to the theme of leadership that is the topic of the coming week. Moses is perhaps, after God, the finest example—the paradigm—of what Jewish leadership is about. Even at the end of his life he does not retire. He tries to make certain the people have learned the lessons of exile and how dire the consequences are for praying to other gods. The book of Deuteronomy is his ethical will, his last chance to teach the people what he tried to teach them all his life. Significantly, he is rarely referred to as "the leader"; we call him Moshe Rabbenu—Moses our teacher.

Leadership, then, is about teaching: by instruction, by example, by using consequences. That also implies Moses living with the consequences himself. He acts incorrectly and is prevented from entering the Land. He too suffers consequences—as did the entire generation of the Exodus, which has completely died out except for Joshua. But he remains a teacher to the end. He uses his own fate as an object lesson: "See—I did wrong. The people I led also did wrong, and as their leader I bear responsibility. Be careful and do the right thing."

He certainly paints a dire picture. But he also holds out hope: "BUT IF YOU ASK THERE FOR ADONAI YOUR GOD, YOU WILL FIND GOD, IF ONLY YOU SEEK GOD WITH ALL YOUR HEART AND WITH ALL YOUR SOUL WHEN YOU ARE IN DISTRESS BECAUSE ALL THESE THINGS HAVE BEFALLEN YOU, AND, IN THE END RETURN TO ADONAI YOUR GOD AND HEAR GOD'S VOICE. FOR ADONAI YOUR GOD IS A COMPASSIONATE GOD AND WILL NOT FORGET YOU AND WILL NOT LET YOU BE DESTROYED AND WILL NOT FORGET THE COVENANT GOD MADE WITH YOUR ANCESTORS" [Deut. 4.29–31].

Part of our job as Jews is to try and emulate Moshe's leadership. We must try to be teachers to ourselves and others. The curriculum is clearly written in the Torah and in the life of our people. ■

Parashat Ekev

Deuteronomy 7.12–11.25

Rabbi Gordon Tucker

Gordon Tucker is Rabbi of Temple Israel Center, White Plains, NY. He is also Adjunct Assistant Professor of Jewish Philosophy at the Jewish Theological Seminary of America.

The literary setting of the book of *Devarim* (Deuteronomy) is Moses' great address to the Israelites in the weeks before his death. As for its historical setting, a number of views exist. Most scholars consider *Devarim* to be a product of the late stages of the Israelite monarchy, and it is generally connected to the book found by the High Priest Hilkiah in the Temple in Jerusalem in the year 622 B.C.E. (see II Kings 22.8ff). Many believe it to have flowed originally from prophetic circles in the Northern Kingdom of Israel (which, beginning in the tenth century B.C.E., after the reign of Solomon, incorporated ten tribes that became separate and distinct from the Jerusalem-based Kingdom of Judea).

Indeed, the book of *Devarim*, whatever its origin, has much in common with the milieu of the Northern Kingdom in the last decades before its unraveling and ultimate destruction at the hands of the Assyrians in the year 722 B.C.E. Those decades prior to the demise were marked at first by a good deal of prosperity. It took a prophetic eye (such as that of the prophet Hosea) to be able to see beyond short-term political and economic gains to the collapse that would be brought about not only by external pressures, but also by the underlying corruption of the society. *Parashat Ekev*, which brings almost to a close the lengthy preamble of *Devarim*, treats, in two separate sections marked by high oratory, a theological/psychological problem that makes even more probable the connection between *Devarim* and the Ten Tribes.

But one need not take a critical, historical stance *vis-à-vis* the Torah to appreciate this parashah. It is unquestionably also a valid reading to understand Moses, in the last weeks of his life, looking beyond the Plains of Moab, across the Jordan River, to a land rich in potential and the promise of prosperity and foreseeing some of the very problems that would plague Israelites of future centuries. The snag, put simply, is the tendency of human beings and the societies they form to convert prosperity into complacency. It is the tendency to infer from prosperity one's moral

והיה עקב תשמעון את

rectitude. Doing *well* is not always the same as doing *good*, but many people, societies, and religious traditions have failed to make that distinction. We are perplexed when those who do good do not do well (i.e., we often ask "Why do the righteous suffer?"), yet circumstances force us to accept the fact that the one does not necessarily involve the other. What seems harder for us to catch on to is the fact that doing well—having success, particularly material success—does not mean that we have achieved a moral high point and that we can let our guard down. The less-than-righteous can often prosper, but they are no more righteous for having achieved comfort.

The whole first part of this parashah describes all the blessings that the Israelites will earn if, upon entering the Land, they live up to God's expectations of them, and there is a beautiful and graphic description of the richness of the Land that they are about to inherit:

"...A LAND OF WHEAT AND BARLEY, OF VINES, FIGS, AND POMEGRANATES, A LAND OF OLIVE TREES AND HONEY; A LAND WHERE YOU MAY EAT FOOD WITHOUT STINT, WHERE YOU WILL LACK NOTHING; A LAND WHOSE ROCKS ARE IRON AND FROM WHOSE HILLS YOU CAN MINE COPPER" [Deut. 8.8-9].

And then follows a sentence that we know so well from *Birkat ha-Mazon*, the grace after meals: "WHEN YOU HAVE EATEN YOUR FILL וְאָכַלְתָּ וְשָׂבָעְתָּ *v'Akhalta v'Savata* GIVE THANKS TO THE LORD YOUR GOD FOR THE GOOD LAND WHICH HE HAS GIVEN YOU" [Deut. 8.10].

There's the crucial word in this section, the word וְשָׂבָעְתָּ *v'Savata*—and you shall be full or satisfied. The sense here is not simply that you will be filled with food and drink, but that you will be satisfied with yourselves, that you will be self-satisfied, full of yourselves. Indeed, this extension of the meaning of וְשָׂבָעְתָּ *v'Savata* is borne out by the sequel in the biblical text: "TAKE CARE LEST YOU FORGET פֶּן-תִּשְׁכַּח *Pen-Teshkah* THE LORD YOUR GOD, AND FAIL TO KEEP HIS COMMANDMENTS, HIS RULES, AND HIS LAWS, WHICH I ENJOIN UPON YOU THIS DAY." Be careful that in the midst of this satisfaction, this self-satisfaction, you do not forget God's mandate upon you. "WHEN YOU HAVE EATEN YOUR FILL...BEWARE LEST YOUR HEART GROW HAUGHTY וְרָם לְבָבֶךָ *v'Ram l'vavekha*." Beware of becoming haughty, and of concluding that it was your moral worthiness that brought you this prosperity.

H. L. Ginsberg, the late revered professor of the Bible, pointed

SYNOPSIS: *The review continues with the connection between following God's ways and being blessed, the warning not to be self-righteous, and a reminder of the importance of history.*

RASHI OF THE WEEK: *This sidrah begins incoherently with the word* עֵקֶב *Ekev, which means "heel." The JPS* New Torah Translation (1967) *skips the difficulty and reads:* "AND IF YOU DO OBEY THESE RULES AND OBSERVE THEM FAITHFULLY, THE LORD YOUR GOD WILL MAINTAIN FOR YOU THE GRACIOUS COVENANT THAT HE MADE ON OATH WITH YOUR FATHERS" [Deut. 7.12]. *The verse begins:* וְהָיָה עֵקֶב תִּשְׁמְעוּן אֵת הַמִּשְׁפָּטִים ***v'Ha-Yah EKEV ti'Shmun et ha-Mishpatim.*** The word עֵקֶב *EKEV seems both unnecessary and incoherent. The JPS translation just skips it. It reads as if the word were missing from the verse. It is a problem of both "meaning" and "extra language."*

Rashi centers in on the word and makes midrash. He says: If you do the easy mitzvot, the ones that people just tread on with their heels (and don't get down into) and you observe these, then...*He is saying, "The heel is the part of the foot that feels least. It is hard and callused. We don't notice texture when we step with our heel. We skip a lot of pain when we step with our heel. Some people hop over mitzvot, getting them done but not feeling them. They skip the texture, they skip the pain—and lose the experience." This is especially true of mitzvot that seem easy, which we do on auto-pilot. Rashi is telling us that mitzvot are to experience, not just to get done and check off. They are not matters of the heel. He finds a lesson in the word others skip over.*

out the great similarities between the extended sermon in *Parashat Ekev* and a brief pronouncement by Hosea, the prophet of Northern Israel:

"WHEN THEY GRAZED, THEY WERE SATED; WHEN THEY WERE SATED, THEY GREW HAUGHTY; AND SO THEY FORGOT ME.

כְּמַרְעִיתָם וַיִּשְׂבָּעוּ שָׂבְעוּ וַיָּרָם לִבָּם עַל-כֵּן שְׁכֵחוּנִי

k'Maritam va-Yisba-u Savu va-Yaram Libam Al Keyn Shikhahuni" [Hosea 13.6]. (Notice the appearance of the three critical Hebrew roots we've already seen—**שבע** [TO BE SATISFIED], **שכח** [TO FORGET], **רמה** [TO BE HAUGHTY]).

The admonition here is clear. The possession of the Land of Canaan was God's will for Israel. We may say, by extension, that the possession of the earth is God's will for humankind. We might even say that it is given to us as an advance against our meeting God's expectations. But it is not an unconditional grant. And as soon as we let our moral guard down, as soon as we allow injustice and corruption to creep in, the prosperity that tends to turn our eyes away from that corruption and our minds away from self-scrutiny will not long endure.

When the Religious Kibbutz Movement looked for an appropriate Torah reading for Yom Ha'Atzmaut, Israel's Independence Day, they chose the beginning of *Parashat Ekev*. But they did not choose to read just the first of the seven aliyot into which this parashah is divided, even though that would have had more than enough text and would have ended with the glorious description of the Land cited above. Rather, they chose to continue this reading into the second aliyah and to include this last cited passage, which makes it clear that the success—military, economic, political, material—that the Jewish people have in its land today, as it had in ancient times, must never become a substitute for moral self-examination and refinement. The modern grant of the Land is, like the ancient grant, conditional.

This idea is reinforced in a striking way at the end of our parashah, where the Land of Canaan is again described in flattering terms:

"FOR THE LAND THAT YOU ARE ABOUT TO ENTER AND POSSESS IS NOT LIKE THE LAND OF EGYPT FROM WHICH YOU HAVE COME. THERE THE GRAIN YOU SOWED HAD TO BE WATERED BY YOUR OWN LABORS, LIKE A VEGETABLE GARDEN; BUT THE LAND YOU ARE ABOUT TO CROSS INTO AND POSSESS, A LAND OF HILLS AND VALLEYS, SOAKS UP ITS WATER FROM THE RAINS OF HEAVEN. IT IS A LAND WHICH THE LORD YOUR GOD LOOKS AFTER, ON WHICH THE LORD YOUR GOD ALWAYS KEEPS HIS EYE, FROM YEAR'S BEGINNING TO YEAR'S END" [Deut. 11.10-12].

This passage has, from a literary point of view, a beautiful complexity. On the one hand it seems to speak of some of the virtues of the land that the Israelites are about to enter. It is a varied terrain, it can receive adequate water from rainfall, and elaborate labors on irrigation canals and water drawing systems are not necessary. Moreover, it is a land in which God takes a special interest. On the other hand, it is unlike Egypt in another more grave respect: In Egypt water was available from the Nile's flooding, and human sustenance could always be achieved through the labor of irrigation. In the Israelites' new land, however, there are hills and valleys that cannot be irrigated in that way, and in any event there will be a dependency on rain. And our text tells us that God will be watching this land all year long. Watching for what? The immediate sequel is the very famous second paragraph of the Shema: "If, then, you obey the commandments that I enjoin upon you this day, loving the Lord your God and serving Him with all your heart and soul, I will grant the rain for your land in season, the early and the late. You shall gather in your new grain and wine and oil..." [Deut. 11.13-14].

Rashbam, Rabbi Samuel ben Meir, an important Bible commentator of the twelfth century, caught the meaning of this extended passage perfectly: "This land is the best land for those who keep God's commands, and the worst land for those who do not; for it is not like Egypt, which doesn't depend on rain, and where the hydration of fields can be taken for granted."

We might sum up the message of *Parashat Ekev* as follows: The Israelites are going to be expected to be "rainmakers," in both the literal and widest senses of that term. We may be unable to accept in simple form the Shema's notion that complying with God's will guarantees blessing. But we can and must acknowledge that a world in which prosperity is taken for granted is not a world in which morality is likely to flourish. Good fortune is sometimes unearned; and when it is, prosperity is best seen as an advance that must be continually justified by the ways in which we live. Remembering that is what Hosea expected of his fellow citizens, what Deuteronomy expected of all Israelites, and what we ought to hold ourselves to, wherever on God's earth we live. It is the antidote to self-satisfaction, to haughtiness, and to forgetfulness. It is the way in which we learn that however well we are privileged to do, the Torah is still primarily about the obligation to do good. ■

Rabbi Morley T. Feinstein

Morley T. Feinstein is rabbi of Temple Beth-El, South Bend, Indiana. He is the immediate past Treasurer of the CCAR and the author of *The Jewish Law Review volume 1: The Mishnah on Damages.*

Ekev

Suffering for Love

In *Parashat Ekev* the notion of יִסּוּרִין שֶׁל אַהֲבָה *yisurin shel ahavah,* is promulgated. God forced our travel/travail in the wilderness in order to "TEST YOU BY HARDSHIPS TO LEARN WHAT WAS IN YOUR HEARTS" (Jewish Publication Society), "TO HUMBLE THEE, AND TO PROVE THEE, TO KNOW WHAT WAS IN THY HEART" (Koren), "IN ORDER TO AFFLICT YOU, BY TESTING YOU, TO KNOW WHAT WAS IN YOUR HEART" (Fox, *Schocken*). שֶׁל אַהֲבָה יִסּוּרִין *Yisurin shel ahavah*—chastisements of love—are the Olympics of suffering, as Plaut translates, "IN ORDER TO AFFLICT YOU FOR THE PURPOSE OF TESTING YOU" [Deut. 8.2].

The verb used here, עַנּוֹת *anot,* can refer to both physical and spiritual deprivation. In Exodus 1.11 it refers to the oppression of the Israelites by the Egyptians. Forced labor was indeed an affliction. But it also refers to the self-denial on Yom Kippur [Lev. 16.31], which, though of a physical nature, has a deeply spiritual side to it. While it was the Egyptian taskmasters who afflicted the Jews in Egypt, these chastisements of the desert were of God's doing.

Rabba, although some say Rav Hisda, taught in the *Talmud Berakhot* [5a] that if there really is nothing that's objectionable in behavior, no sin or transgression that has occurred, suffering must be attributed to the neglect of Torah study. And furthermore, if this was really not the cause, the difficulties and afflictions of this world would be considered chastenings of love. This Rabbinic notion suggests that the righteous are visited with such sufferings because they alone can bear יִסּוּרִין שֶׁל אַהֲבָה *yisurin shel ahavah* in love.

Rabba also taught in the name of Rav Sakhorah, in the name of Rav Huna, that the Holy-and-Blessed-One, when pleased with someone, crushes the person with painful sufferings. Rav Haggai, quoting Rav Yitzhak, taught in *Pesikta de Rav Kahana* [24.2] that the awesome nature of God's work in the world to come will make up for the afflictions God brought upon people in this world. The Italian commentator Ovadiah Sforno says that such testing affords the individual an opportunity to do God's will. How difficult a notion to comprehend in light of the burning of churches now! Are these tragedies indeed God's chastisements of love?

As we watch the houses of prayer burn in flames, who would have thought that a place where the name of God was raised in joy and jubilation would be torched by those opposed to the worship within? Since people pray to the same universal God, why would it matter that the words or the customs of the people might be a bit different from those of the arsonists? Sadly, the burning of over thirty black churches in the South hearkens back to the terror the Jewish people felt during Kristallnacht in 1938.

Kristallnacht was a night of horror sanctioned by the Nazi state and its offices, creating a frenzy of violence that shocked the civilized world. Hundreds of synagogues in Germany and Austria were ransacked, leveled, and destroyed. Innocent people were hurt because they were Jews; others were arrested, humbled by the SS, and eventually sent to concentration camps. Those sites return to my mind as I see the churches of African Americans smoldering in flames.

The Holocaust was a period of evil when good people stood by instead of confronting and opposing wicked and inhumane behavior. Shall we, too, stand by as our neighbors' homes for prayer are declared unworthy and torched to the ground? Are these tragedies indeed God's chastisements of love?

How shocking to learn a thirteen-year-old white child was arrested. *South Pacific* had lyrics that went "You have to be taught how to hate"; this student must have been a terrifically competent student. Another defendant arrested for two church burnings in South Carolina allegedly has ties to the Christian Knights of the Ku Klux Klan. Are we at all surprised to learn how much their love of white people is translated into the affliction of others?

We Jews have a long memory stretching back to the time of the Bible. We understand the pain and humiliation our people suffered, and each year during Passover we rekindle the memory and sear the feelings of deprivation into our soul. Because our people perished and burned in synagogues, we have a strong determination that such acts of wanton violence never again be perpetrated, and that the greater cause of justice be served by our words and deeds.

Sadly, our awareness of these tragedies is heightened as we observe *Tisha b'Av,* as we commemorate the destruction of both Temples, the fall of Betar, Bar Kokhba's fortress, the expulsion of the Jews from Spain in 1492. Can we see the destruction of a house of worship and not reflect on our people's own history, the burning of our synagogues, our Temple in Jerusalem in flames? Though most of the Jewish community seek to observe the commemoration of the Shoah on 27 Nisan, there is a minority who would prefer to see the Shoah in light of all the calamities that befell our people, by including its commemoration on Tisha b'Av. How does our people, having experienced such suffering, explain how holy sites can be turned to ashes?

יִשּׁוּרִין שֶׁל אַהֲבָה *Yisurin shel ahavah*—chastisements of love—is a difficult theological notion to accept, living in a post-Shoah world. Can we truly believe that God would cause the suffering of so many or of just a few as a test? Maimonides in the *Guide of the Perplexed III.* 24 logically pummels this view that "God sends down calamities upon an individual, without their having been preceded by a sin, in order that his reward be increased." This principle is not mentioned in the Torah explicitly. The meaning of the trials mentioned in the Torah is that they took place in order to test and to receive information so that one can know the degree of faith or the degree of the obedience of the individual or nation in question. It may suggest that God sometimes makes an individual suffer in order that his reward be greater. But this is not the truth of the matter. It is hard for us in a post-Holocaust world to accept such sufferings as an airplane disaster, cancer, or the burning of a house of worship as God's will.

The prophet Isaiah says, "In all their troubles, God was troubled/in all their afflictions, God was afflicted" [Is. 63.9]. When commenting on this in *Exodus Rabbah* 11.5, the Midrash teaches, "The Holy and Blessed One said to Moses: 'Do you not feel that I am in pain just as

Israel is in pain? Understand this from the place out of which I am speaking to you: the thorns (for God called to Moses from the thorn bush) [Ex. 3.4]. If one could possibly say so, I'm sharing Israel's sufferings.'" God stands with the people in the midst of their distress, their affliction, their trouble. God feels the people's pain even while giving them chastisements of love.

I had a congregant in South Bend who was very hesitant to speak about her experiences during the Holocaust. Somehow I gained her trust, and she invited me to her house to see her photographs from over fifty years ago. In her living room, seated on a couch, she gently opened an old photo album. Inside was a black and white photo whose image gripped me. She explained it as the photograph of her synagogue with her father standing in front—a synagogue that was no more. It had been terrorized during Kristallnacht and burnt to the ground. With a voice haunted by her history, she said to me, "I hope it never happens again." I wonder what she is feeling now seeing churches, houses of worship, places for congregations to gather, safe havens of prayer and study, in flames.

Would she describe these church burnings as chastisements of love, יִשּׁוּרִין שֶׁל אַהֲבָה *yisurin shel ahavah*? Are they the sufferings and disciplines of people who believe in God? I think not. Rather, she would echo the words of Elie Wiesel: "I would like to be able to tell them that in spite of endless disillusionments one must maintain faith in humankind; that one must never lose heart. I would like to tell them that, notwithstanding the official discourses and policies, people do have friends and allies and reasons to advocate hope. But I have never lied to them, I am not going to begin now. And yet...despair is no solution, I know that. What is the solution? Hitler had one. And he tried it while a civilized world kept silent. I remember. And I am afraid." ■

ראה אנכי נתן לפניכם

Parashat Re-eh

Deuteronomy 11.26-16.17

Dr. David Lieber

Dr. David Lieber is President Emeritus of the University of Judaism in Los Angeles and Skovron Distinguished Professor of Biblical Literature. He is the President of the Rabbinical Assembly.

This parashah sets the tone for the whole book of Deuteronomy. It opens with a reference to a covenant ceremony that is to take place as soon as the Israelites enter the Promised Land and closes with the assurance of the Divine blessing if they are obedient to God. In between it highlights what the covenant requires: the total rejection of pagan practices and customs, the establishment of a just and compassionate society, and the proper worship of God. This is what it means for Israel to live up to the Divine call to be a holy people and God's "special treasure."

It is well known that one of the reasons the book found in the Temple during the age of Josiah [II Kings 22.8 ff] is identified with Deuteronomy is the requirement in the parashah for the centralization of the sacrificial cult.

No fewer than sixteen times is the Israelite enjoined to journey to the place God has chosen to bring offerings and tithes. Nor can a festival celebration be complete without a pilgrimage to the place where "God chooses to have His name dwell." This designation appears eight times here and is found in a variety of later texts ranging from Kings to Chronicles. Plainly, it is intended both to affirm and to deny a truth concerning the Temple. Yes, it is God's "place" where God can be encountered and approached. No, God does not "dwell" there since, as Solomon puts it, "Even the heavens, the heavens of the heavens, cannot contain You, how much less this house that I have built" [I Kings 8.27]. It is an ingenious way of resolving both a theological problem and a practical one. The practical problem is the obvious absence of God's presence, God's failure to respond on occasions when people come to the Temple to cry out for help. The theological one is that of God's transcendence of the world in which God is also supposed to be immanent. God does appear at will at Horeb, for example, to pronounce demands to the people and is present for them in the sanctuary when they come to offer sacrifices and rejoice. At the same time, the Temple does not constitute the Divine residence. On the contrary, the one who brings the tithe calls on God to bless Israel from Heaven, which is God's holy abode [Deut. 26.15]. That is possibly why Deuteronomy, despite its concern for ritual purity or defilement, does not pay as much attention to purification rites as does Leviticus, for example.

Re'eh

The priests of the Temple, to be sure, are the seat of authority. They are the guardians of the law and experts in it. It is the prophet, however, who, independent of the Temple, is called by God to convey God's wishes to the people [Deut. 18.18]. The ancient symbols and expressions—the ark, the tabernacle, the כָּבוֹד *Kavod*—the visible manifestation of God—hover in the background, but they are no longer central. What matters most is the covenant with God and obedience to God's will and word, now embodied in the Torah.

That is expressed in a key verse in the parashah that reads: "AFTER YHWH YOUR GOD YOU ARE TO WALK, HIM YOU ARE TO HOLD-IN-AWE, HIS COMMANDMENTS YOU ARE TO KEEP, TO HIS VOICE YOU ARE TO HEARKEN, HIM YOU ARE TO SERVE, TO HIM YOU ARE TO CLING" [Deut. 13.5] (Fox translation). Compare this to Deut. 17.18-19, where the king is explicitly enjoined to write a copy of the Torah in order that he may learn "TO FEAR YHWH HIS GOD."

In his new translation Everett Fox replaces the literal translation "FEAR" with the phrase "HOLD-IN-AWE." It is, of course, an acceptable interpretation but does not convey the primary meaning of the term as it appears in numerous passages of the Bible. "TO FEAR GOD" is more than to stand in awe of God. It is to experience the kind of dread Moses felt when he hid his face for *fear* of looking at the Lord [Ex. 3.6], or that Jacob felt when he realized that he had slept in a place where God had appeared [Gen. 28.17]. In both instances what is represented is a fear of the awesome power of "the holy," which, as Rudolph Otto pointed out a long time ago, both attracts and overwhelms those who are confronted by it.

Interestingly, the injunction to fear God appears earlier in Deuteronomy in the same chapter as the more famous one to LOVE GOD. (Compare Deut. 6.13 with 6.5.) While the former leads to the exclusive worship of the God of Israel, the latter calls for a life devoted to the teaching and fulfillment of God's commandments. Both phrases—to fear God and to love God—as has been pointed out in recent years, refer to faithful obedience to the covenant, following the usage of the terms in Babylonian vassal treaties. This is consonant with Deuteronomy's stress on the centrality of the covenantal relationship between God and Israel and accounts for the renewal of the covenant during the reign of Josiah [II Kings 23.3].

And yet one cannot totally divorce the terms from their primary meaning, as is apparent from the comments of the ancient sages. "Let all your undertakings be for the sake of Heaven," reads a relatively early passage in a rabbinic text [cited in *Derekh Erez Zuta* 2.1]. "Love Heaven and fear Heaven." It is not enough to love God. One must also fear the punishments God has in store for those who disobey, as Rashi puts it. Still, Rabbi Shimon ben Elazar insists, "Greater is one who does (God's will) from love than one who does it from fear" [*B. Sotah* 31a].

What is the love of God? It is illustrated movingly in the words of the psalmist: "WHOM HAVE I IN HEAVEN BUT YOU? AND HAVING YOU, I DESIRE NOTHING ELSE ON EARTH. THOUGH HEART AND BODY FAIL; YET GOD IS THE ROCK OF MY HEART, MY PORTION FOREVER" [Psalm 73.25-26]. Again: "MY SOUL THIRSTS FOR YOU; MY BODY YEARNS FOR YOU, AS A PARCHED AND THIRSTY LAND THAT HAS NO WATER" [Psalm 63.2]. "MY WHOLE BEING CRIES OUT WITH JOY TO THE LIVING GOD" [Psalm 84.2].

These are clearly not conventional assertions. They are heartfelt statements reflecting deep emotion, describing the worshipper's longing for God, his or her sense of joy and feeling of serenity awakened by the Divine presence. No wonder the psalmist can proclaim: "I HAVE SET THE LORD BEFORE ME AT ALL TIMES: WITH HIM AT MY RIGHT HAND I CANNOT BE SHAKEN" [Psalm 16.8-6], perhaps the best all around statement of the meaning of spirituality in the Bible.

Interestingly, the American philosopher Santayana offered a secular definition of spirituality that is reminiscent of this verse: "A man is spiritual when he lives in the presence of the ideal, and whether he eat or drink does so for the sake of a true and ultimate good" [*Reason in Religion*, p. 193]. What is

SYNOPSIS: *Moses presents the great choice: the blessing or the curse. This is followed with prohibitions about eating blood and obeying false prophets—then a restatement of the laws of* shemitah *and* yovel *(Sabbatical and Jubilee years) and the pilgrimage festivals.*

RASHI OF THE WEEK: *This week Rashi teaches us how God teaches. This Torah portion begins with a famous Moses speech*: LOOK! I AM PLACING BEFORE YOU THIS DAY *A STATE OF* BLESSING AND *A STATE OF* CURSE. THE BLESSING—IF YOU HEAR THE MITZVOT OF THE ETERNAL, YOUR GOD, WHICH I MAKE MITZVOT FOR YOU TODAY..." [Deut. 11.26].

*Rashi looks at the first word. "*Re'eh*" "Look!" and asks "*What were we supposed to see?*" For Rashi, the "Look" can't be symbolic—otherwise it was unnecessary (and for him, God is never redundant). Therefore, when God says* Re'eh, *there must be something to see. Rashi therefore comments, "Look ahead to verse 29." Blessings are connected to Mt. Gerezim and curses to Mt. Ebal.* "AND IT WILL BE, WHEN THE ETERNAL, YOUR GOD, BRINGS YOU INTO THE LAND YOU ARE GOING TO INHERIT, THAT BLESSINGS WILL BE GIVEN YOU ON MT. GEREZIM AND THE CURSE ON MT. EBAL." *The Targum understood this, translating this passage into Aramaic and commenting: "Those who pronounced the blessing (the* kohanim*) faced toward Mt. Gerezim and said the words 'Blessed be.' When they were done they turned and faced Mt. Ebal and said the corresponding curse. This still makes no sense to us, till we match this passage with Deuteronomy 27.2-8.* ON THE DAY WHEN YOU CROSS THE JORDAN...YOU SHALL SET UP GREAT STONES AND PLASTER THEM WITH PLASTER, AND WRITE ON THEM THE WORDS OF THE TORAH...WHEN YOU HAVE CROSSED THE JORDAN, YOU SHALL SET UP THESE STONES... ON MT. EBAL... *Mt. Ebal forms the connection. Israel is standing across the Jordan, ready to enter the Land. Moses describes Torah as a life-or-death experience. Mt. Gerizim and Mt. Ebal are in the distance. Twin peaks. Moses is foreshadowing the life-and-death nature of Torah that will be enacted when they enter the Land. The Talmud draws this together into a much clearer scene.*

Sota 32a: Six tribes ascended the summit of Mt. Gerizim, six tribes ascended the summit of Mt. Ebal, and the *kohanim* and Levites with the ark were positioned below in the center, the *kohanim* surrounding the ark, the Levites surrounding the priests, and all Israel on this side and that side, as it is said, AND ALL ISRAEL, AND THEIR ELDERS AND OFFICERS, AND THEIR JUDGES STOOD ON THIS SIDE THE ARK AND ON THAT SIDE, etc. (Josh. VIII, 33).

The *kohanim* turned their faces towards Mt. Gerizim and opened with the blessing: "BLESSED BE THE MAN THAT MAKETH NOT A GRAVEN OR MOLTEN IMAGE" (cf. Deut. 27.15), and both parties on both mountains responded, "Amen." Then they turned their faces towards Mt. Ebal and opened with the curse: "CURSED BE THE MAN THAT MAKETH THE GRAVEN OR MOLTEN IMAGE," and both parties respond, "Amen." So they continue until they completed the blessings and curses. After that they brought the stones [Deut. 27.2ff], built the altar and plastered it with plaster, and inscribed thereon all the words of the Torah in seventy languages used in the world, as it is said, very plainly. Then they took the stones and took apart the altar [Deut. 27.8] and went, and spent the night in their place in Gilgal where they were again set up [Josh. IV, 20]. *The lesson here: Look at those two mountains. They represent the peaks of hearing and not-hearing Torah. Each of us knows what it is like on each summit. Each of us has been in the valley. Choose where you want to stand.*

Re'eh

leading a spiritual life if not eating and sleeping and performing all of our waking activities with a sense that we are doing so in the presence of God, that all of our actions are guided by the desire to keep God in our lives. If this is so, spirituality does not differ from the effort to sanctify life, which, Dr. Finkelstein, *z"l*, pointed out a long time ago, is the defining characteristic of the Jewish religion.

To *believe in* God is to believe that human life is worthwhile, that it is not an accident, that the universe is shaped in such a way as to enable human beings to find meaning and fulfillment for their lives, that the resources for them to do so have been made available as well. This includes their freedom to make choices, to create relationships with others, and to fashion communities of meaning.

To *fear* God is to recognize the danger that threatens those who turn their backs on God in favor of lesser gods—money, fame, pleasure, and power. Ultimately these cannot satisfy, since they offer only transient purposes for living and keep us from enlisting in the service of the God who can sustain in times of crisis as well as joy and provide meaning to our lives that transcends our limited time and space.

To *love* God is to give ourselves to the creative power that keeps our world going, to recognize our own limits, and to live the kind of life that will justify our brief stay on earth and enable us to experience eternity in the ceaseless flow of time.

The parashah opens with reference to blessings and curses that God has set before us. It closes with a reprise of the pilgrimage festivals and the injunction that each individual is to appear before the Lord on them. This provides an opportunity for him and his family to rejoice on the festive occasion together with the entire community. For us, too, they remain a moving experience, since they reprise the great acts of God for our ancestors as well as God's bountiful gifts to us. They remind us of our responsibility to share our good fortune with others, each in keeping with the gifts we have received from God, thereby demonstrating that we seek to remain faithful members of the covenant community and servants of God.

It is noteworthy that the first three sentences in the parashah contain the word אָנֹכִי *Anokhi,* and the last, the phrase יהוה אֱלֹהֶיךָ *Adonai Elohekha*, the opening words of the Decalogue. Is that a chance occurrence, or have they been placed there to remind us that all that comes in between is designed to help us keep the Divine presence ever before us? ■

At the Boundary

Cantor Simcha Prombaum

CANTOR SIMCHA PROMBAUM IS SPIRITUAL LEADER OF CONGREGATION SONS OF ABRAHAM, LA CROSSE, WISCONSIN.

Re'eh

With a little help from the daily liturgy, the most popular imperative in Torah is Shema (listen, comprehend). But our parashah begins with the imperative *Re'eh* (see, perceive). The connection between perception and comprehension is worth exploring in some depth. In the learning process, which comes first? Perception. In the five books of Moses *Re'eh* is used fifteen times and Shema is used only ten. The gap between them narrows in the book of Deuteronomy, where *Re'eh* (seven mentions) and Shema (six mentions) come head to head in dramatic tension.

In Deuteronomy the failure of *B'nei Yisrael* to negotiate its new life on the frontier will result when *Re'eh* perceptions deviate from the Shema comprehension intended by Torah:

"THAT YOU NOT GO SCOUTING-AROUND AFTER YOUR HEART, AFTER YOUR EYES WHICH YOU GO WHORING AFTER"; and "TAKE-YOU-CARE, LEST YOUR HEART BE SEDUCED, SO THAT YOU TURN-ASIDE AND SERVE OTHER GODS AND PROSTRATE YOURSELVES TO THEM" [Numbers 15.39; Deut. 11.16; Fox translation].

As a cultural survivor of Egypt, Moshe is aware of the seductive pull of Canaan. This explains the motherlode of protective mitzvot he drops on the people in the book of Deuteronomy (fifty-five mitzvot in *Re'eh,* forty-two more in *Shoftim,* a total of one hundred and seventy by the end of *Ki Tetze*!). Moshe is gambling that unbridled *Re'eh* experience will be tamed by refraction through the lens of mitzvah, giving Shema comprehension a chance to be heard in Torah terms.

Alas! *B'nei Yisrael,* new driver's license in hand, will not be denied its own experiences within the new, expanding borders. The concept of the expanding border (גְּבוּל *G'vul* [גבל G-V-L root]) as it is developed in Torah sheds important light on the never-ending struggle between individualistic, self-absorbed, *Re'eh* perception and *Shema* comprehension for spiritual/communal good.

A גְּבוּל *G'vul* is a clear demarcation between the acceptable and the unacceptable, mine versus yours. Edom refuses to grant Israel passage through its territory, despite assurances by Moshe: "ON THE KING'S ROAD SHALL WE TRAVEL—WE SHALL NOT VEER RIGHT OR LEFT—UNTIL WE PASS THROUGH YOUR BORDER" [Num. 20.17; Artscroll translation].

But גְּבוּל *G'vul* is not always fixed and outward-looking in Torah. גְּבוּל *G'vul* looks inward on fluid, expandable turf shared by people, their community, and God. The forty-year wilderness encampment was cloistered and self-contained; the people and its holy institutions were one. Now the dynamic, expanding landscape will be different.

The chasm that separates desirable *Re'eh* and Shema connections can be bridged. For our גבל G-V-L root provides more than the hard defining line. It also means mixing and kneading. To get a good *hallah* for Shabbat, for example, the dough must have its diverse elements brought into balance with on another. Competing ingredients become one consistent unit through vigilant hands-on work.

Moshe had faith that we could triumph over our frontier experiences, assimilate them, balance them, and hear the Torah in them through the mediation of mitzvah. And the never-ending frontier beckons us even now. ■

שפטים ושטרים תתן לך

בַּמָּקוֹם אֲשֶׁר-יִבְחַר ה׳

At the Place That the Lord Will Choose

Parashat Shoftim
Deuteronomy 16.18-21.9

Rabbi Don Well

Rabbi Dr. Don Well is an eminent Jewish educator who served formally as the Executive Vice-President on the Board of Jewish Education of Greater New York and as President of the Hebrew Theological College in Skokie, IL.

One of the many enigmas the *Tanakh* presents in its various references to the eternal capital of Israel is the preponderance of Hebrew roots containing the letters [בחר] (*Bet, Het, Resh*) in connection with Jerusalem. Indeed, the very name of Jerusalem appears nowhere in the Torah itself. Instead it is referred to obliquely but repeatedly in *Devarim* simply as the PLACE WHICH THE LORD YOUR GOD WILL CHOOSE יִבְחַר *yiv'har*!

The great Song of Jerusalem in Psalm 122 shuffles the order of the letters, and, in the classic phrase from which our Sages extracted the concept of an earthly Jerusalem paired with a celestial one, Jerusalem is labeled the CITY WHICH IS JOINED TOGETHER חֶבְרָה *Hebrah*. The ultimate destiny of Jerusalem has been tragically designated twice in our history by the same single painful word, destruction חוּרְבָּן *Hurban*.

Through the subtle linguistic transformation of one root, rotating only the order of the same three letters, the entire tapestry of Jerusalem's history, from its initial selection through the articulation of its fundamental mission to its final devastation, is portrayed.

Let us examine the first of these expressions, which is reiterated staccato in *Parashat Shoftim* and its neighboring parshiot. The only other expression that appears with almost the same frequency in these parshiot is THE LAND WHICH THE LORD GIVES TO YOU. One wonders why Jerusalem is camouflaged and left unnamed, and why its as-yet-unrealized sanctity is harnessed to an act of God's choosing at some indefinite point in the future. Why is the Land—*Ha'Aretz*—given now, while the *Makom* to be chosen must await the revelation of its identity at a later date?

One possible answer is that THE PLACE WHICH GOD WILL CHOOSE is not designated by name for the simple reason that there was a succession of such places. The Mishkan was stationed in Gilgal,

Shoftim

Shiloh, Nov, and Givon before being permanently established in Jerusalem. The site chosen for the tabernacle therefore changed places, while the location of the Land was immutable.

Another approach might be to distinguish between Jerusalem, which the Almighty would choose four centuries later, only after it was conquered by King David, and the Land, portions of which were already in Israelite hands when Moshe delivered his historic closing speech, of which *Parashat Shoftim* is a part.

These explanations, however, fall short. A careful reading of the text will show that sometimes the Torah refers to THE PLACE WHICH GOD WILL CHOOSE and sometimes to THE PLACE WHICH GOD WILL CHOOSE TO PUT HIS NAME. If one studies the context of these subtle variations, it will be apparent that the generalized phrase, THE PLACE HE WILL CHOOSE, refers to the entire city of Jerusalem, whereas THE PLACE WHICH GOD WILL CHOOSE TO PUT HIS NAME specifically refers only to the *Bet ha-Mikdash* itself. According to halakhah, for example, the *Korban Pesah̲,* the Paschal Lamb sacrifice, had to be slaughtered in the Temple courtyard; it could, however, be eaten anywhere in the city. Thus the Torah instructs us to perform the sacrifice in THE PLACE WHICH GOD WILL CHOOSE TO PUT HIS NAME [Deut. 16.6] but permits us to eat it at our family seder anywhere in town—in THE PLACE CHOSEN BY THE LORD YOUR GOD [Deut. 16.7].

Without any doubt, therefore, the Torah already had Jerusalem in mind even though the tabernacle was destined to rest for a time in other locations and even though Jerusalem itself would remain a Jebusite fortress for another several hundred years.

To answer our question, then, we must look elsewhere. Let us first take note of a general theme in the book of *Devarim* that provides context for our discussion. That theme is the concept of וְהָלַכְתָּ בִּדְרָכָיו *ve-Halakhta bi'Drakhav*—of walking in God's ways. Recast in Latin as "*Imitatio Dei,*" the injunction to follow the Almighty and imitate the Almighty's behavior, this commandment captures the highest mission assigned to mankind: JUST AS HE IS MERCIFUL, SO MUST YOU BE MERCIFUL. Just as God clothes the naked and buries the dead and engages in a variety of behaviors defined as גְמִילוּת חֲסָדִים *gemilut h̲asadim*—acts of loving kindness—so must we emulate God's ways. The pinnacle of desirable human behavior is patterned after the Almighty's own example, and it is intentionally articulated in a way that implicitly confers the status of striving to be Godlike on one who performs those very acts of kindness the Almighty performs.

Yet over the years I have been repeatedly astonished at the scattered references in classical Rabbinic literature to God's behavior in other experiential spheres unrelated to *gemilut hasadim*, which one would have thought were reserved for people alone. We find sources that indicate that God prays, that God mourns—even weeps—for the destroyed temples, that God learns Torah and creates novel חִדּוּשִׁים *hidushim*—interpretations. We find God enjoying *oneg* shabbat, seeking the blessings of צַדִּיקִים *tzaddikim*, and being satisfied.

All this in the sacred literature of a people who shudder at any hint of anthropomorphism and eschew even the symbolic representation of the Divine in any kind of imagery.

Lulei De'Mistefina, the Rabbis called it: Dare we continue? For we tread here on sacred soil. Yet I believe that a profound insight concerning the preeminent commitments of Jewish life and how they are generated lies hidden within. The Almighty is like a loving parent who wants the best for his children. Like a loving parent, God showers beneficence on them and presents them with generous gifts, the land, its cities and gates, cattle and estates.

But we know there are two ways in which parents bestow their bounty upon their children. The bounty of material possessions by and large is presented in the form of gifts. But the truly transcendent treasures—values, emotional commitments, loyalties and principles, rules to live by, perspectives on life—these must be modeled and acquired through imitation. They cannot be presented. The child learns by seeing and imitating and internalizing. These qualities of character and will and caring are caught, not taught. Of the two alternative modes of conveying parental goodness and blessing—giving and modeling—modeling is by far the more effective and enduring.

This is especially true with reference to the pivotal sancta of Jewish life, many of which had to survive two millennia of displacement and continued to exist only in our imaginations. Our emotional ties to Jerusalem's Temple had to be sustained in the hearts and minds of the Jew and kept alive in his inner core without any external physical reinforcement. The-Holy-One-Who-is-to Be-Blessed knew how to educate effectively. God knew that these commitments could not be transmitted; they had to be voluntarily self-initiated.

God knew the children would ultimately choose that which God chose. They would value and revere that which God valued and revered. That is why Jerusalem is called THE PLACE WHICH GOD WILL CHOOSE. The Land of Israel is a special gift. It was given to Israel to possess and to occupy. Jerusalem, however, is more than a gift and a possession. It is the site for Divine encounter and communion with the Shekhinah,

SYNOPSIS: *The review continues with laws for judges, the prohibition against idols, laws for the king,* kohanim, *Leviim. Also reviewed are some criminal codes and the laws of warfare.*

RASHI OF THE WEEK:

Usually we see Rashi expand the meaning of a passage. Here is a Rashi that develops an understanding by shrinking the meaning of a verse. Deuteronomy 16.20 is one of those famous verses that marched with Martin Luther King and protested the war in Vietnam: **JUSTICE, JUSTICE YOU SHALL PURSUE**—THAT YOU MAY LIVE LONG AND INHERIT THE LAND WHICH THE ETERNAL, YOUR GOD, IS GIVING YOU. *Rather than taking off on the theme of justice, Rashi simply says:* Pursue means pursue. When you have a legal case to have arbitrated, you shall seek a reliable court [*Sifre, San.* 32b] **THAT YOU MAY LIVE LONG AND INHERIT THE LAND.** The appointment of honest judges is enough merit to guarantee that Israel stays alive and settled securely in the Land [*Sifre*].

Justice is not an abstraction. Justice has to do with fair courts and fair trials. Justice starts with the protection of the day-to-day justice system, not with global issues.

for worship, supplication, and self-renewal. It is the supreme object of longing and constant choosing. And in the choosing—a process that has persisted without losing any intensity for two millennia—we emulate not only the deeds of the Holy-One-Who-is-to-Be-Blessed, but the transcendent spiritual priorities and perspectives as well.

If to realize and express the image of God within ourselves by performing acts of loving kindness means to learn to walk in God's ways, how much more so for spiritual priorities and existential imperatives. We have truly learned to pray to our praying God, to learn with our learning God, and to weep with our weeping God. And despite the centuries of separation, we believe profoundly that our acts of choosing the place God has chosen will eventually restore to us the בֵּית הַמִּקְדָּשׁ *Beit ha-Mikdash*, may it be rebuilt speedily in our days. ■

Shoftim

"Justice, Justice Pursue"

Tikvah Frymer-Kensky

TIKVAH FRYMER-KENSKY IS THE AUTHOR OF *IN THE WAKE OF THE GODDESSES* AND DIRECTOR OF BIBLICAL STUDIES AT THE RECONSTRUCTIONIST RABBINICAL COLLEGE.

Shoftim

צֶדֶק צֶדֶק תִּרְדֹּף *tzedek tzedek tirdof,* JUSTICE, JUSTICE SHALT THOU PURSUE. This stirring sentence is one of the great statements of the Bible. To many it has become the great principle undergirding their Jewish identity and, indeed, the motivating principle of their lives. The great involvement of Jews in socialist and democratic movements and their disproportionate involvement in social action and the helping professions show the continuation of the ongoing importance of this pursuit of justice in the life of even secular Jews.

There is another great statement in the Bible, קְדֹשִׁים תִּהְיוּ *kedoshim tihyu,* BE HOLY [Lev. 19.1].

These two main principles of Judaism are the two poles of what reform Judaism has called "the ethical message of the prophets." In halakhic Judaism they are the great metahalakhic principles undergirding the legal system. Together they are also the major elements of the Jewish narrative by which Jews understand their role in history. God who is justice and holiness desires that we establish a world full of justice and holiness. This is the purpose of the Jewish people and the thrust of our history. Achieving it brings on the Messianic times.

Justice and holiness are not separate items. There is no such thing as holiness without justice. וְהָאֵל הַקָּדוֹשׁ נִקְדַּשׁ בִּצְדָקָה *veha-El ha-Kadosh niKdash beTzedaka,* THE HOLY GOD IS SANCTIFIED BY JUSTICE [Isaiah 5.16]. A long line of prophets from Amos to Jeremiah castigated the people for their concentration on the rituals and cults without an equivalent concern with justice. They were not listened to then, and we constantly misunderstand them now. We often seek to understand the prophets by finding something wrong or idolatrous about the cult itself, or by assuming that the worshippers were either totally hypocritical or were simply going through the motions. But as far as we can see, there was nothing wrong with the ritual observances. The religious worship that Amos condemned was a cult of thanksgiving for God's abundant gifts of the land and its fertility and prayer for the continuation of this Divine *hesed.* Nor were people simply "going through the motions." Even Amos acknowledges that they were sincere people who approached God

Shoftim

eagerly and generously. The anger of Amos and Jeremiah is not directed at the people's desire for holiness, but at their lack of understanding that there can be no true holiness without a pursuit of true justice. We have not quite learned this lesson, but nevertheless it has not changed during the millennia since Deuteronomy. Today also, no amount of halakhic observance or ritual participation will create holiness if there is no true search for justice.

The parashah demands that we pursue justice, not that we observe, guard, or remember it. Elsewhere we are told to בַּקֵּשׁ שָׁלוֹם וְרָדְפֵהוּ *Bakesh Shalom ve-Rodefehu,* SEARCH FOR AND PURSUE PEACE [Ps. 34.15], and we remember that Aaron was a אוֹהֵב שָׁלוֹם וְרוֹדֵף שָׁלוֹם *Ohev Shalom ve-Rodef Shalom* LOVER OF PEACE AND A PURSUER OF PEACE [Avot 1.12]. To these pursuits America adds a third, not an obligation but a right: the pursuit of happiness. They are all elusive and never completely or permanently achieved. We are not told how to pursue justice and peace; the ongoing pursuit is part of our obligation and our right.

Parashat Shoftim gives us a road map for the pursuit of justice. It prescribes the establishment of a legal system with magistrates and officials and guidelines for its use. The first requirement is wholeness: just as we should not sacrifice blemished animals, so we should not stand blemished before God. So the blemished, those who have affronted God by idolatrous behavior, must be stoned, but only after a just judicial procedure. The parashah then starts to delineate proper judicial procedure. It requires thorough inquiry and the testimony of two witnesses. Since cases are not always so easily decided, the parashah sets up a judicial hierarchy. Any dispute—capital or not—too difficult for the local court is sent to the central judicial authority, whose verdict is binding on pain of death.

The parashah then turns to this question of authority and seeks to prevent a tyrannical subversion of justice by multiplying various forms of authority and limiting them, a strategy also advocated by the narratives about the passing of authority from Moses to Joshua and the priests. *Shoftim* limits the accumulation of royal wealth and power; it denies the Levites and priests an independent economic well-being; it demands the authority of true prophets but makes it very difficult for a prophet to speak by prescribing death to those whose predictions do not come true. And it also retains some of the authority of the family; the family of a slain man is not the judge who determines the guilt of the slayer (the elders do that) nor the sentencer who demands the death sentence (the law requires it), but it is the executioner, for the elders deliver the killer to the blood-avenger.

Having delineated the powers of authorities other than the *shoftim* and *shotrim* with whom the parashah began, it now turns to the scope of the authority of these officials. It prescribes proper judicial procedure, ordering cities of refuge where killers can be safe while awaiting trial and where accidental homicides remain after their trials. It requires two witnesses for all trials and provides tit-for-tat retribution for false witnesses. It also prescribes proper military procedure. The priests are to exhort the people, the *shotrim* are to exempt those who have recently married or planted and those who are afraid to go. And then the campaign begins. When Israel attacks it must first invite surrender. Only after it is denied can Israel attack. During a siege Israel must spare all food-bearing trees. After the conquest Israel is to kill the men and take the women, children, and animals for booty. But these rules of limited war, says the parashah, do not apply to the seven nations of the land; for them the parashah calls for חֵרֶם *Herem*, total extermination.

The rule of *Herem* shocks us, for it does not seem to be justice in warfare. The question is no longer relevant today, of course, for these peoples have long since disappeared. Actually, these people had long since disappeared by the time when Deuteronomy was written. חֵרֶם *Herem* is not a law for practice but the statement of a principle that these people were dangerous and that to eradicate them would have been just.

But to most of our eyes the חֵרֶם *Herem*, even as a wish statement about something that did not happen, does not seem just. Nor does the "limited" war against other peoples in which all men are killed and all the rest are taken captive. The very idea of an outward campaign of conquest seems unjust to many people. These specifics of justice in war are a dramatic example of how elusive justice can be, and how indeterminate. The beginning of the parashah is equally problematic. *Shoftim* opens with an admonition to the judges to not show partiality and cautions them not to take bribes that might induce partiality. But this is a very different definition of justice from the commandment to vindicate the widow and the orphan. This other view of justice *demands* bias in favor of the underprivileged and is dramatically represented in Psalm 82. There God addresses the heavenly beings who have been overseeing the world and reminds them that God charged them to vindicate the lowly and the poor. But they had never understood, and God eliminates them from the universe, making them die as men do. In this view of justice, justice cannot be pursued simply by strict impartiality. If the law allows oppression, then sticking to the law continues the oppression. There is, after all, no such thing as a neutral court. If the court opts to modify the law in order to create justice, then it undermines the authority of the law and makes it unpredictable; if it decides strictly by the law, it perpetuates the status quo and whatever injustice is encoded in it.

This is not a problem only for judges. In the pursuit of justice, observing the law is not enough. Amos' great complaint is not that the rich were breaking the law, but rather that they did not realize that the law (of debt foreclosure, to name one) was impoverishing the weak and debilitating them. Standing on one's legal rights can get in the way of just behavior.

The view of justice detailed in *Parashat Shoftim* is a view from the top and is concerned with establishing authorities and delineating their functions and procedures. The view of justice in Amos and Psalm 82 is a view from the bottom. It considers what the law looks like to those who have no power. These are two differing views of justice, perhaps two different types of justice: strict procedural justice and social justice. Even though they sometimes contradict each other, the parashah orders us צֶדֶק צֶדֶק תִּרְדֹּף *Tzedek tzedek tirdof,* JUSTICE, JUSTICE SHALT THOU PURSUE. We must pursue both types of justice; we must find a way to make the tension between them a dynamic creative tension. Our attempt at their reconciliation must continually carry us forward in our pursuit of that justice which is the true "JUSTICE, JUSTICE," which makes manifest the holiness of God. ■

Parashat Ki Tetze

Deuteronomy 21.10–25.19

Marc Bregman

Marc Bregman teaches at the Hebrew Union College in Jerusalem. In addition to writing scholarly articles and modern midrash in English and Hebrew, he is the co-author, together with Howard Schwartz, of *The Four Who Entered Paradise* (Jason Aronson, 1995) and the author of a study of the *Tanhuma-Yelammedenu* Midrashim entitled *The Sign of the Serpent and the Plague of Blood* (Mohr-Siebeck).

The Captive Woman

This week's parashah begins on an ominous note: כִּי-תֵצֵא לַמִּלְחָמָה עַל-אֹיְבֶיךָ *Ki-Tetzeh la-Milhamah al-Oy'vekhah,* When you go out to war against your enemies [Deut. 21.10]. The following five verses detail what may be done with a אֵשֶׁת יְפַת-תֹּאַר *Eshet Yefat-Toar,* woman of beautiful appearance captured by an Israelite soldier.

The Torah views this situation from the male perspective and addresses its legislation to the captor. But what, I wonder, might have been the emotional experience of a captive woman as she underwent the transformation described in our passage from alien to Israelite. I have attempted to create an imaginary narrative that encompasses the biblical text and its commentaries (see the end for sources). Of course, the spectrum of possible narrations is limited only by the individual imaginations of those who undertake such an exercise. I invite you to "release the captive" within yourself and see who emerges.

Diary of a Captive Woman

I can't believe that I am alive. The panic and pillage were horrible when yesterday the enemy overran our town. We had been warned how savagely the children of

---

דָּבָר אַחֵר **DAVAR AHER.** You shall blot out the memory of Amalek from under heaven, Do not forget! [Deut. 25.19]. *The Mitzvah of Forgetting.* We Jews are a people committed to remembering what has been. Ingrained in our psyches is this seemingly 614th commandment, "Thou shalt not forget." We say it about Jerusalem (If I forget thee, O Jerusalem, may my right hand lose its cunning); we say it about the Shoah ("lest it happen again"); we say it about our loved ones (through *kaddish* and *yahrzeit*). We are a people with a prodigious memory. And ye, Rabbi Sidney Greenberg has suggested that what we really need to work on is developing our "forgettory"—i.e. the ability to forget and move on.

It is a unique human trait that we cannot remember physical pain. We remember that we were in pain, but

כי תצא למלחמה על

Abraham deal with the children of Lot his kinsman, who was also our forefather. The soldiers made us lie down with our faces in the dust, roped together in three lines—men, women, and young ones like me. I could only hear the piteous cries of my people being slaughtered—my own father and mother and my bridegroom, to whom I had not yet borne a child. Then we who were left alive were made to parade past the enemy warriors. I saw one cast his eye on me and grin. He said something to one of their officers, and I was taken out of the line. Those of us chosen spent the night huddled together for warmth. Since daybreak we have been herded behind the enemy army, marching away down the King's Highway. Leaving behind our home, Rabbat Mo'av, smoldering in the distance. I pray to you, O Kemosh, protect me from these barbarians for I know not where I go nor what is to become of me.

❧ ❧ ❧

We traveled for days and days, huddled together, following the army. I am numb with exhaustion and fear. When we crossed the Jordan I was separated from my companions. I have lost everything I love. I feel so empty, all alone among this alien people. I am watched and cared for by a bunch of old women who are constantly babbling to each other in a language I can somehow understand. Today they came into the tent I am kept in and made me strip off my dress. How bitter it was for me to hear them call this last remnant of my home "her garment of captivity"! At first I was sure they were finally preparing me to be raped by the man who seemed to have singled me out for his own. But then they

---

the pain itself cannot be recaptured. And for that we "Thank God!" Imagine how terrible life would be if at any moment we could remember and experience again the many pains long passed. There are many times when forgetting is preferable to remembering. As we approach the coming *Yamim Noraim* we are emboldened to forgive and forget the hurt done to us by others so that our relationships can be repaired, rebuilt, and reinvigorated.

The real challenge is determining when we are best served by our memory and when by our "forgettory." *Parashat Ki Tetze* provides some clues about the values of remembering and forgetting in two seemingly unrelated passages in the parashah: Shekhikhah [The

SYNOPSIS: *And yet more laws are reviewed. This time we have family laws, laws of kindness, laws of lost property, and a potpourri of other legal concerns.*

RASHI OF THE WEEK:

Here is a Rashi that reveals a transformation in thinking between his time and ours. The Torah says: A MAN'S CLOTHING SHALL NOT BE ON A WOMAN. *Rashi asks, "Why?" Then he answers his own question. He learns from the midrash in Sifre and the Talmud, Nazir 59a*: Because she would then look like a man, and she would do this only in order to consort with men, so cross-dressing will lead to adultery. *The Torah continues:* NEITHER SHALL A MAN PUT ON WOMEN'S CLOTHING. *Why would he do that? The answer:* In order to go and stay unnoticed among women... *The Torah reaches its denouement with the warning:* BECAUSE DOING SO IS AN ABOMINATION BEFORE THE ETERNAL [Deut. 22.5]. *Rashi asks: "What makes this an abomination?" Reading the same passage in Sifre, he answers:* It is not the wearing of the clothes but the adultery that follows that is the abomination. *A differing understanding of why cross-dressing is forbidden in the Torah doesn't forgo traditional halakhah or undo the force of a Torah—but we do learn a lot about the difference between rabbinic fears and our own.*

made me shave my head and cut off my fingernails! How could anyone think I look more attractive this way? What strange people I have been captured by. I weep constantly for my mother and my father; their cries are still in my ears.

❧ ❧ ❧

Weeks have passed since I was taken from my home. The numbness and emptiness I feel seem only to deepen. All that came before is beginning to fade, like another lifetime lived by someone else. The old women realized I understand their speech and have been telling me old stories. They say that generations ago there was a Moabite woman like me, named Ruth, who came to live among them and became the ancestor of their King David. They say I must not pray to Kemosh but, like Ruth, accept their God, whose image I have not yet seen and whose name I have not heard. They tell me I may become like their matriarchs Rachel, Leah, and Tamar, the wives of men descended from Abraham, their patriarch, who was the ancestor of our patriarch Mo'av. I cannot deny who I was. Yet I cannot escape what is happening to me. And I cannot hold out against whatever is to be.

❧ ❧ ❧

Soon the full moon will emerge again, as it did on the night after I was captured. I have not seen again the man who brought me here. Moabite men would certainly not treat a captive woman this way! The old women have told me that tonight he is finally permitted to come and lie with me. And after that I will be not his slave but his wife, and I will then be considered one of them. I can see them outside making preparations for the wedding feast. And I can hear them beginning to sing their songs, which seem to beckon me to sing with them:

> Sing, O barren one, you who did not bear... Cry aloud you who

---

Ki Tetze

forgotten sheaf, Deut. 24.19] and Amalek [Deut. 25.17-19].

The Amalek passage recalls the events that transpired during the wanderings (first described in Ex. 17.8-13) when Amalek achieved notoriety as the "archenemy" of the Israelites by attacking them from the rear. Although such cowardice suggests why the text speaks with the tone of moral outrage, in fact the real core of Amalek's offense was, as our parashah clearly states: *v'lo Yarei Elohim*—and he feared not God. On Shabbat *Zakhor*, as on this Shabbat, we read the commandment to blot out the memory of Amalek from under heaven. Do not forget! It is paradoxical: Remember...forget Amalek, let his memory cease, blot out his name. It is because of his audacious stance toward God, because his relationship with God was based on hubris

HAVE NOT TRAVAILED WITH CHILD... ENLARGE THE PLACE OF YOUR TENT AND STRETCH FORTH THE CURTAINS OF YOUR HABITATIONS...FOR YOUR SEED SHALL POSSESS NATIONS. FEAR NOT, FOR YOU SHALL NOT BE ASHAMED...YOU SHALL FORGET THE HUMILIATION OF YOUR YOUTH...FOR HE WHO POSSESSES YOU IS YOUR MAKER; THE LORD OF HOSTS IS HIS NAME. AND YOUR REDEEMER IS THE HOLY ONE OF ISRAEL. THE GOD OF THE WHOLE EARTH HE IS CALLED.

Sources for Further Study

II Samuel 8.2 tells that when David conquered Moab he made the captives lie down on the ground in three "lines" (חֲבָלִים *Havalim*), two of which he put to death and one of which he kept alive. This despite the fact that, according to Genesis 19.36-37, Moab (the progenitor of the Moabites) was the first son of Lot, the nephew of Abraham. The national god of the Moabites was Kemosh [see for example Num. 21.29], who seems to have represented a threat to the Israelite religion [I Kings 11.7]. Their language was remarkably similar to biblical Hebrew. A Moabite inscription found in 1868 in the town of Dibon (Transjordan) contains a proclamation of Mesha, King of Moab, who is mentioned in the Bible. See for example the story of how he sacrificed his own son to prevent his capital from being conquered by Yehoram, King of Israel, and Yehoshafat, King of Judah, together with the King of Edom [II Kings, Ch. 3].

Deuteronomy 21.12 prescribes in detail what must be done with a woman taken in war. The Sifre [section 212] to this verse records a difference of interpretation between early sages. Rabbi Eliezer argued that "DOING" HER NAILS (וְעָשְׂתָה אֶת-צִפָּרְנֶיהָ *Ve-Astah et-Tzipornehah*) means to pare them down, just as she was to SHAVE THE HAIR OFF HER HEAD (וְגִלְּחָה אֶת-רֹאשָׁהּ *Ve-Gilhah et-Roshah*). Rabbi Akibah argued that since shaving her head was a form of disfigurement, her nails should be allowed to grow untended, since this was even more disfiguring. It seems that shaving the head, and perhaps the other practices as well, were intended to make the female captive as unattractive as possible and prevent her being exploited sexually during the month allowed to her to mourn having been forcefully taken from her parental home and native people. Ancient exegetes (see *Sifre Deut.* section 213, *Babylonian Talmud Kiddushin* 21b, and traditional Jewish commentators) and modern ones as well understood the legislation recorded in Deuteronomy 21.10-14 as designed primarily to prevent the rape of women captured in war. Some commentators suggest that the rituals specified in our passage were intended to facilitate the transition of such women from the status of foreigners and their assimilation into Israel as the wives of Israelite men. See Carolyn Pressler, *The View of Women Found*

---

and not humility, that we are commanded to forget him. It takes an active, purposeful use of our "forgettory" to blot him from our memory.

By contrast, the section of the parashah dealing with the Shekhikhah teaches us about the merit of that which is inadvertently forgotten. The mitzvah of leaving the forgotten sheaf depends upon a lack of deliberate intention. The *Tosefta* [*Peah* 3.8] highlights this: "Even though a person has no deliberate intention of performing a mitzvah, yet it is reckoned to him/her as having successfully observed the commandment. How much the more so when the mitzvah is done with intention." *Sefer ha-Hinukh* teaches that the thrust of performing a mitzvah that one did not intend to fulfill helps us to "acquire a generous nature." The very core of this mitzvah is that one cannot purposefully forget the sheaf; it is only by actually forgetting and then resisting the temptation to return and collect it that the mitzvah is fulfilled.

How then can we resolve the conflicting nature of these two passages? The Amalek passage depends upon purposeful forgetting in order to fulfill the instruction, whereas the Shekhikhah commandment is invalidated if done with intention. The solution to this

in the Deuteronomic Family Laws [Berlin-New York: Walter de Gruyter, 1993], pp. 9-15.

When Boaz marries Ruth, the Moabite, the people express the hope and expectation that the woman he is wedding be like Rachel, Leah, and Tamar through the offspring she will bring into his house. Their son Oved was the father of Yishay, who was the father of David. See the conclusion of the book of Ruth.

The final song is taken from the special haftarah read in conjunction with *Parashat Ki Tetze*, beginning with Isaiah 54.1. This is the fifth of the seven special haftarot of Consolation *(sheva de-nehemta)* read on the seven shabbatot between Tisha B'Av and Rosh ha-Shanah. ■

Ki Tetze

conundrum is found in the last few words of Deuteronomy 24.19, ...IN ORDER THAT THE LORD YOUR GOD MAY BLESS YOU. The performance of the mitzvah of the forgotten sheaf molds our character so as to make us fitting receptacles for God's blessing. It is in its unintentionality that the mitzvah trains us to be more giving and urges us to affirm that God is the one who provides food to all, and that we must work in partnership with the Holy Provider and thus merit Divine blessing. As enumerated before, the very purposeful forgetting of Amalek serves the same end: to teach us of an appropriate relationship with God lest we emulate Amalek's audacious lack of FEAR/AWE.

In the final analysis, there are times to remember and times to forget, both purposefully and unintentionally. In every instance the use or misuse of memory must be determined by the higher purpose that is being served. In what we choose to remember and what we choose to forget, may we be guided by our desire to draw nearer to the One from whom all blessing flows, and may we truly merit the gift of that blessing. **Rabbi Michael Torop, Leo Baeck Centre for Progressive Judaism, Victoria, Australia, <rabbimt@netspace.net.au>**

והיה **כי תבוא** אל ארץ

Parashat Ki Tavo

Deuteronomy 26.1–29.8

Daniel Boyarin

Daniel Boyarin is Taubman Professor of Talmudic Culture at the University of California at Berkeley. He is the author of *Unheroic Conduct: The Rise of Heterosexuality and the Invention of the Jewish Man* (Berkeley: 1997).

The opening section of the Torah portion *Ki Tavo* presents itself as a definition of what it means for Israel to be an עַם *Am* (the word conventionally translated means "nation"). The parashah begins by announcing that its purpose is to inform Israel what it is that is expected of us upon entering into the Land that God gives us. (Note well: not the land that God *gave us*, but the Land that God *gives us*; the giving is every day renewed and conditional, as we shall see.) If we look carefully at the components of this expectation, we will see that they consist of several different elements.

The first is the preservation of memory and especially the memory of God's grace to Israel in the past.

We are to take from the first fruits of the land [Deut. 6.2], place them in a basket, take them to Jerusalem, and offer them to the priest. However, the most striking part of the liturgy for this ritual (the *bikkurim*) consists of the text that we are enjoined to recite as we bring the offering. This hymn (וְעָנִיתָ *v'anita* וְאָמַרְתָּ *v'amarta*, in v. 5, best translated, "And you shall say in song") consists of a brief recital of all of Jewish history from its foundation by Jacob until the present moment, including, of course, the sojourn in Egypt as slaves, and all of God's merciful response to the Jews' crying out in pain there. God saw our poverty, and our travail, and our oppression [Deut. 26.7] and brought us out of there. Now we are coming to the Promised Land [Deut. 26.8], and we owe several debts of duty to that God, our Redeemer.

In addition to denoting our gratitude through bringing the fruits and reciting the song, we are expected to behave in particular ways that are expressive of our recognition of God for our miraculous deliverance from oppression. We bow before God [Deut. 26.10], feel joy at all the good that God has given us [Deut. 26.11], and do it together with the Levite and the stranger who dwells in our midst.

Inclusion of the stranger is accordingly marked precisely as a vitally important part of the inheritance of the Land. This point is underlined further in the next section, which details yet another ritual act connected with the produce of the Land of Israel. According to this ritual

Ki Tavo

[vs. 12–15] we are commanded to take a tenth of all of our produce and to distribute it to the Levite, the stranger, the orphan, and the widow who are within our gates, that they might be satisfied.

Levites, orphans, widows; these categories are clear. The Levite is landless because he has been dedicated to the service of God and the temple and therefore must be supported by the public; the orphan and the widow are classical examples of people who might be lacking any means of support. But who is the stranger, the גֵּר *ger*?

If we look for other occurrences of this term in the Torah, we will very quickly find that the frequent understanding of it as "convert" is not sufficient. The very first use of the term STRANGER refers to the situation of the Jews in Egypt. In Genesis 15.13 God informs Abram that his descendants will be STRANGERS in a land that does not belong to them. At least two more verses utilize the same motif. In Exodus 18.3 we learn that Moses' wife named her child גֵּרְשֹׁם "Gershom" because Israel had been a גֵּר *Ger* שָׁם *Sham*, i.e., there in the land of Egypt. Furthermore, Exodus 22.20 informs us that we must not oppress the גֵּר *Ger* who dwells among us, because we have been גֵּרִים *Gerim* ourselves in the land of Egypt. Even more compelling is Exodus 23.9, which tells us that "YOU WILL NOT OPPRESS THE גֵּר *GER*, BECAUSE YOU ARE EMPATHETIC WITH THE SOUL OF THE גֵּר *GER*, SINCE YOU HAVE BEEN גֵּרִים *GERIM* IN THE LAND OF EGYPT." It is obvious that the Israelites were not converts in the Land of Egypt; indeed, one of the main virtues of the Jews during their sojourn was their faithfulness to God and to the traditions of their ancestors. It follows that the word גֵּר *Ger* cannot be translated as "convert" but must mean precisely one who is not part of the group, who remains outside of the Jewish people. Not only are we commanded not to oppress this stranger, but special care of him or her is required by the Torah, precisely because he or she does not belong to the "in group."

Thus we are enjoined to feed this stranger [see also Lev. 19.10] as part of the justification for being given the Land of Israel and in response to which the verse informs us that "TODAY YOU HAVE BECOME A PEOPLE UNTO THE LORD, YOUR GOD" [Deut. 23.9].

If we are not a people unto the Lord, a special people [Deut. 26.18], a holy people [Deut. 26.19], there is no reason for us to have been given the Land, and indeed, as the end of the Torah portion informs us, the Land will be taken away from us.

These reflections seem particularly relevant given the current situation in Israel, into which I have just returned after several years away. The Palestinians (who, according to many halakhic authorities, are precisely the גֵּרִים *Gerim* of whom the Torah speaks) are bereft of any means of support owing to the political situation. To be sure, it was the actions of a few Palestinian extremists that led the Israeli government to take the actions that it has taken, closing off all entry into Israel for most Palestinian workers and importing 200,000 Thai, Romanian, and other foreign workers to fill their places in the Israeli economy. But nevertheless, it is the vast majority of Palestinians, those who were willing to accept the peace agreements and accords, however unfavorable, as well as those who opposed them and those who had no choice in the matter at all because they are infants and children, who are suffering. "Liberal" Israelis say things like: "We are not responsible for them. Let them worry about themselves. We want to separate from them. The closure is good; it will lead to separation." But the Torah tells us differently. When you have come into the Land you must take a tenth of your produce and set it aside for the poor, the Levite (of "your own" people), the orphan and the widow (unspecified ethnicity), and the stranger (the non-Jew who dwells among you because you have entered the Land). Once political responsibility—sovereignty—has been gained by a people over a land and those who dwell in it, the language of Diaspora—"We will take care of ourselves; let them take care of themselves"—is no longer adequate. כִּי-תָבוֹא אֶל-הָאָרֶץ *Ki Tavo el Ha'aretz*! You must take moral responsibility as a sovereign people for all who dwell within your midst and who are dependent on you, whether you love them or not. Then you will be a Nation unto the Lord, show yourself worthy of the Land, and God will give it unto you each and every day. ■

SYNOPSIS: *And still the review continues, with laws of tithing and the preparation for crossing the Jordan.*

RASHI OF THE WEEK:
Usually we have seen Rashi work as a seeker of exegetical meaning. This citation shows Rashi working in a very different mode. Here he is using his Talmudic knowledge to clarify the application of a Torah Law as it has been filtered through the Rabbinic tradition. The Torah says [Deut. 26.2]: YOU SHALL TAKE THE FIRST OF ALL FRUIT OF THE LAND. When the Torah says ALL THE FRUIT OF THE LAND the Torah actually means that you only have to bring the first fruits of "the seven kinds" of symbolic key products of the land of Israel. We learn this via a word link with the word ERETZ (Land), which is used in this verse and in Deuteronomy 8.8. (That verse reads: FOR THE ETERNAL YOUR GOD IS BRINGING YOU INTO A GOOD LAND.) An ERETZ (land) OF (1) WHEAT, (2) BARLEY, (3) GRAPEVINES, (4) FIG TREES, (5) POMEGRANATES, AN ERETZ (land) OF (6) OLIVE OIL, AND (7) HONEY [*Sifre, Men.* 84b]. *By bringing these two verses together we clarify the parameters of the mitzvah of* bikkurim.

Peninnah Schram

Peninnah Schram, associate professor at Stern College of Yeshiva University, is a storyteller and author of *Jewish Stories One Generation Tells Another* and *Chosen Tales: Stories Told by Jewish Storytellers.*

Ki Tavo

MIRROR IMAGES—BLESSINGS AND CURSES IN TORAH AND FOLKTALES

"I don't like curses. May the curses fall into deep waters." This was my mother speaking with intensity, in Yiddish, whenever she heard someone curse. After all, words are viewed in Jewish tradition as synonymous with actions. Thus she viewed curses as having power and so felt they should not be used lightly or in anger. In Yiddish there are some very imaginative and earthy curses, such as, "May beets grow in your belly!" "May you grow like an onion, with your head in the ground and your feet in the air!" "May he have a sweet death...run over by a sugar truck."

However, blessings were definitely part of my parents' speech: my father in his ritual functions as cantor/*shokhet*/ mohel; my mother, whenever she conversed with people. This was their way of life. Since our many prayers begin with *Barukh,* Blessed, Jews are always expressing gratitude to God. And in the folk idiom we also have creative and earthy blessings, such as "A blessing on your head." "May what should be open be open and what should be closed be closed." "May you have a good year, a sweet year filled with health and a livelihood."

So how did we Jews learn to bless so well and also to curse? Throughout Leviticus and Deuteronomy we have a record of God telling Moses what blessings and curses we will receive conditionally, depending on whether or not we will follow the commandments given to us by God. As I was reading the parashah *Ki Tavo*, examining the parallel structure of blessings and curses, I was struck by the analogous repetition of blessings and curses found in Leviticus 26 (*Be-Hukkotai*), in Deuteronomy 11 (*Re'eh*), and in Deuteronomy 30 (*Nitzavim*). Sometimes we need to hear things over and over. But, interestingly, the blessings and curses were pronounced alternately from different places: blessings from Mt. Gerizim and curses from Mt. Ebal. From this we see that blessings and curses must never be combined. However, we must always try to transform a curse into a blessing.

So why do we have these blessings and curses? On one hand, blessings cause us to pause, often turning mundane moments of life into sacred moments and allowing us to express gratitude for God's creation. (The Talmud states that we should recite one hundred blessings a day.) It is at those moments that we experience the presence of God and the beauty of life itself. We see things with "open eyes." When we bless someone we enter into a sacred ritual that binds us together. On the other hand, curses are warnings of doom that cause us to shudder with fear and dread.

In reading *Ki Tavo* I rediscovered that the Torah serves as the most original and imaginative source for folktales and folk sayings. In the Torah, in folklore, and in our daily conversations, the blessings as well as the curses, both imaginative, colorful, earthy, sometimes humorous, and varied, demonstrate who we are as a people from another perspective—a mirror image reflecting and revealing ourselves.

Let us examine two references in Deuteronomy 28 that focus only on blessings.

In Deuteronomy 28.6 we find the blessing of safety as we go about our business, BLESSED SHALT THOU BE WHEN THOU COMEST IN, AND BLESSED SHALT THOU BE WHEN THOU GOEST OUT. I recall my mother saying in Yiddish "*For gezunt un kumpt tzurik gezunt*" as anyone was about to leave on a trip. "Travel in good health and return in good health." In Hebrew there is the same expression, סַע לְשָׁלוֹם וְתַחְזוֹר לְשָׁלוֹם *Sa l'shalom ve ta<u>h</u>zor l'shalom.* Our goings and comings should be blessed—a wonderful blessing indeed. I have continued the family tradition of giving this blessing to my family and friends as they embark on a journey.

In Deuteronomy 28.13: AND THE LORD WILL MAKE THEE THE HEAD, AND NOT THE TAIL;...IF THOU SHALT HEARKEN UNTO THE COMMANDMENTS OF THE LORD THY GOD, WHICH I COMMAND THEE THIS DAY, TO OBSERVE AND TO DO THEM. This verse of head versus tail may be a puzzling reference, perhaps a blessing in disguise, but it all becomes clear with the midrashic parable from *Yalkut Deuteronomy* 802. It is the story of a serpent's tail that wants to lead for a change. "How much longer will you go first? I want to go first," complains the tail. So the head finally agrees, and the tail begins to lead. But since the tail has no eyes or other ways to see the obstacles on the ground, the poor tail falls into the waterhole, flinging the snake's head into the water, then into a fire, then into a thorn bush. Finally the poor battered tail realizes that it is not fit to lead, only to follow. So we too must realize our potential to see where we can go by observing God's commandments.

Perhaps the most potent way to avoid curses is to live positively with blessings. Like my mother, I dislike curses. I long for blessings and realize that each of us has the capacity to give blessings, not just receive them. It is this hope for blessings that has kept us longing for Elijah the Prophet and choosing life. One of the most meaningful blessings we toast each other with is לְחַיִּים *L'<u>H</u>ayim*! May our prayers be for good and not for evil. לְחַיִּים *L'<u>H</u>ayim*! ■

Parashat Nitzavim

Deuteronomy 29.9-30.20

Deborah Lipstadt

Deborah E. Lipstadt is Dorot Professor of Modern Jewish and Holocaust Studies at Emory University in Atlanta.

P*arashat Nitzavim* is read every year on the Shabbat before Rosh ha-Shanah. It does not matter if Rosh ha-Shanah comes out "early" or "late" on a particular year. On the Shabbat before the *Yamim Noraim,* the Days of Awe, we read *Nitzavim.* Rambam believes it is immaterial when some sections of the Torah are read during the year, but that five particular parashiot have to be read on specific dates. *Nitzavim* is one of them. If the *Yamim Noraim* constitute a period when we take account of our actions and our souls—the April 15th of the Jewish year—*Nitzavim* serves as the final reminder that it is time to prepare our tax returns.

The most overt connection between *Nitzavim* and the *Yamim Noraim* is in the parashah's multiple references to תְּשׁוּבָה *Tshuvah,* repentance. You shall return to God and to all the mitzvot which God commands you on this day [Deut. 30.8]. Return to the Lord your God with all your heart and soul [Deut. 30.10]. But this is not just a one-way street. Engaged in a reciprocal relationship with us, God also returns to us even as we return to God. God will return to again delight in your wellbeing, as God delighted in the wellbeing of your ancestors [Deut 30.9]. But this is not the only connection between *Nitzavim* and the time of the year.

Basic to the *Yamim Noraim* is the notion that we are judged as individuals and as a community. The liturgy emphasizes this point. Virtually the entire liturgy, including the confessional—אָשַׁמְנוּ, בָּגַדְנוּ *Ashamnu, Bagadnu,* we have sinned, we have rebelled—and our supplications for a good year—חָתְמֵנוּ בְּסֵפֶר הַחַיִּים *Hat'meinu be-Sefer ha-Hayim,* inscribe *us* in the Book of Life—are in the plural. Even if there is a sin listed in the confessional that we know we could not have committed, we recite it because someone in our midst might have done so. The first verses of *Nitzavim* explicitly demonstrate the individual's intimate interconnection with the community. אַתֶּם נִצָּבִים הַיּוֹם כֻּלְּכֶם *Atem Nitzavim ha-Yom Kulkhem* [Deut. 29.9], You are **all** present here today.

אתם **נצבים** היום כלכם

Who is present? Your leaders and your hewers of wood and drawers of water, your elders and your young, your men, women, and children. But another group also joins this covenant. Even THOSE WHO ARE NOT WITH US HERE THIS DAY are included [Deut. 29.14]. Past, present, and future generations are linked. On Yom Kippur, during *Yizkor,* we echo this act and invoke the memories of those WHO ARE NOT WITH US HERE THIS DAY. We ask that they too stand with us during a pivotal moment of our lives.

This parashah, with its memorable verse **וּבָחַרְתָּ בַּחַיִּים** *u'vakharta ba-hayim,* THEREFORE CHOOSE LIFE [Deut. 30.19], also echoes one of the quandaries that beset many of us during these days: How much control do we ultimately have over the coming year? Can we really choose life? Many of us grew up with the image of a book of life in which our fate is inscribed, believing that if we prayed, repented, and performed charitable acts we and those we love would be inscribed in this heavenly book. Now we know that life is far more arbitrary. Though we tend to think of ourselves as solidly in control of our future, we are well aware that each year that looms ahead constitutes a great unknown. With it comes much we cannot control. The liturgy of the Days of Awe does not shy away from confronting that. In the *U'Netaneh Tokef* we ask **מִי יִחְיֶה וּמִי יָמוּת** *Mi Yehiyeh u'Mi Yamut,* who will live and who will die; **מִי בְקִצּוֹ, וּמִי לֹא בְקִצּוֹ** *Mi b'Kitzo u'Mi Lo b'Kitzo,* who in their time and who before their time; who will be strong and who will be ill, who will perish in floods, fires, and earthquakes? We have no control over these "acts of nature." Anyone who has had a serious illness or watched someone they love bravely but vainly fight for their life; anyone who has felt the earth undulate beneath his feet as if it were water and not something solid; anyone who has known someone who boarded a bus to go to work and instead was blown to bits by a terrorist's ghastly deed knows that in many respects our ability to choose life is illusionary.

We then liken God to the shepherd separating the flock, **כְּבַקָּרַת רוֹעֶה עֶדְרוֹ** *k'Vakarat Roeh Edro;* so are we separated. So is our fate decreed. We hope that the shepherd's actions will be rational and fair, but we know that often they will seem—and sometimes be—arbitrary. During Yom Kippur musaf we read about the goat for Azazel. It was dispatched to the wilderness as symbolic expiation for Israel's sins. Rav Soloveitchik *z"l* says that the goat is chosen by lots to remind us how much of our lives is controlled by chance and fate.

SYNOPSIS: *Moses' "State of the Union Address," which begins with a restatement of the covenant.*

RASHI OF THE WEEK: *In this sermon God gives a warning of a forthcoming exile:* THE ETERNAL *VA-YITASEM* (UPROOTED) THEM FROM THEIR SOIL IN GREAT ANGER, WRATH, AND GREAT FURY, AND HE CAST THEM INTO ANOTHER LAND, AS IT IS IN THIS DAY [Deut. 29.27]. *The meaning of the word Va-Yitasem (uprooted) is unclear; the* Targum *(the Aramaic translation) understands it as "uprooted." This is similar to Jeremiah 12.14:* BEHOLD I UPROOTED THEM (*NO-T'SHAM*) FROM THEIR LAND. *When we check out that context we find this:* THE ETERNAL SAID: "MY WICKED NEIGHBORS WHO ENCROACH ON MY INHERITANCE WHICH I GAVE MY PEOPLE ISRAEL—I AM GOING TO UPROOT THEM FROM THEIR SOIL, AND I WILL UPROOT THE HOUSE OF JUDAH OUT OF THEIR MIDST. THEN, AFTER I HAVE UPROOTED THEM, I WILL TAKE THEM BACK INTO FAVOR AND RESTORE TO EACH OF THEM THEIR INHERITANCE." *Rashi is teaching us two lessons: (1) This passage is connected to Jeremiah's prophecy; (2) Enclosed in every exile is the seed of our return. That concept will be explicated a couple of verses hence in Deuteronomy 30.1–3:* AND IT SHALL COME TO PASS WHEN ALL THESE THINGS HAPPEN TO YOU... THAT THE ETERNAL YOUR GOD WILL TURN YOUR CAPTIVITY...

Nitzavim

Can we convincingly say we can choose life?

This notion of our lack of control over the coming years stands in dramatic opposition to the concept of the *Yamim Noraim* as a period of self-empowerment. According to Rambam, תְּשׁוּבָה *tshuvah* is not designed to convince God to change a harsh decree to a benign one. Such a notion would suggest that we have power over God. For Rambam this was utterly irrational. Rather, *we* are changed by the process. Engaging in תְּשׁוּבָה *tshuvah* means we take account of what we have done during the year; try to right our wrongs; apologize to our victims; and resolve to try not to repeat these errors. After engaging in this process a person is no longer the same. Repentance becomes, therefore, an ontological act, something that changes our very sense of being. It is a "different" person who is נִצָּב *nitzav,* present before God, not the person who has committed the wrongs.

This theology is exquisitely expressed in Rambam's interpretation of

הֵן הָאָדָם הָיָה כְּאַחַד מִמֶּנּוּ לָדַעַת טוֹב וָרָע.

Hein ha'Adam haya k'E<u>h</u>ed memnu la'Da'at Tov ve'Ra [Gen. 3.22]. Instead of reading NOW ADAM IS LIKE ONE OF US KNOWING THE DIFFERENCE BETWEEN RIGHT AND WRONG, Rambam puts a period after *k'e<u>h</u>ad* and reads it הֵן הָאָדָם הָיָה כְּאַחַד *Heyn ha'Adam haya k'E<u>h</u>ed.* NOW ADAM IS UNIQUE. מִמֶּנּוּ *Memnu,* FROM WITHIN HIMSELF, ADAM KNOWS THE DIFFERENCE BETWEEN RIGHT AND WRONG.

How then do we reconcile the arbitrary aspects of the year faced with a process through which we are self-empowered? In the *U'Netaneh Tokef,* after acknowledging what faces us, after listing the things we do not control, after enumerating the fearful calamities looming in the void; we proclaim:

וּתְשׁוּבָה וּתְפִלָּה וּצְדָקָה
מַעֲבִירִין אֶת רֹעַ הַגְּזֵרָה

u'Tshuvah, u'Tefilah, u'Tzedakah ma'Averin et Roah ha-Gezarah, repentance, prayer, and *tzedakah* avert the severe decree. Rather than reading this as "avert the severe decree" we can read it, as Rabbi Sidney Greenberg has taught, as "avert the *severity* of the decree." Herein lies the crux of the matter. There is much that is in our control: how we live our lives, relate to one another, function as part of the community, perform good deeds, and practice וּתְשׁוּבָה וּתְפִלָּה וּצְדָקָה *tshuvah, tefillah,* and *tzedakah* in their broadest manifestations. The manner in which we do all this helps determine how we handle that which is out of our control.

Long before the *U'Netaneh Tokef* was composed, *Nitzavim* taught us this lesson. We are told לֹא בַשָּׁמַיִם הִוא *lo va'shamayim hee.* THIS TORAH, THIS COVENANT IS NOT IN THE HEAVENS, וְלֹא-מֵעֵבֶר לַיָּם *v'lo ma-ever la-yam,* NOR IS IT ON THE OTHER SIDE OF THE SEA. You need not ascend to the heavens to find it nor

cross the sea to retrieve it.
כִּי בְּפִיךָ וּלְבָבְךָ לַעֲשֹׂתוֹ *Kee b'fekha, u'veLevavkha l'Asoto.* IT IS IN YOUR MOUTH, AND IN YOUR HEART TO OBSERVE IT [Deut. 30.11-14]. There is a wonderful linguistic connection to the *Yamim Noraim* in this last verse. פִּיךָ *Peekha* (your mouth), which is the equivalent of תְּשׁוּבָה *Tshuvah,* repentance, is something that must be done verbally. בִּלְבָבְךָ *B'Levavkha* (your heart), which is the equivalent of תְּפִלָּה *Tefillah,* prayer, which the rabbis describe as עֲבוֹדָה שֶׁבַּלֵּב *Avodah sheba-Lev,* service of the heart, and לַעֲשֹׂתוֹ *la-Asoto* (to do), which is the equivalent of צְדָקָה *Tzedakah,* righteous actions.

There are things we don't control. But there is much that we do. We do not control life and death, but we do control the kind of life we lead. We know, מִמֶּנּוּ *mimenu,* FROM WITHIN OURSELVES, the difference between right and wrong. That is why on Yom Kippur, when our prayers for a good life reach their crescendo, the symbols of the day are symbols of mourning. Many wear no leather and don a *kittel,* the white robe reminiscent of the burial shroud. These symbols remind us of life's fleeting nature. Even *Yizkor* reminds us that our actions today become the next generation's memories. As we remember those who preceded us we cannot help but ask ourselves, how will we be remembered? When we are no longer in the book of life, will we be listed in the books of the living?

Just as the events at Sinai were "reenacted" in *Nitzavim,* during the יָמִים נוֹרָאִים *Yamim Noraim* we once again stand at Sinai. The Talmud says that on Yom Kippur the children of Israel are [Yoma 8.24] as pure from sin as angels. Yom Kippur is the only day when we chant
בָּרוּךְ שֵׁם כְּבוֹד מַלְכוּתוֹ לְעוֹלָם וָעֶד
Barukh Shem Kavod Malkhuto l'Olam va'Ed (Blessed is God's glorious name for ever and ever) aloud. When we do we supposedly emulate a chorus of angels. Starting with Shabbat *Nitzavim* until the shofar is blown at the conclusion of Yom Kippur we stand as individuals, but we do not stand alone. We stand together with a chorus, not of angels but of our community, family, friends, and memories of those no longer here on this day. They stand with us, even as, one day—when the measure of our years has been filled—we will stand with others. We stand as individuals. We stand on our own record, a record shaped by our mouths, hearts, and actions, by our
וּתְשׁוּבָה וּתְפִלָּה וּצְדָקָה *Tshuvah, u'Tefillah, u'Tzedakah.* But we do not stand alone.

אַתֶּם נִצָּבִים הַיּוֹם כֻּלְּכֶם
Atem Nitzavim ha-Yom Kulkhem. ■

Robert Bleiweiss

ROBERT BLEIWEISS IS THE EDITOR OF THE MAGAZINE *JEWISH SPECTATOR*.

Nitzavim

A participant in my Shabbat morning minyan once likened Torah to God's user manual for human beings. Just as their creators provide guides for how to operate your car, computer, or lawn mower, so has God in God's nurturing kindness provided humanity with Torah so that we may live well and sustain from generation to generation in accordance with God's design.

Should you choose to ignore the dos and don'ts in your easy-to-understand automobile guidebook, which is presented by geniuses to be understood by quite ordinary folks, there will be serious consequences sooner or later. The more that is ignored and the longer, the more extreme the failings of your machine will be, up to and including a calamitous end.

That's why you are urged to refer to the manual frequently and to obey its advice and commands punctiliously.

So it is with Torah and your life, the life of your family, and ultimately the fate of humanity.

God, in *sidrat Nitzavim*, recognizes the human tendency to ignore the ultimate guidebook (Torah) and its crucial rules and recognizes that there will be unavoidable disaster. "BUT YOU WILL RETURN (TSHUVAH) AND HEARKEN TO THE VOICE OF GOD AND CARRY OUT ALL HIS COMMANDMENTS THAT I COMMAND YOU TODAY, AND GOD, YOUR GOD, WILL MARK YOU FOR THE GOOD IN ALL THE WORK OF YOUR HANDS....FOR YOU WILL THEN HEARKEN TO THE VOICE OF GOD, YOUR GOD, WHICH IS WRITTEN IN THIS BOOK OF THE TEACHING, TO KEEP ALL HIS COMMANDMENTS AND HIS LAWS....FOR THIS COMMANDMENT THAT I COMMAND YOU TODAY IS NOT BEYOND YOUR UNDERSTANDING, NOR IS IT FAR AWAY" (Deut. 30.8–11].

Read, internalize, and execute the guidebook given by the Ultimate Manufacturer to provide you the good life, meaning, and an assured future for those who come after. Don't imagine for a moment that Torah's contents have meaning only for *hakhamim* (learned Jews).

"FOR THE WORD IS VERY NEAR TO YOU, TO CARRY IT OUT WITH YOUR MOUTH AND YOUR HEART. SEE, I HAVE SET BEFORE YOU TODAY LIFE AND GOOD, AND ALSO, DEATH AND EVIL; INASMUCH AS I COMMAND YOU TODAY...TO WALK IN HIS WAYS AND KEEP HIS COMMANDMENTS, HIS STATUTES, AND HIS SOCIAL ORDINANCES, SO THAT YOU MAY LIVE AND MULTIPLY." [Deut. 30.14–16].

God, for all our inability to know God directly, is easily accessible through the words of Torah. When God's wisdom is consistently ignored, inevitable and unavoidable disaster results. Understood, acted upon, and lived, the life prescribed by Torah will help you get from birth to the *Olam ha-Ba*, the world to come, with maximum joy, meaning, and peace. ■

הדברים האלה

Parashat Va-Yelekh

Deuteronomy 31.1-31.30

Everett Fox

Everett Fox holds the Allen M. Glick Chair in Biblical and Judaic Studies at Clark University in Worcester, Massachusetts. He is the translator and commentator of *The Five Books of Moses*, published by Schocken Books in 1995.

The reading of *Va-Yelekh* this year occurs a mere twelve days short of the two hundredth anniversary of George Washington's famous Farewell Address. This may be pure coincidence, but it is an old Jewish trait to find meaning in what appears to be fortuitous. So we may take advantage of the date to draw a comparison with Moses' own famous last words, which begin in this parashah.

Washington's speech does not make for easy reading today. Full of the expansive sentences and flowery phrases of eighteenth-century English, it presents a tempting target for an editor who wants to make it understandable to contemporary high school students.

Once we get past the difficulties of language, however, the content of the speech is of great interest.

Washington opens by giving the reasons for his retirement and thanks his countrymen for their support and the honors they have showered upon him. He then exhorts them to preserve good relations with each other and to keep the Constitution, to the end that other nations will see its wisdom and adopt an identical form of government. This latter thought contains biblical echoes reminiscent of Deuteronomy.

Washington goes on to plead passionately for a number of points: (1) to preserve the Union as the best guarantee of freedom and peace; (2) to obey the government and to fight opposition to it; (3) to be careful not to change the Constitution too much or too fast, but rather to trust the findings of experience; (4) to beware of partisanship; (5) to bear in mind the importance of religion and morality; (6) to encourage institutions that will spread knowledge among the electorate; and (7) to develop peaceful relations with other countries, while taking care not to favor or hate one above all others. This last point, Washington's famous (and oft-misunderstood) advice to avoid "entangling alliances," comprises an appreciable percentage of the speech.

On the whole, the farewell address is a rather conservative document that puts faith in the twin pillars of common sense and trust in the central document that the Founding Fathers have drawn up. The biblical model of a leader's last words is rather different. The protagonist, be he Jacob, Moses, or David, speaks immediately before death (retirement does not seem to have been much of an option in a culture where the aged were revered), and his words, in their typical garb of poetry, tend to be more akin to a prophetic vision than to a dinner speech. This should not be surprising, given that religious traditions often identify ancestors as visionaries with a close relationship with the Divine. So on his deathbed, in Genesis 48–49, Jacob blesses his sons and grandsons with a prediction of what will become of them in the future. Moses, in Deuteronomy 32 and 33, envisions the future rebellions and punishment of Israel, then parallels Jacob's blessing of the tribes. David, in Samuel 22 and 23, recounts God's protection of him and vengeance on his enemies, ending with a flourish about how God has established an eternal covenant with him. In a narrative postscript, David's actual last words occur on his deathbed in I Kings I, with his blood-curdling advice to his son Solomon to eliminate Joab and Shimei.

In all of the poetic passages it is rhetorical urgency and not calm reason that is primary. The leader speaks not as an equal or fellow aristocrat (as in the case of Washington), but as a man who is inspired by God and who is imparting to the people an emotionally charged vision of their relationship to God. Yet the prologue to Moses' two great poems, which makes up this week's parashah, is rather like Washington's address in that it deals with highly practical matters: the issue of succession and provisions for the future success of the political enterprise.

Washington, of course, did not have to worry about a successor in the way that European royal regimes did, thanks to the ultimately workable system set up by the Constitution. In contrast, the entire book of Judges and much of Samuel are deeply concerned with the stability of Israelite leadership. Moses, for his part, is able to solve the problem by appointing a tried and true successor, approved by God, in his own lifetime.

The heart of the parashah, however, concerns how Israel will avoid straying from God in the future, and here we are introduced to something quite remarkable. Beginning in verse 9, we are told how Moses writes down the "Instruction" (we are not told

SYNOPSIS: *The beginning of the end. Joshua is announced. The law is handed to the* kohanim.

RASHI OF THE WEEK:

Things are wrapping up. Moses begins this speech by saying: "TODAY I AM ONE-HUNDRED-AND TWENTY. *Lo U'khal* (I CAN NO MORE) GO OUT OR COME IN. ALSO THE ETERNAL HAS SAID TO ME: 'YOU SHALL NOT CROSS OVER THE JORDAN' [Deut. 31.2]. (*Among other things) Rashi is bothered by the phrase:* I CAN NO MORE GO OUT OR COME IN. *He says* one might think that this was because he was frail and his physical strength was gone, but we know this cannot be true, because the Torah will say about Moses just before his death: HIS EYES WERE NOT DIM, HIS MOISTURE HAD NOT DRIED [Deut. 34.7]. Then what is the meaning of *Lo U'khal*? It actually means not permitted because the power of leadership is being taken away from him and given to Joshua. *There is much midrash behind this simple Rashi, but the bottom line is that Moses succeeds in learning the meaning of emeritus.*

Va-Yelekh

exactly what that includes, so it may be only parts of Deuteronomy rather than everything) beginning with Genesis, hands it to the priests for safekeeping, and establishes the practice of reading the document once every seven years to the people. Rather unusually, the audience is to comprise the entire populace—not only the landholding males or those of fighting age, as we might expect, but everybody, including women, children, and foreigners— "THAT THEY MAY HEAR AND THAT THEY MAY LEARN, AND HAVE AWE FOR YHWH YOUR GOD" [Deut. 31.12–13]. Here, of course, the groundwork is laid for what became a central institution in Judaism, the public reading of the Torah, an institution that implies that the way of life embodied in the Torah should be open to all in the community. It is clear that Judaism's emphasis on study as a universal community activity (ironically, despite the above, restricted to males for much of our history) stems in some ways from this practice of community "reading." It should be mentioned that parallel to the public reading of the instruction in this chapter is the provision for writing down Moses' ominous poem in the next chapter, so that "IT MAY SERVE AS A WITNESS FOR ME AGAINST THE CHILDREN OF ISRAEL" [Deut. 31.19]. In both cases writing serves to ensure that documents will be publicly recited, and such recitation is to lead to positive behavior and the avoidance of negative behavior.

It is intriguing, if we think back to Washington's address, that the first president also suggested establishing institutions that would lead to the spread of knowledge. But that is a far cry from a periodic ritual in which the nation's founding document is read in the hearing of the entire populace. I have often wondered what the United States would be like if we had such a ritual. What would happen if, every July 4th, television stations were obliged to broadcast readings of the Constitution, whose text, after all, is not very well known to the majority of people in this country? Or what would happen if there were large gatherings in which the document were read from a podium (through the smoke of barbecues)? Or even if, Heaven forbid, the Constitution were broadcast or read weekly? Such suggestions may well strike us as silly, and indeed our gut reaction to them may tell us something very serious about American society. But I lay them out for consideration here to pose the question of what values in fact drive a society, and how that society chooses to preserve and promulgate them. The situation we currently have, where high school students are required to study the Constitution, obviously does not go far enough toward producing the kind of citizens that Washington hoped for.

Suggestions parallel to Deuteronomy's have occasionally been made in modern times. Following Germany's defeat in

World War II, the aged and distinguished German historian Friedrich Meinecke proposed that "Goethe centers" be set up all over the country. At these centers the master's works would be read and would somehow inspire Germans to recover the true greatness of their culture. Meinecke's plan was, of course, misguided and almost laughable; Goethe, great as he was, is hardly a moral model on which a society can be built or rebuilt. Art is no substitute for morality, and it was the breakdown of Western morality and moral discourse that was at the heart of the Nazi enterprise.

But the document with which Washington is linked and the one associated with the name of Moses are different matters entirely. In societies for whom a founding document is central and where that document is not only revered but tested by time, public reading— the actual hearing of the words—is crucial. Reading leads to study and discussion; discussion sends us back to the process of living legislation for a living society engaged with life issues. In this season, as the Torah draws to a close and we get ready to concern ourselves with renewal, we would do well to bear in mind what is at stake in our founding documents and consider how we may best go about keeping our supposedly cherished values and ideals alive. ■

Va-Yelekh

Jenais Zeitland

Jenais Zeitland is a teenager and lives in Mendocino, CA.

In my family's book of Torah and commentary it says poems and songs are interchangeable. Does that mean that when Moses delivered his very powerful farewell poem to the people he might have actually been singing? Imagine, Moses emerges from the tent of meeting and stands before the Israelites near the shore of the Jordan River, then breaks into song, some enchanting melody that has the people hushed and listening.

I'm not sure Moses actually sang to the people, but if it had happened, it probably would have made the people listen. How often do leaders want you to understand well enough that they sing or recite poetry?

How is poetry different from narrative writing? Poetry uses rhythm, repetition, image, and metaphor to further illustrate points being made.

It makes analogies and comparisons weighing one thing against the next. Today poetry is frequently used because it stays with you and doesn't just fade into every other speech or lecture you might have heard over the course of your lifetime. At the inauguration of President Clinton, Maya Angelou hit home the blessing of a new beginning in a beautiful poem called *On the Pulse of Morning*. "Lift up your eyes upon/This day breaking for you./Give birth again/To the dream." Basically saying we should renew hope in our original dream and give it another chance. She could have said it the way I did, but the form she chose is so much more beautiful, it sticks with you and makes you have feelings for the words as she compares renewed hope to birth.

Poetry is found frequently in prayer, one of my favorites being the *Nishmat*. It contains detailed images that grab you and can easily be visualized. "Though our mouths should overflow with song as the sea, our tongues with melody as the roaring waves, our lips with praise as the heaven's wide expanse; and though our eyes were to shine as the sun and the moon, our arms extend like eagles' wings, our feet speed swiftly as deer...." The basic wish that our minds be full of prayer and song are compared to beautiful and awesome everyday things such as the roaring waves, the sea, the heaven's wide expanse, the sun and the moon, eagle's wings, and swift deer. These natural phenomena still draw a breath of wonder from us at every sighting. There has always been something magical about the sun and the moon, mysterious about the sea. I suppose people don't often compare themselves to such awestriking beauties of nature.

I think Moses probably knew the general message he was trying to get across to the people, but I think he was struggling with how to make them really understand. In the end he delivered his farewell as a poem. His goal was to let the people get the message, and so he illustrated it with rhythm and detailed examples and comparisons to their lives so far, so that his words would stay with them for a long time. In this way, after Moses' death, they could create guidelines for their lives so that they would be appreciative to God for everything that was and would be done for the Israelites.

Being a poet (or rather a person who likes to write poetry as a form of expression), I know that a poem can be very powerful. I imagine that part of Moses' goal was to make sure the poem stuck with the people; I think he accomplished his goal quite well. His first two lines alone grab you: "Give ear, O heavens, let me speak;/Let the earth hear the words I utter!/May my discourse come down as the rain."

The poem is full of emotion. Moses is angry with the people and openly expresses it. He criticizes the people and calls them "children unworthy of Him,/That crooked and twisted generation," saying that the people are undeserving of such an awesome God, whom Moses refers to many times as a "Rock." Moses also showers God with praise using poetry, saying what a support God is and how God took Jacob "like an eagle who rouses his nestlings,/Gliding down to his young,/So did He spread His wings and take him." Over the course of the poem you basically see Moses going back and forth between saying how horrible and unworthy the people are and how appreciative he is for everything God has done. He does so by supporting each point with an image or metaphor to make the ideas real to the people.

Poetry is an effective vehicle to make ideas stand out. It is a different medium than simple speech. It places images where they wouldn't necessarily be, and it puts forth a more mystical message. It adds rhythm, metaphor, and repetition not normally found in everyday language. No wonder God told Moses to deliver his words in the form of a poem. ■

ותשמע הארץ אמרי פי

Parashat Ha-azinu

Deuteronomy 32.1–32.52

Rabbi Lawrence A. Hoffman

Rabbi Lawrence A. Hoffman is Professor of Liturgy at Hebrew Union College in New York. His books include a thorough revision of the classic introduction to Judaism by Rabbi Morris N. Kertzer, *What Is a Jew?* (Collier Books) and most recently *Covenant of Blood: Circumcision and Gender in Rabbinic Judaism* (Univeristy of Chicago Press).

"I don't do school work on Wednesday nights," my student said. "I spend Wednesdays with my daughter. It is not a lot, I know, but it is at least quality time." As the last two words escaped her lips she smiled, recognizing the debate over whether there even is "quality time" when it comes to raising a child. Is it quality or quantity that matters?

A recent survey suggests that quality had better count for something. Most American parents, even those with lots of time at home, spend their free time watching television. Most of us recollect special moments, cradled in our parents' arms, for instance, that came but rarely kept us going in the long arid period between sustaining hugs. They were like spiritual oases spread out through the years.

"Aridity" and "oases" are part of the larger metaphor of water, which figures prominently in this week's sidrah. There, too, we hear echoes of the quality/quantity debate. "My doctrine shall drop as rain," says Moses of God's word; "My speech shall be strained as dew; As the gentle rain upon the tender grass." Isaac Abravanel of Spain (1437-1508) explains, "Torah is compared to rain because even though it is abundant, it arrives in small doses, like the well-chosen words of a great orator. It is therefore strained as dew. Though small in quantity, however, Torah is great in quality."

By Torah, Abravanel meant the wisdom of even one piece of insight that keeps us going through a difficult week. But he meant acts of Torah, too. "Talk is not crucial; action is," goes a well-known adage that Abravanel had surely memorized and internalized. He was commending qualitative deeds of lovingkindness, the rainlike gifts that we bestow on one another—like a hug from a friend that we never expected but will never forget; flowers that arrive at our sickbed from people who didn't really have to send them; a letter we write to thank someone who helped us; or a dinner invitation to welcome a new family on the block or down the hall. In the vernacular of today, these are random acts of Torah, which may be infrequent, but, if they are fully given, generously offered, and passionately provided, drop into our lives "AS THE GENTLE RAIN UPON THE TENDER GRASS."

None other than William Shakespeare supplies a similar message for the English-speaking world at large, possibly derived from the Torah! Writing in 1594, he consulted new Bible translations that were becoming the rage in an era marked by reformation and the new technology of print. In the first Bible (1525), written by William Tyndalek, and in its successor, the 1539 "Great Bible" by Miles Coverdale, he read words that we now take for granted, but were new back then—"LONG SUFFERING," and "LOVING-KINDNESS"; whole expressions like "A LAND FLOWING WITH MILK AND HONEY"; and even basic holiday names and terms like "PASSOVER" and "SCAPEGOAT"—newly coined at the time.

We must imagine Shakespeare coming across our sidrah, too, with its image of life's sustenance arriving "STRAINED...AS THE GENTLE RAIN UPON THE TENDER GRASS." But England and Spain were in constant diplomatic and cultural contact then, so he may even have heard Abravanel's explanation to the effect that sustenance from heaven may be strained in quantity, but we are sustained thereby anyway, because, to put it simply, "The *quality* is not strained."

Out came Shakespeare's famous soliloquy of *The Merchant of Venice* (of all places): "The *quality* of mercy is not strained; It droppeth as the gentle rain from heaven upon the place beneath." It is the *quality*, not the *quantity* of life's precious moments that matters, says the bard, citing, whether he knew it or not, the standard medieval interpretation of our Torah.

Eternal truths are eternal truths; they never diminish in value. Today, too, we suffer from a dearth of quality. We tend to titillate, not to touch. We hint to parents or those who raised us (but never really tell them outright) how much we love them; we chat to but do not converse with neighbors, lest they burden us with their affairs; and they say they are fine even as their marriages cave in, their businesses go sour, and their children run off in youthful rebellion. We get veneer-deep soundbite information on the news that will scarcely move us to change the world. No quality there, thank you.

Parashat Ha'azinu anticipates Sukkot, a holiday that reminds us of the sustaining power of rain. Precipitation seems random, and it is often sparse, but it saves us anyway if, when it comes, it comes with quality, saturating the ground, not just wetting the surface. By metaphoric extension, we, too, have the power to water

SYNOPSIS: *The Song of Moses—his final words to the people.*

RASHI OF THE WEEK:
Here is Rashi relaying a wonderful midrash. It takes little commentary. AND THE ETERNAL SAID TO MOSES... "GO UP THIS MOUNTAIN, UP TO NEBO...AND DIE ON THE MOUNT WHERE YOU ARE GOING, AND BE GATHERED UNTO YOUR PEOPLE, AS AARON YOUR BROTHER DIED ON MT. HOR, AND WAS GATHERED TO HIS PEOPLE" [Deut. 32.48-50]. *And how did Aaron die? God is telling Moshe:* You witnessed Aaron's death. It is the kind of death you want. For Moses undressed Aaron before his death, one garment at a time. First the upper garment. Then the next. Then the third. He then dressed Eliezer, Aaron's son, in each of these garments. Aaron got to see his son in his new uniform and his new dignity. Moses then said to him: "Aaron, my brother, climb up on the bier." He ascended. "Stretch out your hand." He stretched it out. "Close your eyes." He closed them. "Close your mouth." He closed it. That is how he died. Then Moses said, "Happy is one who will die a death like this." *And such is an ideal way to die, with dignity, with tranquillity, and with a sense of posterity.*

parched souls if, once in a while, we saturate the barren lives of others with random acts of Torah.

Sukkot services feature הוֹשָׁנוֹת *Hoshanot*, poetry with a distinctive refrain, אָנָּא יְיָ הוֹשִׁיעָה נָּא *Ana Adonai Hoshi'a na*!, "Oh, God, save us!" God will save us at the end of time, say the rabbis; meanwhile, with random acts of Torah, graciously and fully given, we can save one another. The quality of Torah must not be strained. Go out of your way to make your genuine moments of human contact matter, and you will know the joy of renewing life. ■

Ha'azinu

Dr. Jack H. Bloom

Jack H. Bloom, Ph.D., Rabbi and Clinical Psychologist, is a consultant to clergy and conducts a private practice at The Psychotherapy Center in Fairfield, Ct.

Ha'azinu

He was thirteen and pudgy, standing in a suit that itched, bought from Bobby's Clothing Store on Canal Street. Bobby's specialized in outfitting husky boys. He was thinking more about the kiddush that was to follow than about what he was doing at that moment. It was his bar mitzvah day, and he was reading (or, more accurately, reciting from memory) the Torah portion—*Ha'azinu*. Thank God and his birth date, it was really short. The aliyot were just a few verses long. He was doubly lucky because Mr. Rappoport had insisted in his antiquated way that the entire seventh grade, each and every one, learn *Ha'azinu* by heart. As classmate after classmate struggled to recite the right words he could, with just the inkling of a smirk, rattle it off. To be fair to him, he had to learn a special trope for *Ha'azinu*.

That was burden enough, but it had become part of him. And every year thereafter, when he could, he would chant the poem in any synagogue that would have him.

He was chanting Moses' great ode—*Ha'azinu*: "Give ear, O heavens, let me speak; Let the earth hear the words I utter!" [Deut. 32.1]. A visionary's poem! Breathtaking scope! People's destinies decided! The fate of nations hanging in the balance! The bar mitzvah boy understood little of it. Everyone said it was too tough to understand anyway. Even Mr. Rappoport said so. Maybe Mr. Rappoport had assigned it by heart because of the verses at the end of *Ha'azinu:* "Take to heart all the words with which I have warned you this day. Enjoin them upon your children, that they may observe faithfully all the terms of this teaching. For this is not a trifling thing for you; it is your very life" [Deut. 32.46-47]. Mr. Rappoport took such things seriously. This was no trifling matter. He would have it be part of us. Memorized.

When Moses delivered *Ha'azinu* he didn't have to learn it by heart. He knew it by heart. The words came from his heart. They were his. Moses just spoke the poem, teaching as he went. *Moshe Rabeinu*; our peerless teacher who, against all odds, had brought the people Israel to the very edge of the Promised Land. Moses, who maneuvered between an ingrate people and their explosive ally, who had more than once threatened to destroy them all. Moses, master mover of men and, yes, let it be said, of God. God's friend and intimate; awesome leader of God's people. Yet at the end of the ode, in full

Ha'azinu

view of the promise about to be realized, Moses hears the fateful words the bar mitzvah boy dares in his ignorance to recite: "YOU SHALL DIE ON THE MOUNTAIN THAT YOU ARE ABOUT TO ASCEND...FOR YOU BROKE FAITH WITH ME AMONG THE ISRAELITE PEOPLE, AT THE WATERS OF MERIBATH-KADESH IN THE WILDERNESS OF ZIN, BY FAILING TO UPHOLD MY SANCTITY AMONG THE ISRAELITE PEOPLE. YOU MAY VIEW THE LAND FROM A DISTANCE, BUT YOU SHALL NOT ENTER IT..." [Deut. 32.50-52].

The bar mitzvah boy didn't understand it when he stood in his Bobby's suit, and he doesn't understand it now. How could Moses, who envisioned the whole thing, who led the trek through the desert for forty years, be turned away on account of such trivia? Okay, so he hit the rock (probably hurt his hand) instead of talking to it, to get water for his people. Big deal! A small thing! Too great a punishment for a trivial offense, not forgotten by the God of justice nor forgiven by the God of compassion. He is denied the prize for not having sanctified God's name in the midst of the people Israel.

He didn't know if he would understand it if he lived to Moses' one hundred and twenty years. Nor did he care. It was enough just to get to the end of the Torah portion without any mistakes. And to get downstairs for the herring in sour cream.

Fifty years later he understands a bit more, though not very much. There have been glimpses of meanings. Learning it by heart did something. It comes in his dreams and enters his musings from time to time. He knows that though the big vision is crucial, little things matter. They count big time. Kind words he said to others, words others offered him made a difference. A smile, a note, a bit of praise and appreciation all lingered. He knows he liked them when he got them, but though it was so easy, he often failed in giving them. He's learned that we fail when success is in our grasp and succeed when failure is at the door. And that we are magnificent in both. He's seen that we're both holy and mundane, saint and sinner, generous and stingy, incredibly vicious and supremely kind, each of us and all of us. He's recognized that though we get lost in the little things, we dare not ignore them. For it's in the little things that we sanctify God's name in the midst of our people.

He understands a bit more, and then only sometimes. Like Moses we're destined to die without the prize; the prizes we do get are often not worth pursuing. He has seen big prizes lost by small acts. He's noticed that for brief shining moments we succeed, and that we make promises to ourselves that we intend to keep and don't. That things we can't help impede us. And that that's just the way it is. We're more human than not. Over the fifty years he has learned something—sometimes.

He had learned *Ha'azinu* by heart. Mr. Rappoport's pedantic vision and the luck of his birth date had seen to that. Long after his bar mitzvah he was reading *Ha'azinu* in synagogue with the confidence of having done it fifty times. Pretty soon it would be kiddush time, and he could have herring in sour cream. But now his wife's caring concern about animal fat would deny him that prize, too. Still, he could taste the herring as the words, planted in him long ago, came out of his mouth. He had never guessed how they would bloom. ■

משה איש האלהים

Parashat V'Zot ha-Brakhah
Deuteronomy 33.1–34.12

Rabbi Benjamin J. Segal

Rabbi Benjamin Segal is the President of the Seminary of Judaic Studies (Bet Midrash) in Jerusalem, the Academic Center of Conservative/Masorti Judaism in Israel.

This parashah, וְזֹאת הַבְּרָכָה *V'Zot ha-Brakhah,* too often escapes our attention. Never read in the Diaspora on Shabbat but only on Simhat Torah, it is sometimes lost among *Hakafot, Hallel,* the honorees of חֲתַן-תּוֹרָה *hatan-Torah* and חֲתַן-בְּרֵאשִׁית *hatan-Bereshit,* the re-beginning of the Torah reading.

It deserves much more. Certainly Moses' death is one of the most moving sections of the Bible.

The penultimate section, Moses' blessing, the subject of this study, is relatively early literature, attested both by the language and by the fact that its framework looks forward to achievements that were never fulfilled. This is much less a retrospective than a record of dreams.

The framework, in particular, bears the ring of authenticity: Moses looks back at the desert experience as assurance for what is to come. A people of history even then, Israel turned to the ideal past to chart the ideal future.

Immediately before the blessings of the individual tribes, the ideal totality is described.

וַיְהִי בִישֻׁרוּן מֶלֶךְ בְּהִתְאַסֵּף רָאשֵׁי עָם יַחַד שִׁבְטֵי יִשְׂרָאֵל

va-Yehi ve-Yeshuron Melekh b'hitAsaif Roshai Am Yahad Shivtai Yisrael, THEN HE BECAME KING IN JESHURUN, WHEN THE HEADS OF THE PEOPLE

דָּבָר אַחֵר **DAVAR AHER.** NEVER AGAIN DID THERE ARISE IN ISRAEL A PROPHET LIKE MOSES—WHOM THE LORD SINGLED OUT, FACE TO FACE, FOR THE VARIOUS SIGNS AND PORTENTS THAT THE LORD SENT HIM TO DISPLAY IN THE LAND OF EGYPT, AGAINST PHARAOH AND ALL HIS COURTIERS AND HIS WHOLE COUNTRY, AND FOR ALL THE GREAT MIGHT AND AWESOME POWER THAT MOSES DISPLAYED BEFORE ALL ISRAEL [Deut. 34.10-12]. Reading an article about Thomas Jefferson on the same day on which I was studying *V'Zot ha-Brakhah,* I was struck by a possible oddity of the concluding lines of Torah. Just as Jefferson omitted his presidency from his epitaph, the Torah, in establishing what is essentially Moses' epitaph, focuses not on the task that had occupied his time for the past forty years and that most of us would consider his most significant accomplishment—the giving of

וזאת הברכה אשר ברך

ASSEMBLED, THE TRIBES OF ISRAEL TOGETHER [Deut. 33.5].

The past is ideal. Once there was a king…

Indeed there was a king, and later interpretation reflects the obvious implication of the verse: Just as God's kingship was achieved at the moment of national unity, so it will be in the future a direct reflection of such unity.

Unity is also the emphasis of several midrashim: YOU ARE GOD'S CHILDREN, states Deuteronomy 14.1—לֹא תִתְגֹּדְדוּ *lo titgodidu*—the Hebrew referring to nothing more than the ban on gashing ourselves in funeral or mourning ceremonies. The word, however, was used for a well known midrash: Do not תִתְגֹּדְדוּ *titgodidu*: do not make yourselves אֲגֻדּוֹת אֲגֻדּוֹת *agudot agudot,* into small sub-groups. "Rather, you must all be as one group and not the way the others break into sub-groups" [*Sifre*].

Similarly, the *Sifre* comments on our verse: "THEN HE BECAME KING IN YESHURUN—when the people of Israel are of a single mind in the world below, and when is that? WHEN THE HEADS OF THE PEOPLE ASSEMBLED…THE TRIBES OF ISRAEL TOGETHER, when they join into a single group and not when they make themselves into little sub-groups."

But our text itself testifies to the complexity of this goal. No sooner is unity held up as ideal than Moses proceeds to bless the people tribe by tribe, each in its own way. The return to a unified blessing of peace does not erase the impression that the people are divided.

In emphasizing the unity of the people as a necessary condition for God's kingship, however, the rabbis were aware of the

SYNOPSIS: *The closing sidrah. Moses blesses each tribe and then goes up Mt. Nebo to die.*

RASHI OF THE WEEK:

Here is our last Rashi, and it is on a major theological issue—revelation. The Torah says: SO MOSES, THE SERVANT OF THE ETERNAL, DIED THERE [Deut. 43.5]. *Rashi asks:* How could Moses have died and then written "SO MOSES, THE SERVANT OF THE ETERNAL, DIED THERE?" He couldn't have. Rather, Moses wrote up to this point, and Joshua wrote from this verse to the end of the Torah. That is an extant theory, but it makes little sense that the Torah would still be short of anything important and yet would still state (before the death of Moses): TAKE THIS BOOK OF THE TORAH [Deut. 31.26]. *This is the only reasonable explanation.* The Holy One dictated this passage, and Moses wrote it in tears [*Sifre, B. Bathra* 15a, *Men.* 30a]. *In one way or another, each of us is like Moses, writing the story of our own death.*

Torah—but rather on the events surrounding the Exodus. What could be the reason for this?

Having posed the question, I would like to propose a tentative answer. In paying tribute to Moses, the text emphasizes his uniqueness. Since the Exodus was a one-time event, there was no harm in suggesting that God would never again give someone the power to duplicate the ten plagues. However, the giving of Torah is an ongoing process. If the Torah had emphasized Moses' uniqueness in this area, it would have undermined the leaders of later generations and hampered the development of Rabbinic Judaism. For the sake of later generations, the Torah appears to have deliberately downplayed the significance of the man behind the most profound code of ethics in human history. **Stu Lewis, Prairie Village, KS.**

diversity of the people. In fact, the desirability of that diversity was emphasized in many instances. They stated that there are "seventy faces to the Torah" [*Numbers Rabbah* 13.15]. "The Torah...was written so that one could argue in forty-nine ways for impurity and forty-nine ways for purity" (and one decides by majority opinion) [*Masekhet Sofrim* 16.5, with many parallels]. It is preferable that any rabbinic student learn from more than one teacher [*Avodah Zarah* 19a].

At the same time, disagreement had its limits. All members of court had to accept the decision of either the majority or the Head of the Court. Thus did Rabbi Yehoshua have to accept Rabban Gamliel's decision as to when Yom Kippur fell, and even appear before him on the day that was Yom Kippur by Rabbi Yehoshua's calculation with money and walking stick, in order to demonstrate his acceptance [*Rosh Hashanah* 11.8-9]. Thus was Akavia ben Mahalalel banned for insisting that his memory of earlier decisions was correct, not the memory of the majority [*Eduyot* v.6]. And thus did the Rabbinic court take no heed of miracles or voices from heaven in halakhic matters, but decided only by majority vote [*Bava Metzia* 59a].

No group of sources better reflects the unity–diversity tension than the stories of Beit Shamai and Beit Hillel, the two early "schools of thought." They are filled with well-known references of respect and even willingness to live in accordance with the other group's pronouncements [*Yebamot* 1.4]. Still, we are aware that once tensions rose even to the point of killing [*Yerushalmi Shabbat* 1.4].

Of greatest interest is that section wherein later rabbis looked back and tried to determine whether Beit Shamai, presumed to be the minority, actually acted upon their conclusions or simply differed in argument. Both opinions are put forth and logically supported—with reference both to before Beit Hillel being declared normative halakhah (through a voice from heaven) and even after! Toward the end the *Gemorrah* challenges that even if one rejects direct communications from heaven in matters of Jewish law, still we all certainly accept the ban on splitting into sub-groups. How, then, could Beit Shamai have acted upon their own opinion? In response Rava severely restricts the prohibition. The ban on forming sub-groups is restricted to a single court, which may not give a mixed decision because the judges cannot agree. However, even within the same city, if two courts disagree, one does not consider *that* an infraction of the ban of forming sub-groups! Reflected, then, is a wide range of opinion on the acceptable limits of diversity.

Disagreement, the rabbis further declared, could be good or bad. If it is for its own sake or for the sake of power, it is to be condemned. If it is for the sake of heaven, not only is it desirable—it is destined to exist forever [*Avot* v.17].

Diversity and unity form the grid on which much of Jewish history is written. The observer is fascinated as analyses of this interplay in history continue to proliferate. But while observation can be fascinating, living the challenge can be demanding, even painful.

Certainly in Israel today the potential involvement of state power in such matters raises the level of concern for the successful integration of unity and diversity. The results of the recent elections in Israel (in terms of backing parties that support, to varying degrees, religious coercive legislation), street violence to force closing traffic throughways on Shabbat, and political attacks by some religious circles on the Supreme Court (a bastion of democracy and individual rights) have led to talk of a cultural war. Many unfortunate things have been said, among them the analysis that an out-and-out struggle is necessary because religion is, by its nature, theocratic and therefore antithetical to democratic processes.

Once again the role of modern, enlightened approaches to Judaism becomes clear in Israel. Judaism itself has struggled with differences for thousands of years and reflects not only a demand for unity, but also a clear recognition that differences of opinion and of action are to be tolerated, even encouraged. The same tradition even warns that matters can, on occasion, get out of control. Any objective reading of our history, then, is illustrative of both of the desire and the necessity to find a peaceful, honorable, positive *modus vivendi*, alongside the necessity for unity in decision-making. That reading of our history is authentic, and it must be communicated to the Israeli public as the religious position. Only religious outlooks sensitive to the pluralistic nature of tradition will be able to bear that message.

For Rosh ha-Shanah our verse was chosen as one of the three Torah verses to reflect God's Kingship. The goal of unity must remain ever with us, even if conceived as a framework in which divisions exist. The ultimate guiding principle to achieve that is reflected in the name of the people as used by the verse—יְשׁוּרוּן *Yeshurun*. According to most, the word echoes the more common name, Israel (יְשׁוּרוּן *Yeshurun* and יִשְׂרָאֵל *Yisrael*), but because it is derived from the root יָשָׁר *Yashar,* straight, it is a counterweight for Israel's other name, Jacob (יַעֲקֹב *Ya'akov*)—from the root "to deceive." We need not only unity, but also a "straight," an ethical approach to life. If we achieve that, and build our unity while allowing for diversity of opinion and action, we might indeed be blessed, and our unity might help allow for God's Kingship on high and on earth. ■

INDEX

INDEX

INDEX